In Search of America's Soul

Conversations with Americans about
the declining power of the US empire
and the politics of race and racism
in the Presidential Elections of 2012

OWEN BAPTISTE

A Douens Publication

ALSO BY OWEN BAPTISTE

Crisis
Duprey
The Seagulls Won't Come Down
Benedict Wight and Other Writings

DOUENS
P R E S S

ISBN – 13: 978-9628616602
ISBN – 10: 9628616609

Published by Douens Press Hong Kong

Printed by CreateSpace owned by Amazon.com Inc

Photography by She Xiuling

Cover and book design by She Xiuling

Dedication
For my sons
Marc and Simon

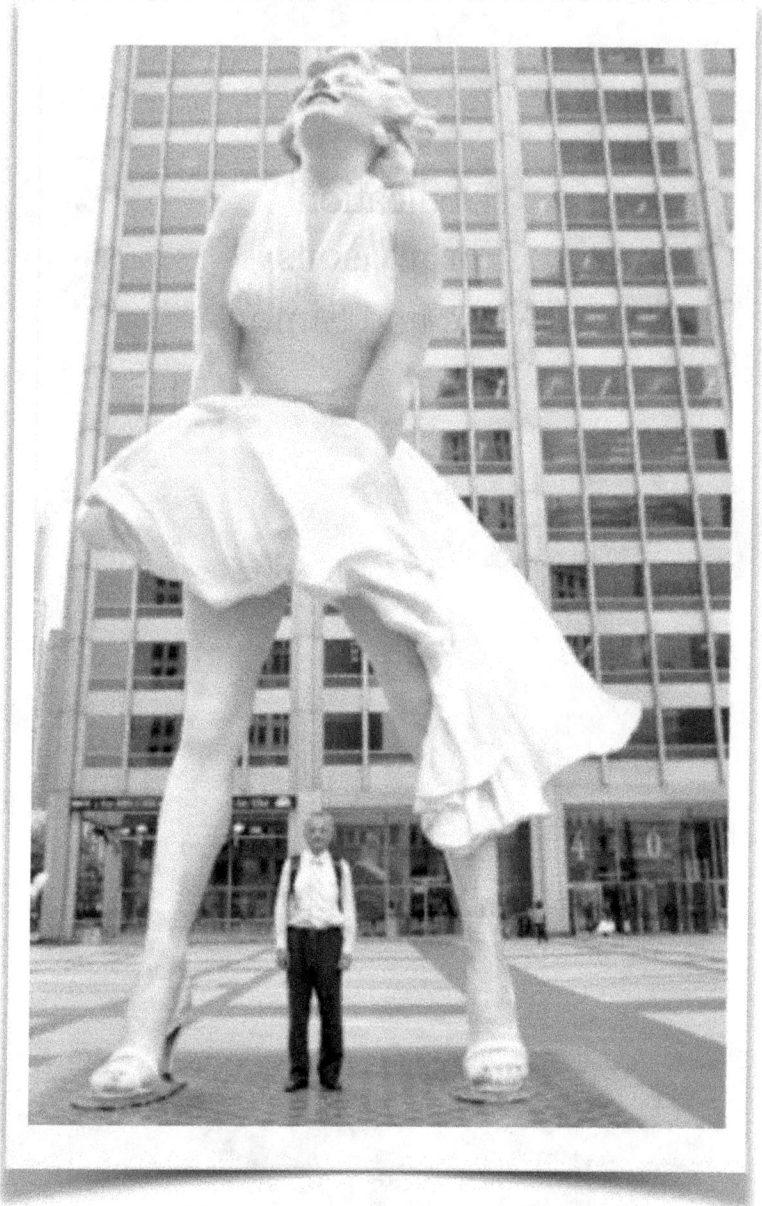

Author with Marilyn Monroe in Chicago

Contents

Note to Readers

FROM OUR first meeting at a McDonald's restaurant in New York City on Lexington Avenue on 1 September 2011 it was clear that all we had hoped to achieve in the month of travel across the United States was unlikely to happen and that we would have to come up with a secondary plan to do what we set out to accomplish. Time and the willingness of Americans to discuss the myths and mythology of US superiority in the world today were not on our side and in many cases we believed we would be forcing our way against closed minds. This however did not deter us; it was the reporter's natural thinking that ours is a crusade to discover truth and that the result would gladden the hearts of men and women everywhere. Ask Anderson Cooper. Ask Christiane Amanpour. Ask Thomas L. Friedman.

I recalled that when we had reached Los Angeles, Trinidad-born Davan Maharaj, then Managing Editor of the *Los Angeles Times,* had asked us who was sponsoring our travel and stay in the United States and we had said, "No one. We are doing this on our own." I could see the incredulity on Davan's face and I was sure that Davan who had started his career in journalism at the *Trinidad Express* was thinking his old editor was naïve or crazy. Or that we had just won a multi-million-dollar lottery that would enable us to spend enough time in the United States to get the work done.

Davan's surprise brought something else to mind and this was the astonishment of Prime Minister Basdeo Panday when he had first come to the Caribbean Basin Exhibit at Caribbean Information Systems & Services building at Frederick Street in Port of Spain in the mid-1990s and he had asked, not understanding why anyone would invest so much in a program to inform and educate the children of Trinidad and Tobago on social, political and economic matters, "Why did you do it?" It was inconceivable to him that a pair of journalists working on their own and without financial support from the Government or Big Business would introduce touch-screen technology to fire the interest of primary school students in the electronic world in which they lived. Fifteen years later the Government was giving laptops to teenagers who had successfully completed the SEA (Secondary Entrance Assessment) exams. But this had been our style: to jump into the deep and to swim against the current.

The truth was our appeal to Ms. Dawn Thomas, who is CEO of One Caribbean Media at Express House in Port of Spain, to underwrite the project had fallen on barren ground. "What would we get from the book?" she had asked, the businesswoman trumping the journalist. I had thought that our plan to examine what issues galvanize Americans before a U.S. Presidential Election was something that would be of interest to her readers and which would be irresistible to the head and heart of a Caribbean Communications Group that had interests in newspapers, television and radio and which should have had as well a mission to improve the intellectual lives of citizens who supported its ambitious growth plan. But as we talked with Davan about her unwillingness to explore this new path in journalism, the Chinese idiom, *Yu hu mou pi*, came to mind. It was as if I was "asking a tiger for its skin". It was obvious that she didn't want to blaze any new literary path. Her thrust it seemed lay in the acquisition of other commercial activities and this was probably why the *Express*, once an aggressive watchdog in the country, was now the focus of skepticism and ridicule. I remembered that Ken Gordon, the former Chairman of the Express, had said to me when I was writing my paper about the need for a School of Journalism that the NAR (National Alliance for Reconstruction) Government had opened up the Communications Media by making it possible for the explosion in the number of media houses in the country today. But to many Trinidadians and Tobagonians it simply opened the way for a lot of babble on radio and garbage on television. It had in no way added to the integrity and importance of print journalism.

There was of course a lot about America in books, newspapers, magazines and on the Internet that could provide evidence of *Homo sapiens americanus* after the Flood, but would any or all of it reveal the divinity in the breast of Sally Ride or the devil in the heart of Bernard Madoff when we examined their images in the press? It seemed that we had Hobson's choice. We could use and acknowledge the public records of saint and sinner and could do this successfully without arousing accusations of plagiarism, but it meant that we would be putting our trust in The Associated Press, in Reuters, in Agence France Presse, in US television networks, in Yahoo! News and in Wikipedia to complete our search for America's Soul. Was this the way we should go? We weren't worried about the integrity or relevance of the information since we would be casting a wide net. The danger was the possibility that we would miss a news report or a dissenting view that could be vital to judgments we would make for the inclusion of news and views in our work even as we listened to native-born Americans and new immigrants in New York, in Washington DC, in Chicago, in Detroit, in San Francisco, in Los Angeles, in Las Vegas and in Miami.

And there was also the uneasiness of an old newspaperman. How much do the media reveal the *soul* of a country? Or, is it just a mirror of activities and opinions in the life of communities? Is journalism what Truman Capote said of literature – just gossip? How much, for example, does the work of Bob Woodward, associate editor of *The Washington Post*, influence Americans' choices for a President, from Nixon to Obama? Or, are his books like many newspapers only a written record of the activities in politics, business, sport, entertainment, science and war? This is not to deny that journalism has a role to play in the development of societies by shining a light where there is darkness. But how much of the character of a people does it reveal apart from the fact that in a democracy people can say and write whatever they like? Or, think that they could do so. How does news on examination bare a nation's soul? And how important is it to keep in mind the uneasiness of a President that the "amplifications of conflict" by the media contribute to an atmosphere of suspicion and unreality?

Any other route seemed pointless to consider if we were to find answers to the question before the 6 November 2012 election. The interviews we had planned with state officials, with university administrators and with members of the media and the public would be insufficient in the four weeks we had to provide us with the answers to our inquiries about what it is to be an American in these times of acute financial worry and growing international distrust of Washington's ability to safeguard the Nation and the World. It was easy to think that we had bitten off more than we could chew and perhaps the thing to do was to enjoy the visits to eight of America's fascinating cities as tourists. But then the Chinese idiom, *Yu gong yi shan*, came to mind. It is the story of a Foolish Old Man whose house faced two mountains that obstructed his way. One day he called his family together and said, "Let's work together, remove the mountains and open a road." His wife protested. "You can hardly level a small mound," she said. But the Foolish Old Man was not discouraged and the following day the family began to dig to achieve his goal.

That is why we did not give up and revelations of the Soul of America in this book come as much from written records as from our own observations and from friends. We scoured the Internet for news and information that would enhance our comprehension of America and Americans and we would like to acknowledge the news sources that facilitated this ambitious undertaking. The list includes The New York Times, The Washington Post, The Chicago Tribune, The Wall Street Journal, The Los Angeles Times, and USA Today. It is not our intention to suggest anywhere in these pages that all the reporting is original and indeed we acknowledge the journalists whose reports we have quoted, including the work of The Yahoo! News Politics Team. We knew however that we had to be vigilant. Gore Vidal had warned in *Dreaming War* that U.S. newspapers often played the game of "follow the leader" so we couldn't afford to be gullible. Vidal shared another concern: Americans were "dumbed down" he was told and one should write only about what readers already knew. We knew much more was required of us and that we would have to claw our way through tensions, fears and prejudices to get to the soul of the country and we had to do so without compromising our integrity.

And as I have written I quoted from sources online and I acknowledged every source. I was not familiar with many of the developments in the United States, especially during our twelve years in China, and I relied a lot on published accounts to complete my understanding of America and Americans. My aim was to present enough evidence from media reports to help with the revelation of the *Soul* of America and the event of a Presidential election provided me with information I would not have had at another time. What I could be accused of is an excess of liberty in quoting from these sources but I had no intention to pass off all the reporting as my own. There are some long passages that I have reproduced because I didn't want to change or to corrupt the work of the journalists and academics but in no instance was I trying to present others' research and writing as my own. The reason was they were on the ground and were better able to present the material that described the situation. I was thousands of miles away. Thus readers might find fault with the selection of material but not with the transparency of my motive. I tried real hard to give a kaleidoscopic view of the American experience and what influences the American character when I searched the news media and the Internet for an understanding of America's Soul. At most times I was doing unabashedly the work of a reviewer or a historian, and the contents in this book provided me with intimate knowledge of the US government, US business, US race relations and the US media.

Is this revelation something that would raise doubts about the integrity of the work and would inhibit its publication? In fact in November 2012 it did just that. Did I have *written* consent, CreateSpace asked, to use reports from the Internet? Well, I didn't and I felt I had to spend time in re-writing some of the news material to make them feel more comfortable with the contents of the book. It took me longer than I had hoped because when I started the work I didn't count on illness and surgery to remove a wretched gall bladder to shut me down for months. "For some time," Rhona wrote a troubled Xiuling, "I didn't think he would make it, but his doctors and the nurses at the WestShore Medical were magnificent and he pulled through all right, celebrating his 80th birthday with all kinds of tubes attached to him and with countless visits from nurses to stick needles in him." For several nights I had told her that as I lay helpless in bed I had chased away the boatman on the River Styx. I wasn't finished with my work I explained and he went in search of less troublesome passengers. But the truth is the care and attention I got from Doctors Dexter Thomas and Michelle Trotman and their staff of nurses was what brought me back to the land of the living.

In addition my sincere thanks go today to Kerry Luft of the *Chicago Tribune* and Davan Maharaj of the *Los Angeles Times*, to Carole Mussarachia, Beverly Nunez, Yolanda Singh, Denise Singh, Simone Long, Carl Sturken, Ray and Myrna Boddie, Jawaharlal Ramnarace, David Harold, Philip Lomenzo, Joyce Hunter, and Chester and Lynette Morong who spent hours talking with us about what it is to be an American and what it is to live in the United States at this time when the American sun seems to be setting.

We hope that both Democrats and Republicans will judge this work kindly for our efforts to present an understanding of the risks and hopes that enhance Americans' love of country and the creativity that sustains the unbroken American Spirit.

One final word, Vidal passed away on 31 July 2012. He was 86. We know that America has lost one of its noblest minds and an outstanding man of letters.

OWEN BAPTISTE
Port of Spain, Trinidad

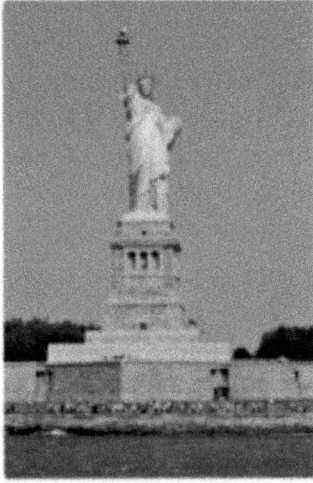

Introduction — God Bless America!

Give me your tired, your poor,
Your huddled masses yearning to breathe free,
The wretched refuse of your teeming shore.
Send these, the homeless, tempest-tost to me,
I lift my lamp beside the golden door!

– From the inscription on the Statue of Liberty.

PORT OF SPAIN, Trinidad – There are times when the United States is insane and on the evening of 26 February 2012 when George Zimmerman shot and killed Trayvon Martin it was an example of the insanity that has been tearing America apart for centuries. I believe if the black teenager had smashed in the head of Zimmerman who had stalked him in the rain it would have been as clearly a case of "standing his ground" as the law implies in Florida. However what I believe – even if it is also the opinion of millions of Americans and people around the world – has no influence on the matter before the court and on the verdict; but the killing was the reason that my wife Rhona and I were going back to Detroit, Michigan, in May 2012. This time She Xiuling, who had been one of our graduate students in China, was not with us. She was back in her hometown of Chaozhou getting ready for her job at the London Olympics.

I hadn't planned to retrace the steps we had taken nine months before in our quest to discover America's Soul. The city had lacked signs of prosperity and building after building was barred, vandalized or unoccupied – startling proof of a disabled economy and the reason Republicans were insisting that Barack Obama should be removed from the White House this November. Red-brick luxury townhouses on the river, across from which we watched the skyline in Windsor, Canada, were empty – the hope for home-owners abandoned. They were like tombstones of a once gracious age. The truth is we should not have been surprised the day before we left Chicago when Scott Stantis, the political cartoonist at the *Chicago Tribune,* blurted out the word "Death!" when we told him that Detroit would be our next stop. We could see that Kerry Luft, the *Tribune*'s Nation and World Editor, who had brought Stantis to our meeting, was surprised by his colleague's swift denunciation of the city, but he didn't contradict him.

Detroit was an old newspaper story of foreclosures and neglect and in an interview that week with *The Detroit News* the city's new Chief Financial Officer, Jack Martin, appeared to be unsure of how to keep the city from further decay and was appealing to the Obama Administration for executive help. Still, we were in no position to refute Stantis' gloomy forecast and the lack of hope he held out for us. The economic news was grim even if the Page One lead story in the *Michigan Chronicle* of 23-29 May 2012 was "Restoring Hope" that focused on the Mackinac Policy Conference to take place and which stated that the Conference aimed to put Michigan's urban cities "front and center". Despite the dwindling of population as shown in the recent Census report, wrote the *Chronicle* Senior Editor Bankole Thompson, "the city still remains a political and economic fortress in Michigan." What was necessary now, Mayor Dave Bing told Thompson, "is to transform the city to a place where people can come in and want to live and work." And according to Governor Rick Snyder the change was a work in progress and what the city needed was "people coming together in the new culture we need for our state. You don't change a culture overnight, but I think we've made tremendous progress."

The statistics did not support this cheerfulness however. On 25 January 2012 a report on five American cities nearly destroyed by the recession included Flint, Michigan, the birthplace of General Motors.

The report authored by Michael B. Sauter, Ashley C. Allen, and Charles B. Stockdale of 24/7 Wall St. stated that the nation continues to be mired in an anemic, jobless recovery. Commissioned by the United States Conference of Mayors and prepared by IHS Global Insight, the report exposed regions in the country that continue to lose jobs. Of the 363 U.S. metropolitan regions reviewed by IHS, only 61 it stated will fully recover all the jobs that were lost during the recession by the end of this year. The rest will recover far fewer – the average city will recover only about 40 per cent of jobs lost from peak employment.

24/7 Wall St. had examined nine metropolitan regions that are projected to recover less than 5 per cent of the jobs lost during the recession by the end of 2012. These five cities, in particular, were hurt by the housing crash, the loss or decline of an industry, and a reduction in government services and jobs. According to the Conference of Mayors' report, many cities that rely heavily on merchandise exports, such as automotive-based Flint, have been suffering as manufacturing businesses continue to move overseas. In 2005, nearly 10 per cent of the Flint, Michigan's economy was based on exported goods. As of 2009, the number dropped to just 3.2 per cent. Over that time, the value of the city's annual exports dropped by roughly $850 million, or 70 per cent of its original value. Flint's economy, which is primarily based on auto manufacturing, has been suffering for a number of years. In the first quarter of 2007, employment reached its peak with over 151,300 residents employed. By the end of the first quarter of 2012, IHS projects employment to reach a floor, after a loss of over 20,000 positions. Recovery, it seems, will also be slow as only 600 jobs are projected to be recovered by the end of the year, or just 2.8 per cent of jobs lost. The value of exports from the region has dropped 81.9 per cent since 2005 – one of the largest decreases in the country. This, of course, has had a bruising effect on Flint's economy and population. Poverty rate in the area has risen to 21 per cent, one of the worst rates in the country.

Was the forecast less ominous for Detroit, the state capital? A Reuters report by Julie Halpert in July reminded readers of an April deal between Detroit and the state of Michigan in which Snyder was finalizing a plan to tear down thousands of abandoned houses in a bid to make the city safer. Detroit, as the story goes, has been hard-hit over the past four decades by a steep drop in population, a steadily eroding tax base and crippling budget deficits, resulting in countless barren streets punctuated by vacant lots and burned-out buildings. The state plan is likely to be announced early in August 2012, wrote Ms. Halpert, and is part of a financial stability agreement that headed off the appointment of an emergency city manager, which Detroit had opposed.

Bing's administration had promised to demolish by July 4,500 "dangerous and abandoned buildings", according to press secretary Naomi Patton, and plans were to tear down another 1,500 vacant structures by the end of September – part of Bing's pledge three years ago to demolish 10,000 derelict buildings by the end of his term in late 2013. In a statement, the mayor said, "We welcome the governor's efforts ... Tangible assistance from the state is critical to our efforts to transform Detroit." As Detroit struggles with a $197 million budget deficit, Snyder has looked at a variety of state actions to support the city. The financial stability agreement outlined a plan to improve the quality of life and safety for Detroiters, including demolition as a way to address blight. "We're working with a variety of state departments and agencies to coordinate in an unprecedented way the work that gets done," said Sara Wurfel, Snyder's press secretary.

This was not the end of the city's troubles however; there was looming turmoil in education. Keith Johnson, the president of Detroit Federation of Teachers, said that the union that represents 4,300 teachers who were laid off by Detroit Public Schools should consider suing the district if its members were not re-hired in September because of what it called "drive-by evaluations". Under a new teacher tenure law in Michigan, every district will use evaluation results to make personnel decisions for the upcoming school year, with a goal of removing ineffective teachers. But the union promised to fight any move by the state because it said the state-mandated evaluation process in April was an inadequate test as evaluators sat in classrooms for as little as four minutes. "A drive-by is not indicative of how effective a teacher is or is not, and is an insult to the profession," Johnson told *The Detroit News*.

But the problem is bigger than the test for teachers that Johnson thinks is unfair; the problem is the quality of education itself and what it achieves. In their book, *That used to be us*, Michael Friedman and

Michael Mandelbaum write that a May 2011 study by the Detroit Regional Workforce Fund found that 47 per cent of adult Detroit residents, or about 200,000 people, are functionally illiterate – which means that nearly half the adults in the city can't perform simple tasks such as reading an instruction book, reading labels on packages or machinery, or filling out a job application. Depressingly, about 100,000 of those functionally illiterate adults have either a high school diploma or the GED equivalent. "You can stimulate the Detroit economy all you want, but even if jobs come back, people who can't read won't be able to do them," they warned.

It was obvious that talk of an economic, social and psychological turnaround was still premature so what miracle did we expect to find there? Clearly, as a Republican, Stantis did not think that the government's $80 billion bailout of the auto manufacturers had been successful in reviving expectations for the city's transformation. He was sure that our attempt to find the meaning of what it is to be an American today would be futile, blocked at every turn by disillusionment with an administration that had failed to deliver on its promises. But rooted in this pessimism was the fact that Republicans, who often looked the same in Washington as Democrats, did not have always the identical vision for the country as Democrats. And the situation had deteriorated with the financial institutions' failures and the poor man's protests that continued to divide America. It was as Obama had lamented some years ago that the country was more divided politically than at any time since before World War II and when we looked at the issues that Americans disagreed on – taxes, guns, abortions, gay marriages and immigration – as Obama did, there was for us the same presentiment that something terrible would come to pass.

However, we were not about to turn back. The senseless killing of Trayvon Martin had renewed in us searing doubt that the United States had learnt benevolence since its historic voting in 2008 for a black president. There was instead a growing mountain of evidence that this thinking was reckless and naïve and a result of our own belief in political commonsense and in the arguments for survival because as Shaw had stated there could be "no hope for the world unless power can be tamed, and brought into the service, not of this or that group of fanatical tyrants, but of the whole human race, white and yellow and black, fascist and communist and democrat, for science has made it inevitable that all must live or all must die." However this warning seemed to have fallen on deaf ears because there are leaders in the United States who cannot put aside the bigotry that denies fellow Americans the rights to their pursuit of peace, justice, equality and happiness. And there is no doubt, as Condoleezza Rice told a Super PAC fundraiser in Washington in June that the election in November is a crucial one for the country. "This is a truly consequential election," the former Secretary of State and National Security Adviser who was introduced as "the smartest woman in the world", told her audience. "This is perhaps a turning point for the country," Rice insisted before briefly listing a series of challenges abroad. "There are many foreign policy issues on the agenda, but we are not going to address any of those international challenges unless we get it right at home. And it's not right at home right now, and the American people know it."

America is clearly in a crisis and every report we read in the newspapers and watched on television pointed to the absence of forbearance and hope. There must scarcely be a day indeed when Barack Obama could be comfortable about the nation's waning authority and feel secure in the White House if even a year ago he had cut off the head of al-Qaeda. Too many Americans, from prominent Republicans who still kept alive the farcical issue of his birth to ordinary citizens who continued to embrace the dangerous creed of "Have Gun, Will Shoot", were unrelenting in putting blame on the President and the Democratic Party for the miserable state of American lives. Mitt Romney, the Republicans' choice for President, for example, had said in April that President Obama is "in over his head and swimming in the wrong direction" when it comes to the nation's economy and that his policies are "putting in peril" America's future. But speaking to voters nationwide from the pivotal battleground of Ohio, President Obama defiantly defended his record on the economy and painted Romney as the standard-bearer for those who would bring back George W. Bush's policies. "I want to speak to everybody who is watching who may not be a supporter, may be undecided, or thinking about voting the other way," Mr. Obama said. "If you want to give the policies of the last decade another try, then you should vote for Mr. Romney."

Was it a sign that he was fed up with the politics of 1600 Pennsylvania Avenue and that Republicans' bigotry and spite were undermining his hopes and plans to bring change to Washington and to the rest of America? And did we get his answer to that question three months later, on 15 July 2012, when the Associated Press reported him as saying that Washington "feels as broken as it did four years ago" when he took office. He was most frustrated he said by the inability "to change the atmosphere" in the capital "to reflect the decency and common sense of ordinary people" who want leaders to solve problems. He told CBS' *Sunday Morning* that there's no doubt that he underestimated how much "politics trump problem-solving." And when asked if he was prepared for the November election, Mr. Obama said, "Well, I get a little depressed." He too, one felt, was seeing the nation's madness and was growing weary of the lies, the distrust, the bickering and the malevolence.

But this surrender, as the President knew, is the way that evil triumphs over good and the fight against ignorance and deceit has no time-out and it is sometimes necessary to enlist the support of outside forces. First Lady Michelle Obama showed she understood this when she offered a rare public reflection on her religious faith, telling a conference of the African Methodist Episcopal church at the Gaylord Opryland Resort in Nashville, Tenn. in June that the life of Jesus Christ is a model for democratic organizing. "We see that in the life of Jesus Christ. Jesus didn't limit his ministry to the four walls of the church," she said. "He was out there fighting injustice and speaking truth to power every single day. He was out there spreading a message of grace and redemption to the least, the last, and the lost. And our charge is to find Him everywhere, every day by how we live our lives." Mrs. Obama said citizenship like the practice of faith is not a once-a-week kind of deal. "Democracy is also an everyday activity," she said. "And being an engaged citizen should once again be a daily part of our lives." Such engagement she said involved "the tireless, the thankless, relentless work of making change, you know, the phone-calling, letter-writing, door-knocking, meeting-planning kind of work."

In Charlotte, N.C., just blocks from where Obama would accept his party's nomination at the Democratic National Convention, Romney had delivered in April what his campaign described as a "prebuttal" to Obama's nomination speech, focusing on "what you won't hear" this September. He accused the president of not doing enough to encourage job creation and for running up the nation's debts. And he lambasted Obama for not delivering on the promises he made in his 2008 convention speech, vowing to remind voters of the president's "failures" when it comes to issues like unemployment. Forgotten were the wretched administration of George W. Bush and his infamous wars in Afghanistan and Iraq and the financial meltdown that started in the years of his presidency.

The truth is after three and a half years it did not appear that there was anyone in the Republican Party who was willing to accept the burden of conciliation that Al Gore had shown in his concession speech in 2000 when he quoted the words of Senator Stephen Douglas to Abraham Lincoln that "Partisan feeling must yield to patriotism." To hardnosed Republicans that notion was weakness itself and there would be no truce. Thus, day after day the Democrats seemed to be fighting a war with an enemy that did not have the interests and expectations as the people who had lost their jobs, their pensions and their hope for a better life. Their goal was how to re-take the power they had lost at the end of eight mangled years. That is why *The New York Times* could report on 16 May that Mr. Romney had described the economy as "a prairie fire of debt (that) is sweeping across ... our nation and every day we fail to act we feed that fire with our own lack of resolve." It was how the Republicans saw their strategy: to scare Americans into believing that Obama Rule is the cruelest and dumbest thing that ever happened to America. The newspaper also reported that Speaker John A. Boehner had said that the stage was set for a bruising election-year showdown on fiscal policy and vowed to hold up another increase in the federal debt-ceiling unless it was offset by larger spending cuts. "It clearly does not bother (Mr. Boehner)," said the paper in an editorial on 16 May 2012, "that he pushed the United States to the brink of default last year. It does not matter that the deep spending cuts in the resolution he demanded to end that crisis will hurt economic growth. It does not even matter that the House he leads is determined now to break that agreement with even deeper cuts in vital programs. No, Mr. Boehner wants to do it all over again."

But here on the morning of 25 May 2012 Rhona and I were on an Amtrak train leaving Chicago and heading for what was once the auto industry capital of the world and the home of the Fords, the Dodge Brothers, the Olds and the Chevrolets. Nine months before, on the morning of 15 September 2011, we had taken the train to Dearborn where we were to stay at the Hyatt Regency, clearly a victim too of the financial crisis. For the five days we spent there the hotel had appeared to be deserted and the nearby shopping mall with Sears and JCPenny stores seemed barren compared to similar malls in Guangzhou. What were we seeing – the coming death of the city? Was this what Chris Christoff writing in the *Bloomberg News* meant when he said that "Detroit, whose 139 square miles contain 60 percent fewer residents than in 1950, will try to nudge them into a small living space by eliminating nearly half of its streetlights"? Was it sarcasm or a prophecy? But the hotel's distance from downtown Detroit afforded us with the adventure of travelling by bus to the city and so we joined every morning the queue at the bus-stop and watched the grim faces of Detroiters waiting for transport to parts of the city.

II

DETROIT WAS the fourth city in our eight-city odyssey of the United States to find out how Americans felt about their lives and about the United States' declining power in the world. We hoped then that in Detroit, as in the cities we had visited and those we planned to visit, we would learn what Americans, black, yellow and white, had to do to cope with the economic blight that was strangling their city, their state, and the rest of America and that we would come away, more importantly, with a sincere understanding of race and racism in America. The journey, always daunting because the world was not any more a safer place, was nevertheless inspiring as we tested Americans' faith in their Constitution and even when Americans still saw America as falling behind the rest of the world and especially behind China, even if profits and salaries for CEOs at big U.S. companies had broken records in 2011. But to maintain American greatness, wrote two well-known and respected Americans in 2011, "The right option for us is not to become more like China. It is to become more like ourselves." These are men who say that the Chinese still suffer from large and potentially debilitating problems like a lack of freedom, rampant corruption, horrible pollution and an education system that historically has stifled creativity, and who continue to think that China does not have better political and economic systems than the United States. But right now they say China is "getting 90 per cent of the potential benefits from a second-rate political system while the United States has strayed from our own best practices and are getting only 50 per cent of the potential benefits from our first-rate system."

What were we really seeking to find out? I remember Alan Greenspan, the former chairman of the US Federal Reserve Board, quoting Winston Churchill's doctrine that the further backward we look, the further forward we can see. And Greenspan himself had written in *The Age of Turbulence* that "the principle of individual freedom touches a deep cultural chord in Americans: the belief embodied in our Constitution of the basic equality of all citizens before the law." He had regretted however that reality has not always matched this ideal, and discrimination against African Americans in particular forces Americans periodically to revisit the early constitutional debates about slavery and its violent resolution in the Civil War. "We have come a long way," he said, "but we have a distance yet to travel." This was the reality even in cosmopolitan New York City that is the choice still of many immigrants. "I hate the fact that there is still such blatant racism," said Trinidad-born Simone Long, Assistant Director of Columbia University's International Students and Scholars Office. "You would think that after all these years race relations would be different but it is not."

We hadn't succeeded that first time in 2011 to look as far back as we could because, perhaps, we were too polite to raise the matter of race and racism when we met our host at a birthday party to celebrate four generations of the Harold clan: Dave who was 80, Theresa who was 70, Larry who was 60, and Patrice who was 50. The invitation that had come to Rhona from Dave had stated that it would be "a Garden Party at a lovely location with the Detroit River as the backdrop" and, indeed, the evening was perfect with food, drink and carefree conversation that rendered it impossible for us to want to question the group about the disagreeable past, to remind them of prejudice and embarrassment, and even of pain, as we thought that life in the deep south and even in the state of Michigan might have been for them. I realized of course that recalling the past had not seemed to bother Dave

Harold when he spoke of his youth in Biloxi, Mississippi, of living in foster homes, and even when he described his brother as a "dumpster diver" and pointed to some of the articles he had secured for himself and members of his family. He was amused to relate the story but that account had been of his own volition; we hadn't been asking questions. We were friends from afar with no knowledge of the life he, his brother and sister had lived and he probably figured he was satisfying some kind of latent curiosity in us. It was obvious that more than twenty years of working at Detroit Edison in Affirmative Action had removed from him self-conscious pride, what in China our students used to call "face".

But I had wondered what did our attention to race and our embarrassment to pursue it mean? When we spoke about the journey we were preparing to take a second time our son Simon reminded us of an incident in the eighties when we were shopping at a K-Mart store in Miami, Florida. A soccer fan, he was aware of present-day racist remarks in European soccer and in American basketball. "Race," he said, "is still an unresolved issue in the world" and he recalled that Juventus had been fined 30,000 euros and were warned about the future conduct of their fans after they made racist chants during a 2-1 win at home to Lazio. I had read the Reuters report. Chants were heard on five occasions during the match but the club and other supporters tried to silence the offenders. "Juventus," said Simon, "were forced to play a game behind closed doors three years ago after then-Inter Milan player Mario Balotelli was racially abused." His concern was a warning to us of the possibility of racial discrimination while on our visit. "Dad," he said, "I had tried on a belt and came looking for you to approve my choice." Just eight at the time he saw a store attendant following him closely, almost accusingly. He had not experienced this kind of intimidation in Trinidad; racial discrimination was always a hidden vice in the country. "You quickly picked up on the situation, which was clearly a form of racial profiling, and spoke to the attendant who apologised and went back to her station." I did not recall the incident but I know I was careful whenever we shopped and I guess it was because I did not trust Americans to be able to regard every shopper as honest, especially if the face of the shopper, young or old, was not white. I knew it was not the fault of K-Mart's employees; it was the culture they had grown up in, as Anderson Cooper had been stressing in his CNN program on race after the Trayvon Martin killing.

Discrimination in various shapes and sizes is a story that haunts media. Bill Kovach and Tom Rosenstiel discussed one of its forms in *The Elements of Journalism*, pointing out that most types of discrimination were like a plant that grows in the dark. "Discrimination doesn't happen while you're there," a TV producer tells a young reporter who felt that he had never experienced discrimination. "It happens the moment you leave." And I wondered how often I was just like that young, disabled reporter who had felt that he had never been discriminated against. It was probably how Harvard University professor Henry Louis Gates, Jr. felt on 16 July 2009 when he was arrested while entering his Cambridge, Massachusetts, home by a local police officer responding to a 9/11 call from a neighbour. Surprise followed by outrage. And then revolt – the feeling not to comply with the law.

This must have been the defiance of most slaves after the revolutionary war and was probably why, according to the Tuskegee Institute, 3,446 of them were lynched between 1882 and 1968. Or, maybe they were just the wrong colour. In the Introduction to the *Narrative of the Life of Frederick Douglass*, the writer says, "The world and the United States have changed dramatically since Douglass first wrote the *Narrative* (and) in the fight for civil rights and citizenship, thousands upon thousands of men and women have struggled and sometimes triumphed over injustice. Yet the struggle against racism, oppression and systematic cruelty in America continues. The difficulty of claiming what it is to be American in the midst of this struggle also continues." However, Carole Musaracchia, a New Yorker who makes pet clothes for a living, does not see this anguish and says that "an American is not one race, sexuality, creed or belief. He or she is all different entities smushed into one nation and we basically tolerate each other as we go along striving for what makes us content."

The more I reflected on our reluctance to address the subject of racism with Dave Harold, the more I saw it as something like the Heisenberg Uncertainty Principle that Sir Courtney Blackman described in his book, *The Practice of Economic Management*. It did appear odd even eccentric to be defining our racial discomfort with a mathematical formula but I found the similarity striking. We had run into Sir Courtney, the former Governor of the Barbados Central Bank and his country's Ambassador to Washington, and his wife Gloria in New York in September and the next day at lunch he had given us a copy of the book. The Heisenberg Uncertainty Principle is the problem that confronts many social scientists – the problem of observing and analysing data of which one is a part and of separating one's own value set from the values of the subject one is observing. Did I see myself as a black man and a victim of discrimination that black Americans had experienced and would I be able to discern what could be examples of institutionalised racism? I had not grown up in the United States among slaves and the sons and daughters of slaves and I could never think that I could identify with the horrors, past or present, of black Americans. I could not, except as a fool or a charlatan, pretend to feel their pain. I believe this was the point that author and MSNBC contributor Touré was trying to make to Piers Morgan after his interview with the brother of George Zimmerman. The two had quarrelled on Twitter after Touré had criticised Morgan's handling of the interview on CNN and the insults they traded reminded me of the public outcry during the British Parliamentary inquiry into the phone hacking charges of Morgan's former employers.

Thus the evening passed uneventful and we were left with certain criteria, food, drink, carefree conversation and laughter, to draw a conclusion, perhaps the wrong conclusion, of the conditions of blacks in America. On the ground it appeared that the rule of law was not intended to discriminate between white and black and that more people were friendly rather than hostile. Whatever hardships had attached themselves to other people in Detroit this group of black Americans might have mortgages to pay and children to send to university, but they did not have those things to study now, as Trinidadians, planning for the next Carnival, say. It was definitely, we thought, not the time to invite discussions on Medgar Evans, Rosa Parks, and Rodney King. And so we left Detroit the next day with the questions of race and racism unstated and the perils of social disorder unaddressed. But I was remembering another warning from Greenspan in the chapter he called *The Delphic Future*. "Will the rule of law still be firm in 2030? To be largely free of fear of a secret police arbitrarily hauling us off for interrogation for 'crimes' we never knew existed is something not to be taken for granted." This is not the kind of pessimism one would expect from a high-ranking American bureaucrat and Americans could ignore the warning at their own peril.

When we finally reached Los Angeles, Davan Maharaj, Trinidad-born managing editor of the *Los Angeles Times* could answer our inquiries at lunch at a Mexican grill house with optimism. "The United States," he said, "appears to be blessed by Providence and whenever the country seems to be on the brink of disaster, something miraculous happens to fix the lives of Americans." I thought of the tech-stock bubble that on 18 December 2000 had forced Greenspan to tell President-elect George W. Bush that the short-term outlook for the United States was not good. "For the first time in years, we seemed to be faced with the real possibility of recession," Greenspan recalled telling Bush after his court victory. But the US had weathered this storm and others and was going blithely along to another election with the promise to remake America. And yet, it was not possible to escape the shiftless feeling that the United States was a tinderbox and that any day the streets could erupt into chaos and anarchy. There was too much hate fanned by the rage of Republicans against Democrats and the President.

After the January shooting of Democratic Congresswoman Gabrielle Giffords during a meeting with constituents in a supermarket parking lot in Arizona, Republicans of the Tea Party ilk appeared however to be suddenly aware of the risks they were taking with a population that was stressed out over the loss of jobs and homes and the insecurity of retirement. But the disrespect towards President Barack Obama had not been replaced by the spirit of compromise and the willingness for bipartisan leadership that he called for in Congress. And this was the case even up to April 2012 when rocker Ted Nugent denounced Obama and his top advisers as "evil" and urged National Rifle Association members to help "chop their heads off in November." Nugent was speking at the NRAs annual gathering and he urged his listeners "to clean house in this vile, evil, America-hating administration". No American hearing him could fail to understand what evil he himself had espoused and was advocating.

The simple truth is this was not an example of the right to free speech that so many of our respondents identified as the soul of America; it was a message of hate. And the US Secret Service in

Oklahoma must have recalled Timothy McVeigh and the city bombing that had killed 168 people on 19 April 1995. They understood that it was time to question Nugent and the agency did meet with him and said later that the issue had been "resolved." There is undoubtedly a problem in the country with the irrational hate of Americans and all good Americans must be able to see that America is not dealing with loonies and pranksters but with people who are sick and who lack respect for their neighbours and for themselves. The Secret Service rampage in Colombia was another sign that Americans are faced with a national disease and with individuals who put their own interests before everything else, before service, self-sacrifice and honour. It is clear that early Americans were too arrogant to learn anything from the demeanour and nobility of the slaves they brutalised and Americans today are as consumed by violence and depravity as their ancestors were.

On 4 April 2012, for example, *Good Morning America* reported that gun sales were booming and asked whether it was because of President Obama or zombies. Buyers in record numbers, retailers said, were flooding into gun stores. Ammo, too, was flying off the shelves the network said. The reasons for the spike included fears that a second Obama administration might restrict gun ownership and the popularity of TV shows devoted to doomsday preparation and the killing of zombies. "He's never been pro-gun," said the owner of a Texas gun purveyor called the Houston Armory. The President, the man insisted, has been "pretty coy" about his antipathy toward guns and that he likely would remain so during the campaign because to do otherwise would "upset a lot of people." But Alan Korwin, author of nine books on gun laws, including *Gun Laws of America*, said gun owners were worried that the President, as a lame duck, will clamp down as never before on gun ownership.

There were also reports that stocks of gun makers were surging. Sturm, Ruger's share price was up 55 per cent this year. Smith & Wesson soared 91 per cent. Sporting goods and hunting retailer Cabela's was up 53 per cent. Other forces besides politics, though, explained the current boom. "There are the preppers," explained one seller, "and then there is this whole Zombie Apocalypse thing." It was a reference to two trends in popular culture. The first is a National Geographic TV show called "Doomsday Preppers" that chronicled the preparations being made by people convinced that a doomsday of some kind is coming. A whole industry in fact had sprung up to sell preppers survival and self-defense goods, including guns and ammo. Then there are the zombies – zombie movies, zombie comics, zombie novels, zombie TV shows. Americans' fascination with all things zombie has grown to such proportions that arms manufactures have come out with zombie-specific firearms and ammo.

An Associated Press report by Eileen Sullivan and Jack Gillum on 19 October 2012 said that President Barack Obama has presided over a heyday for the gun industry despite predictions by the National Rifle Association four years ago that he would be the "most anti-gun president in American history." Gun buyers fear that Obama wants to restrict their purchases, especially if he were re-elected. But the analysis by The Associated Press of data tracking the health of the gun industry shows that sales are on the rise, so much that some gun manufacturers can't make enough guns fast enough. Major gun company stock prices are up. The number of federally licensed, retail gun dealers is increasing for the first time in nearly 20 years. The NRA is bursting with cash and political clout. And Washington has expressed little interest in passing new gun laws, despite renewed calls to do so after recent deadly shootings in Colorado and Wisconsin.

The report stated that Obama has made no promises to impose new gun control legislation and doesn't have the support in Congress or among voters even if he did. During his second presidential debate, Obama suggested renewing a U.S. ban on assault weapons and coming up with an overall strategy to reduce violence, but both Obama and Republican presidential nominee Mitt Romney said the government needs to enforce gun laws already on the books. "The driver is President Obama. He's the best thing that ever happened to the firearm industry," said Jim Barrett, an industry analyst at C.L. King & Associates Inc. in New York.

Tennessee lawyer Brian Manookian said he never considered himself a gun enthusiast like others in his state. He owns only one handgun. But the firearms industry has proved so lucrative for him that he's enthusiastic now. Manookian and his business partner, Gary Semanchik, opened a $5 million firearms retail and training complex in September in Nashville. Inventory is selling three to four times faster than they expected since the facility opened. "It is a very strong investment," Manookian said. Others agree. For the first time since 1993, the number of federally licensed retail gun dealers in the U.S. increased slightly in 2010 and 2011, as the country added 1,167 more licensed retail gun dealers, according to Bureau of Alcohol, Tobacco, Firearms and Explosives records. After the assault weapons ban in 1994, the number of gun dealerships dropped annually until 2010. As of October 2012, there were 50,812 retail gun dealers – that's 3,303 more than in 2009. "Business has been very good," said Frederick Prehn, who a year ago opened a small gun store above his dentistry practice in Wausau, Wis. In the past year, Prehn has relocated twice to larger spaces and gone from one employee to eight.

It is easy of course to read the statistics of guns and crime and to see the United States on the edge of a precipice. However crime is not an American invention and no single individual in any other part of the world could find pride to gloat at Americans. Greed, drugs and hate have made it a flat world too. In India, for example, and in the same spring, Bollywood actress Meenakshi Thapar was kidnapped by two fellow actors, who then beheaded her after extorting money from her family. Thapar, 26, had appeared in an Indian horror film in 2011, where she met her alleged killers. In Norway people are still horrified over the killing of 77 people, mostly teenagers, by Anders Behring Breivik, who has been described as an anti-Islamic fanatic and who has said in court that he would do it all over again. In London a British diplomat, George Fergusson, 56, lost sight in his left eye after being attacked as he walked through Hammersmith in West London. And in Trinidad, the 18-year-old daughter of an attorney, Nikita Ramischand, died from stabbing injuries. And yet the stories of crime in the United States still shock and traumatize. In Las Vegas, a 10-year-old girl was sexually assaulted before she died in a bludgeoning attack that also killed her mother and left her father with critical head injuries in a blood-splattered home. Officers found the bodies after the girl's 9-year-old brother arrived at school saying that his mom and sister were dead.

III

THINKING AMERICANS must be at once worried and scared however. The surge in gun sales is abnormal and points to a disturbing development in U.S. life. There have been police reports of threats made against the President and the First Lady and the talk and terror is widespread and involves civilians as well as government representatives who are expected to uphold the law. Federal agents in Washington State, writes Devin Dwyer of ABC OTUS News, arrested an armed man accused of making threats against President Obama. "A threat against the president was delivered via email to a general FBI inbox," said Cathy Schrock with the Federal Way Police. "The Secret Service went down to investigate and the defendant was found to be armed when they arrived at the apartment." Another report came from Jason Sickles of Yahoo! / The Lookout who stated that a Texas judge warned about possible "civil war" if President Obama is re-elected. And on 4 October 2012 the chief federal judge for Montana said he would step down from the post after forwarding a racist joke involving President Obama. U.S. Courts spokeswoman Karen Redmond said U.S. District Judge Richard Cebull of Billings asked the 9th U.S. Circuit Court of Appeals to review his conduct after he was criticized for an email that included a joke about bestiality and Obama's mother. After one hundred and fifty years the country seems to have stepped back into the dark abyss of the past and on some days there is diminishing hope that white and black Americans are on their way to find respect and common ground.

When we look back there might have been a case for the presence of so many guns at the dawn of America when Americans were involved in wrongfully seizing the land from indigenous tribes of Indians bent on protecting their lives and their rights. Some film-makers have reminded us of this evil as the 1967 film *Hombre* with Paul Newman did and the 1986 made-for-Television *Stagecoach* with Willie Nelson playing the role of Doc Holiday showed. But the country moved away from its bloody past and now lays claim to a civilized code of conduct and to the rule of law. Today however all these gains seem like an invention and there is wonder if the peace was a lie and the respect was a fraud. Was there any change in the fate of black Americans? Lincoln, for example, was forced to send a warning to Lt. Col. John Glenn on 7 February 1965 that complaints were made to him that Glenn was forcing Negroes into the military service and even torturing them. "You must not force Negroes," Lincoln wrote, "any more than white men." The war indeed did not produce a level playing field for black Americans and time has not erased the discrimination that white Americans always harbored against black Americans and at no time is this not more evident than nowadays when there are signs that Barack Obama will still be in the White House after 6 November 2012.

And the evidence of bad blood mounts. On 24 October 2012, Gregory J. Krieg of ABC OTUS News wrote that former vice presidential candidate Sarah Palin released a statement on her Facebook page accusing President Obama of engaging in "shuck and jive shtick" regarding September's attack in Benghazi, Libya. "Why the lies? Why the cover up? Why the dissembling about the cause of the murder of our ambassador on the anniversary of the worst terrorist attacks on American soil? We deserve answers to this. President Obama's shuck and jive shtick with these Benghazi lies must end," Palin wrote. For those who aren't familiar with the phrase said Krieg, "shuck and jive" is a racially-tinged expression. According to the user-submitted Urban Dictionary, the term "originally referred to the intentionally misleading words and actions that African-Americans would employ in order to deceive racist Euro-Americans in power, both during the period of slavery and afterwards." And as Politico points out, this isn't the first time the phrase has come up and inspired controversy. Several years ago, Andrew Cuomo, then New York's Attorney General, used the expression while campaigning for Hillary Rodham Clinton. "You can't shuck and jive at a press conference. All those moves you can make with the press don't work when you're in someone's living room." Cuomo was promptly blasted by CNN's Roland Martin, who wrote, "Shucking and jiving have long been words used as a negative assessment of African Americans, along the lines of a 'foot shufflin' Negro.' In fact, I don't recall ever hearing the phrase used in reference to anyone white." Earlier, conservative pundit Ann Coulter inspired outrage when she called President Obama a "retard" following his Florida debate with Mitt Romney. An athlete with Down Syndrome wrote an open letter to Coulter in response. "Come on Ms. Coulter," he wrote. "You aren't dumb and you aren't shallow. So why are you continually using a word like the R-word as an insult?" wrote Krieg.

Here too Lincoln might have been right about the problems of race: they will not go away. And nowadays it is difficult for any intelligent man to recall the horrors of the Ku Klux Klan and to believe that the campaign of terror against blacks, which included arson, beatings and the nasty habit of shooting and hanging black Americans, was intended only to protect themselves and their property as the men who shot Summer Moody have claimed. The evidence shows that they were a blood-thirsty lot and their crimes against people who were often in the wrong place at the wrong time destroyed the hope of any real trust between white and black as most Americans read today in the Trayvon Martin shooting. From the beginning the soil of the country was soaked with the blood of indigenous Indians and uprooted Africans and the horror of these crimes had sometimes escaped the public conscience of George Washington, Thomas Jefferson and George Mason IV who had all kept slaves and by this act had legitimized the abomination of slavery. But as Lincoln had said in Springfield, Illinois, quoting the Scriptures, "a house divided against itself cannot stand." It was not until the civil rights movement of the 1960s however that the illusion of a homogeneous American society was questioned and for the first time in the 20th century concerns about national identity, about a multiracial, multicultural society, were debated.

Thus it was good sense not to assume the equality and comfort of black Americans as we moved from city to city and to shrug off the reports about the unstable character of American life and its dismal destiny. It might not be Armageddon, but the warnings were not to be ignored, nor the tattoos and graffiti slighted. Years ago when we were visiting Aunt Bessie Porter in Jamaica, Long Island, she said she was about to call the New York Police Department when we were late returning from a shopping trip and she feared that something horrible had happened to us. She had lived long enough to know that Providence did not always shield the innocent. We had been going to the United States for more than half a century – and indeed Rhona had graduated from Marygrove College in Detroit and our sons, Marc and Simon, had graduated from Dartmouth College in New Hampshire and from the University of Miami in Florida – and we believed that we had not experienced attacks of racism or crime. But we were not so naïve to think that while we were in the United States we had earned ourselves immunity by our good looks or good manners and we would be safe from every type of mischief the Devil puts in the hearts and hands of men.

As we walked the streets of Detroit and shuddered at the ramshackle state of buildings, the pestilence of foreclosures, and the depressed and despairing looks of Detroiters, we realized that in New York, Washington DC, and Chicago we had tended to close our eyes to the plight of black Americans and possibly saw them, as the writers of American textbooks had done up to the 1960s, as a footnote of contemporary America. The truth is the civil war had not made life a better proposition for black Americans and according to the view of some Americans, Andrew Johnson was the wrong man for the presidency after the war. He was said to have lacked dignity and judgment and was without concerns for the rights of the freed slaves. It was hardly surprising however. "There is a natural disgust in the minds of nearly all white people," Lincoln had said, "to the idea of an indiscriminate amalgamation of white and black races." But there was the view too, espoused by Democrats said Lincoln, that "slavery is as good as freedom". It is clear that Andrew Johnson was not the only villain in America's history; the system of slavery had tarnished other prominent Americans.

In Washington DC we had visited the ancestral home and estate of George Mason IV with Ray Boddie, a native of North Carolina, and I had wondered about his role in showing white Americans the luxury lifestyle of a man who had built his 5,500-acre plantation of tobacco and corn on the backs of slaves. The father of four boys, Ray Boddie is friendly, cheerful and god-fearing and is married to Trinidad-born Myrna Porter who had served in the US army as a nurse. Did he see himself as an Uncle Tom I wondered when we visited Gunston Hall where he worked as a guide?

I remembered that the question drew a rebuke from Rhona and Xiuling. I hadn't asked 82-year-old Jawaharlal Ramnarace who was from Fyzabad, Trinidad, if *he* was an Uncle Tom they said even though his life, from his own accounting, was an example of a black man living out his fantasies of a white man and hoping for the rewards his imitation would bring him. Ramnarace had left Trinidad in the nineteen-fifties and had lived and worked with white Americans earning he thought their respect; but now as a retired person he was outside of the old circle of colleagues whom he once counted as friends. His story was that he had spent years with the U.S. Military perfecting rockets and flares that he said were used in Vietnam and in other wars.

In *Rocket and Space Science Series*, a publication of the Amateur Rocket Association, Ramnarace is described as a Project Engineer with the Badger Army Ammunition Plant. He recalled the shock he suffered in 1968 when a million pounds of explosion a day he said was dropped on Vietnam, killing men, women and children. "We burnt their houses, destroyed their fields, and killed their animals. When I asked my superior officer why we did these gruesome things, he said, *They are communists*." But the atrocities did not bother him. "I didn't kill anybody," he says defensively.

Ramnarace's skills assisted however the "Imperial Grand Strategy", to use the description of Noam Chomsky in *Hegemony or Survival*, and were employed to develop "forces that would be strong enough to dissuade potential adversaries from pursuing a military build-up in hopes of surpassing, or equaling, the power of the United States." This is how Ramnarace sees it, so why now the indifference that borders on a lack of respect, ingratitude and discrimination? It was impossible not to discern in his manner and his voice, as he barbequed chicken and pork on an outside fire, that "white adults teach you how to hate and what to hate." And now he says, not entirely with pleasure, "all my friends are black." After spending two days interviewing him for a documentary that was planned of his life, it was obvious that "Uncle Ram", as everyone called him, believed that he had served his masters with distinction but he was not given the recognition he should have got for his work and patents because of his race. "If I were white," he insisted, "I am sure it would have made the difference between prominence and anonymity." It was easy to see that he was bitter and resented being black, though he insisted he was Indian and believed that Indians had done much better than "a lot of the white people in America. Now they were investing in the United States, especially in motels." Though he didn't get the respect he felt he deserved, he was happy in the U.S. "I was treated worse in Trinidad by white-skinned Negroes," he said telling of his days at Queen's Royal College during the period of colonialism that followed slavery in the Caribbean and before the country became an independent nation.

His concern with his own fate made me wonder if he had ever really suspected what it was to be black in the United States and what it had been to be a slave or the son or daughter of parents who were slaves. I was thinking of Dave Harold whose resistance to black profiling in the U.S. Navy had landed him in the brig of his warship. Or, had he read the Harriet Beecher Stowe novel, *Uncle Tom's Cabin*, which in 1851 had exposed the ruthlessness of slavery? Reading did not seem to be a passion with him however as it had been for an old schoolmate named V.S. Naipaul. "I write to the newspapers," he said gloomily at one time, "but they won't publish what I write about Jews in the *Washington Post*."

When we left him, Xiuling asked what he meant by "white-skinned Negroes".

"Do you think it is an oxymoron?" Rhona said.

"In the West Indies," I explained, "color, that is the color of one's skin, plays a big part in society. Judgments are made all the time on the character of someone who is black or brown skinned. Before the black power movement of 1970 for instance you couldn't find a black girl or woman working in one of our banks. Bank jobs were reserved for white girls and for Chinese. Young black males and females went into the Public Service. Prime Minister Eric Williams did a lot to remove this color bar but he did not do it on his own. He was helped by what became known, after 1970, as Black Power protests that were organized by the National Joint Action Committee and which held Stokely Carmichael as one of its poster models. But don't place any bets on the likelihood that the age of discrimination has passed and that racial slurs like the N word and the C word have been put to rest. When we applied for new ID cards in 2010, for example, Rhona was described as *brown* while I who was not well at the time and looked miserably pale was described as *light-brown*. People still see color and genuflect to it. But this is not a problem only for Trinidadians. It is obvious that the problems of race never went away after emancipation and the presence today of a black president is often a red flag to many Americans."

The point is race creates a brittle and hostile environment and distrust is read in every unusual word or group of words. According to *Globe* correspondent Callum Borchers, for example, the Obama campaign offered no apology for Vice President Joe Biden's "chains" remark, refusing even to call it a poor choice of words as Republicans accused the President's re-election campaign of race baiting. At a rally in Virginia, Biden told an audience that included hundreds of African-Americans that Republican challenger Mitt Romney and his running-mate, Paul Ryan, are "going to put y'all back in chains." Biden made the comment while talking about bank regulations and later said he was referencing to Ryan's promise to "unshackle" the economy, but critics have accused him of inappropriately using a slavery metaphor and a *Globe* editorial called for Biden to apologize.

Obama's deputy campaign manager, Stephanie Cutter, said on CNN's *State of the Union* that Biden had nothing to apologize for. "Let's look at what the Vice President said. Speaker [John] Boehner and even Paul Ryan have been traveling this country talking about the need to unshackle the private sector, to unshackle the financial industry," Cutter said. "And the vice president was just taking that metaphor a step further and talking about wanting to put other people in shackles. And the word that he used, chains, is a distraction from the larger argument." Asked by host Jim Acosta whether the Obama campaign would acknowledge Biden made a poor choice of words, Cutter said it is the Romney campaign that has chosen its words poorly. "If we want to talk about words on the campaign trail that are poor choices of words, let's talk about Mitt Romney's, when he's been traveling for the last few years basically calling the President un-American, that the President wanted to make this a less Christian nation," Cutter said. "Those are poor choices of words, and that's what we find completely offensive."

Later on the same program, former Republican presidential candidate Rick Santorum said Biden's remark was offensive. "You saw Vice-President Biden play the race card in Virginia," Santorum said. The former Pennsylvania senator said, based on his own experience at similar rallies, that Biden was likely "trying to develop [an] affinity" with a Southern audience by using the word "y'all" but that "he did so in a very horrendous way. And he should apologize," Santorum added. Former New York City Mayor Rudy Giuliani, a GOP presidential candidate in 2008, said on CBS's *Face the Nation* that Biden was guilty of an "absolutely blatant appeal to racism" and called on Democrats to say Biden had gone too far. Illinois Senator Dick Durbin, appearing with Giuliani, said Biden's remark "may have been a misuse of words" but defended the vice president, saying "there isn't a racist bone in Joe Biden's body." On NBC's *Meet the Press*, Maryland Governor Martin O'Malley used the exact same phrase to defend Biden but said the vice president had made an "indelicate choice of words."

Had I been guilty also of an indelicate choice of words?

However Ray Boddie was not upset with the question. I recalled a book I had seen on the coffee table in his home in Woodbridge, Virginia: *The Boddies in America: From 1790 to 1997*. It was a collection of Boddie census records. "When I went there at first," Ray said in answer to my query, "I had worried about this stereotype being attached to me, but as soon as I started to work I never saw myself as an Uncle Tom. I am aware that racial and ethnic prejudices still exist in the United States today but I am learning a lot about America's history and how to deal with its uglier aspects from the questions people ask me." I had no doubt that he would see that the life of this American patriot was blemished because of his role in slavery and even though George Mason IV had shown a willingness to free his slaves before his death in 1792, this was not the wish of his family and it was his grandson who wrote the heinous Fugitive Slave Act of 1850. There is a lot about the "uglier aspects" of American history that Ray would discover I was sure. And his journey of discovery would take him past the relentless war waged against the Indians and their confinement to reservations – a grotesque part of the madness that corrupts still today America and American values. A country is not as Ms. Musaracchia says only about food, money, real estate and power. It is also about justice and allowing men to live with dignity.

Obama has pointed to the destructive nature of American administrations in his *Audacity of Hope*. "As American soldiers and settlers moved steadily west and southwest, successive administrations described the annexation of territory in terms of 'manifest destiny' – the conviction that such expansion was pre-ordained, part of God's plan to extend what Andrew Jackson called 'the area of freedom' across the continent. Of course, manifest destiny also meant bloody and violent conquest – of Native American tribes forcibly removed from their lands. It was a conquest that, like slavery, contradicted America's founding principles and tended to be justified in explicitly racist terms, a conquest that American mythology has always had difficulty fully absorbing but that other countries recognized for what it was – an exercise in raw power."

In her 1979 classic, *America Revised*, Frances FitzGerald wrote that in the texts of the 1830s and 1840s, "The North American Indians are presented as interesting, important people in spite of the fact that there are not Christians." But later writers referred to the Indian nations as "savage", "barbarous", and "half-civilized" even as Americans plundered their villages and destroyed their civilization. When I read the FitzGerald texts I thought of Dave Harold's Choctaw mother, beautiful in the portrait on the desk where he worked, and belonging to a class of blacks called Creoles and considered a rank above the rest of the colored population as mulattoes were in the West Indies. There had been equal or angrier resentment against Africans and Black Americans that did not enter American textbooks until the mid-sixties. In the nineteen-thirties wrote Ms. FitzGerald the most progressive of social histories identified 'the Negro' as a 'social problem' and few books published then or earlier noted the existence of blacks in America. Still fewer recorded the name of an individual and "in the vast majority of books there were only 'the slaves' – slaves who had appeared magically in this country at some unspecified time and had disappeared with the end of the Civil War. The textbooks made many discoveries about Americans during the 1960s and "the country conceived as male and Anglo-Saxon turned out to be filled with blacks, ethnics, Indians, Asians and women." The shattering of the image of homogeneous American society she wrote occurred not because of pressure from Irish-Americans, Italian-Americans or Jews but because of the black civil rights movement.

But apart from race there is another urgent problem that is undermining American stability. It is the economic future of the United States. On 17 July 2012 Jeffe Macke wrote in Breakout that according to CEO and Chief Global Strategist of Euro Pacific Capital Peter Schiff, "the U.S. economy is heading for an economic crash that will make 2008 look like a walk in the park." Stimulus programs can delay this day of reckoning, but only for so long and only at the expense of making the eventual meltdown much worse. Schiff, who had warned investors about the housing and financial crisis in his 2007 book *Crash Proof*, says the Fed's palliative efforts during the housing meltdown have made the next crisis inevitable. "We've got a much bigger collapse coming, and not just of the markets but of the economy," Schiff said. "It's like what you're seeing in Europe right now, only worse."

Macke writes that in this nightmare scenario detailed in *The Real Crash: America's Coming Bankruptcy*, the current economic pause is actually the beginning of a material slowdown or recession into year-end. At that point, the Federal Reserve will unleash a third round of Quantitative Easing – weakening the dollar without jump-starting the economy. As a result of dollar weakness, import prices rise, pressing the margins of corporate America. Lower margins lead to heavy layoffs; sending millions of workers into unemployment during a time when they can least afford it. Banks fail, housing collapses, and taxes are raised in a futile effort to give the government the capital to try more futile stimulus. "That's when it really is going to get interesting, because that's when we hit our real fiscal cliff, when we're going to have to slash government spending," says Schiff. Those cuts he insisted would not be unlike the draconian austerity measures in Greece, with programs like Social Security and Medicare being dramatically cut or possibly disappearing entirely. "Alternatively, we can bail everybody out, pretend we can print our way out of a crisis, and, instead, we have runaway inflation, or hyper-inflation, which is going to be far worse than the collapse we would have if we did the right thing and just let everything implode," he said.

It was the kind of scenario we were grappling with on 17 September 2011 when we were discussing the problems of the economy with Dave Harold on the bank of the Detroit River. A new movement had erupted in New York City when a group of young Americans started the Occupy Wall Street protest. Several days before when we left Ellis Island we had walked to Wall Street and had taken pictures in front of Wall Street's charging bull that characterizes the American Stock Exchange. We were sure as we toasted the health of the four generations of Harolds that the protest struck a chord in the hearts of most Americans who with few exceptions had not been taught anything about the subject of money. The nineteenth century writers, according to Ms. FitzGerald, had paid no attention to economics at all; their interest had lain in earthquakes, wars and presidents.

This failure to teach Americans about the economy was a serious misstep; another equally serious faux pas was the assertion that Americans are all alike, no matter what their color or their background might be. In fact, Daniel P. Moynihan and Nathan Glazer's sociological study, *Beyond the Melting Pot*, tends to mislead Americans when it speaks about an ethnic truth in describing the "wonderful variety of life in America". And to side with Ms. FitzGerald the textbooks' doctrine of American homogeneity is nowhere more false than in the reporting of economics in American life. "In this most economically successful of societies," she wrote, "a child can hardly discover what a corporation is, to say nothing of the nature of the economy. And it has always been that way." Wood, Gabriel and Biller in their *America, Its People and Values*, stated clearly that "closely related to the problems of minority groups and civil rights was the problem of poverty in America. Many Americans were affected by poverty, or being poor, but minority groups were especially affected."

And in the years after World War II when American prosperity had reached an all-time high and when economists had declared that America was an "affluent society", there was another part of America writes Ms. FitzGerald where large numbers were classified as poor – those lacking enough income to buy the products and services needed for an adequate standard of living. As Wood, Gabriel and Biller discovered, in the 1970s the American poor were found throughout the nation, in rural areas as well as urban areas. Some of them had no skills and were unable to get jobs. Many were workers who had lost their jobs because new methods of production had wiped out many jobs in their industries. Clearly the widening gap between the rich and the poor, and the sense that their lives were no better after Jimmy Carter's fumbling presidency, had moved Americans to put their trust in an actor who had achieved moderate success in films. But the truth is politics is never enough to change a nation's destiny and Ronald Reagan's greatest achievements were the wooing of Margaret Thatcher and the collapse of the Berlin Wall, both events outside of main street America.

The Wall Street protests of September 2011 that have led to Occupy protests and movements around the world are the result of one Administration after another's failure to unite Americans under the banner that identifies and encourages justice and self-sacrifice. The main issues for the nation had not changed under a Democrat or Republican White House and they are still social and economic inequality, greed, corruption and the undue influence of corporations on government. And yet the world's consensus is that America has built "the world's most vibrant economy and democracy precisely because in every historical turn since its founding, it has applied its own particular formula for prosperity." But even if Wall Street analysts and journalists think so, these successes are not enough and the protest group's slogan, *We are the 99%*, for example, addresses the growing income inequality and wealth distribution in the U.S. between the wealthiest 1 per cent and the rest of the population.

So the writing was on the wall for CEOs with their inflated packages and seven months after the first Wall Street protest their ire struck at the heart of Citigroup's CEO Vikram Pandit who was refused a bonus of millions of dollars. Citi shareholders didn't think that Mr. Pandit should be paid an extra $15 million. They gave a vote of no confidence to Pandit's board-approved compensation package, snubbing Pandit and sounding a clarion call to other investors that it was time to fight excessive executive pay. This was only the beginning for Americans' fight in modern times for a fairer slice of the economic pie.

IV

BUT EVEN though Americans might be squeamish about the subject of race and money, they are never squeamish about sex and it is fairly true to say that the Kardashians – Kourtney, Kim and Khloe – did not start a trend but they are equipped with the goods and the brass to take part in the public display and discussion of sex. It is of course a subject that is always in your face wherever you are in the United States and over time one's appetite for it is honed by popular news magazines, popular television shows, popular films, popular artistes and popular marketing strategies. And in Guangzhou, in Beijing and in Shanghai, young Chinese audiences are as familiar with scenes and dialogue from *Sex and the City* as they were at one time with the precepts of Chairman Mao's *Little Red Book*. There is enough in *Sex and the City* and on nearly every new sitcom to make Americans think that sex like cereals for breakfast is an American institution and is never to be refused. As Carrie in *Sex and the City* says, waving the Stars and Stripes for promiscuity, "There are 1.3 million single men in New York, 1.8 million single women, and of these more than 3 million people, about 12 think they're having enough sex." It is supposed to be a joke, a classic line of dialogue, but it adequately describes the American addiction for sex.

This was the audacity behind Meghan McCain's assertion to *Playboy* that "I love sex and I love men." Dyland Stableford had written in The Cutline on 16 March 2012 that Ms. McCain was at the time at a book party for Perez Hilton and according to the Associated Press she gave a revealing interview to *Playboy*. "I'm not private about anything," the daughter of Arizona Sen. John McCain told the magazine. She said that had her father won the 2008 election, the White House would certainly be a different place with her in it. "You would have the craziest first daughter ever, who'd be making ridiculous headlines and hurting the administration every step of the way. That aside, I think Dad would have made an incredible president. The recession wouldn't have been as bad as it is now. We wouldn't be pulling troops out of Afghanistan and Iraq. I think morale in the military and in the country at large would be higher, and we'd be much further on the road to recovery." While she supports same-sex marriage, she's not gay, she said. "I'm strickly dickly... It might simplify my life if I were gay, but no. ... For me, it's an issue of civil rights. Who people want to sleep with and who they want to love should not have anything to do with government politics at all. And if you see me in a gay bar, it's only because they play the best music and my gay friends like to dance. Gay guys love me. It's the big boobs and blond hair."

Not all Americans are into gay bars, big boobs and blond hair, however, and from Los Angeles Joshua L. Weinstein of Reuters had reported on 2 February 2012 that "One Million Moms", a project of the American Family Association, were angry at JC Penney because the Texas-based department store has hired Ellen DeGeneres as a spokeswoman. Why? Well because DeGeneres is gay, and open about it. "Funny that JC Penney thinks hiring an open homosexual spokesperson will help their business when most of their customers are traditional families," One Million Moms wrote on their website. "DeGeneres is not a true representation of the type of families that shop at their store. The majority of JC Penney shoppers will be offended and choose to no longer shop there." One Million Moms asked people to call JC Penney to complain. With this campaign, One Million Moms, which claims to be "the most powerful tool you have to stand against the immorality, violence, vulgarity and profanity the entertainment media is throwing at your children," was going after one of the country's most-beloved television hosts Reuters said. The moms wanted JC Penney to replace Ellen DeGeneres as their new spokesperson. The Gay and Lesbian Alliance Against Discrimination disagreed. "A vast majority of Americans today support Ellen as well as their LGBT friends and family members," Herndon Graddick, a GLAAD spokesman said in a written statement. "Selecting an out performer who has inspired and entertained millions, is not only a smart business practice, but a reflection of how LGBT Americans today are an integral and valued part of the fabric of our culture." DeGeneres' daytime talk show it pointed out has more viewers than the American Family Association has moms. Between January 16 and January 22, *Ellen* averaged 3.38 million viewers – or 2.38 million more people than the AFA has mothers.

The fact is Americans' appetite for sex is inexhaustible as 11-year-olds given notebook computers by the People's Partnership Government in Trinidad and Tobago after the 2010 general elections could be finding out. And the narrative about sex on television is unending. On 18 October 2012, for example, Christina Aguilera was telling Access Hollywood that she didn't like to wear underwear. Ms. Aguilera told Chelsea Handler on *Chelsea Lately* that she likes a little freedom under her clothes. "I don't like to wear underwear. I like to be as free as possible at all times. It's just who I am. It's empowering," Ms. Aguilera added.

When I began researching this book in 2012 the Internet was buzzing with stories about Jenny McCarthy's *Playboy* cover that had debuted online in June. Ms. McCarthy was not a stranger to posing nude; she first posed in 1993. She is now 39 and a mother to a 10-year-old son. And then there was Charlize Theron who was reported by *Us* magazine to have made "slutty" comments about being naked. She said that she has no qualms about taking her clothes off. The

Academy Award winner, who is 36, shares the cover of *W*'s August issue with her *Prometheus* costar Michael Fassbender, who is 35. The magazine spread features the scantily-clad actors fondling each other in a warehouse. When asked if it's harder to film a death scene or a sex scene, Theron quipped, "It depends on who you're doing the sex scene with. I don't have issues being naked. That sounds very slut. What I mean is, I'm not hung up on my body."

What effect does all this have on teenagers in Trinidad and Tobago who in 2010 were given laptop computers on their entry into secondary schools? "Computers do enrich our lives," says 13-year-old Giovanna de Souza, a student of Holy Name Convent in Port of Spain. "The Internet has introduced me and my sisters to show people and lifestyles we would not have known unless we had travelled to the United States. Every one of my school friends has applauded the government's decision to give students notebooks." It could be too early to judge the effect that the lead singer in the band, *My Chemical Romance*, would have on her studies and the studies of her younger sisters, Genevieve, aged 11, and the twins, 9-year-old Shania and Shakira. But right now music is their passion and their hope is to go to the US to meet stars like Justin Beiber, Frank Iero and Gerard Way whom they say unabashedly they love. Frankly, I have no problem with that and I would prefer them to watch sex shows than *Criminal Minds*. It's a matter of parental guidance and discretion. And it's the same as years ago, long before the Internet, when the grandmothers of today's teenagers used to say they had a crush on Jeff Chandler, James Dean and Elvis Presley. Language and feelings then were more discreet, less a problem for parents and psychologists, but the teenage obsessions were the same.

V

LET ME say straight away that I have nothing against sex. I like women and I have always enjoyed making love. And I believe that consensual sex between adults in the privacy of their home is not anyone else's business. From time to time because of the incidence of rape, child assault, pornography and pedophilia there have been complaints about the high visibility of sex in the media, in films and on television but usually they are storms that blow away leaving no casualty. But this is so too because the protagonists, the defenders of open sex, wage unconditional war against every conservative attempt to bridle sexual activity. In the May 2012 issue of *Playboy*, for example, Hugh Hefner took up his pen to fight off a new threat he sees. Hefner re-asserts his leadership in the sexual revolution with an editorial headlined, "The War Against Sex" in which he blasts conservatives for wanting to pound on America's bedroom doors. Hefner clearly enjoys the openness in the country about sex, the candor with which actors and entertainers talk about their love affairs and their bodies. It is also clear that Hefner has always seen the magazine and the Playboy Mansion as the Alamo in his fights against attempts to introduce any standard of prudery or strict old-fashioned morality. These are battles we have already fought and soundly won, he wrote, but "I want to believe that what we are hearing is the death knell of a desperate minority clinging to a fading ideology." Decades ago, said Hefner, "we fought back against these moral charlatans because your sex life, your fantasies and desires, your plans to have or not have a family, none of that is anyone else's business, especially not the government's."

I have not been so militant and I hadn't kept in touch with news of American sex idols during the twelve years I was in China and knew nothing, for example, of Jennifer Love Hewitt until I came across a report about her this year in Yahoo News. According to the report Ms. Love Hewitt got a big surprise during an appearance on *Jimmy Kimmel Live*. I had never even heard of Jimmy Kimmel. On the late night talk show to promote *The Client List*, a new Lifetime series in which she plays a single mom who turns to prostitution to support her children, Kimmel told the 33-year-old actress that a huge billboard for the show – with her cleavage front and center – had been placed directly outside of his office window. The host then had a staffer carry a "gift" for the star – a square section of the billboard, which had recently been taken down, featuring just a close-up shot of her breasts. And in another recent share on Twitter, the actress posted a photo in which she appears without makeup. While she was all about her bare face in the photo, she said she has no plans to share her exposed body on camera – ever. "I wouldn't have done nudity," she said while promoting the show at a press event. "That's not something that I feel particularly comfortable with… I also think that it's sexier not to show everything. I feel like imaginations can do more."

This was not the feeling of Heidi Klum. I had seen online in an ABC News report Ms. Klum baring all in a cover shoot for the May issue of *Allure*. Klum, a mother of four, had said that she had no issue with posing nude. "I think you just have to be comfortable in your skin," said the 38-year-old. "But I'm a nudist in any case, I've never had a problem with my body and I don't really care what people think." She said she had never had any cosmetic surgery. "Ask me again when I'm 65, but I'm proud to be able to say, in this day and age, I haven't done anything. Everyone has a view of what's pretty and what's not pretty, and surgery just doesn't look pretty to me." Ms. Klum discussed her husband of seven years from whom she had filed for divorce. "I don't resent anything that ever happened," she said. "Things just turn out the way they turn out."

This openness about sex didn't take place when I was a young man and I am aware that teenagers like Giovanna de Souza could easily access these conversations even with the strictest of mothers. In my time girls were expected to be modest and virtuous; they did not feel the need to compete with boys as they appear to do today and think that it is even a challenge to become pregnant as students in an American school once confessed. It is possible that times have changed since the Internet and the record of this sexual revolution is always there no matter how many years have passed. "Once you have pasted something on the Internet," Victor Goden warned me, "it's there forever." And to show easy access to all these websites, he insisted that I could find on YouTube "Granny Quilla talks about Kamla", the obscene two-year-old posting of a teenager denouncing the first woman Prime Minister of Trinidad and Tobago, Kamla Persad-Bissessar. "It's on record and it will be there for years to come," Goden who is married to my daughter, Deborah, said, "unless the Internet crashes."

There is no doubt that the Internet could be a Pandora Box. For a time I had my own version of Heidi Fleiss who tried to get me to eat the forbidden fruit and to swear that I had the means to make her time in bed financially profitable. Then I went to the United States and when I came back I lost contact with Hetty Aron who used to tell me how horny she was. Her last words to me were, "Gonna change my clothes. Wanna watch." We were not linked up by cam, however, so I had to miss this opportunity of a lifetime. Then out of the blue I had this spam from something called F***book. "We can't make it any easier to get laid tonight," it boasted. "There are literally millions of horny woman (sic) waiting to have sex. These woman (sic) are easily searchable and available in YOUR area. We cannot make it any easier to get laid every day of the week." I took a peek at them and saw that they were all white with beautiful young bodies: Brooke 32, Sara 28, Daniela 25. I guess I didn't lose anything by being dumped by Ms. Aron if this was my fantasy. But while I was flirting with Ms. Aron this was not what New York Congressman Anthony Weiner was doing. He wasn't engaged in a harmless dialogue with an Internet whore. Instead he used the social website Twitter to send sexually suggestive pictures to a 21-year-old Washington woman that precipitated his resignation in June 2011.

But the temptations to reveal their bodies are irresistible for some women as *Playboy* has shown over the years. After watching Kathy Griffin stripping down on the David Letterman show, Dave Nemetz asked what is it about David Letterman that makes women want to take their clothes off? *What is it about David Letterman?* I have a different question. "Following in the grand tradition of Drew Barrymore's memorable 1995 flashing of Dave," wrote Nemetz, "comedienne Kathy Griffin decided to show a little skin last night on CBS's *Late Show*. But while the Barrymore incident was fun and spontaneous, Griffin's striptease was... well, a little awkward." Griffin he recalled was explaining how she shocked her CNN New Year's Eve co-host Anderson Cooper by stripping down to her underwear on live TV and after the clip played, she offered to do the stunt for Letterman, saying "I'll do it right now." But Griffin had trouble getting out of her black cocktail dress, struggling with the zipper while the 64-year-old host stood to the side.

Dave eventually helped her unhook the dress, which Kathy peeled down to reveal her bra, but it was all a little anticlimactic.

There are of course limits to what is amusing and what is in good taste and it is sometimes shocking what gets on the Internet and on television. Katie Zezima of the Associated Press reports for example that a New Jersey mother was suing an Iowa production company after an instructional breast-feeding video she appeared in was taken by a third party and used to create pornography. A federal court judge had ruled that MaryAnn Sahoury's lawsuit against the Meredith Corp. could proceed. In January 2010, Sahoury agreed to demonstrate breast-feeding techniques with her month-old daughter in a video for Parents TV, which broadcasts original videos on parenting. Sahoury, who had had trouble breast-feeding, wanted to help women who faced similar difficulties, she said. "I didn't get paid to do this. I didn't want to be some sort of celebrity," Sahoury, 35, told The Associated Press. "I did this to help other moms."

Sahoury claims she was told by a producer that only first names would be used in the video. When filming was over, Sahoury was asked to sign a piece of paper; she was juggling her daughter and signed it without reading. Months later Sahoury Googled herself. She was shocked by the results: numerous links to pornographic sites and videos containing her name. She clicked on one and saw the breast-feeding video spliced with a woman of "similar features and stature" performing sex acts. Sahoury also Googled her infant daughter's name and this also returned links to pornographic sites and videos. "It was terrifying," Sahoury said. Her full name was used in the video, the lawsuit states, yielding the Google results. The lawsuit also claims the video was placed on YouTube, when Sahoury was told it would appear only on Parents TV and cable television. Her lawsuit is seeking an order prohibiting the defendants from using the video featuring her and her daughter for any purpose; it also seeks attorney fees. Sahoury said she hopes the lawsuit leads to greater Internet protections. "I never want this to happen again," she said.

And in August, Greg Wyshynski writing in Fourth-Place Medal said that the 2012 London Olympic Games have been labeled "the women's Olympics" thanks to record-setting performances and watershed moments like the dawn of women's boxing as well as the participation of female athletes from Saudi Arabia. But how did NBC decide to help celebrate this incredible time for women in sports? With meaningless objectification, says Wyshynski. *Bodies In Motion* was an online video produced by NBC in which women competing in various Olympic sports were featured in softcore, fetishist slow-motion highlights, while porn-tastic jazz music played on the soundtrack. It looked like something a testosterone-filled teenager with a DVR would have spliced together for YouTube; instead, it was the official rights holder of the Olympics in the U.S. that produced it. I am quoting Wyshynski.

However the video was removed from NBCOlympics.com, according to the Huffington Post. Erin Gloria Ryan of Jezebel had called the clip creepy. "I guess I'm not plugged in to the hip, with language of the youths nowadays or on board with the notion that Olympic bodies are at their most noteworthy when they're female, (mostly) white, stereotypically feminine, and thin," she wrote.

VI

IN AUGUST 2011 She Xiuling was in Hong Kong after her work at the Universities Games in Shenzhen. Our plan was to meet in New York on 1 September. She was flying by China Eastern Airlines from Shanghai and Rhona and I were flying by Caribbean Airways from Port of Spain. Our planes would land at different terminals at John F. Kennedy Airport but through the wonders of the cellphone we would confirm our arrival, get together and take a yellow cab to the Hotel Affinia 50 in midtown Manhattan. It never worked out that way, however. We did not make contact with her and thinking there was a Plan B we left the airport with fellow Trinidadian Sean Padmanabman, one of Simon's friends from the University of Miami who had come to New York on the same flight to attend a friend's wedding in Manhattan. The world is a global village as Marshall McLuhan said. But his phone also did not work. It was hours after we had checked in and awaited her arrival that a furious She Xiuling turned up at the hotel. The poor child had roamed the airport looking for us.

"Are you serious about this project?" she stormed. "I just wasted four hours of my life trying to find you at the airport."

I understood her anger. I would have been mad like hell too.

"I will buy you dinner," I said. I knew how important it was for the Chinese to have their three meals every day. I had learnt that from my students in Guangzhou who never passed up a meal in the school canteen even when they complained that the vegetables had worms in them. They paid pennies for their meals and for their lodging but they were as fussy as if they were in a five-star hotel. "There is a McDonald's down the street."

She laughed. "Let's go," she said, dropping her backpack on the floor.

Xiuling was one of the students we had met from our first year in Guangzhou and on graduating she had travelled with us to Hong Kong, to Shanghai, to Hangzhou, to Beijing, to Xi'an, to Harbin, to Tianjin, to Jinan, to Qingdao, to Chengdu and to Wuhan. We had been so impressed with her diligence and discipline when we taught her at Guangdong Teachers' College of Foreign Language and Arts that we had given her a scholarship in 2005 to study for an MA degree at Warwick University in England. She selected Comparative Literature as her study and she later introduced us to the works of Liu Hong and Timothy Mo. We had great confidence in her and allowed her to make all the arrangements for travel and accommodation whenever we planned a getaway.

Having thus diffused the row, we went to eat and I recalled our online conversation some days before. I began it all over again.

"All this stuff about sex that we read on the Internet could be intriguing but are we selling America short," I said over a Big Mac and fries. I didn't want to sound ungrateful but I didn't want her to waste her time with stories of sexual conduct or misconduct. "There must be other things Americans are doing that are as interesting and which define the American personality more than *Dancing with the Stars* does. What is this drink you ordered for me?"

"It is a kind of mocha or frappé. You like it. In Chinese it is *mai le ku*. I looked it up on line once and it is called Melody Cool in English. It is very similar in sound with the Chinese. It is not an aphrodisiac, if that is what you mean."

I didn't sense any ire. I said, "An America that leads the world – the complexity of Lincoln, the wizardry of Walt Disney, the heroism of Martin Luther King, the innovativeness of Steve Jobs and

Bill Gates, the passion of Oprah Winfrey, the daring of Joseph Pulitzer, the audacity of Marilyn Monroe and Madonna, the vision of Warren Buffett, and the spectacular talents of Miami Heat's LeBron James and gymnast Gabrielle Douglas who seems to be on her way to the London Olympics next year."

"I am not surprised that you don't have any of politicians on your list."

"You have said time and time again that you are not interested in politics but this is an election year in America and it would not be possible to ignore the news about the campaigns. I was coming to that and I had in mind Bill Clinton."

"You would and he was at one time a huge part of the sexual landscape."

"What?"

"Sex American style."

"Sex American style?"

"I am pointing you to what you will find in your search for America's Soul. I am not sure that you have the character to resist the temptation to let it lead you to more explicit porn sites after your affair with Ms. Aron but I am going to take the chance."

"I don't really believe that all Americans have on their minds is sex," I said, remembering however that Walter Lippmann had written nearly a hundred years before that what we have in the U.S. is a life that is swamped by sex and that Barbara Walters_when she had interviewed Monica Lewinsky all she seemed interested in was finding out if Bill Clinton was a passionate lover. "I am aware that the crimes of Wall Street have alienated many Americans from the New York Stock Exchange and pushed them to the point of repudiating the American Dream, but Barack Obama wrote a book about reclaiming the American Dream and it was a *New York Times* bestseller."

"You mean *The Audacity of Hope*? He has to be a cheerleader for the Dream Team but he did say – didn't he? – that in the world's greatest deliberative body, meaning the Senate I believe, that no one is listening."

"I think he did. Do you see an alternative to sex in America?"

"You must be joking! This is the United States. *American Idol* and *Dancing with the Stars* have better ratings than most of the networks' regular programs. Their audiences are the people you will be interviewing. I am not familiar with the Fox network or with Rush Limbaugh, but everything I read on line points to an America that glorifies sex and everybody wants to be a star. And you shouldn't underestimate and speak ill of Kim Khadashian. Her face and bod earn her as much as $25,000 for an appearance at a function. I won't be surprised to learn that only Bill Clinton makes more than she does and the truth is Mr. Clinton is in a special category. His private life is as fascinating to his audiences as Ms. Khadashian's covetous statistics are fascinating to Americans."

"I am not slighting Ms. Khadashian and her assets. As Rhona says, I might be displaying an astonishing astigmatism with my lukewarm interest in the Internet's fabulous possibilities and my old-fashioned view of today's social values. But don't blame me. Blame the lady I had for a mother."

"I wouldn't dare do that, but the Internet is there for our use and I am sure that the lady in question would be happy to know that you are making use of all your assets. You will have access not just to Yahoo News but to a variety of news sources, from The Onion to The Daily Beast to The Huffington Post. You will find also The Sideshow, The Ticket and The Lookout. You could lift your head from the pages of the *Chicago Tribune* and the *Los Angeles Times*."

"You left out *The New York Times,* the *Washington Post,* the *Wall Street Journal* and *USA Today*. But what are you getting at, Xiuling?"

"We wouldn't have the time to do all the interviews you need for this project of yours so why don't you use the resources I named to help you? I remember what you used to say to us. 'There are journalists who spend two days in a new country and return home to write a magazine article. There are those who spend a week and return home to write a book.' This is how they do it. They use newspaper sources, they explore Google and Wikipedia, and they scan the Associated Press, Reuters and Agence France Presse."

"I think you are making a wrong assumption but anyway it's not my first visit."

"You are not listening."

"I am listening and you are giving me an idea."

"I hope you are not taking us on another adventure," Rhona said.

"You have to trust me. Xiuling is right. When we get back home we could make use of the Internet to keep our eyes on news, trends and events."

"Are you forgetting what you used to tell your students about copying things from the Internet?"

"I am not talking about copying anything *and* presenting it is as *our* work. That is what some of your classmates did with the essays they handed to me. But it is clear as you say that we cannot do all the interviews we want to do and we might have to come back to the United States next year."

"I can see that but why should we proceed with our original plan? Isn't it like a waste of time and money?"

"Are you saying, Rhona, that we should abandon the search for America's Soul?"

"Yes. I don't see an alternative. To do the project in the way you say could be stepping in a hornet's nest. Journalists are as sensitive and self-righteous as politicians are. And the less creative they are the more jealous they will be about your work. You will be quoting them at your peril. I am sorry if you think I am being too negative."

"Oh, I think you are being cautious and conservative but I understand. And yet, think. If we had got the help we asked for we could have done the job over a longer period of time rather than the rush that we are in to meet our publication deadline of 31 August 2012. Even this will be difficult because Xiuling will be at the London Olympics. But the heads of media in Trinidad, like the politicians and businessmen they condemn, still look to the North for ideas and validation. They are all afraid of taking risks and they don't see the merits of a new idea until it is presented to them wrapped and tied with ribbons and marked *Made in USA*. I really should not have expected Dawn Thomas to sponsor this work; there is hardly any precedence for it in the country and nothing in her past suggests a literary interest outside the Bocas project that OCM helps to sponsor. Do you remember the Chinese idiom, *Hong hu zhi zhi?*"

"Could a goose ever know the aspirations of a swan?"

"That's right."

"You don't have to be a practicing journalist to run a successful, *read*, profitable, newspaper. It doesn't mean you have no instincts about journalism and the importance of the Fourth Estate. How many Beaverbrooks have there been on Fleet Street."

"I agree with Xiuling and there are even fewer Al Neuharths in the United States."

"Who's he?"

"Al Neuharth started *USA Today* in 1982 when he worked with the Gannett Company. I know that in the newspaper world there have been more great editors than great businessmen, but Ken Gordon did say that the One Caribbean Media group owed me something when we spoke about the books I was doing."

"It is clear to me that Ms. Thomas does not share Ken Gordon's view and the truth is she didn't keep her word with you the first time you two agreed on a training programme for *Express* staff. But it does not mean she has no skill in running a successful business operation. Look around you: women are in top political and financial positions all over the world, from Brazil and Argentina in the south to France and Germany in the north. It is only in the Vatican that women are still barred from holding the top office."

"So we must solve the problems we face in gathering information by our own skills and initiatives. What I am suggesting is a way to accomplish what we set out to do. I will be quoting material from the wire services and from other sources to supplement the interviews we do. I will be crediting all of it. I won't be writing as though the information originated with me. We will see through all the forms of media, print and electronic, what Americans think about America – its genius, its genitals and its geo-politics."

"I would not have put it that way but I know you need access to more news sources than what you have in Thomas Friedman and Anderson Cooper."

"You mean let the work speak for itself?" said Rhona. "Let the reporting describe the Soul of America?"

"Yes. I think it will be presumptuous of us to say what America's Soul is especially when we are not working in the field."

"I think I understand what you are saying. The news reports you quote – facts about the economy, the politics, the courts and the society, the examples of everyday life in the United States that you give – will be the testimony that reveals the Soul of America. If it doesn't work out that way and it seems to be only a work of grand larceny we might end up sharing space with Allen Stanford."

"Who is Allen Stanford?" asked Xiuling.

"One of America's big-time swindlers," I said. "But don't let Rhona frighten you. This is not a Ponzi scheme we are putting together."

VII

AMERICA'S OPENNESS about sex, as She Xiuling was discovering, is not confined to America but goes beyond its borders. Hollywood and network television had conspired to make the doctrine spread even to countries where there are indescribable taboos against women and in places where the hijab and the burka have a significance of sanctity not unlike the nun's habit of yesteryear. In a report from Pakistan, for example, Bollywood actress Veena Malik has said she would pose nude for *Playboy* for $1million dollars. The model confessed that she would bare all for the magazine's centerfold if she was asked. She said: "Why would I say no? It's a great opportunity. I'd definitely go for that." But in Pakistan it was widely viewed as a bad decision, given the enemies she made by appearing nude before. A call for her citizenship to be revoked was the least of her worries when Lashkar-e-Taiba, a Pakistani militant group behind the 2008 attack on Mumbai, made it known they were not happy with her. "She has made fun of all Muslim women and brought shame to the entire nation," the group said, clearly seeing neither beauty nor humor in Mr. Hefner's bunnies.

Or, was it resentment against something deeper? Breivik, the Norwegian killer, revealed the squalid quality of hate that warps men's souls when he was arrested, showing no sign of remorse. His cause was the eradication of Muslims in his country, something like the hate white Protestant Americans bore African slaves.

In *Lincoln*, Gore Vidal recalled a moment when the President told John Hay, "Why would any colored man want to live in this country, where there is so much hatred of him?" Perhaps, said the young man, they think that that will change, once slavery's gone. "There are passions," said Lincoln, "too deep for even a millennium to efface." As Vidal wrote Lincoln was averse to the institution of slavery but he was no abolitionist and supported "the policy of colonizing the blacks elsewhere."

Norman Mailer in his 2003 critique of George W. Bush and his quest for empire makes this point for the hatred of American values and identifies the West's cultural invasion into Islam. "The Muslim reaction is that Islam is endangered," he wrote in *Why Are We At War?* "by modern technology and corporate capitalism. Muslims see everything in America as aiming to destroy the basis of Islam. The huge freedom given to women in American culture is seen as an outrage by orthodox Muslims and they find that American television is licentious in the extreme. They feel that all that Islam stands for is going to be eroded by American culture." The core of the hatred of Muslims toward us, writes Mailer, is "the fear that they're going to lose their own people to Western values."

How is this demonstrated in the United States? On 30 August 2010, *TIME* magazine included an analysis of what it called, *Islamophobia: Does America have a Muslim problem?*, in which it asked readers to experience what it feels like to be a Muslim in America today (by walking) in the shoes of Dr. Mansoor Mirza of Sheboygan County, Wisconsin. "It's a February evening, and you're at a meeting of the planning commission of Wilson, which is considering your application to open a mosque in the nearby village of Oostburg. You're not expecting much opposition: you already own the property, and having worked in the nearby Manitowoc hospital for the past five years, you're hardly a stranger to the town. Indeed, some of the people at the meetings are like most of your patients – white Americans who don't seem to care about their doctor's race or creed when they talk to him about their illnesses. But when the floor is opened to discussion, you hear things they would never say to you even in the privacy of an examination room. One after another, they pour scorn and hostility on your proposal, and most of the objections have nothing to do with zoning regulations. It's about your faith. Islam is a religion of hate, they say. Muslims are out to wipe out Christianity. There are 20 jihadi training camps hidden across rural America, busy even now producing the next wave of terrorists. Muslims murder their children. Christian kids have enough problems with drugs, alcohol and pornography and should not have to worry about Islam too. "I don't want it in my backyard," says one. Another says, "I just think it's not America."

Is it bigotry and is it really *not* America?

As we have learnt from the founders of *TIME,* there could be more than one side to a story and the editors of the Southern Poverty Law Center in their spring 2012 issue of *Intelligence Report* state that hate groups are at record levels and that the so-called "patriot" movement grew explosively in 2011. In fact says Morris Dees, founder, the Department of Homeland Security reported that between

1990 and 2010, far-right extremists were involved in more than 345 "homicide incidents". In its cover story, *The year in Hate & Extremism*, Mark Potok reported that "the number of hate groups counted by the Southern Poverty Law Center last year reached a total of 1,018, up slightly from the years before but continuing a trend of significant growth that is now more than a decade old." The truly stunning growth came in the anti-government "Patriot" movement – conspiracy-minded groups that see the federal government as their primary enemy. The report is evidence that hate and intolerance have not changed in the US since 1692 when the first woman described as a witch was hanged in Salem and even since 1882 when the first black American was lynched in the South by mobs as enthusiastic about killing as white Americans had been in the North about burning women at the stake. The swelling of the Patriot movement has been astounding, the *Intelligence Report* states, and from 149 groups in 2008, the number of Patriot organisations skyrocketed to 512 in 2009, shot up again in 2010 to 824, and jumped to 1,274 in 2011. Islam-bashing organisations like Pamela Geller's Stop Islamization of America that organised major rallies against what was falsely depicted as a Ground Zero Mosque helped ratchet up resentment that ultimately translated into a hate crime spike.

This situation was dramatized in August when, as Dylan Stableford reported for Yahoo! News / The Lookout, seven people were killed, including the suspected gunman, in a mass shooting at a Sikh temple in Oak Creek, Wis., south of Milwaukee. According to police, 911 dispatchers received multiple calls from the temple at approximately 10:25 a.m. local time. An officer who responded to the scene was treating a victim when he was "ambushed" by the suspected gunman in the parking lot, Oak Creek Police Chief John Edwards said. The veteran officer was shot multiple times and rushed to Milwaukee's Froedtert Hospital where he underwent surgery, Edwards said. The suspect was shot and killed by a second officer, police said. The gunman was not identified, and no motive was released. But according to Thomas Ahern, spokesman for the ATF Chicago bureau, the gunman was a white male in his early 40s. Sources told ABC News the suspect was a "white supremacist" or "skinhead." And officials told NBC News he had "some kind of radical or white supremacist views," but was apparently not a member of any kind of radical organization. His past run-ins with law enforcement were described as minor.

Law enforcement officials treated the case as an "act of domestic terrorism", police said, and the FBI was leading the investigation. According to the Milwaukee *Journal Sentinel*, Satwant Kaleka, the president of the temple, was one of the victims taken to Froedtert Hospital. Dozens of worshipers, including women and children, were gathered for a meal before an 11:30 a.m. prayer service at the temple, or gurdwara, when the shooting occurred. There are about 500 members in the congregation, officials said. And in a later report, Liz Goodwin and Stableford said that the man suspected of opening fire in the Sikh temple in Oak Creek, Wis., was identified by police as Wade Michael Page, a 40-year-old former member of the U.S. Army. The six victims identified by police – five men and one woman – ranged in age from 39 to 84. According to Edwards, Lt. Brian Murphy, a 51-year-old officer was the first to arrive at the temple shortly after 10:25 a.m. Sunday. He began to render aid to one of the victims in the parking lot when he was "ambushed", Edwards said at a news conference the next day. Murphy was shot eight or nine times at close range with a handgun, Edwards said. Two other officers exchanged gunfire with Page after they arrived, Edwards said, killing him. The officers then found Murphy in the parking lot. Murphy was carried to a squad car and rushed to Milwaukee's Froedtert Hospital where he underwent surgery. Three shooting victims, including the officer, were listed in critical condition at the hospital. Murphy, a 21-year veteran of the force, was wearing a bullet proof vest when he was shot, Edwards said. "There is no doubt in my mind the heroic actions of our police officers prevented an even greater tragedy," Oak Creek Mayor Steve Scaffidi said.

According to the Southern Poverty Law Center, Page "was a frustrated neo-Nazi who had been the leader of a racist white-power band." The band, called End Apathy, was formed in 2005. And according to the group's MySpace page, its music "is a sad commentary on our sick society and the problems that prevent true progress." The Montgomery, Ala.-based law center said it had been tracking Page since 2000, when he "attempted to purchase goods from the neo-Nazi National Alliance, then America's most important hate group." The Milwaukee *Journal Sentinel* reported that Page is believed to have worked as a truck driver between 2006 and 2010 while living in Fayetteville, N.C. There were initial, unconfirmed reports of multiple shooters and a hostage situation, though police said they believe Page was the lone shooter. Tactical units performed a three-square-mile grid search of the area around the temple. Law enforcement officials were treating the case as an "act of domestic terrorism" police said, and the FBI was leading the investigation.

President Obama was notified of the shooting shortly before 1 p.m. (ET) by chief counterterrorism adviser John Brennan, a senior administration official told Yahoo News. "Michelle and I were deeply saddened to learn of the shooting that tragically took so many lives in Wisconsin," Obama said. "At this difficult time, the people of Oak Creek must know that the American people have them in our thoughts and prayers, and our hearts go out to the families and friends of those who were killed and wounded. My administration will provide whatever support is necessary to the officials who are responding to this tragic shooting and moving forward with an investigation. As we mourn this loss which took place at a house of worship, we are reminded how much our country has been enriched by Sikhs, who are a part of our broader American family." Mitt Romney released a statement, too. "This was a senseless act of violence and a tragedy that should never befall any house of worship," Romney said. "Our hearts are with the victims, their families, and the entire Oak Creek Sikh community. We join Americans everywhere in mourning those who lost their lives and in prayer for healing in the difficult days ahead." And Wis. Gov. Scott Walker said his office was working with the FBI and local law enforcement in its investigation. "Our hearts go out to the victims and their families as we all struggle to comprehend the evil that begets this terrible violence," Walker said. "At the same time, we are filled with gratitude for our first responders, who show bravery and selflessness as they put aside their own safety to protect our neighbors and friends."

Sikhism, the Associated Press told its readers, is a 500-year-old monotheist faith with about 27 million followers worldwide, including about 300,000 in the United States. Since 9/11, Sikh groups in the United States have reported a rise in bias attacks. There have been more than 700 reports of hate-related incidents against Sikhs since the 11 September 2001 terror attacks. "Sikhs don't practice the same religion as Muslims," the AP noted, "but their long beards and turbans often cause them to be mistaken for Muslims, advocates say." Since the September 11 attacks, Sikhs have sometimes been mistaken for Muslims and have increasingly found themselves the target of anti-Muslim hate crimes in America. It's possible, reporters surmised, that Page could have mixed up the temple with a mosque and started his attack as a way to make a political statement against Muslims – another political act that seems to fit the bill of terrorism. Prabhjot Singh, the co-founder of the Sikh Coalition in New York, told Yahoo News that he thinks it's too soon to talk about whether the attack should be treated as terrorism or a hate crime. "How we categorize it is not so important right now," Singh said. "It's that the nation comes to heal collectively."

The coalition was founded when hate crimes against Sikhs escalated after 2001, including the murder of gas station owner Balbir Singh Sodhi in Mesa, Ariz., by Frank Roque. The killer was reportedly out for "revenge" for the 9/11 attacks and wrongly assumed Singh Sodhi was a Muslim. The discussion around what counts as terrorism has been charged since 9/11, when Muslim-American communities were subjected to surveillance and heightened scrutiny out of fear that more terror attacks were on the way. Domestic terrorism is actually at a four-decade low, according to Gary LaFree at the University of Maryland's National Consortium for the Study of Terrorism and Responses to Terrorism. Between 1980 and 2001, non-Islamic American extremists carried out about two-thirds of all terrorism in the United States, according to FBI statistics cited by the Council on Foreign Relations. Between 2002 and 2005 that figure jumped to 95 percent. In the 10 years following 2001, only 6 percent of terrorist acts in America have been the work of Islamic extremists. Even so, some scholars say the common perception is that most home-grown terrorists in America are Muslims adhering to a violent brand of Islamist extremism. People are less likely to understand that violent white supremacism can also be terrorism. "I think that [white supremacist attacks] should quality as terrorism just as much as an individual who's a Muslim who abuses that faith to say 'I want to kill these people to further my political agenda,'" said Sahar Aziz, an associate professor at Texas Wesleyan University School of Law.

VIII

ON 11 OCTOBER 2011 the Chinese Twitter, Sina Weibo, reported that kindergarten kids in China were chanting, "*Fly a plane. Drop a bomb. Kill the assholes in the USA.*" It was scary and to them, as it is to many, the United States of America is now a paper tiger, as Mao Zedong had said in the nineteen fifties. At a meeting in Moscow in 1957, Mao criticized U.S. imperialism as he saw its expansion and authority in the Third World and told his comrades that US administrations would be overthrown in spite of the fact that they had the bomb. "I have said that all the reputedly powerful reactionaries are paper tigers," he said. "The reason is they are divorced from the people."

Is this what we are seeing today – the end of the American empire as some people in the Western world have been saying since George W. Bush was in the White House? In *The New Republic* of 11 January 2012, Robert Kagan asks how much truth there is to the talk that the U.S. has lost its power and influence. Much of the commentary on American decline he wrote rests on rather loose analysis, on impressions that the United States has lost its way, that it has abandoned the virtues that made it successful in the past, that it lacks the will to address the problems it faces. "Americans look at other nations whose economies are now in better shape than their own, and seem to have the dynamism that America once had, and they lament, as the title of Thomas Friedman and Michael Mandelbaum's latest book says, *That used to be us.*" But Kagan admits that the perception of decline today is certainly understandable, given the dismal economic situation since 2008 and the nation's large fiscal deficits, which, combined with the continuing growth of the Chinese, Indian, Brazilian, Turkish, and other economies, seem to portend a significant and irreversible shift in global economic power. "Some of the pessimism is also due to the belief that the United States has lost favor, and therefore influence, in much of the world, because of its various responses to the attacks of September 11. The detainment facilities at Guantánamo, the use of torture against suspected terrorists, and the widely condemned invasion of Iraq in 2003 have all tarnished the American 'brand' and put a dent in America's 'soft power' – its ability to attract others to its point of view."

And Kagan points too to the difficult wars in Iraq and Afghanistan, which many argue proved the limits of military power, stretched the United States beyond its capacities, and weakened the nation at its core. "Some compare the United States to the British Empire at the end of the nineteenth century, with the Iraq and Afghanistan wars serving as the equivalent of Britain's difficult and demoralizing Boer War." With this broad perception of decline as the backdrop said Kagan "every failure of the United States to get its way in the world tends to reinforce the impression. Arabs and Israelis refuse to make peace, despite American entreaties. Iran and North Korea defy American demands that they cease their nuclear weapons programs. China refuses to let its currency rise. Ferment in the Arab world spins out of America's control. Every day, it seems, brings more evidence that the time has passed when the United States could lead the world and get others to do its bidding."

Some Americans might think that Kagan is right and the fact is the image of a weak America continues to spread in the world and in America and it is just as easy I think to believe that it is the end of the American Empire and to look to see who will be the next World Leader. This is not a betrayal of Washington; it is the lesson of history.

There is always a Caesar or a Cromwell whose time has come. In Fairfax, Virginia, the perception as elsewhere is that American power is on the decline and it is largely because, despite enormously expensive military efforts that lasted for many years, the U.S. has not been victorious. Indeed, the growing unpopularity in America of fighting wars has resulted in U.S. forces leaving Iraq at the end of 2011, and beginning their withdrawal from Afghanistan, which is due to be completed at the end of 2014, and neither the American public nor the American government seems likely to countenance major military intervention anywhere else any time soon.

It is no wonder that the debate is under way on whether the United States has already seen its best days. The fact is the United States is saddled with historic debt after a decade of war and its leaders are rarely able to agree on much other than that the political system is dysfunctional. Unemployment rates in recent years have been at their worst in three decades and income inequality is by some accounts at modern highs. For a tangible case study in the theory of decline, one needs only to fly from an aging US airport to one of Asia's glittering new air hubs. Few observers would argue that the country is short of innovation and creativity or would doubt the staggering gap in military spending between the United States and every other country in the world today but the question of the decline and fall of the American empire is shaping out to be a defining national debate in this election year. Mitt Romney has relentlessly attacked President Obama for what he charges is a focus on managing decline instead of asserting the "exceptionalism" of the United States. However in January, Obama said that his commitment to working with other nations had restored "a sense of America as the sole, indispensable power." In a recent speech, Secretary of State Hillary Clinton offered a robust defense of an active US role in the world and assured that 2012 "is not 1912", when friction between a declining Britain and a rising Germany set the stage for global conflict.

But decline has become a favorite theme for prominent US scholars as the media continue to point out. Former national security adviser Zbigniew Brzezinski argues like Kagan that the U.S. decline is exaggerated and that the world is far better off with a strong United States. Yet whatever the reality, the very perception of U.S. decline has effects. In a widely read recent essay, Wang Jisi, one of China's top experts on the United States, said that Chinese policymakers are convinced of U.S. decline and increasingly see U.S. actions – even longstanding policies such as urging more respect for human rights and selling weapons to Taiwan – as signs of a diminished power trying to keep down a rising China. However many Chinese support a strong United States – if nothing else, as a consumer market for its products. On the other side of the Pacific, meanwhile, any leader who openly renounces the country's role as a world leader is seen as committing political suicide.

The idea of U.S. decline has its defenders but the debate itself is at no risk of declining. On 22 February 2012, Christiane Amanpour put the same question to Kagan with the added spin, Is the U.S. Committing Superpower Suicide Against China? While there has been growing concern that the United States is slowly losing ground as the world's dominant Superpower, Kagan insisted once more on national television that it's all in our head. "I think that the basic measures of power indicate that the United States really is just as strong as it's ever been," he said. "People have talked themselves into this notion that we no longer have the capacity to play the role we've been playing." But as the United States begins to pull troops out of Afghanistan, after already pulling out of Iraq, there are questions as to whether America has the resources to assert its power in future conflicts, including the brewing situation with Iran. "I don't think it's a question of whether we can afford it," said Kagan, "we certainly have that capability." Kagan doesn't deny that countries like China, whose international power is clearly growing, are a threat to America. Rather, his point is that the threat is nothing new. "We tend to sort of fantasize about the past, a past when the United States was allegedly able to do whatever it wants whenever it wanted to, and that past never existed."

And yet there are signs today that tell another kind of story – the thinking among some of America's allies that the U.S. can be bullied. Pakistan's ambassador to the United States, for example, says her country will not relent from demanding that the CIA end its drone strikes, wrote Kimberly Dozier of the Associated Press from Aspen, Colo. on 27 July 2012. In a debate with White House war adviser Douglas Lute at the Aspen Security Forum, Sherry Rehman said drone attacks have damaged al-Qaida but are now only serving to recruit new militants. "I am not saying drones have not assisted in the war against terror, but they have diminishing rate of returns," Rehman said by video teleconference from Washington. With Pakistan's spy chief, Lt. Gen. Zaheerul Islam, expected to hold his first meeting with CIA Director David Petraeus at CIA headquarters in Virginia the first week of August, the ambassador said, "We will seek an end to drone strikes and there will be no compromise on that."

Lute would not comment on the drone program. U.S. officials have said privately that it will continue because Pakistan has proved incapable or unwilling to target militants the U.S. considers dangerous. A long-sought U.S. apology to Pakistan over a deadly border incident cleared the way to restart counterterrorism talks. In addition to the end to drone strikes, Pakistani officials say they will ask the U.S. to feed intelligence gathered by the pilotless aircraft to Pakistani jets and ground forces so they can target militants. While neither side expects much progress, officials from both countries see the return to dialogue as a chance to repair a relationship dented by a series of incidents that damaged trust on both sides. U.S. officials remain angry over what they say is Pakistan's support of Taliban groups, including the militant network, that the U.S. contends are taking shelter in Pakistan's tribal areas and attack troops in neighbouring Afghanistan. But Rehman dismissed as "outrageous" the claim that Pakistan is harboring al-Qaida or other militants who intend to harm the U.S. She said Pakistan's army was working hard to combat the militants, including reporting 52 times to NATO in recent months when militants were spotted crossing into Afghan territory. "Pakistan is maxed out on the international border with Afghanistan," she said. "Sovereignty has privileges but also comes with responsibilities," countered Lute who called for Pakistan to step up its efforts and to cease "hedging its bets" by supporting the Afghan Taliban.

The two did agree, however, that Pakistan could help broker an eventual peace deal with the Taliban. When asked why the Taliban would surrender ahead of the 2014 drawdown of U.S. troops, Lute said a recent security agreement with Afghanistan ensures a long-term U.S. commitment to Afghan security. "The agreement we've made with Afghanistan signals to Taliban that they can't wait us out," Lute said. "If they want another decade of this, to get hammered every day and every night," U.S. and Afghan forces can provide. If the Taliban are willing to disarm and respect the laws of the Afghan government, "the door will remain open to negotiation," Lute said.

A major grievance for Pakistan remains last year's U.S. Navy SEAL raid that killed Osama bin Laden on Pakistani soil. The operation was conducted without Pakistan's permission. Rehman defended Pakistan's arrest of Dr. Shakil Afridi, who has been sentenced to more than three decades in prison for aiding the CIA in tracking down bin Laden. Afridi conducted a vaccine program in the military town where the terrorist mastermind turned out to be hiding. U.S. lawmakers have threatened to halt millions of dollars in aid to Pakistan unless Afridi is released, in recognition of his contribution. Afridi is appealing his sentence. "He had no clue he was looking for Osama bin Laden," Rehman countered. "He was contracting with a foreign intelligence agency." She added that Afridi's actions put thousands of children at risk because some vaccine programs had to be ended after Pakistani aid workers were targeted by the Taliban.

Was Mailer wrong to voice his concern and criticism? "When you have a great country," Mailer said, "it's your duty to be critical of it so it can become even greater. But culturally, emotionally,

Americans are growing more arrogant. We are losing a sense of the beauty not only of democracy but also of its peril." What is left I believe is a hunger for war; the craving to test one's physical strength. And other Americans, seeing the end of democracy, have joined the war against bureaucratic arrogance. In September 2002 the Bush Administration writes Noam Chomsky in *Hegemony or Survival* announced its National Security Strategy, which declared the right to resort to force to eliminate any perceived challenge to US global hegemony. The new grand strategy aroused deep concern worldwide, even within the foreign policy elite at home. By October 2002, said Chomsky, it was beginning to be hard to ignore the fact that the world was "more concerned about the unbridle use of American power than … about the threat posed by Saddam Hussein."

To quote Mailer once more: "Questions about our nature as a country were being asked that most good American men and women had never posed to themselves before. Questions such as, "Why are we so hated?" The question was not so unexpected as some Americans thought; it had been on the public agenda for years. The flower people of the sixties, dreading war and the consequences of war, had popularized the slogan, "make love not war". They were the sons and daughters of men and women who had found themselves in the jungles of Vietnam and Burma, the children of many Americans who did not return home. But even then young Americans were late in presenting their protest. Ever since 1941, Gore Vidal wrote in *Dreaming War*, "when Roosevelt got us out of the Depression by pumping federal money into re-arming, war or the threat of war has been the principal engine to our society." In January 2001 after the Supreme Court justices had declared that George W. Bush had won the election, Vidal asked the question, "What will the next four years bring?" and he answered, "Expect a small war or two in order to keep military appropriations flowing."

It was not just pique and cynicism. The American war machines were never at rest for long. American taxpayers' money was constantly in use to get a war or a revolution going. In *Obama's Wars*, Bob Woodward writes, "One important secret that had never been reported in the media or elsewhere was the existence of the CIA's 3,000-man covert army in Afghanistan. Called CTPT, for Counterterrorism Pursuit Teams, the army consisted mostly of Afghans, the cream of the corp in the CIA's opinion. These pursuit teams were a paid, trained and functioning tool of the CIA that was authorized by President Bush." The revelation of this in 2010 could have made Obama say to one of his closest advisers, "I'm inheriting a world that could blow up any minute in half a dozen ways, and I will have some powerful but limited and perhaps even dubious tools to keep it from happening."

IX

RACE, MONEY, sex, crime and war: Did these things define Americans and America more than the freedom to live and to speak one's mind? There was not a Chinese teenager who had not said to us during the years we lived and taught in Guangzhou and Beijing that the United States was the place they would want to visit more than any other place on earth. And yet, it had not been kind to the African slaves and to immigrants who were not white Anglo Saxon protestants and during World War II, as Ms. FitzGerald recalled, Japanese-Americans were interned. The truth is, minorities in the US have always faced risks and the difficulties so many of the immigrants encountered when they got off the boats were "brutalizing labor in factories and mines, slum conditions in the cities, prejudice against them, and the shock of entering another culture." There was, she wrote, "a remarkable disparity between their treatment of European ethnic groups and their treatment of all other ethnic minorities."

We had gone to Ellis Island to see for ourselves, to put ourselves in American shoes to confront and to welcome or to turn away the huddled masses yearning to breathe free, the wretched refuse of Europe's teeming shores. In his own harrowing account of Ellis Island, the British journalist Alistair Cooke reported on 25 June 1993 that "the routine procedure employed with the fourteen and a half million immigrants who arrived here, mainly New York or Boston, in the first two decades of the twentieth century and who must have looked up in awe to the bosom of the colossal lady peering out towards Europe would soon find out that the physical routine of getting into the United States was not quite what a poor foundling might expect of a new compassionate mother." Coming across the

Atlantic, Cooke wrote, "they were not so much allotted space as stowed aboard, (and were) as many as nine hundred in steerage. Sailing slowly up the lower bay of New York City, they would spot their first Americans climbing aboard from a Coast Guard cutter, two men and a woman; immigration inspectors whose first job was to look over the ship's manifest and see if the captain had recorded cases of contagious disease. Considering the frequency and unpredictability at the time of ravaging epidemics across the continent of Europe, they looked out first for signs of cholera, typhoid, and tuberculosis. If any of them showed any sign of these fearsome diseases, he or she was taken at once off to quarantine on an island in the bay and got ready for early deportation." It was with a heart full of sadness for these early immigrants that I had trudged about the large reception hall on Ellis Island, peering at the photographs and other memorabilia and seeing the multitude of hopeful immigrants tagged with numbers and grouped according to their native tongues. They were too many to wonder what had been their fate as they moved past a doctor in a blue uniform and past a man with chalk in his hand.

But the stories of Ellis Island reminded me of the Giuseppe Tornatore film, *The Legend of 1900*, and my students in China who had watched the film with me and who were always touched by the drama of the migrations from Europe to America, a journey I always suspected they yearned to make and to see for the first time the Lady in New York harbor. I knew however that it would not be an easy passage for them even if Ellis Island was just a historical fact as it was for us when we visited New York years ago with our sons where they had smelled, not just sung, chestnuts roasting in an open fire and had ridden in a horse-driven carriage through Manhattan.

She Xiuling had her own disappointment in getting a visitor's visa to land in the United States. In 2002 when she was a junior at South China Normal University, we had made arrangements to take her on a holiday with us to Washington, DC, where Bessie Porter, Rhona's aunt, was celebrating that year her one hundredth birthday. But the US Visa Officer in Guangzhou spent less than five minutes with her and declared her an unwanted alien. He never looked at any of the documents she had with her explaining her visit and showing that she would not be a liability on the taxpayers of the United States. He did not have to; he held the power of a Caesar. Section 214(b) of the U.S.

Immigration and Nationality Act (INA) presumes that every applicant for a non-immigrant visa is an intending immigrant to the United States unless he or she can provide credible evidence of strong family, social, professional and economic ties that would compel him or her to leave the United States after a temporary stay. This was the reason too I assumed that my daughter Deborah was refused a visa to travel to the U.S. with us. Twice before when she had travelled to Los Angeles and to New York she had stayed the six months she had been allowed. Though married and living with her husband in Trinidad, the visa officer felt that there was something awkward in her length of stay in the U.S. The decision cost me the price of air tickets for the two for their travel in the U.S.

In other words, visa applicants must demonstrate that they do not intend to abandon their residence in China or in Trinidad and Tobago. All applicants must overcome the presumption of Section 214(b) regardless of their reason for travel. At the interview, Xiuling did not overcome the presumption of an intending immigrant. She was at the time just twenty and we supposed the visa officer might have thought that she was going to the United States to find a husband and never to return to Mao Zedong's China of pandas, concubines and acupuncture.

This arrogance had slammed the door in the faces of Chinese travelers before and what Xiuling met was the presumption of every visa officer in an American embassy or consulate that prospective tourists are barbarians waiting to get inside the hallowed gates at any cost. However Americans may not be the only government guards with this feeling. I had sometimes felt that China, especially at the time of the 2008 Olympics, had its own hostile policy towards immigrants and officers who thought as maniacally about their country. And so it was not until 2010, after graduating from Warwick University in England, that Xiuling had better luck with the Americans in Guangzhou, this time a female visa officer. I remembered the day she telephoned us in Trinidad and said breathlessly, "God Bless America!" She was, like some of her classmates, about to realize her dream to see America, the new Promised Land.

Still it was not that the United States was opening its arms to welcome bona fides travelers, as Fareed Zakarias, the CNN correspondent, lamented in a recent interview with Frits Van

Paasschen, CEO of Starwood Hotels and Resorts that owns the Sheraton, Western and W. Hotels brands. Travel companies like his are anticipating a boom in global tourism. "You see millions of people from emerging economies like China," said Zakarias, "who are entering the middle class and are becoming tourists. Already there are fifty million of them. Chinese are traveling outside their home country. In just four years that number should double to 100 million. And America is one of their top destinations." When we think of creating jobs, Zakarias said, "we tend to think of new factories or software start-ups or solar energy spin-offs. But there's one industry that's big, growing and could be made much bigger. That's Tourism. There is a gold mine of new customers and new jobs for the taking."

Van Paasschen saw the same golden opportunity. "Chinese travellers or people coming from other countries," he said, "are walking stimulus packages. They spend an average of $4,000 per visit in the US. People want to come to America. And when they come, they create jobs." The fact is while the government appears to be blind to the windfall from tourism, corporate America is acting on the assumption that this myopia will change. She Xiuling believed she had come across proof of this when she was on her way back to China. "When I was passing through New York City in April on my way home, Macy's offered a 10 per cent off a visitor's card. Any visitor with a passport could get it from their customer service centre. When I went to get mine, the guy at the counter even said this in Chinese, *San shi tian you xiao*. You could see that they are all out to attract potential customers, even by learning their language."

Zakarias and Van Paasschen agreed that tourism is already one of America's biggest industries, supporting over eight million US jobs. Plus, jobs in this industry often don't require an advanced education, making them attainable for Americans without a high school degree. The good news is, "you can't download a hotel. You can't outsource a hotel and you can't put a hotel in a low wage factory somewhere else. So these are jobs that will stay in America." There is a major problem, however. Foreigners who want to visit America continue to face a barrier that makes it difficult to do so: the hassle of getting a visa. After 9/11 America tightened its visa policies to address security reasons. Partly as a result, the U.S. share of the international travel market plummeted by more than one-third over the last 10 years. According to the industry, that's an estimated 78 million visitors lost to other countries.

If America had maintained its share of the market, the industry estimates that almost half a million more jobs would have been supported annually. That squandered opportunity is referred to as the lost decade. "If we're going to get those jobs back," said Zakarias, "America will need to reform its visa process. Because trying to get one is like entering an obstacle course. In Brazil, for example, a Brazilian can pay for a visa only through a certain bank. The online visa applications are only in English. Scheduling an interview at a U.S. consulate can take months. The lines at those consulates can go on for hours, even days."

The story is the same in Trinidad and Tobago and in China, but was the US State Department listening to these complaints and was it putting the cart before the horse when it announced that fees for visas were going to cost more even though there seemed to be no new procedures in place to make the obtaining of a visa easier for bona fide travelers. In Port of Spain after decades of complaints Trinidadians with their eye to travel still huddle outside the US embassy on Marli Street in droves and in any weather – men, women, children and mothers with babies in arms. No power on earth it seemed could deter them from being interrogated, photographed, and finger-printed to have a page in their passports that declares them fit to enter the sacred portals of the United States in Florida or New York.

When, for instance, the US Embassy in Port of Spain said that fees for visas would be increased because clerical costs had gone up, it seemed a wretched joke. Trinidadians and Tobagonians applying for non-immigrant visas to the United States, the press release said, will have to pay more for the appointment as of 13 April, as the US enforces a worldwide increase in the fee, as the demand for visas increases. The US State Department that had posted the notification of the increased fees for the processing of visas stated that the Bureau of Consular Affairs is required by law to recover the cost of processing non-immigrant visas through the collection of visa application fees. "Certain categories of non-immigrant visas," it said, "cost more to process than other categories of non-immigrant visas. The new fees reflect the costs of each visa service." Is this revelation what we should expect from the country that gave birth to Warren Buffett and to the Rockefellers? The embassy explained that items that impact the cost of visa processing includes an increase in the number of visas processed or new regulations requiring additional security screening.

Years ago the embassy in Port of Spain was transformed into a fortress and you wouldn't be wrong if you thought the top of Marli Street opposite the Queen's Park Savannah was considered in CIA handbooks to be a prime target of terrorists. Even with the old fees I didn't think there would be a problem in meeting the embassy's costs in Trinidad but I am aware that costs were escalating everywhere in the free world. The increase was said to be based on US law that requires the Consular Offices to recover the cost of processing non-immigrant visas through visa application fees; and the US Department of State had said that for a number of reasons, the current fees no longer cover the actual cost of processing non-immigrant visas. "The non-immigrant visa fee increase will support the addition and expansion of overseas facilities, as well as additional staffing required to meet increased visa demand," an official said. I thought of my students in Guangzhou who had paid two or three times for the chance of a visa interview and who were denied their dream of going to the United States for a holiday every time. Do they still think it is worth it?

I welcomed the notion of efficiency and safety, but apart from the fact that fees were going up, nothing had changed on the street outside the embassy. Trinidadians and Tobagonians who wished to travel to the United States were still being treated like undesired immigrants. Perhaps it was the standard all over the world though I could not recall being made to feel this humiliation in Hong Kong in 2003 when Rhona and I applied for new U.S. visas.

In Trinidad, we had taken Xiuling to the embassy for a 9.00 appointment but two and a half hours later she was still to see an officer. "When I looked at my watch," she told us later when she met us at Rituals in Newtown for a cup of coffee, "it was after 11:30. The waiting room seemed to quiet down with about 50 applicants left. And I saw that some 9:30 applicants were being called. So I was more focused on the environment. The Indian boy who was in the line ahead of me came out from Window E and passed the TTPost without stopping. I had been observing all the applicants and I knew that was a bad sign. It meant he had failed to get his visa. I remembered him because he was quite cheerful outside, and was letting 9:00 applicants go before him. We kind of exchanged a sentence or two. But now I was getting a bit worried. Was it because it was getting late and the visa officers were getting tired, so they started to fail people? I told myself to stay away from Window E, and more than willed to be called by the nice Window B.

"Then I saw that the man immediately before me was called, but the next one was not me; then some families, not me; then the man who presented the 'essential four pieces' (passport, appointment confirmation sheet, DS160 application form confirmation sheet, and the two TTPost application fee receipts) was called, not me. I was getting more worried. By this time, there were about twenty applicants left. Were they going to keep me for last, because my case was complicated? I was willing in my mind for Window B to become vacant and to hear my name called. Then it happened; I heard my name but my prayer was answered only halfway. It was for Window E and it was a male visa officer who greeted me. He was thirty-ish, with glasses. He told me to print my fingers. I had gone through the process before in Guangzhou, China. I hope he could tell that I was a genuine tourist not someone wishing to immigrate."

I know that I am presenting a bleak case here for the next applicant for a US visa and for the opportunity to live, study and work in the United States. Perhaps it doesn't have to be so grim and I should repeat what Dr. Merle Hoyte, a former President of the College of Science, Technology and Applied Arts of Trinidad and Tobago, told me about her choice of studying and living in the US. We were on our way to COSTAATT at Melville Street in Port of Spain when I turned to her and asked, "What do you think is America's soul?" She didn't hesitate. "It's the freedom to think and do and say what's in your mind and in your heart."

Months later, I saw that this was the response of nearly everyone in the United States that I had asked the question. "I like the freedom," Simone Long said. "By that I mean you could go on the subway wearing a costume and no one will pay any attention to you." Ms. Long had gone to New York when she was twenty-five because she felt that she had reached her full potential working at Republic Bank in Trinidad. "I thought that I could come to the US and go back to school. That was as far ahead as I was thinking and it took me about five years to actually get myself to the point where I could get into college. That was twenty-three years ago and I can think today of no place I would rather live than in New York." And Carole Musaracchia, a native-born New Yorker, expressed the same opinion. "What makes an American," she said, "is pride in the freedom that we have to express ourselves, as an explorer, an inventor, a creator of positive change."

"This is surely not what all Americans think," I had told Dr. Hoyte in July 2011.

"No," she said, unperturbed. "Mostly white Americans think this. But when immigrants do not believe this, and a lot of immigrants go to the United States with a lot of baggage, they should just do what they came to the US to achieve – a better education, a better quality of life – and, if they cannot cope, they should just go back home."

But I was remembering what Barack Obama had written in *The Audacity of Hope*, which I felt was nearer to the truth of life in the United States today. "We need to understand," he wrote, "just how we got to this place, this land of warring factions and tribal hatreds. And we need to remind ourselves, despite all our differences, just how much we share: common hopes, common dreams, a bond that will not break." And yet he had written too that he found it "hard to shake the feeling these days that our democracy has gone seriously awry."

William A. Galston in a Brookings Institute study published on 10 May 2012 hinted at this 'bad blood' between the parties when in his study of the Presidential Election he had said that the historic level of partisan polarization ensured that it would be a hard-fought and divisive battle. The 2012 election he wrote has unfolded against a backdrop of public anxiety and discontent and he drew attention to four recent surveys that found on average only 28 per cent of Americans who are satisfied with conditions in the country while 70 per cent are dissatisfied. Four other surveys he said found that only 33 per cent think that the country is heading in the right direction, compared to 61 per cent who think that the country is on the wrong track. But these findings tell nothing of the hostility of American businessmen to the policies of the Democratic Party and the President. Galston wrote that "the sense that America is going in the wrong direction reflects not only current economic realities, but also pervasive worries about the future." According to one national survey, he said, 69 per cent of Americans fear that their children's standard of living will be lower than their own.

These opinions seemed to energize corporate America's distaste for the President and in the weeks before 6 November there were heads of American companies who made no secret of their wish to regain the White House. According to Dylan Stableford, of Yahoo! News / The Ticket, Koch Industries, the Wichita, Kan.-based company run by the billionaire Koch brothers, sent a voter information packet to 45,000 employees of its Georgia Pacific subsidiary in September that contained a letter, dated 1 October from Koch Industries president Dave Robertson implicitly warning that "many of our more than 50,000 U.S. employees and contractors may suffer the consequences" of voting for President Obama and other Democrats in the 2012 elections, a list of conservative candidates the company's political action committee endorses and a pair of editorials: one, by David Koch, supporting Mitt Romney, and the other, by Charles Koch, condemning Obama.

"While we are typically told before each Presidential election that it is important and historic, I believe the upcoming election will determine what kind of America future generations will inherit," Robertson's letter, first published by InTheseTimes.com begins. "If we elect candidates who want to spend hundreds of billions in borrowed money on costly new subsidies for a few favored cronies, put unprecedented regulatory burdens on businesses, prevent or delay important new construction projects, and excessively hinder free trade, then many of our more than 50,000 U.S. employees and contractors may suffer the consequences, including higher gasoline prices, runaway inflation, and other ills. This is true regardless of what your political affiliation might be." Robertson's letter continued: "To help you engage in the political process, we have enclosed several items in this packet. For most of you, this includes information about voter registration deadlines and early voting options for your state. At the request of many employees, we have also provided a list of candidates in your state that have been supported by Koch companies or by the KOCHPAC, our employee political action committee. I want to emphasize two things about these lists. First, and most important, we believe any decision about which candidates to support is – as always – yours and yours alone, based on the factors that are most important to you. Second, we do not support candidates based on their political affiliation. We evaluate them based on who is the most market-based and willing to support economic freedom for the benefit of society as a whole. If you are concerned about our economy, our future and enhancing the quality of life for all Americans, then I encourage you to consider the principles of your candidates and not just their party affiliation. It is essential that we are all informed and educated voters. Our future depends on it."

The Koch letter was not the only assault on Obama by titans in business. The week before David Siegel, the founder and CEO of Florida-based Westgate Resorts, sent an email to employees informing them that layoffs are likely if Obama is re-elected: "It's quite simple. If any new taxes are levied on me, or my company, as our current President plans, I will have no choice but to reduce the size of this company. Rather than grow this company I will be forced to cut back. This means fewer jobs, less benefits and certainly less opportunity for everyone. So, when you make your decision to vote, ask yourself, which candidate understands the economics of business ownership and who doesn't? Whose policies will endanger your job? Answer those questions and you should know who might be the one capable of protecting and saving your job. While the media wants to tell you to believe the '1 percenters' are bad, I'm telling you they are not. They create most of the jobs. If you lose your job, it won't be at the hands of the '1%'; it will be at the hands of a political hurricane that swept through this country." Siegel and his wife were the subjects of *The Queen of Versailles*, a recent documentary "about their ongoing quest to build the largest house in America." And Siegel has often claimed credit for George W. Bush's victory over Al Gore in the 2000 presidential race. ("I had my managers do a survey on every employee [8,000 total]," Siegel told Bloomberg BusinessWeek. "If they liked Bush, we made them register to vote. But not if they liked Gore.")

Siegel and the Koch brothers were not alone in issuing anti-Obama missives to employees. According to MSNBC, Arthur Allen, chief executive of ASG Software Solutions, wrote a similar email to his staffers on 30 September: "Many of you have been with ASG for over 5, 10, 15, and even 20 years. As you know, together, we have been able to keep ASG an independent company while still growing our revenues and customers. But I can tell you, if the US re-elects

President Obama, our chances of staying independent are slim to none. I am already heavily involved in considering options that make our independence go away, and with that all of our lives would change forever. I believe that a new President and administration would give US citizens and the world the renewed confidence and optimism we all need to get the global economies started again, and give ASG a chance to stay independent. If we fail as a nation to make the right choice on November 6th, and we lose our independence as a company, I don't want to hear any complaints regarding the fallout that will most likely come."

In the May/June 2012 issue of *Foreign Affairs*, the editors published "campaign tips" from Quintus Tullius Cicero that emphasized among other advice the need of politicians to "pay special attention to businessmen and moderately wealthy citizens." Their special interests, as Siegel and the Koch brothers, were to indicate in their letters to employees, what must be taken into account, even if it sounded as whitemail, by their votes for Governor Mitt Romney. As one read the admonitions it was easy to think that the story was modern and not more than two centuries old and that it was Washington DC and not Rome. Or, that it was London, Athens or Port of Spain. "Our city," wrote the editors, "is a cesspool of humanity, a place of deceit, plots, and vice of every imaginable kind. Anywhere you turn you will see arrogance, stubbornness, malevolence, pride and hatred." It was an indisputable description of the capitals we know at election time and readers must have wondered at the similarities of evil after two thousand years of Christianity. As James Carville remarked, *Plus ça change, plus c'est la même chose.*

X

THE POINT of a political campaign is to bring hope to people and this is true in the United States as it was in Rome and as it is in Trinidad and Tobago. Thus as a conscientious believer in good governance and in efficient government I had agreed in 2010 when I returned to Trinidad to take part in the formation of a Debates Commission that the Trinidad and Tobago Chamber of Industry and Commerce was in the mood to set up with help from a similar movement in Jamaica and with the support of the U.S. Commission of Presidential Debates. But the debates that were planned before Election Day 2010 did not materialize because the then Prime Minister Patrick Manning felt he should not debate Ms. Kamla Persad-Bissessar. Did he send the wrong message to the country? As it turned out on 24 May Ms. Persad-Bissessar's People's Partnership party, a collection of mismatched politicians, trounced Mr. Manning's People's National Movement, winning twenty-nine of the forty-one seats in the House of Representatives.

However the Chamber did succeed in hosting a debate during the campaign for Local Government Elections that were held in July 2010; but it was never clear that the event had had any impact on the Trinidad and Tobago electorate. And what is worse is that since that time there has been excruciating silence from the Chamber offices at Westmoorings as it waits for an announcement of the Tobago House of Assembly's elections due in 2013. Meanwhile the Commission on Presidential Debates had not forgotten the dream of the Chamber and in May 2012 Janet Brown, Executive Director, and Matt Dippell, Debates Program Advisor and Deputy Director for Latin America and the Caribbean, sent an invitation to Ms. Catherine Kumar, CEO of the Trinidad and Tobago Chamber, to attend the Second Presidential Debate that took place at Hofstra University in New York on 15 October 2012.

This was the debate that President Barack Obama was reported to have won over Governor Mitt Romney after a disastrous showing in his first debate. According to CBS News the first Presidential debate in Colorado on 3 October 2012 sparked a new_round of opinions about the election. CBS contributor Ben Stein had this to say, "The first Presidential debate this year was one of those great moments. In a campaign that's been alternately boring and nasty, this was a night of civility, information, and genuine learning about the men who might be our President. In President Obama, whom I have often criticized, I saw a man of dignity, deference and politeness, extremely well-informed and quick with a quip that expressed his point of view. I admired his demand for more detail, and his noting the contradictions in Governor Romney's different plans over the years. In Governor Romney, as to whose chance to win I have been skeptical, I saw a man who still lacks specifics, but who is facile with concepts and numbers, extremely adroit at mixing practicality and ideology. I also saw a man of good humor, who began the evening with congratulations to Mr. Obama on his anniversary and a joke about how he was sure Mr. Obama wanted to spend his big day on a stage with Romney. I saw a Presidential dignity. Both are men of power and material comfort. Yet I saw what seemed to me to be genuine concern for the less well-off among us. I saw two men who seemed to me to want the job to help people in need and to defend the nation."

The table was turned the next time Obama and Romney debated however. This is the way that Jeff Greenfield, a Yahoo! News columnist and the host of *Need to Know* on PBS, reported it: "When the evening began, one observation dominated the conversation: 'If President Barack Obama has another debate like the last one, the election's over.' When the evening ended, I was struck by a different thought: If Obama had performed this way at the first debate the election would have been over. In every debate, whatever the format, whatever the questions, there is one and only one way to identify the winner: Who commands the room? Who drives the narrative? Who is in charge? More often than not on Tuesday night, I think, Obama had the better of it."

But at the end of the debate I was still reflecting on our own Debates Commission and the Trinidad and Tobago Chamber's hopes to change Trinidadians and Tobagonians' thinking on political matters. I have no doubt that the work of the Chamber staff is well-meaning but a revolution requires more than good intentions; it requires that something must be done to change Destiny. And this demands giving up old systems and old ideas that worked for just a few. It is time I thought for the Chamber to give up its protective custody of the Debates Commission and put the Debates Commission in the hands of someone whose industry and independence will drive the development of the Debates Commission to inspire the Trinidad and Tobago community and win its respect. Was this something that Ms. Kumar could have learnt in the days she spent at Hofstra University? Will she speak bluntly of the TTDC when she gets back and be willing to change the course of the Debates Commission and make a case for an independent and experienced Executive Director? The program agenda I recalled included discussions with individuals involved in the CPD presidential debate such as the CPD leadership and staff, television production specialists, candidate representatives, the debate moderator, journalists, Hofstra University leaders and law enforcement officials. It is true that at first glance the Chamber could believe that it does not have the resources to fire and fund the development of the TTDC in this way; but if it does think this and remains in a state of intellectual paralysis, it should abandon its dream to improve the politics in Trinidad and Tobago with thoughtful and stimulating debate. Anything else is a sham.

XI

I DIDN'T THINK my unwillingness to believe that it was a level playing field for black Americans bothered Dr. Hoyte. As Ms. FitzGerald had noted before the black civil rights movement of the 1960s Americans thought their country was a nation of immigrants and in the textbooks published there were hardly any mention of blacks. "The blacks were never treated as a group at all; they were quite literally invisible." And in one textbook, Charles Garrett Vannest and Henry Lester Smith's *Socialized History of the United States*, most other immigrants were doing quite well. However "in the sixties New Left historians introduced evidence to show that the Republicans had not gone far enough in the Radical Reconstruction period after the civil war, and their failure to deliver on their promises to give the free slaves economic independence had doomed the blacks to inferior status and the country to racial conflict for generations to come. The Jews, for instance, were said to be doing well in politics and the Germans were farming successfully; in fact no one was causing any trouble except the Japanese and the Chinese, who according to Harold Rugg's *An Introduction to Problems of American Culture*, had brought a race problem to the Western states." And yet, since the 1930s writers dared to describe the United States as "a melting pot" and called on the foreign born to appreciate American ideals and make a responsible effort to help realize the dreams of Americans.

Is there a solution to the racial problems we see in the United States? Remember the dream of Martin Luther King Jr. on the 28 August 1963 in Washington DC? "I have a dream," Dr. King said, "that my four little children will one day live in a nation where they will not be judged by the color of their skin but by the content of their character." That dream it seems still eludes American society. "I hate the fact that there is still such blatant racism," said Ms. Long. "You would think that after all these years things would be different but it is not. It is illegal to discriminate but that doesn't stop some people and when we have groups like the Tea Party reinforcing these stereotypes I realize that we still have a long way to go before we can believe in any changes."

But there is a problem too with the economic state of the US as the 25-page analysis of the state of the country by Galston makes the point that "to an extent that Americans have not seen for at least two decades, the election of 2012 will revolve around a single defining issue – the condition of the economy." The long, bitter fight over the debt ceiling, wrote Galston, antagonized voters across the political spectrum, and the failure of the economy to maintain its spring momentum sapped confidence in the recovery. And the sense that America is going in the wrong direction "reflects not only current economic realities, but also pervasive worries about the future (and) according to one national survey, 69 percent of Americans fear that their children's standard of living will be lower than their own."

The Republicans' squabble over who should be the Party's choice to oppose President Obama, bitter at times, did not help to clarify the state of American politics and, more importantly, the quality of the country's fiscal policies. And while the debates raged, toppling first Herman Cain, then Michele Bachmann, Jon Huntsman and Texas governor Rick Perry in the same month, followed by Rick Santorum, Newt Gingrich and Ron Paul, the consensus was that economic growth began to slow and consumer sentiment stopped rising and the pace of job generation fell. "After averaging 252,000 per month from December 2011 through February 2012," wrote Galston, "the economy created 154,000 jobs in March and only 115,000 in April." The feeling among economists was that it was the third consecutive spring in which hope of a broader recovery gave way to disappointment said Galston.

This was definitely not the place President Obama had hoped to be six months before Election Day on 6 November and it was not surprising that in this negative environment the way was clear for a new range of attacks on him. In June, for example, when he called a press conference to chide Republicans he said that the private sector was doing fine. Was it politically incorrect for Obama to say this? Does the opposition expect him to make no mention of the private sector, good or bad? And should Americans, in particular Democrats, be bewildered when Republicans react as though the remark had come from the mouth of a communist or a terrorist, someone they think they cannot trust?

The President, to use the words of one Republican, was "lurching" America towards a European-style socialism. It was what Judith Jones, a Republican activist, had insinuated the President might be doing when we were at a Pompano Beach restaurant in Florida in May. "We have a President," the conversation around the dinner table went, "who has a socialist agenda for the American people." As a Trinidadian couple, Simon Rambaran and his wife, Gail, entertained us with Bob Marley's songs and Kitchener's calypsoes, I had to remember that we were in so-called Republican country. "People in this town," said our Haitian driver who drove us from the Fort Lauderdale Airport to our hosts, Phil Lomenzo and Joyce Hunter's beach-front home, "are out of touch with reality. They hate Obama so much you'd think he's the anti-Christ." But this hadn't been the finding of Ms. Jones who reluctantly confessed that in several days of phone calls she had been unable to contact more than just three persons who expressed support for Mitt Romney.

The truth is it is as difficult a race for Romney and in spite of the millions he is pouring into his campaign it could be money going down the drain. He could draw, for example, no support from a CNN/ORC International poll released on 8 June that found President George W. Bush with a low favorable rating when he left office, and he was still not popular. In fact Bush is the only living president with a favorable rating that's lower than 50 per cent. The poll showed that 54 per cent of people questioned had an unfavorable opinion of him, and with only 43 per cent saying they had a favorable view. So is Romney following in the footsteps of an American president who has been reviled by allies and foes all over the world? This was a poll in fact that gave strength to Obama's warning that, "The economic vision of Mr. Romney and his allies in Congress was tested just a few years ago. Their policies did not grow the economy. They did not grow the middle class. They did not reduce our debt. Why would we think that they would work better this time? We can't afford to jeopardize our future by repeating the mistakes of the past. Not now. Not when there's so much at stake."

And yet, Louisiana's Indian-American governor Bobby Jindal seized the opportunity to denigrate Obama when he attended a meeting in Washington on 9 June and called the President "the most liberal, most incompetent president" in the White House since Jimmy Carter. "The Obama administration is at the nexus of liberalism and incompetence and together that's a deadly combination," said Jindal in a scathing criticism of Obama at the Chicago Conservative Political Action Conference. Responding to Obama's statement that the private sector was doing fine, he added, "Mr. President, I've got a message for you: The private sector is not doing well when 23 million Americans are unemployed and underemployed in this great country."

Obama, nettled by this negativism, accused Republicans of playing "political games" by turning his earlier words against him. And, in a brief photo opportunity, Obama revisited the issue. "It is absolutely clear that the economy is not doing fine," he said. "That's the reason I had the press conference." He said he had called reporters together to press Congress to pass his stalled jobs program. "That's why I spent yesterday, the day before yesterday, this past week, this past month, and this past year talking about how we can make the economy stronger," he said. "The economy is not doing fine. There are too many people out of work. The housing market is still weak and too many homes are under water. And that's precisely why I asked Congress to start taking some steps that can make a difference." But he also insisted that "we've actually seen some good momentum in the private sector." And the president renewed his criticisms of Republicans, underlining their rejection of his jobs plan. "Now, you can't give me a good reason as to why Congress would not act on these items other than politics – because these are traditionally ideas that Democrats and Republicans have supported," he said. "And one of the things that people get so frustrated about is that instead of actually talking about what would help, we get wrapped up in these political games. That's what we need to put an end to."

In spite of this explanation and plea, Romney still released a Web video hammering Obama for his assertion that "the economy is doing fine." The Romney campaign paid for the 54-second spot, which opened with the president at a White House press conference. The ad showed eight people talking about their experiences: staff cuts, job loss, personal bankruptcy, a two-year job hunt, no healthcare and a slashed pension and other concerns. The ad closed with, "No, Mr. President, we are not doing fine." The economy with its stubborn 8.2 per cent unemployment remained the biggest issue for voters and a weak spot for Obama.

Addressing this problem of the economy recently, Harvard professor Niall Ferguson said the US has lost its competitive edge and there's only one place to put the blame. In an interview with Bloomberg TV, Ferguson, who has warned about the US faltering economy for years, cited a new Harvard Business School study that claims the US has fallen behind in global economic competitiveness. For instance, the January study found that for "Harvard alums personally involved in a company relocation decision, 57 per cent said the decision involved the possibility of moving existing activities out of the US," according to Rob Wile of *Business Insider*. "Meanwhile, only 9 per cent considered moving existing activities from another country into the US," he added. A US-based respondent was three times more likely to consider moving business activity out of the US than a non-US respondent was likely to consider moving an activity into the US, wrote Professor Michael Porter, the study's author. Why the dismal outlook? Apparently, US businesses hate the US economy for a couple of simple reasons: "[T]hey can't stand the tax code and they can't stand politicians," *Business Insider's* Joe Wiesenthal writes.

In Elyria, Ohio, President Obama had said in April that his Republican rivals are sincere, patriotic and absolutely wrong about how to reinvigorate the economy. He said they didn't seem to remember how America was built. The President was speaking in politically pivotal Ohio before rolling into neighboring Michigan for an evening of fundraising. Pounding home the theme of his re-election run, Obama said the rich should pay higher taxes to support priorities, such as education, that help the entire nation. "In this country, prosperity doesn't trickle down," Obama told an audience of roughly 400 people at Lorain County Community College. "Prosperity grows from the bottom up and it grows from a strong middle class out. That's why I'm always confused when we keep having the same argument with folks who don't seem to remember how America was built," We have two competing visions of our future, Obama said. "The choice could not be clearer. Those folks running on the other side, I'm sure they are patriots, I'm sure they are sincere in terms of what they say, but their theory, I believe, is wrong."

There is, however, another group of patriots that the President will have to confront in any plan he has for the economy. This is the group that came out in 2011 to challenge the country's richest 1 per cent and which was looking to build on the Occupy Wall Street movement. The movement is not dead and its activists say they are turning to corporate shareholder meetings to vent their anger over economic disparity in the United States and to promote an assortment of other causes. The group calling themselves 99% Power – a reference to those not among the top 1% of earners – says it plans actions at 36 shareholder meetings. The protests could give another jolt to the 2012 annual meeting season, which has already featured a shareholder vote of no confidence in Citigroup's executive compensation plan. Organizers said they expected hundreds of protesters to target a broad range of issues from foreclosures to financing of "dirty energy" to immigrant rights to corporate taxes. Activists are expecting more protesters than in past years and are buoyed by grass-root campaigns last fall that led banks to cancel proposed debit card fees and moved disgruntled customers to shift their deposits to credit unions.

The struggle for a better sharing of the American economic pie goes on even as a report that the 40 richest individuals on earth had lost a combined $6.2 billion one day in April as stocks dropped amid disappointing US earnings, according to the Bloomberg Billionaires Index that measures the world's wealthiest people based on market and economic changes and Bloomberg News reporting. The combined wealth of the index is $1.1 trillion, and the 40 billionaires gained a combined $88.2 billion since the beginning of the year. But this vast treasury of wealth, even when it places Americans among the richest people in the world, fails to dispel the apprehensions that all's not well with America and I am reminded instead of the warnings of Doomsday and I question if the United States would be the spark that triggers Armageddon more than any uprising in the Middle East could do.

In his 2000 bestseller, *The Coming Anarchy*, Robert D. Kaplan urges us to "think of a stretch limo in the potholed streets of New York City where homeless beggars live. Inside the limo are the air-conditioned post-industrial regions of North America, Europe, the emerging Pacific Rim, and a few other isolated places, with their trade summitry and computer-information highways. Outside is the rest of mankind, going in a completely different direction." And Kaplan doesn't end his gloomy view of the world with this snapshot only. "We are entering," he writes, "a bifurcated world. Part of the globe is inhabited by Hegel's and Fukuyama's Last Man, healthy, well-fed, and pampered by technology. The other, larger, part is inhabited by Hobbes' First Man, condemned to a life that is "poor, nasty, brutish, and short."

And on the afternoon of 25 May, as the Amtrak train made its way to Detroit, I asked myself the question Abraham Lincoln had asked himself on 10 November 1864, whether any government that is not too strong to safeguard the liberties of its people can be strong enough to maintain its own existence, in great emergencies?

There is a second view of Apocalypse that Thomas Friedman and Michael Mandelbaum describe in *That used to be us* that should worry Americans. In America today they said there is something that poses a greater threat to America's national security and well-being than al-Qaeda does. "We have seen a country with enormous potential falling into disrepair, political disarray, and palpable discomfort about its present condition and future prospects." As I read this searing acknowledgement of America's problems I felt that Detroit fitted the description of plunder, indifference and decay and I understood more the pessimism of the *Tribune*'s cartoonist. But could Republicans really extricate themselves from the horror of America today? What we are seeing, said Dave Harold, is the end of a civilization.

As our train travelled through the heartland of the state of Michigan I knew that the answer for America's salvation was given by Russell Simmons, who with Rick Rubin had founded the pioneering hip-hop label Def Jam. "We are at the beginning of a very exciting time for America," said Simmons. "I started GlobalGrind.com because I believed that young people inspired by the President and of course by hip-hop as well, yearned for a post-racial America – an America that celebrates our diversity but also recognizes the wounds that we have suffered. It is this younger generation that I put my most faith in to lead our country to this inspirational place. I may be supporting Obama, but that's just my choice. If young people really get involved and support the candidate that really speaks to them, I know that whoever wins on Election Day will have to spend the next four years working for them. That is the incredible power that they hold!"

Were Republicans seeing it this way too and did they think it a fairly good chance that Barack Obama would win a second term in the White House? Was it something that House Speaker John Boehmer believed after the Republicans' bruising primaries? In what he called a frank interview, Boehner, a Republican from Ohio, said there's a "one-in-three chance" that Democrats could take control of the House of Representatives in the next election. "I would say that there is a two-in-three chance that we win control of the House again," Boehner said during a Fox News interview, "but there's a one-in-three chance that we could lose and I'm being myself, frank." Whenever I read the news I never thought that he saw himself and the Grand Old Party as partners with President Obama to build a strong, happy, prosperous and unified nation. Bigotry like hell, to misquote Thomas Paine, is not easily conquered but serious Americans still have the consolation that the harder the conflict, the more glorious the triumph.

I know that the mistake men often make, as Albert Camus said, is thinking that a situation is tragic because it is wretched and because we do not have the heart to forgive the perpetrators of this wretchedness. I hoped we were not going down that road as we disembarked and walked into the sunlight to greet Dave Harold, an American who had defied the odds in Mississippi, in the University of Detroit, and in the United States Navy, a man who was not, as far as I had seen, going through an identity crisis, and a man who is proud of his accomplishments and the successful revolt of his soul. I was confident of learning the truth and I felt a sense of lucidity that I hadn't felt before.

Chapter One – The American Dream

Greed is good. Now it's legal. Everyone is drinking the same kool aid. The mother of all evil is speculation. It's systematic, malignant and it's global. – Michael Douglas in the Oliver Stone film, *Wall Street – Money Never Sleeps*.

NEW YORK. – His name was Andrew Johnson he said and he was from North Carolina. We had got in his cab at Kennedy Airport and he was taking us to our destination in Brooklyn. "Sit back and relax," he said. "I know where you are going. I have been doing this work for seventeen years, from the first day I came to New York, and I know the city better than most New Yorkers." As the yellow cab gathered speed in the afternoon traffic I was sure he did.

His aplomb reminded me of another Andrew Johnson back in Trinidad. He was one of several journalists who had joined the PP (People's Partnership) Government service after the 2010 general election. But though the shape and size of the head was like Andy's I didn't think they were related except through the incident of slavery and because of Lincoln's desire to give the slaves freedom after the Civil War and south Trinidad became the home of many of the African slaves who had fought Lincoln's war. Andy was from Siparia, the hometown of Prime Minister Kamla Persad-Bissessar, and like his namesake in the United States his name had no likeness to the name of his African ancestry. It was one of the ways, like making him bend his knees in worship of a new god, that slavery stripped the African of his true identity.

As I watched the afternoon traffic I remembered too that She Xiuling did not like New York as much as she liked some of the other cities we had visited. It was not just because of the habit of slavery that Afro-Americans in the Big Apple seemed unable to escape even in the twenty-first century; it was because the unmistakable smell of money and power was too much for a heart that treasured the mysticism of Beijing and the unpretentiousness of London. "It's a kind of sumptuous depravity", she was to say when we stopped for lunch with Sir Courtney Blackman at one of the city's Brasserie restaurants. But it sounded like intellectual snobbery and she was in a minority she knew. Her research had revealed that the Big Apple draws every year more visitors than any other city in the United States, more even than Los Angeles with Hollywood and Disneyland, more even than Orlando with Disneyworld and Circus World. And whenever she walked Manhattan's famous avenues, with its stores and homes for the rich, she flinched from the city's attempts to pull her into the swirling waters of the American Dream. Her antagonisms, however, would not blind her from seeing New York, what the Founding Fathers called New Amsterdam, as the most famous commercial city in the modern world.

I remembered that Rhona had said, "When you are in New York the flavor of the day, week and month is Money with a capital M. Every store and restaurant owner, every waitress and shop-clerk, every taxi-driver, every panhandler seems to have his or her eyes on your wallet. This primordial greed is sure to challenge Xiuling's modest village upbringing. Linxi, Chaozhou, is light years away from Fifth Avenue, Manhattan."

"It is the same in China," I said. "You forgot what Margaret Thatcher once said. There are more capitalists in China than in any other part of the Western World."

She shook her head. "It's nothing like this. New York is the world's capital of Capitalism. It's the cradle of the American Dream. People don't disguise their predatory instincts and intentions in this town. They go for the jugular. China is a pussy cat."

"If you keep this up you are not going to make this a pleasant visit for Xiuling."

"Why? Is it because she was born on Hainan Island and grew up in a village in Chaozhou? Don't be naïve. She's a different person from the shy and innocent student we met in 1998. Travel and Warwick University have changed her. You will see that for yourself when you take her walking around Manhattan. She forms opinions of her own."

"You could be right."

What I wondered did Andrew Johnson think about the city. Taxi-drivers are a race that arouses suspicion in me whether I am in New York or Beijing, but I thought we could trust him. I had no idea where we were going. In all my years of going to New York I had seldom been out of Manhattan. One time I spent a night in White Plains City where Nelson Foote lived. It was in 1976 and I had been looking for funds to print *Crisis* and Wendell Mottley who was in Toronto at the time suggested that I should ask Foote to assist me. God knows why. I had never met Foote but I recalled that he had been working as a consultant with the Telephone Service of Trinidad and Tobago. I was grabbing at straws so I did fly to New York from Toronto but I didn't get any help from Foote. He was however a good host and a great talker and we spent the evening analyzing the politics of Trinidad and Tobago and the character of people he had met. In the end it was John Jepson, an Englishman who was married to my youngest sister, Barbara, who loaned me the CAN$9,000 I needed to get *Crisis* printed. There was another time that I went to a White Plains City newspaper with *Express* Production Manager Malcolm Smith and Marketing Manager James Persaud to observe the front-end system we planned to invest in. But most of the time I had been to New York I seldom went out of Manhattan, captivated by its savage energy and cosmopolitan character.

"How long will it take to get to Brooklyn?" Rhona asked. "The friends we are going to said it was a 30-minute drive."

He must have seen that she was looking at the meter.

"It depends on the traffic," he said calmly. "At this time it could be 40 or 45 minutes. But don't worry. I know where we are going. We won't get lost." Then, "Did they tell you how much the fare would be?"

"Thirty or thirty-five dollars," she said.

He nodded. "Have they been living here for a long time?"

"Yes," she said.

"And this is not your first visit to New York?"

"It is not," she said.

I knew that Rhona was thinking of the tip at the end of the ride. Like most people she resented the assumption that it was the public's duty to supplement the wages of employees in the service industry. "People should be paid a fair wage," she insisted, "and should not expect handouts from customers." When we first went to China it was impossible to find porters or taxi-drivers who would accept a tip from you and after twelve years in China to do so in the West was often an unexpected burden on our goodwill and our pockets. But the point is a tip was not any more what you would graciously give for what you considered good service; now it was part of the transaction even if you hated the attitude of workmen and the service they delivered. The fact is tipping is one of the symptoms of the capitalist economy and we just had to live with the custom though most people see it as a fee you paid to avoid a nasty row with waiters, baggage handlers and taxi-drivers. "How much do I tip?" I once asked Ray Boddie at an Italian restaurant in Woodbridge, Virginia, where we had a delightful dinner and had been served by a young waitress who was probably working to pay her way through university. "Seventeen or twenty percent of the bill," he said. But at the Sheraton Hotel in New York some years before I had questioned the waiter on the money he had brought back for me and he had said coolly, "Oh, I took my tip." The sonofabitch! It was my son Marc who prevented me from exploding. I see recently that Americans are questioning their responsibility to tip or how much to do so and I have hope for a change in workers' expectations to be compensated by the public for the work they do. The Chinese, poor as they are, do not expect you to pay their wages and this independence is part of their dignity. I remembered the airline baggage employee who told me in Detroit that he depended on tips to support him and I wondered if his work was a source of humiliation for him and his family. I knew that not all jobs brought in sufficient income but one shouldn't have to beg. Find a second job. My father worked at two jobs, kept bees and learnt tailoring and shoe-making to take care of my mother and their eleven children. It was for him a heroic life but it was an example other men could emulate.

"Seventeen per cent," I said to no one. Would it be what Andrew Johnson was expecting? Or would ten per cent be enough?

"Here we are," he said, positioning the vehicle in the middle of the street to turn right on Ocean Avenue and pointing to a brown-stone building at the corner. It was an old building that the gentrification program that was changing the face of Brooklyn had not as yet touched. The fare on the meter I saw was thirty-three dollars.

I took out a $50 bill and told him, "Give me back ten dollars."

He did. "Thanks," he said. "Enjoy your vacation."

"I think you tipped too much," Rhona said when he drove away. "I am glad that come tomorrow we will be using the subway."

"Me too. But he was an all-right guy. He got here very quickly."

"He did. Now how are we going to get in if the girls are not at home?"

"Yolanda said she would leave the keys with the doorman."

"She's been living here for a long time?"

"I have no idea but the apartment is hers."

"Good for her! She must be doing very well in her job."

"Her father said she lost her job with one of the television companies. The failing economy is affecting everyone. You see the figures – 18, 19 million people unemployed. It's not going to be easy for Barack Obama. Anyway I am not sure what she's doing."

"It must be hard to survive and to be successful in America. Why do people still come to the United States? I remember that Alistair Cooke wrote that New York is a bad town and America is a bad country to be poor in."

"We have had this conversation before. They are all hooked into the American Dream and want piece of the American Pie. That's what Hollywood, Entertainment TV and Macy's Thanksgiving Parade have done to them. But I am sure it is so in every country for the new immigrant. You have to be tough and focused to overcome the problems of food, shelter and work. Think of Charlie Chaplin."

"He was white."

"Okay. Think of Rihanna and Obama's Attorney-General. They are both from Barbados by the way."

"Eric Holder? You are right. But I think Yolanda has done very well to buy her own apartment. It shows she's enterprising and she's probably not taking crap from anyone. No wonder her father is so proud of her. Are you listening to me? Stop admiring the neighbourhood I know it's your first time in Brooklyn but we are behaving like new immigrants. Let's go in."

"Remember she said to forgive the state it's in. She's re-modeling."

"Don't worry. I am happy that she could accommodate us. And the weather is better than it was last year when we were here."

"I thought you loved the cold."

"It wasn't cold. It was wet."

II

NINE MONTHS before, on the morning of Friday 1 September 2011 when we left our Petit Valley home to catch Air Caribbean's flight 425 to John F. Kennedy Airport in New York winds and rains from Hurricane Irene were lashing the East Coast of the United States. More than a thousand flights into Kennedy and La Guardia had been cancelled but there had been no word from Air Caribbean that our flight was one of them. I had called Kevin Livingston, the taxi-driver who was to take us to Piarco International Airport to make sure that he would be on time. The flight was scheduled to leave at 7:05 and I had no wish to be late. I didn't trust the airline's efficiency. Since coming back to Trinidad from China I had been finding out that simple business transactions had a way of going painfully wrong and people did not care anymore about being professional or courteous. They did not care period. I was still to be paid National Insurance benefits and this was holding up my claim for Old Age pension. I thought that people were waiting for me to pass on even though my claims were more than twelve years late. Judy Thomas was like public servants of old however; she had tended to me with diligence. I felt that if I were to live long enough I would be able to receive the $3,000 pension that the Government promised to pay old folks.

But Air Caribbean was only a part of the problem. I was beginning to dislike air travel. I knew that the security searches at airports all around the world are necessary for our safety since the hijacking of four American planes that crashed into the Twin Towers in New York, into the Pentagon in Washington DC, and into a field in Pennsylvania killing more than 3,000 people on the morning of 11 September 2001. And I knew that Richard Reid, the so-called shoe-bomber who pleaded guilty to terrorism charges in October 2002 and is serving a life sentence in Florence, Colorado, and Omar Farouk Abdulmutallab, the 25-year-old engineer of Lagos, Nigeria, who became known as the underwear bomber and who pleaded guilty to the attempted use of a weapon of mass destruction by placing a destructive device on an aircraft and who is also incarcerated at the penitentiary in Colorado, are responsible for the long and relentless searches at airports.

Two months after 19 jihadists hijacked airplanes and flew them into the World Trade Center, the Pentagon and a Pennsylvania field, Richard Reid who was born in Jamaica attempted to detonate explosives hidden in his sneakers on an American Airlines flight from Paris, France, to Miami, Florida. Passengers thwarted his plan, and the plane landed safely in Boston, Massachusetts. Reid pleaded guilty to terrorism charges in October 2002 and is serving a life sentence at the nation's super-maximum security prison in Florence, Colorado. American Airlines Flight 63, carrying 197 people from Paris to Miami was diverted to Boston on December 22, 2001, after passengers and crew saw Reid trying to light a fuse and subdued him by tying him to his seat. A doctor on board administered a tranquilizer. FBI bomb technicians and explosives experts found explosives in Reid's shoes. Reid, a British citizen and convert to Islam, pleaded guilty to all eight counts against him – including attempted use of a weapon of mass destruction, attempted homicide and placing an explosive device on an aircraft.

Zacarias Moussaoui, the only person convicted in the United States for his role in the 11 September 2001 terror attacks, said during his 2006 sentencing trial that he and Reid were supposed to be part of the attacks on U.S. targets. But Reid testified that although he knew Moussaoui, he knew nothing about the 2001 attacks. Moussaoui was arrested in August 2001 in Minnesota after instructors at the flight school he was attending reported he was acting suspiciously and did not have much flying experience. He pleaded guilty to terrorism conspiracy and is also serving a life sentence.

Umar Farouk Abdulmutallab pleaded guilty to the attempted use of a weapon of mass destruction, the attempted murder of 300 people, the attempted destruction of a civilian aircraft, placing a destructive device on an aircraft, and possession of explosives. Incarcerated at the

United States Penitentiary in Florence, Colorado, Abdulmutallab confessed to and was convicted of attempting to detonate plastic explosives hidden in his underwear while on board Northwest Airlines Flight 253, en route from Amsterdam to Detroit, Michigan, on December 25, 2009. Al-Qaeda in the Arabian Peninsula claimed to have organized the attack with Adbulmutallab saying that they supplied him with the bomb and trained him. On February 16, 2012 he was sentenced to life in prison without the possibility of parole by a U.S. federal court.

These are the men who make flying such a chore nowadays but they are not the sum total of the pain we get from air travel. The airlines one could think exploit passengers' powerlessness to strike back at the increasing costs of travel. And it was in response to this exploitation that on 1 September 2011 I had my first row with an airline when I protested its incompetence and lack of concern for passengers. The truth is I have been developing a contempt for airlines and for their supercilious and hypocritical concern for passengers. We are expected to feel a special relationship with the airline we are on when the captain and flight attendants say they know that we have a choice of travel and they are grateful for our business; but it's all insincere and platitudinous. I think that I prefer the honest humor of Southwest Airlines flight attendants who say, "We like your money. Come fly with us again."

I know the exploitation is calculated to sound as if the airline industry is in a worse economic situation than Greece and needs our sympathy and support. In fact on 11 June 2012, airline industry group IATA warned that global profits would more than halve this year owing to surging oil prices and the Eurozone crisis, with European carriers suffering losses of $1.1 billion. Tony Tyler, head of the International Air Transport Association, also hit out at a controversial carbon tax scheme put in place by the European Union, calling it a "polarizing obstacle to real progress". Tyler told the group's annual general meeting in Beijing that "2012 is another challenging year. We expect revenues of $631 billion but a profit of just $3.0 billion." That compares with a profit of $7.9 billion in 2011, IATA figures show. Tyler cited the cost of oil as a reason for "anemic global profitability" and IATA said it predicted an overall average price of $110 a barrel this year using Brent crude oil as a basis, warning political risks could push this up.

It has become normal to read reports that most of the world's airlines are facing very difficult times and because of the increases in fuel costs profitability is at an all-time risk. The Department of Transportation's Bureau of Transportation Statistics (BTS) reported that U.S. airlines collected almost $5.7 billion from baggage fees and reservation change fees in 2010. American passenger airlines made an estimated profit of $2.6 billion in 2010, according to the ATA. More than $2.1 billion of that profit came from fees. Baggage fees and reservation change fees were the two largest chunks at $906 million and $646 million respectively. Carry-on luggage has reached ridiculous proportions as a result and it seems it is the only way passengers could save on travel costs. But the no-frills policy has taken the fun out of flying and I think that the policy behind non-refundable tickets is scandalously unfair.

The Middle Seat scorecard ranks major carriers each year on a number of key measures important to travelers: on-time arrivals, long delays, canceled flights, mishandled bags, passengers bumped from flights and complaints filed with the Department of Transportation. Data come from DOT and FlightStats.com, a flight-tracking service that collects real-time flight information from airlines, airports and the Federal Aviation Administration. Alaska, which launched an operational overhaul in 2007 after several years of dismal reliability, was first among major airlines in on-time arrivals. The carrier has set internal standards: There are 50 different check points on a timeline for each departure, with data collected on each one. Flight attendants have to be on board 45 minutes before scheduled departure; customer-service agents board the first passenger 40 minutes before departure, and 90 per cent of passengers need to be boarded 10 minutes before departure. What time the fuel truck hooks up and what time it disconnects its hose are measured. When flights arrive, the time the belt-loader pulls up to the plane is tracked. The cargo door is supposed to be opened three minutes after arrival; the first bag needs to be dropped on the carousel before 15 minutes after arrival. "There are so many moving parts. You just can't tell people to get the airplane out on time," said Ben Minicucci, Alaska's chief operating officer.

Delta engineered a major operational turnaround last year. In 2010, Delta was second-worst in punctuality and baggage handling among rival airlines and it had the highest rates of canceled flights and consumer complaints filed with the DOT. For 2011, Delta ranked in the top three in five of six categories. In the past two years, Delta opened maintenance operations in nine cities that aren't hubs for the airline, such as Miami, Portland, Ore., and Philadelphia, to keep more of its fleet ready to fly. Once it was done integrating with Northwest Airlines, Delta invested in new baggage systems in Atlanta, plus new technology in its operations control center and retraining for customer-service workers. "There are a lot of side benefits to running a good, clean operation," said David Holtz, Delta's vice president of operations control.

American, which filed for bankruptcy-court re-organization in November 2011, has struggled with its operation for several years. United and Continental merged in 2010, but the two carriers still operate on separate reservation systems. JetBlue Airways had both the most-frequent delays and the longest delays. Nearly one out of every eight JetBlue flights was at least 45 minutes late last year, according to DOT and FlightStats data. The average delay for a JetBlue flight that ran late was 65 minutes, according to DOT data for the first 10 months of the year. JetBlue says the New York and Boston areas, which are departing or arriving points for 73 per cent of all its flights, got slammed last year with a few severe weather events that led to long delays and canceled flights. Hurricane Irene and severe snowstorms in January and October hurt performance. "We don't have hubs in more favorable weather areas to balance it out," said Rob Maruster, JetBlue's chief operating officer.

Southwest Airlines, the only major airline that doesn't charge fees to check two pieces of luggage, had the second-worst rate of mishandled bags, better than only American. In addition to added volume, Southwest's baggage operation has struggled with complexity of connecting lots of different flights in lots of different cities. Southwest said it made a major push to improve its on-time reliability in the second half of 2011. Currently, the carrier is studying use of hand-held scanners to improve accuracy in routing bags. Still, Southwest customers aren't complaining. The airline had the fewest complaints per passenger, according to DOT stats. The overall rate of cancellations among major carriers was unchanged in 2011 from 2010 at 1.4 per cent of all flights, according to DOT data covering 10 months and FlightStats data for November and December.

III

FOURTEEN YEARS before, when I left Trinidad to teach Oral English and English Writing in Guangzhou, China, my favorite choice of airline was British West Indian Airways (BWIA), which like Trinidad and Tobago Television (TTT) underwent a change in identity during the prime ministership of Patrick Manning. BeeWee is now flying as Caribbean Airlines but after our September experience I am sure that the flying public has lost something that is more valuable than an old familiar name. They lost an airline with a heart. There is a story that Trinidad and Tobago's Prime Minister Eric Williams once asked Cyril Duprey to change the name of Colonial Life Insurance Company. But to this request Duprey replied, "When you change the name of British West Indian Airways, I will consider changing Colonial Life." Duprey, the founder of the company, knew what it is to maintain a corporation's identity with a brand name that was well-known. But two generations after the demise of these leaders, the government gave up the reputation and legacy of both TTT and BWIA.

Much else had befallen BWIA however; it had sold its rights to fly into Heathrow and the chairman of its Board was young George Nicholas II who it is assumed inherited business skills from a father who had developed overnight from a haberdashery store-owner to an innkeeper and real estate mogul. I wondered how all these changes had affected efficiency and loyalty at the airline. This was the reason that in June 2011 we thought we should secure our tickets to the U.S. and not wait to do so in August. We did and regularly up to the week we were to travel we called the airline for assurance that we were confirmed to travel. I felt at times that we were showing too much anxiety but it was important we believed to have the airline's assurance because we didn't want to disappoint She Xiuling who was coming from the other side of the world. She too had been pushing us to make sure that our flight was confirmed.

Then a lady named Irene came calling and it was bad news.

According to the Weather Channel, Irene was a powerful Category 3 storm and an extreme threat from eastern North Carolina to southern New England. Irene had been expected to hit the Carolinas, moving through the northeast. As of 8:00 p.m. eastern time on 30 August a map showed Irene over the Caribbean islands with winds of 120 mph, moving northwest at 12 mph. Major airlines were still operating as normal, but were already offering compensation to those whose travel plans had been affected. This applied to those with flights into or out of Caribbean airports. American Airlines and US Airways said they would waive fees for one ticket change; Delta said it would allow a refund or one-time flight change without penalty; United travelers said it would make one change to their trip without penalty, and those with already canceled flights would be entitled to a refund; Continental offered refunds to those whose Caribbean flights had been cancelled or delayed more than two hours. Penalty-free rescheduling was also being offered.

As Hurricane Irene slammed into North Carolina on 27 August commuters and travelers across the United States felt its impact. More than 8,300 commercial airline flights had to be cancelled over the weekend and that number was expected to rise, according to the website, Flightware.com. In fact, all airports in the New York area – Newark, John F. Kennedy and LaGuardia – stopped accepting domestic and international arrival flights and public transportation in New York City signaled that they would stop running if Irene turned out too powerful to ignore. Airport officials explained that they did not want arriving passengers to be stranded at the airports. And as the days passed, most airlines began to give out travel waivers, which meant they did not charge any fees for changing your flight. In many cases, passengers would have to book their next flight within a short window. But on 25 August, airlines were expanding the scope of their Hurricane Irene waivers, now offering assistance to passengers traveling to or from Caribbean airports and those on the U.S. East Coast.

Hundreds of thousands of residents and vacationers were evacuating from Irene's path, starting in east North Carolina where the hurricane, now packing winds of 100 miles per hour, was expected to make landfall on Saturday 26 August. Tropical storm winds were already arriving along the coast of the Carolinas, the National

Hurricane Center said. A quarter of a million New Yorkers were ordered to leave homes in low-lying areas as authorities prepared for dangerous storm surge and flooding on Sunday in the city and farther east on Long Island. Some New York hospitals in flood-prone areas were already evacuating patients. "We've never done a mandatory evacuation before and we wouldn't be doing it now if we didn't think this storm had the potential to be very serious," New York Mayor Michael Bloomberg told a news conference. Federal and state leaders, from President Obama downward, urged the millions of Americans in the hurricane's path to prepare and to heed evacuation orders if they received them. "All indications point to this being a historic hurricane," Obama said.

Irene, the first hurricane of the 2011 Atlantic season, had already caused as much as $1.1 billion in insured losses in the Caribbean, catastrophe modeling company AIR Worldwide said, with more losses expected to come. New York City's mass transit system, which serves 8.5 million riders a weekday, was expected to shut around noon on Saturday ahead of Irene's arrival, Governor Andrew Cuomo said in a statement. The NHC said hurricane force winds extended outward up to 90 miles from Irene's center, while tropical storm force winds extended out to 290 miles, giving the storm a vast wind field width of nearly 600 miles. "The wind field is huge," U.S. National Hurricane Center Director Bill Read told Reuters. In earlier comments, NHC chief Read said Irene, which would be the first significant hurricane to affect the populous U.S. Northeast in decades, would lash the eastern seaboard with tropical storm-force winds and a "huge swath of rain" from the Carolinas to New England. He said North Carolina would start seeing tropical storm conditions on Friday afternoon. Cities like Washington, Baltimore, Philadelphia and New York could experience heavy rain and wind and power outages from the weekend.

Homeland Security Secretary Janet Napolitano urged East Coast residents not to delay precautions. "The window of preparation is quickly closing," Napolitano said. "This is a big, bad storm," North Carolina Governor Bev Perdue told CNN. Maryland Governor Martin O'Malley told the TV network: "Anyone who thinks this is just a normal hurricane and they can stick it out is being ... selfish and stupid." Wall Street firms scrambled to raise cash in case Irene causes major disruption in trading. Bond trading volume dropped precipitously by noon on Friday. Traders were "watching that big white swirl" on their television sets, said Guy LeBas, chief fixed income strategist at Janney Montgomery Scott in Philadelphia.

Irene would be the first hurricane to hit the U.S. mainland since Ike pounded Texas in 2008. In Washington, Irene forced the postponement of Sunday's dedication ceremony for the new memorial honoring civil rights leader Martin Luther King Jr. Tens of thousands of people, including President Obama, had been expected to attend.

Flooding from Irene had killed at least one person in Puerto Rico and two in the Dominican Republic. The storm knocked out power in the Bahamian capital, Nassau, and blocked roads with trees. But the hurricane had not affected Trinidad and Tobago. However Air Caribbean flights to New York were affected; so too were China Eastern Airlines flights from Shanghai to Kennedy.

But what emergency measures did Caribbean Airlines take? In China, said She Xiuling, passengers were offered a sum of money to give up their flight on 1 September and to fly at another time. In Trinidad this is what happened. When we reached the airline counter after about an hour in the queue, the ticketing clerk said to us, sotto voce: "You are not on flight 425. We are putting you on an afternoon flight." I hit the roof.

For several days as Irene moved north I had been in touch with the airline's Port of Spain ticketing office because I wanted to make sure that we would be flying to New York on the first of September. In fact, we had checked up to the day before we were to travel that we were on the flight. So why were we bumped from the flight and why didn't the airline called to tell us that was all they could do because of accommodating passengers from earlier flights because of Irene? But I was so mad at their inefficiency and indifference that I made a terrible scene and only then was I offered a sum of money to fly later in the day. But this was not what I wanted so the arrangements were made finally to get us on the flight.

IV

I HAD GOT a window seat and as our plane flew into New York on 1 September I peered at the flood water on the ground from Hurricane

Irene now on her way to the New England states. I had been thinking of She Xiuling and how she would feel about New York. What did she expect to find and how would she spend the time? Most people go to New York for the shopping, the entertainment, and the food. They also do so for the sightseeing and 50.6 million of them who did so in 2011 made New York the No. 1 tourist city in the United States because of their wish to see the United Nations headquarters, Radio City Hall, Fifth Avenue, Harlem and Brooklyn. The year before Xiuling had been to Los Angeles and to Miami but this would be her first time in the Big Apple. What would be her reaction to Manhattan's concrete canyons, to Macy's, to Broadway, to Wall Street, to Central Park? Would she be surprised or disappointed? I was sure she had read everything about the city she could find on the Internet.

My first impressions of New York were from the writings of Damon Runyon who was a sports columnist and short story writer. I remember buying *Guys and Dolls* from Fogarty's Bookstore when I started out at the *Trinidad Guardian* in the fifties. I never considered whether his romantic view of New York was true or not; I was just fascinated by the people he wrote about, whether they were gangsters or whores. When Runyon died in 1946 Alistair Cooke said that his death marked the end of an era. "I have noticed that insight into American ways has nothing much to do with intellect or education. Most people find in a foreign country what they want to find," Cooke told his BBC audience in England. So what did I think She Xiuling would discover? If she had looked it up on the Internet, she was bound to know that New York is the most populous city in the United States and the center of one of the most populous metropolitan areas in the world and that it exerts a significant impact upon global commerce, finance, media, art, fashion, research, technology, education, and entertainment. The home of the United Nations Headquarters, New York is an important center for international diplomacy and has been described as the cultural capital of the world. The city is also referred to as New York City or The City of New York to distinguish it from the State of New York, of which it is a part.

In the 19th century, the city was transformed by immigration and development. A visionary development proposal, the Commissioners' Plan of 1811, expanded the city street grid to encompass all of Manhattan, and the 1819 opening of the Erie Canal connected the

Atlantic port to the vast agricultural markets of the North American interior. Local politics fell under the domination of Tammany Hall, a political machine supported by Irish immigrants. Several prominent American literary figures lived in New York during the 1830s and 1840s, including Washington Irving, Herman Melville and Edgar Allan Poe. Public-minded members of the old merchant aristocracy lobbied for the establishment of Central Park, which became the first landscaped park in an American city in 1857. A significant free-black population also existed in Manhattan and Brooklyn. Slaves had been held in New York through 1827, but during the 1830s New York became a center of interracial abolitionist activism in the North. New York's black population was over 16,000 in 1840. The Great Irish Famine brought a large influx of Irish immigrants, and by 1860, one in four New Yorkers, over 200,000, had been born in Ireland. Anger at military conscription during the American Civil War led to the Draft Riots of 1863, one of the worst incidents of civil unrest in American history.

What is New York's history? In 1898, says Wikipedia, the modern City of New York was formed with the consolidation of Brooklyn, until then a separate city, the County of New York which then included parts of the Bronx, the County of Richmond, and the western portion of the County of Queens. The opening of the subway in 1904 helped bind the new city together. Throughout the first half of the 20th century, the city became a world center for industry, commerce, and communication. However, this development did not come without a price. In 1904, the steamship General Slocum caught fire in the East River, killing 1,021 people on board. In 1911, the Triangle Shirtwaist Factory fire, the city's worst industrial disaster until the 9/11 World Trade Center disaster, took the lives of 146 garment workers and spurred the growth of the International Ladies' Garment Workers' Union and major improvements in factory safety standards. Aunt Bessie was part of its later history, a union leader and devotee of Ronald Reagan when he was in the White House.

New York's non-white population was 36,620 in 1890. In the 1920s New York City was a prime destination for African Americans during the Great Migration from the American South. By 1916, New York City was home to the largest urban African diaspora in North America. The Harlem Renaissance flourished during the era of

Prohibition, in keeping with a larger economic boom that saw the skyline develop with the construction of competing skyscrapers. Thus, New York became the most populous urbanized area in the world in early 1920s, overtaking London, and the metropolitan area surpassed the 10 million mark in early 1930s. The difficult years of the Great Depression saw the election of reformer Fiorello LaGuardia as mayor and the fall of Tammany Hall after eighty years of political dominance. Returning World War II veterans created a postwar economic boom and the development of large housing tracts in eastern Queens. New York emerged from the war unscathed as the leading city of the world, with Wall Street leading America's place as the world's dominant economic power. The United Nations Headquarters emphasized New York's political influence, and the rise of abstract expressionism in the city precipitated New York's displacement of Paris as the center of the art world.

Its popularity however brought it problems. In the 1960s New York City began to suffer from economic problems and rising crime rates, which extended into the 1970s. While a resurgence in the financial industry greatly improved the city's economic health in the 1980s, New York's crime rate continued a steep uphill climb through the decade and into the beginning of the 1990s. By the 1990s, crime rates started to drop dramatically due to increased police presence and gentrification, and many American transplants and waves of new immigrants arrived from Asia and Latin America. Important new sectors, such as Silicon Alley, emerged in the city's economy, and New York's population reached all-time highs in the 2000 Census and then again in the 2010 Census. Ivy Peters was one of the new immigrants that came in that year. Born in St. Catherine's, Jamaica, she came to be with her mother who had lived and worked a number of years in New York. But she had come to the U.S. too late she said. Jobs had dried up and the only kind of work she could find was baby-sitting.

The Big Apple is a nickname for New York City. Again according to Wikipedia, it was first popularized in the 1920s by John J. FitzGerald, a sports writer for the New York *Morning Telegraph*. Its popularity since the 1970s is due to a promotional campaign by the New York Convention and Visitors Bureau. The earliest citation for "big apple" is the 1909 book, *The Wayfarer in New York* by Edward Martin who wrote: "Kansas is apt to see in New York a greedy city. ...

It inclines to think that the big apple gets a disproportionate share of the national sap." William Safire considered this the coinage, but the Random House Dictionary of American Slang considers the usage "metaphorical or perhaps proverbial, rather than a concrete example of the later slang term". By the late 1920s New York writers other than FitzGerald were starting to use "Big Apple" and were using it outside of a horse-racing context. Walter Winchell and other writers continued to use the name in the 1940s and 1950s. By the 1960s, "the Big Apple" was known only as an old name for New York. In the early 1970s, however, the New York Convention and Visitors Bureau, the official marketing and tourism organization for New York City, under the leadership of its president, Charles Gillett, began promoting "the Big Apple" for the city. It has remained popular since then. Mayor Rudolph W. Giuliani in 1997 signed legislation designating the southwest corner of West 54th Street and Broadway, the corner on which John J. FitzGerald lived from 1934 to 1963, as "Big Apple Corner."

Manhattan, also according to Wikipedia, is the most densely populated of the five boroughs of New York City. Located primarily on the island of Manhattan at the mouth of the Hudson River, the boundaries of the borough are identical to those of New York County, an original county of the U.S. state of New York. The borough and county consist of Manhattan Island and several small adjacent islands: Roosevelt Island, Randall's Island, Wards Island, Governors Island, Liberty Island, part of Ellis Island, Mill Rock, and U Thant Island; as well as Marble Hill, a very small area on the mainland bordering the Bronx. The original city of New York began at the southern end of Manhattan, expanded northward, and then between 1874 and 1898, annexed land from surrounding counties. It is the third-largest of New York's five boroughs in population, and its smallest borough in land area. Manhattan is the major commercial, financial, and cultural center of the United States. Anchored by Wall Street in Lower Manhattan, New York City functions as the financial capital of the world and is home of both the New York Stock Exchange and NASDAQ. Many major radio, television, and telecommunications companies in the United States are based here, as well as many news magazines, books, and other media publishers. Manhattan has many famous landmarks, tourist attractions, museums, and universities. It is also the location of the United Nations Headquarters. It is the center of New York City and the New York metropolitan region, hosting the seat of city government and a large portion of the area's employment, business, and entertainment activities.

I knew that Xiuling would be comparing New York City with Beijing, formerly known as Peking, the capital of the People's Republic of China and one of the most populous cities in the world, with a population of 19,612,368 as of 2010. Located in northern China, it is governed as a direct-controlled municipality under the national government, with 14 urban and suburban districts and two rural counties. Beijing is China's second largest city by urban population after Shanghai and is the country's political, cultural, and educational center and home to the headquarters for most of China's largest state-owned companies. It is a major transportation hub in the national highway, expressway, railway and high-speed rail network and Beijing's Capital International Airport is the second busiest in the world by passenger traffic. Few cities in the world have been the political and cultural center of an area as immense for so long. However Beijing is one of the Four Great Ancient Capitals of China and has been the heart of China's history for centuries. There is scarcely a major building of any age in Beijing that does not have at least some national historical significance. The city is renowned for its opulent palaces, temples, and huge stone walls and gates. Its art treasures and universities have long made it a center of culture.

In 2007 when she had returned from England and her studies at Warwick University, Xiuling had lived in Beijing and in 2008 she had worked at the Beijing Olympics. She had worked as a tourist and cultural guide and had taken visitors to the Forbidden City, to the Great Wall and to the sites of the terra cotta warriors in Xi'an; she had used China's bullet trains to go from the capital to Tianjin.

This is how Thomas L. Friedman and Michael Mandelbaum begin their recent book on *How America fell behind in the world it invented and how we can come back*. "This is a book about America that begins in China. In September 2010, Tom attended the world Economic Forum's summer conference in Tianjin, China. Five years earlier, getting to Tianjin had involved a three-and-a-half hour car ride from Beijing to a polluted, crowded Chinese version of Detroit, but things had changed. Now, to get to Tianjin, you head to the Beijing

South Railway Station – an ultramodern flying saucer of a building with glass walls and an oval roof covered with 3,246 solar panels – buy a ticket from an electronic kiosk offering choices in Chinese and English, and board a world-class high-speed train that goes right to another roomy, modern train station in downtown Tianjin. Said to be the fastest in the world when it began operating in 2008, the Chinese bullet train covers 115 kilometers, or 72 miles, in a mere twenty-nine minutes."

Xiuling had been on that train. What would she find in New York to be as significant to the city and country's growth? Would she see anything that would make her believe that the United States would be coming back any day soon?

V

IT WAS the bad experience with Caribbean Airlines that made Rhona and me fly by American Airlines on 16 May 2012 to Miami on our way to New York. This too was a mistake because the ninety minutes between flights were barely enough to clear immigration and customs and face another set of security personnel, the able-bodied men and women of the Department of Homeland Security that was established in 2000 and whose "vital mission it is to secure the nation from the many threats we face. This requires the dedication of more than 230,000 persons." The number is correct; I looked it up. But this was how we met Lauren Browne, a Peace Corps worker from New York on her way home from Guatemala. Lauren said she was returning to be present at her 22-year-old sister's college graduation. A native New Yorker from Long Island has been working in Guatemala. She said that she is from German-Italian roots and became interested in the Peace Corps after graduation from college and believed that she could spread the good name of the United States in neighboring Latin American countries. But more and more nowadays, she said, the news was bad for Peace Corps workers and in Latin America women in the Peace Corps are maligned as "floozies". This public defamation did not make easy their work of convincing foreigners to see America's good side. The insults and resentment are indeed the opposite of what the Peace Corps hopes to achieve.

As one example of the negative history they meet, Lauren said, the Peace Corps in Honduras was closed because of violence. Overall Peace Corps members have dwindled and in Guatemala there were only 37 Americans while just three were working in the town where she was. What does she do? She prepares educational material for teachers and leaders in health education. "You could look up the Peace Corps website to find the raison d'etre for its establishment," she said. "Our mission is to go out and show the good side of America; to offer technical support; and to help countries to share in networking." For her it was an opportunity to work even for minimal wages and to serve her country. But Western influence was "very great" on native people who watch a lot of Hollywood movies and network shows. As a result most people think Americans are stereotyped in their attitudes to sex. Latin men are very macho, she said, employing a similar stereotype, and think all American girls are "floozies". This however was "the least risk when you work in foreign countries even though it was not unusual that some girls who went on hikes had to fight off men who wanted to rob them." These risks hadn't deterred her from believing that the job she was doing was worth the trouble of getting people to see America in a positive way.

The Peace Corps of America Rhona discovered from her search of Wikipedia has an annual budget of $374.25 million. It is a volunteer program run by the United States Government, as well as a government agency of the same name. The stated mission of the Peace Corps includes three goals: providing technical assistance; helping people outside the United States to understand US culture; and helping Americans to understand the cultures of other countries. The work is generally related to social and economic development. Each program participant (aka Peace Corps Volunteer) is an American citizen, typically with a college degree, who works abroad for a period of 24 months after three months of training. Volunteers work with governments, schools, non-profit organizations, non-government organizations, and entrepreneurs in education, hunger, business, information technology, agriculture, and the environment. After 24 months of service, volunteers can request an extension of service.

The program was established by Executive Order, issued by President John F. Kennedy on March 1, 1961, announced by televised broadcast March 2, 1961, and authorized by Congress on September

22, 1961, with passage of the Peace Corps Act. The act declares the program's purpose as follows: To promote world peace and friendship through a Peace Corps, which shall make available to interested countries and areas men and women of the United States qualified for service abroad and willing to serve, under conditions of hardship if necessary, to help the peoples of such countries and areas in meeting their needs for trained manpower. Since 1961, over 200,000 Americans have joined the Peace Corps and have served in 139 countries.

While Kennedy is credited with the creation of the Peace Corps as president, the first initiative came from Senator Hubert H. Humphrey, Jr. (D-Minnesota), who introduced the first bill to create the Peace Corps in 1957, three years prior to the University of Michigan speech. In his autobiography, *The Education of a Public Man*, Humphrey wrote, "There were three bills of particular emotional importance to me: the Peace Corps, a disarmament agency, and the Nuclear Test Ban Treaty. The President, knowing how I felt, asked me to introduce legislation for all three. I introduced the first Peace Corps bill in 1957. It did not meet with much enthusiasm. Some traditional diplomats quaked at the thought of thousands of young Americans scattered across their world. Many senators, including liberal ones, thought it silly and an unworkable idea. Now, with a young president urging its passage, it became possible and we pushed it rapidly through the Senate. It is fashionable now to suggest that Peace Corps Volunteers gained as much or more, from their experience as the countries they worked. That may be true, but it ought not demean their work. They touched many lives and made them better."

It was not until 1959, however, that the idea received serious attention in Washington when Congressman Henry S. Reuss of Wisconsin proposed a "Point Four Youth Corps". In 1960, he and Senator Richard L. Neuberger of Oregon introduced identical measures calling for a non-governmental study of the idea's "advisability and practicability". Both the House Foreign Affairs Committee and the Senate Foreign Relations Committee endorsed the study, the latter writing the Reuss proposal into the pending Mutual Security legislation. In this form it became law in June 1960. In August the Mutual Security Appropriations Act was enacted, making available US$10,000 for the study, and in November ICA contracted with the Maurice Albertson, Andrew E. Rice, and Pauline E. Birky of Colorado State University Research Foundation for the study. John F. Kennedy first announced his idea for such an organization during the 1960 presidential campaign, at a late-night speech at the University of Michigan in Ann Arbor on October 14, 1960. On November 1, he dubbed the proposed organization the "Peace Corps".

Kennedy's opponent, Richard M. Nixon, predicted it would become a "cult of escapism" and "a haven for draft dodgers." Others doubted whether recent graduates had the necessary skills and maturity. The idea was popular among students, however, and Kennedy pursued it, asking respected academics such as Max Millikan and Chester Bowles to help him outline the organization and its goals. During his inaugural address, Kennedy again promised to create the program: "And so, my fellow Americans: ask not what your country can do for you, ask what you can do for your country." President Kennedy in a speech at the White House on June 22 1962 acknowledged that Operation Crossroads for Africa was the basis for the development of the Peace Corps. The Peace Corps website answered the question "Who Inspired the Creation of the Peace Corps?", acknowledging that the Peace Corps were based on Operation Crossroads Africa founded by Rev. James H. Robinson. President Jimmy Carter, an advocate of the program, said that his mother, who had served as a nurse in the program, had "one of the most glorious experiences of her life" in the Peace Corps. In 1979, he made it fully autonomous in an executive order. This independent status was further secured by 1981 legislation making the organization an independent federal agency.

But the news has not always been good. In 1976, Deborah Gardner was found murdered in her home in Tonga, where she was serving in the Peace Corps. Dennis Provan, a fellow Peace Corps worker, was later charged with the murder by the Tonga government. He was found not guilty by reason of insanity, and was sentenced to serve time in a mental institution in Washington D.C. Provan was never admitted to any institution, and the handling of the case has been heavily criticized. The main criticism has been that the Peace Corps seems to have worked to keep one of its volunteers from being found guilty of murder, due to the reflection it would have on the organization. And in 2009, Casey Frazee, who was sexually assaulted while serving in South Africa, created First Response Action, an advocacy group for a stronger Peace Corps response for volunteers who are survivors or victims of physical and sexual violence. In 2010, concerns about the safety of volunteers were illustrated by a report, compiled from official public documents, listing hundreds of violent crimes against volunteers since 1989. In 2011, a 20/20 investigation found that "more than 1,000 young American women have been raped or sexually assaulted in the last decade while serving as Peace Corps volunteers in foreign countries."

After the 11 September 2001 attacks alerted the US to growing anti-U.S. sentiment in the Middle East, President George W. Bush pledged to double the size of the organization within five years as a part of the War on Terrorism. For the 2004 fiscal year, Congress passed a budget increase at US$325 million, US$30 million above that of 2003 but US$30 million below the President's request. As part of an economic stimulus package in 2008, President Barack Obama proposed to double the size of the Peace Corps. However, as of 2010, the amount requested was insufficient to reach this goal by 2011. Congress raised the 2010 appropriation from the US$373 million requested by the President to US$400 million, and proposed bills would raise this further for 2011 and 2012. According to former director Gaddi Vasquez, the Peace Corps is trying to recruit more diverse volunteers of different ages and make it look "more like America". A Harvard International Review article from 2007 proposes to expand the Peace Corps, revisit its mission and equip it with new technology. In 1961 only 1 per cent of volunteers were over 50, compared with 5 per cent today. Ethnic minorities currently comprise 19 per cent of volunteers.

Currently, Peace Corps Volunteers are working in 68 countries. They are in the Dominican Republic, in Jamaica, in Central America and Mexico, in Belize, Costa Rica, El Salvador, Guatemala, Honduras, Mexico, Nicaragua, and Panama; and in Colombia, Ecuador, Guyana, Paraguay, Peru, and Suriname. They are in Eastern Europe and Central Asia, in Albania, Armenia, Azerbaijan, Bulgaria, Georgia, Macedonia, Moldova, Romania, Ukraine, Kyrgyz Republic, Turkmenistan[. They are in North Africa and the Middle East; in Jordan and in Morocco. In Africa the Peace Corps is in Benin, Botswana, Burkina Faso, Cameroon, Cape Verde, Ethiopia, The Gambia, Ghana, Guinea,

Kenya, Lesotho, Liberia, Madagascar, Malawi, Mali, Mozambique, Namibia, Rwanda, Senegal, Sierra Leone, South Africa, Swaziland, Tanzania, Togo, Uganda, and Zambia. In Asia it is in Cambodia, China, Indonesia, Mongolia, Philippines, Thailand, and in the Pacific Islands of Fiji, Micronesia and Palau, Samoa, Tonga, and Vanuatu.

It is no surprise that many people in all these countries think that the United States is using the Peace Corps to spy on them and to strengthen its role as "the world's policeman." But why not says Carole Musaracchia. "In my personal, family and work life, I try to figure out who is going to do a job on me, how will they try to do it, and what do I do to circumvent a disaster waiting to happen. It's all relative yet on a bigger scale. So I believe that America should watch for situations that may harm her balance. As my Sicilian father would say, keep your friends close but your enemies closer."

VI

DURING THE days we spent with Phil Lomenzo and Joyce Hunter in their Pompano Beach home in Florida at the end of May 2012, I came across an autobiography written by a 78-year-old Italian-born businesswoman. "I am blessed to have jumped into that proverbial melting pot and come out an American," Emilia Zecchino wrote in *Only in America*. "Countless success stories," she wrote, "make up the fabric of this country. No wonder everyone wants to come and live in America. Only in America could I have found the opportunities I have had. Those opportunities are still abundant." What is Ms. Zecchino's story? In 1983 with just $1,000 she started a small catering business and in January 2006 she sold her company, Holiday Foods, to a multi-billion company, Schwan Food Company. She was convinced that her success is the American Dream: To start out with very little or nothing and to make a fortune. This too was the lesson Barack Obama hoped to share when he wrote *The Audacity of Hope* and said that the book was his idea of how to reclaim The American Dream.

But this is not how young Americans view their lives, said Bill O'Reilly on the Fox Network about the same time I was reading Ms. Zecchino's story. "Young people are losing their imagination," he said. "They want instant gratification." Was this how he viewed the Wall

Street protests? And did he think the same of the 27-year-old Mark Zuckerberg who when he went public with Facebook in 2012 made hundreds of millionaires and billionaires? Or, was there something happening in the United States that Bill O'Reilly was missing? Hadn't the US economy led by Wall Street lost its way and wasn't the old notion of hard work undermined by greed as Michael Douglas had said in the films about Wall Street? Had O'Reilly forgotten the stories of Bernard Madoff, Raj Rajaratnam and Allen Stanford? Was this trio the real examples of the American Dream? The truth was from New York to Davos to Rio de Janeiro to Los Cabos, Capitalism, aka the American Dream, was on trial and the old principles of taking a number and your place in the line were being questioned, not just by the young and impatient but also by the middle-aged and wise. People were tired of the rigmarole of the market that had the power to make thieves of honest men.

As Joseph E. Stiglitz was to write, showing the naiveté or hypocrisy of peddlers of this Dream, "There's not much mobility up and down" in the American economy. Stiglitz pointed out that America has the least equality of opportunity of any of the advanced industrial economies. "In short, the status you are born into – whether rich or poor – is more likely to be the status of your adult life in America vs. any other advanced economy, including Old Europe." Stiglitz says, for example, that just 8 per cent of students at America's elite universities come from households in the bottom 50m per cent of income and admission to those universities isn't predicated on your ability to pay. "The chances of someone from the top who doesn't do very well in school are better than someone from the bottom who does well in school." And because the children of those at the top of society tend to do better than those at the bottom – thanks, in part, to better education, health care and nutrition – "the income inequality that's slowly emerged over the past 30 years will only widen in the next 10 to 20 years."

But if the root causes of income inequality go unaddressed, Stiglitz warns, America will truly become a two-class society and look much more like a third world economy, and he adds, "People will live in gated communities with armed guards. It's an ugly picture. There will be political, social and economic turmoil." At a meeting of businessmen and government officials in Hong Kong in January 2012

Stiglitz, who won the Nobel Prize for his work on how markets work inefficiently, had warned that imposing austerity measures as countries slow towards recession is a fundamentally flawed response. However Stiglitz believes this "nightmare we're slowly marching toward" can be avoided, and he cites Brazil's experience since the early 1990s as an example of a country that has reduced income inequality. Among other things, he recommends improving education and nutrition for those at the bottom of society, and eliminating "corporate welfare" and other policies which "create wealth but not economic growth." Stiglitz believes inequality of wealth and opportunity are hurting the overall economy, by limiting competition, promoting cronyism and keeping those at the bottom from reaching their potential. "What I want is a more dynamic economy and a fairer society," he says, suggesting income inequality is ultimately detrimental to those at the top, too. "My point is we've created an economy that is not in accord with the principles of the free market." This brings me to Bernard Madoff.

The Madoff investment scandal broke in December 2008 when former NASDAQ chairman Bernard Madoff admitted that the wealth management arm of his business was an elaborate Ponzi scheme. He founded the Wall Street firm Bernard L. Madoff Investment Securities LLC in 1960, and was its chairman until his arrest. Alerted by his sons, federal authorities arrested Madoff on December 11, 2008. On 12 March 2009, Madoff pleaded guilty to 11 federal crimes and admitted to operating what has been the largest Ponzi scheme in history. On 29 June 2009, he was sentenced to 150 years in prison with restitution of $170 billion. According to the original federal charges, Madoff said that his firm had "liabilities of approximately US$50 billion". Prosecutors estimated the size of the fraud to be $64.8 billion, based on the amounts in the accounts of Madoff's 4,800 clients as of 30 November 2008. The U.S. Securities and Exchange Commission has also come under fire for not investigating Madoff more thoroughly; questions about his firm had been raised as early as 1999. Madoff's business, in the process of liquidation, was one of the top market makers on Wall Street and in 2008, the sixth-largest. Madoff's personal and business asset freeze has created a chain reaction throughout the world's business and philanthropic community, forcing many organizations to at least temporarily close, including the Robert

I. Lappin Charitable Foundation, the Picower Foundation, and the JEHT Foundation.

What is Raj Rajaratnam's story? The Galleon Group was one of the largest hedge fund management firms in the world, managing over $7 billion, before closing in October 2009. The firm was founded by Raj Rajaratnam, a former equity research analyst and eventual president of Needham & Company in 1997, and was the center of a 2009 insider trading scandal. The firm was named for the galleon, a large sailing ship used from the 16th to 18th centuries in Europe, and headquartered in New York City. In October 2009 Rajaratnam and five others were arrested and charged with multiple counts of fraud and insider trading. Rajaratnam pleaded not guilty and remained free on $100 million bail, the largest in United States history. He was indicted by a grand jury in December 2009 and found guilty in U.S. District Court on 14 charges in May 2011. He was sentenced by U.S. District Judge Richard Sullivan to 11 years in prison on the 13 October 2011.

But is that the nature of the beast? According to a Reuters report on 9 July 2012 if the ancient Greek philosopher Diogenes were to go out with his lantern in search of an honest man today, a survey of Wall Street executives on workplace conduct suggests he might have to look elsewhere. A quarter of Wall Street executives see wrongdoing as a key to success, according to a survey by whistleblower law firm Labaton Sucharow. In a survey of 500 senior executives in the United States and the United Kingdom, 26 per cent of respondents said they had observed or had firsthand knowledge of wrongdoing in the workplace, while 24 per cent said they believed financial services professionals may need to engage in unethical or illegal conduct to be successful. Sixteen per cent of respondents said they would commit insider trading if they could get away with it, according to Labaton Sucharow. And 30 per cent said their compensation plans created pressure to compromise ethical standards or violate the law. "When misconduct is common and accepted by financial services professionals, the integrity of our entire financial system is at risk," Jordan Thomas, partner and chair of Labaton Sucharow's whistleblower representation practice, said in a statement. And it should be no surprise to Americans when The Lookout reported that there is a manhunt for Georgia money manager, Aubrey Lee Price, who is accused of embezzling $17 million. According to the Lowndes

County Sheriff's Office, the 46-year-old disappeared in mid-June "after telling acquaintances that he had lost a large amount of money through trading activities and that he planned to kill himself." The *Atlanta Journal-Constitution* reported that Price told some people he planned to jump to his death off a ferry. The FBI said he was last seen boarding a ferry boat in Key West bound for Fort Myers on June 16. However a Coast Guard search has not turned up a body.

The Department of Justice has charged Price with embezzling millions from a small southern Georgia bank he took over in December 2010. "The complaint alleges that, instead of investing the money as promised, Price fraudulently wired the bank's funds to accounts that he personally controlled at other financial institutions and provided bank management with altered documents to make it appear as if he had invested the bank's money in Treasury securities," the justice department said in a statement. But in the alleged suicide note obtained by the *Atlanta Journal-Constitution*, Price maintained he did nothing illegal. "I hid many things fraudulently and deceptively, to try and give myself more time to pull some positive returns together," the note said. "To be clear, nothing has been taken, only lost through stressful periods of trading in bad investments ... I am emotionally overwhelmed and incapable of continuing in this life." The FBI believes Price may own real estate in Venezuela and Guatemala. They are asking for the public's help in solving the mystery. Wendy Cross, an Atlanta woman who reportedly lost $364,000 in the alleged scheme, says Price is fooling folks again. "I don't believe he's dead. I believe he planned for this exit," Cross told the Atlanta newspaper. "This guy," she said, "was the best actor."

And finally there is the case of the former jet-setting Texas tycoon R. Allen Stanford, whose financial empire once spanned the Americas. He was sentenced to 110 years in prison for bilking investors out of more than $7 billion over 20 years in one of the largest Ponzi schemes in U.S. history. U.S. District Judge David Hittner handed down the sentence during a court hearing in which two people spoke on behalf of Stanford's investors about how his fraud had affected their lives. Prosecutors had asked that Stanford be sentenced to 230 years in prison, the maximum sentence possible after a jury convicted the one-time billionaire in March on 13 of 14 fraud-related counts. Stanford's convictions on conspiracy, wire and mail fraud charges followed a seven-week trial.

During sentencing hearing, Stanford gave rambling statement to the court in which he denied he did anything wrong. Speaking for more than 40 minutes, Stanford said he was a scapegoat and blamed the federal government and a U.S. appointed receiver who took over his companies for tearing down his business empire and preventing his investors from getting any of their money back. "I'm not here to ask for sympathy or forgiveness or to throw myself at your mercy," Stanford told Hittner. "I did not run a Ponzi scheme. I didn't defraud anybody." Stanford was once considered one of the richest men in the U.S., with an estimated net worth of more than $2 billion. His financial empire stretched from the U.S. to Latin America and the Caribbean. But after his arrest, all of his assets were seized and he had to rely on court-appointed attorneys to defend him. The jury that convicted Stanford also cleared the way for U.S. authorities to go after about $330 million in stolen investor funds sitting in the financier's frozen foreign bank accounts in Canada, England and Switzerland. But due to legal wrangling, it could be years before the more than 21,000 investors recover anything, and whatever they ultimately get will only be a fraction of what they lost.

This was New York and the American Dream She Xiuling was coming to and the truth is in her own country corruption and the misappropriation of public and private funds was as rampant. Economic fraud has been dispelling the notion of riches and fame waiting for every ambitious and hard-working American. Among the dissenting voices in the United States was that of Stiglitz whose latest book, *The Price of Inequality*, states that America is "no longer the land of opportunity" as Ms. Zecchino claimed. While we all know stories of people who have moved up the social stratosphere, Stiglitz wrote, the statistics tell a very different story. In the last 30 years Stiglitz points out the share of national income held by the top 1 per cent of Americans has doubled; and for the top 0.1 per cent, their share has tripled. Meanwhile, median incomes for American workers have stagnated.

And, as we saw in 2012, the problem with Facebook's IPO did not make the American Dream seem more easily attainable. Reuters reported in fact that Facebook Inc. is facing a raft of lawsuits from investors seeking to recoup losses from its botched IPO, and how cascading NASDAQ trading glitches might have stoked the confusion that marred its May 18 debut. The No. 1 social network and lead underwriters Morgan Stanley, Goldman Sachs Group Inc. and JPMorgan Chase & Co have filed a motion requesting that dozens of shareholder lawsuits over its $16 billion initial public offering be grouped together in Manhattan federal court. The filing, while standard in cases with multiple lawsuits, gives a glimpse at how Facebook may choose to structure its defense and represents the social networking company's first public response to the chaos that engulfed its high-profile debut. But the eight-year-old company founded by Mark Zuckerberg in his Harvard dorm room has shed a fifth, or $20 billion, of its value from the $38 IPO price.

However the IPO market is settling into a deep freeze following Facebook's troubled initial public offering. At least five companies have postponed their IPO plans. Among them: travel company Kayak.com, which planned to debut on the NASDAQ; Formula One, which was set to go public in Singapore; and London Jeweler Graff Diamonds, which had been planning a $1.5 billion IPO in Hong Kong. "Facebook alone froze the pipeline. It was done so poorly by the underwriters, and there had been so much hype around this deal that it (has) produced so much angst and fear about the IPO market," said Scott Sweet, managing director of IPO Boutique. The "bloodbath" on Wall Street following a dismal U.S. jobs report makes it even more unlikely that companies will want to test the public market anytime soon. Investors are still dealing with the aftermath. Corsair Components and Tria Beauty, which were both expected to go public before Memorial Day, put their IPO plans on hold indefinitely. Online firewall provider Palo Alto Networks, risk management Software Company Reval Holdings, craft retailer Michael's and cloud computing firm ServiceNow were among some of the other highly anticipated IPOs that were expected to launch after Memorial Day.

Why the freeze? The records show that first there were worries that large and small investors who got burned by Facebook's errant first-day of trading on NASDAQ won't even consider buying into an IPO right now. In the Facebook blame game, lead underwriter Morgan Stanley has come under attack for overvaluing the stock, which is now trading nearly 29 per cent below its IPO price. New companies are now worried that underwriters may significantly underprice their shares to simply get investors interested in this environment, according to several experts. "Underwriters are going to have to price the next IPO so reasonably to force it to work," said Sweet. Companies appear to be wary of becoming that market test case. The sea change signals a retrenchment for a market that was finally starting to open up. The IPO market ground to a near halt in 2008 and 2009 with just eight venture capital-backed companies tapping the public markets in each year, raising $562 million and $904 million respectively, according to Dow Jones VentureSource. By 2010, 47 venture-backed U.S. companies went public, raising $3.2 billion, and last year 45 companies went public, raising $5.3 billion. The IPO market was on track to beat both prior years in 2012, with 28 companies filing by the time of Facebook's May 18 IPO. So far, companies have raised $8.9 billion.

The fact is Facebook has created a New Millionaire's Club and a Few Billionaires too. Morgan Korn in The Daily Ticker wrote on 2 February that the millionaire's club has to make room for a few more hundred people, at least. When Facebook filed to go public he said many current and former employees expected huge paydays. The public offering could value the social media titan between $75 billion to $100 billion he said and for those employees who received stock options their personal worth could equal several hundred million dollars. Facebook's Co-Founder Mark Zuckerberg, 27, was slated to become one of the richest people in the world with a personal fortune of at least $28 billion. His salary was to be cut to $1 from $1.48 million last year, effective 1 January 2013. Facebook's Chief Operating Officer Sheryl Sandberg, who made $30.8 million in 2011, would enter the billionaire's club for the first time and early Facebook investors like Peter Thiel and venture capital firm Accel Partners were both expected to net profits in the billions. Even Facebook's biggest foes, Tyler and Cameron Winklevoss, would become richer, thanks to the 1.2 million shares they owned. Zuckerberg had dropped out of Harvard to concentrate on expanding Facebook, which he started with a few friends in his sophomore college dormitory eight years ago. Facebook now has 845 million users worldwide.

The *New York Times* profiled graffiti artist David Choe as one example of how Facebook's public offering would change the lives of thousands of people. Choe was hired to paint murals on the walls of Facebook's Palo Alto office in 2005; instead of taking cash as payment, he accepted several hundred stock options. Those shares could be now worth more than $200 million. Zuckerberg's father Edward, a dentist in New York, will also greatly benefit from the IPO. He was given two million shares "in satisfaction of funds provided for our initial working capital," according to Facebook's S-1 filing. One person left out of the Facebook filing is estranged Co-Founder Eduardo Saverin. Zuckerberg's former best friend and roommate, and the one who provided the company's early financing, Salverin has sold a majority of his stake (worth five percent) of the company on the secondary market. Business Insider's Nicholas Carlson joined The Daily Ticker's Aaron Task to discuss the Facebook IPO and how the newly-minted Facebook millionaires will be spending their money. Google's IPO in 2004 made many people rich, but Facebook's public offering takes it to another level. "It's a monument to capitalism," Carlson says.

VII

IN CNNMONEY.COM Jeanne Sahadi reminded Americans in December 2011 that President Obama wanted the wealthiest to pay more in taxes. Noting the rise in income inequality in recent years and the need to reform the U.S. tax system, the president said that some of the wealthiest in America pay far less in federal taxes as a percentage of their income than many lower down the income scale. "A quarter of all millionaires now pay lower tax rates than millions of middle-class households. Some billionaires have a tax rate as low as 1 per cent," Obama said in a speech in Kansas.

What are the facts behind the claim: In 2006 roughly 25 per cent of those with adjusted gross incomes over $1 million paid a smaller portion of their income in federal taxes – income, payroll and corporate – than 10 per cent of those with AGIs below $100,000, according to a recent study from the Congressional Research Service. As for the president's assertion that some billionaires have a tax rate as low as 1 per cent, Robertson Williams, a senior fellow at the Tax Policy Center, said that it's definitely possible but hard to verify. "Billionaires are still rare enough that we cannot get data for them without running afoul of privacy rules," he said. But for a lot of reasons, Chris Bergin, president and publisher of Tax Analysts, said, "It is certainly not implausible." However in 2011 4,000 households with incomes over a million dollars owed no federal income tax whatsoever, according to Tax Policy Center estimates. What's more, of the top 400 federal tax returns with the highest adjusted gross incomes in 2008, 30 had an effective tax rate of less than 10 per cent, noted Mark Luscombe, the principal federal tax analyst at CCH. A big reason is that a large percentage of wealthy Americans' income comes from investments, which are often taxed at lower rates than ordinary wages and salaries.

Of course, the wealthy aren't the only ones who enjoy what Obama refers to as "loopholes and shelters." Anyone who deducts their mortgage interest, saves money for retirement, realizes a capital gain or loss, or gets health insurance from their employer is enjoying a tax break. The difference is that the rich use a broader array of tax-preferred investments, such as partnerships. Or they may invest in dividend-paying foreign stocks and can claim a foreign tax credit for the tax withheld from them by the foreign government. Typically, too, the wealthiest are more likely to be retired or self-employed and are in a position to make big charitable contributions – all of which come with distinct tax advantages. And the wealthy can afford to be more risk-averse and park a lot of money in bonds, often tax-free.

To Obama, the fact that the wealthy can so whittle down their tax burden is "the height of unfairness." Fairness in the tax code is a real issue, but there is no absolute answer to the question "what's fair?" And that's one reason why reforming the tax code will be a tough fight. Earlier, Obama proposed what he dubbed the Buffett Rule, named after billionaire investor Warren Buffett, who has urged Congress to tax the rich more. The Buffett Rule is intended as a guiding principle for tax reform to ensure that millionaires pay a higher percentage of their income in federal taxes than those who make less. That may not be as easy to implement as it sounds.

And yet it was not time for Americans to think that all's well on the economic front and with the American Dream. As the Associated Press reported shares of JPMorgan Chase & Co. tumbled recently as a published report said that the bank's losses on a bad trade may reach as much as $9 billion – far higher than the estimated $2 billion loss disclosed in May. Then, JPMorgan said, the loss came from trading in credit derivatives designed to hedge against financial risk, not to make a profit for the New York bank. The New York Times, citing sources it did not identify by name, said that the losses have grown recently as JPMorgan has been unwinding its positions. The newspaper said its sources were current and former traders and executives at JPMorgan, which is the largest bank in the U.S. by assets. The *New York Times* story cites an internal report that JPMorgan made in April that showed the losses could reach $8 billion to $9 billion, in a worst-case scenario. But the newspaper added that because JPMorgan has already been unwinding its positions, some expect that the losses will not be more than $6 billion to $7 billion.

VIII

THE FINANCIAL crisis was global and not just an American tragedy involving American banks and investment companies. In Europe Andre Lehmann of Agence France Presse reported in January 2012 that the Davos elite claimed that capitalism has widened the income gap and this group of economic and political elites meeting at the Swiss resort of Davos aimed to seek reforms of "outdated" capitalism and were asked to find ways to reform a capitalist system that has been described as outdated and crumbling. "We have a general morality gap, we are over-leveraged, we have neglected to invest in the future, we have undermined social coherence, and we are in danger of completely losing the confidence of future generations," said Klaus Schwab, host and founder of the annual World Economic Forum. "Solving problems in the context of outdated and crumbling models will only dig us deeper into the hole. We are in an era of profound change that urgently requires new ways of thinking instead of more business-as-usual," the 73-year-old said, adding that "capitalism in its current form has no place in the world around us."

Some 1,600 economic and political leaders, including 40 heads of states and governments, were asked to come up with new ideas as they converge at eastern Switzerland's chic ski station for the 42nd edition of the five-day World Economic Forum. The Eurozone's failure to get a grip on its debt crisis and the specter this is casting over the global economy will dominate discussions. "The main issue would be the pre-occupation with the global economy. There will be relatively less conversation about social responsibility and environment issues – those tend to come to the fore when the economy is doing well," John Quelch, dean of the China European International Business School, told AFP. "The main conversation will be about a deficit of leadership in Europe as a prime problem," he added. The annual talk-shop came barely a week after the Eurozone's reputation took a further battering, as ratings agency Standard and Poor's downgraded the credit-worthiness of nine Eurozone countries, including stripping France of its triple-A grade. While saved from the downgrade embarrassment, the region's economic powerhouse Germany has nevertheless been forced to lower its growth forecast, dragged down by its neighbors' debt woes and weaker demand from emerging markets.

The forum centered on the issue from the beginning, as German Chancellor Angela Merkel opened with a keynote speech. European Central Bank chief Mario Draghi, US Treasury Secretary Timothy Geithner and International Monetary Fund chief Christine Lagarde also gave a broader insight into the international economic impact of the Eurozone crisis. The World Bank slashed its global economic growth forecasts to 2.5 per cent for 2012 and 3.1 per cent in 2013 – sharply lower than previous estimates of 3.6 per cent for both years. Beyond economic issues, the forum will address a plethora of other subjects. Sessions will range from scientific discoveries expected to shape 2012 to a discussion on how virtual games can be harnessed for innovation in the real world. It also heard about the profound changes in the Arab world after a series of revolutions swept across the region in 2011. New Tunisian Prime Minister Hamadi Jebali and Egyptian presidential candidate Amre Moussa were both present at the meeting. Political issues in other regions were addressed, with the participation of Mexican Felipe Calderon, his Nigerian counterpart Goodluck Jonathan, and Salva Kiir Mayardit, President of the fledgling South Sudan.

Up to 5,000 Swiss soldiers were mobilized to secure the location, and the air space around eastern Switzerland's Davos region was also severely restricted during the week of talks. But anti-capitalist demonstrators had planned to make their presence felt. The Occupy WEF protestors had built igloos in the middle of the village perched 1,500 meters above sea level and had planned a protest against those they call "self-proclaimed elites." The Associated Press reported that three topless Ukrainian protesters were detained while trying to break into an invitation-only gathering of international CEOs and political leaders to call attention to the needs of the world's poor. Separately, demonstrators from the Occupy movement marched to the edge of the gathering and engaged in a brief standoff with police. After a complicated journey to reach the heavily guarded Swiss resort town of Davos, the Ukrainians arrived at the entrance to the complex where the World Economic Forum takes place every year. With temperatures around freezing in the snow-filled town, they took off their tops and tried to climb a fence before being detained. Davos police spokesman Thomas Hobi said the three women were taken to a police station and told that they weren't allowed to demonstrate without a permit – or to do so naked. They were released later. The activists are from the Ukrainian group Femen, which has staged small, half-naked protests to highlight a range of issues including oppression of political opposition.

Protesters from the Occupy movement that started with opposition to practices on Wall Street held a separate rally in Davos. A small group of protesters camped in igloos in Davos and called for more help for the needy. About 100 Occupy protesters gathered in front of the town hall. Some held placards with slogans such as "If voting would change anything, it would be illegal" and "Don't let them decide for you, Occupy WEF." Later, a small group split from the rally and marched toward the forum, prompting about a dozen police officers to hastily erect a mobile barrier as shoppers looked on with bemusement. The demonstrators chanted anti-capitalist slogans and engaged in a brief violent standoff with police that resulted in a car's rear window being smashed. Officers used pepper spray against the protesters and detained seven people, Hobi said. Nobody was injured. One member of the Occupy camp was invited to speak at a special event outside the forum to discuss the future of capitalism. Soon after the panel discussion began, some activists in the audience jumped up and started chanting slogans, and the protester panelist walked off the stage.

The Associated Press said in January that financial leaders in Davos had conceded that the four-year economic crisis has left societies battered and widened the gap between the haves and have-nots – with one suggesting that Western-style capitalism itself may be endangered. As Europe struggles with its debt crisis and the global economic outlook remains gloomy at best, there's a sense free markets are on trial. Many at the elite economic gathering in the Swiss Alps accept that more must be done to convince critics that Western capitalism has a future and that it can learn from its massive failures. For David Rubenstein, the co-founder and managing director of asset management firm Carlyle Group, leaders must work fast to overcome the current crisis or else different models of capitalism, such as the form practiced in China, may win the day. "As a result of this recession that lasted longer than anyone predicted and will probably go on for a number more years ... we're going to have a lot of economic disparities," Rubenstein said. "We've got to work through these problems. If we don't in three or four years ... the game will be over for the type of capitalism that many of us have lived through and thought was the best type." Some 2,600 of the world's most influential people came for the forum amid increasing worries about the global economy and social unrest due to rising income inequalities. Many economists think that China has reaped the rewards of its transition to a more market economy and is now the world's second-largest economy. Unlike the capitalist systems in the U.S. and Europe, China's market transformation has been heavily guided by a state apparatus that continues to balk at widespread democratic reforms. Latin America, too, has seen success in the development of "state capitalism" in certain industries. "You combine elements of private enterprise with public responsibility," said Colombia's mining and energy minister, Mauricio Cardenas.

Although Rubenstein's stark appraisal might have been a surprise, there was a clear defensive posture among many participants on the opening day of the forum. There were numerous references to the need to innovate, the need to consult with employees and the realization that power in the world is shifting from the West to the East. While the traditional industrial economies of the United States and Europe have limped through the last few years, often from one crisis to another, many economies in Asia and Latin America have been booming. But Raghuram Rajan, a professor at the University of Chicago, doubted that the Chinese model was likely to last for too long. State capitalism, he said, may be good if you're playing "catch-up" but it reaches its "natural limits" once that's been accomplished.

Others worried about conflicts of interest as the same government officials run the companies and set industry regulations. Mark Penn, global CEO of the public relations firm Burson-Marsteller, told the Associated Press that "the whole crisis has raised larger questions about how is capitalism working, how do you re-define fairness in the 21st century?" Many rejected the suggestion by Sharan Burrow, the general secretary of the International Trade Union Confederation, that capitalism has lost its "moral compass" and needed to be "re-set." Business leaders insisted they were learning from the mistakes that dragged the world into its deepest economic recession since the World War II.

Bank of America's CEO Brian Moynihan said bank excesses in the run-up to the credit crunch of 2008 reflected the economies the banks were operating in, so it is important now that policymakers don't overreact. Moynihan, whose bank had to back down on charging a $5 debit card fee after protests by the Occupy movement and others, said banks have "done a lot" to reduce earlier excesses. He also noted that boom and bust cycles are a part of the Western capitalist structure. Many outside the confines of the Davos conference center disagree, after years of crisis in which hundreds of millions have lost their jobs even as top executives still reap huge pay packets.

Protesters had sent aloft big red weather balloons carrying a huge protest banner reading "Hey WEF, Where are the other 6.9999 billion leaders?" The activists were from the Occupy WEF movement, a small group camping out in igloos at Davos and following in the footsteps of the Occupy Wall Street movement that spread around the world. Experts said protests must be expected after the excesses of the last decade. "When you have a financial sector which is a casino, that's putting at risk taxpayers' money, you have a reaction," said Guillermo Ortiz, a former governor of the Bank of Mexico. Policymakers around the world have sought to rein in the excesses of the banking sector by introducing new regulations requiring them to keep bigger capital buffers, but those measures did not do much to appease those voicing their discontent around Davos. Although some protesters clearly had revolutionary goals like the overthrow of the capitalist system, many just wanted their aspirations and objectives met by an often-distant political and business elite. The CEO of accounting giant Deloitte, Joe Echevarria, talked about developing compassionate capitalism.

"You're going to have to deal with regulation – balancing the need to protect society along with stifling growth," he told AP in an interview. "I think that has to manifest itself through the choices that governments and businesses make."

While the bigwigs debated at Davos, key Greek bondholders were holding closed-door meetings in Paris to discuss how to continue discussions central to resolving Europe's debt crisis that would forgive 50 per cent of Greece's enormous debt. German Chancellor Angela Merkel in an interview with six European newspapers drove home the need for reform in debt-troubled Eurozone nations instead of spending more to beef up the region's bailout fund. Surveys ahead of the meeting had showed pessimism among world CEOs, plunging levels of public trust in business and government leaders and concerns that fragility in the U.S. and European economies could hurt the global economy. In Brazil thousands of critics of capitalism called for a worldwide protest in June to press for concrete steps to tackle the global economic crisis. The World Social Forum wrapped up a five-day meeting in the southern Brazilian city, urging citizens to "take to the streets on June 5" for the global action, which would be in support of social and environmental justice. The forum also announced a "peoples' summit" of social movements to be held in parallel with the high-level UN conference on sustainable development next June 20-22 in Rio de Janeiro. The Rio+20 summit, the fourth major gathering on sustainable development since 1972, will press world leaders to commit themselves to creating a social and "green economy" with priority being given to eradicating hunger.

But World Social Forum participants, including representatives of the Arab Spring, Spain's "Indignant" movement, Occupy Wall Street, and students from Chile, sharply criticized the concept of "a green economy" that would allow multinational corporations to reap the profit. "The political and economic elites are the one per cent who controls the world and we are the one per cent seeking to change it. Where are the (other) 98 per cent?" said Chico Whitaker, one of the Forum's founders. "There are many who are happy because each time they get more consumer goods, but many are concerned and unsatisfied. The challenge for us is to speak with them." If we do not raise the issue of inequality, we won't solve the problems, said Venezuelan sociologist Edgardo Lander. "If the system is not capable of re-distributing and dealing with inequality, we have to do it ourselves," agreed Sam Halvorsen, of the Occupy London movement.

The Forum is an alliance of social movements opposed to the World Economic Forum, the annual gathering of the world's economic and political elites held at the same time in the Swiss resort of Davos. Addressing the gathering, Brazilian President Dilma Rousseff appealed for "a development model that articulates growth and job creation, battles poverty and decreases inequalities," and advocated for the "sustainable use and preservation of natural resources." Candido Grzywoski, one of the founders and a coordinator of the Forum, said the urgency of the global economic crisis and the popular indignation around the world "gave us more unity in diversity." The Forum, which drew around 40,000 participants this year, has its roots in 1999 street protests in the US city of Seattle during a World Trade Organization meeting but it settled in Porto Alegre as its regular venue 12 years ago when it drew 20,000 activists from around the world. Next year, it will be held in Cairo.

IX

BACK IN New York the signs of the financial protest were gone by mid-year, but the movement according to the Associated Press lives on. What nobody knows is just how long it can survive without a literal place to call home. For Occupy Wall Street, Zuccotti Park was a rallying cry, a symbol of defiance. But the park itself unwittingly had become a mirror image of the world it was trying to change: a microcosm of society rife with crime, drug problems and fights over things like real estate and access to medical care. That's why, after protesters were hauled out of the park during a police raid, some organizers believe the loss of their camp was actually a blessing in disguise. "This is much bigger than a square plaza in downtown Manhattan," said Han Shan, an organizer who was working with churches to find places for protesters to sleep. "You can't evict an idea whose time has come." The protesters had camped out in the privately owned park since mid-September and had vowed to stay put indefinitely. Mayor Michael Bloomberg said he ordered the sweep because health and safety conditions had become "intolerable" in the crowded plaza. The raid was conducted in the middle of the night "to reduce the risk of confrontation" and "to minimize disruption to the surrounding neighborhood," he said. Some protesters were allowed back into the park two by two. But they could each take only a small bag after a judge ruled that their free speech rights do not extend to pitching a tent and setting up camp for months at a time.

Pete Dutro, head of the group's finances, said the loss of the movement's original encampment will open up a dialogue with other cities and take the protest to the next level of action. "We all knew this was coming," Dutro said. "Now it's time for us to not be tucked away in Zuccotti Park, and have different areas of occupation throughout the city." But without a place to congregate, protesters will have a difficult time communicating with each other en masse. For now, they are planning to move forward with plans for a day of civil disobedience and marches. And they will be joined by angry city leaders who publicly denounced Bloomberg for the nighttime raid. Robert Harrington, owner of a small importing business in New York, stood outside the barricade with a sign calling for tighter banking regulations. "To be effective it almost has to move out of the park," Harrington said. "It's like the antiwar movement in the 1960s which started as street theater and grew into something else." The issues, he added, "are larger than just this camp." The next challenge is figuring out how to decentralize the movement and give it staying power. "People are really recognizing that we need to build a movement here," Shan said. "What we're dedicated to is not just about occupying space. That's a tactic."

The raid seemed to mark a shift in the city's dealings with the Wall Street protests. Only a week before Bloomberg privately told a group of executives and journalists that he thought reports of problems at the park had been exaggerated and didn't require any immediate intervention. However it was the third raid of a major camp in a span of three days, as police broke up camps in Portland, Oregon, and in Oakland, California. Authorities acknowledged that police departments across the nation consulted with each other about nonviolent ways to clear encampments. Officers in as many as 40 cities participated in the conference calls. When New York police began their crackdown at 1 a.m., most of the Occupy Wall Street protesters were sleeping. Officers arrived by the hundreds and set up powerful klieg lights to illuminate the block. They handed out notices from Brookfield Office Properties, the park's owner, and the city saying that the plaza had to be cleared because it had become unsanitary and hazardous. Many people left, carrying their belongings with them. Others tried to make a stand, locking arms or even chaining themselves together with bicycle locks.

Around 200 people were arrested, including a member of the City Council and dozens who tried to resist the eviction by linking arms in a tight circle at the center of the park. At least half-dozen journalists were arrested later in the day, including a reporter and photographer from the Associated Press who were held for four hours before being released. In contrast to the scene weeks ago in Oakland, where a similar eviction turned chaotic and violent, the police action was comparatively orderly. But some protesters complained of being hit by police batons and shoved to the ground. The police commissioner said officers gave the crowd 45 minutes to retrieve their belongings before starting to dismantle tents, and let people leave voluntarily until around 3:30 a.m., when they moved in to make mass arrests. "Arresting people is not easy," he said, adding that he thought the officers "showed an awful lot of restraint in the face of "an awful lot of taunting, people getting in police officers' faces, calling them names."

The ouster at Zuccotti Park came as a rift within the movement had been widening between the park's full-time residents and the movement's power players, most of whom no longer lived in the park. Some residents of the park have been grumbling about the recent formation of a "spokes council", an upper echelon of organizers who held meetings at a high school near police headquarters. Some protesters felt that the selection of any leaders whatsoever wasn't true to Occupy Wall Street's original anti-government spirit: That no single person is more important or more powerful than another person. "Right now we're in the organizing stages of building a national movement," said protester Sandra Nurse. "I think this is going to serve as more momentum to draw people in."

It was unlikely that the problems would go away and that Capitalism and the American Dream would regain their old respect. In April, CNBC was asking the question if the world's biggest economy, China's largest export market and the top contributor to the

International Monetary Fund, was in danger of disintegrating. While its politicians and citizens may feel some sense of belonging to the European Union, few people identify with Europe. Since the credit crunch hit, flaws in the European economic model have been exposed. Many countries in the region are now among the biggest beneficiaries of IMF funds, causing concern for investors on all continents. Fifty-five years after the signing of the Treaty of Rome which founded what is now the European Union, the EU finds itself at odds with the very countries that make it up: politicians increasingly put national interest and popularity at home first and blame the EU and the single currency, the euro, for most of their countries' economic troubles. If that trend continues, analysts fear that the union that was built painstakingly over decades and brought peace and prosperity to the continent is in danger of disintegrating. "Clearly I am very worried because the movement towards European cooperation or integration seems to have stalled at the moment and the aftermath of the euro crisis is going to make the movement towards disintegration more powerful," Stephen Tindale, Associate Fellow at the Centre for European Reform in London told CNBC.com. "There's a clear need for some imaginative and inspiring European political leadership and there's no obvious figure willing or able to play that role," Tindale added.

The current and most of the aspiring political leaders in Europe seem to be doing just the opposite. Nicolas Sarkozy had said that he was going to push for more trade protectionism in Europe and tighter external border controls. France's new Socialist President Francois Hollande has promised to re-negotiate the fiscal pact agreed last December, which ensures that countries in the EU take the issue of tackling their debt seriously. And far-right leader Marie Le Pen had focused her campaign on "economic patriotism", which she sees as "the only way to revive employment without the inhumane austerity measures" that other European countries have had to face. In other parts of the European Union, outbursts of anger from German politicians against Greeks and other southern Europeans are notorious, and Spain's Prime Minister Mariano Rajoy had called on other EU leaders to be more cautious when they talk about Spain, reminding them that "what is good for Spain is good for the Eurozone."

In an article in the *Financial Times*, billionaire investor George Soros warned that the EU was unlikely to continue to exist unless extraordinary steps are taken to save it from the consequences of the debt crisis, after measures such as injecting more liquidity in the markets failed. "Latin American countries suffered a lost decade after 1982, and Japan has been stagnating for a quarter of a century; both have survived. But the European Union is not a country and it is unlikely to survive. The deflationary debt trap threatens to destroy a still-incomplete political union," Soros wrote. This is the union's main problem: the lack of a common political identity; and it cannot be solved overnight. According to Tindale, there is no European political identity because the European Parliament, which is made of members elected by citizens in each country, does not have substantial political power and the European Commission, the executive body of the EU, is not an elected organization.

The trend towards divergence, rather than convergence, is not only visible in politics. In economics, too, more often than not national interests take precedence. The German central bank, the Bundesbank, recently announced that it would reject bank bonds guaranteed by states that received aid from the EU and the IMF, after the European Central Bank gave national banks more flexibility on picking collateral. The Austrian central bank followed suit. The amounts involved are small and unlikely to cause problems for the periphery countries, but analysts said they were watching to see if these moves signal that worse things are to come. "If it is a sign of things to come, if it is a sign that the Bundesbank and other banks are going to demand more assurance on loans to Greece and other countries, then it is a very worrying sign," Jennifer McKeown, senior European economist at Capital Economics, told CNBC.com. "We've argued for some time now that the euro zone is likely to break up. Greece is likely to leave, possibly as soon as this year, and may be followed by Portugal, maybe by Ireland," McKeown added. The periphery countries might be pushed out of the euro zone by their electorates, sick of the austerity measures that have plunged Greece, Spain and Portugal into deep recessions, or Germany might get tired of having to foot the biggest part of the bill for bailouts and get out, she said.

Since the beginning of the debt crisis, analysts have argued that European legislation does not allow a country to leave the euro zone and remain in the EU – the single currency was designed as a one-way street, to ensure its credibility. But McKeown pointed out that the ECB was prohibited from printing money and it still did. Although the central bank insists that it is sterilizing the cash it injects in markets when it buys government bonds, it is difficult to check whether all the liquidity has been drained.

Politicians' statements do not mean all is lost for the EU, but the union must reform quickly or face disintegration, analysts said. "The EU is not much threatened by rhetoric but by action or rather lack of action," Daniel Gros, director at the Centre for European Policy Studies in Brussels, told CNBC.com. "I would like to see in Spain recognition of the severity of problems in the housing market and liberalization of the labor market, and the same in Italy," Gros added. In northern Europe, people in Germany, the Netherlands, Sweden and Denmark and, in Central Europe, Austria, save too much and consumers in these countries should be encouraged to spend more, he said. The French model, although it still has some life left in it, is not sustainable in the long term, Gros warned, adding: "You cannot live forever running a current deficit and consuming more than you produce." For the EU to survive, "the current constellation of economic imbalances" must be fixed over the next decade, Gros said. "The idea of having a unified economic government of the EU or of the euro zone is something that is 50 years away. We don't have that much time to get the euro situation under control," he added.

In Stone Mountain, Georgia, Federal Reserve Chairman Ben Bernanke said that banks need to have more capital at hand in order to ensure the financial system is stable. Bernanke said regulators were taking steps to force financial institutions to hold higher capital buffers, even if they allow for a long period of implementation to prevent any market disruptions. "We need to have higher capital, and that's what Basel III does," he said in response to questions at an Atlanta Fed conference, referring to the latest international effort to tighten bank oversight. "That's essential for a stable financial system." Bernanke made the comments the same day that an international bank lobby group, the Institute of International Finance, urged policymakers to pause in regulating the industry. Toughened capital standards, new liquidity requirements and rules that limit activities all restrict banks' ability to provide businesses and households with the credit needed to lift economic growth, the IIF said in a letter to central bankers and finance ministers. Whether big banks have sufficient levels of capital to protect against possible losses has been an ongoing source of contention. A call by the head of the International Monetary Fund, Christine Lagarde, last year for European banks to raise up to 200 billion euros in new capital was quickly rejected by European politicians.

In his prepared remarks, Bernanke said the U.S. economy has yet to fully recover from the effects of the financial crisis, and regulators must continue to find new ways to strengthen the banking system. "The heavy human and economic costs of the crisis underscore the importance of taking all necessary steps to avoid a repeat of the events of the past few years," Bernanke said. Although he did not touch directly on the outlook for economic growth or monetary policy, Bernanke focused on the lingering blind spots for financial authorities trying to prevent a repeat of the 2008-2009 meltdown. He said financial stability matters had historically played second fiddle to monetary policy issues in the list of central bank priorities, but the crisis changed that. "Financial stability policy has taken on greater prominence and is now generally considered to stand on an equal footing with monetary policy as a critical responsibility of central banks," he said.

Bernanke said recent bank stress tests will become a regular feature of the supervisory landscape, and for that reason the latest round of tests is being reviewed to identify possible areas of improvement in execution and communication. He reiterated a worry that he and other top policymakers have expressed about the continued vulnerability of money market funds. "Additional steps to increase the resiliency of money market funds are important for the overall stability of our financial system and warrant serious consideration," Bernanke said. "The risk of runs ... remains a concern, particularly since some of the tools that policymakers employed to stem the runs during the crisis are no longer available," he said.

In Washington the commissioner of the U.S. tax-collecting Internal Revenue Service warned of "a real disaster" for taxpayers next year should Congress miss a December 31 deadline to decide on billions in major tax provisions. Congress is expected to wait until after Election Day, November 6, to take up whether to extend the individual income tax cuts passed under former president George W. Bush that expire at the end of 2012. Most Democrats and President

Obama want to extend all but the top two tax brackets, allowing taxes to increase for high-income earners. Republicans want to extend the lower rates for all income groups. A 2010 "lame duck" session deadlock to extend the Bush tax cuts delayed the start of the tax filing season in early 2011. Allowing the pending tax decisions to lapse into 2013 will cause confusion for taxpayers, said Douglas Shulman, IRS commissioner, speaking at the National Press Club in Washington. "We're going to have real risk in the system" if Congress delays, Shulman said. "You could have a real disaster in the filing season where there's total confusion," especially for the alternative minimum tax "patch" he said.

The alternative minimum tax is a parallel tax system that applies to higher-income taxpayers. A legislative fix to index it for inflation must be approved before year's end to prevent the tax from hitting taxpayers in lower income brackets. In the absence of congressional action by January 1, the IRS might be forced to delay the tax-filing season, which begins promptly with the New Year, Shulman said. As it is, Congress faces a huge workload for the two-month lame-duck period after the elections when about $650 billion of tax and spending provisions expire. Shulman, appointed by President George W. Bush is now in the last year of a five-year term. He defended IRS's regulation of 501(c) 4 groups, including Tea Party organizations, which have received IRS letters asking questions about their political work. For any non-profit group that raises a red flag, the IRS will "go out and do an audit and gather more facts," Shulman said in response to a question about IRS investigations into the non-profit groups. Shulman also touted stronger IRS international enforcement efforts for businesses and individuals. The agency has hired private-sector experts to catch businesses that aggressively shift assets and profits offshore. The new enforcers will help the IRS keep pace with corporations' evolving tax strategies, Shulman said. Tax professionals have doubted whether the IRS has the muscle to enforce these "transfer pricing" disputes. Transfer pricing is a booming field of global tax law. It involves multinational corporations moving goods, services and assets from one subsidiary to another in different countries and how they account for these "transfers".

X

AS THE price of oil trades near 2008-highs and the average price of gasoline hovers around $4 a gallon, world leaders are considering adding more supply to the market. In recent days, the United States along with the United Kingdom, France and Japan have been in talks to ease the shock of rising oil and gas prices by releasing billions of emergency reserves onto the market. The laws of supply and demand dictate that when supply is great, prices should fall. But the rise in the price for fuel is not an issue of supply and demand, says former Senator Byron Dorgan (D-ND), who helped shape the nation's energy policy as chairman the Senate Indian Affairs Committee. "There is no justification for the current gas prices. This is all about speculation by the people who are speculating on the price of oil and gas," he says. "We could shutdown excess speculation in commodity markets. This government should do that."

Fadel Gheit, senior energy analyst at Oppenheimer, said he blames speculators for adding "at a minimum" $20 per barrel to the price of oil. In a study of oil prices over the last five years, the St. Louis Federal Reserve determined speculation drove up oil prices by 15 per cent. The CEO of ExxonMobil believes speculation could be driving up oil prices by as much as 40 per cent a barrel. "These are people who will never buy oil and never sell oil. They are actually buying and selling things they will never have from people who never had it," says Dorgan. "They are making money by driving up the price at the pump and the American people are the victims." But for all the lambasting of Wall Street speculators for driving up energy prices, economists at IHS said they believe new regulation of commodity markets could adversely affect the U.S. economy as a whole. "The regulations, as currently envisioned, could create a significant ripple effect through the energy economy that would reduce production, increase the cost of electricity and gasoline and ultimately affect jobs," said Kurt Barrow, vice president at Purvin & Gertz, a division of IHS. Why? By limiting commodity trading, IHS says it would make it more difficult for companies that hedge against future oil prices to manage risks.

Half a decade into the deepest U.S. housing crisis since the 1930s, many Americans are hoping the crisis is finally nearing its end.

House sales are picking up across most of the country, the plunge in prices is slowing and attempts by lenders to claim back properties from struggling borrowers dropped by more than a third in 2011, hitting a four-year low. But a painful part two of the slump looks set to unfold: Many more U.S. homeowners face the prospect of losing their homes this year as banks pick up the pace of foreclosures. "We are right back where we were two years ago. I would put money on 2012 being a bigger year for foreclosures than 2010," said Mark Seifert, executive director of Empowering & Strengthening Ohio's People (ESOP), a counseling group with 10 offices in Ohio. "Last year was an anomaly, and not in a good way," he said.

In 2011 the "robo-signing" scandal, in which foreclosure documents were signed without properly reviewing individual cases, prompted banks to hold back on new foreclosures pending a settlement. Five major banks eventually struck that settlement with 49 U.S. states in February. Signs are growing the pace of foreclosures is picking up again, something housing experts predict will again weigh on home prices before any sustained recovery can occur. Mortgage servicing provider Lender Processing Services reported in early March that U.S. foreclosure starts jumped 28 per cent in January. Watchdog group, 4closurefraud.org which helped uncover the "robo-signing" scandal, says it has turned up evidence of a large rise in new foreclosures between March 1 and 24 by three big banks in Palm Beach County in Florida, one of the states hit hardest by the housing crash

Although foreclosure starts were 50 per cent lower than for the same period in 2010, those begun by Deutsche Bank were up 47 per cent from 2011. Those of Wells Fargo's rose 68 per cent and Bank of America's, including BAC Home Loans Servicing, jumped nearly seven-fold – 251 starts versus 37 in the same period in 2011. Housing experts say localized warning signs of a new wave of foreclosure are likely to be replicated across much of the United States. Online foreclosure marketplace RealtyTrac estimated that while foreclosures dropped slightly nationwide in February from January and from February 2011, they rose in 21 states and jumped sharply in cities like Tampa (64 per cent), Chicago (43 per cent) and Miami (53 per cent). RealtyTrac CEO Brandon Moore said the "numbers point to a gradually rising foreclosure tide as some of the barriers that have been holding back foreclosures are removed."

The national unemployment rate fell to 8.3 per cent from its peak of 10 per cent in October 2009, but nearly 13 million Americans remained jobless, meaning many are struggling to keep up with their mortgage payments. Real estate company Zillow Inc. says more than one in four American homeowners were "under water" or owed more than their homes were worth in the fourth quarter of 2011. The crisis has wiped out some $7 trillion in U.S. household wealth. "We're seeing more people coming through who have good loans with reasonable interest rates," said Ed Jacob, executive director of non-profit lender Neighborhood Housing Services of Chicago Inc., which provides foreclosure counseling. "But in many households only one person works now instead of two, or they had their hours cut. The answer to the housing crisis now is job creation." Zillow expects the resurgence in foreclosures this year, combined with excess inventory of unsold, bank-owned homes will contribute to a 3.7 per cent national decline in prices before the market hits bottom in 2013 and stays there until 2016. "The hangover from this crisis will far outlast the party of the boom years," said Zillow chief economist Stan Humphries. Getting through the remaining foreclosures and dealing with the resulting flood of homes on the market in the wake of the bank settlement is a necessary part of the healing process for the U.S. housing market, he added. According to leading broker dealer Amherst Securities, some 9.5 million homes are still at risk of default and in February it said it expected to see the uptick in foreclosures start to hit in March and April. There is other evidence that many of the foreclosures that did not happen in 2011 will happen this year.

A January report by the Neighborhood Economic Development Advocacy Project in New York found that in the first half of 2011 the number of 90-day pre-foreclosure notices in New York City outnumbered court foreclosure actions by a ratio of 14 to one, indicating that while proceedings were initiated against many homeowners, they were left incomplete. "Now the banks have a settlement, foreclosure numbers for 2012 are going to be high," said NEDAP co-director Josh Zinner.

A recent survey by the California Reinvestment Coalition, an umbrella group of nearly 300 non-profit groups in the state, of member agencies found 75 per cent of respondents expected increased demand for their foreclosure prevention services in 2012 but more than a third had to scale back services because of funding cuts. "Funding is a major concern given what our members expect for this year," said associate director Kevin Stein. All this has non-profits intensifying calls for the Federal Housing Finance Agency to drop its opposition to allowing the government-backed mortgage giants Fannie Mae and Freddie Mac it regulates to reduce principal for underwater homeowners. Principal reduction involves reducing the amount borrowers owe in order to make a loan modification affordable for struggling homeowners. ESOP in Ohio engages in "hits" on Chase branches – they say Chase is the least accommodating major bank when it comes to working with struggling homeowners – where they try to hand letters to bank mangers calling on chief executive Jamie Dimon to lobby FHFA head Edward DeMarco for principal reductions. A Chase spokeswoman said the bank has made "extensive efforts" to work with homeowners, helping 775,000 borrowers stay in their homes since early 2009, and avoiding foreclosure "more than twice as often as we have had to foreclose." Housing groups like ESOP maintain, as they have throughout the housing crisis, that unless the FHFA embraces extensive principal reduction, many more under water borrowers face losing their homes. "Until banks engage in meaningful principal reduction as a matter of course," ESOP's Seifert said after a recent protest at a Chase branch in Cleveland, "this crisis will not end."

And according to the Associated Press, a big shift is happening in Big Oil: an American giant now ranks behind a Chinese upstart. ExxonMobil is no longer the world's biggest publicly traded producer of oil. For the first time, that distinction belongs to a 13-year-old Chinese company called PetroChina. The Beijing company was created by the Chinese government to secure more oil for that nation's booming economy. PetroChina announced that it pumped 2.4 million barrels a day last year, surpassing Exxon by 100,000. The company has grown rapidly over the last decade by squeezing more from China's aging oil fields and outspending Western companies to acquire more petroleum reserves in places like Canada, Iraq and Qatar. The company's output increased 3.3 per cent in 2011 while Exxon's fell 5 per cent. Exxon's oil production also fell behind Rosneft, the Russian energy company. PetroChina's rise highlights a fundamental difference in how the largest petroleum companies plan to supply the world as new deposits become tougher to find and more expensive to produce.

Every major oil company has aggressively pursued new finds to replace their current wells. But analysts say Western oil firms like ExxonMobil have been more conservative than the Chinese, mindful of their bottom line and investor returns. With oil prices up 19 percent in 2011, they still made money without increasing production. PetroChina Co. Ltd. has a different mission. The Chinese government owns 86 per cent of its stock and the nation uses nearly every drop of oil PetroChina pumps. Its appetite for gasoline and other petroleum products is projected to double between 2010 and 2035. "There's a lot of anxiety in China about the energy question," says energy historian Dan Yergin. "It's just growing so fast." While PetroChina sits atop other publicly traded companies in oil production, it falls well short of national oil companies like Saudi Aramco, which produces nearly 8 million barrels a day. And Exxon is still the biggest publicly traded energy company when counting combined output of oil and natural gas. PetroChina ranks third behind Exxon and BP in total output of oil and natural gas. PetroChina is looking to build on its momentum in 2012. "We must push ahead," PetroChina chairman Jiang Jiemin said in January.

PetroChina has grown by pumping everything it can from reserves in China, estimated to contain more than 6.5 billion barrels. It drilled thousands of oil wells across vast stretches of the nation's northern grasslands. Some of those fields are ancient by industry standards, dating close to the beginning of China's communist government in the 1950s. The commitment to aging fields distinguishes PetroChina from its biggest Western rivals. Exxon and other major oil companies typically sell their aging, low-performing fields, or they put them out of commission. PetroChina also has been on a buying spree, acquiring new reserves in Iraq, Australia, Africa, Qatar and Canada. Since 2010, its acquisitions have totaled $7 billion, about twice as much as Exxon, according to data provider Dealogic.

Several other Chinese companies have become deal makers around the globe as well. Total acquisitions by Chinese energy firms jumped from less than $2 billion between 2002 and 2003 to nearly $48 billion in 2009 and 2010, according to the International Energy

Agency. More times than not, the companies are paying above the industry average to get those deals done. It's making some in the West nervous. In 2005, for example, CNOOC Ltd., a company mostly owned by the Chinese government tried to buy American oil producer Unocal. U.S. lawmakers worked to block the deal, asking President Bush to investigate the role the Chinese central government played in the process. Chevron Corp. eventually bought Unocal for $17.3 billion. "There's a resistance to Chinese investment in (U.S.) oil and gas," Morningstar analyst Robert Bellinski says. "It's like how Japan was to us in the 1980s. People think they're going to take us over. They're going to buy all of our resources."

"China's oil companies have been willing to outspend everyone and that drives up the price of fields and makes it more expensive for everyone to expand. You now have to outbid them," says Argus Research analyst Phil Weiss. "If you can't, you're going to have access to fewer assets." Longer term, Chinese expansion globally will bring benefits to the U.S. and other economies. By developing as many oil wells as possible – especially in Africa, Iraq and other politically unstable regions – China will help expand supply. "Frankly, the more risk-hungry producers there are, the more oil will be on the market, and the cheaper prices are," says Michael Levi, an energy policy expert at the Council on Foreign Relations. Despite its swift expansion, PetroChina and other Chinese companies still have much to prove to investors, analysts say.

PetroChina's parent, China National Petroleum Corp., for example, has spent millions of dollars in Sudan to provide highways, medical facilities and shuttle buses for the elderly. Oil companies typically don't do that. All of that increases the cost of business and minimizes the returns for shareholders. In 2009 and 2010, PetroChina's profit margins for its exploration and production business were only about two-thirds that of ExxonMobil's. Its stock price has climbed less than 1 per cent, in the past year, compared with a 3.7 per cent rise in the stock of ExxonMobil Corp. "You have to ask yourself: What is the purpose of PetroChina?" Bellinski says. "It is to fuel China. That's it. Although they're a public company, I'm very skeptical that they have any interest in shareholder value creation."

In another area, China took a milestone step in turning the yuan into a global currency by doubling the size of its trading band against the dollar, pushing through a crucial reform that further liberalizes its nascent financial markets. The People's Bank of China said it would allow the yuan to rise or fall 1 per cent from a mid-point every day, compared with its previous 0.5 per cent limit. The timing of the move underlines Beijing's belief that the yuan is near its equilibrium level, and that China's economy, although cooling, is sturdy enough to handle important, long-promised, structural reforms, analysts said. The move it was said would help China deflect criticism of its controversial currency policy ahead of the annual spring meeting of the International Monetary Fund in Washington.

A slowing world economy that has pared investor expectations of a steadily rising yuan also gave Beijing the confidence to proceed, knowing that a larger band would not necessarily lead to a stronger currency. "The Central Bank chose a good time window to enlarge the trading band. The market's expectation for a stronger yuan is weakening," said Dong Xian'an, chief economist at Peking First Advisory in Beijing. "The move partially clears away doubts on whether China can manage a soft landing in its economy, and makes clear China's reform road map." Investors have widely expected China to widen the yuan's trading band this year, thanks to repeated hints from Beijing that the change would take China one step closer to its financial goal: a basically convertible yuan by 2015. Having a currency that trades with fewer restrictions also enhances Shanghai's status as a financial center.

The yuan, also known as the renminbi or "people's money", hit a record high of 6.2884 against the dollar on 10 February, but is little changed against the U.S. currency for the year, softening 0.14 per cent since January. Analysts say its listless showing is likely to persist through 2012, as expectations of future gains are dulled by China's easing economic growth, and speculation that the yuan is near equilibrium. As China this year heads into its biggest leadership changeover in a decade, it would be in Beijing's interests to avoid dramatic fluctuations in the yuan that could hurt exporters, many of whom are battling rising costs and tepid demand as it is. "The yuan is close to an equilibrium. We expect it could only gain 1.4 per cent against the dollar this year, so the time is right to widen the band," said Lan Shen, an economist at Standard Chartered Bank in Shanghai.

But the truth is more Americans than Chinese can't put food on the table. Zachary Roth of The Lookout reported in October 2011 that the number of Americans who lack access to basic necessities like food and health care was now higher than it was at the peak of the Great Recession, according to a survey released then. And in a finding that could worsen fears of U.S. decline, the share of Americans struggling to put food on the table is now three times as large as the share of the Chinese population in the same position. The United States' Basic Index Score, a Gallup measure of access to necessities, fell to 81.4 in September, even lower than the 81.5 mark it reached in February and March, 2009. The recession officially ended in June of that year, but the halting recovery hasn't given a sustained boost to the number of Americans able to provide for themselves. The government reported also that a record number of Americans is living in poverty.

Between September 2008 and October 2011, the share of Americans with access to a personal doctor plummeted from 82.5 per cent to 78.3 per cent. The share with health insurance fell from 85.9 per cent to 82.3 per cent. And the population saying they had enough money to buy food for themselves and their family dropped from 81.1 per cent to 80.1 per cent. Gallup found that just 6 per cent of Chinese said there were times in the past 12 months when they lacked enough money for food for themselves or their family, compared to 19 per cent of Americans. Just three years ago, those results were almost reversed: 16 per cent of Chinese couldn't put food on the table at times, compared to 9 per cent of Americans.

In December 2011 Jeffrey Goldberg told Tim Worstall of *Forbes* magazine that six members of the Walton family, the original owners of Wal-Mart, have more wealth than the bottom 30 per cent of Americans. In 2007, according to the labor economist Sylvia Allegretto, the six Walton family members on the *Forbes* 400 had a net worth equal to the bottom 30 per cent of all Americans. It's a telling indictment of American wealth inequality, and it suggests to Wall Street protest movements around the world that something must be done about rising inequality. The Waltons are now collectively worth about $93 billion, according to *Forbes*. Total U.S. household wealth is in the $50 trillion to $70 trillion range. So these Waltons have, between the family members, 0.13 per cent of US wealth. But, as Worstall points out, for the people who inherited the world's largest and most successful retailer it doesn't sound like a particularly terrible concentration of wealth and it is less than John D. Rockefeller had when he was at his peak.

XI

ON 18 JUNE 2012 President Obama said that G-20 nations must "do what's necessary" to boost world economy. Obama welcomed the results of the Greek election as he prepared to join other world leaders at a summit in Los Cabos, Mexico, aimed at boosting a sluggish global economic recovery. Officially, the G-20 Summit would largely focus on one of the primary causes of the recovery's lethargy – the threat of a European currency collapse that would undermine the already fragile economies of most of the 17 countries that use the euro. "The world is concerned about the slowing of growth that has taken place," Obama said before the start of the summit, following one-on-one-talks with host President Felipe Calderon of Mexico. "A lot of attention has been centered on Europe. Now is the time, as we've discussed, to make sure that all of us join to do what's necessary to stabilize the world financial system, to avoid protectionism, to ensure that we are working hand-in-hand to both grow the economy and create jobs while taking a responsible approach long term and medium term towards our fiscal structures."

However, the summit was not expected to produce concrete commitments, and European Union President Jose Manuel Barroso made clear that European nations were not there to be lectured on how to proceed. "This crisis was not originated in Europe. ... This crisis was originated in North America," Barroso said. "And many of our financial sector were contaminated by – how can I put it – unorthodox practice from some sectors of the financial market. But we are not putting the blame on our partners. What we are saying is let's work together when we have a global problem like the one we have today." He called for the G-20 leaders to back steps the European Union is taking, such as possible further bailouts of struggling economies such as Greece and Spain. "Frankly, we are not coming here to receive lessons in terms of democracy or in terms of how to handle the economy because the European Union is a model that we may be very proud of," Barroso said. "We are not complacent about the difficulties. We are extremely open. I wish that all our partners were so open about their own difficulties."

As usual for any summit, Obama also has bilateral meetings with other leaders, including his first direct talks with Russian President Vladimir Putin since Putin recently returned to the post for a second time. Obama and Putin began their one-on-one meeting after Obama and host President Felipe Calderon of Mexico held that talks that included the announcement that Mexico would join the United States and eight other countries in negotiations on the Trans Pacific Partnership, an economic union to boost trade. In addition to the United States, the current countries of the partnership are Australia, Brunei, Chile, Malaysia, New Zealand, Peru, Singapore, and Vietnam. A main topic of the summit was the elections in debt-ridden Greece, where the center-right New Democracy party won the most votes and was asked to try to form a coalition government. The vote was widely seen as a Greek referendum on staying in the euro, and the narrow victory for New Democracy over Syriza – a leftist party that opposes conditions that accompany an international bailout for the country – brought initial ease to world markets troubled by the prospect of a possible European currency collapse.

After his talks with Calderon, Obama expressed optimism that the new Greek government would remain committed to a solution that would keep the country in the European monetary union. "I think the election in Greece indicates a positive prospect for not only them forming a government, but also them working constructively with their international partners in order that they can continue on the path of reform, and do so in a way that also offers the prospects for the Greek people to succeed and prosper," Obama told reporters. A rocky election in Greece that would result in its departure from the Eurozone was one of the greatest fears coming into the summit, and while that fear appears to have been averted for now, the United States still expects European leaders to lay out a plan for dealing with the effects of the distressed Greek economy. "We expect to hear more of this in Los Cabos, showing that they are fundamentally committed to evolving the euro area in a way that makes the monetary union much stronger by virtue of having a more banking union, more fiscal union, more political union," Treasury Under Secretary for International

Affairs Lael Brainard told reporters in a briefing just days before the start of the summit. Mike Froman, Obama's deputy national security adviser for international economics, told the advance briefing that "this isn't a meeting where we expect Europeans to make decisions about Europe."

While avoiding an economic contagion is central to the G-20s formal mission, many eyes were trained on the bilateral meeting between Obama and Putin. Russia has recently blocked two resolutions in the U.N. Security Council targeted at putting a stop to Syrian President Bashar al-Assad's brutal attacks on civilians, deepening a divide that has darkened an otherwise resurgent relationship between the United States and its former Cold War foe. Prior to the summit, U.S. Deputy National Security Adviser Ben Rhodes told reporters that the United States continues to work to get Russia to agree with its position that al-Assad must relinquish power. "We've been working to get the Russians to come in line with, frankly, the broad international community," Rhodes said. "This is not just an issue between the United States and Russia, it's really an issue between the international community, on the one hand, that is expressing support for a real transition in Syria, and the Syrian government, which has, of course, resisted those steps. So we'll continue to work through that area of difference with the Russians because we believe that they can play a role, again, in pressing the Assad regime and supporting a political transition."

Obama met with German Chancellor Angela Merkel and then with Chinese President Hu Jintao. Obama and Hu are expected to discuss China's role in ongoing talks with Iran over its nuclear program, as well as China's role in spurring growth. The members of the G-20 are the United States, the European Union, Germany, Great Britain, France, Italy, Japan, Russia, China, Canada, Argentina, South Korea, South Africa, Mexico, Brazil, India, Indonesia, Saudi Arabia, Turkey and Australia.

But all these international issues and events did not mean that the Occupy protests had gone away. In Los Angeles more than 480 tents were erected on the lawns of City Hall. The camp has remained largely peaceful since police and city officials established a relationship early on based on dialogue instead of dictates. "We are thankful that we are, first and foremost, in a country where we can protest," said the Rev.

Cecil Williams, the founder of Glide and a fixture in the city's activist community. Oakland police said however that when a truck driver tried to deliver a portable restroom to protesters at Frank Ogawa Plaza, officers ordered the driver to leave because he had no permit. Police and about 150 protesters squared off; one person was arrested. In Maine five people face charges in Portland after police were called to investigate four separate assaults at the OccupyMaine encampment in Lincoln Park. The arrests were announced amid growing concerns over health and safety issues at the park, where OccupyMaine protesters have been camping since early October. In Massachusetts, a judge has banned a Framingham woman from the Occupy Boston camp after she allegedly interfered with a domestic violence investigation at the site, failed to appear in court and punched two police officers and kicked another. Nineteen-year-old Jade Anderson was arraigned on charges of disorderly conduct and several assault offenses. A Boston Municipal Court judge set bail at $850 and ordered Anderson to stay away from any Occupy Boston activities in the city.

In Minnesota, heavy security kept a close eye at anti-Wall Street protesters who showed up at Republican Michele Bachmann's Black Friday book signing at the Mall of America in Bloomington. The GOP presidential candidate signed copies of her *Core of Conviction* autobiography in a private area of the megamall. At least a dozen members from the Minnesota offshoot of the Occupy Wall Street movement bought copies so they could approach her. Several uniformed and plain-clothed officers prevented the protesters from bringing in signs and let them into the room one at a time. Bachmann foes and fans alike were subject to bag searches and pat-downs before entering. Reporters were not allowed in the room when the protesters came through. Anti-Wall Street protesters in Minneapolis plan to erect 99 tents in defiance of Hennepin County rules and a federal judge's decision. The Occupy Minneapolis Events Committee says the protesters have the right to assemble and the right to shelter. The 99 tents relate to an Occupy slogan suggesting that 1 per cent of the nation's population controls the wealth and the other 99 percent suffers the consequences.

It was clear that the protests were not frivolous but the 99 per cent are up against what Shaw would have described as evidence of "naked power" that has grown every year in astonishing ways. For example, in 1992 the 400th richest person in America made $24 million. In 2007, the 400th richest person in America made $138 million. In all of the 1990s, only 25 per cent of *Fortune*'s 400 made more than one appearance, but the overall message is the same: The rich keep getting richer. The average income of a top-400 earner grew by 650 per cent between 1992 and 2007 to a whopping $344 million. Over that time, the average salary didn't even double. But the average capital gains haul increased by 1,200 per cent. And what of Mark Zuckerberg who at 28 is the world's 40th wealthiest person, with a net worth of $15.7 billion, according to the Bloomberg Billionaires Index? His company Facebook went public in a $16 billion initial public offering in May that made millionaires of many young Americans. Their influence in the financial world will be daunting and it will be tempting for the 99 per cent to believe if their movement fails to bring about meaningful change that justice, as Plato said in *The Republic,* is simply the interest of the stronger.

XII

IN HIS State of the Union address President Obama had said that the nation's middle class is at risk because of growing economic inequality, and argued that the government must do more to preserve the basic American Dream. He said the basic American promise that hard work can allow one to own a home and support a family are at risk if the government doesn't do more to balance the scale between the nation's rich and poor. "The defining issue of our time is how to keep that promise alive. No challenge is more urgent. No debate is more important," Obama declared. "We can either settle for a country where a shrinking number of people do really well, while a growing number of Americans barely get by. Or we can restore an economy where everyone gets a fair shot, everyone does their fair share, and everyone plays by the same set of rules. What's at stake are not Democratic values or Republican values, but American values. We have to reclaim them."

In his third such address to the Congress, Obama's focus was not just on the future as he laid out broad proposals to boost an "economy built to last, where hard work pays off and responsibility is rewarded."

But in a message that was unmistakably aimed at voters in the upcoming presidential election, Obama reminded his audience that the nation's economic troubles began long before he arrived at the White House, starting with the collapse of the nation's leading banks in 2008 due to lax regulation and bad behavior. "In the six months before I took office, we lost nearly four million jobs. And we lost another four million before our policies were in full effect," Obama said. But he argued that the country is turning around under his policies, pointing to 3 million jobs created in the last 22 months. In a sign that Obama will campaign against the Republican-led Congress as much as his eventual GOP presidential rival, the president indicated he will take a hard stand against lawmakers determined to block his economic agenda. "The state of our union is getting stronger, and we've come too far to turn back now," Obama insisted. "As long as I'm president, I will work with anyone in this chamber to build on this momentum. But I intend to fight obstruction with action, and I will oppose any effort to return to the very same policies that brought on this economic crisis in the first place." The president argued that he's laying out a "blueprint for an economy that's built to last" based on four main themes: American manufacturing, American energy, skills for American workers and "a renewal of American values."

Among other things, Obama called for a rollback for tax breaks for American companies that outsource jobs overseas and proposed new tax cuts for manufacturers that build their products stateside – a proposal that generated muted applause among Republican lawmakers in the House chamber. He also announced the creation of a "trade enforcement unit" that would investigate unfair trade practices in countries including China – an issue that has been a big issue on the 2012 campaign trail. "Our workers are the most productive on Earth, and if the playing field is level, I promise you, America will always win," Obama declared.

Tackling an issue that will be big in the general election, Obama called on Republicans to pass immigration reform, including the DREAM Act. "If election-year politics keeps Congress from acting on a comprehensive plan, let's at least agree to stop expelling responsible young people who want to staff our labs, start new businesses, and defend this country," Obama said. "Send me a law that gives them the chance to earn their citizenship. I will sign it right away." Obama also called for aid to boost the nation's struggling housing market – proposing new tax incentives to help homeowners save $3,000 a year on their mortgages. He also announced the creation of a federal task force to monitor banks, mortgage lenders and credit card companies for fraud. "Millions of Americans who work hard and play by the rules every day deserve a government and a financial system that do the same," Obama said. "It's time to apply the same rules from top to bottom: No bailouts, no handouts, and no copouts. An America built to last insists on responsibility from everybody."

Obama sounded familiar themes on energy calling for a rollback of tax cuts on oil companies in favor of investments in clean energy sources. He announced a federal incentive to build clean energy projects on government land. On education, he called on states to pass laws to mandate that all minors stay in school until they graduate or turn 18. He also called on Congress to enact measures to ensure student aid – but he also warned higher education institutions to crack down on skyrocketing education costs. "If you can't stop tuition from going up, the funding you get from taxpayers will go down," Obama said. "Higher education can't be a luxury – it's an economic imperative that every family in America should be able to afford." He repeated a call for investment in the nation's crumbling infrastructure, announcing that he will sign an executive order to clear the red tape slowing federal construction projects. "But you need to fund these projects. Take the money we're no longer spending at war, use half of it to pay down our debt, and use the rest to do some nation-building right here at home," Obama said.

The White House has been signaling for weeks that Obama would embrace populist themes about the economy, as a way of drawing a line in the sand between him and his Republican rivals ahead of his 2012 re-election push. Like other presidents before him, he was joined in the House chamber by individuals aimed at personifying elements of his speech, including Debbie Bosanek, the secretary to billionaire financier Warren Buffett, whose argument that he shouldn't be paying a lower tax rate than average workers has become a rallying cry for the White House. "We don't begrudge financial success in this country. We admire it," Obama insisted. "When Americans talk about folks like me paying my fair share of taxes, it's not because they envy the rich. It's because they understand that when I get tax breaks I don't need and the country can't afford, it either adds to the deficit, or somebody else has to make up the difference."

But the larger message of Obama's remarks was obvious, as the president at one point returned to one of the major themes of his 2008 presidential bid of rising above cynicism and partisan gridlock to enact real change in Washington. He noted that the "greatest blow to confidence in our economy" came during last year's combative debt ceiling talks. "Who benefited from that fiasco?" Obama asked. "I've talked tonight about the deficit of trust between Main Street and Wall Street. But the divide between this city and the rest of the country is at least as bad – and it seems to get worse every year." He called for lawmakers to "lower the temperature" and "end the notion" that Democrats and Republicans must be locked in a "perpetual campaign of mutual destruction." At the same time, he warned again that he wouldn't wait for Congress to enact major reforms in Washington. "With or without this Congress, I will keep taking actions that help the economy grow," Obama said. "But I can do a whole lot more with your help. Because when we act together, there is nothing the United States of America can't achieve."

He was not the only one calling on Americans to act together. As Americans began observing Independence Day 2012, Starbucks CEO Howard Schultz wrote an open letter to the nation, *How Can America Win this Election*, in which he spells out his concern about the economy and specifically unemployment. In the letter he asks politicians to stop fighting and for business leaders to step up. "I love America, but we all know there is something wrong. The deficits this country must reconcile are much more than financial, and our inability to solve our own problems is sapping our national spirit. We are better than this," he writes. Schultz ran the letter in an advertisement in national newspapers and websites in July. He previously voiced his unhappiness with the state of the union last summer during the deadlocked federal budget debate.

"We are drifting towards mediocrity," Schultz told Andy Serwer, managing editor of *Fortune* magazine. The letter is a continuation of the concern that he shared with many Americans about the economy and unemployment and the lack of political leadership to address the problem. "Since I took this position a year ago things really haven't gotten better, they have gotten worse. I'm not trying to criticize the President or the Republican Party; I just want to try with civility and respect to use the scale of Starbucks for good. Business leaders need to change too. We all have a stake in this. In the letter, you can see we are trying to create a platform using social media and digital to give people a place to elevate the conversation."

What motivates Schultz is the fact he said that Americans cannot be bystanders anymore. "It's a dangerous time. We deserve a better America. You probably read that Stockton, California just declared bankruptcy. What was incredible to me was how it was reported in such a de minimus fashion. Like it was not a big deal. I don't want to sound like I'm preaching, but we need to try to do everything we can to create confidence and stimulate the economy. I hasten to think what might happen if we end up in another budget deadlock in a few months and S&P lowers the U.S. debt rating again. I was just in Europe. We don't want that to happen to us. We need real leadership from Washington and from the business community. I've been the ultimate beneficiary of the American Dream and that dream is now in jeopardy. I can't just stand by."

On 13 June 2012 The Associated Press reported that JPMorgan Chase said that its loss from a highly publicized trading blunder had grown to $4.4 billion in the most recent quarter, more than double the bank's original estimate of $2 billion. The bank also said that it was reducing its net income for the first quarter by $459 million because it had discovered information that "raises questions about the integrity" of values placed on certain trades. "We don't take it lightly," CEO Jamie Dimon told Wall Street analysts on a conference call. He added: "We're not making light of this error, but we do think it's an isolated event." Dimon said the bank had closed the division of the bank responsible for the bad trade and moved the remainder of the trading position under its investment banking division. Overall, JPMorgan said it earned $5 billion, or $1.21 per share, for the second quarter, which covers April through June and includes the bank's disclosure of the trading loss on May 10.

JPMorgan has lost about 15 per cent of its in market value since the loss came to light. The bank could take back pay from executives in charge of the division where the losses occurred. That procedure is known as a "clawback". It would be the first time JPMorgan exercised such a procedure. The most likely candidate would be Ina Drew, JPMorgan's chief investment officer, who oversaw the division responsible for the loss and left the bank days after the disclosure. In 2011, her pay package totaled $15 million. The *Wall Street Journal* reported that three other employees of the bank tied to the trade, including one who was known as the "London whale", had left the bank. Under close questioning from lawmakers in June about his own role in setting up the investment division responsible for the mess, Dimon declared: "We made a mistake. I'm absolutely responsible. The buck stops with me." The trading loss has raised concerns that the biggest banks still pose risks to the U.S. financial system, less than four years after the financial crisis erupted in the fall of 2008.

Meanwhile Reuters reported that Visa Inc., MasterCard Inc. and banks that issue their credit cards have agreed to a $7.25 billion settlement with U.S. retailers in a lawsuit over the fixing of credit and debit card fees in what could be the largest antitrust settlement in U.S. history. The settlement, if approved by a judge, would resolve dozens of lawsuits filed by retailers in 2005. The card companies and banks would also allow stores to start charging customers extra for using certain credit cards in an effort to steer them toward cheaper forms of payment. Swipe fees – charges to cover processing credit and debit payments – are set by the card companies and deducted from the transaction by the banks that issue the cards, essentially passing on the cost to merchants, the lawsuits said. The proposed settlement involves a payment to a class of stores of $6 billion from Visa, MasterCard and more than a dozen of the country's largest banks who issue the companies' cards. The card companies have also agreed to reduce swipe fees by the equivalent of 10 basis points for eight months for a total consideration to stores valued at about $1.2 billion, according to lawyers for the plaintiffs.

The deal called for merchants to be allowed to negotiate collectively over the swipe fees, also known as interchange fees. Merchants would also be required to disclose information about card fees to customers, and credit card surcharges would be subject to a cap, according to the settlement papers. Surcharge rules would not affect the 10 states that currently prohibit that practice, which include California, New York and Texas. An additional $525 million will be paid to stores suing individually, according to the documents. "This is an historic settlement," said Bonny Sweeney, a lawyer for the plaintiffs. The settlement "will help shift the competitive balance from one formerly dominated by the banks which controlled the card networks to the side of merchants and consumers," said Craig Wildfang, who also represented the plaintiffs. Noah Hanft, general counsel for MasterCard, said the company believed its interests were "best served by an amicable resolution" of the case. Visa Chief Executive Officer Joseph Saunders said the settlement was in the best interest of all parties and did not expect the settlement to impact its current guidance.

Not everyone was pleased with the proposed settlement, however. One class plaintiff, the National Association of Convenience Stores, rejected the settlement in a statement from its president, Tom Robinson, who is also president of Robinson Oil Corp. "Not only does the proposed settlement fail to introduce competition and transparency, it actually provides Visa and MasterCard with the tools to continue to shield swipe fees from market forces," Robinson said. The proposed considerations are in fact a far cry from the $50 billion in swipe-fees paid each year by U.S. retailers, he said. The American Bankers Association, a trade group whose members include the bank defendants, said retailers, not consumers, stood to gain the most from the proposed settlement. "Big-box retailers will likely seize this opportunity to ask Congress for even more handouts," said ABA President Frank Keating in a statement, referring to the Durbin amendment passed by Congress in 2010 limiting debit-card swipe fees – a move that banks say resulted in an $8 billion windfall for retailers. "The legal process worked and should send a signal to Congress that it is wrong to pick winners and losers in a complex dispute between two industries," the Electronic Payment Coalition, which represents payment networks, said in a statement.

The plaintiffs charged that Visa and MasterCard colluded directly and indirectly through the issuing banks to keep merchants from finding ways to mitigate credit-card costs. Plaintiffs in the case include supermarket chain Kroger Co, pharmacy chain Rite-Aid Corp and shoe retailer Payless ShoeSource, as well as trade associations such as the National Association of Convenience Stores, National Grocers Association and the American Booksellers Association. The National Retail Federation, a trade group representing retailers, said that "the test will be whether the injunctive relief is meaningful. Unless it is, the card market will stay broken and neither merchants nor their customers will achieve a long-term benefit." A number of banks that issue Visa and MasterCard cards, including JP Morgan Chase & Co, were also named as defendants in the lawsuit, along with Visa and MasterCard's payment networks. A spokeswoman for Bank of America NA said it believed the terms of the settlement were fair. JP Morgan declined to comment. Citigroup Inc. acknowledged its role in the deal and declined further comment. A spokesman for Wells Fargo said the company was pleased to put the matter behind it.

An estimated 7 million retailers will be affected by the settlement, according to lawyers for the plaintiffs. Visa and MasterCard have been plagued by legal problems over their payment-card policies for the last decade. In 2003, the companies paid a combined $3 billion to settle a lawsuit by stores over their "honor all cards" policies, which tied acceptance of credit to debit cards. The U.S. Department of Justice brought and settled a civil antitrust suit against Visa and MasterCard in 2010. As part of the consent decree, the companies agreed to drop certain policies that kept stores from steering their customers to cheaper forms of payment. But the decree left intact policies that prohibit stores from charging customers more when they use certain payment cards, according to a July 2011 court filing from plaintiffs. The defendants denied that any collusion took place. Visa said its share of the settlement is $4.4 billion, and MasterCard said its share is $790 million. In December, Visa announced it set aside an additional $1.57 billion to cover the cost of a potential settlement in the case, bringing its litigation reserve balance to $4.28 billion, according to a regulatory filing. MasterCard in the fourth quarter of 2011 recorded a $770 million pretax charge, as an estimate of its potential liability in the case, a filing with the U.S. Securities and Exchange Commission showed. MasterCard said in a statement that it expected to incur an additional $20 million pre-tax charge in its 2012 second quarter financial statements to cover its portion of the settlement. Visa and MasterCard together accounted for more than 80 percent of U.S. credit and debit card purchases by volume in 2011, according to data from the Nilson Report, a California trade publication.

Albert Foer, president of think-tank the American Antitrust Institute, said that the settlement should create more transparency for consumers at the cash register. Because merchants had been forbidden from charging customers extra for costlier payment forms, they often built that cost into the retail price, he said. While it may not lead to lower prices, "it gives the consumers some choice and it should ultimately mean a better deal for everybody," Foer said. "In the longer run, it should help keep retail prices under better control." It may also be the last time retailers are allowed to take Visa and MasterCard to court over interchange fees. The proposal provides for extensive litigation releases that would keep stores that join the settlement from suing over a wide range of issues relating to fees and anti-steering restraints. Reporting on the case was Jessica Dye.

And from Orlando, Fla. and New York, Reuters reported that Coca-Cola Co. was dropping its membership in a conservative national advocacy group that supports "Stand Your Ground" laws such as the one being used as a defense in the Florida killing of Trayvon Martin. The move by the world's biggest soft drink maker comes as corporate America faces increased scrutiny from consumers and shareholder activists over lobbying and political spending. PepsiCo Inc. ended its relationship with the group – the American Legislative Exchange Council (ALEC) – in January.

There were problems too for the American taxpayer abroad. Robert Burns of The Associated Press wrote that after years of following the paper trail of $51 billion in U.S. taxpayer dollars provided to rebuild a broken Iraq, the U.S. government can say with certainty that too much was wasted. But it couldn't say how much. In what it called its final audit report, the Office of the Special Inspector General for Iraq Reconstruction Funds spelled out a range of accounting weaknesses that put "billions of American taxpayer dollars at risk of waste and misappropriation" in the largest reconstruction project of its kind in U.S. history. "The precise amount lost to fraud and waste can never be known," the report said. The auditors found huge problems accounting for the huge sums, but one small example of failure stood out: A contractor got away with charging $80 for a pipe fitting that its competitor was selling for $1.41. Why? The company's billing documents were reviewed sloppily by U.S. contracting officers or were not reviewed at all. With dry understatement, wrote Burns, the inspector general said that while he couldn't pinpoint the amount wasted, it "could be substantial."

Asked why the exact amount squandered can never be determined, the inspector general's office referred The Associated Press to a report it did in February 2009 titled "Hard Lessons" in which it said the auditors – much like the reconstruction managers themselves – faced personnel shortages and other hazards. "Given the vicissitudes of the reconstruction effort – which was dogged from the start by persistent violence, shifting goals, constantly changing contracting practices and undermined by a lack of unity of effort – a complete accounting of all reconstruction expenditures is impossible to achieve," the report concluded. In that same report, the inspector general, Stuart Bowen, recalled what then Defense Secretary Donald H. Rumsfeld asked when they met shortly after Bowen started in January 2004: "Why did you take this job? It's an impossible task."

As proof, the General Services Administration is back in Congress's crosshairs after the GSA's inspector general reported to Congress on another installment of "egregious waste of taxpayer dollars" at the beleaguered government agency. John Parkinson of ABC OTUS News said just months after the agency was rocked when a lavish 2010 Las Vegas conference was exposed by the agency's inspector general, GSA was now facing scrutiny for wasteful spending at another performance awards ceremony for its employees. This time, the agency is being investigated for spending $268,732 on a one-day conference for its Federal Acquisition Service division on 17 November 2010, in Arlington, Virginia. More than $20,000 of taxpayer money was spent on drumsticks for 4000 attendees, more than $8,500 for an appearance by someone called "Agent X", according to the preliminary findings of the Inspector General. The event, which was held at the Crystal City Gateway Marriott just outside Washington, D.C., also included expenses of more than $35,000 for picture frames, $20,000 in catering charges as well as additional funding for a violinist and guitarist. "This is another sad day for the taxpayers in the United States," Rep. John Mica, the Republican chairman of the Transportation and Infrastructure committee, said. "This sounds almost unbelievable to have this kind of waste reported when we're running trillions in dollars in deficit makes absolutely everyone's blood boil."

Last April, the GSA Inspector General revealed that the agency had spent $822,751 of taxpayer funds to conduct the Western Regions Conference in Las Vegas, Nevada. Martha Johnson, the former administrator of GSA, resigned abruptly in the wake of the scandal and was replaced by Acting Administrator Dan Tangherlini. GSA noted that "under the new GSA leadership, this event and type of spending is not tolerated" and the agency continues a "rigorous top-to-bottom review of all agency operations" as it considers further reforms. "These events indicate an already recognized pattern of misjudgment which spans several years and administrations. It must stop," GSA communications director Betsaida Alcantara wrote in an email. "The new leadership at the GSA is leaving no stone unturned in investigating any misuse of taxpayer dollars. When we find serious issues we refer them to the Office of Inspector General, as we did in this case. We look forward to the recommendations and findings of the OIG's investigation."

Earlier, Tangherlini cut executive bonuses and instituted a hiring freeze across GSA. Additionally, Tangherlini has cancelled 36 conferences so far, according to GSA, saving millions in taxpayer dollars. The committee was notified of the latest spending spree in a letter from IG Brian Miller, who was informed of the incident by Tangherlini on 11 July 2012. Still, Rep. Jeff Dehnam, the chairman of the Transportation and Infrastructure subcommittee on oversight, said that his panel will conduct hearings to further examine the incident. "It's still a blatant abuse of taxpayer dollars and it's going to stop," Dehnam, R-Calif., said. "The taxpayers can't afford it and they're not going to stand for it any longer." President Obama had written that "it's time we acknowledge that a defense budget and force structure built principally around the prospect of World War III makes little strategic sense. The U.S. military and defense budget in 2005 topped $522 billion, more than that of the next thirty countries combined. The United States' GDP is greater than that of the two largest countries and fastest-growing economies, China and India, combined. We need to maintain a strategic force posture that allows us to manage threats posed by rogue nations…"

By law, Bowen's office reports to both the Secretary of Defense and the Secretary of State. It goes out of business in 2013. Bowen's office has spent more than $200 million tracking the reconstruction funds, and in addition to producing numerous reports, his office has investigated criminal fraud that has resulted in 87 indictments, 71 convictions and $176 million in fines and other penalties. These include civilians and military members accused of kickbacks, bribery, bid-rigging, fraud, embezzlement and outright theft of government property and funds. Much, however, apparently got overlooked. Example: A $35 million Pentagon project was started in December 2006 to establish the Baghdad airport as an international economic gateway, and the inspector general found that by the end of 2010 about half the money was "at risk of being wasted" unless someone else completed the work.

Of the $51 billion that Congress approved for Iraq reconstruction, about $20 billion was for re-building Iraqi security forces and about $20 billion was for re-building the country's basic infrastructure. The programs were run mainly by the Defense Department, the State Department and the U.S. Agency for International Development. A key weakness found by Bowen's inspectors was inadequate reviewing of contractors' invoices. In some cases invoices were checked months after they had been paid because there were too few government contracting officers. Bowen found a case in which the State Department had only one contracting officer in Iraq to validate more than $2.5 billion in spending on a DynCorp contract for Iraqi police training "As a result, invoices were not properly reviewed, and the $2.5 billion in U.S. funds were vulnerable to fraud and waste," the report said. "We found this lack of control to be especially disturbing since earlier reviews of the DynCorp contract had found similar weaknesses."

In that case the State Department eventually reconciled all of the old invoices and as of July 2009 had recovered more than $60 million. The report touched on a problem that cropped up in virtually every major aspect of the U.S. war effort in Iraq, namely, the consequences of fighting an insurgency that proved more resilient than the Pentagon had foreseen. That not only made reconstruction more difficult, dangerous and costly, but also left the U.S. military unprepared for the grind of multiple troop deployments, the tactics of an adaptable insurgency and the complexity of battlefield wounds. It also left the U.S. government short of the expertise it needed to monitor contractors.

However, Schultz was not the only American that sees America is in a crisis. In a wide-ranging conversation between current Secretary of State Hillary Clinton and former Secretary of State James Baker that focused on American foreign policy, some of the liveliest comments centered on what's happening in the United States. Baker made it clear that in his view the biggest threat to America right now isn't Iran or China or the Middle East uprisings, but the economy. "We better damn well get our economic house in order," he told the crowd to which Clinton responded with "Amen to that!" She told the audience that she's spent much of her tenure as Secretary of State "reassuring" the world's leaders in government and in business that the U.S. economy is moving forward, and that the American government recognizes "We have to put our economic house in order."

It was what everyone was saying. Mrs. Clinton, for example, told a story about one Hong Kong visit where she encountered nervous billionaires. "I was in Hong Kong during the debt ceiling debate and all these billionaire moguls were at this event, lining up with anxiety asking if the United States of America was going to default on its debt." I said, "Oh nooo." Clinton talked about how during the last three administrations, despite often heated rhetoric, when it came to issues of foreign policy and the economy ultimately the two parties would find a compromise with the President. Not so with this administration Clinton observed. "We have to get back into the political work of rolling up our sleeves and solving these problems," she said. Though a staunch Republican, Baker backed her up. "I don't disagree with that at all," the former secretary said dead-panned to an amused audience. "I hate to tell you this but based on my political and civil service experience, it ain't happening before November."

As the U.S. continues to rack up more than $1 trillion of new debt every year, Americans are beginning to worry about who they owe this money to and how much power their creditors have over them. According to Barry P. Bosworth, a senior fellow at the Brookings Institution, the U.S. two biggest foreign creditors are Japan and China. Although it may seem as though our debt to these countries renders us a puppet on strings, Bosworth said, this fear is overblown. The U.S. market is very important to China's economy, so China would be loath to do anything that might exacerbate tensions or disrupt trade between the two countries. And the same can be said for Japan.

China owns $1.15 trillion of U.S. government debt – more than any other country – but U.S. taxpayers actually owe less money to China compared to recent years. China holds 10 per cent of U.S. Treasuries, down from 12 per cent two years ago.

And what about all the anti-China rhetoric that Americans hear about on the campaign trail? Republican Presidential Nominee Mitt Romney has been promising the country that he will declare China a "currency manipulator" on the first day of his presidency – and then enact tariffs as necessary until he forces China to level the trading playing field. Is that something that Romney is actually likely to do if he gets elected? No, says Bosworth. Tough talk with respect to China has become standard rhetoric for any presidential challenger. If and when Romney becomes president, his position will likely mellow.

Bosworth also says that the problem with the U.S.-China trade relationship is not, as is commonly believed, that China doesn't play fair. China has actually addressed lots of its unfair practices over the past decade, Bosworth says, while the U.S. is still pursuing the same old self-destructive habits. Until we stop consuming so much and start producing more, Bosworth says, we're in no position to demand anything.

Chapter Two – Superpower

Almost as if according to some natural law, in every century there seems to emerge a country with the power, the will, and the intellectual system in accordance with its own values... In the twentieth century, no country has influenced international relations as decisively and at the same time as ambivalently as the United States. – Henry Kissinger in *Diplomacy*

WASHINGTON, DC – One World Trade Center, the so-called Freedom Tower currently under construction in Lower Manhattan, technically became New York City's tallest building in May 2012, as workers erected steel columns on the 100th floor, 1,271 feet above the street, to make it stand 21 feet higher than the Empire State Building's observation deck. The Freedom Tower, which is being built to replace the twin towers that suffered the worst of the 11 September 2001 attacks, is a new complex, that includes One World Trade Center, a 9/11 memorial and museum, and three other office towers. It is being built on the site and is scheduled for completion by the year 2014. When it is completed, it will be 104 stories and likely declared the tallest building in America, surpassing Chicago's 1,451-foot Willis Tower at 1,776 feet. The achievement isn't without controversy because a 408-foot-tall needle will sit on the tower's roof to give the Freedom Tower its supremacy. It is something of a hoax but New Yorkers don't mind. Count this needle and the World Trade Center is on top. Otherwise, it will be behind the world's tallest building, Burj

Khalifa in Dubai, which stands at 2,717 feet. On two occasions however Rhona and I were barred from getting close to Ground Zero. Barricades made it hallowed ground.

New York Mayor Mike Bloomberg marked the milestone with this statement: "The New York City skyline is once again stretching to new heights. The latest progress at the World Trade Center is a testament to New Yorkers' strength and resolve and to our belief in a city that is always reaching upward. This building has been a labor of love for many, and I congratulate the men and women who have worked together to solve the challenges presented by this incredibly complex project. Today our city has a new tallest building and a new sense of how bright our future is." And in a public-spirited statement the Empire State Building offered its congratulations. For ten years as New Yorkers licked their wounds it was clear that many of them and Democrats and Republicans in Washington would have liked to get their hands on more than the men who were sent to Guantanamo Bay for carrying out the raid on Manhattan Island. The question is, who are these villains?

George W. Bush did not hide his hand and he had identified, as Ronald Reagan had done, the countries he had damned as an evil empire. It was no surprise that in 2008, as Barack Obama and John McCain fought for the White House, the Chinese were accused of hacking into the Obama campaign computers and moving files and documents out at an astonishing speed. China has always denied the charges brought against it by US Administration after US Administration, insisting that the United States was harassing it with Cold War strategies after the Americans had made peace with the weakened Soviet Union and launched it on the perilous road to democracy. But according to Mike McConnell, Director of National Intelligence, the Chinese were clumsy in their hacking and had got caught. This is the story that Bob Woodward tells in his latest book on American presidents, *Obama's Wars*. But as every 10-year-old American child knows it was not the much maligned Chinese that led the terrorists' attacks on New York and Washington but Saudi Arabians, the rich oil friends of the United States.

I was in China when the attacks on the World Trade Center and the Pentagon took place and I remember my Chinese college students discussing the flight plans of the four hijacked aircraft that seemed to be aimed at the heart of American trade, the heart of American military and, in the case of the fourth plane that crashed in a field in Pennsylvania, the heart of American politics. So was the mission of the Saudi Arabian terrorists to attack the enemy that most Islamic people perceived: American business, American military and American politics? In other words, was the plan to deliver a death blow to Capitalism, Militarism and Imperialism? These were the three stout ropes, Mao Zedong had said, that bound the feet of people in the developing world and he had urged the Chinese people never to give up the struggle against the imperialist, militarist and capitalist United States. But in 2001 the Chinese were not involved in any way in this dismal adventurism to dent America's dominance in the Third World and none of the conspiracy theories that have surfaced after 9/11 has implicated China.

It was always clear to our Chinese students that New York, not the Hong Kong that was returned to the People's Republic of China in 1997, is the financial capital of the world, the soul of capitalism and the womb that gave birth to the American Dream and therefore was correctly targeted by al-Qaeda as the heart of American capitalism. The notion had come as well to Alan Greenspan, the chairman of the Federal Reserve Bank of the United States on Swissair Flight 128 when he was returning home from a bankers' meeting in Switzerland. "I doubted that physically disrupting the financial system was what the hijackers had in mind," wrote Greenspan in his memoir, *The Age of Turbulence*. "Much more likely, this was meant to be a symbolic act of violence against capitalist America."

There was hardly any evidence in college and in the city of Guangzhou of Chinese grief or sympathy and I recalled what it was like on 7 May in 1999 when US planes bombed the Chinese Embassy in Belgrade, killing three Chinese nationals, because as it was said its pilots had used an outdated map of the city. This is the kind of disingenuousness that makes distrustful American pleas for world peace. I remember one white American teacher saying that he had tried to enter a bus in downtown Guangzhou to return to our college and he was barred from doing so by the bus-driver. And when he had attempted to take a taxi none would stop for him. In the end he had to walk back to the campus. But Rhona did not have this trouble when she was out on the same day. As one of my weekend students, a bank manager, told me, "The attack on the twin towers was a horrible incident but you are not going to find many Chinese who will tell you they are sorry that it took place." The United States in fact had put itself in a place where the feeling everywhere was that it deserved to be hurt or destroyed. According to Norman Mailer in *Why are we at war?* John Le Carre had told the *The Times of London* that "America has entered one of its periods of historic madness", and Harold Pinter had said that "The American administration is now a bloodthirsty wild animal."

I had no trouble thinking indeed that Wall Street and the American Stock Exchange were the places that were identified as the proper targets long before the idea of hijacking the two American airliners and the two United airliners entered the heads of the 19 terrorists engaged in this plot. On the Swissair plane that was heading back to Zurich, Greenspan recalled the bomb in the parking garage of the World Trade Center eight years earlier. "What worried me," he wrote, "was the fear such an attack would create." It was he thought the psychology that leads to panics and recessions. And in the days to come he was informed that all across the country people had stopped spending on everything except on items bought in preparation for possible additional attacks, sales of groceries, security devices, bottled water. From the West coast to the East coast businesses were disrupted by the suspension of air freight. The shutdown of the airspace and the tightening of borders led to shortages, bottlenecks and cancelled shifts and in the end to the decision by Ford Motor to shut down temporarily five of its factories. And on 14 September, three days after the terrorists' attacks, Congress passed an initial emergency appropriation of $40 billion that authorized President Bush to use force against the nations, organizations or persons who had taken part in the attacks.

Who were the *real* villains that had disrupted the world's markets and terrorized Americans into thinking that Armageddon was on their doorsteps? The European edition of *TIME* magazine that had conducted a poll on its website that asked, "Which country poses a greater danger to world peace in 2003?" found after 318,000 votes were cast, that the responses were: North Korea, 7 per cent; Iraq, 8 per cent; and the United States, 84 per cent. In a 2008 global poll of 17 countries, 46 per cent of those surveyed believed al-Qaeda was responsible for the attacks, 15 per cent believed the U.S. government was responsible, 7 per cent believed Israel was and another 7 per cent believed some other perpetrator, other than al-Qaeda, was responsible. China was nowhere in the equation but tensions between the two countries had not disappeared over China's reluctance to re-evaluate the yuan and to take notice of calls to address complaints of human rights.

II

ON 22 JULY 2011 Olivier Knox wrote that President Obama was addressing negotiations on a deal to avert a ruinous early August debt default. Obama said he was confident the United States would not default on its debt, after tough negotiations on a budget deal with Republicans had collapsed. New White House talks to avert a disastrous early August debt default teetered on the edge of collapse as Republican House Speaker Boehner abruptly quit the negotiations. The President had condemned Boehner's decision and called top lawmakers to the White House for emergency negotiations. "I expect them to have an answer in terms of how they intend to get this thing done over the course of the next week. The American people expect action," the president said at a hastily called public appearance. Obama said Boehner, House Minority Leader Nancy Pelosi, Democratic Senate Majority Leader Harry Reid, and Republican Senate Minority Leader Mitch McConnell must have some answers to re-assure skittish global markets.

"I cannot believe that Congress would end up being that irresponsible that they would not send a package that avoids a self-inflicted wound to the economy at a time when things are so difficult," Obama said. His remarks came just a half-hour after Boehner telephoned him to say he was backing out of often acrimonious negotiations that had centered, Republican aides said, on a plan to cut $3-$3.5 trillion from US debt over ten years. Boehner said in a letter to members of the House of Representatives that he was walking away because the Democratic president was insisting on increasing tax revenue collected from the rich and wealthy corporations. "I have decided to end discussions with the White House and begin conversations with the leaders of the Senate in an effort to find a path forward," Boehner wrote in a letter to members of the House of Representatives.

Washington hit its debt ceiling on 16 May but has used spending and accounting adjustments, as well as higher-than-expected tax receipts, to pay its bills and continue operating up to 2 August. Finance and business leaders had warned failure to raise the US debt ceiling by then would send shock waves through the world economy, while Obama had predicted a default would trigger economic "Armageddon". Boehner and Obama had been at odds on a range of issues, but a key sticking point was the White House's push for increasing tax revenues from the rich and wealthy corporations, something Republicans fiercely opposed. "A deal was never reached, and was never really close. In the end, we couldn't connect. Not because of different personalities, but because of different visions for our country," Boehner said in his letter to the House. "The president is emphatic that taxes have to be raised. As a former small businessman, I know tax increases destroy jobs."

The response from the other congressional leaders did little to fuel expectations that a deal could quickly be reached. McConnell called the collapse "disappointing" and vowed to tackle "the nation's unsustainable debt" but "without job-killing tax hikes." Reid stressed that "we must avert a default at all costs" but condemned Republicans for an "ideological opposition to ending taxpayer-funded giveaways for millionaires, corporate jet owners and oil companies." Reid and Pelosi flatly opposed any short-term deal, said it was time for Boehner to act like an "adult" and vowed to protect social safety net programs dear to Democrats but targeted by Obama and Boehner alike for savings. Boehner said at a press conference later that "no one wants to default on the full faith and credit of the United States government. And I'm convinced that we will not."

Three days later on 25 July 2011 President Obama decided to tell the nation about the national debt, a debate he said that directly affects the lives of all Americans. For the last decade, he said, we have spent more money than we take in. In the year 2000, he pointed out, the government had a budget surplus but instead of using it to pay off our debt, the money was spent on trillions of dollars in new tax cuts, while two wars and an expensive prescription drug program were simply added to our nation's credit card. As a result, the deficit was on track to top $1 trillion the year he took office. To make matters worse, the recession meant that there was less money coming in, and it required the government to spend even more – on tax cuts for middle-class families; on unemployment insurance; on aid to states so we could prevent more teachers and firefighters and police officers from being laid off. These emergency steps also added to the deficit.

"Now, every family knows that a little credit card debt is manageable. But if we stay on the current path, our growing debt could cost us jobs and do serious damage to the economy," he said. "More of our tax dollars will go toward paying off the interest on our loans. Businesses will be less likely to open up shop and hire workers in a country that can't balance its books. Interest rates could climb for everyone who borrows money – the homeowner with a mortgage, the student with a college loan, the corner store that wants to expand. And we won't have enough money to make job-creating investments in things like education and infrastructure, or pay for vital programs like Medicare and Medicaid. Because neither party is blameless for the decisions that led to this problem, both parties have a responsibility to solve it. And over the last several months, that's what we've been trying to do. I won't bore you with the details of every plan or proposal, but basically, the debate has centered around two different approaches.

"The first approach says let's live within our means by making serious, historic cuts in government spending. Let's cut domestic spending to the lowest level it's been since Dwight Eisenhower was President. Let's cut defense spending at the Pentagon by hundreds of billions of dollars. Let's cut out the waste and fraud in health care programs like Medicare – and at the same time let's make modest adjustments so that Medicare is still there for future generations. Finally, let's ask the wealthiest Americans and biggest corporations to give up some of their tax breaks and special deductions. This balanced approach asks everyone to give a little without requiring anyone to sacrifice too much. It would reduce the deficit by around $4 trillion and put us on a path to pay down our debt. And the cuts wouldn't happen so abruptly that they'd be a drag on our economy, or prevent us from helping small business and middle-class families get back on their feet right now. This approach is also bipartisan. While many in my own party aren't happy with the painful cuts it makes, enough will be willing to accept them if the burden is fairly shared.

"While Republicans would have liked to see deeper cuts and no revenue at all, there were many in the Senate who had said, 'Yes, I'm willing to put politics aside and consider this approach because I care about solving the problem.' And to his credit, this is the kind of approach the Republican Speaker of the House, John Boehner, was working on with me over the last several weeks.

"The only reason this balanced approach isn't on its way to becoming law right now is because a significant number of Republicans in Congress are insisting on a cuts-only approach – an approach that doesn't ask the wealthiest Americans or biggest corporations to contribute anything at all. And because nothing is asked of those at the top of the income scales, such an approach would close the deficit only with more severe cuts to programs we all care about cuts that place a greater burden on working families. So the debate right now isn't about whether we need to make tough choices. Democrats and Republicans agree on the amount of deficit reduction we need. The debate is about how it should be done. Most Americans, regardless of political party, don't understand how we can ask a senior citizen to pay more for her Medicare before we ask corporate jet owners and oil companies to give up tax breaks that other companies don't get.

"How can we ask a student to pay more for college before we ask hedge fund managers to stop paying taxes at a lower rate than their secretaries? How can we slash funding for education and clean energy before we ask people like me to give up tax breaks we don't need and didn't ask for? That's not right. It's not fair. We all want a government that lives within its means, but there are still things we need to pay for as a country – things like new roads and bridges; weather satellites and food inspection; services to veterans and medical research.

"Keep in mind that under a balanced approach, the 98 per cent of Americans who make under $250,000 would see no tax increases at all. None. In fact, I want to extend the payroll tax cut for working families. What we're talking about under a balanced approach is asking Americans whose incomes have gone up the most over the last decade – millionaires and billionaires – to share in the sacrifice everyone else has to make. And I think these patriotic Americans are willing to pitch in. In fact, over the last few decades, they've pitched in every time we passed a bipartisan deal to reduce the deficit. The first time a deal passed, a predecessor of mine made the case for a balanced approach by saying this: Would you rather reduce deficits and interest rates by raising revenue from those who are not now paying their fair share? Or would you rather accept larger budget deficits, higher interest rates, and higher unemployment? And I think I know your answer. Those words were spoken by Ronald Reagan. But today, many Republicans in the House refuse to consider this kind of balanced approach – an approach that was pursued not only by President Reagan, but by the first President Bush, President Clinton, myself, and many Democrats and Republicans in the United States Senate. So we are left with a stalemate.

"Now, what makes today's stalemate so dangerous is that it has been tied to something known as the debt ceiling – a term that most people outside of Washington have probably never heard of before. Understand, raising the debt ceiling does not allow Congress to spend more money. It simply gives our country the ability to pay the bills that Congress has already racked up. In the past, raising the debt ceiling was routine. Since the 1950s, Congress has always passed it, and every President has signed it. President Reagan did it 18 times. George W. Bush did it 7 times. And we have to do it by next Tuesday, August 2nd, or else we won't be able to pay all of our bills. Unfortunately, for the past several weeks, Republican House members have essentially said that the only way they'll vote to prevent America's first-ever default is if the rest of us agree to their deep, spending cuts-only approach. If that happens, and we default, we would not have enough money to pay all of our bills – bills that include monthly Social Security checks, veterans' benefits, and the government contracts we've signed with thousands of businesses.

"For the first time in history, our country's Triple A credit rating would be downgraded, leaving investors around the world to wonder whether the United States is still a good bet. Interest rates would skyrocket on credit cards, mortgages, and car loans, which amounts to a huge tax hike on the American people. We would risk sparking a deep economic crisis – one caused almost entirely by Washington. Defaulting on our obligations is a reckless and irresponsible outcome to this debate. And Republican leaders say that they agree we must avoid default. But the new approach that Speaker Boehner unveiled today, which would temporarily extend the debt ceiling in exchange for spending cuts, would force us to once again face the threat of default just six months from now. In other words, it doesn't solve the problem. First of all, a six-month extension of the debt ceiling might not be enough to avoid a credit downgrade and the higher interest rates that all Americans would have to pay as a result. We know what we have to do to reduce our deficits; there's no point in putting the economy at risk by kicking the can further down the road."

Six months later, the Associated Press reported that a government watchdog had pointed out that U.S. taxpayers are still owed $132.9 billion that companies haven't repaid from the financial bailout, and some of that will never be recovered. The bailout launched at the height of the financial crisis in September 2008 will continue to exist for years, says a report issued by Christy Romero, the acting special inspector general for the $700 billion bailout. Some bailout programs, such as the effort to help homeowners avoid foreclosure by reducing mortgage payments, will last as late as 2017, costing the government an additional $51 billion or so.

The gyrating stock market has slowed the Treasury Department's efforts to sell off its stakes in 458 bailed-out companies, the report says. They include insurer American International Group Inc., General Motors Co. and Ally Financial Inc. If Treasury plans to sell its stock in the three companies at or above the price where taxpayers would break even on their investment – $28.73 a share for AIG, $53.98 for GM – it may take a long time for the market to rebound to that level, the report says. AIG's shares closed at $25.31, while GM ended at $24.92. Ally isn't publicly traded. It will also be challenging for the government to get out of the 458 companies as the market remains volatile and banks struggle to keep afloat in the tough economy, it says.

Congress had authorized $700 billion for the bailout of financial companies and automakers, and $413.4 billion was paid out. So far the government has recovered about $318 billion. The bailout is called the Troubled Asset Relief Program, or TARP.

"TARP is not over," Romero said in a statement. She said her office will maintain its commitment to protect taxpayers for the duration of the program.

Treasury spokesman Matt Anderson said the department made substantial progress winding down TARP and has already recovered more than 77 per cent of the funds disbursed for the program, through repayments and other income. "We'll continue to balance the important goals of exiting our investments as soon as practicable and maximizing value for taxpayers," Anderson said. The government has unwound its investments in four of the companies that received the most aid: Bank of America Corp., Citigroup Inc., Chrysler Group LLC and Chrysler Financial, the automaker's old lending arm and the Treasury announced that it had sold the final batch of securities under its $368 million Small Business Administration loan program under TARP.

In Romero's quarterly report to Congress, she said her office has uncovered and prevented fraud related to TARP. Investigations by her office resulted in criminal charges against 10 people and three convictions in the quarter ended 31 December, the report notes. Altogether, the investigations have resulted in criminal charges against 61 people, including 45 senior company executives, according to the report. Thirty-one of the 61 individuals have been convicted. Civil charges have been filed against 38 people.

III

THESE PROBLEMS however did not block Americans from focusing on the "enemy" in the East. The Blaze said on 15 December 2011 that it had discovered one of China's Secret Weapons when a commercial U.S. satellite company told reporters it has captured a photo of China's first aircraft carrier in the Yellow Sea off the Chinese coast. DigitalGlobe Inc. said one of its satellites photographed the carrier on 8 December. A DigitalGlobe analyst found the image while searching through photos. Stephen Wood, director of DigitalGlobe's analysis center, said he was confident the ship is the Chinese carrier because of the location and date of the photo. The aircraft carrier has generated intense international interest because of what it might portend about China's intentions as a military power. The story is that former Soviet Union started building the carrier, which it called the *Varyag*, but never finished it. When the Soviet Union collapsed, it ended up in the hands of Ukraine, a former Soviet republic. China bought the ship from

Ukraine in 1998 and spent years refurbishing it. It had no engines, weaponry or navigation systems when China acquired it.

"Is this the same aircraft carrier the college took us to see in Shenzhen?" asked a skeptical Rhona. "Do you remember how we tramped about the vessel and gawked at pictures of Yuri Gagarin?"

"I have no idea if it is the same aircraft carrier," I said. I had never understood why the college had felt that its teachers would find a day in Shenzhen on a Russian aircraft carrier was the inspiration we needed to teach students when according to our contracts we couldn't talk with them about politics or religion. I remembered the case an English teacher had to make to discuss the nature and habit of Jews when she taught Shakespeare's *Merchant of Venice*.

"But we have pictures of the time we spent on a Russian aircraft carrier," she said. "Do you think we should send them to DigitalGlobe Inc.?"

"Do you want to spend the rest of your life at Guantanamo Bay?"

The day before, on 14 December, 2011, the House had passed a massive $662 billion defense bill after last-minute changes placated the White House and ensured President Obama's ability to prosecute terrorist suspects in the civilian justice system. The vote was 283-136 and reflected the strong support for annual legislation that authorizes money for the men and women of the military as well as weapons systems and the millions of jobs they generate in lawmakers' districts. It was a rare instance of bipartisanship in a bitterly divided Congress. The House vote came just hours after the administration abandoned a veto threat over provisions dealing with the handling of terrorism suspects. Applying pressure on House and Senate negotiators working on the bill, Obama and senior members of his national security team, including Defense Secretary Leon Panetta and Secretary of State Hillary Rodham Clinton, had sought modifications in the detainee provisions.

Negotiators announced the changes, clearing the way for White House acceptance. In a statement press secretary Jay Carney said the new bill "does not challenge the president's ability to collect intelligence, incapacitate dangerous terrorists and protect the American people." Specifically, the bill would require that the military take custody of a suspect deemed to be a member of al-Qaeda or its affiliates and who is involved in plotting or committing attacks on the United States. There is an exemption for U.S. citizens. House and Senate negotiators added language that says nothing in the bill will affect "existing criminal enforcement and national security authorities of the FBI or any other domestic law enforcement agency" with regard to a captured suspect "regardless of whether such ... person is held in military custody." The bill also says the president can waive the provision based on national security. "While we remain concerned about the uncertainty that this law will create for our counterterrorism professionals, the most recent changes give the president additional discretion in determining how the law will be implemented, consistent with our values and the rule of law, which are at the heart of our country's strength," Carney said.

Uncertainty was a major concern of FBI Director Robert Mueller who expressed serious reservations about the detainee provisions. Testifying before the Senate Judiciary Committee, Mueller said a coordinated effort by the military, intelligence agencies and law enforcement has weakened al-Qaeda and captured or killed many of its leaders, including Osama bin Laden and Anwar al-Awlaki, the U.S.-born radical Islamic cleric. He suggested that the divisive provision in the bipartisan defense bill would deny that flexibility and prove impractical. Unnerving many conservative Republicans and liberal Democrats, the legislation also would deny suspected terrorists, even U.S. citizens seized within the nation's borders, the right to trial and subject them to indefinite detention. House Republican leaders had to tamp down a small revolt among some rank-and-file who sought to delay a vote on the bill. Some of the Republicans were concerned that the "president would use the military to round up American citizens," said Rep. Allen West, R-Fla., a member of the Armed Services panel. It continued to be an astonishing fear of the Republican Party that the people would devour them one day.

The fight over whether to treat suspects as prisoners of war or criminals has divided Democrats and Republicans, the Pentagon and Congress. The administration insists that the military, law enforcement and intelligence officials need flexibility in the campaign against terrorism. Obama pointed to his administration's successes in killing bin Laden and al-Awlaki. Republicans countered that their efforts are

169

necessary to respond to an evolving, post-September 11 threat, and that Obama has failed to produce a consistent policy on handling terror suspects. And in a reflection of the uncertainty, House members offered differing interpretations of the military custody and indefinite detention provisions and what would happen if the bill became law. "The provisions do not extend new authority to detain U.S. citizens," House Armed Services Chairman Howard "Buck" McKeon, R-Calif., said during debate. But Rep. Jerrold Nadler, D-N.Y., said the bill would turn "the military into a domestic police force." Civil rights groups were outraged by the legislation, however, and the White House's decision to drop the veto threat. "As a former constitutional lawyer, the president should know better," said Raha Wala, advocacy counsel for Human Rights First. "This legislation not only undermines the Constitution, it compromises national security. The president needed to show leadership on this, and he's failed."

Highlighting a period of austerity and a winding down of decade-old conflicts, the bill is $27 billion less than Obama requested and $43 billion less than Congress gave the Pentagon. The bill also authorizes money for the wars in Iraq and Afghanistan and national security programs in the Energy Department. Frustrated with delays and cost overruns with the troubled F-35 Joint Strike Fighter aircraft program, lawmakers planned to require the contractor, Lockheed Martin, to cover the expense of any extra costs on the next batch and future purchases of the aircraft. The Pentagon envisions buying 2,443 planes for the Air Force, Marine Corps and Navy, but the price could make it the most expensive program in military history – $1 trillion. The legislation freezes $700 million for Pakistan until the defense secretary provides Congress a report on how Islamabad is countering the threat of improvised explosive devices. It would impose tough new penalties on Iran, targeting foreign financial institutions that do business with the country's central bank. The president could waive those penalties if he notifies Congress that it's in the interest of national security.

The bill begins a reduction in defense spending, a reality the Pentagon hasn't faced in the decade since the September 11 attacks. Pentagon spending has nearly doubled in that period, but the deficit-reduction plan that Obama and congressional Republicans backed in 2011 set the Defense Department on a budget-cutting course. Arizona

Sen. John McCain, the top Republican on the Senate Armed Services Committee, and several other GOP defense hawks pledged to return to Washington with a plan to avoid automatic across-the-board cuts to defense required in 2013. The failure of Congress' deficit super committee means $1.2 trillion in cuts over the next 10 years, with half from defense. Defense hawks said the 10 per cent cut would hollow out the Pentagon and devastate U.S. military readiness. McKeon introduced legislation to avert the cuts for one year by reducing the federal workforce by 10 per cent. The savings would go to defense and non-defense spending.

IV

WHEN PRESIDENT Obama cited cost as a reason to bring troops home from Afghanistan, he referred to a $1 trillion price-tag for America's wars. Staggering as it is, that figure grossly underestimates the total cost of wars in Iraq, Afghanistan and Pakistan to the U.S. Treasury and ignores more imposing costs yet to come, according to a study released in June 2011. The final bill will run at least $3.7 trillion and could reach as high as $4.4 trillion, according to the research project *Costs of War* by Brown University's Watson Institute for International Studies. In the 10 years since U.S. troops went into Afghanistan to root out the al Qaeda leaders behind the 11 September 2001 attacks, spending on the conflicts totaled $2.3 trillion to $2.7 trillion. Those numbers will continue to soar when considering often overlooked costs such as long-term obligations to wounded veterans and projected war spending from 2012 through 2020. The estimates do not include at least $1 trillion more in interest payments coming due and many billions more in expenses that cannot be counted, according to the study.

On Memorial Day this year, the *Detroit News* carried an Associated Press story that said nearly half of returning veterans seek disability. "America's newest veterans", wrote Marilynn Marchione, "are filing for disability benefits at a historic rate, claiming to be the most medically and mentally troubled generation of former troops the nation has ever seen." A staggering 45 per cent of the 1.6 million veterans from the wars in Iraq and Afghanistan, said Ms. Marchione, are now seeking compensation for injuries they say are service-related. That is more than double the estimate of 21 per cent who filed such claims after the Gulf War in the early 1990s, top government officials told the Associated Press. As the nation commemorates the more than 6,400 troops who died in post 9/11 wars, the problems of those who survived also draw attention. These new veterans are seeking a level of help the government did not anticipate and for which there is no special fund set aside to pay.

The White House says the total amount appropriated for war-related activities of the Department of Defense, intelligence and State Department since 2001 is about $1.3 trillion, and that would rise to nearly $1.4 trillion in 2012. Researchers with the Watson Institute say that type of accounting is common but too narrow to measure the real costs. In human terms, 224,000 to 258,000 people have died directly from warfare, including 125,000 civilians in Iraq. Many more have died indirectly, from the loss of clean drinking water, healthcare, and nutrition. An additional 365,000 have been wounded and 7.8 million people – "equal to the combined population of Connecticut and Kentucky" – have been displaced. *Costs of War* brought together more than 20 academics to uncover the expense of war in lives and dollars, a daunting task given the inconsistent recording of lives lost and what the report called opaque and sloppy accounting by the U.S. Congress and the Pentagon. The report underlines the extent to which war will continue to stretch the U.S. federal budget, which is already on an unsustainable course due to an aging American population and skyrocketing healthcare costs. It also raises the question of what the United States gained from its multitrillion-dollar investment. "I hope that when we look back, whenever this ends, something very good has come out of it," Senator Bob Corker, a Republican from Tennessee, told Reuters in Washington.

In one sense, the report measures the cost of 9/11, the American shorthand for the events of 11 September 2001. Nineteen hijackers plus other al Qaeda plotters spent an estimated $400,000 to $500,000 on the plane attacks that killed 2,995 people and caused $50 billion to $100 billion in economic damages. What followed were three wars in which $50 billion amounts to a rounding error. For every person killed on 11 September, another 73 have been killed since. Was it worth it? That is a question many people want answered, said Catherine Lutz, head of the anthropology department at Brown and co-director of the study. "We decided we needed to do this kind of rigorous assessment of what it cost to make those choices to go to war," she said. "Politicians, we assumed, were not going to do that kind of assessment." The report arrived as Congress debated how to cut a U.S. deficit projected at $1.4 trillion this year, roughly a 10th of which can be attributed to direct war spending.

What did the United States gain for its trillions? Strategically, the results for the United States are mixed. Osama bin Laden and Saddam Hussein are dead, but Iraq and Afghanistan are far from stable democracies. Iran has gained influence in the Gulf and the Taliban, though ousted from government, remains a viable military force in Afghanistan. "The United States has been extremely successful in protecting the homeland," said George Friedman, founder of STRATFOR, a U.S.-based intelligence company. "Al Qaeda in Afghanistan was capable of mounting very sophisticated, complex, operations on an intercontinental basis. That organization with that capability has not only been substantially reduced, it seems to have been shattered," Friedman said. Economically, the results are also mixed. War spending may be adding half a percentage point a year to growth in the gross domestic product.

During his 2008 campaign, Obama promised to increase foreign aid dramatically, raising the national total to $50 billion. Today, that core message is being rejected. GOP hopeful Rick Perry had called for a complete elimination of foreign aid, and Mitt Romney had agreed with Mr. Perry during the debate. Today the United States spends about $25 billion a year on foreign aid, about 50 per cent of which goes to countries that assist in the war on terror and the drug trade including Iraq, Afghanistan, Sudan, Colombia, Egypt, Nigeria, Pakistan and The Congo. Critics of foreign aid argue that as America continues to struggle financially, critical resources are sent abroad without a noticeable return on the investment, with some funds even indirectly ending up in the wrong hands. On the other side, advocates point out that foreign aid makes up only 1 per cent of the United States annual budget and what we get out of that investment is critical to our own national security and economy. Mr. Perry and Mr. Romney did not necessarily speak for the entire GOP either. Henry Kissinger and Condoleezza Rice, along with three other former Secretaries of State, have signed an appeal of support for foreign aid, calling it "a strategic investment in our nation's security and prosperity". On *Around the World* Christiane Amanpour spoke with Deputy Secretary of State Tom Nides who argued that foreign aid protects our nation's security and is a smart investment, returning $5 for every $1 spent.

On 14 January 2012 Reuters reported that the United States said it would offer Bangladesh close to $1 billion in aid over the next five years. A U.S. Embassy statement said that the money would go towards alleviating poverty and malnutrition, as well as family planning and the fight against infectious diseases. The funds will also be used to support research in improving farm productivity and deal with the impact of climate change. As of 2011, the U.S. government has provided over $5.7 billion in development assistance to Bangladesh. Commenting on this in the Yahoo Contributor Network, Susan Culver-Graybeal writes that "It always shocks me when I hear – amid all the noise about how broke our government is – that we're giving billions to help other countries. It's not that I'm against helping, mind you. I tend to think charitable giving is something better left in the hands of private organizations, with private dollars, however. But it isn't. What's more, according to a June Fox News report, we're giving hundreds of millions of dollars in aid to countries we're borrowing billions of dollars from, including China, Brazil, Russia, India, Mexico and Egypt. As a side note, I did not realize we were borrowing money from Mexico, but according to the report, it holds $28.1 billion of U.S. Treasury bonds."

The Fox News article states much of this money is going to preventing tuberculosis and AIDS/HIV, combating weapons of mass destruction and counterterrorism. But that's not all. The Census Bureau compiles foreign aid information, with reports that can be found in PDF format on its website. According to the 2012 statistical data, in 2009, the U.S. provided almost $45 billion in foreign aid, including about $34 billion in economic aid and a little over 11 billion in military aid.

Of the U.S. economic aid in 2009, the largest recipients were Afghanistan and Iraq, followed by Pakistan and Sudan. The West Bank/Gaza tops of the list of the five countries receiving the most economic aid from the U.S., with a little over $1 billion worth. In military aid, more than $5.7 billion went to Afghanistan. Over $2 billion went to Israel. Egypt received more than $1 billion. "The list of countries the U.S. sends money to is daunting," complained a contributor to Yahoo News. "According to the figures, since 2001, that amount has increased from $16,836,000,000 to $44,957,000,000. And we don't have enough to pay our own bills. And we listen to our Congress talk about cutting our spending. I think we need to cut down on the high-priced gifts and loans we're giving to everyone else."

Lawmakers were under pressure to agree by Thanksgiving on where they can cut $1.2 trillion over the next decade. If they could not, automatic cuts to Medicare, defense spending and other critical areas of the budget would go into effect in January 2013. For 2011, the government had to borrow 36 cents of every dollar it spent. The string of massive debts has made interest on that debt the fastest growing budget category. For 2011, net interest payments rose 15.7 per cent to $227 billion. A slightly improved job market helped boost income tax revenue this year. From October 2010 through June, the economy added 1.3 million net jobs. That compares with only 339,000 net job gains in the previous 12-month period. Still, that hasn't been enough to bring the millions of Americans who lost jobs during the recession back into the work force.

The government also lost revenue because of the 2 percentage point cut in Social Security taxes, and also it had to pay for an extension of emergency unemployment benefits. Congress approved both in December to boost the sluggish economy. Total revenues increased 6.5 per cent to $2.3 trillion for the budget year that ended September 30; spending rose 4.2 per cent to $3.6 trillion. The nation's debt is now $14.8 trillion. The enormity of that figure has stoked intense partisan debate in Congress over spending and taxes. Polls show growing voter anger with the inability of both parties to reach solutions to the country's budget problems. Congress reached a last-minute deal in August to raise the government's borrowing limit in stages. But as part of the deal, lawmakers tasked a 12-member deficit-cutting panel with finding at least $1.2 trillion in savings over the next decade.

The committee, which is evenly split between Democrats and Republicans, had until Thanksgiving to come up with a plan. It would then go before the House and Senate in December for up-or-down votes. Administration officials said that Congress needs to reach an agreement through the super committee process but also should approve President Obama's $447 billion jobs plan. But the measure fell short of gaining the 60 votes required to be called up for debate in the Senate. All 46 Republicans in the chamber opposed the measure, which sought to pay for the plan by boosting taxes on the wealthy and corporations. As members of the super committee deliberate in secret, party leaders have jousted in public over their conflicting priorities. For Republicans, that means no tax increases. For Democrats, it means no curbs on popular entitlement programs, such as Medicare, without tax increases. The August budget deal is projected to trim future deficits by $2.1 trillion. That includes the cuts made by the super committee and another $900 billion in savings from caps on discretionary spending. The cuts are expected to begin in the 2012 budget year. CBO estimates $21 billion in cuts to this year's deficit, which is estimated to be $973 billion. The Obama administration is estimating that the 2012 deficit will total $956 billion.

On 31 December 2011 Will Lester of The Associated Press reported that the United States has reached a deal to sell $3.48 billion worth of missiles and related technology to the United Arab Emirates, a close Mideast ally, as part of a massive buildup of defense technology among friendly Mideast nations near Iran. Pentagon spokesman George Little announced the Christmas Day sale. He said the U.S. and U.A.E. have a strong defense relationship and are both interested in "a secure and stable" Persian Gulf region. The deal includes 96 missiles, along with supporting technology and training support that Little says will bolster the nation's missile defense capacity. The deal includes a contract with Lockheed Martin to produce the highly sophisticated Terminal High Altitude Area Defense, or THAAD, weapon system for the U.A.E. Tom McGrath, vice president and program manager for Lockheed Martin's THAAD program in Dallas, said in a statement it was the first foreign military sale of the THAAD system. THAAD interceptors are produced at Lockheed Martin's Pike County Facility in Troy, Alabama. The launchers and fire control units are produced at the company's Camden, Arkansas, facility.

Wary of Iran, the U.S. has been building up missile defenses of its allies, including a $1.7 billion deal to upgrade Saudi Arabia's Patriot missiles and the sale of 209 Patriot missiles to Kuwait, valued at about $900 million. The Obama administration announced the sale of $30 billion worth of F-15SA fighter jets to Saudi Arabia. Under the fighter jet agreement, the U.S. will send Saudi Arabia 84 new fighter jets and upgrades for 70 more. Production of the aircraft, which will be manufactured by Boeing Co., will support 50,000 jobs and have a $3.5 billion annual economic impact in the U.S. All the sales are part of a larger U.S. effort to realign its defense policies in the Persian Gulf to keep Iran in check. The announcement came as U.S. officials weighed a fresh threat from Tehran, which warned it could disrupt traffic through the Strait of Hormuz, a vital Persian Gulf oil transport route, if Washington levies new sanctions targeting Iran's crude exports.

V

IN THE MIDST of all this, the Obama administration was weighing an unprecedented diplomatic act – whether to bar a friendly president from U.S. soil. American officials were evaluating an awkward request from Yemeni strongman and longtime U.S. counter-terrorism partner Ali Abdullah Saleh. Saleh had said he planned to come to the United States for medical treatment for injuries suffered in a June assassination attempt, and he asked for a U.S. visa for entry to the country. Fearful of appearing to harbor an autocrat with blood on his hands, the Obama administration was trying to ensure that Saleh visits only for medical care and doesn't plan to stay, U.S. officials said.

Washington's hesitation reflected the shifting alliances and foreign policy strategy prompted by a year of upheaval in the Arab world. Saleh has served as an American ally against al-Qaeda and would soon transfer power under a U.S.-backed deal with Yemen's opposition aimed at ending months of instability. He isn't subject to any U.S. or international sanctions; but he also is accused of committing gross human rights violations during a year of internal conflict, and the U.S. was trying not to burn any bridges with Yemeni political groups likely to take part in future governments. Political asylum for Saleh in the United States, or the appearance of preferential treatment from an administration that has championed peaceful and democratic change, would be highly unpopular with Yemenis who have fought to depose their dictator of 33 years.

Officials close to the Saleh said Washington's suspicion that he may seek political asylum was delaying approval of his trip. But American officials appeared to substantiate those concerns and said they were troubled by Saleh's recent comments portraying his trip as a move designed to ease the political transition. "What we're looking at now is a request to come to the United States for the sole purpose of medical treatment," State Department spokesman Mark Toner said, refusing to go into the specific of the evaluation. "That permission has not been granted yet." Toner declined to elaborate on the assurances the United States wanted from Saleh or offer a timetable for a decision. He also couldn't say whether any provisions existed under U.S. law to prevent the Yemeni leader from visiting the country – provided he assures officials he would stay only temporarily. In that case, Saleh almost surely would be granted entry, U.S. officials said. It was unclear when, if ever, the last time the head of state of a friendly government was blocked from visiting the United States. One official went so far as to say Saleh's exit from Yemen might be beneficial by lowering the risk of disruptions in the lead-up to planned February elections. The U.S. is committed to doing everything it can to ensure those elections take place, the official said, but President Barack Obama's national security team was expected to make the final decision on Saleh's request. Obama was being briefed on developments while on vacation in Hawaii.

The Obama administration's attempts to tightly contain its internal debate over whether to allow Saleh into the country were quickly thwarted. With Obama vacationing, the administration waited almost two days before responding to Saleh's assertion that he would be traveling to the U.S. Officials at the White House and State Department initially insisted that while Saleh's request was being considered, no decision had been made. However reports that the U.S. already had decided to approve Saleh's request quickly surfaced, forcing officials in both Washington and Honolulu to issue repeated denials.

The botched handling of the sensitive debate frustrated some officials, who worried about fallout in the Middle East. Demonstrators began protesting against Saleh and calling for his ouster in February. The Yemeni government responded with a bloody crackdown, leaving hundreds of protesters dead, and stoking fears of instability in a nation grappling with burgeoning extremism. A June rocket attack on his compound had left him badly burned and wounded, and led Saleh to seek medical treatment in neighboring Saudi Arabia for three months. American officials had hoped he would remain there, but the Yemeni leader returned and violence worsened anew. Saleh later agreed to a Saudi-backed deal to hand power to his vice president and commit to stepping down completely in exchange for immunity.

The deal further angered Saleh's opponents who demanded he be tried for his attacks on protesters and the protests expanded to include labor strikes, calls for Saleh to be put on trial and demands that his loyalists to be removed from office. Activists said troops commanded by Saleh's relatives attacked protesters in the capital of Sanaa, killing at least nine people. Tens of thousands demonstrated the following day. Saleh's immediate plans are unclear. The wily leader has maintained his rule over a country divided by tribal and regional loyalties by consistently outsmarting his opponents, but Toner said the U.S. is trying to remind everyone of the "importance of continuing along this agreed-upon path of political transition that will lead to the next election. We need to see that process continue regardless of where President Saleh is," Toner said.

An American official said Saleh's office informed the U.S. Embassy in Sanaa that the outgoing leader would leave Yemen soon and travel elsewhere abroad first, before possibly coming to the U.S. The situation offered an eerie parallel to three decades ago, when President Jimmy Carter allowed the exiled Shah of Iran into the U.S. for medical treatment. The decision contributed to rapidly worsening relations between Washington and Ayatollah Ruhollah Khomeini's revolution in Teheran, with Iranian students occupying the U.S. Embassy in Iran a month later. Fifty-two American hostages were held for 444 days in response to Carter's refusal to send the Shah back to Iran for trial.

There was another kind of problem for the US in March. The Taliban had vowed revenge against "sick-minded American savages" after a U.S. soldier was accused of going on a deadly shooting rampage, Muhammad Lila and Martha Raddatz related on *Good Morning America*. The group said it would "take revenge from the invaders and the savage murderers for every single martyr," according to a statement posted on its website, *The Times* of London reported.

An Army veteran of three tours in Iraq who left his base in the middle of the night is suspected of methodically killing 16 Afghan civilians, most of them children and women. The soldier's name has not been released, but a U.S. official told ABC News he is a 38-year-old staff sergeant who is married with two children. He is apparently based at Fort Lewis in Washington State. The story was that the soldier wore night-vision goggles during the alleged rampage and has "lawyered up" and declined to talk, according to a source. The fear now is that this latest incident could set off a fresh wave of violence.

The attack came just as outrage stemming from burning of several Korans by members of the U.S. military seemed to be calming down. The U.S. Embassy in Kabul warned foreigners to keep a low profile. Afghan President Hamid Karzai called it "an assassination, one that cannot be forgiven." The Afghan parliament passed a resolution in protest of the killings, and asked for a public trial of the U.S. soldier. U.S. officials were quick to condemn the attack. "I offer my profound regret and deepest condolences to the victims and their families," Gen. John Allen, head of NATO forces in Afghanistan, said in a statement. "This deeply appalling incident in no way represents the values of ISAF [International Security Assistance Force] and coalition troops or the abiding respect we feel for the Afghan people."

The shooting had taken place at 3 a.m. in two villages in the Panjwai district of southern Kandahar province, a hotbed for the Taliban insurgency against U.S .forces. The two villages are a short walk away from the U.S. base where the soldier was stationed. Nine of the victims were children and three were women, all were shot while they slept in their beds, according to villagers and the Afghan president's office. Photos from the scene show blood-splattered floors and walls inside a villager's home, one of three believed to have been attached, and blood-soaked bodies of victims, including the elderly and young children, wrapped in blankets and placed in the backseat of a van. John Kirby, a Pentagon spokesman said officials "don't know what his [soldier's] motivation was, we are looking into that." After the alleged shooting spree, it's believed the soldier returned to the base and calmly turned himself in. He remains in NATO custody. It's unclear whether the soldier knew the victims or whether the alleged attack was spontaneous and unprovoked. It is also unknown whether he had any accomplices. This was his first tour in Afghanistan, where he has been since early December, the official said. NATO has launched its own investigation, and Karzai has sent his delegation to Kandahar for its own inquiry.

The White House said that President Obama called President Karzai "to express his shock and sadness at the reported killing and wounding of Afghan civilians." President Obama extended his condolences to the people of Afghanistan, and made clear his "Administration's commitment to establish the facts as quickly as possible and to hold fully accountable anyone responsible." The president re-affirmed "our deep respect for the Afghan people and the bonds between our two countries."

In China on 11 October 2011 the Associated Press reported that Russian Prime Minister Vladimir Putin likened the U.S. to a parasite following his meetings with Chinese leaders to push ahead energy deals and draw the once wary neighbors closer. In an interview with Chinese state media, Putin said that the U.S. itself is not a parasite for the world economy but that its dollar monopoly is. Putin said his criticism was meant to help find a solution to problems in the world economy. Putin's reproach came after a half-day of talks in Beijing in which he and Chinese Premier Wen Jiabao reportedly agreed on the pricing of oil shipped to China and vowed to push ahead on gas prices.

And on 23 March 2012, Russia issued new warnings over US missile defense. This time the warning came from Russian President Dmitry Medvedev and it was aimed at the U.S. led NATO missile defense plan that Washington says is aimed at deflecting potential Iranian threats. According to the Associated Press Medvedev warned that it will break existing nuclear parity with Russia and prompt it to retaliate. Moscow had rejected Washington's claim the plan is solely to deal with any Iranian threat and voiced fears it will eventually become powerful enough to undermine Russia's nuclear deterrent. "No one has explained to me why we should believe that the new missile defense system in Europe isn't directed against us," Medvedev said in a speech at a security conference, adding that the shield will "break the nuclear parity."

NATO has said it wants to cooperate with Russia on the missile shield, but has rejected Moscow's proposal to run it jointly. Without a NATO-Russia cooperation deal, the Kremlin has sought guarantees from the U.S. that any future missile defense is not aimed at Russia and threatened to retaliate if no such deal is negotiated. "I will say honestly that no matter how warm relations between me and my colleagues are, no matter how advanced relations between Russia and NATO member states are, we will have to take that into account and, under certain circumstances, respond," Medvedev said. Earlier, he told the top Russian military brass that the armed forces must prepare to counter U.S. missile defense plans even as talks between Moscow and Washington are continuing. "By 2017-2018, we must be fully prepared, fully armed," Medvedev said, referring to his earlier threat to aim missiles at the U.S.-led NATO missile shield if no agreement is reached. Speaking at the conference, he re-affirmed that Russia isn't "shutting the door to dialogue" but warned that "time is running out. It's in our mutual interests to quickly reach mutually acceptable agreements," he said.

Dmitry Rogozin, a deputy prime minister in charge of the military industries, was more hawkish in his remarks at the conference, saying the NATO shield has an "openly anti-Russian vector." The system that is being developed is intended to intercept heavy intercontinental missiles blasting off from the Russian territory, Rogozin said. "Missile defense isn't the best way to ensure security," he added. "Those who are smart know that the defensive arms race is no better than the offensive arms race. Strengthening of the shield entails strengthening of the sword." Rogozin claimed the new Russian missiles have been fitted with systems that would allow them to penetrate any prospective missile defense. "They would allow Russia to feel absolutely calm, even if the missile defense becomes global and affects our interests," he said.

Tensions over the missile shield, which long have tarnished ties between Moscow and Washington, are expected to flare again in May when Vladimir Putin heads to the U.S. for the Group of Eight summit shortly after being sworn in for his third presidential term. NATO Secretary-General Anders Fogh Rasmussen said that Putin would unlikely attend NATO's summit in Chicago that follows the G-8 summit. The NATO chief cited Putin's busy domestic political calendar, but many observers believe the Russian leader would not come to Chicago because of the missile defense rift.

In Moscow in November 2011, Russia's chief military officer had said the nation is facing an increased threat of being drawn into conflicts at its borders that may grow into an all-out nuclear war. Gen. Nikolai Makarov, chief of the General Staff, pointed at NATO's expansion eastward and said that the risks for Russia to be pulled into local conflicts have "risen sharply." He added, according to Russian news agencies wires, that "under certain conditions local and regional conflicts may develop into a full-scale war involving nuclear weapons." A steady decline of Russia's conventional forces has prompted the Kremlin to rely increasingly on nuclear deterrent. Its military doctrine says it may use nuclear weapons to counter a nuclear attack on Russia or an ally, or a large-scale conventional attack that threatens Russia's existence.

These are some of the headaches of the nation that has taken on the role of the World's Policeman as students in China used to say. Not all Americans agree with this view however and Ray Boddie made it clear that he didn't think it is accurate to call America the world's policeman. "I believe," he said, "our resources and belief in the value of mankind put America in a special category and that she must continue to promote justice in whatever form." When I asked Beverly Nunez, a Trinidadian who teaches in Brooklyn, the same question she said, "I don't think America should continue to be the world's policeman. I think there are other countries, such as England, that I feel are more sophisticated to make better decisions." Simone Long was doubtful too that it is a good idea. "There have been too many blunders," she said. "America should pay more attention to its citizens and to its own problems. We continue to spend so much money on fighting wars that should not even take place." But this is what President Obama has said, "(T)here will be times when we must again play the role of the world's reluctant sheriff. This will not change – nor should it."

On 29 February 2012 the U.S. announced a diplomatic breakthrough with North Korea. Senior Foreign Affairs Reporter for The Envoy, Laura Rozen reported that U.S. negotiator Glyn Davies spoke with journalists in Beijing on 23 February 2012 ahead of talks with North Korea and said that the United States had a diplomatic breakthrough with North Korea. Under an agreement reached in direct talks in Beijing, North Korea agreed to allow the return of nuclear inspectors from the International Atomic Energy Agency, and agreed to implement a moratorium on long-range missile tests, nuclear tests, and nuclear activities at Yongbyon, including uranium enrichment activities, the State Department said. In return, the United States will provide North Korea with a large food aid package. "To improve the atmosphere for dialogue and demonstrate its commitment to denuclearization, the DPRK has agreed to implement a moratorium on long-range missile launches, nuclear tests and nuclear activities at Yongbyon, including uranium enrichment activities," State Department spokeswoman Victoria Nuland said in a press statement. "The DPRK has also agreed to the return of IAEA inspectors to verify and monitor the moratorium on uranium enrichment activities at Yongbyon and confirm the disablement of the 5-MW reactor and associated facilities."

Despite the breakthrough, "the United States still had profound concerns regarding North Korean behavior across a wide range of areas," Nuland's statement cautioned. But she added that "today's announcement reflects important, if limited, progress in addressing some of these." In return, the United States will "move forward with our proposed package of 240,000 metric tons of nutritional assistance along with the intensive monitoring required for the delivery of such assistance," she said. Ms. Davies held the first face-to-face talks with his North Korean counterpart Kim Kye Gwan since the death of North Korean leader Kim Jong-Il in December. Davies' February 23-24 discussions in Beijing asserted several points, Nuland's statement said. Among them, "the United States re-affirms that it does not have hostile intent toward the DPRK" and that U.S. sanctions are not targeted against the livelihood of the North Korean people.

Arms control experts welcomed the signs of progress in U.S. efforts to engage Pyongyang but U.S. North Korea experts and foreign policy hands advised high caution in assessing Pyongyang's intent, given its track record of abrupt reversals. "These steps are modestly significant," Richard Bush, director of Northeast Asian studies at the Brookings Institution, said in a statement. However, he noted, they "are only what negotiators call 'confidence-building measures'. They could indeed be an initial step on a path towards serious negotiations ... Or they could simply be a ploy to get nutritional assistance and meddle in South Korean politics. North Korea's record suggests the latter, but we shall see." While the new agreement "appears to be an important step," Rep. Howard Berman (D-CA), ranking Democrat on the House Foreign Affairs Committee, told Secretary of State Hillary Clinton at a hearing, "I'm sure you don't need me to remind you that we've been down this road before, and it remains to be seen whether the North will keep its promises this time."

The return of nuclear inspectors to North Korea for the first time in three years would be a "very positive development," Sen. John Kerry (D-Mass.), chairman of the Senate Foreign Relations panel, said in a statement. And he added the United States has a humanitarian interest in helping the North Korean people receive food aid. "Resuming nutritional assistance to the DPRK is the right thing to do if we can ensure our aid will reach those in need." The announced measures are "an important step toward a verifiable freeze of the most worrisome North Korean nuclear activities," Daryl Kimball, of the Arms Control Association, wrote in an analysis of the announced agreement. President Barack Obama and Ambassador Glyn Davies, he said, "need to maintain the momentum in the weeks and months ahead."

VI

HOWEVER THE problems with Israel continued for the Obama Administration. In November 2011, the French President Nicolas Sarkozy had told President Obama that he was fed up with dealing with Israeli Prime Minister Benjamin Netanyahu and considered him a liar. Sarkozy made the comment in a private conversation with Obama during a G20 summit in the French Riviera town of Cannes in November and the remarks were overheard by a small number of journalists but not initially reported. "I cannot bear Netanyahu, he's a liar," Sarkozy told Obama during an exchange where the US president took him to task for backing a Palestinian request for membership of the UN cultural heritage agency UNESCO. And in March 2012, the White House was coy on a reported Israeli request for bombs and planes.

According to Olivier Knox of The Ticket, the White House tap danced around questions about news reports that Israeli Prime Minister Benjamin Netanyahu asked the Obama administration for massive "bunker-buster" bombs and long-range refueling planes that could play a role in a strike on Iran. Israeli media accounts said that Washington agreed in return for a pledge that any such attack would not happen in 2012. "In the meetings the president had, there was no such agreement proposed or reached," spokesman Jay Carney said. "It's possible that there's a report out there in a news outlet that might not be accurate. We have provided a lot of cooperation with the Israeli military. We have provided material to the Israeli military in the past, and I'm sure we will continue to do that as part of our cooperation with and partnership with the Israeli military," Carney said. As Yahoo News reported on the day of Obama's talks with Netanyahu, the prime minister's schedule included "a potentially telling bit of logistics." After his midday talks at the White House, Netanyahu sat down separately with Defense Secretary Leon Panetta, who then crossed the street from the Blair House for visiting dignitaries to see Obama at the White House.

But what would happen to the US if Israel attacks Iran? Brian Ross of ABC News reported on 5 March 2012 that President Obama was meeting with Prime Minister Netanyahu at the White House trying to talk him out of an immediate strike on Iran's nuclear sites. If Israel does decide to bomb Iran, however, what will it mean for the United States? Former White House counter-terrorism official Richard Clarke said that Americans should brace for a painful impact. Within a week of the first Israeli attack, says Clarke, a worst case scenario would bring soaring gas prices, terror attacks in U.S. cities, worldwide cyber war, dead and wounded U.S. sailors, and the real possibility of broad American military involvement.

According to U.S. government estimates, about 20 per cent of the oil traded worldwide passes through the Persian Gulf, bordered by Iran, Iraq, Kuwait, Saudi Arabia and the Gulf states. If Israel were to bomb Iran, oil prices would immediately go up. If Iran responded by attacking oil tankers going through the Persian Gulf, says Clarke, gasoline prices for U.S. consumers could double. "You could see very quickly Iranian commandos and their small boats attacking tankers, attacking oil platforms," said Clarke. "You could see mines being laid in the Gulf." The result, said Clarke, "would be a huge crisis in energy." President Obama would tap the U.S.'s strategic petroleum reserve, alleviating some of the price rise. The spike in prices "might not last long if the U.S. and its allies are able to take control of the

Gulf," said Clarke. "But that could take more than a week and under some scenarios it could take almost a month."

If Israel were to bomb Iran, American officials fear there could be a new wave of terrorism directed by Teheran, especially if the U.S. gets pulled in to the conflict. "If we, the United States, we're bombing Iran, then I think they'd certainly want to try to do something on our homeland because we were bombing their homeland," said Clarke. Iran and its Lebanese proxy Hezbollah have already shown a willingness to act outside their own borders, both with deadly attacks on Jewish targets in Argentina in the 1990s and the apparent attempted hits on Israeli targets in a number of countries earlier this year. "Both have strong inroads in Asia, Europe, and Latin America, where they could strike Israeli, Jewish, and U.S. targets," said Clarke.

An Israeli attack on Iran would likely set off the world's first international cyber war. Before striking, Israel would try to blind the air defenses of Iran and its neighbors with cyber warfare. And the U.S. might end up using capabilities it has kept secret until now. "The United States has a very powerful ability to cause this sort of disruption to electric power grids, communications networks," said Clarke. "It hasn't done it because it doesn't like to expose its tricks as it's afraid once it does it, people will figure out how the United States does it. But in a war with Iran, they would be willing to run that risk." Iran would also attempt to hit back. "Iran also has a cyber command, which might try to retaliate by attacking U.S infrastructure such as the power grid, trains, airlines, refineries," said Clarke.

But should the U.S. become involved in an Israeli-Iran conflict militarily, says Clarke, it will be impossible to avoid American casualties. "The Iranians have hundreds if not thousands of small boats, armed small boats, commando small boats that will operate in the Gulf," said Clarke. "They can get in, they can swarm a U.S. destroyer. The Iranians now also have cruise missiles, anti-ship cruise missiles." Clarke said there is a potential for the U.S. to sustain significant damage to a few ships and lose some sailors, just as it did during the war between Iran and Iraq in the 1980s. Two U.S. ships were hit during that conflict, with a loss of nearly 40 American lives. According to Clarke, Israel can't do long-term, severe damage to Iran's nuclear infrastructure, so its chief purpose in bombing Iran would be to trigger Iranian retaliation and draw the U.S. into the war to defend

Israel, and to finish off what Israel started. If Israel bombs Iran, Clarke says the cascade of events will lead to attacks on Israeli cities. "Advisors to Prime Minister Netanyahu and Defense Minister Barak are saying that if Israel bombed Iran, the retaliation on Israel would be tolerable," said Clarke. "But if Hezbollah in Lebanon launched thousands of extended range, improved accuracy rockets on Israel, hundreds of Israelis would die. In such a small country, that would be devastating." The casualties, in turn, would bring the inevitable call to Washington for help. "You will very quickly see a phone call from Prime Minister Netanyahu to the President," said Clarke, "and he will say to him, Only the United States, Mr. President, can find and destroy these mobile missile launchers. Only you can save the lives of Israelis who are dying as I speak in our cities." Clarke said that message would probably spur any U.S. president into action – but especially one who is up for re-election within months. "It's likely to get a yes answer from the president," predicts Clarke, "and bring the U.S. into the war."

According to Josef Federman of the Associated Press on 19 February 2012 the U.S. and Britain urged Israel not to attack Iran's nuclear program as the White House's national security adviser arrived in the region, reflecting growing international jitters that the Israelis are poised to strike. In their warnings, both the chairman of the U.S. Joint Chiefs of Staff, Gen. Martin Dempsey, and British Foreign Secretary William Hague said an Israeli attack on Iran would have grave consequences for the entire region and urged Israel to give international sanctions against Teheran more time to work. Dempsey said an Israeli attack is "not prudent," and Hague said it would not be "a wise thing." It was not known whether their messages were coordinated.

Both Israel and the West believe Iran is trying to develop a nuclear bomb – a charge Teheran denies. But differences have emerged in how to respond to the perceived threat. The U.S. and the European Union have both imposed harsh new sanctions targeting Iran's oil sector, the lifeline of the Iranian economy. With the sanctions just beginning to bite, they have expressed optimism that Iran can be persuaded to curb its nuclear ambitions. Iran's Oil Ministry said it has halted oil shipments to Britain and France in an apparent pre-emptive blow against the European Union. The semi-official Mehr news agency said the National Iranian Oil Company has sent letters to some European refineries with an ultimatum to either sign long-term contracts of two to five years or be cut off. The 27-nation EU accounts for about 18 per cent of Iran's oil exports.

Israel has welcomed the sanctions but it has pointedly refused to rule out military action and in recent weeks sent signals that its patience is running thin. Israel believes a nuclear-armed Iran would be a threat to its very existence, citing Iran's support for Arab militant groups, its sophisticated arsenal of missiles capable of reaching Israel and its leaders' calls for the destruction of the Jewish state. Israel accused Iran of being behind a string of attempted attacks on Israeli diplomats in India, Georgia and Thailand. There is precedent for Israeli action. In 1981, the Israeli air force destroyed an unfinished Iraqi nuclear reactor. And in 2007, Israeli warplanes are believed to have destroyed a target that foreign experts think was an unfinished nuclear reactor in Syria. Experts, however, have questioned how much an Israeli operation would accomplish.

With Iran's nuclear installations scattered and buried deep underground, it is believed that an Iranian strike would set back, but not destroy, Iran's nuclear program. There are also concerns Iran could fire missiles at Israel, get its local proxies Hezbollah and Hamas to launch rockets into the Jewish state, and cause global oil prices to spike by striking targets in the Gulf. In an interview broadcast on CNN, Dempsey said Israel has the capability to strike Iran and delay the Iranians "probably for a couple of years. But some of the targets are probably beyond their reach." He expressed concern that an Israeli attack could spark reprisals against U.S. targets in the Gulf or Afghanistan, where American forces are based. "That's the question with which we all wrestle. And the reason that we think that it's not prudent at this point to decide to attack Iran," Dempsey said. Describing Iran as a "rational actor", Dempsey said he believed that the international sanctions on Iran are beginning to have an effect. "For that reason, I think, that we think the current path we're on is the most prudent path at this point."

The arrival of White House National Security Adviser Tom Donilon was the latest in a series of high-level meetings between Israel and the U.S. Dempsey visited Israel, and Prime Minister Benjamin Netanyahu is expected to visit the White House. Donilon was set to meet with Netanyahu and with Israeli Defense Minister Ehud Barak before leaving. Asked whether he believed Israel could be deterred from striking, Dempsey said: "I'm confident that they understand our concerns, that a strike at this time would be destabilizing and wouldn't achieve their long-term objectives. But, I mean, I also understand that Israel has national interests that are unique to them." Hague delivered a similar message in Britain. Speaking to the BBC, he said Britain was focused on pressuring Iran through diplomatic means. "I don't think a wise thing at this moment is for Israel to launch a military attack on Iran," he said. "I think Israel like everyone else in the world should be giving a real chance to the approach we have adopted on very serious economic sanctions and economic pressure and the readiness to negotiate with Iran."

In a sign that the diplomatic pressure might be working, Iran's foreign minister said that a new round of talks with six world powers on the nuclear program will be held in Istanbul, Turkey. Ali Akbar Salehi didn't give any timing for the talks. The last round of talks between Iran and the five permanent members of the U.N. Security Council and Germany were held in Istanbul in January 2011 but ended in failure.

On 1 March 2012 according to an AFP report the White House warned that any military action against Iran would create "greater instability" that could threaten the safety of Americans in Afghanistan and Iraq. "Any military action in that region threatens greater instability in the region," said White House spokesman Jay Carney. "We have civilian personnel in Iraq. We have military personnel as well as civilians in Afghanistan." So far, the United States has no conclusive evidence the Iranians are building a nuclear weapon, he said.

The Obama administration is advocating for a political solution to the crisis that includes International Atomic Energy Agency monitoring of Iran's nuclear program. "We continue to ratchet up the pressure on Teheran," Carney said. "And I think it's important to note that, while Teheran does not and has not lived up to its international obligations... we do have visibility into their programs."

VII

THE U.S. CALL for Assad's exit – which was immediately followed by a chorus of similar declarations from the leaders of Canada, the United Kingdom, France, Germany and the European Union foreign policy chief – stressed that the United States does not plan for any sort of international military intervention in Syria on the order of the NATO-led action that aided rebel forces to oust Libya's Muammar Gadhafi. "The United States cannot and will not impose this transition upon Syria," Obama said. "It is up to the Syrian people to choose their own leaders, and we have heard their strong desire that there not be foreign intervention in their movement." But in fact the call for Assad to step down came as a United Nations' human rights team announced in Geneva that it had determined the Syrian regime may have committed war crimes in its brutal crackdown on anti-government unrest. The UN panel said it may recommend the referral of Syria to the International Criminal Court in The Hague. The Security Council was also scheduled to discuss Syria. The Obama administration also announced a new, fifth round of sanctions on Syria.

The new sanctions prohibit U.S. persons from having any financial dealings with the Syrian regime and in particular with Syria's petroleum industry, and called on other countries to follow the U.S. action. The European Union receives some 90 per cent of Syria's petroleum exports, analysts estimate, and the United States has been pressing European allies to curtail their Syrian energy imports to further financially choke off and pressure the Damascus regime. The sanctions were "in part symbolic and in part significant," said Douglas Jacobson, an attorney who specializes in international trade law, to The Envoy, noting that the U.S. "imports more petroleum products from Trinidad and Tobago than it does from Syria." Symbolically, however, Jacobson added, the further U.S. sanctions put Syria in the unwelcome category of such shunned regimes as those of Iran, Cuba and Sudan.

U.S. officials cautioned that his toppling may be neither swift nor easy. "We can't predict how long this will take, and it's not likely to be easy," one senior U.S. diplomat told journalists in a call organized by the White House to explain the escalation of coordinated international actions on Syria. "But we are certain Assad is on the way out, and we are certain his isolation will increase." Syria is in effect emerging from forty years of an induced coma, the senior official continued, referring to the four-decade reign of Bashar al-Assad and his father Hafez al-Assad before him. "People are not afraid any more, and that is when regimes start to crumble." As the fighting continues, the prophecy now appears in 2012 to be premature.

On 11 March 2012 Alexander Jaffe wrote in the *National Journal* that Sen. John McCain had harsh words for President Obama on foreign policy, calling the president's refusal to engage in the Syrian conflict "disgraceful and shameful." It is a violation of the United States national security policy made by the president of the United States that we would prevent massacres wherever they take place, McCain said on Fox News. McCain had called for the use of U.S. air power in Syria. Obama responded in a press conference, arguing that Syria is a more complicated situation than Libya, where the U.S. intervened to help topple Libyan President Muammar Gaddafi. McCain also slammed the president on his position on Iran. He said that the U.S. request for Israel not to use military force against Iran has hurt relations. "Relations between the United States and Israel have never been worse," he said. But the slaughter of women and children has not stopped in Africa and there is no talk of having no-fly zones or of putting American boots on the ground.

I am as yet unable to find two national leaders more stupid than Saddam Hussein and Muammar Gadhafi who allowed western armies to destroy their ancient cities, killing thousands of Iraqis and Libyans under the sanction of the United Nations and the North Atlantic Treaty Organization and with the promise that they were assisting the Iraqis and the Libyans to overthrow a dictatorship and to establish a democracy. I had always viewed the invasions and the deaths of Hussein and Gadhafi as a felony and Bishop Desmond Tutu's recent blast against Bush and Blair was not unexpected. An Associated Press report by David Stringer from London said that the Nobel Peace Prize Laureate had called for Tony Blair and George W. Bush to face prosecution at the International Criminal Court for their role in the 2003 U.S.-led invasion of Iraq. Tutu, the retired Anglican Church's archbishop of South Africa, wrote in an op-ed piece for *The Observer* newspaper that the ex-leaders of Britain and the United States should be made to "answer for their actions." The Iraq war "has destabilized and polarized the world to a greater extent than any other conflict in history," wrote Tutu, who was awarded the Nobel Prize in 1984. "Those responsible for this suffering and loss of life should be treading the same path as some of their African and Asian peers who have been made to answer for their actions in The Hague," he added.

The Hague, Netherlands, based court is the world's first permanent war crimes tribunal and has been in operation for 10 years. So far it has launched prosecutions in Africa, including in Sudan, Congo, Libya and Ivory Coast. While the International Criminal Court can handle cases of genocide, war crimes and crimes against humanity, it does not currently have the jurisdiction to prosecute crimes of aggression. Any potential prosecution over the Iraq war would likely come under the aggression category. However the U.S. is among nations which do not recognize the International Criminal Court. And while I have no love for Bashar al-Assad and wish him out of the way, if it means that there will be an end to the killing, I find it difficult to open my heart to Mr. McCain when I recall the Chinese idiom of putting a wolf to guard the sheep. But, seriously, did Americans think he was sincere and felt torn apart by Syrian deaths when he said what he did? Or was it just out of the need to criticize Mr. Obama's decision this time not to interfere in the chaos in Syria and to hope that Mr. Kofi Annan's peace mission would work?

The truth is more and more Americans are seeing that it is a risk to put their trust in politicians as a record 64 per cent of American adults surveyed by Gallup in a poll that rated the honesty and ethical standards for members of Congress as "low" or "very low". Those numbers mark the lowest rating that Gallup has measured for any profession since it began polling the question in 1976, wrote Rachel Rose Hartman of The Ticket in December 2011. The 64 per cent rating ties members of Congress with the 64 per cent low rating that lobbyists received in Gallup's 2008 survey. Historical trends indicate that it's not surprising Congress ranked so low on ethics. But the more noteworthy trend is that a growing number of Americans are labeling their rating "low" or "very low" with a corresponding decline in "high" or "very high" ratings. The low ethics rating is in line with the overall low regard the American public has for its lawmakers. Many of the Republican presidential candidates have seized on those sentiments and are floating ideas to institute new restrictions, such as term limits for members of Congress. Lobbyists, car salespeople, and telemarketers round out the bottom tier of professions ranked by public perceptions of their ethics in the Gallup survey. The professions earning high ethics marks in the poll were nurses, pharmacists, medical doctors and high school teachers.

The mistrust goes deep and on 8 January 2012 David Alexander of Reuters reported that Defense Secretary Leon Panetta cautioned global rivals not to misjudge U.S. plans to slash military spending over the next decade, saying America would still field the world's strongest military and nobody should "mess with that." Panetta, speaking on CBS's *Face the Nation* program ahead of the New Hampshire primary, also reminded Republican presidential contenders who have criticized the Pentagon's new military strategy that the decision to cut $487 billion in defense spending was made by a bipartisan Congress. Some Republicans have expressed concerns about the cuts and their impact. Leading Republican presidential candidate Mitt Romney charged that President Barack Obama's new military strategy unveiled in that week was "inexcusable and unthinkable" because it would reduce U.S. global military capability. The new strategy, which is meant to guide defense spending over the next decade as the military cuts back, calls for greater emphasis on Asia even as the Army and Marines shrink to become smaller and more agile forces.

Some Republicans have been concerned about a shift away from the Pentagon's Cold War-era goal of being able to fight two major ground wars simultaneously. Pentagon officials have downplayed the shift, saying the military will still be configured to fight more than one conflict at a time. "I think this country has to deal with the reality of the situation that we're confronting," Panetta said in a pre-recorded interview. "We're coming out of a decade of war. We're facing a huge budget crisis in this country. The Congress said ... we have to reduce the defense budget by $487 billion." General Martin Dempsey, the top U.S. military officer as chairman of the Joint Chiefs of Staff, told *Face the Nation* he worried that some countries might misunderstand the debate Americans are having over changing strategy and the need to cut defense spending. "There may be some around the world who see us as a nation in decline, and worse, as a military in decline. And nothing could be further from the truth," Dempsey said. He said such a miscalculation could be "troublesome" in dealing with countries like

Iran or North Korea but it could also cause close friends to wonder if the United States would continue to be a consistent ally. "What I'd like to say right now is we're the same partner we've always been, and intend to remain that way," Dempsey said.

Panetta said U.S. rivals should not misunderstand the situation. "I think the message that the world needs to understand is: America is the strongest military power and we intend to remain the strongest military power and nobody ought to mess with that," he said. Asked whether it would be difficult to take out Iran's nuclear capability, Dempsey said it was his job to plan and understand the risks associated with any military option and "all those activities are going on. They need to know that ... if they take that step, they are going to get stopped," Panetta said.

Obama and Congress agreed in August 2011 to cut some $487 billion in defense spending over the next decade as part of efforts to bring of the nation's $14 trillion debt under control. Defense spending could be cut by another $600 billion as part of the August deal unless Congress compromises on an alternative. Congress missed the deadline for reaching an agreement but could still take action to override the cuts before they are due to go into force next year. Obama, in unveiling the new defense strategy at a Pentagon news conference noted that even with the $487 trillion in cuts to projected spending, the defense budget would continue to grow in nominal terms. He also noted that the U.S. defense budget also would still be by far the world's largest – roughly the size of the next largest defense budgets combined.

In Lakewood, Washington, Peter Henderson and Bill Rigby reported that around the home base of the American soldier accused of killing 16 Afghan civilians there is a sense of dedication to a tough job, but stress from years of battle in repeated tours in the "sand box" of Iraq and Afghanistan is eating away at troops. "A lot of the guys, especially those with a lot of deployments, have built up a numbness to people being killed or hurt," said one veteran of six tours abroad, including Iraq and Afghanistan, to the Reuters pair, describing his own reaction to the weekend shooting. "The people who hate us are going to put a bad spin on us no matter what we do." The 33-year-old sergeant says he suffers from post-traumatic stress disorder, or PTSD. He asked not to be identified, since the base has told soldiers not to speak with media. "These things happen," Vietnam veteran John

Haddick, an elder at Lake City Community Church in Lakewood, Washington, said of the weekend killings in Afghanistan. "It's not going to change individuals that much, this one incident, or their attitude to deployment. They understand it's a hazardous place," said Haddick, who speaks to many serving soldiers and veterans in his role at the church, a 10-minute drive from Joint Base Lewis-McChord, and helps them overcome their ordeal.

Lewis-McChord, 10 miles southwest of Tacoma, Washington, is the largest military base on the West Coast, with about 40,000 military personnel, swelled to more than 60,000 by civilians and families. Currently, 5,955 troops – including 5,400 Army, 500 Air Force and 55 Air Force Reserve troops – are serving in Afghanistan from the base. That accounts for about 7 per cent of the 90,000-strong U.S. force in Afghanistan. "They are not going to be normal again," said Alicia Underberg, 60, a retiree, in an interview at the nearby Veterans Affairs hospital, where she was helping a retired Marine sniper with PTSD who takes 11 medications daily and sleeps away most of his days. "They serve so many tours," she said. "What is it going to be like when they try to integrate with society?" There are concerns that the Army does not always take care of soldiers damaged – physically or mentally – by the rigors of war. "It's like they break them, and don't want to fix them. So they just find anything to shut them out," said the wife of a sergeant who has served multiple tours of duty in Iraq over a 17-year Army career.

More than 4,000 Army combat soldiers from Lewis-McChord's 2nd Stryker Brigade, 2nd Infantry Division, were scheduled for deployment to Afghanistan in April and May. "If I was to go to Afghanistan, I would be scared," said 23-year-old Alyssa Patrick, a reservist who left her full-time post in the Army in 2010 after serving at a big base in Iraq, which she said felt normal in comparison. Together the two countries are called "the sand box", she said. Patrick said a male friend of hers who is single was getting ready to deploy and excited by the prospects of higher pay and a new experience. "Some people are addicted to war, some are moderate, and some people don't want to go," said a second soldier who declined to be identified. A third, who once served near the place of the civilian shooting in Kandahar, said his unit had struggled to establish a rapport with locals. "I put in blood, sweat and tears, and I mean that literally.

It just makes it harder. We can't leave like we left Vietnam, scrambling from the embassy rooftop," he said. The 33-year-old sergeant who spoke of numbness toward violence said the main hit to morale after the Kandahar shooting was dealing with more training about PTSD. "Everyone was like, Really? Are you kidding me," he said. "Somebody screwed up, and we have to do additional training."

VIII

ON 2 FEBRUARY 2012, Eileen Sullivan of the Associated Press wrote that even as the Obama administration says it's close to defeating al-Qaeda, the size of the government's secret list of suspected terrorists who are banned from flying to or within the United States has more than doubled in the past year and according to the Associated Press the no-fly list jumped from about 10,000 known or suspected terrorists one year ago to about 21,000. Most people on the list are from other countries; about 500 are Americans. The flood of new names began after the failed Christmas 2009 bombing of a Detroit-bound jetliner. The government lowered the standard for putting people on the list, and then scoured its files for anyone who qualified. The government will not disclose who is on its list or why someone might have been placed on it. The surge in the size of the no-fly list comes even as the U.S. has killed many senior members of al-Qaeda. That's because the government believes the current terror threat extends well beyond the group responsible for the September 2001 attacks. "Both U.S. intelligence and law enforcement communities and foreign services continue to identify people who want to cause us harm, particularly in the U.S. and particularly as it relates to aviation," Transportation Security Administrator John Pistole said in an interview.

The Nigerian who pleaded guilty in the Christmas 2009 attack over Detroit, Umar Farouk Abdulmutallab, was listed in a large U.S. intelligence database that includes partial names and relatives of suspected terrorists. That database is a feeder to the broad terror watch list, of which the no-fly list is a component, but only when there is enough information linking the person to terrorism. Officials believe the U.S. had enough information about Abdulmutallab at the time to put him on the broader terror watch list, which would have helped the intelligence community catch him. The Christmas attack led to significant changes in how the U.S. assembles its watch list. Intelligence agencies across the government reviewed old files to find people who should have been on the government's terror watch list all along, plus those who should be added because of the new standards put in place to close security gaps. A senior Homeland Security Department official, Caryn Wagner, told senators during an oversight hearing, "We have been able to harness the intelligence from the intelligence community to inform our instruments to keep people out at our borders, to make sure that the wrong people are not getting on airplanes at last points of departure and to make sure that people who shouldn't get them are not receiving immigration benefits from the department." After the Christmas attack, "We learned a lot about the watch-listing process and made strong improvements, which continue to this day," said Timothy Healy, director of the Terrorist Screening Center, which produces the no-fly list.

Among the most significant new standard is that now a person doesn't have to be considered only a threat to aviation to be placed on the no-fly list. People who are considered a broader threat to domestic or international security or who attended a terror training camp also are included, said a U.S. counter-terrorism official who spoke on condition of anonymity to discuss sensitive security matters. As agencies complete the reviews of their files, the pace of growth is expected to slow, the counter-terrorism official said. The American Civil Liberties Union has sued the government on behalf of Americans who believe they are on the no-fly list and have not been able to travel by air for work or to see family. "The news that the list is growing tells us that more people's rights are being violated," said Nusrat Choudhury, a staff attorney working for the ACLU's national security project. "It's a secret list, and the government puts people on it without any explanation. Citizens have been stranded abroad."

The government will not tell people whether they are on the list or why they are on it, making it impossible for people to defend themselves, Choudhury said. People who complain that they are unfairly on the no-fly list can submit a letter to the Homeland Security Department, but the only way they will know if they are still on the list is to try to fly again, she said. While the list is secret, it is subject to continuous review to ensure that the right people are on it and that the ones who shouldn't be on it are removed, said Martin Reardon, former chief of the Terrorist Screening Operations center and now a vice president with the Soufan Group. If a person is nominated to be on the no-fly list, but there is insufficient information to justify it, the Terrorist Screening Center downgrades the person to a different list, he said. "You can't just say: 'Here's a name. Put him on the list.' You've got to have articulable facts."

On average, there are 1,000 changes to the government's watch lists each day, most of which involve adding new information about someone on the list. The no-fly list has swelled to 20,000 people before, such as in 2004. At the time people like the late Senator Ted Kennedy were getting stopped before flying, causing constant angst and aggravation for innocent travelers. But much has changed since then. While thousands more people are on the list, instances of travelers being mistaken for terrorists are down significantly since the government – not the airlines – became responsible for checking the list, Pistole said. Travelers must now provide their full name, birthdate and gender when purchasing an airline ticket so the government can screen them against the terror watch list. But with the nature of the terrorism threat, it's not likely that the list will dwindle, even as al-Qaeda's core leadership is defeated, Reardon said. "I would argue that even if (al-Qaeda) as we know it ceased to exist as of tomorrow, other terrorist organizations or lone wolves with both the intent and capability of carrying out attacks against the U.S. would fill the void," Reardon said. "The consolidated terrorist watch list exists for that very reason. Once they are identified and placed on the list, we have a much greater chance of keeping them from entering the country." However the threats of terrorists and the forces that have been massed against them have robbed even Americans of a sense of freedom and forgiveness.

IX

IN WASHINGTON DC whenever Rhona and I are with Ray and Myrna Boddie, we always attend Sunday service at Fort Belvoir and we did so on 11 September 2011 with She Xiuling, going through the routine of showing the sentry at the gates our passports. On that day we heard the sermon on "Hard Times but not Hard Hearts" and I remembered that in all the years we were in China, I hadn't met any student or adult who spoke of the Japanese in a way that suggested that they were unforgiving and wanted to destroy Japan and the Japanese for the Nanjing Massacre in 1937. Was it the same with Americans after 9/11? The Nanking Massacre or Nanjing Massacre, also known as the Rape of Nanking, was a mass murder and war rape that occurred during the six-week period following the Japanese capture of the city of Nanjing (Nanking), the former capital of the Republic of China, on 13 December 1937 during the Second Sino-Japanese War. Hundreds of thousands of Chinese civilians and disarmed soldiers were murdered by soldiers of the Imperial Japanese Army. Widespread rape and looting also occurred. Historians and witnesses have estimated that 250,000 to 300,000 people were killed. Several of the key perpetrators of the atrocities, at the time labeled as war crimes, were later tried and found guilty at the Nanjing War Crimes Tribunal, and were subsequently executed. In fact whenever I asked the question which country they would like to visit the most, it was rare that I didn't get Japan as the answer.

That is why I was curious about what Col. Arthur C. Pace would say on that morning. Would he show that in his heart he had forgiven the hijackers who had slammed their planes in the World Trade Center and into the Pentagon killing 3,000 people? In *Why Are We At War?* Norman Mailer wrote that "A mass identity crisis for all of Americans descended upon us after 9/11, and our response was wholly comprehensible. We were plunged into a fever of patriotism." Looking at the skyline from Brooklyn, said Ms. Musaracchia, "I can still see a huge gap where the buildings stood, where a friend lost her husband. As a driver many roads have been closed and you can't get around as easily as before. Now it's just an excuse for more bike lanes and pedestrian seating areas in the middle of the road. As a weekend biker, I love it. As a week-day driver, I don't like it so much." It has been near impossible indeed to find any American who could bring himself or herself to forgive the hijackers.

When he was finished speaking, I didn't think I got my answer but I felt that Chaplain Pace understood that hard hearts would not help Americans to be better Americans. "In the spiritual challenges that many of us face every day," Chaplain Pace said, "the genuineness of our faith is revealed not only to us, but to all those around us. And the tougher the times, the clearer others can see the true depth of our devotion to Christ. It is in these tough times that we may find ourselves, in whole or in part, allowing our hearts to become hardened. But we don't like to admit that. We know it is wrong. The good news is that we can fix it. Ten years ago today, groups of Jihadist Muslims deeply wounded America, and changed our lives forever. For the weeks following the attack, America's churches were filled. In hard times, we opened our hearts to God. This matches what Carl Sandberg once said: *I see America not in the setting sun of a black night of despair. I see America in the crimson light of a rising sun fresh from the burning, creative hand of God.* If this is true for our nation as a whole, it is equally true for us as individuals as well."

It didn't mean however that the United States should not be prepared and, according to David Alexander of Reuters, to make sure that the country had the men and arms to protect it, the House of Representatives approved $606 billion in defense spending for next year after two days of debate that saw lawmakers from both parties line up to condemn the ongoing war in Afghanistan as a waste of lives and money. The Republican-dominated House voted 326-90 to approve the annual defense appropriations bill, which includes a Pentagon base budget of $518 billion plus $87.7 billion in spending for the Afghanistan war and other overseas operations, according to the House Appropriations Committee. Lawmakers proposed dozens of bills over two days of debate seeking to reduce spending by cutting war funding or trimming programs, but the measure remained relatively unchanged until the final moments of voting. In a last series of amendments, lawmakers agreed to freeze Pentagon spending at 2012 levels, effectively cutting $1 billion from the base budget appropriation. They also approved an amendment switching $5.6 billion between accounts for technical reasons. Even with the spending freeze, the House measure is $2 billion more than requested by President Obama, whose administration issued a veto threat against the bill because it exceeded budget caps imposed last year. The president and Congress had agreed last autumn to cut projected Pentagon spending by $487 billion over 10 years as part of a budget deal aimed at reducing the government's trillion-dollar annual deficits. The budget proposed by the Pentagon would have cut defense spending for the first time in more than a decade.

The House appropriations bill, which covers the 2013 fiscal year beginning in October, will have to be reconciled with the Senate's version of the measure before it can be sent to President Obama for his signature. The Senate is not expected to debate its bill until August. "This bill supports and takes care of our troops at the highest possible level, keeps America at the forefront of defense technologies and boosts key training and readiness programs to prepare our troops for combat and peace-time missions," Appropriations Committee Chairman Hal Rogers said.

War-weary lawmakers from both parties voiced frustration during debate with the Afghanistan war and submitted a series of amendments trying to reduce war spending to speed the return of U.S. forces. They also expressed anger over corruption in the government of Afghan President Hamid Karzai, skepticism about any lasting progress toward resolving the conflict, and exhaustion over the unending cost in lives and treasure. But the bill easily passed the House.

Chapter Three – Politics and Government

"You seem like a nice enough guy. Why do you want to go into something dirty and nasty like politics?" – Barack Obama in *The Audacity of Hope*

CHICAGO. – As the Southwest Airlines' flight started its descent into O'Hare Airport, She Xiuling said, "You really have never been to Chicago?"

"That's right."

"So I guess you don't know anything of its history and politics."

"When I was in primary and secondary school in Trinidad we were a British colony. Geography and History lessons focused on the British Commonwealth and not the Americas. It seems absurd seeing that the Caribbean has been described as the American Lake, but absurdity is often what politics is about and we all learn to live with this absurdity. You learn the language and ways of the conquerors and you have no real identity of your own. And even though we are an independent nation today no politician appears to be desirous or willing to break emotional ties with England. We are still waiting for a Mao or a Castro or a Mandela to come along and lead us out of our bondage."

"What about Williams?"

"Eric Eustace Williams? Oh yes. He led the country for twenty-five years and has been called the Father of the Nation. But I think he gave up on Trinidadians. He gave up on the two races that constitute the majority races in the population."

"You mean Africans and Indians?"

"Not Africans, as my son-in-law will insist. Negroes. Negroes and Indians."

"Aren't they all Trinidadians? Trinidadians and Tobagonians?"

"Technically, but they seem to want to be Africans and Indians. Williams did try to get them to think as Trinidadians and Tobagonians when he urged that there must be no Mother Africa and no Mother India but this did not suit a lot of politicians who saw their constituencies as made up of one or the other race. That's why our politics has always been tribal since the dawn of party politics in 1956."

"Doesn't this cause a problem for national unity and for development?"

"Of course it does. In fact it is a recipe for disaster. That is, the distrust that exists between the two races. I think sometimes it's a time-bomb waiting to happen."

"I suppose it is a similar distrust you see in the United States between white Americans and black Americans and that is why you believe that the peace we see in the cities is a brittle one."

"It is. Lincoln believed this too and the solution he suggested was to export the problem, which was African slaves, to a Central American country. I don't believe that the wounds of slavery would ever heal. Every morning that Americans awake they know that they will see the face of the enemy on the street, on trains and buses, and in their offices, work places and playing fields. The marvel is that the blood-shedding has not as yet taken place and this is due primarily because of the nobility, or cowardice, of black Americans. But this abomination is enough to cause us to hold the United States in contempt. The injustices start at the top with the white oligarchy and it is necessary to remember what Thomas Paine wrote. Government with insolence he said is despotism but when contempt is added it becomes worse and to pay for contempt is the excess of slavery."

"You are frightening me. I used to see America in a different way."

"So many people do. But you come from a country that has a history that is as violent as the history of places in the Bible as Sima

Qian's *Records of the Historian* shows and this violence starts with the power brokers in the dynasties and their contempt for the people. In fact this is what struck me when I read the *Records of the Historian*. It was so much like the Old Testament with its inhuman and brutal laws. And in less than five centuries Americans have succeeded in equaling the treachery, strife and murder we find in centuries of European and Eastern histories. They have no moral credibility to accuse any other country of human rights violations."

"So do you think we are on a wild goose chase?"

"That's a good question. Ask me it again when we get to Miami."

She Xiuling had been looking forward to visit the United States as much as she looked forward to explore the city that Barack Obama had made his home. I knew she wasn't impressed by the ramshackle state of New York as much as she was by the geometric orderliness of Washington DC. How would she find Chicago? I knew there was hardly anything I could tell her that she would not have read on the Internet. But I knew too that she had an insatiable appetite for information.

With a population of 3 million, Chicago is Illinois' largest and the country's third most populous city. In addition, the greater Chicago area that encompasses northeastern Illinois and extends into southeastern Wisconsin and northwestern Indiana is the country's third largest metropolitan area and the dominant metropolis of the Midwest. It is often referred to as the "Windy City", though the origin of the term remains unknown. The nickname has at times been attributed to the city's windswept location on Lake Michigan. As children of the 30s and 40s and members of the British Commonwealth, our attention was not fixed on the United States but we used to say, "How do you spell Chicago? And the childish answer would be, *A chicken in a car and the car can't go, that's the way to spell Chicago.*" As a man I recalled the name of Al Capone and the Valentine's Day massacre and more recently the political event of 1968 when the mayor, Richard J. Daley, unleashed his police force on Democrats at their convention. But that was as much as I knew.

"I am sure Kerry Luft could fill in the blanks when we meet him at the Chicago Tribune," Rhona, in the row of seats ahead of us, said.

"I hope we could sit in on his editorial meetings," Xiuling added. "By the way if you have never been to Chicago how do you know Mr. Luft?"

"Davan Maharaj who works at the Los Angeles Times put me in touch with him. The Times and the Tribune are sister newspapers. But why would you want to sit in at their editorial meetings?"

"Maybe it could help me to make up my mind about Columbia University. Isn't that what you want me to do?"

"No, no. Don't put that burden on me. You must decide on your career. Rhona and I did our part already when we sent you to Warwick University."

"And I am grateful. I realize how lucky I was – how lucky I am to be on this trip also and be given the opportunity to work with you on this project."

II

IN THE DAYS that we spent in the "Windy City" I enjoyed our walks around the shopping district and pier, learning quickly that we were not to consider dinner at any restaurant that offered valet parking. "We just can't afford the prices," a disappointed Xiuling quipped as we searched for an establishment that was neither a bar nor a fast-food place. These culinary problems did not diminish her affection for Chicago however and instead made her anxious to reach the other cities we had planned to visit in our search for America's Soul – to discover what America's core values were.

The *Chicago Tribune* had said that *The Audacity of Hope* was Barack Obama's "upbeat view of the country's potential and a political biography that concentrates on the senator's core values." Were these values sufficient to keep him in the White House for a second term? It was clear that Republicans did not think so and Bill Maher had the answer to their opposition and hostility. During an appearance on *The Tonight Show* with Jay Leno, he had one takeaway piece of advice for President Obama: "Stop trying to make everyone like you." This advice came on the heels of Maher's decision to give a million dollars to Obama's presidential campaign. "He's got to understand that with the Republicans," Maher told Leno, "it's not the entrée they don't like. They don't like the waiter." When he was pressed for his reaction to Obama's jobs speech, Maher said, "You could give all the money to the rich, and they would still call you a socialist." Maher admitted however that he was impressed by Obama's speech, but was interested to see how the president will follow through and put his plan into action. Like most Obama watchers, Maher wasn't seeing the streak of ruthlessness that is common in all great world leaders, from Alexander to Lincoln.

It is never though cruelty for cruelty's sake. Even in a democracy we have to learn to use power and to direct it to the best ends. These are times however when the freedom to think and to talk, to rant and to rave has made all men equal before the law – university   professor, journalist, janitor and your friendly neighborhood watch – and with the right to support any political agenda he chooses. The chaos that comes from this universal rule is thus our real problem and one that always brings about uneasiness and pending change. So behind the jokes Maher was saying something we all know: every opposition party in government believes that voters made the wrong decision and that they can do the job of managing the affairs of the country better than the people's choice. And fortified with this supercilious belief, every Republican since 2008, whether it is Mitt Romney from Massachusetts or Bobby Jindal from Louisiana, has sought to undermine the wisdom and rule of Barack Obama.

This arrogance is not characteristic only of the leaders of the Party however; it is manifest as well in members of the media who seem to think that their ethereal views as a liberal or a conservative absolve them of the journalistic law to be fair and protect them from public criticism or condemnation. That is why Rush Limbaugh could dare to call Sandra Fluke a "slut" and a "prostitute" for her support of women having access to birth control and no member of Mr. Romney's Party of White Anglo-Saxon Protestants could feel ashamed of his behavior and apologize for his obnoxious attack on American women.

It took Mr. Obama to do so and as Dylan Stableford reported in The Ticket on 2 March 2012 the President called the Georgetown law student and defended her in the face of Limbaugh's "reprehensible ... personal and crude" attacks on her. The conversation, which lasted for "several minutes", wrote Stableford, came because Mr. Obama "wanted to offer his support to her." According to Jay Carney, the

President wanted "to express his disappointment that she had been the subject of inappropriate personal attacks, and to thank her for exercising her rights as a citizen to speak out on an issue of public policy." Ms. Fluke, when she appeared on the *Today* show to talk about the incident, said, "I think my reaction was the reaction a lot of women have had historically when they've been called these types of names. Initially to be stunned by it, and then to quickly feel outraged and very upset," she said. "[It's] an attempt to silence me, to silence all of us from speaking about the health care we need." That is what it was: a wish to isolate the government from its public by threats and abuse.

I was surprised that Michelle Bachmann decided to stay out of the fray even though her husband Dr. Marcus Bachmann is the President of Bachmann and Associates, a Christian counseling center in Minnesota, according to a source on the Internet. What I wondered do they tell their five children about sex and sexuality and about their responsibility not to be irresponsible in spite of the foolishness of politicians and journalists. The question is does politics trump all and rob us of decency and the need to apologize for gross misconduct by our friends and associates? The public record of Rush Limbaugh, even from this distance in the Caribbean, is one of a disgrace to the country that advocates freedom of the press more than any other country in the western world. And it was no surprise that Republicans' silence on this abomination encouraged Limbaugh to continue his verbal assault on Ms. Fluke and on every American woman, from Eleanor Roosevelt to Rosa Parks, whose example has been to act responsibly in society.

In *The National Journal* of 6 March 2012, Jonathan Miller wrote that Michele Bachmann had ample opportunity to offer critical words about Rush Limbaugh, but the most she came up with was, "I think we need to be respectful on both sides." Speaking on CNN's *Newsroom*, the Republican House member from Minnesota and a former presidential candidate was repeatedly asked about the still-simmering controversy over Limbaugh's calling Georgetown law student Sandra Fluke a "slut" and a "prostitute" on his show. Bachmann said: "I think Rush Limbaugh has already addressed this issue. He came out, and he very forcefully said that he was wrong. He apologized not just once but several times. I think he's put that issue to bed." Limbaugh had tendered what he has since called a sincere apology and labeled his own statements "wrong". But critics continued to rip him for the comments, and advertisers pulled funding from his program. When pressed on the issue, Ms. Bachmann continued to demur, saying that she was "called name after name after name" on the campaign trail, and that no media firestorm ensued. "I think we need to be respectful on both sides," she said, refusing to see any difference in the case between herself and Ms. Fluke.

The fact is Ms. Fluke is not an aspiring politician, a point that Maher used in his defense of his battle with Sarah Palin. Ms. Bachmann also said she was busy concentrating on her role on the House Intelligence Committee, and that "the media's been focusing on these little pinprick issues when really we should be focusing on bigger issues." It was as if she was waiting on a cue from members of the Tea Party or from some other quarter in the Republican Party to direct her steps and I recalled what Bertrand Russell had written about *Leaders and Followers*: "Some men's characters lead them always to command, others always to obey; between these extremes lie the mass of average human beings, who like to command in some situations, but in others prefer to be subject to a leader."

At the hearing where Ms. Fluke originally spoke about the issue of birth control, she argued that women should have free access to contraceptives, complaining that Georgetown, a Catholic university, won't cover it for her. "Contraception can cost a woman over $3,000 during law school," she said. "For a lot of students like me who are on public interest scholarships, that's practically an entire summer's salary." After her comments, Limbaugh lashed out: "What does it say about the college co-ed Fluke, who goes before a congressional committee and essentially says she must be paid to have sex? What does that make her? It makes her a slut, right? It makes her a prostitute. She wants to be paid to have sex. She's having so much sex she can't afford the contraception." Limbaugh later suggested that in exchange for contraceptives paid for by taxpayers, Fluke should produce a sex tape. "If we are going to pay for your contraceptives and thus pay for you to have sex, we want something for it," Limbaugh said. "We want you to post the videos online so we can all watch."

I am having trouble dealing with this asshole. Walter Lippmann had said that he had learned from Herbert Croly at *The New Republic* that the ability to get away with impertinence is almost the best quality a political journalist can have. But Limbaugh has never succeeded to do this; he has always been insulting and boorish. And I am thinking that George Zimmerman showed as much contempt for the high school student he shot and killed and hoped that a stupid law in Florida that had its roots in racial discrimination would free him of murder just as Limbaugh must think that America's commitment to freedom of the press would absolve him of the insults he flung at Ms. Fluke and free him of the need to apologize for his gross behavior. And the slow and slack response from Republicans was as pathetic. It was not until House Democrats called on House Speaker John Boehner to denounce Limbaugh's comments, that his office did so. "The Speaker obviously believes the use of those words was inappropriate," Boehner spokesman Michael Steel told CNN.

The apology did not seem appropriate enough however and even after Limbaugh himself had apologized twice for his remarks about Ms. Fluke more than a dozen companies pulled sponsorships of his program including AOL, Tax Reform, ProFlowers, Quicken Loans, Sleep Number, The Sleep Train, Citrix, LegalZoom and Carbonite. Hawaiian radio station KPUA ended its support of Limbaugh also and dropped his show, which is broadcast across more than 600 markets, reaching between 13 million and 20 million weekly listeners. And later more than two dozen companies pulled their ads from Limbaugh's program, including NetFlix, Capitol One, and John Deere. The Atlantic Wire reported the reaction from the growing number of advertisers that pulled their ads stems largely from consumer comments made in social media circles, says Brad Adgate, SVP of Horizon Media. "Consumers can now directly talk to sponsors and advertisers, one-on-one... It is no longer a top-down approach where marketers tell consumers what to think. It is now a level playing field and consumers can tell marketers what they think," Adgate notes. "This is a great opportunity for consumers to voice their opinion." And voice their opinion they did.

In addition more than 7,000 people wrote comments on ProFlowers' Facebook page to voice their displeasure with Limbaugh. The CEO of Carbonite used social media to explain why the company pulled its sponsorship. "No one with daughters the age of Sandra Fluke, and I have two, could possibly abide the insult and abuse heaped upon this courageous and well-intentioned young lady," wrote

Carbonite CEO David Friend on the company's Facebook page. "Mr. Limbaugh, with his highly personal attacks on Miss Fluke, overstepped any reasonable bounds of decency. Even though Mr. Limbaugh has now issued an apology, we have nonetheless decided to withdraw our advertising from his show. We hope that our action, along with the other advertisers who have already withdrawn their ads, will ultimately contribute to a more civilized public discourse."

Limbaugh, the highest paid radio host with a $400 million 8-year contract, is often hailed as a top Republican voice outside of Washington. He is credited with setting the tone for the Republican Party and obviously did not have any misgiving that Republican candidates would come out against him for his squalid remarks – with the exception of Ron Paul whom I thought from the beginning of the Republicans' debates was there on a personal mission to lift the standard of Republican thinking in spite of the presence of Newt Gingrich. But Americans, affected with a lust for power and a kind of invincible ignorance, have turned politics into an expensive circus and made cowards of men and women whose desire is to preserve the integrity of the U.S. political system. Their goal is to create all over again a servile community where all decisions of life and death are determined by an oligarchy with guns and tanks and drones waiting for the next war in Asia, in the Middle East, or in Africa.

What is it that prevents politicians from believing that other politicians are not afflicted with invincible ignorance and are incapable of coming up with plans and policies to make a difference in our lives? Alexandra Jaffe, writing in the *National Journal* on 23 January 2012, reported that House Speaker John Boehner had called President Obama's policies pathetic and implored him to "go in a new direction" to improve the economy. "It sounds to me like the same old policies," Boehner said on Fox News. "More spending and higher taxes and more regulations – the same policies that haven't helped our economy, they've made it worse. And if that's what the president's going to talk about Tuesday night, I think it's pathetic." Boehner brandished a list of 30 jobs bills passed by the House that he says Obama should consider folding into his agenda for the upcoming year, and he blamed Congress' inactivity on the Senate, which hasn't taken up any of those bills. Boehner also dismissed claims that he's often been stymied in his attempts to make deals with Obama by a small coalition of stubborn

GOP freshmen, particularly those affiliated with the Tea Party. "We have some members who always want to do more," he said, but "the problem is getting the president to say yes."

Two weeks later on 8 February 2012, Chris Moody wrote in The Ticket that from the Republican presidential candidates to top GOP lawmakers in Washington, party leaders are engaging in a full-court press against the Obama Administration's decision to force employers affiliated with religious groups to offer health care insurance plans to workers that cover birth control free of charge, even if the action contradicts the employer's religious beliefs. In a rare move for someone in his office, Boehner took to the floor of the chamber to discuss a legislative plan to overturn the decision. Calling the rule "an unambiguous attack" on faith-based groups, Boehner said the House would begin work on a bill immediately. "If the president does not reverse the department's attack on religious freedom, then the Congress, acting on behalf of the American people, and the Constitution that we're sworn to uphold and defend, must," Boehner, a Catholic, said. "The House will approach this matter fairly and deliberately through regular order and appropriate legislative channels." Boehner said that the chamber's Energy and Commerce committee will take the lead in drafting the legislation to overturn the decision.

In January, Health and Human Services Secretary Kathleen Sebelius announced that certain faith-based groups would have one year to comply with the requirement, enacted when Congress passed a federal health care overhaul in 2010. "Nonprofit employers who, based on religious beliefs, do not currently provide contraceptive coverage in their insurance plan, will be provided an additional year, until 1 August 2013, to comply with the new law," Sebelius said in the statement. The rule still exempts houses of worship from having to provide insurance that offers free contraceptives, but it applies to non-profit organizations funded by churches, including universities, hospitals and charities. The decision not to exempt those groups resulted in an uproar from religious groups – particularly the Catholic Church – who say the federal mandate to pay for birth control infringes on their religious beliefs.

The Republican National Committee rolled out a new ad in March 2012, wrote Dylan Stableford of The Cutline, called "Obama's

War on Women," linking comedian and Obama campaign backer Bill Maher's controversial comments about Sarah Palin to the administration. The 90-second spot featured several TV news personalities, including ABC's George Stephanopoulos, MSNBC's Chris Matthews and CNN's Erin Burnett. "At first I was kind of amused I was included," Burnett said. "Then I was annoyed. I certainly don't agree that Democrats are in a war on women."

Conservatives have criticized liberals for attacking Rush Limbaugh over his comments about Sandra Fluke but failing to denounce Maher. But neither party, Burnett said, "came out hard enough when the offender was one of its own." To say an entire party, either party, is at war with women? This is all just politics," she said. "Frankly, we've seen many references to a War on Women recently – from Dems and GOP. Both sides need to be honest that the words used, like the s-word and the c-word, are not acceptable. Not by someone who is a pundit, an entertainer, a broadcaster ... or a co-worker. Not by anyone. There isn't any defending it. This isn't political; this should be personal for all Americans. If you're a woman, you get it because you deal with sexism, in both its mundane and offensive forms. If you're a man, you have women in your life whom you respect and you don't want to hear those words used to describe them. When my father ran for Congress during a special election in 1969, the slogan he used was 'Let's End Politics As Usual.' And that still holds true today. Let's end this talk about a war on women and name calling ... and instead have substantive conversations about the real issues: like women's pay and reproductive rights."

Earlier in the program, Burnett interviewed Democratic National Committee chairman Bill Burton about Maher. "I'm not going to stand here and defend vulgarity no matter who's using it," Burton said. "I'm just not going to. But I'm also not going to accept the Republicans' selective outrage when they get mad over who uses what terms. And to listen to Rush Limbaugh or Ted Nugent, I think that Republicans are very happy to ignore that and just try to use this as an issue to distract from what are actually important issues that we're trying to discuss in this election."

III

THERE WAS never it appeared any attempt at any time to find middle ground. As far back as 6 October 2011, Ben Feller, AP White House Correspondent, reported that Barack Obama was defiant and frustrated at a press conference in which he aggressively challenged Republicans to get behind his jobs plan or explain why not, declaring that if Congress fails to act "the American people will run them out of town." The president used the White House news conference to attempt to heighten the pressure he's sought to create on the GOP by traveling around the country, into swing states and onto the home turf of key Republican foes including House Speaker Boehner and Texas Governor Rick Perry. And giving a bit of ground on his own plan, he endorsed a new proposal by Senate Democrats to tax millionaires to pay for his jobs program. "This is not a game," he said. As Feller reported, Obama made no apologies for his decision to abandon seeking compromise with Republicans in favor of assailing them, sometimes by name. He contended that he had gone out of his way to work with the GOP since becoming president, reaching hard-fought deals to raise the government's borrowing limit and avert a government shutdown, and had got nothing in return. "Each time, what we have seen is games playing," Obama said.

However the president predicted dire political consequences for his opponents if they don't go along. "I think the American people will run them out of town because they are frustrated and they know we need to do something big, something bold. We will just keep on going at it and hammering away until something gets done," he said. "And I would love nothing more than to see Congress act so aggressively that I can't campaign against them as a do-nothing Congress."

Republicans are resolutely opposed to much of Obama's jobs initiative, both for its tax increases for wealthier people and small businesses and its reprise of stimulus spending on roads, bridges and schools and grants to local governments to pay the salaries of teachers and first responders. They criticize his bill as another version of his $825 billion stimulus of 2009, one that this time would rely on raising taxes. But Obama insisted that the economy was weaker now than at the beginning of the year. Citing economists' estimates, he said his $447 billion jobs bill would help the economy grow by 2 per cent and create 1.9 million jobs. "At a time when so many people are having such a hard time, we have to have an approach, we have to take action that is big enough to meet the moment," he said.

Obama addressed the disaffection with politics pervasive among the public that's driven down his approval ratings – and even more so Congress' – as he seeks a second term. Appearing fed up, Obama blamed it on Republicans who he said refuse to cooperate with him even on issues where he said they once agreed with him. He talked about the ugly debate over raising the government's borrowing limit that consumed Capitol Hill and the White House over the summer, until Obama gave in to Republican demands for deep spending cuts without new taxes. "They don't get a sense that folks in this town are looking out for their interests," Obama said of Americans in general. "So if they see that over and over again, that cynicism is not going to be reduced until Congress actually proves their cynicism wrong by doing something. What the American people saw is that the Congress didn't care."

Obama also said the "Occupy Wall Street" demonstrators protesting against Wall Street and economic inequality are expressing the frustrations of the American public. He said he understands the public's concerns about how the nation's financial system works. And he said Americans see Wall Street as an example of the financial industry not always following the rules.

On 25 January 2012 Elspeth Reeve wrote in The Atlantic Wire that Boehner dismissed President Obama's campaign against a do-nothing Congress by saying "most Americans think we've got too many laws already," but Boehner's underlings don't think so. House Republicans "worry they're going to go home to campaign with a light legislative résumé," Politico's Jake Sherman reported. "That's funny, because their strategy since the 2010 elections has been to do as little as possible so Obama can't pad his résumé either. And with Congress's approval ratings in the gutter, Republicans are sick of blaming the Senate for their inaction," Sherman wrote. "They want real legislative victories, not just GOP bills that pass out of the House and go nowhere on the other side of the dome."

In his State of the Union address, Obama listed a number of bills he promised he'd sign right away: reform of the tax code, tax breaks for companies who bring back jobs from overseas, bills on energy and

215

infrastructure, a ban on congressional insider trading. But *The New York Times* Jonathan Chait wrote that "Obama knows full well that Republicans in Congress will block everything." He can't pass anything, but he can be populist. Obama's "agenda is dead, but his public standing has benefited," Chait said. "Perhaps one day Republicans will wish they had been a little more flexible, and had kept the old, wonky, bargaining Obama rather than the slashing populist who's cutting their throats."

But when Fox News' Chris Wallace asked Boehner why Congress has been one of the least productive ever – 80 laws were passed and a fifth of them were formalities –-the Speaker said he was just concentrating on "quantity over quality." But Republican lawmakers are unconvinced. "We need to get more done," said Rep. Steve Stivers told Politico. "House Republicans need to work with [conservative] Senate Democrats, not just Republicans, because we need 60. We not only have to work with Senate Republicans, we have to work with some conservative Senate Democrats because frankly, conservative Senate Democrats aren't that far away from Senate Republicans."

In the heat of a US presidential election year, with Americans immune to the polarized and bitter nature of political discourse, it takes a lot to shock them, especially in Washington, reports the Agence France Presse on 2 March 2012. But one ad at a DC Metro station – which starts off criticizing Obama's health care reforms and ends up telling the president to "go to hell" – goes beyond the pale, says Jim Moran, a Democratic congressman from Virginia. The advertisement is for "Sick and Sicker: When the Government Becomes Your Doctor," a documentary that interviews Canadian doctors and patients in the hope of showing how dangerous "Obamacare" is for the American people. "Barack Obama wants politicians and bureaucrats to control America's entire medical system. Go to hell Barack," the ad says. Moran wrote a letter to Metro general manager Richard Sarles calling for the removal of the advertisement. "The ad is deeply disrespectful of the President of the United States and does not belong in the Washington Metropolitan Area Transit Authority (WMATA) network," he wrote. It turns out that such language is within the accepted limits of American law and such advertisements are protected under the First Amendment of the US

Constitution, guaranteeing free speech. "WMATA advertising has been ruled by the courts as a public forum protected by the First Amendment of the Constitution, and we may not decline ads based on their political content," the Metro authority said in a written statement. "WMATA does not endorse the advertising on our system, and ads do not reflect the position of the Authority."

Democrats have accused Republicans of lowering the tone of the political discourse in the United States during this election season, in particular with highly personal attacks on the president. Arizona Governor Jan Brewer, a Republican, was widely condemned recently by Democrats for poking her finger at the president during an angry exchange on the tarmac after she greeted his arrival in Phoenix. But conservatives argue that the treatment Obama gets is no worse than what liberals dished out to former president George W. Bush, especially in his second term after the US-led invasion of Iraq.

The battle for Americans Lippmann wrote almost a century ago is not against crusted prejudice but against the chaos of a new freedom. We must give our attention not so much to the evils of authority, he said, but to the weaknesses of democracy. But how does a man go about such a task? he asked. "He faces an enormously complicated world, full of stirring and confusion and ferment. He hears of movements and agitations, criticisms and reforms, knows people who are devoted to causes, feels angry or hopeful at different times, goes to meetings, reads radical books, and accumulates a sense of uneasiness and pending change." Is it any different today than it was in Lippmann's time? I don't think so.

On 30 November 2012 Jeff Poor reported in The Daily Caller that former Speaker of the House Newt Gingrich acknowledged on the Hugh Hewitt Radio Show that his front-runner status would open up his political record to the same level of scrutiny that has already torpedoed other candidates. And presuming he is eventually debating President Obama instead of other Republicans, Gingrich said, he would emulate former President Ronald Reagan, whose catch-phrase, "There you go again", was the standard response to attacks from President Jimmy Carter in the 1980 presidential campaign. "Reagan thought for a long time about it," Gingrich said. "He came up with a very simple phrase, 'There you go again.' And during the debate between Reagan and Carter, every time Carter started lying (?), Reagan would just smile and say, 'There you go again.' And everybody in the country said, 'Got it. He's lying.' So, I'm happy to say I've already memorized 'There you go again.'"

Gingrich said he had other tactics, including challenging Obama to seven three-hour Lincoln-Douglas-style debates with a time-keeper and a moderator to combat negative attacks. But he said Obama would be forced to go "negative" if the electoral options were "positive." "I want him to have to stand on a platform and defend a billion dollars' worth of lies and smears," Gingrich said. "This is a president who cannot get re-elected with a positive campaign. If it's two positive choices ending up in food stamps with Obama versus paychecks with Gingrich, everybody knows we will beat him very badly. So we have to expect they're going to run a miserable, negative, vicious attack campaign. They'll be proud of it. They'll sit around on the evening telling each other how clever they are."

Was this why Obama believed he is the underdog in the 2012 election campaign and believes that the faltering economy is a drag on his presidency and is seriously impairing his chances of winning? As Russell Goldman reported on 3 October 2011, "Absolutely," he said in response to a question from ABC News' George Stephanopoulos about whether the odds were against him come November 2012, given the economy. "I'm used to being the underdog. But at the end of the day people are going to ask, who's got a vision?" The American people, he conceded, are "not better off" than they were four years ago. Obama said his proposed American Jobs Act will put construction workers, teachers and veterans to work and give "more consumers more confidence." Foreign affairs, the wars in Iraq and Afghanistan, and social issues like gay marriage will all be fodder on the campaign trail, but with the first caucus and primaries less than 100 days away, no issue looms larger for 2012 than the economy and jobs. The latest unemployment figures for the month of September will be released (shortly), but the jobless rate is not expected to significantly improve. And next year, leading up to the fall elections, the unemployment rate is expected to climb to its highest level since 1940.

With an approval rate that was hovering at around 40 per cent, Obama objected to New Jersey Governor Chris Christie's comments that he divided people more than united them. Republicans, he said, have stood in the way of working with him time and again to fix the economy. "At every step of way, I have tried to get the Republican Party to work with me on the biggest crisis of our lifetime. And each time we've gotten 'No'" he said. Obama called the 2012 race a "contest of values and vision" and a referendum on whether Americans believed the government should invest now in long-term improvements in education and infrastructure. The questions featured in an online interview, the first under a new alliance between ABC News and Yahoo! News, were generated by Internet users. More than 40,000 questions, including one from former Massachusetts Governor Mitt Romney, were submitted online. Asked which sites he visits to get the news, Obama noted that former Apple CEO Steve Jobs gave him an iPad to surf the Web. "You know I'm pretty eclectic," the president said. "I read a lot of news that I used to read in print, I read on the Web now. I go to ABCNews.com, of course, and also Yahoo! Typically, I read on the web what I read in hard copy."

In the *National Journal* of 3 January 2012, Naureen Khan in Sioux City, Iowa, wrote that Rick Santorum added a twist to the Republican argument that President Obama wants to make people more dependent on the federal government. He singled out blacks as people whose lives he would improve without using "somebody else's money." The comment came in response to a man's question about foreign influence on the U.S. economy. "How do we get off this crazy train? We've got so much foreign influence in this country now," the man said. "Where do we go from here?" In a lengthy answer, Santorum talked about reviving U.S. manufacturing and then pivoted to the government-dependency theme. "What President Obama wants to do, his economic plan is to make more people dependent upon government. To grow the government, to make sure we have more food stamps, and more SSI, and more Medicaid. Four in 10 children are now on government-provided health care. It just keeps expanding," Santorum said. He talked about how Iowa is going to get fined if more people don't sign up for Medicaid and then said, "They're pushing harder and harder to get more and more of you dependent upon them so they can get your vote. That's what the bottom line is. So I don't want to make black people's lives better by giving them somebody else's money. I want to give them the opportunity to go out and earn the money and provide for themselves and their families."

But there was a sense of a blight over what politicians were saying and more and more Americans felt an unwillingness to put their hearts into any new promise of fixing the problems. In an op-ed article published on the *Washington Post* website on 2 March 2012, Senator Olympia Snowe, R-Maine, detailed the factors that led her to announce that she won't run for re-election in November. The institution, she said, "is not living up to what the Founding Fathers envisioned." The Senate is supposed to be an "institutional check that ensures all voices are heard and considered," but it is not "living up to its billing." She criticized the Senate for brinksmanship and said each party works to block the other, instead of working together. "I do not believe that, in the near term, the Senate can correct itself from within … [but] I look forward to helping the country raise those voices to support the Senate returning to its deserved status and stature – but from outside the institution," Snowe concluded. Citing Ronald Brownstein's analysis of the *National Journal*'s vote ratings, Snowe said Congress is becoming more like a parliamentary system. "Everyone simply votes with their party and those in charge employ every possible tactic to block the other side."

Two months before on 13 January 2012, a Reuters report from Alex Dobuzinskis stated that late night comedian Stephen Colbert hinted that he was exploring a run in the Republican presidential primary in South Carolina, although the deadline has passed to get on the ballot. But that may not be the point. His announcement on his satirical *The Colbert Report* on Comedy Central gave Colbert an avenue for poking fun at how well-funded political action committees, operating at arm's length from a candidate, can spend to support that candidate. To a cheering studio audience, Colbert joked on his show that "for over a day now" residents of South Carolina had been crying out for someone who can restore our nation's former greatness to its current perfection. "Well, America, that someone is now," he said. "I am proud to announce that I am forming an exploratory committee to lay the groundwork for my possible candidacy for the president of the United States of South Carolina."

The point is, as Associated Press writer Tammy Webber had reported on 22 December 2011, Americans are frustrated by Congressional stalemates. As Americans watch yet another political drama play out on Capitol Hill – this time over whether to extend the payroll tax cut and jobless benefits – they have a question for Congress: Can't you all just get along? For once? "It's like, 'Kids, kids, kids,'" said Brenda Bissett, a lawyer from Santa Clarita, Calif., as she waited for coffee at a Starbucks in downtown Los Angeles. "It's just frustrating that there's no compromise. I think that both parties have been listening too much to their far ends."

Regardless of their backgrounds, incomes or political leanings, people say they are angry and downright disgusted by the posturing in Washington after the Senate approved a two-month extension of the payroll tax cut and adjourned for the holidays. Then House leaders balked at it. If lawmakers didn't act by 1 January, payroll taxes would jump almost $20 a week, or $1,000 a year, for a worker earning $50,000, and as much as $82 a week, or $4,272 a year, for a household with two high-paid workers. What's more, about 6 million people could lose unemployment benefits, and Medicare payments to doctors would be slashed. "The Senate ... should have tried to stay and resolve this for the American people," said Jorge Gonzalez, an accounting clerk at a law firm in Miami. "Partisan politics should be set aside for the best interest of the country."

IV

PRESIDENT OBAMA had urged congressional leaders to return to Washington to pass a short-term payroll tax cut extension before New Year's Day, promising in return to start working immediately on a full-year extension. House Republicans have insisted that both chambers instead negotiate a full-year agreement by the end of the year. Meanwhile, the public can only wait and wonder as even a quick perusal of the news shows. "I wish those guys would come and finish the job they started and deserted," said Sandi Dumich, a retired teacher from Schaumburg, Ill., who has taken a part-time job in a neuropsychologist's office to help pay bills. At Augie & Ray's, a popular eatery in East Hartford, Conn., the consensus among several diners was that the partisan bickering was eroding their already shaky faith in Congress. To some, that was just as frustrating as the idea that their paychecks could shrink. "It's us, the average Joe, that's getting caught in the middle," said Ray Ramsey, a retired utility meter technician who works part-time for a medical-supply company. Fellow diner Richard Longo, who owns a building-maintenance business, said he worries about the effect of the taxes on himself and his 30-plus employees. But he thinks there's a lot of blame to go around.

"I truly believe that if the sides were reversed, if we had a Republican president and a Democratic Congress, we'd still be going through the same thing," he said. But Scott Gessner, a Boston man who works with homeless women and children, said he's suspicious of House Republican demands for a yearlong extension. "We can't repeal Bush's tax hikes for the extremely wealthy, but we are going to let this one expire, which affects millions of millions of millions of more people and the middle class?" Gessner said. "What I'd like to know is ... what do the Democrats have to give up to get the one-year bill?"

A payroll tax increase would come at a vulnerable time for some people who already have been affected by falling property values and, in some cases, state tax increases, and some said they would spend less on non-essential things, like dining out. Others, though, said they were willing to pay more if it means reducing the deficit. "I understand every dollar is every dollar, but I think there are some bigger problems that we have here that can put a lot more money in your pocket than a $20 payroll tax," said Thomas Lowndes, who owns a real estate investment business in Charleston, S.C., and was in Louisville, Ky., for a basketball game. But almost all agreed that the partisan acrimony and 11th-hour crises in Washington are getting old. "It seems they want to bring down everything to the last minute and then figure it out," said David Kaiser, a researcher at a Miami college who said a tax increase wouldn't affect him significantly. Kaiser wanted "some way to send that message to them: That's not what they're hired for."

The tax cut lowered the Social Security tax on incomes of up to $106,800 from 6.2 per cent to 4.2 per cent. It has meant a maximum savings of $2,136 for an individual. Without a deal, Americans would begin 2012 facing a tax increase just as an election year begins. And many say the bickering has more to do with elections than economic ideals. "It's a fight between the parties. It's really not about the citizens," said Sandra Robinson, an administrative officer at the Department of the Interior in Little Rock, Ark., who depends on the extra money to help pay her daughter's college tuition. "They don't care about us." Greg Kirksey, a pastor in Little Rock, Ark., said a payroll tax increase would be little more than an inconvenience for him, but others are "talking about whether to buy dried beans or ground beef to get their protein. I'm not thinking anybody's really got the guts to make the hard decisions," he said. "They just keep putting a Band-Aid on, putting a Band-Aid on, kicking the can down the road a little farther."

In an election year, it's hard to turn on the television or read a newspaper without getting the sense that Americans are becoming ever more divided into red versus blue. But a new study finds that perception may be downright wrong, wrote Stephanie Pappas in LiveScience.com on 29 January 2012. In fact, she says, political polarization among the public has barely budged at all over the past 40 years, according to research presented on 27 January at the annual meeting of the Society for Personality and Social Psychology. But, crucially, people vastly overestimate how polarized the American public is – a tendency toward exaggeration that is especially strong in the most extreme Democrats and Republicans. "Strongly identified Republicans or Democrats perceive and exaggerate polarization more than weakly identified Republicans or Democrats or political independents," said study researcher John Chambers, a professor of psychology at the University of Florida. The people who see the world split into two opposing factions are also most likely to vote and become politically active, Chambers said in a talk at the meeting. This means that while real growing polarization is illusory, the perception of polarization could drive the political process.

Inspired by polling data showing that two-thirds of Americans believe the United States is becoming more politically polarized, with the gap between the political parties widening, Chambers and his colleagues looked at nationally representative data stretching from 1970 to 2004. More than 43,000 respondents over the years have participated in the large-scale American National Election Survey, though not all answered all questions. So the researchers had between 4,000 and 26,000 individuals to work with on various questions. The respondents indicated their political beliefs by answering questions on their opinions on a wild variety of issues, from government-provided health care to defense spending to women's equality. They also reported how they believe a "typical" Republican and Democrat would feel about these same issues. "Using these two measures, we were able to look at actual and perceived differences in polarization," Chambers said.

They found that actual polarization has remained steady since the 1970s. The historical responses also showed that people have always over-estimated polarization. Even decades ago, in times now remembered as cooperative and cordial, people pegged political disagreements much more than they really were. When the researchers broke down the respondents by political positions, they found that not everyone judges polarization in the same way. Everyone over-estimates it, but political independents are much closer to the mark than strong Republicans or strong Democrats, who tend to see the gulf between themselves and the other party as impossibly wide. Moderate Republicans and moderate Democrats were in-between, perceiving more polarization than independents but less than the extreme ends of the parties.

In a separate study, University of Colorado, Boulder, psychology professor Leaf Van Boven looked at why people at the political extremes might over-estimate polarization. The answer seems to be that they project their own strong, emotional thought processes onto others, Van Boven and his colleagues concluded. In their study, they presented students with a fictional policy that would try to lure out-of-state students to campus with preferential treatment, including first pick of classes and dorms. Unsurprisingly, this fake proposal yielded polarized views. "This proposal is bulls ...!" one student wrote. Another indicated support, adding, "I am biased, because I am out of state, and I want the sweet hookups." When the researchers asked students to indicate how they thought other students felt about the proposal, those who themselves opposed or supported it most strongly assumed that others would also feel strongly, in support or opposition. When asked how they came to their conclusions about the proposal and how they believed others came to their conclusions, the students gave themselves credit for more fairness and less self-interest than they did others. But they also assumed that everyone gave equal weight to emotion and extensive thought. "If someone has a strong moral reaction and says 'This is a moral issue', they may reasonably think that others, both on their side and other side, will think in the same way," Van Boven explained. "Although we tend to see the world as divided between blue and red, in reality, the world has much greater shades of purple," Chambers said. "There is more common ground than we realize."

But on 28 February 2012 Natalie Wolchover wrote in LiveScience.com that scientists say people aren't smart enough for democracy to flourish. The democratic process, they say, relies on the assumption that citizens (the majority of them, at least) can recognize the best political candidate, or best policy idea, when they see it. But a growing body of research has revealed an unfortunate aspect of the human psyche that would seem to disprove this notion, and imply instead that democratic elections produce mediocre leadership and policies. The research, led by David Dunning, a psychologist at Cornell University, shows that incompetent people are inherently unable to judge the competence of other people, or the quality of those people's ideas. For example, if people lack expertise on tax reform, it is very difficult for them to identify the candidates who are actual experts. They simply lack the mental tools needed to make meaningful judgments.

As a result, no amount of information or facts about political candidates can override the inherent inability of many voters to accurately evaluate them. On top of that, "very smart ideas are going to be hard for people to adopt, because most people don't have the sophistication to recognize how good an idea is," Dunning told Life's Little Mysteries. He and colleague Justin Kruger, formerly of Cornell and now of New York University, have demonstrated again and again that people are self-delusional when it comes to their own intellectual skills. Whether the researchers are testing people's ability to rate the funniness of jokes, the correctness of grammar, or even their own performance in a game of chess, the duo has found that people always assess their own performance as "above average" – even people who, when tested, actually perform at the very bottom of the pile.

We're just as undiscerning about the skills of others as about ourselves. "To the extent that you are incompetent, you are a worse judge of incompetence in other people," Dunning said. In one study, the researchers asked students to grade quizzes that tested for grammar skill. "We found that students who had done worse on the test itself gave more inaccurate grades to other students." Essentially, they didn't recognize the correct answer even when they saw it. The reason for this disconnect is simple: "If you have gaps in your knowledge in a given area, then you're not in a position to assess your own gaps or the gaps of others," Dunning said. Strangely though, in these experiments, people tend to readily and accurately agree on who the worst performers are, while failing to recognize the best performers. The most incompetent among us serve as canaries in the coal mine signifying a larger quandary in the concept of democracy; truly ignorant people may be the worst judges of candidates and ideas, Dunning said, but we all suffer from a degree of blindness stemming from our own personal lack of expertise.

Mato Nagel, a sociologist in Germany, recently implemented Dunning and Kruger's theories by computer-simulating a democratic election. In his mathematical model of the election, he assumed that voters' own leadership skills were distributed on a bell curve – some were really good leaders, some, really bad, but most were mediocre – and that each voter was incapable of recognizing the leadership skills of a political candidate as being better than his or her own. When such an election was simulated, candidates whose leadership skills were only slightly better than average always won. Nagel concluded that democracies rarely or never elect the best leaders. Their advantage over dictatorships or other forms of government is merely that they "effectively prevent lower-than-average candidates from becoming leaders."

And then there was on 22 March 2012 the Etch A Sketch remark. Eric Fehrnstrom, Romney's senior campaign adviser, was asked in a CNN interview whether the former Massachusetts governor had been forced to adopt conservative positions in the rugged race that could hurt his standing with moderates. "I think you hit a reset button for the fall campaign. Everything changes," Fehrnstrom responded. "It's almost like an Etch A Sketch. You can kind of shake it up, and we start all over again."

Rival candidates Rick Santorum and Newt Gingrich, who were vying for conservative support against the more moderate Romney, seized on the comment as indicative of their longstanding criticism that Romney shifts his positions on issues such as health care reform and abortion to suit his political needs. Gingrich brought out an Etch A Sketch at a campaign appearance in Louisiana, where the next primary was to take place that weekend. "You have to stand for something that lasts longer than this," Gingrich said at the Lake Charles event, holding the drawing toy invented in 1959. "You could not have found a more perfect illustration of why people distrust Romney than to have his (adviser) say that the Etch A Sketch allows you to erase everything in the general election," Gingrich added. "You have to read the guy's quote to realize if he had set out to highlight for everybody why we distrust Romney. I think he couldn't have done a better job."

Santorum's campaign posted a photo on Twitter of the candidate using an Etch A Sketch, saying it showed him "studying up on (Romney's) policy positions." Romney "will say what he needs to say to win the election before him, and if he has to say something different because it's a different election and a different group of voters, he will say that, too," Santorum said while campaigning in Harvey, Louisiana. "Well, that should be comforting to all of you who are voting in this primary."

Fehrnstrom later said he was referring to the campaign as a whole and Romney spoke to reporters after an afternoon event to try to exercise some damage control. "Organizationally, a general election campaign takes on a different profile," Romney said. "The issues I am running on will be exactly the same. I am running as a conservative Republican. I was a conservative Republican governor. I will be running as a conservative Republican nominee, at that point hopefully, for president. The policies and positions are the same." However, the Etch A Sketch remark – coming on what should have been a triumphant day that happened to be Romney's 43rd wedding anniversary – threatened to sap attention from his growing momentum toward winning the nomination.

Romney's Illinois victory showed "the writing's on the wall" for the rest of the field, said CNN analyst Erick Erickson, a longtime Romney critic. "This comes down to Mitt Romney," Erickson said. "Not only is he the front-runner but the nominee. This is a clear win for Mitt Romney tonight in a state with blue-collar voters, with industrial voters and suburban voters." The Illinois result followed established patterns in the Republican race, with Romney doing well in urban and suburban areas while Santorum, the former Pennsylvania senator who is his main conservative rival, ran strong in rural areas. Romney had 55 per cent of the total with 99 per cent of precincts reporting in Chicago while Santorum notched 25 per cent according to the city's election website. In Lake County, one of the surrounding counties near Chicago, Romney had 56 per cent with all precincts reporting, according to the clerk's office website, and Santorum had 28 per cent. The results gave Romney at least 41 of the 54 delegates up for grabs in the state, increasing his total to 562, according to CNN's estimate. Santorum is second with 249, Gingrich third with 137 and Paul last with 69. A total of 1,144 delegates is needed to clinch the GOP nomination.

Romney's campaign trumpeted the Illinois showing as a broad-based triumph, seeking to overcome questions about the candidate's ability to win over the conservative GOP base. "Romney won with tea party voters. He won with Catholics," campaign spokeswoman Andrea Saul said. "There are a lot of groups within the Republican Party, and Gov. Romney has won their votes." In remarks to cheering supporters, Romney resumed his front-runner attacks on Obama's economic, health care and spending policies. "The simple truth is, this president does not understand the genius of this economy," Romney said, adding that "the American economy is fueled by freedom."

Santorum skipped Illinois on primary night and awaited the results in Gettysburg in his home state of Pennsylvania. In his concession speech, below a banner that proclaimed "Freedom," he said he was staying in the race to battle a government that he complained was "trying to order us around." This is an election about fundamental and foundational things, Santorum said, attacking Romney's claim of greater business and government management experience. "This is an election about not who's the best person to manage Washington or manage the economy. We don't need a manager, we need someone who's going to pull government up by the roots and do something to liberate the private sector in America."

Romney's Illinois victory followed an overwhelming triumph in Puerto Rico, where Romney got 83 per cent of the vote and picked up all 20 delegates at stake.

Gingrich, who appeared increasingly unlikely to mount another comeback after two previous campaign surges, issued a statement blasting Romney for relying on his vast financial resources rather than offering "solutions that hold the president accountable for his failures." To defeat Barack Obama, he said, Republicans can't nominate a candidate who relies on outspending his opponents 7-1.

V

ON THE OTHER side of the world, the war continued in Afghanistan and White House Correspondent Olivier Knox wrote in The Ticket on 23 February 2012 that President Obama had apologized in a letter to Afghan President Hamid Karzai for the burning of Korans at the largest American military base in Afghanistan, according to the White House and Karzai's office. The incident at Bagram Air Base fueled days of angry protests in the war-torn country. "I wish to express my deep regret for the reported incident," Karzai's office quoted Obama as saying in the message. "The error was inadvertent; I assure you that we will take the appropriate steps to avoid any recurrence, to include holding accountable those responsible."

Three days of protests over the incident left 14 people dead, including two American soldiers shot dead when an Afghan soldier turned his weapon on them at their base in Khogyani in eastern Nangarhar province, district governor Mohammad Hassan told AFP. US Ambassador Ryan Crocker had delivered the letter to Karzai, according to US National Security Council spokesman Tommy Vietor. Obama "expressed our regret and apologies over the incident in which religious materials were unintentionally mishandled at Bagram Airbase," Vietor said in an emailed statement. The incident led the Taliban to call on Afghans to retaliate against the US-led coalition forces in Afghanistan and drew a stern rebuke from Karzai himself.

This was the second time this year that the U.S has apologized to Karzai. The first time was on 12 January 2012. According to Associated Press writers Robert Burns in Washington and Slobodan Lekic in Kabul, Karzai condemned a video depicting what appears to be four U.S. Marines urinating on the corpses of Taliban fighters. A presidential statement described the act as "completely inhumane" and called on the U.S. military to punish the Marines. The Marine Corps said it is investigating the YouTube video but had not yet verified its origin or authenticity. The case was referred to the Naval Criminal Investigative Service, the Navy's worldwide law enforcement organization. The Afghan Ministry of Defense also condemned the actions in the video, which it described as "shocking".

The NATO-led security force in Afghanistan released a statement later saying, "This disrespectful act is inexplicable and not in keeping with the high moral standards we expect of coalition forces." The International Security Assistance Force said the actions "appear to have been conducted by a small group of U.S. individuals, who apparently are no longer serving in Afghanistan." The statement did not identify the personnel or explain why the ISAF thought they had left the country. Sen. John McCain, a Navy veteran who fought in the Vietnam War, said the incident "makes me so sad." McCain, the top Republican on the Senate Armed Services Committee, called the Marine Corps one of America's strongest institutions and said its image has apparently been tarnished by "a handful of obviously undisciplined people." Appearing on CBS *This Morning*, the Arizona Republican said, "There should be an investigation and these young people should be punished."

The Council on Islamic-American Relations, a prominent Muslim civil rights and advocacy group based in Washington, protested the video in a letter faxed to Defense Secretary Leon Panetta. "We condemn this apparent desecration of the dead as a violation of our nation's military regulations and of international laws of war prohibiting such disgusting and immoral actions," the group wrote. "If verified as authentic, the video shows behavior that is totally unbecoming of American military personnel and that could ultimately endanger other soldiers and civilians," the letter said. Marine Corps headquarters at the Pentagon said: "The actions portrayed are not consistent with our core values and are not indicative of the character of the Marines in our Corps. This matter will be fully investigated." A Marine Corps spokesman, Lt. Col. Stewart Upton, added, "Allegations of Marines not doing the right thing in regard to dead Taliban insurgents are very serious and, if proven, represent a failure to adhere to the high standards expected of American military personnel."

But according to Anne Flaherty of the Associated Press Republican presidential hopeful Rick Perry accused the Obama administration of "over-the-top rhetoric" and "disdain for the military" in its condemnation of the video that purportedly showed the four Marines urinating on corpses in Afghanistan. Perry's comments put him at odds with McCain, the top Republican on the Senate Armed Services Committee, who had said the images could damage the war effort. "The Marine Corps prides itself that we don't lower ourselves to the level of the enemy," McCain said when asked about Perry's position. "So it makes me sad more than anything else, because ... I can't tell you how wonderful these people (Marines) are. And it hurts their reputation and their image."

No one has been charged in the case, but officials in the U.S. and abroad have called for swift punishment of the four Marines. Defense Secretary Leon Panetta said that he worried the video could be used by the Taliban to undermine Afghan peace talks. A military criminal investigation and an internal Marine Corps review are under way. The Geneva Conventions forbid the desecration of the dead. Perry said the Marines involved should be reprimanded but not prosecuted on criminal charges. "Obviously, 18-, 19-year-old kids make stupid mistakes all too often. And that's what's occurred here," the Texas governor told CNN's *State of the Union*.

But Perry was not the only Republican protesting the President's action. GOP presidential candidate Rick Santorum slammed President Obama for apologizing to Afghans for the burning of Korans at a U.S. military base on 26 February 2012 on ABC's *This Week*. "There was nothing deliberately done wrong here. This was something that happened as a mistake. Killing Americans in uniform is not a mistake," said Santorum. "Say it's unfortunate... but to apologize for something that was not an intentional act is something that the president of the United States in my opinion should not have done." Protests erupted in Afghanistan after the accidental burning and two American troops were killed by an Afghan soldier. "I think it shows weakness," said Santorum on the apology. However Santorum was not the first Republican to criticize President Obama for his actions. Republican presidential candidate Newt Gingrich said it was "an outrage" for the president to issue an apology.

It's clear that Americans don't feel as comfortable as they were before all the talk about a weak America and in the *National Journal* of 26 February 2012, Chris Frates reported that former national security adviser Zbigniew Brzezinski, who served under President Carter, said the United States has to make clear to Israel that an Israeli attack on Iran is not in U.S. interests. "We don't need to go to war," he said in an interview on CNN's Fareed Zakaria GPS. "And we have to make that very clear to our Israeli friends. We're not going to go to war. They're not going to go to war by flying over our airspace over Iraq. We're not going to support them. If they do it, they will be on their own. The consequences will be theirs, because the price we'll all pay if they start a massive war, which the Iranians interpret as being done with our connivance, will be disastrous for us in Afghanistan, in Iraq, in the terms of oil, stability in the Middle East more generally."

As tension mounted between the U.S. and its allies and Iran over the country's nuclear program, with economic sanctions dragging on and a European Union oil embargo pending this summer, there has been a great deal of speculation over whether the U.S. or Israel will mount a military strike against nuclear targets in Iran. Gen. Martin Dempsey, chairman of the Joint Chiefs of Staff, spoke out against a military option right now, saying that diplomacy and sanctions may yet work. Brzezinski said that Israel will be tempted to attack Iran before the elections because it will be politically difficult for President Obama to oppose. He said the Israelis are pushing the United States to offer the Iranians a compromise that the Iranians cannot accept "and then, prior to the election, they'll be tempted to strike." Obama, he said, should tell Israel that "the Iranians would blame us for it. They'll take action against us. We'll be paying the price. This is not acceptable and we want you to know that. ... Most Israelis, we also have to remember, most Israelis don't support a war," he said. "The American Jewish community in the majority is not for it. ... So when the president speaks, he speaks with some degree of political credibility, not only here, but also among the Israelis."

On Syria's civil war and President Bashar al-Assad's brutal crackdown, Brzezinski said the United States shouldn't get out front, but rather support any solution put forward by Turkey and Saudi Arabia, who are the U.S. allies in the region. "I think it's far from clear yet that Assad can, in fact, be overthrown at this stage," he said. And as Syria's bloodshed deepens, the British-born first lady has become an object of contempt for many, a Marie Antoinette figure who shopped online for crystal-encrusted Christian Louboutin stilettos while her country burned. The European Union slapped sanctions on Asma Assad, the 36-year-old wife of the president who for the past decade offered a veneer of respectability to one of the world's ruthless dictatorships. The Syrian government's crackdown on the year-old uprising has shattered the image of her as a glamorous, reform-minded woman who could help bring progressive values to a country that has been ruled by the Assad family dynasty for more than 40 years. The European action – the latest punishment imposed by world leaders on Syria for its crackdown – bans her from traveling to EU countries and freezing any assets she may have there. "She is one of the regime's deceptions," said Amer Mattar, a 26-year-old Syrian who recently fled the country because of the violence that has killed 8,000 people in the past year.

VI

WAS PRESIDENT Barack Obama back in the good graces of women? He was. This was the view of two Associated Press writers, Jennifer Agiesta and Laurie Kellman on 27 February 2012. The President's support had dropped among this critical constituency just before the New Year began and the presidential campaign got under way in earnest. But his standing with female voters is strengthening, polls show, as the economy improves and social issues, including birth control, become a bigger part of the nation's political discourse. "Republicans are making a big mistake with this contraception talk, and I'm pretty sure that they are giving (the election) to Obama," said Patricia Speyerer, 87, of McComb, Miss., a GOP-leaning independent. "It's a stupid thing."

The recent furor over whether religious employers should be forced to pay for their workers' contraception is certainly a factor but hardly the only reason for women warming up to Obama again after turning away from him late last year. For Obama, there is no more crucial constituency than women. They make up a majority of voters in presidential elections, and a bit more of them identify with his party. He would not be president today without topping Republican John McCain in that group in 2008. And Republicans would need to win a sizable share, more than about 40 percent, of female voters to beat him. Though the economy remains the top concern among both women and men, an array of social issues – gay marriage, access to birth control and whether cancer research should be kept separate from the issue of abortion – have returned to the nation's political conversation since December. And both parties have snapped up those issues to awaken their staunchest supporters.

Republicans from Capitol Hill to the presidential campaign trail focused particularly on a requirement in Obama's health care law for some religious employers to pay for birth control. Obama then adjusted that policy by instead directing insurance companies to pay for birth control and Democrats are running with a message that Republicans want to upend long-established rights for women. "Women are used to making decisions and running their lives," said Linda Young, president of the National Women's Political Caucus, which favors abortion rights. "To hear their right to contraception questioned in 2012 is shocking, and it's gotten a lot of people's attention."

Republicans say the economy will again overtake that discussion and it will be clear the GOP offers families more once Republicans choose a nominee, turn their fire from each other to Obama and make their case on issues such as gas prices and the deficit. "The economic indicators, we have to admit, are very slowly improving, and that is something that has always affected the female vote," said Rae Lynne Chornenky, president of the National Federation of Republican Women. "Until we get a candidate I don't think the full story can be told." People in both political parties are keeping this (cultural narrative) alive because they're trying to excite their bases, said Republican Brian Flaherty, who served as a Connecticut legislator for 15 years. An AP-GfK poll conducted on 16-20 February showed that on overall approval Obama has gained 10 percentage points among women since December, from 43 per cent to 53 per cent, even though his administration seemed to stumble over whether religious employers should be forced to pay for contraception. Women also are the reason behind Obama's lead over Republican hopefuls Mitt Romney and Rick Santorum: In one-on-one matchups, Obama beats Romney 54 per cent to 41 per cent and tops Santorum 56 per cent to 40 per cent among women, but virtually ties each Republican among men. Women are Obama's to lose: They are more apt to identify with Democrats and give that party higher favorability than are men.

Over time, there hasn't been much shift in women's views of the Democratic Party, but views of the GOP have become more polarized since the AP last asked about the issue in January 2011. Thirty-nine per cent of Republican women hold a "very favorable" view of the party, compared with 27 per cent a year ago. At the same time, 57 per cent of Democratic women now give the GOP a deeply unfavorable rating, the first time that figure has topped 50 per cent. Republicans insist their objections to Obama's policy on birth control coverage are about government infringing on the freedom of religion, not about contraception, which is supported by a broad majority of Americans. "Well, I'm a Roman Catholic, too," said Speyerer. She recalls that in the 1940s New Orleans, where she was born and married, it was illegal to publish anything about birth control, "and I don't want to see that happen again."

Democrats already have sought to capitalize on that sentiment, holding a faux hearing with a single woman denied the chance to testify about contraception to a Republican-controlled House committee. Senate Democrats have agreed to debate a measure by Republican Sen. Roy Blunt of Missouri that would allow health plans to deny coverage for any service that violates the sponsor's beliefs. And a coalition of women's groups called HERvotes is holding a news conference in Washington to protest the renewed questioning of long-established rights for women.

However according to a Reuters report on 28 December 2011 voter turnout will likely drop substantially in the 2012 election, due in part to decreased interest among young people who flocked to the polls in 2008 to help elect President Barack Obama. A report by the Center for the Study of the American Electorate at American University predicted that the drop in turnout among young people will likely contribute to a decline in overall voter turnout in the November election after near record numbers in the last two presidential elections. "The election is likely to offer a minimum of hope and a maximum of televised invective – likely between the perception of a failed president and a party of failed ideas magnified by an unprecedented level of scurrilous and vitriolic and often ad hominem television advertising," wrote Curtis Gans, director of the center. "Against this backdrop, it is hard to envision anything other than a substantial decline in turnout." Gans said the 2008 election had the highest turnout since 1960 due in part to a sharp increase in voting by college-educated youth and record numbers of African-Americans going to the polls. But he said the 2012 election would be different amid reduced enthusiasm for all of the candidates.

Olivier Knox writing in The Ticket on 5 July 2012 stated that President Obama's re-election campaign charged that Mr. Romney hoped to use word of his eye-popping $100-million June fundraising haul as, essentially, a staggeringly expensive and carefully orchestrated smokescreen. The remarkable total, if confirmed, was sure to fan the flames of fears, frequently and publicly expressed by team Obama, that Romney will out-raise him. But Obama campaign spokesman Ben LaBolt said Romney's leaked total was aimed to "distract" voters from a pair of news reports about the Republican's personal finances and renewed focus on his health care plan after the Supreme Court upheld "Obamacare". Politico's Mike Allen first reported the total, which includes contributions to both Romney's campaign and the Romney Victory Fund, a joint account between the Romney campaign and the Republican National Committee.

"Mitt Romney is trying to distract from a week when he took contradictory positions on the freeloader penalty in the Affordable Care Act and we learned more about his offshore finances in Switzerland, Bermuda, and the Cayman Islands," LaBolt said in an email statement. The Obama and Romney camps have struggled to respond to the Supreme Court's ruling that the fine, imposed on Americans who do not buy health care, is a tax – a provision in both of their health care overhauls. Obama aides have insisted it is a penalty. Romney's camp initially agreed, but Romney himself later said it was a tax when imposed at the federal level but not at the state level. LaBolt was also referring to news reports in *Vanity Fair* and by the Associated Press regarding Romney's offshore holdings. The Obama campaign has frequently used the former Massachusetts governor's personal finances to paint him as out of touch with struggling Americans. "Americans are less concerned about how much money he raised to get himself elected and more interested in what he would do after repealing health reform, which he has refused to share, and why he won't disclose the necessary tax returns that prove whether or not he paid any U.S. taxes on his shell corporation in Bermuda," LaBolt said.

On 8 July 2012 David Espo of the Associated Press wrote that Republicans and Democrats in Congress who congratulated themselves for passing relatively routine legislation before July 4 are returning to the Capitol for a summer stocked with political show votes and no serious role for bipartisanship. Any thought of compromise on major issues – taxes, spending, deficit control or immigration among them – would have to wait until after the election or the New Year, he wrote. So, too, with a farm bill. It cleared the Senate on a bipartisan vote and is now at risk for becoming sidetracked in the House.

Senate Democrats are not without their own July agenda, beginning with a business tax cut that is set for a test vote. They also want to end existing tax breaks for the costs businesses incur in moving jobs overseas. This measure dovetails nicely with Obama's attempts to cast Romney as a champion outsourcer of jobs during his career as a businessman. In addition, they may set up a vote on legislation to require disclosure for individuals making high-dollar contributions to political organizations that spend millions on campaign commercials. Whatever the merits of these proposals, Republican and Democratic aides say there is no expectation any of them will pass this summer. Instead, they say, each is designed to make lawmakers on the other side of the political aisle choose between a popular position on the one hand and political orthodoxy within their own party on the other.

By their own count, House Republicans have voted more than 30 times to repeal, defund or erode the health care overhaul that stands as Obama's signature domestic achievement yet fares poorly in public opinion polling. "The law I passed is here to stay," the president said, brushing aside the latest Republican assault. But if anything, Republicans are more eager than ever to hold a vote to repeal it, following a majority opinion from Chief Justice John Roberts that said the law was constitutional because it imposes a tax, not a penalty, on anyone who refuses to purchase insurance. The vote will take place in the midst of a $9 million television advertising campaign by the conservative Americans for Prosperity.

The commercial includes a video of Obama saying the law "is absolutely not a tax increase." Referring to the court's ruling, the announcer rebuts him, saying, "Now we know that's not true," and the ad calls for repeal of the legislation. On tax cuts, Obama and Republicans compromised once, and they may again – after the election. But for now, the president has pledged he won't agree to another renewal of the reductions on individuals earning over $200,000 or couples making more than $250,000 a year. The dispute is one of the main issues to be presented to voters this fall. It's a showdown Republicans are eager to have. "Working families and small business should not be saddled with the uncertainty of a looming tax increase as they attempt to invest and grow for the remainder of the year," House Majority Leader Eric Cantor, R-Va., wrote this spring in a memo to the rank and file.

More disclosure for political contributions generally enjoys public support in the polls, but Republican outside groups, more than Democratic ones, are awash in large donations from anonymous donors. The Senate Republican leader, Mitch McConnell of Kentucky, calls the Democratic legislation a threat to the Constitution's guarantee of free speech. Its supporters "have a simple view: If the Supreme Court is no longer willing to limit the speech of those who oppose their agenda, they'll find other ways to do it," he said. Nor is there much prospect for immediate compromise on the farm bill, meaning the likeliest outcome is a one-year or two-year extension of current programs that puts off difficult decisions over spending cuts. Bipartisan legislation passed the Senate to cut $23 billion over a decade. The bill before the House Agriculture Committee would chop $35 billion.

Some conservatives want to slice more; other Republicans, as well as Democrats, prefer less. Several officials say it's unlikely the GOP leadership will permit the full House to vote on the bill with their own rank and file divided. That means deferring politically difficult decisions about food stamps, commodity programs and other accounts until after the election. Lawmakers produced a short-term, one-year, solution to prevent an increase in interest rates on federal student loans for an estimated 7.4 million new borrowers. Another portion of the same bill pays for highway construction and other transportation programs for two years. Its approval ended an unbroken string of nine short-term extensions dating back three years – evidence itself of Congress' chronic difficulty in compromising.

Sounding every bit like the candidate he is, President Obama called for a one-year extension of Bush-era tax cuts on annual income up to $250,000, while letting those that chiefly benefit the very wealthy expire on schedule at year's end. The proposal re-ignited an election-year fight designed to polish his credentials as a champion for middle-class Americans. "It's time to let the tax cuts for the wealthiest Americans, folks like myself, to expire," he said in the East Room of the White House, surrounded by people he warned could see a $2,200 jump in their tax bill if the rates expire. "I'm not proposing anything radical here," he insisted, casting the move as a return to the tax rates in force under President Bill Clinton, who presided over an era of robust job growth. Obama's announcement echoed his core campaign message on the economy, the top issue on voters' minds. He did not refer to Mitt Romney by name, but tried to make the debate over the upper-bracket tax cuts central to the election. "The fate of the tax cut for the wealthiest Americans will be decided by the outcome of the next election. My opponent will fight to keep them in place, I will fight to end them," he said. "The American people are with me on this." Obama aides say they hope that the "tax fairness" argument will win over voters struggling in the fitful economy three and a half years after he took office vowing to fix it.

With national unemployment at 8.2 per cent and little relief expected between now and 6 November, the Obama campaign has sought to convince struggling Americans that he has their best interests at heart. He has urged voters to see the election as a choice between his approach and Romney's, not as a referendum on his record. The White House and Congress will face the issue in earnest after the election, with the expiration looming. But even before Obama spoke, Republicans declared it dead on arrival. "President Obama is still asleep at the switch when it comes to our economy and jobs," Republican House Speaker John Boehner said in a statement that mocked the initiative as quixotic. "How will these small business tax hikes create jobs? Even Democratic congressional leaders and former President Clinton have turned their back on this proposal," Boehner said. That was an apparent reference to Democratic House Minority Leader Nancy Pelosi and Democratic Sen. Chuck Schumer's call for extending the tax cuts that affect income below $1 million.

Mitt Romney's campaign also blasted the proposal, with spokeswoman Andrea Saul calling it "a massive tax increase" and saying "it proves again that the president doesn't have a clue how to get America working again and help the middle class." Unlike President Obama, "Governor Romney understands that the last thing we need to do in this economy is raise taxes on anyone," Saul said in a statement emailed to reporters.

The president's proposal would extend tax cuts on annual income up to $250,000. Americans making more would still see benefits up to that level. Obama has said that failing to raise taxes on the wealthiest will mean cash-strapped state and federal governments have to make deeper cuts to education, infrastructure and scientific research. ABC News, citing the Tax Policy Center, reported that raising taxes in line with the president's approach would affect 2.5 per cent of small businesses, a total of 894,000 businesses. Obama called the upper-bracket tax cuts "a major driver of our deficit" yet "the least likely to promote growth." And, he noted, "It's not like I like to pay taxes. I might feel differently if we were still in surplus."

Obama signed legislation in December 2010 to extend all of the Bush-era tax cuts to the end of this year. But even then he made clear that he favored letting the reductions for the highest-income Americans expire. He has consistently said since then that the wealthiest should pay more in taxes. Republicans have cast this as Obama pushing a tax increase on investors, and warned that it will smother already weak job growth. But Republican opposition may only boost the initiative's political value to the president, who has told voters that the chief obstacle to the recovery is a Republican-engineered "stalemate" in polarized Washington. "The choice in this election is between the President's plan to build this economy from the middle class out, promoting job creation and reducing the deficit in a balanced way, or Mitt Romney's plan to return to the same top-down policies that crashed our economy and decimated the middle class in the first place," Obama campaign spokesman Ben LaBolt said in a statement. "Today, Mitt Romney made that choice even more crystal clear."

Several Democratic senators facing difficult re-election fights have signaled that they will break with the president on the issue. But with Republicans pointing to Pelosi's past comments as evidence of a Democratic schism at the very top, a senior Democratic House aide told reporters by email that "Democrats support immediate extension of the middle-income tax cuts." Republicans are very clear: they continue to hold tax cuts for the middle class hostage to costly and unnecessary tax breaks for the wealthiest Americans, even though tax cuts for the rich have created more debt and won't produce jobs, the aide said on condition of anonymity. "Democrats say pass the extension of the middle income tax cuts now and end the uncertainty."

Girls seeking abortions in New Hampshire must first tell their parents or a judge, some employers in Alabama must verify new workers' U.S. residency, and California students will be the first in the country to receive mandatory lessons about the contributions of gays and lesbians under state laws set to take effect at the start of 2012, Andrew Welsh-Huggins of the Associated Press reported on 28 December 2011. Many laws reflect the nation's concerns over immigration, the cost of government and the best way to protect and benefit young people, including regulations on sports concussions. Alabama, with the country's toughest immigration law, is enacting a key provision requiring all employers who do business with any government entity to use a federal system known as E-Verify to check that all new employees are in the country legally.

Georgia is putting a similar law into effect requiring any business with 500 or more employees to use E-Verify to check the employment eligibility of new hires. The requirement is being phased in, with all employers with more than 10 employees to be included by July 2013. Supporters said they wanted to deter illegal immigrants from coming to Georgia by making it tougher for them to work. Critics said that changes to immigration law should come at the federal level and that portions of the law already in effect are already hurting Georgia. "It is destroying Georgia's economy and it is destroying the fabric of our social network in South Georgia," Paul Bridges, mayor of the onion-farming town of Uvalda, said in November. He is part of a lawsuit challenging the new law.

Tennessee will also require businesses to ensure employees are legally authorized to work in the U.S. but exempts employers with five or fewer workers and allows them to keep a copy of the new hire's driver's license instead of using E-Verify.

A South Carolina law would allow officials to yank the operating licenses of businesses that don't check new hires' legal status through E-verify. A federal judge blocked parts of the law that would have required police to check the immigration status of criminal suspects or people stopped for traffic violations they think might be in the country illegally, and that would have made it a crime for illegal immigrants to transport or house themselves. California is also addressing illegal immigration, but with a bill that allows students who entered the country illegally to receive private financial aid at public colleges. Many laws aim to protect young people. In Colorado, coaches will be required to bench players as young as 11 when they are believed to have suffered a head injury. The young athletes will also need medical clearance to return to play.

The law also requires coaches in public and private schools and even volunteer Little League and Pop Warner football coaches to take free annual online training to recognize the symptoms of a concussion. At least a dozen other states have enacted similar laws with the support of the National Football League. People 18 and under in Illinois will have to wear seat belts while riding in taxis for school-related purposes, and Illinois school boards can now suspend or expel students who make explicit threats on websites against other students or school employees. Florida will take control of lunch and other school food programs from the federal government, allowing the state to put more Florida-grown fresh fruit and vegetables on school menus. Agriculture Commissioner Adam Putnam says the change will help children eat healthier. A California law will add gays and lesbians and people with disabilities to the list of social and ethnic groups whose contributions must be taught in history lessons in public schools. The law also bans teaching materials that reflect poorly on gays or particular religions.

Opponents have filed five potential initiatives to repeal the requirement outright or let parents remove their children while gays' contributions are being taught. In New Hampshire, a law requiring girls seeking abortions to tell their parents or a judge first was reinstated by conservative Republicans over a gubernatorial veto. The state enacted a similar law eight years ago, but it was never enforced following a series of lawsuits. In Arkansas, facilities that perform 10 or more nonsurgical abortions a month must be licensed by the state Health Department and be subject to inspections by the department; the same requirements faced by facilities that offer surgical abortions in the state. It affects two Planned Parenthood facilities that offer the abortion pill, though they are not singled out in the statute.

Among federal laws, a measure Congress passed to extend Social Security tax cuts and federal unemployment benefit programs raises insurance fees on new mortgages and refinancings backed by Fannie Mae, Freddie Mac and the Federal Housing Administration by 0.1 per cent beginning 1 January. That covers about 90 per cent of them and effectively makes a borrower's monthly payment on a new $200,000 mortgage or refinancing about $17 a month more than it would have been if obtained before the first of the year. Nevada's 3-month old ban on texting while driving will get tougher, with tickets replacing the warnings that police have issued since the ban took effect 1 October. In Pennsylvania, police are preparing to enforce that state's recently enacted ban on texting, scheduled to take effect by spring.

Election law changes in Rhode Island and Tennessee will require voters to present photo ID, a measure that supporters say prevents fraud and that opponents say will make it harder for minorities and the elderly to cast ballots. In Ohio, a measure that creates one primary in March, instead of two that would have cost the state an extra $15 million, goes into effect later in January. Ohio is also one of eight states with automatic increases in the minimum wage taking effect 1 January. The others, with increases between 28 and 37 cents, are Arizona, Colorado, Florida, Montana, Oregon, Vermont and Washington. A few laws try to address budget woes. In Delaware, new state employees will have to contribute more to their pensions, while state workers hired after 1 January in Nevada will have to pay more for their own health care costs in retirement. The first of January is the effective date in many states for laws passed during this year's legislative sessions. In others, laws take effect 1 July, or 90 days after passage.

In another Associated Press report from Phoenix, Arizona, Jacques Billeaud wrote on 27 December 2011 that an administrative law judge had ruled that a Tucson school district's ethnic studies program violates state law, agreeing with the findings of Arizona's public schools chief. Judge Lewis Kowal's ruling marked a defeat for the Tucson Unified School District, which appealed the findings issued in June by Superintendent of Public Instruction John Huppenthal. Kowal's ruling, first reported by *The Arizona Daily Star*, said the district's Mexican-American Studies program violated state law by having one or more classes designed primarily for one ethnic group, promoting racial resentment and advocating ethnic solidarity instead of treating students as individuals. The judge, who found grounds to withhold 10 per cent of the district's monthly state aid until it comes into compliance, said the law permits the objective instruction about the oppression of people that may result in racial resentment or ethnic solidarity. "However, teaching oppression objectively is quite different than actively presenting material in a biased, political and emotionally charged manner, which is what occurred in (Mexican-American Studies) classes," Kowal wrote. The judge said such teaching promotes activism against white people, promotes racial resentment and advocates ethnic solidarity. Huppenthal has 30 days to accept, reject or modify the ruling. If he accepts the judge's decision, the district has about 30 days to appeal the ruling in Superior Court. "I made a decision based on the totality of the information and facts gathered during my investigation – a decision that I felt was best for all students in the Tucson Unified School District." Huppenthal said.

The battle over the ethnic studies program escalated shortly after Arizona's heavily scrutinized immigration enforcement law was passed in April 2010. The program's supporters have called challenges to the courses an attack on the state's Hispanic population, while critics say the program demonizes white people as oppressors of Hispanics. Huppenthal ordered a review of the program when he took office in January after his predecessor, Tom Horne, said the Mexican-American Studies program violated state law and that Huppenthal would have to decide whether to withhold funding. Huppenthal, a Republican, had voted in favor of the ethnic studies law as a state senator before becoming the state's schools chief.

VII

DR. DOOM aka Nouriel Roubini said the perfect storm scenario he forecast for the global economy earlier this year is unfolding right now as growth slows in the U.S., Europe, and China. In May, Roubini predicted four elements that are stalling growth in the U.S. – debt troubles in Europe, a slowdown in emerging markets, particularly China, and military conflict in Iran – would come together to create a storm for the global economy in 2013. "(The) 2013 perfect storm scenario I wrote on months ago is unfolding," Roubini said on Twitter. Chinese inflation data suggested that the economy is cooling faster than expected, while employment data out of the U.S indicated that jobs growth was tepid for a fourth straight month in June. Roubini said that unlike in 2008 when central banks had policy bullets to stimulate the global economy, this time around policymakers are running out of rabbits to pull out of the hat. Policy easing moves by the European Central Bank (ECB), Bank of England (BoE) and the People's Bank of China (PBoC) did little to inspire confidence in global stock markets. "Levitational force of policy easing can only temporarily lift asset prices as gravitational forces of weaker fundamentals dominate over time," he said. Bill Smead, CEO of Smead Capital Management, agreed that there is little central banks can do arrest the global slowdown. He told CNBC that there is virtually zero chance that pump-priming by central banks will succeed, suggesting that policymakers should instead let the economic bust work itself through the system.

President Obama called on Congress to pass a one-year extension of Bush-era tax cuts on income on annual income up to $250,000, while letting those that chiefly benefit the very wealthy expire on schedule at year's end. The proposal reignited an election-year fight designed to polish his credentials as a champion for middle-class Americans. "It's time to let the tax cuts for the wealthiest Americans, folks like myself, to expire," he said in the East Room of the White House, surrounded by people he warned could see a $2,200 jump in their tax bill if the rates expire. "I'm not proposing anything radical here," he insisted, casting the move as a return to the tax rates in force under President Bill Clinton, who presided over an era of robust job growth. Obama's announcement echoed his core campaign message on the economy, the top issue on voters' minds. He did not refer to Mitt Romney by name, but tried to make the debate over the upper-bracket tax cuts central to the election. "The fate of the tax cut for the wealthiest Americans will be decided by the outcome of the next election. My opponent will fight to keep them in place, I will fight to end them," he said. "The American people are with me on this." Obama aides say they hope that the "tax fairness" argument will win over voters struggling in the fitful economy three and a half years after he took office vowing to fix it.

With national unemployment at 8.2 per cent and little relief expected between now and 6 November, the Obama campaign has sought to convince struggling Americans that he has their best interests at heart. He has urged voters to see the election as a choice between his approach and Romney's, not as a referendum on his record. The White House and Congress will face the issue in earnest after the election, with the expiration looming. But even before Obama spoke, Republicans declared it dead on arrival. Obama has said that failing to raise taxes on the wealthiest will mean cash-strapped state and federal governments have to make deeper cuts to education, infrastructure and scientific research. ABC News, citing the Tax Policy Center, reported that raising taxes in line with the president's approach would affect 2.5 per cent of small businesses, a total of 894,000 businesses.

Obama called the upper-bracket tax cuts a major driver of our deficit yet the least likely to promote growth. And, he noted, "It's not like I like to pay taxes. I might feel differently if we were still in surplus." The president was to do a series of interviews with local and regional television anchors from six battleground states: Florida, Iowa, Nevada, New Hampshire, North Carolina and Wisconsin. He will also sit down for chats with anchors from Kentucky and Louisiana, which are not seen as tossups in November.

The president signed legislation in December 2010 to extend all of the Bush-era tax cuts to the end of this year. But even then he made clear that he favored letting the reductions for the highest-income Americans expire. He has consistently said since then that the wealthiest should pay more in taxes. Republicans have cast this as Obama pushing a tax increase on investors, and warned that it will smother already weak job growth. But Republican opposition may only boost the initiative's political value to the president, who has told voters that the chief obstacle to the recovery is a Republican-engineered stalemate in polarized Washington. "The choice in this election is between the President's plan to build this economy from the middle class out, promoting job creation and reducing the deficit in a balanced way, or Mitt Romney's plan to return to the same top-down policies that crashed our economy and decimated the middle class in the first place," Obama campaign spokesman Ben LaBolt said in a statement.

Several Democratic senators facing difficult re-election fights have signaled that they will break with the president on the issue. But with Republicans pointing to Pelosi's past comments as evidence of a Democratic schism at the very top, a senior Democratic House aide told reporters by email that Democrats supported immediate extension of the middle-income tax cuts. "Republicans are very clear: they continue to hold tax cuts for the middle class hostage to costly and unnecessary tax breaks for the wealthiest Americans, even though tax cuts for the rich have created more debt and won't produce jobs," the aide said on condition of anonymity. "Democrats say pass the extension of the middle income tax cuts now and end the uncertainty."

In a commentary on the Yahoo Contributor Network on 17 February 2012, Elizabeth Danu wrote that as Presidents' Day approaches and as Americans reflect on the challenges faced by past presidents, we note that Barack Obama has taken office during one of the toughest times in history. Most importantly, he began his term during an "economic free-fall," according to *Forbes*, which is one of several outlets predicting an Obama victory this year. And according to *Forbes* contributor Peter Cohan, Obama has done an excellent job in the face of extraordinary obstacles. The economy is recovering, which is undermining the Republican strategy of blaming Obama for the current mess. Cohan calls his handling of foreign policy "masterful". The end of Osama bin Laden and the war in Iraq are significant accomplishments. Yahoo! News experts are also predicting victory for the president based on many indicators, which have continually evolved over past elections. While things could change over the next months, the current direction of Obama's term is positive. The economy continues to improve, unemployment is decreasing, and the president's approval ratings are solid. According to the Yahoo! News Signal forecast, the current state of the economy is less important than the direction it is going.

Why do I think that President Obama will win in 2012? Ms. Danu asked and gave her reasons: None of the GOP candidates has what it takes to galvanize the Republican Party. Rick Santorum's sudden rise is similar to other rallies this election year. All of the GOP candidates at one time or another had a surge. I believe this has more to do with voter indecision than passion for any candidate. GOP voters appear to be struggling to find a candidate they can get excited about. The United States has been in an economic mess for some time, which President Obama had to step into and try to clean up, understanding that somebody was always going to be unhappy. He has persevered despite tremendous obstacles, including obvious racism that doesn't generally get discussed. Most presidents who seek re-election get a second term. I doubt American voters will interrupt now and risk everything. There is no moderate on the GOP ticket. Romney is accused by his rivals of being a moderate, but his wealth and his repeated verbal gaffes show that he cannot relate to the average struggling American. Voters in this election year have a choice between an incumbent president who is getting the job done over enormous obstacles or whoever the GOP decides is conservative enough. There is no middle ground. All of the GOP candidates scare me. We have a rich guy, a mean guy, or a homophobic guy. No thanks. Come November, Obama should expect to see more Presidents Days from the Oval Office concluded Ms. Danu.

On 18 January 2012 Warren Buffett said he would be writing a check made out to the United States Treasury for just over $49,000 to help pay down the national debt. He's matching voluntary contributions made this year and last year by Rep. Scott Rigell, a Republican representing Virginia. In a letter to Rep. Rigell released by Berkshire Hathaway, Buffett writes he's "particularly impressed that you took this action before my challenge." In his challenge, issued in a *TIME* magazine interview, Buffett promises to match voluntary contributions aimed at reducing the deficit by "all Republican members of Congress, and I'll even go three for one with (Senate Minority Leader Mitch) McConnell." McConnell, and other critics of Buffett's call for higher tax rates on the super-rich, have been suggesting that if Buffett thinks he's not taxed enough then he should "send in a check" to the Treasury. In his letter to Buffett, also released by Berkshire, Rep. Rigell writes, that he "appreciates" and "gladly accepts" Buffett's "generous offer". Rigell says he makes it a practice to donate 15 per cent of his Congressional salary "to pay down the debt." That amounted to $23,103.33 in 2011 and about $26,100 in 2012. Rigell adds, "Though we differ on tax policy, as fellow Americans and businessmen I know that we share this common bond: a deep concern over the state and trajectory of our country's finances." Buffett writes back that he hopes Rigell's action "spurs an intramural rivalry between Republicans and Democrats ... a form of competition between the two parties that the American people would applaud" as a "small step" toward "better cooperation between the two parties."

Dylan Stableford in The Cutline reported on 23 February 2012 that just as he did following the death of *The New York Times* reporter Anthony Shadid in Syria, White House press secretary Jay Carney began his daily briefing by praising the work of Marie Colvin, the *Sunday Times* reporter who also was killed there. Carney called their deaths "tragic", and "a reminder of the incredible risks that journalists take ... in order to bring the truth about what is happening in a country like Syria to those of us at home." But Obama's press secretary seemed unprepared for a hard line of questioning from ABC News senior White House correspondent Jake Tapper, who took issue with the administration's applause of aggressive reporting abroad while trying to silence it at home in the United States.

On 16 October 2011 Neil Munro had written in The Daily Caller that two hours after President Obama had cited the Rev. Martin Luther King's advice that Americans not question each other's love of country, Deputy Press Secretary Josh Earnest demanded that GOP legislators "put country before party" by ending their opposition to the president's spending plans. The demand came during an afternoon press conference called to tout the president's three-day bus tour through counties in swing-states Virginia and North Carolina. The bus tour was intended to magnify the media's coverage of poll-tested provisions in Obama's proposed $446 billion, one-year stimulus bill, the American Jobs Act. For example, the measure seeks the expenditure of $35 billion to employ up to 400,000 teachers for the year prior to Obama's re-election vote.

But GOP legislators say the stimulus is an inefficient use of borrowed funds, that its tax-boosting provisions would stymie economic growth and that it would be followed by a recessionary cut-off of spending unless the federal government continued to borrow more funds. They say the economy, and teachers' employment prospects, would be increased by a rollback of federal regulations and an increased emphasis on free-market growth. The bus tour will pressure legislators to "pass the bill, this week, to protect the job of a North Carolina teacher, or come down here, look her in the eye, and explain why ... [they] don't want to ask millionaires and billionaires to pay a little more," Earnest said. It is time, Earnest demanded, that legislators "put country before party". Earnest told The Daily Caller that his demand did not violate the president's call for comity during the formal unveiling of the new statue of Rev. King. "If [King] were alive today ... he would want us to know we can argue fiercely about the proper size and role of government without questioning each other's love for this country," Obama declared. "The word patriotism did not come out of my mouth ... what the president is calling on Democrats and Republicans to do [is support] the best interests of the country," Earnest said.

Since GOP legislators rebuffed his demands in August for additional taxes, the president has repeatedly denounced GOP opposition to his progressive policies as putting "party before country". On August 20, for example, Obama said his "commonsense ideas" are being held back by "the refusal by some in Congress to put country ahead of party. That's the problem right now. That's what's holding this country back. That's what we have to change." On 4 October in a speech at the Democratic fundraiser in St. Louis, Missouri, Obama accused his opponents of putting partisan interests before the country's good. "We need to pass this [stimulus] bill now. And if the American people see Washington putting their needs first, putting country before party, thinking about their constituencies, that's going to give people confidence, that's going to restore a sense of hope," he said.

Olivier Knox, the White House correspondent for Yahoo News, writing in The Ticket on 15 February 2012 said it was "not even close". By a lopsided margin of 66 per cent to 26 per cent, Americans support President Barack Obama's proposal to require private health insurance plans to cover the full cost of birth control for women, according to a new CBS/New York Times public opinion poll. Re-phrasing the question to ask specifically about "religiously affiliated employers, such as a hospital or university," barely moved the needle, to 61 per cent to 31 per cent. Those numbers, which come with a margin of error of plus or minus 3 percentage points, are better for Obama than his numbers on foreign policy (50 per cent approve, 36 per cent disapprove), Afghanistan in particular (51 per cent approve, 36 per cent disapprove) and are nearly the mirror image of public opinion on his handling of the federal budget deficit, where he loses 32 per cent to 59 per cent.

House Speaker John Boehner blasted new U.S. rules requiring most insurance plans to cover contraception for women over the objections of some religious groups, Agence France Press reported on 2 February 2011. "I think this mandate violates our constitution, I think it violates the rights of these religious organizations and I would hope that the administration would back up and take another look at this," said Boehner. But a senior Obama administration official said that the measures had been decided after "very careful consideration of legal and policy" questions. U.S. Health and Human Services Secretary Kathleen Sebelius rolled out the new rules in late January, saying that "very careful consideration" had been given to "the important concerns some have raised about religious liberty." The move, brought in under Obama's landmark health care reform law, offers an exemption for churches and other houses of worship. Other religious groups can qualify for a one-year exemption before they are covered by the new measures until August 2013 when they will have to comply with the law. Sebelius said when she announced the new procedures that they struck "the appropriate balance between respecting religious freedom and increasing access to important preventive services." The final rule, which followed an interim decision announced in August 2011, was applauded by women's rights advocates but denounced by the U.S. Conference of Catholic Bishops and political conservatives. Boehner cited "a lot of opposition" to the announced rules, which he charged amounted to "requiring religious organizations to violate their beliefs."

VIII

THE NEW procedures have generated heated political debate, with some commentators questioning whether Obama could face a loss of support among Catholic voters when he seeks re-election in November. Some commentators have suggested any loss of support among Catholics could be balanced by support for the measures among women voters and the young – a crucial constituency Obama needs to win re-election. Among the services to be covered are FDA-approved contraception methods and contraceptive counseling; breast-feeding support, supplies, and counseling; and domestic violence screening and counseling. Also included are annual office check-ups, screening for gestational diabetes, human papillomavirus (HPV) testing for women 30 and older, sexually transmitted infection counseling and human immunodeficiency virus (HIV) screening and counseling.

Elizabeth Warren, the Democrat who is running for Scott Brown's U.S. Senate seat in Massachusetts, is nearly keeping pace with Mitt Romney's astronomical fundraising levels, according to the latest figures released by each campaign. If the measurement is money raised per voter, rather than total dollars, that is. In the month of June, according to calculations performed by Yahoo News, Romney raised 77 cents per registered voter in the United States. Warren is right behind him, pulling down 75 cents for every registered voter in Massachusetts. Here's the math: Romney's campaign and a joint committee the candidate formed with the Republican National Committee together reported raising $106 million in June. Using census data for the 2010 election, there are more than 137 million registered voters in the United States. Divide those numbers together and you get the per-voter number: 77 cents. In Massachusetts, Warren raised $3.1 million in June. There are more than 4.1 million voters in Massachusetts, according to state totals released earlier this year. Dividing $3.1 million by the 4,111,128 voters in Massachusetts gets you Warren's dollars-per-voter number: 75 cents.

Democrats who are aiming to cast Mitt Romney and Republicans as out of touch with average Americans, writes Holly Bailey of Yahoo! News and The Ticket, are seizing on comments an unnamed GOP donor made to a reporter outside a Romney campaign fundraiser in the Hamptons suggesting "common people" don't understand what's at stake in the upcoming election. "I don't think the common person is getting it," the Romney supporter, who declined to give her name, told the *Los Angeles Times*' Maeve Reston outside the Romney event. "We've got the message," she said. "But my college kid, the baby sitters, the nails ladies – everybody who's got the right to vote – they don't understand what's going on. I just think if you're lower income – one, you're not as educated, two, they don't understand how it works, they don't understand how the systems work, they don't understand the impact." The donor was described only as a New York City resident riding in the passenger seat of a Range Rover stamped with East Hampton beach permits. But her words quickly became fodder for Democrats amid a larger effort by

President Barack Obama's re-election campaign to define Romney as a wealthy man who can't relate to everyday Americans. In a fundraising email to supporters, Kelly Ward, political director at the Democratic Congressional Campaign Committee, called the donor's comments "the kind of thinking we're up against in this election. If you don't think our country should be run by people who think you need a yacht for your opinion to count, then now's the time to show it," Ward wrote in the email.

Meanwhile the Associated Press reported that the U.S. budget deficit grew by nearly $60 billion in June, remaining on track to exceed $1 trillion for the fourth straight year. Through the first nine months of the budget year, the federal deficit totaled $904.2 billion, the Treasury Department said. Obama and congressional Republicans remain at odds over how to lower the deficit. Unless their disagreement is broken, a series of tax increases and spending cuts could kick in next year. Economists warn that could dramatically slow an already weak U.S. economy and even tip it back into a recession. The Congressional Budget Office predicts the deficit for the full year, which ends on 30 September, will total $1.17 trillion. That would be a slight improvement from the $1.3 trillion deficit recorded in 2011, but still greater than any deficit before Obama took office.

One positive sign this year is the deficit is growing more slowly than last year. In June it was 6.8 per cent behind the pace for the same period in budget year 2011. And a key reason for that is that revenues are up 5.2 per cent this year, while spending is down by 0.9 per cent. But the modest improvement has not cooled the budget debate in Washington. Obama submitted a budget request to Congress in February that sought $4 trillion in deficit reduction over the next decade through a combination of spending cuts and tax hikes. A key part of his proposal is to allow tax cuts to expire for couples earning more than $250,000. He has called for extending similar cuts for people earning less than that. Obama would also set a 30 per cent tax rate on taxpayers making more than $1 million.

Republicans have rejected the tax increases. They want more cuts in government programs. The GOP-controlled House has approved a budget that calls for deep cuts in Medicare and other programs and a new round of tax cuts that would favor wealthy Americans. The House-approved spending plan has no chance of passing in the Senate, where Democrats hold a slim majority. That sets the stage for gridlock until after the November elections when lawmakers will be faced with a number of end-of-the-year deadlines. Romney has proposed broad but largely unspecified spending cuts. He would reduce the federal work force by 10 per cent and keep the tax cuts for all incomes, not just families making less than $250,000. Romney also wants to drop all tax rates by 20 per cent. He would curtail deductions, credits and exemptions for the wealthiest to pay for the lower rates, but he does not specify what tax breaks would be trimmed.

Tax cuts approved during President George W. Bush's administration are scheduled to expire at the end of December. In addition, a set of automatic spending cuts totaling about $1.2 trillion over 10 years are scheduled to kick in. Both parties oppose the automatic spending reductions because they include deep cuts in defense. However, they have been unable to reach an agreement so far on alternate spending cuts or tax increases that would keep the automatic cuts from taking effect. The International Monetary Fund warned that the U.S. economy could suffer another recession if Congress doesn't do something to avert the so-called "fiscal cliff". The impact could shave 4 percentage points off U.S. growth, the IMF said.

It was not good news for the President who told reporters in July 2012 that his biggest mistake since getting to the White House has been his tendency to tackle the job as national policy week rather than the inspiring figure he cut in the 2008 campaign. Call it "too much substance and not enough style," Olivier Knox, White House Correspondent for Yahoo News and The Ticket wrote. "When I think about what we've done well and what we haven't done well," the president told CBS television in an interview, "the mistake of my first term – couple of years – was thinking that this job was just about getting the policy right. And that's important. But the nature of this office is also to tell a story to the American people that gives them a sense of unity and purpose and optimism, especially during tough times," Obama said in an excerpt of the exchange with Charlie Rose.

Mitt Romney hit out hard at Obama: "Being president is not about telling stories. Being president is about leading, and President

Obama has failed to lead. No wonder Americans are losing faith in his presidency," Romney said in a statement.

Obama also seemed to make the argument that he just can't catch a break. "It's funny – when I ran everybody said, 'Well he can give a good speech but can he actually manage the job?'" he said. "And in my first two years I think the notion was, 'Well, he's been juggling and managing a lot of stuff but where's the story that tells us where he's going?' And I think that was a legitimate criticism. So getting out of this town, spending more time with the American people, listening to them and also being in a conversation with them about where do we go together as a country, I need to do a better job of that in my second term," the president said. Rose pressed him, asking whether he means explaining, and Obama replied: "Explaining but also inspiring."

"Because hope is still there," First Lady Michelle Obama added. But Mrs. Obama is also a target of anger and abuse. Z. Byron Wolf of ABC OTUS News reported in July that Washington, D.C., police are investigating a D.C. Metro Police officer for making inappropriate comments about First Lady Michelle Obama. "We received an allegation that inappropriate comments were made. We are currently investigating the nature of those comments," a statement from the D.C. Metro Police department said. The officer works as a motorcycle escort with the agency, but has since been moved to administrative duty, according to the *Washington Post*, which first reported the incident. The newspaper described the alleged incident that led to the investigation: The motorman allegedly made the comments as several officers from the Special Operations Division discussed threats against President Obama. It was not immediately clear where the alleged conversation took place or exactly how many officers took part in the conversation. During that conversation, the officials said, the officer allegedly said he would shoot the First Lady and then he used his phone to retrieve a picture of the firearm he said he would use. It was not immediately clear what type of firearm was allegedly shown. Secret Service spokesman Ed Donovan told ABC Radio, "We're aware of the situation and taking the appropriate steps."

The truth is democrats continue to draw the ire of the far-right in the opposition. Eric Pfeiffer of Yahoo News and The Ticket reported on 31 May 2012 that the Republican campaign spokesman for Republican Nan Hayworth (NY-19) ignited a controversy after he said, "Let's hurl some acid" at female Democratic senators. The comments were alleged to have been posted on a local Facebook discussion forum for New York's 19th congressional district. The comments were made during an online debate over gas prices. The campaign for Rich Becker, who is running to unseat Hayworth, posted a statement online calling for Townsend to be fired. "I'd be fired —immediately and with cause – if I said stuff like this. Which begs the question: why is Jay Townsend still Nan Hayworth's spokesman," wrote Becker campaign spokesman Barry Caro. "Does she agree that bin Laden is dead in spite of Obama? Does she agree that we should 'hurl some acid' at politicians her campaign disagrees with? These comments are simply unprofessional and should never cross the lips of a Congressional spokesman."

But the abuse stops at Condoleezza Rice's door. According to Chris Moody of Yahoo! News / The Ticket the Drudge Report ran a blaring headline in July 2012 that sources within Mitt Romney's presidential campaign say Professor Rice, who served as Secretary of State and National Security Adviser under President George W. Bush, is a "front-runner" for the running mate slot. Matt Drudge, the founder of the site, has close ties to members of Romney's inner circle says Moody and runs one of the most popular news aggregation sites on the Web. For the past few days, President Obama's campaign has hammered Romney by questioning his business record at Bain Capital so it's not surprising that Romney would want to change the conversation to speculation about his vice presidential choice. The question remains, however: Is Romney actually considering Rice, or was the "leak" just a distraction?

Romney is not telling but according to Steve Peoples of the Associated Press he is calling for "something dramatic" to help the economy recover, but he's not saying exactly what. The Republican presidential candidate says he opposes another federal stimulus package and new government programs. He also says that if the Federal Reserve were to undertake another "massive" program of buying government bonds and mortgage-backed securities, with the goal of driving long-term interest rates even lower, it wouldn't help the recovery. "I can absolutely make the case that now is the time for something dramatic and it is not the time to grow government. It's the time to create the incentives and the opportunities for entrepreneurs and businesses big and small to hire more people and that's going to happen," Romney said an interview aired on CNN's *State of the Union.* "You're going to see that happen in this country but not under this president."

Democrats tried to cloud Romney's message by renewing calls for the former businessman to release years of personal tax returns. Romney insisted that he won't release more than two years of returns, although most presidential candidates, including his father, released many more. "What is it that he is hiding?" Obama senior adviser David Axelrod said on *Fox News Sunday.* He also addressed Senate Democratic leader Harry Reid's recent decision to share an anonymous claim that Romney hasn't paid taxes for 10 years. Axelrod said Romney and his campaign "can resolve this in 10 seconds. They can release the tax returns."

As each side debated Romney's personal taxes, the Republican candidate is trying to promote an economic agenda he said repeatedly would create 12 million jobs in his first term. Pushed to explain how, Romney said in the CNN interview, "That's what happens in a normal process. When you come out the kind of recession we've had you should see this kind of job creation," he said. "Good things happen when you have a private sector that's thriving." The former Massachusetts governor so far has been slow to release specifics for his economic plans. He repeated his opposition to Obama's tax plan that would preserve tax cuts passed in the George W. Bush era for all Americans but those who earn more than $250,000. Romney would preserve the tax cuts for everyone, although he has not detailed how he would pay for the plan. "I also hope people understand when they talk about raising taxes on the wealthy – as the president does – he is also talking about the same tax rate that applies to small business," Romney said. "The great majority of small businesses pay taxes at the individual rate so as he raises these taxes 'on the wealthy' he is raising taxes on small business."

Mitt Romney's campaign estimates it will raise at least $800 million in its quest to defeat President Barack Obama this fall, according to a fundraising memo circulated among top supporters. This report is from Holly Bailey of Yahoo News and The Ticket on 17 April 2012 and is from a memo, obtained by the *New York Times*' Nicholas Confessore. It says the campaign hopes to raise $500 million in high-dollar donations for the campaign and for the joint fundraising account it has set up with the Republican National Committee. Romney aides hope to bring in another $300 million from small donors – an area where the former Massachusetts governor has lagged during the GOP primary. In addition to the $800 million raised directly by the campaign, the memo estimates super PACs supporting Romney's candidacy will raise at least another $200 million to support his general election bid, bringing the GOP's overall fundraising target to at least $1 billion to defeat President Obama.

That's on par with what Obama's campaign has estimated it plans to spend in the 2012 election. Last year Obama aides estimated the president would raise at least $750 million for his re-election bid, though that total is now likely to be far more given that Obama has signed off on several Democratic super PACs to raise and spend millions to help him win a second term. Obama enters the general election with a major fundraising advantage. Through February Obama had raised nearly $160 million for his re-election campaign, not including another $126 million he's raised for a joint fundraising account between his campaign and the Democratic National Committee. In April the Obama campaign announced it had raised another $53 million for the campaign and the DNC. The Romney campaign has not yet disclosed its March fundraising totals.

On 10 July 2012 Chris Moody reported in Yahoo! News | The Ticket that a *Wall Street Journal* analysis of political spending found that organized labor groups dropped a combined $4.4 billion on political activities between 2006 and 2011, about four times more than previously estimated. The *Journal* cast a wide net to determine what counted as "political spending" including activities that range from traditional candidate donations to the cost of hot dogs for union demonstrators at political rallies. To find the additional costs the newspaper added spending reports filed with the Labor Department to Federal Election Commission spending data. The usual measure of unions' clout encompasses chiefly what they spend supporting federal candidates through their political-action committees, which are funded with voluntary contributions, and lobbying Washington, which is a cost borne by the unions.

These kinds of spending, which unions report to the Federal Election Commission and to Congress, totaled $1.1 billion from 2005 through 2011, according to the nonpartisan Center for Responsive Politics. The unions' reports to the Labor Department capture an additional $3.3 billion that unions spent over the same period on political activity. The costs reported to the Labor Department range from polling fees to money spent persuading union members to vote a certain way, to bratwursts to feed Wisconsin workers protesting at the state capitol last year. Much of this kind of spending comes not from members' contributions to a PAC but directly from unions' dues-funded coffers. There is no requirement that unions report all of this kind of spending to the Federal Election Commission, or FEC. Union spending goes overwhelmingly to Democratic candidates and liberal causes. According to the Center for Responsive Politics, which tracks political spending, 92 per cent of the $58.5 million in direct candidate donations from 1990 to 2012 went toward Democratic candidates. Jeff Hauser, a spokesman for the AFL-CIO, responded to the *Journal* report, arguing that much of the union political activity on the local and state level cannot be equally compared to spending by super PACs:

The *Wall Street Journal* treats all advocacy for working people at the local, state and federal levels as "political" work. Everything from someone writing policy proposals to create jobs to working in a local community to elect a working families-friendly City Council is viewed as equivalent to corporations anonymously attacking President Obama. Providing expert input for the formulation of mine safety rules, assisting the civil rights community – be it the 1963 March on Washington or voting protection efforts year-round – everything labor works on is said to be a counter-weight to the Super PACs of Karl Rove, the Koch Brothers and more shadowy figures. By this definition, the entire budget of the Chamber of Commerce would be considered political, but the Chamber doesn't report its spending on Department of Labor forms or anywhere else. The *Journal* says Moody misses the central point that unions are advocacy organizations. The job of a union is to advocate on behalf of working men and women. Moreover, the *Journal* ignores the fact that corporations outspend unions by more than 10 to one but are free to hide their spending while unions disclose everything.

IX

AS THE economy shapes voters' attitudes, the Election Day outcome for President Obama and Republican challenger Romney may be decided on the margins by narrower issues that energize small but crucial slivers of the population, wrote Jim Kuhnbenn of the Associated Press in July. For three months, the economy by most measures has faltered. Yet the White House contest has remained locked in place, with the incumbent holding on to a slight national lead or in a virtual tie with his rival. Analysts from both parties have no doubt that, without a defining, unpredictable moment, the race will remain neck and neck until November. That, several strategists say, means secondary issues such as health care, immigration, education, even little mentioned social issues such as abortion, guns or gay rights could make a difference when targeted to the right audiences. Under those conditions, the advantage, these strategists say, rests with Obama. "Part of the power of the presidency, part of the power of incumbency, is having the ability with an executive order to make rules, make effective law that is deeply satisfying to a large group of supporters," said Steve Schmidt, Republican John McCain's presidential campaign manager in 2008 and top aide in President George W. Bush's re-election operation. "Being able to deliver if you're an incumbent president is an enormously important thing."

Obama already has moved to shore up his support with certain voting blocs, with directives on birth control and immigration. He's given his backing to gay marriage and brawled with congressional Republicans on behalf of lower student loan rates. Each issue won praise from disparate groups of voters, many of whom had voiced frustration with the president or whose enthusiasm for Obama had been waning. "In every single state there will be micro-targeted advertisement, direct mail, or online campaign to get voters out there to kind of hit them on those personal issues that are important to them," said Rodell Mollineau, president of a pro-Obama political organization, American Bridge. "Whether you're pro-choice or anti-choice, pro-immigration or anti-immigration, you will be touched one way or the other." The role of these secondary issues is similar to the part that gay marriage ballot initiatives played in the 2004 contest between President George W. Bush and Democratic nominee John

Kerry. That election was dominated by the war in Iraq and national security issues. Though the extent to which 11 ballot issues, especially ones in Michigan and Ohio, helped turn out Bush voters eight years ago is a matter of debate, many analysts believe the initiatives at least primed the vote for the incumbent.

As for Romney and Obama, "neither of them seems to be delivering a knockout blow on the economy, and that's what does raise these issues and their salience," said Daniel Smith, a political scientist at the University of Florida who researched the role ballot initiatives played in the 2004 election. For three months, the economy has created jobs at a snail's pace and the unemployment rate has inched up from 8.1 per cent to 8.2 per cent. Economic growth has slowed, consumer confidence is down, and a strong majority of the public views the country heading in the wrong track. For all that, an Associated Press/GfK poll had Romney and Obama in a statistical tie and a *Washington Post*-ABC poll had them even at 47 per cent each. More remarkable, a majority in both polls – 56 per cent in the AP poll and 58 per cent in the *Post*-ABC survey – said they believed Obama would win re-election. The Romney camp says the contest is still taking shape and Romney is just now beginning to garner a national profile. "You still have a president who is enjoying the benefits of incumbency," said Kevin Madden, a senior Romney adviser. "He gets a lot more attention, and has a higher profile with voters." Ever disciplined, Romney has kept his campaign message exclusively on economic themes, casting the election as a referendum on Obama's economic stewardship. Even when he has strayed into side issues such as health care and the Supreme Court's decision to uphold Obama's signature law, Romney has kept his argument focused on the economics of the law.

At Obama campaign headquarters in Chicago, the election is being framed as one of choices between Romney and Obama on economic themes. "The fact that Romney hasn't gotten traction is not a reflection that there is stasis on economic issues," said Obama senior political adviser David Axelrod. "It's a reflection of the fact he hasn't offered a plausible alternative. I think that's why he's running into problems." Still, Axelrod said: "There's no doubt that people will consider other things, and if it's a close call for them I think some of these other things matter." Axelrod cited education as an important factor, particularly with women, and he contrasted Obama's desire to finance education programs with Romney's wish to cut taxes for millionaires. "For these folks, it's part of the economic discussion, not separate from it," Axelrod said. Axelrod also mentioned Romney's position on immigration and his pledge to defund Planned Parenthood as issues that are important to certain groups of voters. "How Romney has handled himself on those issues is meaningful," he said. "People have broad concerns, and some of these issues will be influential," he added. "Other issues may move some who are on the bubble, but rebuilding the economy and the middle class is the overwhelmingly the top concern."

No side issue stands out more than immigration in its ability to energize and mobilize a bloc of voters. Obama had promised a comprehensive overhaul of the immigration system when he ran in 2008. But Obama put the issue on the back burner after support for immigration changes failed to gel, and Hispanic voters grew resentful. But last month he acted on his own, expanding the authority of the federal government to exempt certain immigrants from deportation and making them eligible for work permits. The stance contrasted sharply with Romney's. During the Republican primaries, he took a hard line against illegal immigration. One ad this past week aired in Nevada by the Service Employees International Union and the pro-Obama Priorities Action political action committee states that Romney "has not demonstrated that he respects the Latino community."

Romney is running Spanish language ads himself and Madden says the challenge for Obama is that until he issued an administrative directive five months before the election Obama had not acted on his promise to Hispanics. But Schmidt says Republicans are in a bad position with Hispanics these days. "Nevada and New Mexico are going to be very, very important states," he said. "The numbers aren't where you want them to be if you're a Republican wanting Mitt Romney to win." Four years after Barack Obama won the support of 66 per cent of voters aged 18 to 29, Republicans are working on a fresh approach to bring younger voters and candidates into the fold, using a coalition of traditional campaign organizations, super PACs, nonprofit advocacy groups and policy-based think tanks. And even Republicans organizing these efforts admit it's going to take some work, writes Chris Moody of Yahoo News.

Two groups, the Young Guns Action Fund and Maverick PAC – the latter was co-founded by George P. Bush, nephew of former President George W. Bush and son of former Florida Governor Jeb Bush – will focus on finding young Republican political talent and supporting them with money. The two organizations announced a strategic partnership that organizers hope will increase engagement with voters that were lost to Obama in 2008. One short-term goal, of course, is to narrow the enthusiasm gap between young Republicans and Democrats, but ultimately they are looking far beyond the next election. "The relationship is about developing something for the long-term that looks past just this November," Young Guns Action Fund President John Murray told reporters during a breakfast meeting in Washington, D.C. "By the midterms in 2014, perhaps we've made a little more progress; by the next presidential we've made some more progress, and [we've gained] the capacity to build that over time because it's going to take time."

The Young Guns Action Fund, a super PAC, plans to scour the country looking for new young Republican House and Senate candidates. The Action Fund will support these new GOP candidates and independently bolster their campaigns. Meanwhile, MavPAC will build its own base of young, new donors and fundraising bundlers, whom they plan to connect with the new recruits. The two groups will share data based on the information they gather from new supporters. They plan to spend $5 million this election cycle on the joint project. Young Guns Action Fund will recruit the pilots and cover the air war, while MavPAC rallies the boots on the ground. Organizers say they hope to make some headway with younger voters this cycle, but they aren't promising a Republican revolution by November. "We want to manage expectations," said MavPac co-founder Bush. "We don't want to say it's going to swing 180 degrees to the other side. I think it's worth the effort. I think to leave a complete demographic group like this uncontested is a mistake for the Republican Party." To reach the goal, MavPAC and Young Guns Action Fund leaders both pointed to Obama's success four years ago, and how he was able to "capture the imagination" of young people in his speeches. Now, they say, many of those same voters have graduated from college, are struggling to find work and are disappointed. Republicans plan to capitalize off that frustration. "I am not here to say that there's some magic wand we're going to wave and all these voters are going to suddenly vote Republican," Murray said. "I think what we recognize is that there's a unique moment in time where there's a real choice being presented in this country, and many of these voters, once you articulate that voice, tend to say, 'You know, I want this freedom and opportunity, and I'm concerned about it.'"

MavPAC and Young Guns Action aren't the only groups focused on shoring up the Republican base of young voters this cycle. American Crossroads, a group co-founded by Republican operatives Karl Rove and Ed Gillespie, announced the formation of Crossroads Generation earlier this year. In 2010, conservative operatives launched Generation Opportunity, which conducts nationwide voter registration drives targeting the younger set. Free from the restrictions of campaign finance laws, those independent groups will work to amplify the efforts of traditional party organizations. Said Young Guns Action Fund spokesman Brad Dayspring: "There's an opportunity to capture the imagination of those voters."

24/7 Wall St. has examined public companies' political contributions in the current election cycle. According to Douglas A. McIntyre and Alexander E.M. Hess on 5 July 2012 the donations include monies given to political parties, candidates, and political action committees. The figures are staggering and have prompted many to ask whether money can buy a seat in the House, Senate, or even the presidency itself. The Republican presidential candidate, Mitt Romney, the Romney Victory Fund, and the Republican National Committee raised more than $76.8 million in May alone. This one month does not include what Romney and his supporters raised for the primaries, or the growing amount he will need as the presidential election shifts into high gear. While President Obama has raised more overall, his campaign and the Democratic Party only raised $60 million for his re-election effort in May.

Political contributions, which used to go directly to candidates, now often flow to Super PACs, independent organizations that can raise money to either help or defeat a political candidate. Historically, traditional political action committees have been prohibited from accepting donations from unions and companies. However, following rulings by the U.S. Supreme Court and the Court of Appeals, Super PACs are now allowed to accept unlimited donations from unions and companies, provided the money does not go directly to the campaign. The rise of the Super PAC has opened the door to a new generation of fund-raising, changing how money is used to elect candidates and increasing the amount candidates need to raise to be competitive as they seek office.

Already, there is evidence of the influence large corporations and their senior managements can have. At one point in January, Las Vegas Sands' CEO, billionaire Sheldon Adelson, gave then GOP's presidential hopeful Newt Gingrich $5 million. Gingrich could not have remained a candidate for the Republican nomination without the money. Adelson went so far in February as to say he might pass an additional $100 million to Gingrich and the PACs that supported him. Adelson, with his activist posture, won't likely go away this political season as Gingrich did. His total contributions this election cycle already total nearly $12 million. Some of his contributions have been given through a tiny methadone clinic owned by him and his wife Miriam. It is perhaps not surprising then to find Las Vegas Sands, which is run by Adelson, at the top of the list of the ten public companies with the largest political contributions. The companies on the list operate in different industries. While one might think financial firms, tethered to the federal government by the financial crisis bailout, and defense companies, which count on billions of dollars in government contracts, would dominate the list, they do not entirely. Microsoft is on the list, as is AT&T, cable company Comcast, and film studio DreamWorks.

Based on data collected and published by the Center for Responsive Politics on its website, opensecrets.org, 24/7 Wall St. has identified the ten publicly traded companies contributing the most to candidates, political parties, and PACs. The Center for Responsive Politics calculates total political contributions made by either companies' PACs or employees within a given election cycle (beginning in January 1, 2011 for the 2012 cycle) that are over $200. 24/7 Wall St. also examined lobbying expenditure data, also published by the Center for Responsive Politics. Finally, it relied on the 2012 Washington Technology Top 100 for revenue earned by the top government contractors.

X

THE TOP Republican in the Congress criticized Representative Michele Bachmann and four other fellow House Republicans for making "pretty dangerous" accusations when they questioned the security clearance of a Muslim aide to Secretary of State Hillary Clinton, Thomas Ferraro of Reuters reported on 19 July 2012. The comments of House of Representatives Speaker John Boehner came after Senator John McCain, the 2008 Republican presidential nominee, blasted the five lawmakers for seeking an investigation into whether Huma Abedin, Clinton's deputy chief of staff, had connections to the Muslim Brotherhood, an Islamist political organization. Boehner, speaking at a regular news briefing, said "accusations like this being thrown around are pretty dangerous." He said he did not know Abedin, but "from everything I know of her, she has a sterling character."

McCain took to the Senate floor to accuse the lawmakers of making a "sinister" attack on Abedin. Following the custom in Congress, he did not name them but left no doubt he was talking about Bachmann, as well as Representatives Louie Gohmert, Trent Franks, Thomas Rooney and Lynn Westmoreland. They sent a letter in June to the State Department's inspector-general suggesting members of Abedin's family may have connections to the Muslim Brotherhood, which the writers said may be seeking access to high levels of the U.S. government. Most attention has focused on Bachmann, who earlier this year failed in her bid for the Republican presidential nomination. She has long been criticized by fellow Republicans, among others, for controversial comments and factual errors. Bachmann defended her actions on the talk show of conservative host Glenn Beck. "If my family members were associated with Hamas, a terrorist organization, that alone could be sufficient to disqualify me from getting a security clearance," Bachmann said, according to a transcript of her remarks. "So all we did is ask, did the federal government look into her family associations before she got a high level security clearance."

There is no evidence connecting Abedin or her family to any terrorist organization, McCain stressed in his Senate speech. "Rarely do I come to the floor of this institution to discuss particular individuals," McCain said. "But I understand how painful and injurious it is when a person's character, reputation, and patriotism are attacked without concern for fact or fairness." He called Abedin "an intelligent, upstanding, hard-working, and loyal servant of our country and our government, who has devoted countless days of her life to advancing the ideals of the nation she loves and looking after its most precious interests." A State Department spokesman said Clinton "very much values" Abedin's "wise counsel and support" and called the allegations preposterous.

McCain was supported by Edward Rollins, a prominent Republican strategist who worked on Bachmann's primary campaign. On the Fox News website, Rollins wrote that he was "fully aware that she sometimes has difficulty with her facts," but said "this is downright vicious and reaches the late Senator Joe McCarthy level," a reference to the U.S. senator from Wisconsin who rose and then fell accusing government officials and others of being communists in the 1950s. Rollins added that she should apologize to Abedin, Clinton and "to the millions of hard working, loyal, Muslim Americans for your wild and unsubstantiated charges."

The lawmakers' June 13 letter, which they released publicly, asserted that the State Department had recently taken action "enormously favorable" to the Muslim Brotherhood and that its interests could pose a security risk for the United States. The letter cited a security study by an outside group alleging that three members of Abedin's family, including her father, who died two decades ago, and her mother and brother were linked to operatives or organizations of the Muslim Brotherhood. Abedin is married to former U.S. Representative Anthony Weiner of New York, a Jew.

The biggest surprise in the Republican presidential campaign in Iowa has been the relative sluggishness – until this week – of the TV propaganda battle, wrote Seth Stevenson on 12 January 2012. "The Iowa ads started later this year than last time around," Ken Goldstein, the president of Kantar Media's Campaign Media Analysis Group, told Yahoo News. "Things are only starting to heat up now. This has been a pre-primary season driven by debates, not by ads, and the campaigns have for the most part been content to let it play out that way." The sheer frequency of the debates kept them front and center in the conversation. And the key turning points this fall happened either on stage (Rick Perry's deflating "oops") or in news reports (Herman

Cain's losing struggle against the skeletons in his closet). Still, the ads the campaigns have launched across the Iowa airwaves offer insight into each candidate's strategic approach to branding. Just as corporate marketing departments seek to shape consumers' feelings toward products, writes Stevenson, political campaigns try to position their candidates within voters' minds.

Stevenson is a columnist for Slate and the author of *Grounded*. He writes that Newt Gingrich's sole Iowa TV ad this election cycle is titled "Rebuilding the America We Love." The ad he says steals its stylistic approach from the "Morning in America" ad created by the 1984 Ronald Reagan campaign. Both spots feature gentle, string-and-woodwind-driven scores, and scenes of waving American flags and suburban tranquility. But while the Reagan ad celebrated an improving national condition, the Gingrich ad is displeased with the status quo and nostalgic for the brighter days of the past. It's a bit incongruous. If conditions are so dire right now (the Gingrich ad's mission statement – "We can and will rebuild the America we love" – implies that our country needs some serious refurbishing), why does the ad emit such a calm, upbeat vibe? Gingrich needs to fight the impression, Stevenson says, aided by a barrage of negative attack ads aimed at him by rival PACs and campaigns, that he is volatile and prone to zany proclamations. So it made little sense to re-introduce him to Iowa with a scaremongering ad full of bleak imagery. Instead, the Gingrich we meet is almost grandfatherly. He is filmed in a warm light and smiles as he speaks in soothing tones. The financially outgunned Gingrich has used his precious paid TV time to paint himself as a cheerful, conciliatory man of reason. He even strikes a subtly inclusive tone: When his script refers to "respecting one another," the ad shows a white woman and an African-American man walking purposefully together, says Stevenson.

The criticisms do not stop with Gingrich. While Gingrich is costumed in a suit and tie amid the dark, wooden bookshelves of a den, says Stevenson, Rick Perry has opted for open-collared shirts and canvas Carhartt work jackets. Perry's ad titled "Strong" shows him moseying along the grassy banks of a picturesque river. Instead of penning up their candidate indoors and filming him in tight close-ups, the Perry team lets us glimpse the physically fit governor on the move, framing the shot to give us an eyeful of his impressive torso – right down to that macho silver belt buckle that fastens his jeans. Amid a gaggle of candidates whose overarching policy themes can seem indistinguishable (cut taxes, shrink government, dismantle corporate and financial regulations), Perry seized on a more personality-driven marketing strategy to differentiate himself from the pack. The "Strong" ad attempts to position Perry within two key psychological niches. First, it depicts Perry as unabashedly, and unapologetically, Christian. "Notice the choreography of Perry's right hand when he removes it from his pocket midway through the ad. Watch how he makes a pushing-away, 'not for me' motion as he says "gays can serve openly in the military" and then turns open his palm as he says "but our kids can't openly celebrate Christmas." Second, by filming Perry in outdoor, non-work settings and in casual clothes, the ad makes a strong play for the want-to-have-a-beer-with-him voting bloc. Newt Gingrich, Mitt Romney, and Ron Paul do not possess the informal charisma and guy's guy bearing that Perry pulls off effortlessly. The "Strong" ad (even its title is suggestive) puts forth Perry as the candidate you want at your barbecue – quaffing a brewski as he espouses traditional, small-town social norms."

Ron Paul has been said to be the demographic outsider in Iowa. In a field of baby boomers, the 76-year-old Paul can look a bit old and slight, overpowered by heartier specimens like Perry and Romney. His ad titled "Big Dog" (again, the title itself gives the game away) attempts to assert Paul's vitality and alpha status as a counter to his somewhat receding, less-than-domineering debate performances. The visual scheme of the ad borrows heavily from a recent series of ads for the Ford F-150 pick-up, voiced by the actor Denis Leary. Note the similar deployment of bold, animated typography, coupled with an aggressive, almost snarly tone. The Paul ad's language is bullying – referring to "sorry" politicians who act like "little Shih Tzus". Its imagery verges on the violent: Federal bureaus literally poof into smoke as the announcer assures us of Ron Paul's animosity toward government. A photo of a nerdy government worker is crumpled up and thrown into the path of a honking, rumbling 18-wheeler. The aim here is to appeal to the same sort of male, working-class voters who might be swayed by the Ford spots, while re-shaping Paul's image as a take-no-prisoners tough guy who will rough up Washington elites. The ad never shows Paul himself – his comparative physical frailty would hinder the image-crafting effort.

The knock on Romney has been that he's a shape-shifter, scrambling his identity to align it with the fashion of the moment. Thus it's notable that the first sentence of his ad titled "Leader" has Romney asserting, "I think people understand that I'm a man of steadiness and constancy." The other personal quality Romney struggles with is his inability to connect with voters on a personal level. He can seem ill at ease, and voters seem to understand that while Romney is qualified to be president, they're just not sure they like him. To address this failing, the ad shows us a bevy of home-movie clips from the Romney family's archives. The voice-over eschews any mentions of policy positions or political bona fides. Instead, we see scenes of Mitt as a young dad and husband. There are multiple shots of his photogenic wife and children. The Mitt we see here, playing with his kids, is anything but robotic. The ad even allows in a verbal slip from Romney to make him seem less programmed. More recently, the campaign has let Mitt's wife, Ann, do his humanizing for him.

XI

LAWMAKERS WERE outraged in July after an ABC World News report revealed that the U.S. Olympic team's opening ceremony outfits were made in China. Some suggested making a bonfire with the outfits, which include berets and blazers. "I think they should take all the uniforms, put them in a big pile and burn them and start all over again," Senate Majority Leader Harry Reid, D-Nev., said when asked by ABC News *Today*, "If they have to wear nothing but a symbol that says USA on it, painted by hand, that is what they should wear." Team USA will be marching into the 2012 Olympic Opening Ceremony wearing Ralph Lauren blazers and berets, much as they did four years ago when Lauren dressed them. ABC's Sharyn Alfonsi reported that every clothing item that the U.S. athletes will be wearing at the opening ceremony in London will carry an overseas label. Reid said today that the U.S. Olympic committee should be "ashamed of themselves and embarrassed" that the items were made in China, especially with people in the textile industry in America who are looking for jobs.

The Congressional reaction on Capitol Hill extended to both houses and both parties. "You'd think they know better," Speaker of the House John Boehner said in response to a question from ABC News *Today*. House Minority Leader Nancy Pelosi said that since the Olympic athletes represent the very best in America they should be wearing uniforms made in America. "They work so hard. They represent the very best, and they're so excellent. It's all so beautiful. And they should be wearing uniforms that are made in America." Already there is a movement on Capitol Hill to make changes so this does not happen again at future Olympic Games. Sen. Kirsten Gillibrand, D-N.Y., and Rep. Steve Israel, D-N.Y., wrote a letter to the chairman of the U.S. Olympic Committee, Lawrence Probst, calling this revelation "shocking and deeply disappointing" and asking all U.S. teams' uniforms be made in America in the future. "We are asking that the Committee and its Board of Directors take immediate steps to guarantee that this embarrassment does not happen again by voting that any future contracts for Olympic uniforms are made in America," Gillibrand and Israel write in their letter, "This would ensure that U.S. Olympians are supporting American jobs. As American fans cheer for our Olympians, we should also be cheering for the American manufacturers and laborers reflected in the red, white and blue on their uniforms."

Sen. Sherrod Brown, D-OH., who has legislation pending in Congress to strengthen "Buy America" provisions for federal tax dollars, also sent a letter to U.S. Olympic Committee calling for the group to scrap this year's uniforms and find a domestic manufacturer to remake them. "The USOC holds its athletes to a high moral and ethical standard, and has a no tolerance policy for cheating or violating rules," Sen. Brown wrote in his letter to Chairman Probst, "But China continues to cheat when it comes to international trade. As we work to achieve a level playing field for American manufacturers and workers, the USOC should act immediately to find a domestic manufacturer for this year's uniforms." Brown calls for the USOC to enact policies to ensure that America's athletes wear only clothing that is Made-in-America in the next 2014 games. ABC News reached out to Ralph Lauren and the U.S. Olympic Committee and asked why American-made clothing had not been selected for the athletes. The committee responded with a statement: "The U.S. Olympic team is privately funded and we're grateful for the support of our sponsors. We're proud of our partnership with Ralph Lauren, an iconic American company."

Olivier Knox of Yahoo! News / The Ticket reported that President Obama had notified Congress on 13 July 2012 that he was suspending for six months a measure that would let any American whose property was seized in the Cuban Revolution of 1959 sue anyone of any nationality using the property today. "I hereby determine and report to the Congress that suspension, for 6 months beyond August 1, 2012, of the right to bring an action under title III of the Act is necessary to the national interests of the United States and will expedite a transition to democracy in Cuba," Obama said in a letter to top lawmakers. Obama's announcement was not a surprise – every president since Bill Clinton has suspended that provision of the Cuban Liberty and Democratic Solidarity Act of 1996, better known as the Helms-Burton law. The legislation empowers presidents to waive that section for six-month intervals. Critics of the law have warned that allowing such lawsuits could pit Americans against individuals and entities from countries that are allied with the United States but who do not respect the U.S. embargo on trade with Cuba. Several large European hotel chains have built establishments in Cuba, where tourism is critical to the economy. But Obama recently seemed to rule out the further easing of trade restrictions if he wins a second term unless the island embraces democratic reforms. The announcement came on the anniversary of a 13 July 1994, incident in which Cubans fleeing the island aboard the tugboat 13 de Marzo died when the vessel sank as it was being chased by Castro's gunboats. Of the roughly 72 people on board, 41 died.

Obama planned a campaign swing through Florida, which is home to a thriving Cuban exile community. While anti-Castro sentiment runs high, younger Cuban-Americans have gradually become less fired-up by the issue than the generations that recall the revolution. Obama has eased some aspects of the five-decade-old American embargo, which initially aimed to pressure Castro over the nationalization of American property, then grew gradually tighter as Havana lined up with Moscow in the Cold War. Supporters of the embargo say it remains Washington's best tool for pressuring Cuba into adopting democratic reforms. But in recent years, a growing chorus of American critics of the sanctions has noted that the punitive measures did nothing to prevent Castro from outlasting American president after president. And they have charged that Washington is guilty of hypocrisy when it embraces trade with China as a democratizing force but blocks trade with Cuba. They have also called the embargo pointless at a time when Europeans and others are investing in Cuba.

Another voice in Tampa was that of Condoleezza Rice who called for a "compassionate" immigration policy. "We must continue to welcome the world's most ambitious people to be a part of us. In that way we stay young and optimistic and determined," Rice said. "We need immigration laws that protect our borders; meet our economic needs; and yet show that we are a compassionate people."

But there is a widening racial chasm for both parties reported Ronald Brownstein in the *National Journal*. Romney, he says, could run as well among whites as any Republican presidential challenger in the history of polling and still lose. That equation carries threats for both parties.

Meanwhile Devin Dwyer of ABC OTUS News reported that for the third consecutive month, the Obama campaign spent more than it raised in July, assumed new debt and substantially depleted its cash-on-hand reserves, according to the organization's Federal Election Commission filing for July. Obama for America collected $49.1 million between July 1 and 31 – a modest increase over June and on pace to match the president's fundraising record of $746 million from four years ago. But a rapid summertime expansion of grassroots organizing operations in swing states and an aggressive advertising blitz against rival Mitt Romney has begun to drain resources. Obama for America spent $58.8 million over the same period, according to the filing. The top five expenditures last month were media buys ($39 million), online ads ($8.7 million), payroll ($2.9 million), payroll taxes ($1.2 million) and polling ($900,000). Obama's available cash on hand fell $10 million in July from $97 million to $87.7 million. Debts owed by the campaign rose to $2.8 million.

However, the Romney campaign and affiliated groups are on track to out-raise and out-spend Obama with an expected $1 billion on advertising. "I will be outspent in this election. And we will not win the ad wars on TV and radio. Right now the other side is outspending us on TV by at least 2-to-1 in most battleground states," Obama said in an email to supporters earlier in the month. "That's OK. But only if we're able to keep the spending gap close enough so that our investments in a truly grassroots campaign pay off," he said.

Joint fundraising accounts with the Democratic National Committee will help keep Obama competitive with Romney. The Obama Victory Fund raised $30.4 million in July. The party itself reported raising $9.9 million. All official entities raising money for a second Obama term had a combined $126.7 million cash on hand as of July 31. The Romney campaign and its affiliated groups reported $185.9 million.

As the focus on money continued, Aaron Smith of CNNMoney.com reported that *The Hill*, a political news site, unveiled its annual list of the 50 richest lawmakers and Rep. Michael McCaul, a Republican from Texas, held on to the top slot with a cool $290.5 million. "McCaul remains in the stratosphere of the very richest members of Congress," said *The Hill*, noting that his wealth "stems from several family trusts," and that his father Lowry Mays founded Clear Channel Communications. His value actually rose by $3 million in 2011, the time period covered in the list. McCaul is far ahead of his challenger, Sen. John Kerry of Massachusetts, the wealthiest Democrat in Congress, who reported a net worth of $198.8 million last year. That's a $5 million increase from the year before, even though in 2010 he made only No. 3. Much of Kerry's wealth comes from his wife, an heir to the Heinz Ketchup estate.

Rep. Darrell Issa, a Republican from California, dropped one notch from 2010 but still placed third. *The Hill* said his wealth plunged about $80 million to $140.6 million. He is the founder of Directed Electronics, a maker of car security systems and also has a high-yield trust worth $50 million as well as bond holdings. He took on $50 million worth of personal loans last year, which *The Hill* said was the main reason his estate took such a big hit. Rep. Jared Polis, a Democrat from Colorado, come in fourth, with $91.1 million, after his wealth soared by $25 million last year. His portfolio includes a blind trust and tech company holdings. The fifth richest lawmaker is Sen. Mark Warner, a Democrat and former Virginia governor, with $85.9 million. *The Hill* said his assets include investment funds, bonds and a

$1 million life insurance policy. Rep. Paul Ryan, a Republican from Wisconsin and a candidate for the vice presidency, is worth a relatively paltry $2.2 million and didn't make the cut. Even though Democrats make up three of the top five on *The Hill*'s list, Republicans outnumber Democrats, 31 to 19.

XII

WADING INTO a debunked conspiracy theory in Commerce, Mitt Romney raised the issue of President Obama's citizenship, wrote Beth Fouhy and Julie Pace of the Associated Press, by joking that "no one's ever asked to see my birth certificate." At a rally in the suburbs of Detroit, Romney told a crowd of about 5,000 that he and his wife were happy to be back near their childhood home. "They know that this is the place that we were born and raised," Romney said. The remark was a clear reference to the discredited claims that Obama was not born in the United States and thus ineligible to be president. Hawaii officials have repeatedly verified Obama's citizenship, and courts have rebuffed lawsuits over the issue. The Obama campaign decried the remark, saying Romney was embracing "the most strident voices in his party instead of standing up to them."

Obama has been dogged throughout his presidency by question about his birthplace. He released a long form copy of his birth certificate last year, showing he was born in Hawaii in 1961. Romney has been careful to steer clear of the birth certificate issue, even while enthusiastically accepting support from Donald Trump. Whenever he was asked about the issue in interviews, Romney always demurred and said it was a settled issue. But among a segment of the conservative, anti-Obama movement, the issue is a rallying cry that continues to persist despite evidence to the contrary. For Romney, raising the issue at this point runs contrary to his campaigns goal of boosting his support among independent and undecided voters, for whom Obama's birth certificate is presumably a non-issue. It also overshadowed efforts by Romney advisers to establish convention themes that cast him as a compassionate and serious presidential candidate by featuring Romney's personal side and life's experiences. Romney's birth certificate crack comes a day after he gave Democrats another opening by declaring that big businesses in the U.S. were "doing fine" in the current strapped economy in part because they get advantages from offshore tax havens. His comments echoed similar assertions by Obama about the state of the private sector, comments Romney has criticized. They are also a reminder that the GOP candidate himself has kept some of his personal fortune in low tax foreign accounts, including Switzerland and the Cayman Islands.

In a sign Romney was further solidifying his base, former Republican presidential candidate Rick Santorum said he was releasing the delegates he won during the GOP primary race to Mitt Romney. The decision is a formality that frees more than 200 delegates to support Romney at the party's national convention in Tampa, Fla. Santorum became Romney's top opponent for the GOP nomination. His withdrawal from the race in April cleared the way for Romney's general election fight against Obama. However Romney couldn't count on such support from Texas Rep. Ron Paul who declined to speak at the Republican National Convention at Tampa telling a *New York Times* reporter that the planners had offered him an opportunity to speak under two conditions, first that he deliver remarks vetted by the Romney campaign and second that he give a full-fledged endorsement of Romney. According to Chris Moody of Yahoo! News / The Ticket, Paul declined, saying, "It wouldn't be my speech. That would undo everything I've done in the last 30 years. I don't fully endorse him for president."

This was not however the way real estate mogul and former presidential candidate Donald Trump felt. "Get Mitt Romney elected," Trump said after accepting Sarasota County's Statesman of the Year Award. "We need a new president. We need somebody that can really help this country become a great country again. Right now, we're a country in decline, serious decline." During a news conference before the ceremony, Trump called on the GOP to engage in a nastier fight with Obama after fielding questions about anti-Romney advertising and the local vandalizing of a "Repeal Obama" billboard in Sarasota County. A campaign's mistake, Trump said, is to be too politically correct and too nice. It's time for Republicans to get nasty and combat what he called an "unbelievably negative" campaign waged by Barack Obama.

But in spite of the celebration, Romney was not without worry and he was telling some people, according to Holly Bailey of Yahoo! News / The Ticket that "I don't think everybody likes me." Before the day of the Republicans' convention when he would accept the GOP nomination, Romney told *USA Today*'s Susan Page, that his wife, Ann, would offer a glimpse of his personal side to voters in her convention speech. But when he takes the stage, it will be all business.

It's a notable choice even as Romney bluntly acknowledges in both the *USA Today* interview and in a separate interview with Politico that some voters just don't like him. He accuses President Barack Obama and his allies of "personal vilification and demonization" – and admits their attacks have been effective. "There are plenty of weaknesses that I have, and I acknowledge that," Romney tells *USA Today*. "But the attacks that have come have been so misguided, have been so far off target, have been so dishonest, that they surprised me. I thought they might go after me on things that were accurate that I've done wrong, instead of absurd things."

Romney insisted he won't change his focus to appeal more to voters on an emotional basis. "I know there are some people who do a very good job acting and pretend they're something they're not. ... You get what you see. I am who I am," Romney told Politico's Jim VandeHei and Mike Allen. "I don't think everybody likes me. I don't believe that, by any means. But I do believe that people of this country are looking for someone who can get the country growing again with more jobs and more take-home pay, and I think they realize this president had four years to do that. ... He got every piece of legislation he wanted passed, and it didn't work. I think they want someone who has a different record, and I do." But while Romney assailed the Obama campaign for its attacks, the presumptive Republican nominee has grown more aggressive on the trail. Two weeks before, he slammed Obama for running a campaign based on "division and anger and hate." He accused Obama of trying to undo historic welfare reforms requiring recipients to work and of using Medicare funds to pay for so-called "Obamacare" – two lines of attack that have been disputed by independent fact-checkers. He told *USA Today* that Obama and his allies have tried "to minimize me as an individual, to make me a bad person, an unacceptable person."

In Tampa Rudy Giuliani said the election this November is between "Mr. Cool" and "Mr. Competent" wrote Chris Moody of Yahoo! News. Voters should consider "competence" over "cool" when deciding who to support for president in November, former New York Mayor Giuliani said. Giuliani told reporters that voters "made a big mistake" by electing President Barack Obama in 2008. "If I had to select somebody to straighten out my business, I wouldn't necessarily select the cool guy, I'd select the competent guy," Giuliani said in response to a question about Mitt Romney's personal appeal to voters. "And I think maybe we made a big mistake last time."

Chapter Four – Race and Racism

"This is God's curse on slavery! – a bitter, bitter, most accursed thing! – a curse to the master and a curse to the slave! I was a fool to think I could make anything good out of such a deadly evil. It is a sin to hold a slave under laws like ours, – I always felt it was, – I always thought so when I was a girl, – I thought so still more after I joined the church; but I thought I could gild it over, – I thought, by kindness, and care, and instruction, I could make the condition of mine better than freedom – fool that I was!" – Harriet Beecher Stowe in *Uncle Tom's Cabin*

DETROIT. – "What we are seeing here," said Dave Harold, "are the early signs of the end of a civilization." I thought he was cool; his voice hadn't raised an octave to indicate sadness or bitterness as he drove his black SUV through the deserted streets of the city that the motor industry had built. "Should we be surprised? I don't think so. It's what happens in history; rise and fall. It happened to the Greeks and to the Mayans. Now it is Americans' turn."

You couldn't however mistake his acceptance of history for a lack of pride and patriotism. It was a phenomenon that always surprised me – the fierce loyalty of black Americans to the Stars and Stripes. "Why is it," I had asked Ray Boddie, "that knowing the horrible acts of inhumanity that white Americans committed on their slaves – the record is there in Frederick Douglass's *Narrative* – why is it that black Americans are always so *American*?" I was thinking not just of their leadership in sport and entertainment but also of their commitment in the wars that the United States has fought and in their forgiveness of the heinous wrongs of slavery and an acceptance it had often seemed of a second-class citizenship. He had answered simply, "This is our country. We know no other."

We know no other. Eric Williams had said that "Massa Day done", and that there must now be no more Mother Africa and no more Mother India, but Trinidadians and Tobagonians were still dressing as if they had just come off the ships from Freetown and Calcutta and asking the government for millions of oil dollars to celebrate the distant cultures of their forefathers. How many children say in school, "This is *our* Trinidad and Tobago", as the Chinese students we taught used to say, "This is *our* China"? There are times when I think that Emancipation and Independence failed us and did not make us patriots. We are, as Williams condemned us without condemning his politics, transients. But this is not the way of black Americans. Their hope for a better life is rooted in the blood, sweat and tears of the land of their birth, in their suffering. They ceased to be Africans a long time ago and it is this fact that makes their patience with white America a kind of heroism that every day increases the nobility of their hearts.

I was humbled by Dave Harold's history and I didn't feel I could talk with him on an equal footing. My life and the lives of my parents and siblings had been compromised by the benefits colonialism bestowed on us. But I still felt capable of resisting crookedness and corruption and I believe, as Confucius said, that man's existence lies in his integrity and that a man without integrity can exist merely through his luck. It was clear that Lady Luck had played a part in Dave's life but it was also clear that he had never left it to luck alone. In the America in which he had grown up he had to have character and will to overcome the hardship and disease that had killed his parents and so many others like them.

This part of America, the state of Michigan, had always seemed very remote and Detroit was not a city I would visit ordinarily, but it was where Rhona had gone to university on a scholarship that was provided by the venerable Canon Max Murphy in the late fifties. The university was Marygrove College, a small Roman Catholic establishment. In 1986 when we worked at the Trinidad *Express* she had attended her 25th graduation class; but I was unable to accompany her. This time in 2011 she was going to her 50th class reunion and I had no excuse not to meet her graduating class members of 1961. And, indeed, it was because of this celebration and travel that I had come up with the idea of finding out what was the Soul of America – and what was the face of the man whom she said she could have married. Over the past fifty years David Harold had been an unknown quantity and all I knew about him was the fact that he had come from Biloxi, a town in the Mississippi area that we had once driven through on our way to Los Angeles from Miami.

But at that time I had not paid any attention to Biloxi and it was not until I was about to go to Detroit that I read that French explorers first arrived on American shores in 1699, to be greeted by the Biloxi Indians, fabled ancestors of the Harold clan. The Mississippi Gulf Coast has been a year-round destination for rest and relaxation. The mild sub-tropical climate has made the area a golf destination that boasts several championship courses designed by legends like Palmer, Nicklaus and Fazio and singled out by golf writers as among the best in the nation. The area hosts the annual Mississippi Gulf Resort Classic, a PGA Champions Tour event. Over 300 years under eight flags gives Biloxi natives an interesting history, and the culture and heritage is kept alive and celebrated through hundreds of annual events, from Mardi Gras to Seafood Festivals, fishing rodeos, the "Blessing of the Fleet" and re-enactments of the 1699 Landing of D'Iberville and Fall Muster at Confederate president Jefferson Davis' former home, Beauvoir. So this was David Harold's history.

"I feel that his past is not unlike yours," Xiuling said, reading aloud as the Amtrak train sped past farm and town. "And were it not for the fact that Rhona was so reluctant to give up her own Trini nationality you would not be making this trip today."

"I have never had a problem with my birth," Rhona said, "and I think the fuss over the President's is absurd."

"I used to think that it was political," Xiuling said, "but now I think it is racist."

The truth is I never did understand the point of the Obama birther controversy and it is difficult to think that it was anything but racist. Dave Harold was to relate his own experiences when he joined the U.S. Navy and contrary to his application to be a photographer with the

Stars and Stripes he was assigned duties in the galley. His rebellion was simple: he spilled coffee over the impeccable laps of his officers and was promptly removed to solitary and to less hazardous duties. In his *Narrative* Frederick Douglass relates a similar strategy of awkwardness to earn a full meal. "One of my greatest faults was that of letting (my master's) horse run away and go down to his father-in-law's farm. I would then have to go after it. My reason was that I could always get something to eat when I went there." In Dave Harold's case it was not a meal he was after; it was the success of being treated as an equal. The fact is the United States since the end of the civil war should not be a country where there are slaves and slave owners and equal opportunities should be had by both black and white. This fact makes the taunts of Obama's birth, especially after he was elected as President of the United States, both fatuous and a sinister form of racism.

What is more absurd is the fact that the groups of persons who make the accusation and who continue to pour oil on this fire are not nincompoops and in fact occupy prominent positions in the U.S. But we could all realize the folly of this stupid joke when the Republicans' candidate to face Obama in November could say that nobody has asked him to show his birth certificate. I think he should have been the first to put a stop to this ludicrous affair. We should not have been surprised therefore when Chris Matthews lashed out at Republican National Committee Chairman Reince Priebus in Tampa during a live "Morning Joe" segment, with the feisty MSNBC host accusing Mitt Romney and the GOP of playing the race card in their campaign against President Barack Obama, according to Dylan Stableford of Yahoo! News / The Ticket. "It is an embarrassment to your party to play that card," Matthews said. "This stuff about getting rid of the work requirement for welfare is dishonest, everyone (has) pointed out it's dishonest, and you are playing that little ethnic card there. You can play games and giggle about it, but the fact is your side is playing that card. You start talking about work requirements and everyone knows what game you're playing. It's a race card."

But the truth is the campaign was never far from talk about race.

In The Sideshow of 16 March 2012, Eric Pfeiffer was puzzled by a racist, anti-Obama bumper sticker. The sticker that was on the back of a vehicle had been garnering lots of attention on Facebook. It warned: *"Don't Re-Nig in 2012."* And in smaller print below, *"Stop repeat offenders. Don't re-elect Obama!"* The sticker also featured an image of the Obama campaign logo crossed out. It seemed shocking that someone would proudly display an openly racist image on their vehicle in 2012. So, was the image authentic? It was Pfeiffer said. The report reminded me of the wish of the Founding Fathers to see all men as equals and of Lincoln's use of African slaves to defeat Robert Lee's forces to defend the South's intention to maintain and spread slavery. I don't think that Lincoln was a lover of the black man but he hated slavery and acted on the principle that it was wrong. And he saw and warned that a government cannot endure permanently half slave and half free. Do Americans need to be told this again?

On the train from Brooklyn to Manhattan I watched the impassive faces of New Yorkers. Most of them had come to this metropolis to improve their lives. And the young woman from Bangladesh, a lawyer, was as friendly as the young man from Michigan, a musician. "People in New York," Denise Singh had said to me, "are friendly. It is like we are all immigrants in this city and in a crisis as in 2001. We must stand together." She had been living in the city for twelve years and was happy even though she had always worked as a baby-sitter. Times as Ingrid McIntosh, a Jamaican waitress, had said were hard. She had joined her mother in 2001 after the terrorists' attack on the World Trade Centre but hadn't found the streets to be paved with gold. Her mother had worked and saved and sent for her but she doubted that she would be able to do the same for children she had left in Kingston. Being black said Yolanda Singh who had worked with one of the network television stations had at times its own problems. "You always have to be prepared to show you can do the job as good as white Americans. It is as if many Americans are still living in the past."

We have got to be judged, said Johnnie Cochran, during the murder trial of O.J. Simpson, by how we do in times of crisis. And to make the point obvious to everyone in that odious courtroom that honor was everyone's responsibility Cochran said, "We are all here together, but there's a lot of different views, people sitting here thinking, I don't own any slaves, all the slaves are dead. Why am I responsible? My family were immigrants too." The thinking behind the bumper sticker is the same as the sentiment in the time of Lincoln that a Negro was not a man but a brute, unequalled to the job of managing himself and others. It is what is implied in the birther gossip.

Pfeiffer said that a website called "Stumpy's Stickers" offers the bumper sticker for sale for $3. And the site also offers several other racially insensitive items for sale as well. The urban myth-debunking site Snopes says it cannot yet determine the origins of the photo, but also points out the availability of other similar t-shirts and bumper stickers. There is even an eponymous "Dontre-nig.com" website that appears to have crashed. Going to the page brings up a "Bandwith Limit Exceeded" warning message. Pfeiffer says he checked the domain registration service site WHOIS, which listed the site as belonging to an anonymous owner who purchased the URL through the company DomainsByProxy.com, based in Scottsdale, Arizona. The company specializes in keeping the names of Internet domain owners private. However as one astute Facebook reader pointed out, the bumper sticker is not only offensive, it's pretty dumb. After all, if you take the top message at its literal meaning, to not renege in 2012, would mean to in fact re-elect President Obama. But this too is semantics and a way to avoid responsibility for the obvious racist commentary.

As Lincoln had said the point of all racist commentary was to deprive the Negro, in every possible event, of the benefit of that provision of the United States Constitution which declares that "the citizens of each state shall be entitled to all privileges and immunities of citizens in the several states." And the war that was fought between north and south, between the Union soldiers and the Confederates, was fought to correct this evil. But the mischief has never totally disappeared and the American society faces still convulsion after convulsion based on race. At Simpson's trial Cochran had said that "it was time in America for African Americans to take retribution for the legal crimes that had been committed against them for almost three centuries" and the cause for retribution is still obvious today.

II

I THINK it was inevitable that on 25 March 2012, according to a Reuters report from Jeff Mason and Daniel Trotta, that President Obama would take part in the controversial killing of Trayvon Martin in Florida in very personal terms, comparing the boy to a son he doesn't have and calling for American "soul searching" over how the incident occurred. Seventeen-year-old Martin, dressed in a "hoodie", a hooded sweatshirt, was shot dead on 26 February in Sanford, Florida, by a 28-year-old white Hispanic neighborhood watch volunteer who said he was acting in self-defense. "If I had a son, he'd look like Trayvon," Obama said in his first comments about the shooting, acknowledging the racial element in the case. "Obviously, this is a tragedy," Obama told reporters. "I can only imagine what these parents are going through. And when I think about this boy, I think about my own kids."

The case had galvanized the nation and prompted rallies protesting the failure of police to arrest the shooter, George Zimmerman, and more broadly, a pattern of racial discrimination that black leaders cite in Sanford and elsewhere in the country. Obama, the first black U.S. president, made his remarks at a White House event to announce his pick to lead the World Bank, waiting briefly after the announcement to take a reporter's question about the incident. Martin's parents thanked the president for his words. "The president's personal comments touched us deeply and made us wonder: If his son looked like Trayvon and wore a hoodie, would he be suspicious too?"

Florida's "Stand Your Ground" law allows people to use deadly force in self-defense. Similar laws are in effect in at least 24 states including Florida, according to the Brady Campaign to Prevent Gun Violence. Calls are mounting to repeal them. Earlier this week, a Florida state senator said he was drafting new legislation to drastically change the law in Florida. A South Carolina state representative said he had introduced a bill to repeal his state's law. Bakari Sellers, a black Democrat and gun owner, said he wanted to prevent an incident like the Trayvon Martin shooting happening in his state. "I'm six-five and a black guy," he said. "I just know that it could have been me."

Obama said the "Stand Your Ground" laws should be studied. "I think all of us have to do some soul-searching to figure out how does something like this happen. And that means that we examine the laws and the context for what happened, as well as the specifics of the incident," he said. "Every parent in America should be able to understand why it is absolutely imperative that we investigate every aspect of this, and that everybody pulls together – federal, state and local – to figure out exactly how this tragedy happened." Obama, the son of a white mother from Kansas and black father from Kenya, does not comment frequently on race, a sensitive topic in the United States, which still grapples with a legacy of slavery, segregation and discrimination. Early in his White House tenure, Obama inflamed another racially tinged incident by declaring police had "acted stupidly" when arresting a well-known black documentary filmmaker, Henry Louis Gates, after an altercation at his home. Obama later invited Gates and the white police officer, Sergeant James Crowley, to the White House, where the men shared a drink in what became known as the "beer summit".

In Sanford, Norton Bonaparte Jr., the city's manager, acknowledged tensions between the black community and police "go back many, many years. The trust that existed is gone, so we have to start from ground zero," he said. Sanford's police chief and a Florida state prosecutor overseeing the case stepped aside as criticism grew over police handling of the investigation. The state's new special prosecutor, Angela Corey, arrived in Sanford after Gov. Rick Scott appointed her. "We appreciate that an investigation was already done. We are going to review what was done. We are going to continue to investigate and then we'll proceed from there," Bernie de la Rionda, an assistant state attorney with Corey's team, told reporters outside the police department.

The U.S. Justice Department is also investigating. Senior officials from the department met with the Martin family in Florida, along with their lawyer. A Justice Department spokeswoman said early in the week that they must collect evidence to prove beyond a reasonable doubt that there was or was not intent to violate civil rights laws. And a Florida college announced it had suspended Zimmerman's enrollment. Zimmerman was working toward an associate's degree in arts at Seminole State College in Sanford. He previously earned a vocational certificate in an insurance field, the school said. "Due to the highly charged and high-profile controversy involving this student,

Seminole State has taken the unusual but necessary step this week to withdraw Mr. Zimmerman from enrollment." Florida court records reviewed by Reuters showed Zimmerman was involved in at least two previous legal incidents, including a 2005 domestic violence case with his former fiancée. Zimmerman, who at the time worked at an insurance agency and he and his ex-fiancée both sought restraining orders against each other after getting into a pushing match. In her complaint, Veronica Zuazo said the two had been involved in two physical fights in 2002 and 2003. Zimmerman was also arrested and charged with resisting a law enforcement officer with violence in 2005. The case was eventually dropped after he completed a program to avoid being formally charged.

It is clear that race is a hydra-head monster and is alive and well in spite of the many efforts to confront and kill it. It is as if the supremacy of one race over others was written in the United States Constitution. In every city and state racist attitudes bristle. On 27 December 2011 in Phoenix, Ar., the Associated Press reported that an administrative law judge ruled that a Tucson school district's ethnic studies program violates state law, agreeing with the findings of Arizona's public schools chief. Judge Lewis Kowal's ruling marked a defeat for the Tucson Unified School District, which appealed the findings issued in June by Superintendent of Public Instruction John Huppenthal. Kowal's ruling, first reported by *The Arizona Daily Star*, said the district's Mexican-American Studies program violated state law by having one or more classes designed primarily for one ethnic group, promoting racial resentment and advocating ethnic solidarity instead of treating students as individuals.

The judge, who found grounds to withhold 10 per cent of the district's monthly state aid until it comes into compliance, said the law permits the objective instruction about the oppression of people that may result in racial resentment or ethnic solidarity. "However, teaching oppression objectively is quite different than actively presenting material in a biased, political and emotionally charged manner, which is what occurred in (Mexican-American Studies) classes," Kowal wrote. The judge said such teaching promotes activism against white people, promotes racial resentment and advocates ethnic solidarity. The battle over the ethnic studies program escalated shortly after Arizona's heavily scrutinized immigration enforcement law was passed in April

2010. The program's supporters have called challenges to the courses an attack on the state's Hispanic population, while critics say the program demonizes white people as oppressors of Hispanics. Huppenthal ordered a review of the program when he took office in January after his predecessor, Tom Horne, said the Mexican-American Studies program violated state law and that Huppenthal would have to decide whether to withhold funding. Huppenthal, a Republican, had voted in favor of the ethnic studies law as a state senator before becoming the state's schools chief.

On 12 January 2012 Joe Mandax of the Associated Press filed a report from Pittsburgh that a black man who says racial discrimination forced him to quit working at a Panera Bread restaurant has sued its franchisee, claiming the company doesn't want black employees in positions where they interact with the public. His lawsuit echoes allegations by a white manager of the suburban Pittsburgh store who sued last year, claiming he was fired for defending the employee. The defendant, Warren, Ohio-based Covelli Enterprises, which operates nearly 200 Panera cafes in four states, contends the 21-year-old man walked off the job last year after he was disciplined for violating company dress code, and health and safety policies. A company statement called the new lawsuit filed by Guy Vines and one filed in November by the fired manager, Scott Donatelli, "a coordinated attempt by two disgruntled former employees to discredit the company for a profit motive." Vines' 12-page complaint, filed in federal court in Pittsburgh, echoes Donatelli's, which alleges he was fired by Covelli for objecting to Vines' treatment. The company said in its statement that it investigated Donatelli's claims and called them "completely unfounded." But Sam Cordes, the attorney for both plaintiffs, writes in Vines' lawsuit that the truth is much simpler. "African Americans were routinely assigned to jobs either in the back of the store washing dishes or doing food preparation so customers would not see them," Cordes said. The lawsuit alleges that the company's top managers dictated that "people who are 'Black, Fat, and/or Ugly' should never be permitted to work the cash registers."

The lawsuit contends Vines, of Castle Shannon, would be moved to the back of the store whenever owner Sam Covelli was at the Mount Lebanon location where Vines worked from November 2009 until he quit in August 2011, or whenever local or district managers expected a visit from Covelli. Both lawsuits contend a district manager reprimanded Donatelli and told him Covelli would "(expletive) if he got a look at 'that'" – meaning Vines working anywhere customers could see him. Both lawsuits contend Donatelli found Vines to be a polite, hardworking employee who was willing to work extra shifts and change schedules as needed. Despite that, both lawsuits claim the district manager became upset with Donatelli in February upon seeing Vines working the cash register, telling Donatelli, "You know that is a death sentence for me and you if Sam would walk in and see him on register."

St. Louis-based Panera Bread Co., which offers freshly baked bread, sandwiches and soups in a sit-down setting for slightly higher prices than those at most fast-food chains, said on its website it has about 1,500 company-owned and franchise-operated bakery-cafes in 40 states and in Ontario, Canada, under the Panera Bread, Saint Louis Bread Co. and Paradise Bakery & Cafe names. According to its website, Covelli is the fifth-largest restaurant franchisee in the country and develops and manages the franchise rights of nearly 200 Panera cafes in northeast Ohio, western Pennsylvania, West Virginia and West Palm Beach, Fla.

The Associated Press also reported on 8 January 2012 that Papa John's Pizza is apologizing after an employee typed a racial slur on a receipt to a customer at one of its New York City locations. Customer Minhee Cho posted a message on Twitter along with an image of the receipt from a Manhattan location describing her as "lady chinky eyes." Several hours later after the message had gone viral, the Louisville, Ky.-based company formally apologized on its Facebook and Twitter pages for Cho's experience. The company says the employee was dismissed.

And on 11 January 2012, Sam Hananel of the Associated Press reported that Pepsi Beverages Co. will pay $3.1 million to settle federal charges of race discrimination for using criminal background checks to screen out job applicants – even if they weren't convicted of a crime. The settlement announced with the Equal Employment Opportunity Commission was part of a national government crackdown on hiring policies that can hurt blacks and Hispanics. EEOC officials said the company's policy of not hiring workers with arrest records disproportionately excluded more than 300 black applicants. The policy barred applicants who had been arrested, but not convicted of a crime, and denied employment to others who were convicted of minor offenses. Using arrest and conviction records to deny employment can be illegal if it's irrelevant for the job, according to the EEOC, which enforces the nation's employment discrimination laws. The agency says such blanket policies can limit job opportunities for minorities with higher arrest and conviction rates than whites. The company has since adopted a new criminal background policy and plans to make jobs available to victims of the old policy if they are still interested in jobs at Pepsi and are qualified for the openings. "I commend Pepsi's willingness to re-examine its policy and modify it to ensure that unwarranted roadblocks to employment are removed," EEOC Chairwoman Jacqueline Berrien said in a statement.

Pepsi Beverage spokesman Dave DeCecco said the company's criminal background check policy has always been neutral and that the EEOC did not find any intentional discrimination. He said after the issue was first raised in 2006, the company worked with the EEOC to revise its background check process "to create a workplace that is as diverse and inclusive as possible. We are committed to promoting diversity and inclusion and we have been widely recognized for our efforts for decades," DeCecco said. He said the new policy would take a more "individualized approach" in considering the applicant's criminal history against the particular job being sought. Pepsi Beverages is PepsiCo's beverage manufacturing, sales and distribution operating unit in the United States, Canada and Mexico. Under the settlement, the company will provide the EEOC with regular reports on its hiring practices and offer anti-discrimination training to its hiring personnel and managers.

About 73 per cent of major employers report that they always check on applicants' criminal records, while 19 per cent do so for select job candidates, according to a 2010 survey by the Society for Human Resource Management. But increased federal scrutiny of such policies has led some companies to re-evaluate their hiring process. Pamela Devata, a Chicago employment lawyer who has represented companies trying to comply with EEOC's requirements, said there has been an uptick over the past year in EEOC charges over the use of background checks. "The EEOC has taken a very aggressive enforcement posture on the use of criminal background and criminal history," Devata said, adding that employers have been expecting the EEOC to issue more specific guidance. EEOC officials have said, for example, that an old drunken driving conviction may not be relevant to a clerical job, but a theft conviction may disqualify someone from working at a bank. Julie Schmid, acting director of the EEOC's Minneapolis office, said the EEOC recommends that employers consider the nature and gravity of offenses, the time that has passed since conviction or completion of a sentence, and the nature of the job sought. "We hope that employers with unnecessarily broad criminal background check policies take note of this agreement and re-assess their policies to ensure compliance" with antidiscrimination laws, Schmid said in a written statement.

III

NEW CENSUS data paint a stark portrait of the nation's haves and have-nots at a time when unemployment remains persistently high. It comes a week before the government released first-ever economic data that will show more Hispanics, elderly and working-age poor have fallen into poverty. In all, the numbers underscore the breadth and scope by which the downturn has reached further into mainstream America. "There now really is no unaffected group, except maybe the very top income earners," said Robert Moffitt, a professor of economics at Johns Hopkins University. "Recessions are supposed to be temporary, and when it's over, everything returns to where it was before. But the worry now is that the downturn – which will end eventually – will have long-lasting effects on families who lose jobs, become worse off and can't recover."

Traditional inner-city black ghettos are thinning out and changing, drawing in impoverished Hispanics who have low-wage jobs or are unemployed. Neighborhoods with poverty rates of at least 40 per cent are stretching over broader areas, increasing in suburbs at twice the rate of cities. Once-booming Sun Belt metro areas are now seeing some of the biggest jumps in concentrated poverty. The Associated Press reported that the ranks of America's poorest poor have climbed to a record high – 1 in 15 people – spread widely across metropolitan areas as the housing bust pushed many inner-city poor into suburbs and other outlying places and shriveled jobs and income.

Signs of a growing divide between rich and poor can be seen in places such as the upscale Miami suburb of Miami Shores, where nannies gather with their charges at a playground nestled between the township's sprawling golf course and soccer fields. The locale is a far cry from where many of them live. One is Mariana Gripaldi, 36, an Argentinian who came to the U.S. about 10 years ago to escape her own country's economic crisis. She and her husband rent a two-bedroom apartment near Biscayne Bay in a middle-class neighborhood at the north end of Miami Beach, far from the chic hotels and stores. But Gripaldi said in the past two years, the neighborhood has seen an increase in crime. "The police come sometimes once or twice a night," she said in Spanish. "We are looking for a new place, but it's so expensive. My husband went to look at a place, and it was $1,500 for a two-bedroom, one bath. I don't like the changes, but I don't know if we can move."

About 20.5 million Americans, or 6.7 per cent of the U.S. population, make up the poorest poor, defined as those at 50 per cent or less of the official poverty level. Those living in deep poverty represent nearly half of the 46.2 million people scraping by below the poverty line. In 2010, the poorest poor meant an income of $5,570 or less for an individual and $11,157 for a family of four. That 6.7 per cent share is the highest in the 35 years that the Census Bureau has maintained such records, surpassing previous highs in 2009 and 1993 of just over 6 per cent. Broken down by states, 40 states and the District of Columbia had increases in the poorest poor since 2007, and none saw decreases. The District of Columbia ranked highest at 10.7 per cent, followed by Mississippi and New Mexico. Nevada had the biggest jump, rising from 4.6 per cent to 7 per cent.

Concentrated poverty also spread wider. After declining during the 1990s economic boom, the proportion of poor people in large metropolitan areas who lived in high-poverty neighborhoods jumped from 11.2 per cent in 2000 to 15.1 per cent last year, according to a Brookings Institution analysis. Such geographically concentrated poverty in the U.S. is now at the highest since 1990, following a decade of high unemployment and rising energy costs. Extreme poverty today continues to be prevalent in the industrial Midwest, including Detroit, Grand Rapids, Mich., and Akron, Ohio, due to a renewed decline in manufacturing. But the biggest growth in high-poverty areas is occurring in newer Sun Belt metro areas such as Las Vegas, Riverside, Calif., and Cape Coral, Fla., after the plummeting housing market wiped out home values and dried up construction jobs. As a whole, the number of poor in the suburbs who lived in high-poverty neighborhoods rose by 41 per cent since 2000, more than double the growth of such city neighborhoods.

Elizabeth Kneebone, a senior research associate at Brookings, described a demographic shift in people living in high-poverty neighborhoods, which have less access to good schools, hospitals and government services. As concentrated poverty spreads to new areas, including suburbs, the residents are now more likely to be white, native-born and high school or college graduates – not the conventional image of high-school dropouts or single mothers in inner-city ghettos. The more recent broader migration of the U.S. population, including working- and middle-class blacks, to the South and to suburbs helps explain some of the shifts in poverty.

A study by the Joint Center for Political and Economic Studies found that the population of 133 historically black ghettos had dropped 36 per cent since 1970, as the U.S. black population growth slowed and many blacks moved to new areas. The newest residents in these ghettos are now more likely to be Hispanics, who have more than tripled their share in the neighborhoods, to 21 per cent. Just over 7 per cent of all African-Americans nationwide now live in traditional ghettos, down from 33 per cent in 1970. "As extreme-poverty neighborhoods emerge in more places, that is shifting the general makeup of those populations," said Kneebone, the lead author of the Brookings analysis.

New 2010 poverty data to be released by the Census Bureau will show additional demographic changes. The new supplemental poverty measure for the first time will take into account non-cash aid such as tax credits and food stamps, but also additional everyday costs such as commuting and medical care. Official poverty figures released in September only take into account income before tax deductions. Based on newly released estimates for 2009, the new measure will show a significant jump in overall poverty. Poverty for Americans 65 and older is on track to nearly double after factoring in rising out-of-pocket medical expenses, from 9 per cent to over 15 per cent. Poverty increases are also anticipated for the working-age population because of commuting and child-care costs, while child poverty will dip partly due to the positive effect of food stamps.

For the first time, the share of Hispanics living in poverty is expected to surpass that of African-Americans based on the new measure, reflecting in part the lower participation of immigrants and non-English speakers in government aid programs such as housing and food stamps. The 2009 census estimates show 27.6 per cent of all Hispanics living in poverty, compared with 23.4 per cent for blacks. Alba Alvarez, 52, a nanny in Miami, said she is lucky because her employer rents an apartment to her and her husband at a low rate in a comfortable neighborhood on the bay. But her adult children, who followed her to the U.S. from Honduras, are having a tougher time. They initially found work in a regional wholesale fruit and vegetable market that supplies many local supermarkets. But her youngest son recently lost his job, and since he has no legal status, he cannot get any help from the government. "As a mother, I feel so horrible. There's this sense of powerlessness. I wanted things to be better for them in this country," Alvarez said. "I suggested my youngest go back to Honduras. It's easier for me to help him there than here, where rent and everything is so expensive."

On 15 March 2012, Chris Chase wrote in The Dagger that members of the University of Southern Mississippi band chanted racist taunts at a Hispanic Kansas State player during the schools' NCAA tournament game. After point guard Angel Rodriguez was fouled late in the first half of the second-round game, a few band members showered the freshman with cries of "where's your green card?" Southern Mississippi President Martha Saunders quickly apologized for the incident. "We deeply regret the remarks made by a few students at today's game," she wrote in a statement issued two hours after the game. "The words of these individuals do not represent the sentiments of our pep band, athletic department or university. We apologize to Mr. Rodriguez and will take quick and appropriate disciplinary action against the students involved in this isolated incident."

The basis for the band's racism was itself misguided. Rodriguez was born in Puerto Rico, a commonwealth of the United States. Even if he hadn't grown up in Miami and starred for a high school basketball team in that city, he'd still be an American citizen and have no need for a green card. However, as Jeff Eisenberg wrote in The Dagger on 20 March 2012 the members of Southern Mississippi's pep band who chanted "where's your green card?" at Puerto Rico-born Kansas State guard Angel Rodriguez will pay a stiff price for their poor decision. Saunders announced that five band members have had their scholarships revoked, have been removed from the band and will have to complete a two-hour cultural sensitivity training course. None of the names of the band members were revealed.

Eric Pfeiffer wrote in The Sideshow on 22 March 2012 that a spokeswoman for an elementary school in North Carolina has apologized for a "poorly worded" letter sent to parents in February, which suggested the students wear "animal print" clothing in honor of Black History Month. WSOCTV reported that the Western Union Elementary School in North Carolina's Union County sent the letter, which also suggested dressing in "African-American attire", in celebration of the school's February 28 Black History Day. The letter was published online by the LGBT rights blog UnicornBooty.com. "While it was well-intended, it was poorly worded," Union County Public Schools' Chief Communications Officer Luan Ingram said in a statement. "We are reminding all of our principals to be very sensitive in word choices when communicating with parents concerning different ethnic groups and cultures that make up our world." Ingram said the students had been studying the history of Africans who had been forcibly brought to America as slaves and that the clothing suggestion was meant to honor their cultural heritage, not be a commentary on modern African-American clothing. Ingram told the *Charlotte Observer* that a similar letter had been sent home to students for the past seven or eight years and that none of the students' parents had complained about it.

An image of the letter first appeared on the photo sharing site Imgur and quickly made its way to Reddit. The full text of the letter reads: "Parents, during the month of February, Western Union students have been studying Black History. On Tuesday, February 28, WUES will participate in a Black History Day. We will have speakers from 8-10am. We are encouraging students to dress in 'African American attire'. If you do not have this, students could wear animal print clothing or shirts with animals native to Africa (zebras, giraffes, lions, elephants, etc.). Thank you!"

IV

ON 23 DECEMBER 2011 Mark Hosenball and Samuel P. Jacobs of Reuters wrote that a direct-mail solicitation for Ron Paul's political and investment newsletters two decades ago warned of a "coming race war in our big cities" and of a "federal-homosexual cover-up" to play down the impact of AIDS. The eight-page letter, which appears to carry Paul's signature at the end, also warns that the U.S. government's re-design of currency to include different colors – a move aimed at thwarting counterfeiters – actually was part of a plot to allow the government to track Americans using the "new money". The letter urged readers to subscribe to Paul's newsletters so that he could "tell you how you can save yourself and your family" from an overbearing government. The letter's details emerge at a time when Paul, now a contender for the Republican nomination for president, is under fire over reports that his newsletters contained racist, anti-homosexual and anti-Israel rants. Reports of the newsletters' contents have Paul's campaign scrambling to deny that he wrote the inflammatory articles. Among other things, the articles called the Rev. Martin Luther King Jr. a "world-class philanderer", criticized the U.S. holiday bearing King's name as "Hate Whitey Day," and said that AIDS sufferers "enjoy the attention and pity that comes with being sick." As Paul made a campaign stop in Manchester, Iowa, his Iowa chairman, Drew Ivers, repeated Paul's assertions that he did not write the articles that re-surfaced in a report in the Weekly Standard magazine.

Paul has said that he is not sure who wrote the articles that were published under his name. He has said the articles do not reflect his views, and noted that his public stances – supporting gays in the military for example – have run counter to the incendiary statements in the newsletters. In an interview with CNN's Gloria Borger, Paul said of the newsletter's articles: "I didn't write them. I didn't read them at the time and I disavow them." When Borger continued to pursue the subject, Paul removed his microphone and walked out of the interview.

"It is ridiculous to imply that Ron Paul is a bigot, racist, or unethical," Ivers said. However, Ivers said, Paul does not deny or retract material that Paul has written under his own signature, such as the letter promoting Paul's newsletters. When asked whether that meant Paul believed there was a government conspiracy to cover up the impact of AIDS, Ivers said, "I don't think he embraces that." Paul's newsletters "showed good factual information and investment information," Ivers said. "It was a public service, helping people understand and equip them to avoid an unsound monetary policy." The letter promoting Paul's newsletters was written about 1993. It was during a period in which Paul – who left Congress in 1985 after serving about eight years – returned to Washington after a decade's absence. The letter was provided to Reuters by James Kirchick, a contributing editor for *The New Republic* magazine. He says he found the letter in archives of political literature maintained by the University of Kansas and the Wisconsin Historical Society.

Early in the 2008 presidential campaign – in which Paul was a candidate – Kirchick published an article in *The New Republic* in which he described Paul as "not the plain-speaking antiwar activist his supporters believe they are backing – but rather a member in good standing of some of the oldest and ugliest traditions in American politics." The letter promoting Paul's newsletters claims that Paul – through what he describes as a network of "extraordinary sources" in Congress, the White House, the Treasury and Justice departments, the Federal Reserve and the Internal Revenue Service – had acquired unique insider information that would help his subscribers to "neutralize" the plans of "powerbrokers". Paul's letter went on to describe various plots and schemes that he had "unmasked," including a "plot for world government, world money and world central banking." He also claimed to have exposed a plan by the Federal Emergency Management Agency (FEMA) to "suspend the Constitution" in a falsely declared national emergency.

Despite being "told not to talk," Paul wrote that his newsletters also "laid bare" the "Israeli lobby, which plays Congress like a cheap harmonica," and a "federal-homosexual cover-up on AIDS." Paul claimed that his "training as a physician" helped him "see through" this alleged cover-up. Paul also suggested that a planned U.S. currency with new notes designed to curb counterfeiting and money laundering would result in the distribution of "totalitarian bills" that "were tinted pink and blue and brown, and blighted with holograms, diffraction gratings, metal and plastic threads and chemical alarms." Paul said the money was designed to allow authorities to "keep track of American cash and American citizens." He urged the letter's readers to send in $99, which would buy subscriptions to his monthly political and investment newsletters, a copy of his book, *Surviving the New Money*, an investment manual and access to the "unlisted phone number of my Financial Hotline for fast breaking news."

On 6 January 2012, Juan Carlos Llorca and Linda Stewart Ball of the Associated Press reported that Jakadrien Lorece Turner, a Texas teenager, was back in the United States and at the center of an international mystery over how a minor could be sent to a country where she is not a citizen. The 15-year-old's family has questioned why U.S. officials didn't do more to verify her identity and say she is not fluent in Spanish and had no ties to Colombia. While many facts of the case involving Jakadrien Lorece Turner remain unclear, U.S. and Colombian officials have pointed fingers over who is responsible. The day before, on 5 January 2012 Jakadrien Lorece Turner who had been missing for more than a year had turned up in Colombia. Lorene Turner had told a Fort Worth television station that her granddaughter had run away from home in the fall of 2010 when she was just 14. Jakadrien made her way to Houston, where she was arrested by police. That's when things took a turn toward the Kafka-esque wrote Eric Pfeiffer in The Slideshow. Jakadrien gave the police a false name and her new alias just happened to match up with the name of a 22-year-old Colombian citizen who had been in the United States illegally. And to compound Turner's plight further, the Colombian National had a warrant out for her arrest. The U.S. Immigration and Customs Enforcement (ICE) then deported Jakadrien in April 2011. "They didn't do their work," Lorene Turner said. "How do you deport a teenager and send her to Colombia without a passport, without anything?" Turner said she'd been looking on her computer every night for clues to her granddaughter's location, and had been cooperating with Dallas police as she carried out her search.

It turns out that after Jakadrien was deported she was given a work card in Colombia and released onto the streets. "She talked about how they had her working in this big house cleaning all day, and how tired she was," Turner said. Jakadrien is now being held in a Colombia detention facility while awaiting more information on her case. "ICE takes these allegations very seriously," said ICE Director of Public Affairs Brian Hale. "At the direction of [the Department of Homeland Security], ICE is fully and immediately investigating this matter in order to expeditiously determine the facts of this case." Immigration experts say that while cases of mistaken identity are rare, people can slip through the cracks, especially if they don't have legal help or family members working on their behalf. But they say U.S. immigration authorities had the responsibility to determine if a person is a citizen. "Often in these situations they have these group hearings where they tell everybody you're going to be deported," said Jacqueline Stevens, a political science professor at Northwestern University, who is an expert on immigration issues. "Everything is really quick, even if you understand English you wouldn't understand what is going on. If she were in that situation as a 14-year-old she would be herded through like cattle and not have a chance to talk to the judge about her situation."

On 26 February 2012 Associated Press writer Verena Dobnik reported from New York that potential candidates for Mayor Michael Bloomberg's office are taking stands on the New York Police Department's surveillance of Muslim students, ranging from cautious support to a warning about curtailing civil liberties. Bloomberg, who leaves office after the 2013 election, has said that he finds "worrisome" the idea that his successor might abandon NYPD policies that have kept New Yorkers safe. The NYPD used undercover officers and informants to infiltrate Muslim student groups at a dozen colleges in New York City, upstate New York, Connecticut, New Jersey and Pennsylvania, documents obtained by The Associated Press show. The monitoring was part of the department's anti-terrorism efforts. But Manhattan Borough President Scott Stringer said in a statement to the AP that "it is troubling when people are subject to surveillance and investigation simply because they are members of a particular group."

NYC Comptroller John C. Liu, who is expected to run for mayor, praised "the dedicated men and women of the NYPD" for doing "an extraordinary job of keeping New Yorkers safe." But in a statement, he also warned that "we should not as a matter of policy profile people based on religion or race – it goes against everything this city stands for." Liu, a Queens Democrat, faces a federal investigation into his fundraising operation after reports of inconsistencies in his campaign finances. When asked about the NYPD surveillance, media executive Tom Allon didn't hedge. "I support the tactics that they've used," said Allon, who plans to run as both a Liberal and a Democrat. "I think we've got a much larger problem here, which is making sure there's no terrorist attack on New York."

In Sioux City, Iowa, Rick Santorum added a twist to the Republican argument that President Obama wants to make people more dependent on the federal government. He singled out blacks as people whose lives he would improve without using "somebody else's money," according to Naureen Khan in the *National Journal* on 3 January 2012. The comment came in response to a man's question about foreign influence on the U.S. economy. "How do we get off this crazy train? We've got so much foreign influence in this country now," the man said. "Where do we go from here?" In a lengthy answer, Santorum talked about reviving U.S. manufacturing and then pivoted to the government-dependency theme. "What President Obama wants to do, his economic plan is to make more people dependent upon government. To grow the government, to make sure we have more food stamps, and more SSI, and more Medicaid. Four in 10 children are now on government-provided health care. It just keeps expanding," Santorum said.

He talked about how Iowa is going to get fined if more people don't sign up for Medicaid and then said, "They're pushing harder and harder to get more and more of you dependent upon them so they can get your vote. That's what the bottom line is. So I don't want to make black people's lives better by giving them somebody else's money. I want to give them the opportunity to go out and earn the money and provide for themselves and their families."

On 15 January 2012 Julie Pace of the Associated Press reported from Columbia S.C. that Presidential hopeful Newt Gingrich faced tough questions about his past statements on race and class, making a rare appearance by a Republican primary candidate before a black church. Standing behind the lectern at Jones Memorial A.M.E. Zion Church, Gingrich was peppered with questions about his assertion that poor children lack work ethic and his criticism of President Obama as a "food-stamp president." While the give and take between Gingrich and more than 50 people in the audience was largely respectful, some in the crowd had sharp questions for the former House Speaker. Many centered on Gingrich's remark that poor children as young as nine should work at least part time cleaning their schools in order to learn about work.

Gingrich said his comments were misconstrued. "What I was saying was, in the poorest neighborhoods, if we can find a way to help young people earn some money, we might actually be able to keep the dropout rate down and give people an incentive to come to school," he said. The explanation little satisfied some in the crowd, including a woman who said Gingrich's words came across "so negatively, like we're not doing everything for our young people." Gingrich was also asked if he stood by his assertion that Obama is a "food stamp president", a line the Georgia Republican used often during stump speeches. He responded with a simple, "Yes."

V

AS TRAYVON MARTIN'S supporters marched through downtown Miami on 23 March 2012, before the start of a town hall meeting, Jason Rosenbloom talked to Reuters reporter Tom Brown of an incident on 5 June 2006, not long after Florida enacted the first "Stand Your Ground" law in the United States, when he was shot in the stomach and chest by his next-door neighbor after a shouting match over trash. Exactly what happened that day in Clearwater, Florida, is still open to dispute. Kenneth Allen, a retired police officer, said he shot Rosenbloom because he was trying to storm into his house. Rosenbloom told Reuters in a telephone interview he never tried to enter the house and was in Allen's yard, about 10 feet from his front door, when he was shot moments after he put his hands up.

Now living in Hawaii, Rosenbloom said he had been unaware of the growing outrage the shooting in Sanford, Florida. Trayvon Martin, 17, was shot by George Zimmerman on 26 February while walking back to the house where he was staying with his father in a gated community. Sanford police have not arrested Zimmerman, largely because "Stand Your Ground" requires them, without clear evidence of malice and in the absence of eyewitness testimony to the contrary, to accept Zimmerman's argument he was acting in self-defense. Allen was not arrested in the shooting of Rosenbloom. Sergeant Tom Nestor of the Pinella's County Sheriff's Office said Allen was found to have acted in self-defense when he pumped two rounds into Rosenbloom with his 9mm semi-automatic pistol.

"He meant for me to be dead and he never called 911," said Rosenbloom, 36, adding that Allen, now 65, bent over him and using an expletive, warned him not to tangle "with an ex-cop" as he lay bleeding on the ground. "The police closed it on his words alone," said Rosenbloom, explaining how the case that began with a complaint about him leaving eight trash bags on the curb instead of the regulation six, was closed after what he described as only a summary investigation. "They made me the bad guy," he added. Allen, contacted by phone in rural Georgia, said he had "no regrets" about shooting Rosenbloom, describing him as a "little punk" who was "lucky to be alive." He denied using profanity after shooting his neighbor, who he claimed had forced his way into the house and threatened to "beat my ass."

Police say Florida's "Stand Your Ground" law, which loosened formerly restrictive rules for using deadly force and gives people wide latitude to employ it in self-defense, was never officially cited in the Rosenbloom case. But Rosenbloom considers himself one of the first victims of the new law in Florida and one of the few who has lived to give a first-hand account of how he said it can be used to shoot to kill with impunity. The law, which extended the "castle doctrine" allowing residents to shoot would-be burglars or intruders entering their homes, gives legal protection to anyone, anywhere, to use deadly force in a case where a person is attacked and believes his life or safety is in danger. One of the law's legislative sponsors said it was partly motivated by a rash of looting and theft after a series of hurricanes hit Florida in 2005. Dubbed the "Shoot First, Ask Questions Later" law by critics, the statute extends even beyond self-defense and is seen by some as encouraging vigilante justice. "A person who is not engaged in an unlawful activity ... has no duty to retreat and has the right to stand his or her ground and meet force with force, including deadly force if he or she reasonably believes it is necessary to do so to prevent death or great bodily harm to himself or herself or another or to prevent the commission of a forcible felony," the law says.

"I think it's a very foolish law meant to turn a blind eye," Rosenbloom said, referring to how Stand Your Ground has been criticized in the past for protecting people who might formerly have been prosecuted for assault or murder. The law, approved under former Governor Jeb Bush after a big push by pro-gun advocates led by the National Rifle Association, was passed over numerous objections from the Florida Prosecuting Attorneys Association and state law enforcement officials. Florida's Republican governor, Rick Scott, announced the formation of a task force to "thoroughly review" the law in the wake of the Martin shooting. "Basically it's a law that fixed something that wasn't broken, and then it created a lot of problems," said William "Willie" Meggs, veteran state attorney for the 2nd Judicial Circuit in Tallahassee, the Florida capital. "I have been an outspoken critic of the law since it came into existence and I would suspect we may be doing something about it after all the interest we're seeing in it now," he said.

According to the Brady Campaign to Prevent Gun Violence, at least 23 states have passed laws similar to Florida's since 2005. Florida does not keep comprehensive records to gauge the impact of "Stand Your Ground". But the *St. Petersburg Times* found that in the first five years after the law was enacted, "justifiable homicides" in Florida more than tripled, to more than 100 in 2010 from just over 30. The Stand Your Ground law was invoked in at least 93 cases over that time period, involving 65 deaths. Despite assertions from supporters of the law that it has worked as a deterrent of violent crime, Dennis Henigan, a lawyer and veteran vice president of the Brady Campaign, said the state was still saddled with a "tragic record" on violent crime. "It's quite remarkable how consistently awful Florida's record has been," Henigan said. "It takes some work to finish in the top five in violent crime among all the states every single year for the last 30 years." Supporters of "Stand Your Ground" say it has worked well. "It's not a 007 license to kill," said Sean Caranna, who heads a gun rights group called Florida Carry.

Republican State Representative Dennis Baxley, one of the authors of the "Stand Your Ground" law, said it did not protect people who pursued and confronted their victims, as occurred in Sanford, according to lawyers for the parents of the dead teenager. Defending "Stand Your Ground", Baxley said that while errors may occur, such as the death of Martin, it was important that the law err on the side of those who fear they are facing "a perceived" threat. "That's good public policy. I think we have a good statute and I would hate to lose anything in it that protects people from harm. It saves lives," Baxley added.

Rosenbloom still has health problems stemming from his injuries and a bullet remains lodged in his right hip. "Now I live as far away from Florida in America as you can get," he said, explaining his recent move to Hawaii was aimed at leaving a lot of bad memories behind in what he now calls the "Gunshine State," a play on Florida's nickname "the Sunshine State." His family was struck by a second tragedy only three days after he was shot by Allen. Rosenbloom said his younger brother Joshua was shot and killed by police after threatening to commit suicide by disemboweling himself with a sword. Twenty-year-old Joshua Rosenbloom, a manic depressive, was acting out after hearing his brother was in intensive care in a Tampa hospital, recovering from his gunshot wounds, Rosenbloom said. He was shot three times in his bedroom when police approached while he was still holding the sword in his hands, his older brother said.

VI

ACCORDING TO a report from Hope Yen of the Associated Press on 8 December 2011 affluent black Americans who are leaving industrial cities for the suburbs and the South are shifting traditional lines between rich and poor. The new census data show their migration is widening the income gap between whites and the inner-city blacks who remain behind, while making blacks less monolithic as a group and subject to greater income disparities. "Reverse migration is changing the South and its race relations," said Roderick Harrison, a Howard University sociologist and former chief of racial statistics at the Census Bureau. He said a rising black middle class is promoting a growing belief among some black conservatives that problems of the disadvantaged are now rooted more in character or cultural problems, rather than race. But Harrison said most black Americans maintain a strong racial identity, focused on redressing perceived lack of opportunities, in part because many of them maintain close ties to siblings or other blacks who are less successful. "I don't think suburban blacks are yet driven by their higher income or new locations, although this might have a greater effect in a generation or two," he said.

The typical white person last year earned income roughly 1.7 times higher than that of blacks, the widest ratio since the 1990s. Census figures show that cities such as Detroit, Chicago, Philadelphia, Cleveland and Milwaukee in particular saw increases in inequality, hurt by an exodus of middle-class minorities while lower-skilled blacks stayed in the cities. Low-income blacks also slipped further behind. The share of black households ranking among the poorest poor – those earning less than $15,000 – climbed from 20 per cent to 26 per cent over the past decade; other race and ethnic groups posted smaller increases. At the same time, African-Americans making $200,000 or more a year were unchanged from 2000 at about 1.1 per cent, even after a deep recession.

Many affluent blacks are moving to the South, seeking a return to their ancestral homeland after a decades-long Great Migration to the North. Pursuing a better quality of life, they are opting for more upscale metropolitan locales rather than the traditional rural communities of the old South in places such as Louisiana, Mississippi and Arkansas, which remain home to larger shares of minority farmers, construction and other low-wage workers. Since 1990 blacks living in Southern urban locations such as Atlanta, Dallas, Washington D.C., and Miami, where incomes rose in the last decade, have increased 70 per cent.

The newer Southern arrivals include Marc Harrigan, 42, a physician who grew up in New York and attended college in Rhode Island. Harrigan said he knew he wanted a change once he finished medical school and married, yearning for what he saw as a more progressive culture than Hampton Roads, Va., where he practiced for a few years. Settling on Atlanta, Harrigan described it as a good fit with affordable housing and decent schools despite the culture shift outside the immediate metro area. "It was important that we move where there was a critical mass of African-American professionals," he said. "But in other parts of the state, I'm not sure they have embraced assimilation, if you will."

William H. Frey, a Brookings Institution demographer who did a broad analysis of the race and income data, said the latest numbers reflect a longer-term trend of increased racial integration between blacks and whites. He said the changes could pose challenges in the coming months in political redistricting as well as courting the traditional black vote. Groups in states such as Texas, Florida, California and Maryland have gone to court or are now otherwise grappling with political maps being redrawn based on the 2010 census, considering whether to preserve historically black legislative seats amid slowing population growth and black movement into traditionally white suburbs. The change also complicates strategy for President Obama, who is banking on blacks in key Southern states in the 2012 election.

Obama is pushing a broader re-election theme of middle-class renewal, reciting his jobs agenda and his feud with Congress over extending a Social Security tax cut, while targeting outreach to black communities in hopes of remaining competitive in Southern and other battleground states. "The Democratic Party will surely gain consistent support from these new black suburbanites, but the active support for traditional black issues like civil rights may take a back seat," Frey said, citing issues such as schools, housing and public safety that may rise to the forefront.

According to census data, about 67 million Americans, or nearly 1 in 4, lived in neighborhoods with poverty rates of 20 per cent or higher; that's up from roughly 1 in 5 in 2000. The South in general had higher shares of people living in high-poverty areas, led by states including Mississippi, Louisiana, Texas and Kentucky. Despite some gains for middle-class blacks, African-Americans on average last year still had rising poverty and worsening economic situations compared with whites. The mostly suburban counties where blacks had growing and higher-than-average income make up about 19 per cent of the black population. That's compared with 45 per cent of blacks who lived in urban counties and small towns where black incomes fell relative to whites. Part of the income divide falls along age and education, with higher unemployment rates for young men and those who lack a college degree. Last year, about 19 per cent of men ages 25 to 34 were "idle" – neither working nor attending school – up 5 percentage points from 2007, according to the Population Reference

Bureau. About 31 per cent of young black adults were disconnected from school and work, compared with 27 per cent for Latinos and about 19 per cent each for whites and Asians. Blacks also were more likely than other groups to live in neighborhoods with poverty rates of 40 per cent or more, roughly 1 in 9.

On 17 February 2012 Ryan J. Foley reporting for the Associated Press from Iowa City, Iowa, stated that in a case closely watched by civil rights activists, an Iowa judge will decide whether to grant thousands of black employees and job applicants monetary damages for hiring practices used by Iowa state government that they say have disadvantaged them. Experts say the case is the largest class-action lawsuit of its kind against an entire state government's civil service system, and tests a legal theory that social science and statistics alone can prove widespread discrimination. The plaintiffs —up to 6,000 African-Americans passed over for state jobs and promotions dating back to 2003 – do not say they faced overt racism or discriminatory hiring tests in Iowa, a state that is 91 per cent white. Instead, their lawyers argue that managers subconsciously favored whites across state government, leaving blacks at a disadvantage in decisions over who got interviewed, hired and promoted.

Judge Robert Blink's decision could award damages and mandate changes in state personnel policies or dismiss a case that represents a growing front of discrimination litigation. "Whenever there is a case like this that goes to trial, it's of interest to all of us," said Jocelyn Larkin, executive director of the Impact Fund, a Berkeley, Calif.-based nonprofit that supports employment discrimination lawsuits and has followed the case. Similar cases against local governments have failed because proving broad bias is extraordinarily difficult, with a myriad of possible factors to explain disparities, said David Friedland, a California human resources consultant who is an expert on discrimination in hiring. Success in Iowa could encourage similar lawsuits elsewhere, he said. University of Washington psychology professor Anthony Greenwald, an expert on implicit bias who testified on behalf of the plaintiffs, said the decision will be important nationally because similar cases against corporations have usually been dismissed or settled before trial.

Scholars and employment lawyers have shown a growing interest in implicit bias in the last several years, after Greenwald and other scientists developed the Implicit Association Test to test racial stereotypes. Their research found an inherent preference for whites over blacks – in up to 80 per cent of test-takers and among many people who do not consider themselves racist. The theory hit a legal obstacle last year when the U.S. Supreme Court disqualified a class-action lawsuit against Wal-Mart's pay and promotion practices for women. The court found the class was too broad and failed to challenge a specific hiring practice as discriminatory. Lawyers defending the state have cited that decision in asking Blink to dismiss the case. But the high court's decision did not specifically reject the theory of implicit bias, and dissenting Justice Ruth Bader Ginsburg wrote that such claims can be allowed.

Class attorney Thomas Newkirk said the science and other evidence that shows disadvantaged groups such as blacks face employment discrimination in subtle ways "is becoming overwhelming." Clearly, the problem is not in Iowa alone, but "we believe Iowa is exactly the right place to ask society to take control of this important issue fairly for all races, and to seek a better future for all as a result," said Newkirk, who was recently honored by the Des Moines chapter of the National Association for the Advancement of Colored People for his work on the case. During a month-long trial last fall, experts called by the plaintiffs' lawyers testified that blacks are hired at lower rates than whites with similar qualifications and receive less favorable evaluations and lower starting salaries. An employment consultant hired by the administration of Gov. Tom Vilsack, who served from 1999 to 2007, warned of hiring disparities between whites and minorities in a report issued after he left office. Larkin called that report a strong "and pretty unusual piece of evidence" proving the state was aware of problems. Vilsack's successor Democratic Gov. Chet Culver responded by issuing an executive order requiring agencies to improve the diversity of the workforce. State officials called that evidence of progress, but class lawyers argued it turned out to be ineffective because rules meant to prevent bias still were not followed.

Republican Gov. Terry Branstrad said last fall his administration had ensured agencies were following uniform rules to stop any abuse – but a top state employment official testified days later he had seen no substantive changes to hiring practices in years. Blacks represented

2.9 per cent of the state's population in 2010 and 2.4 per cent of the state workforce. Among those who joined the lawsuit as a plaintiff was Charles Zanders, of Urbandale, who was passed over for an interview for a position with the Iowa Communications Network in 2008 despite having worked 29 years in the telecommunications industry. "I was very angry at that time and felt like I'd been stepped on," Zanders, 60, said.

In a brief submitted in December, the plaintiffs' lawyers sought lost wages of about $67 million minus what they earned in the meantime. But in court documents, Newkirk said it was even more important that Blink order changes in the way state officials train managers, screen candidates and track disparities in hiring. Lawyers working for Attorney-General Tom Miller, a Democrat, argued that the plaintiffs failed to show bias across state government. "The record simply does not support Plaintiffs' charge that some monolithic, immutable force of bias infected the decisions made by every department, at every step, for every job, for every year of the class period," they wrote in a final brief.

VII

ON 29 DECEMBER 2011, Suzanne Gamboa of the Associated Press wrote that almost two centuries before there was a man named Obama in the White House, there was a man named Obama shackled in the bowels of a slave ship. There is no proof that the unidentified Obama has ties to President Barack Obama. All they share is a name. But that is exactly the commonality that Emory University researchers hope to build upon as they delve into the origins of Africans who were taken up and sold. They have built an online database around those names, and welcome input from people who may share a name that's in the database, or have such names as part of their family lore. "The whole point of the project is to ask the African diaspora, people with any African background, to help us identify the names because the names are so ethno-linguistically specific, we can actually locate the region in Africa to which the individual belonged on the basis of the name," said David Eltis, an Emory University history professor who heads the database research team.

So far they say, two men named Obama sit among some 9,500 captured Africans whose names were written on line after line in the registries of obscure, 19th century slave trafficking courts. The courts processed the human chattel freed from ships that were intercepted and detoured to Havana, Cuba, or Freetown, Sierra Leone. Most of the millions of Africans enslaved before 1807 were known only by numbers, said James Walvin, an expert on the trans-Atlantic slave trade. Once bought by slave owners, the Africans' names were lost. Africans captured by the Portuguese were baptized and given "Christian" names aboard the ships that were taking them into slavery. But original African names – surnames were uncommon for Africans – are rich with information. Some reveal the day of the week an individual was born or whether that individual was the oldest, youngest or middle child or a twin. They can also reveal ethnic or linguistic groups.

The president's father was from Kenya, on the eastern coast of Africa, and Eltis said it was rare for captives to hail from areas far from the port where their ships set sail. The unidentified Obamas on the slave ships sailed from West Africa. Walvin, author of *The Zong*, a book about the slave trade, said there were Africans who had been brought great distances before they were forced onto ships. "Often their enslavement had begun much earlier, deep in the African interior, most of them captured through acts of violence, warfare, kidnapping, or for criminal activity." Walvin said in his book, which chronicles the true story of a captain who ordered a third of the slaves aboard his ship thrown overboard due to a shortage of drinking water.

Obama's ancestors, a nomadic people known as the River Lake Nilotes, migrated from Bahr-el-Ghazal Province in Sudan toward Uganda and into Western Kenya, according to Sally Jacobs, author of *The Other Barack*, a book about the president's father. They were part of several clans and sub-clans that eventually became the Luo people of Kenya, Jacobs writes. The president's great-grandfather's name was Obama. The slaves found aboard intercepted ships provided their names, age and sometimes where they were from, through translators, to English and Spanish speaking court registrars who wrote their names as they sounded to them. Body scars or identifying marks also were recorded. The details were logged in an attempt to prevent the Africans from being enslaved again, which didn't always work.

Emory's researchers are including audio clips of the names as they would likely be pronounced in Africa. "These people enslaved were not just a nebulous group of people with no place and no name," said Kwesi DeGraft-Hanson, one of the researchers, who has found variations of his name, his brother's and his children's names in the database. He is originally from Ghana. "That's how a lot of us view slavery. We don't have faces to go with it ... It makes them that much more removed from us."

Eltis and his researchers acknowledge the database may not help African Americans with genealogical research because records on the Africans once they were freed from the ships are harder to find, if they exist at all. However, the project provides another piece in a major jigsaw, and helps put together a bigger picture on slavery, Walvin said. Before this project, Eltis and others assembled a database of 35,000 trans-Atlantic slave ship voyages responsible for the flow of more than 10 million Africans to the Americas. Together, the two databases provide some details on the horrific voyages of the Africans, including the Obamas. The Xerxes, which carried one of the unidentified Obamas, was a 138-foot schooner that began its voyage in Havana with a crew of 44. Five guns were mounted aboard when the ship left on a slave purchasing trip on 10 February 1828. Sailing under the Spanish flag, the ship's captain Felipe Rebel purchased 429 slaves, nearly one third of them children, before setting out on a return trip to the Americas. But on 26 June 1828, the Xerxes was intercepted and forced to dock at an unknown Cuban port. By then, 26 slaves had died.

The other unidentified Obama, 6-foot-3-inches tall, was one of 562 Africans shackled in the belly of the Midas. The vessel was a Brig, a fast, maneuverable ship with two square-rigged masts. It was equipped with eight guns. Midas' captain J. Martinez and a crew of 53 left Cuba on an unknown date. It left Bonny with 562 slaves but was intercepted. It docked in Cuba on 8 July 1829 minus 162 slaves who had died during the voyage. Some slaves freed from seized ships were returned to Africa, but not always to their original homelands. Some were sent to Liberia or were allowed to remain free in the cities where the courts were located. Some may have been re-enslaved and some died on ships that were returning them to Africa.

VIII

TYRA BATTS, according to Piper Weiss of Shine, stood up to her school in a video posted on *Buffalo News'* website on 10 December 2011. Before every game, the girls' basketball team at Kenmore East High School has a disturbing tradition. "The whole team before our game has a ritual of saying 1-2-3 and then the N word," said Tyra Batts, the only African-American member of her Buffalo-area high school team. "It's a tradition that's been going on for years." When Batts joined the team this year, with dreams of going on to play college basketball, she noticed her teammates would secretly huddle up for the alarmingly racist chant before every game. "I would argue about it and say to not say it," Batts said in a home video submitted to the *Buffalo News*, "and they would tell me they're not racist, it's just a word. There was nothing I could do much before the game because I was outnumbered."

After confronting one of her teammates, she says she was verbally attacked with another racial slur. After that, the confrontation got physical and Batts was suspended for five days for initiating a fight. "It was a buildup of anger and frustration at being singled out of the whole team," she said. When school officials didn't dig around enough to find out why the fight took place, Batts' parents called a local radio station and shared her story with the community. Finally, the school got a clue. Kenmore-Town of Tonawanda Superintendent Mark P. Mondanaro launched an inquiry and released a statement saying: "This type of insensitivity to one of our students is wrong, unacceptable, unfortunate, and will never, ever be tolerated." The students who allegedly engaged in the chant were suspended for two days and the entire team was penalized with canceled practices, a game suspension and the return of a sportsmanship award earned last year.

But Batts isn't satisfied. There is the fact that she's considering not playing on the basketball team anymore, and she's still being penalized with three more days of suspension than her teammates. "I'm getting a lot of feedback that the team should be suspended for more than two days, longer than I have, because I actually fought for a reason," she said. "I didn't just do it out of nowhere." While her teammates are now required to partake in "cultural sensitivity training", the administration hasn't commented on changing their own staff policies. According to Tyra Batts, the chant was only a fraction of the racist remarks she'd been subjected to from her teammates. While her principal has personally apologized to the Batts family, officials may want to focus on larger efforts administrators can make to change the school's culture. Why did it take Batts' parents' public plea for this outrageous tradition to be stopped? And how had no coaches or staff members heard this long-standing tradition taking place? School officials claim the students were secretive about their chant and after the fight broke out, administrators didn't get the "full" story because students were only in school one half day. While it's never okay to use physical violence, Batts' reaction was a last-ditch effort in a situation where everyone had turned their backs. The school should be looking at why it had to get that far before a single student's voice was heard. Now, other students at the school are sending their own message on Twitter. "Our school is racist" one student tweeted. Another classmate wrote simply, "I'm so embarrassed to go to Kenmore East."

Would interracial marriages make a difference in Americans' lives? Lylah M. Alphonse, Senior Editor of Yahoo! Shine Love + Sex, reported on 16 February 2012 that new research shows that one out of 12 marriages in the U.S. are interracial. A new study suggests in fact that interracial marriage in the United States has hit an all-time high, with a record 1 in 12 marriages taking place between people from different racial backgrounds. "The rise in interracial marriage indicates that race relations have improved over the past quarter century," Daniel Lichter, a sociology professor at Cornell University, told The Associated Press. "Mixed-race children have blurred America's color line. They often interact with others on either side of the racial divide and frequently serve as brokers between friends and family members of different racial backgrounds."

While ethnicity and race are two different things, for survey and census purposes they are often used interchangeably. In the Pew study, the term "white" referred to Caucasians who did not also identify as Hispanic. The study found that Hispanics and Asians were still most likely to marry someone from a different racial background, but the biggest change took place among African Americans, where interracial marriages increased from 15.5 per cent to 17.1 per cent. Black men were nearly three times as likely as black women to marry someone of a different race, 24 per cent to 9 per cent. Just 17 per cent Asian men, on the other hand, married someone of a different race during that time, compared to 36 per cent among Asian women. The intermarriage rate among Hispanics was about 25.7 per cent, and among whites it was 9.4 per cent. Of the 275,700 new interracial marriages in 2010, 43 per cent were whites marrying Hispanics, 14.4 per cent were whites marrying Asians, and 11.9 per cent were white marrying blacks. Interracial marriages are more prevalent in some parts of the United States than in others. Hawaii was most likely to have mixed-race couples, with 42 per cent of marriages from 2008 to 2010 involving people of different races. Other Western states – including California, Nevada, and New Mexico – and those in the Northeast were most likely to say such marriages are beneficial for society. Vermont, however, had the lowest rate of intermarriage – just 4 per cent. Overall, the public perception of mixed marriages has only grown more positive. About 83 per cent of Americans now say they think it's "all right" for blacks and whites to date one another; in 1987, only 48 per cent of respondents agreed with the idea. Sixty-three per cent now say it "would be fine" if a family member married someone from another race, and 61 per cent of 18- to 29-year-olds said that they felt interracial marriages were changing society "for the better." Twenty-eight per cent of respondents age 65 or older agreed. According to the study, minorities, young adults, college-educated adults, and those who identify as "liberal" were most likely to look at interracial marriage in a positive way.

Thanks to such unions, the number of multiracial Americans is also on the rise. About 9 million people – roughly 8 per cent of the minority population in the United States – identify as multiracial. "Race is a social construct; race isn't real," Jonathan Brent, whose father is white and his mother is Japanese-American, told the Associated Press. It's an idea that more and more young adults agree about. "In the past century, intermarriage has evolved from being illegal, to be a taboo and then to be merely unusual. And with each passing year, it becomes less unusual," Paul Taylor, director of Pew's Social & Demographic Trends project, told the Associated Press. "For younger Americans, racial and ethnic diversity are a part of their lives."

On 26 January 2012, Felicia Fonseca writing for the Associated Press from Flagstaff, Ariz., quoted from US Census data on the American Indian population that showed almost half of American Indians and Alaska Natives identify with multiple races, representing a group that grew by 39 per cent over a decade, Of the 5.2 million people counted as Natives in 2010, nearly 2.3 million reported being Native in combination with one or more of six other race categories, showcasing a growing diversity among Natives. Those who added black, white or both as a personal identifier made up 84 per cent of the multi-racial group. Their situation showed however national neglect. Tribal officials and organizations look to Census data for funding, to plan communities, to foster solidarity among tribes and for accountability from federal agencies that have a trust responsibility with tribal members. The bump in the multi-racial group from 1.6 million in 2000 to nearly 2.3 million in 2010 was higher than that of those who reported being solely of Native descent. "When information comes out and is available for our tribes and tribal communities, we have a lot of issues going back to identity," said Mellor Willie, executive director of the National American Indian Housing Council. "Who is Indian?"

The Census figures, released during a presentation at the National Museum of the American Indian in Washington, D.C., also include people living in the United States who consider themselves indigenous to Central and South America. Tribal officials say it's the best snapshot of Native people available, but the data is often supplemented with tribal enrollment figures or other surveys and studies. Amber Ebarb, with the National Congress of American Indians' Policy Research Center, said the data also is used to track trends among states and regions, determine the mobility patterns of Natives and figure out how best to deliver services to Natives or conduct outreach. "It's kind of a function of geography," she said. "There's this trend where single-race American Indians live in tribal communities and multi-race Natives live farther." The Blackfeet Nation in Montana had the highest proportion of people who reported being part of more than one racial group or tribe at 74 per cent. Among Alaska Native groups, the Tlingit-Haida had the highest proportion of mixed-race Natives at 42 per cent.

The number of Natives identifying with at least one other race increased in all but three states from 2000 to 2010, according to the

Census. Some tribes were less diverse. Of the 34,000 people who identify as Yup'ik, an Alaska Native tribe, 29,000 said they were affiliated with no other race. The Navajo Nation, whose reservation stretches into New Mexico, Utah and Arizona, had the highest proportion of people who identified as Native and nothing else at 86 per cent of its 332,000 population, Census officials said. The Navajo Nation comes in second in population behind the Cherokee's 819,000 population, 65 per cent of whom identify with another race. Census Director Robert Groves said the bureau has projected that the overall Native population will increase to 6.8 million in 2030 and about 8.6 million in 2050. Both multiracial Natives and Natives alone grew at a rate higher from 2000 to 2010 than the U.S. population at large.

Among other findings: Seventy-eight per cent of Natives live off tribal reservations but many live in counties close to reservations, particularly throughout the West, including Oklahoma. The majority of Natives live in 10 states: Arizona, California, Florida, Michigan, New Mexico, New York, North Carolina, Oklahoma, Texas and Washington. The population of multi-racial Natives jumped by more than 50 per cent in 18 states and by more than 70 per cent in North Carolina, Delaware and South Dakota.

However, Christina Ng reported on 1 December 2011 that a small Appalachian church in Kentucky is being called racist for passing a vote that banned interracial couples from the church. The Gulnare Freewill Baptist Church voted 9 to 6 to ban interracial couples from church services or functions, with the exception of funerals. Stella Harville, 24, and her fiancé Ticha Chikuni, 28, are the couple that prompted the church's actions. Harville is white and Chikuni is black. The couple met at Georgetown College in Kentucky where both went to school and were scheduled to marry in July 2012. Harville is in graduate school in Indiana and Chikuni is working at Georgetown College, but when the couple visits Harville's parents in Pike County, Ky., they usually go to church with her parents. Harville's parents Cathy and Dean Harville have been church members for decades. Cathy Harville has taught Sunday school at the church and Dean Harville was a deacon there and is currently the church's secretary. They consider the church's 42 congregants their family.

But after a service in June where Stella Harville and Chikuni participated by singing and playing the piano for a hymn, the family was shocked when then-pastor Melvin Thompson approached them after the service. "There seemed not to be a problem and then all of a sudden the pastor at the time came up to [Chikuni] and told him he could not sing anymore," Harville said. "That floored us. We wanted to know why." The next week, Cathy and Dean Harville met with Thompson and were shocked to hear their pastor say that members of the congregation had said they would walk out if Chikuni sang again. The parents wanted to know exactly who had a problem with their future son-in-law. "Me, for one," Cathy Harville said that Thompson replied. She said he added, "The best thing [Stella] can do is take him back where she found him." She said the pastor would not tell her any names of people who took issue with Chikuni. Cathy Harville was taken aback. "There's no love at all in that and that really hurt me," she said. "They are both Christians and they both try to live a Christian life and serve God. There is nothing in the Bible that we found that tells us that the couple should not be married."

Thompson has since been replaced with a new pastor who said that everyone was welcome at the church and the Harville family said the issue was dropped, but at a recent meeting Thompson, who is still a member of the congregation, brought up the issue again and asked that it be discussed at a business meeting among the church's men. "Grown men cried at that meeting," Cathy Harville said. Three men voted to bring the issue before the church for a vote, and two voted against it, so the matter went before the congregation. Harville said that of 42 members, very few stayed for the meeting after church and even fewer voted. She said most congregants wanted no part in the vote. The motion read, in part: "The Gulnare Freewill Baptist Church does not condone interracial marriage. Parties of such marriages will not be received as members, nor will they be used in worship services and other church functions, with the exception being funerals." Ultimately, nine people voted for the motion and six voted against it and interracial couples were banned. "It hurt," Harville said. "[Stella] knew she was going to face some challenges after she decided she would marry Ticha, but I didn't think it would be from our family."

IX

IN THE LOOKOUT of 19 August 2011 Mike Krumbolz wrote that companies like to push the envelope with their ads. Sometimes the gamble works, sometimes it doesn't, and sometimes, like in the case of a new advertising campaign from Nivea, the whole thing turns into a fiasco. Nivea, a company that specializes in skin-care products, had released a print ad that it has since pulled. How to best describe the ad? It shows an African American man preparing to toss a decapitated head with an afro-style haircut. The ad copy reads: "Re-Civilize Yourself." The underlying message seems to be that afros are not civilized. Almost immediately, the ad met with outrage. The *Los Angeles Times* reported that Facebook users began "posting photos of themselves with Afros on Nivea's wall, saying things such as: "I wear my hair natural and I just graduated with my doctorate! So who needs to be re-civilized?? Nivea no longer welcomed in my household."

Nivea took down the ad and issued an apology via Facebook. "Thank you for caring enough to give us your feedback about the recent 'Re-civilized' Nivea for Men ad. This ad was inappropriate and offensive. It was never our intention to offend anyone, and for this we are deeply sorry. This ad will never be used again. Diversity and equal opportunity are crucial values of our company." While the ad has since been pulled, the massive interest in the controversy it created continues full steam ahead. Over 24 hours, Web searches for "Nivea re-civilize yourself" surged 629 per cent. "Nivea racist ad" spiked 140 per cent. The conventional wisdom is that there's no such thing as bad publicity, but the fallout from the ad might prove otherwise.

According to the Associated Press hundreds of African-American veterans who helped to integrate the Marine Corps during World War II at a time segregation was an everyday reality are now proud recipients of the nation's highest civilian honor. Nearly 70 years after the Marines of Montford Point became the first African Americans in the Corps, Congress awarded them the Congressional Gold Medal. The Corps was the last branch of the U.S. military to allow blacks to serve.

Originally from Washington, D.C., then-19-year-old Charles Manuel Jr. enrolled with the Marines in 1942 straight out of high school. Manuel was sent to Montford Point, a North Carolina base that the Corps created to keep African Americans away from bases where other Marines trained. Roughly 20,000 other African-American Marines trained at the base, which operated from 1942 to 1949. He said that the training at the base was rough, because for many recruits it was their first time experiencing boot training and their instructors were White. "Our drill instructor told us, 'You people want to be Marines, I'm going to make Marines out of you dead or alive.'" Manuel, now in his late 80's, sat next to his daughter, Rosetta Holloway at the ceremony. "It was more than overdue," Holloway said. "I'm very excited and pleased for my father, who's really proud of being in the Marines." William McDowell, who was selected to represent Montford Point, received the medal on behalf of the roughly 400 Montford Point Marines in attendance. "It does sadden me that some of our brothers are not with us today. The upside of it all is that we do remember each and every one of them. They are in our hearts and minds and they should never be forgotten," McDowell said.

The medal will be on display at the National Museum of the Marine Corps in Virginia. The Marines received bronze replicas. President Franklin D. Roosevelt banned racially based employment discrimination by all federal agencies in 1941, and a presidential directive allowed African Americans to serve the Marines in 1942. House Democratic Leader Nancy Pelosi told the Marines: "You served our country at a time that it took an extra dose of patriotism to do so. All of the freedoms that you were fighting for were not afforded to everyone in our country at that time." Speaker of the House John Boehner, Senate Majority Leader Harry Reid and Senate Republican Leader Mitch McConnell also spoke. "Allowing blacks to serve the Marine Corps was seen as an experiment," Boehner told the crowd. "If it was an experiment, it didn't last any long. Before the end of the war, the Marine commandant at the time said the experiment was over. The men trained at Montford were Marines, period."

X

FELICIA FONSECA and Tracie Cone of the Associated Press wrote on 26 February 2012 that just east of Victorville in California's Mojave Desert two bluffs rise 3,000-feet from the valley floor. A 1949 map by the U.S. Geological Survey officially gave them the name locals had called them for as long as anyone could remember: Pickaninny Buttes. The name, a pejorative term that represents a caricature of black children, was likely bestowed because African Americans attempted a settlement near the Lucerne Valley at the turn of the last century. Whatever the reason, it stuck and still has the propensity to shock. "Good grief," moaned Leon Jenkins, president of the Los Angeles chapter of the NAACP, when told about the site. "That is just about as offensive as it gets because nowhere in the English language was that used other than to be a slur at little girls."

The pair of journalists point out that Pickaninny Buttes is one of thousands of places across the United States still saddled with names that are an insight into our divisive past, when demeaning names given to areas settled by ethnic or racial minorities were recorded on official government maps and often stuck. Some, like Wop Draw in Wyoming; Jewtown, Ga.; Beaner Lake, Wash.; Wetback Tank reservoir in New Mexico and Polack Lake in Michigan, can sound rudely impolitic to the ears of a more inclusive society. Others, such as the former Olympic ski resort of Squaw Valley near Lake Tahoe have become so ingrained in the vernacular that they are spoken without a second thought. And yet, nine states are on a mission to scrub "squaw" from their maps, a slang word first given to Native women that came to mean both a part of the female genitalia and a woman of ill repute. "It's so disrespectful I'm not even going to say the name," said Chairman James Ramos of the San Manuel Band of Serrano Mission Indians in Southern California. "Every time I hear that I think of our women elders and my daughters and my wife, and I'm not going to degrade them that way by repeating the name. It's deplorable to all native people across the United States." Ramos was incredulous to learn that a conical mountain peak in his tribal area along Interstate 15 between Barstow and Las Vegas is named "Squaw Tit", one of more than a thousand places across the U.S. with the S-word in it and eight places with the exact name. "It just seems like dominant society is not culturally sensitive to and doesn't take seriously Native American thought and feelings," said Corinne Fairbanks of the American Indian Movement.

In Arizona, tensions flared over a craggy mountain in Phoenix that was historically named Squaw Peak. A former governor made it her personal crusade to have it renamed for the first American Indian woman killed in combat in Iraq for the U.S. military. It was changed to Piestewa Peak in 2008. Some state legislatures take it upon themselves to change names deemed offensive. In 1995 Minnesota was first to pass legislation outlawing "squaw", a process that took five years to complete. Oregon once had 172 places with the name squaw, the most in the U.S., and since 2001 has been engulfed in the tedious process of determining historically accurate new names. Oklahoma has passed a non-binding resolution encouraging the change. Idaho, Montana, South Dakota, Florida, North Carolina and Tennessee also are making state-mandated changes. In September 2011 the last six offensive place names in Maine were changed. Still, there are 297 Savages nationwide and 11 Redskins.

The issue of offensive place names that have stuck despite changing times arises occasionally, as it did when the media reported the name of Texas Gov. Rick Perry's hunting camp: "Niggerhead," and when the N-word was found on headstones at a cemetery near Sacramento where graves were relocated in 1954 to make way for a dam. Last fall in the California Gold Rush town of Rough and Ready, local resident Gail Smith bought property along a babbling creek. When she looked up the county assessors' map she was mortified to learn its name was still listed as something ordered eliminated from all federal place maps almost five decades ago: "Nigger Creek." It is like an obscenity, wrote Secretary of the Interior Stuart Udall in 1963, when he ordered that the N-word be scrubbed from all federal place maps. Three years later he added "Jap", which was a pejorative form of Japanese. They are the only two names officially outlawed by the federal government. In the days before federal databases, all maps had to be changed by hand. So it was up to federal mapping offices to find and change the local features and some were missed.

When Nevada County officials learned about the N-word Creek, they changed it to Negro Creek. The new name did not appease Smith, who wrote to the Geographic Names board asking to make it something that didn't evoke images of racism. When she learned it was named for the men who panned for gold there, she suggested Black Miners Creek. The all-white Board of Supervisors recommended on 6 December that it not be changed, that they did "not view the word 'Negro' as a pejorative." Said the NAACP's Jenkins, "When you stoop so low to have that name and in 2011 you have the audacity not to want to change it with some reason that defies logic, well it's even more offensive."

From Alaska to Florida and Maine to California there are 757 places with Negro in the name, according to an analysis of government records. Many of those place names were not spelled that way originally. There are also 20 places with "Dago" (and many more that have been changed to "Italian"), 1,100 Squaws, six "Polacks", 10 Cripples, 58 named Gypsy, 30 "Chinamans", 8 "Injuns", 1 "Hebe Canyon", 35 "Spooks", 14 "Sambos" – including Black Sambo Mine in California – 30 "Spades", and too many "Coons" to count. There are also at least seven "Darkeys", another offensive name for black people. Darkey Springs, Tenn., was Dark Springs until 1820, when a slave trader began holding auctions at the site, said Betty Tindell Johnson, a seventh-generation resident of the township. "It's just a part of history that you wish hadn't happened," said Johnson, 71. "But there's a lot of stuff right now you wish wasn't happening." Jewtown, Ga. was settled by former plantation slaves from St. Simons Island. It originally was called Levisonton after Robert and Sig Levison, who owned a store there in 1880. A gentle knoll in eastern New Mexico formerly named "Nigger Hill" was renamed for those Buffalo Soldiers who fought in the Army's American Indian wars in the 1870s. During a campaign against the Comanches in July 1877, four members of a 10th U.S. Calvary Company died on the hill in Roosevelt County. A black personnel director at Eastern New Mexico University heard about the name and campaigned to have it changed to Buffalo Soldier Hill in 2005. But just across the state line in west Texas, a creek likely named for the same event still holds the name "Dead Negro Draw."

The Board on U.S. Geographic Names is a department of the U.S. Geologic Survey, whose mapmakers charted the country in intricate detail on a project only recently completed. Historians say it's important to understand the historical context of the names before passing judgment on them, including the 36 Chinamans and two Chinks. The Chinese Historical Society of America in San Francisco is filled with old paperwork and receipts made out to "Chinaman" because it was easier for some pioneer shopkeepers to write that than to figure out the man's name, said executive director Sue Lee. "Are these places offensive on their face? I'd hesitate to say because it's all

322

in the intent," she said. "It's not that simple because they may have started out not offensive. It's site by site."

For some Americans these efforts to clean up the landscape and the language might seem unimportant and trivial as Congresswoman Bachmann felt of the media's focus on criticisms of Limbaugh's slander of Sandra Fluke. "The media (have) been focusing on these little pinprick issues when really we should be focusing on bigger issues," she said, not seeing that the world's mightiest rivers have their start in tiny streams.

XI

IN HOUSTON the Associated Press reported in July 2012 that Mitt Romney isn't going to win the black vote but he's making a pitch to African-Americans at the NAACP's annual meeting, giving a major speech that's also aimed at showing independent and swing voters that he's willing to reach out to diverse audiences – and demonstrating that his campaign and the Republican Party he leads are inclusive. Romney's advisers say he plans to focus, as he usually does, on the economy. The 14.4 per cent unemployment rate among blacks is much higher than the 8.2 per cent national average. He's also likely to mention his plan to increase school choice – he's called education the "civil rights issue of our era." It's a difficult sell – 95 per cent of blacks backed President Barack Obama in 2008. But no matter what Romney tells the NAACP, Republicans and Democrats say he's making a statement just by speaking to the nation's oldest civil rights group. "The first thing you need to do is show up, so I ultimately think he's doing the right thing," said Rep. Tim Scott, R-S.C., one of two black Republicans in Congress. "What he's saying to everyone is that he's (running to become) America's president and not just those folks he thinks he can get votes from right now. I think that's a very important statement." "You've got to get credit for showing up – for being willing to go – no question," said Karen Finney, a Democratic consultant who worked in the Clinton White House. "It's more about your actions than it is about what you say."

Romney offered a direct appeal to African-American voters, arguing in a speech at the NAACP's annual meeting that the black community has been hardest hit by the bad economy and that if elected, he'll seek to improve the quality of life for all Americans, regardless of color. "I believe that if you understood who I truly am in my heart, and if it were possible to fully communicate what I believe is in the real, enduring best interest of African-American families, you would vote for me for president," Romney said. The crowd's reception to the speech was mixed, with Romney's discussion of his desire to repeal Obamacare receiving sustained boos. Romney acknowledged barriers still exist for black Americans even after Barack Obama became the nation's first black president. He argued the struggling economy has only enhanced those challenges and old inequities. "If equal opportunity in America were an accomplished fact, then a chronically bad economy would be equally bad for everyone," Romney said. "Instead, it's worse for African-Americans in almost every way." At 14.4 per cent, unemployment among black Americans is much higher than the 8.2 per cent national average, while the average income and median family income for African-Americans is much lower, Romney noted. While Romney does not expect to win the black vote, the Republican candidate's National Association for the Advancement of Colored People speech was aimed at showing he's at least trying. As he regularly does on the campaign trail, Romney cited his experience as governor of Massachusetts to prove he hasn't led by "just talking to Republicans" and that he will be an inclusive president. "We have to make our case to every voter. We don't count anybody out, and we sure don't make a habit of presuming anyone's support. Support is asked for and earned – and that's why I'm here today," Romney said. If elected, he added, "we will know each other."

He dismissed as nonsense Democratic charges that a Romney presidency would only help the rich. "The president wants to make this a campaign about blaming the rich," Romney said. "I want to make this a campaign about helping the middle class." If he didn't believe his policies would help "families of color" and all Americans more than Obama's, Romney said, "I would not be running for president." Romney also appealed to the NAACP audience by touting his proposal to increase school choice. The presumptive GOP nominee has repeatedly described education as the civil rights issue of our era and he argued that mediocre schools are setting up kids for failure. In a dig at Obama, he argued that candidates can't have it both ways by arguing they will protect kids while also protecting the interests of teachers unions. "If equal opportunity in America were an accomplished fact, black families could send their sons and daughters to public schools that truly offer the hope of a better life," Romney said. "Instead, for generations, the African-American community has been waiting and waiting for that promise to be kept. Today, black children are 17 per cent of students nationwide but they are 42 per cent of the students in our worst-performing schools."

Romney briefly touched on gay marriage pledging that he would work to defend traditional marriage. While the Republican candidate received polite applause throughout most of the speech, Romney received a few boos, including when he repeated his pledge to repeal Obama's health care law. As the audience jeered the health care line, Romney paused and smiled before continuing on. But Romney emphasized that if elected, his focus would be almost exclusively on job creation. "If I am president, Job One for me will be creating jobs. I have no hidden agenda. If you want a president who will make things better in the African-American community, you are looking at him," Romney declared, as a few audience members booed.

As his campaign readily acknowledges, Romney faces an uphill battle in appealing to black voters. The latest Quinnipiac poll found Obama leads Romney 92 per cent to 2 per cent among African-Americans. But Romney cast himself as someone who is still willing to reach out, even to those who don't agree with him. Closing his speech, the former Massachusetts governor spoke about his father, former Michigan Gov. George Romney, a supporter of the civil rights movement during the 1960s. Romney called his father's leadership an example in his own life. "It wasn't just that my dad helped write the civil rights provision for the Michigan Constitution, though he did. It wasn't just that he helped create Michigan's first civil rights commission or that as governor he marched for civil rights in Detroit, though he did those things, too," Romney said. "It was the kind of man he was, and the way he dealt with every person, black or white. He was a man of the fairest instincts, and a man of faith who knew that every person was a child of God."

Romney rarely speaks to a predominantly black audience at political events. One exception was a May visit to a charter school in Philadelphia, where he cast fixing the education system as a way to help blacks and other minorities. In framing education as a civil rights issue, Romney is following in George W. Bush's footsteps. At a sweeping address to the NAACP in 2000, Bush, then the Republican presidential nominee, said the education system should leave no child behind and he labeled the soft bigotry of low expectations as part of the problem facing black students. The 2012 Republican nominee has a personal history with civil rights issues. Romney's father, George, spoke out against segregation in the 1960s and as governor of Michigan toured his state's inner cities as race riots wracked Detroit and other urban areas across the country. He went on to lead the Housing and Urban Development Department, where he pushed for housing reforms to help blacks. Mitt Romney invoked that legacy during a 2007 interview on NBC's *Meet the Press*. "My dad's reputation ... and my own has always been one of reaching out to people and not discriminating based upon race or anything else."

Speaking before the NAACP, Attorney General Eric Holder departed from his prepared speech, decrying voter ID laws that have been proposed in 10 states so far, according to Conor Skelding of Yahoo! News and The Ticket on 10 July 2012. Talking Points Memo reports: "Under the proposed law, concealed handgun licenses would be acceptable forms of photo ID, but student IDs would not," Holder said. "Many of those without IDs would have to travel great distances to get them, and some would struggle to pay for the documents they might need to obtain them. We call those poll taxes." Holder isn't the first to say such laws are racist. Benjamin Todd Jealous, CEO and president of the NCAAP, evoked the civil rights movement comparing the moment to "Selma and Montgomery times." Jealous unilaterally opposed the laws, saying, "Simply put, the NAACP will never stand by as any state tries to encode discrimination into law."

Jealous, who posits that Romney could garner more votes from African Americans than John McCain did in 2008 when Barack Obama received 96 per cent of the black vote, believes Romney's economic message has not played well so far. "If he's going to pick up more support in the black community," Jealous told the *Times*, "he has to send a message that he's prepared to lead on issues that we care about." For Jealous, that means opposing voter ID laws. Romney has so far been reticent to discuss the issue. Andrea Saul, a campaign spokeswoman, told the *Times* only, "Gov. Romney believes that every legal vote should count."

In recent months, Obama has approached race from an intensely personal perspective. After the shooting of Trayvon Martin Obama spoke directly to Martin's parents from the Rose Garden. "If I had a son, he'd look like Trayvon," Obama said. However diminished enthusiasm for the president in the wake of the economic downturn could dampen black turnout. And that could make the difference in Southern states Obama won in 2008, particularly North Carolina and Virginia. Other factors could keep blacks away from voting booths. Romney's address to the group comes as Democrats and minority communities are expressing concern over a series of tough voter identification laws in a handful of states. Critics say the laws could make it harder for blacks and Hispanics to vote. "He'll be standing in that room asking people for their votes at the same time that Republican legislators are trying to disenfranchise minority communities," said Finney, the Democratic consultant. Romney expressed support for such laws during a late April visit to Pennsylvania, which now has one of the toughest voter identification statutes in the nation. "We ought to have voter identification so we know who's voting and we have a record of that," Romney said then.

If President Barack Obama wins a second term, he may have to thank all the single ladies: A new poll out in July showed Obama crushing Mitt Romney among unmarried women by a lopsided 60 per cent-31 per cent margin. Overall, though, the Quinnipiac University survey found the incumbent barely edges out the Republican standard-bearer 46 per cent to 43 per cent. Romney enjoys what Quinnipiac called a "yawning marriage gap" – he clobbered Obama among voters who put a ring on it by 51 per cent to 38 per cent. The Democrat beats his rival 54 per cent to 34 per cent overall among the unmarried. In 2008, Republican Sen. John McCain beat Obama 52 per cent to 47 per cent among married voters, according to exit polls, while the Democrat thumped him 65 per cent to 33 per cent among unmarried people. That suggests Obama has lost ground among married voters and unmarried voters alike. A drop would hardly be a surprise: Americans are unhappy about the sour economy three and a half years after the president took office vowing to fix it.

The Quinnipiac survey found Romney up 54 per cent to 35 per cent among married men and 49 per cent to 42 per cent among married women. Obama led 47 per cent to 38 per cent among single men and 60 per cent to 31 per cent among single women. Among the other findings, the poll showed Supreme Court Chief Justice John Roberts scoring better than Obama on job approval/disapproval – 46 per cent to 34 per cent for Roberts, and 45 per cent to 49 per cent for Obama. Quinnipiac University Polling Institute assistant director Peter Brown said in a statement about the poll that while the gender gap grabs headlines, "the marriage gap is actually larger and more telling. The marriage gap may be related to the different priorities and economic situations of married and single people," said Brown. "Married people are more likely to be older, more financially secure and more socially conservative than unmarried voters. The married column includes more Republicans and more white voters. Married voters are more likely to focus on the economy and health care, while single voters are more focused on issues such as gay rights and reproductive issues," Brown said.

The survey found that voters disapprove of Obama's handling of the economy by a 55 per cent to 40 per cent margin. But they don't seem particularly enthused about their choices in November, dividing 45 per cent to 46 per cent on whether Obama or Romney would do a better job. The poll queried 2,722 registered voters the first week of July. It has a margin of error of plus or minus 1.9 percentage points.

XII

FIRST LADY Michelle Obama is challenging assertions she has forcefully imposed her will on White House aides and says people have inaccurately tried to portray her as "some kind of angry black woman." The denial was reported by the Associated Press on 11 January 2012. Mrs. Obama told CBS News she had not read the *New York Times* reporter Jodi Kantor's new book that characterizes her as a behind-the-scenes force in the Executive Mansion, whose strong views often draw her into conflict with President Barack Obama's top advisers. "I never read these books," she told CBS's Gayle King in an interview. "So I've just gotten in the habit of not reading other people's impressions of people." In the book, Mrs. Obama is said to have occasionally bristled at some of the demands and constraints of life in the White House. In the interview, Mrs. Obama said, "I love this job. It has been a privilege from day one. And she added, "Now there are challenges. If there's any anxiety that I feel, it's because I want to make sure that my girls come out of this on the other end whole."

The Kantor book portrays a White House where tensions developed between Mrs. Obama and former White House chief of staff Rahm Emanuel and former press secretary and presidential adviser Robert Gibbs. The book, titled The Obamas, describes Mrs. Obama as having gone through an evolution from struggle to fulfillment in her role at the White House, while labeling her an "unrecognized force" in pursuing the president's goals. Neither the president nor his wife agreed to be interviewed for the book. "I do care deeply about my husband," Mrs. Obama said in the CBS appearance. "I am one of his biggest allies. I am one of his biggest confidants." But she sought to put aside this notion that "I sit in meetings. I guess it's just more interesting to imagine this conflicted situation here," she said. "That's been an image people have tried to paint of me that I'm some kind of angry black woman. There will always be people who don't like me," Mrs. Obama added, and said she could live with that. Mrs. Obama said that she's "just trying to be me, and I just hope that over time, that people get to know me."

Asked specifically about an assertion of dissension between herself and Emanuel, now the mayor of Chicago, the first lady said she has "never had a cross word" with him. The same, she said, applies to Gibbs, whom she described as "a good friend, and remains so. I'm sure we could go day to day and find things people wished they didn't say to each other," Mrs. Obama said. "And that's why I don't read these books. ... It's a game, in so many ways, that doesn't fit. Who can write about what I feel? What third person can tell me what I feel?" Mrs. Obama said that when questions or conflicts arise involving her and the White House staff, her East Wing staff resolves the issue with her husband's staff in the West Wing. "If there's communication that needs to happen, it's between staffs," she said.

The world of politics is not without misunderstanding, intrigue and malice. Betsy Rothstein reported on 21 December 2011, for example, that Jim Sensenbrenner (R-Wisc.), was overheard at the Delta

Crown lounge at Reagan National Airport talking on his cellphone about an incident he said occurred three weeks before while at an Episcopal church auction. Rothstein's source, a Democratic operative who heard the whole thing, said he was "very loud". Sensenbrenner was overheard saying that after buying all their "crap" a woman approached him and praised First Lady Michelle Obama. He told the woman that Mrs. Obama should practice what she preaches – "she lectures us on eating right while she has a large posterior herself." It is not what a superior man would say but it is behavior that is common today among many white Americans who feel threatened by the changing face of America.

But the journalist's job is also to find the lighter side of life to report on. And so, Ms. Rothstein on 21 December 2011 said the First Lady had found the time to engage her host, Ellen DeGeneres, in an impressive push-up challenge and completed 25 push-ups on the *Ellen DeGeneres Show* beating the TV host. The challenge began when daytime Ms. DeGeneres asked Mrs. Obama on her show, "How many push-ups can you do?" Thus challenged, Mrs. Obama teased the TV show host saying, "Can you? I know you've got these back issues?" The ladies then took off their jackets and began the challenge which Mrs. Obama won after completing an impressive 25. During the show, Mrs. Obama also revealed some bedroom secrets regarding husband Barack. He doesn't pick up his socks. "He thinks he's neat but he has people who help him. I'm like it's not you that's neat. It's the people who pick up your socks. Those are the neat people," she told DeGeneres.

Mrs. Obama was in California promoting healthy lifestyles for all Americans. She told Jay Leno "I can't sing", but claimed that her husband was in the habit of serenading her. She revealed that the President loves to serenade her by singing songs from Al Green, Marvin Gaye and other R&B greats. "He does have a beautiful voice, and he sings to me all the time," Mrs. Obama told Mr. Leno on *The Tonight Show*. The President gained attention in January for breaking out a bar of an Al Green song during a fundraiser at the Apollo Theater in New York City. But he also sings Marvin Gaye and even "a little Stevie." That's Stevie Wonder. "He likes the classics," she explained.

Michelle Obama also cajoled Mr. Leno into nibbling on apples, sweet potato fries and a pizza made with eggplant, green peppers and zucchini, breaking his long-held aversion for all-things-healthy in his diet. Mr. Leno once told a magazine he hadn't eaten a vegetable since 1969, and he insisted he tasted his last apple in 1984. That didn't dissuade the First Lady, who was promoting her "Let's Move!" campaign to get kids excited about fitness and healthy eating habits. Earlier, Mrs. Obama poked at him in a Twitter post, hinting she'd get Jay to eat some veggies on the NBC show. "That does smell very good. I assume this is sausage-pepperoni," the comedian quipped as he eyed the pizza made with a whole-wheat crust. She convinced Mr. Leno to dip an apple in honey made from beehives in the White House garden: "It will help it go down easier," she assured him. "White House honey? That sounds bad," Mr. Leno told her. "You know, with a different president that could mean a whole different thing, a little White House honey."

Lylah M. Alphonse, Senior Editor of Yahoo! Shine | Work + Money reported on 11 June 2012 that people are usually reluctant to admit their real feelings in surveys, but there's no doubt that our experiences and our prejudices play a part in the way we vote. In order to figure out whether racial bias affected Barack Obama's results in the 2008 presidential election, Seth Stephens-Davidowitz, a doctoral candidate in economics at Harvard University, passed over easy-to-manipulate surveys and looked at data from another source: online searches. When most people are searching for information online, he said, they're likely to be alone and less likely to censor their thoughts. "You may have typed things into Google that you would hesitate to admit in polite company," he writes in a *New York Times* article. "I certainly have. The majority of Americans have as well: We Google the word 'porn' more often than the word 'weather'."

He chose a common racial insult that starts with "N" and looked for searches that used the singular and plural forms of the word. "The most common searches including the epithet... return websites with derogatory material about African-Americans," he writes in his study. "The top hits for the top racially charged searches are nearly all textbook examples of antilocution, a majority group's sharing stereotype-based jokes using coarse language outside a minority group's presence." That held true for searches from 2004 through 2007 (searches for "n**ga" led mostly to rap lyrics, which he disregarded for this study). "I used data from 2004 to 2007 because I wanted a measure not directly influenced by feelings toward Mr. Obama", he writes in *The New York Times*. But from 2008 on, he discovered, "Obama" was one of the most prevalent search terms in racially tinged online searches. After gathering information on the racially charged search queries, Stephens-Davidowitz took a look at voting data from around the country and compared each area's 2008 results, when Obama was running for president, to voting results from 2004, when all of the candidates were white.

Though many people believe that our first African-American president won the election thanks in part to increased turnout by African-American voters, Stephens-Davidowitz's research shows that those votes only added about 1 percentage point to Obama's totals. "In the general election, this effect was comparatively minor," he concludes. But in areas with high racial search rates, the fact that Obama is African American worked against him, sometimes significantly. "The results imply that, relative to the most racially tolerant areas in the United States, prejudice cost Obama between 3.1 percentage points and 5.0 percentage points of the national popular vote," Stephens-Davidowitz points out in his study. "This implies racial animus gave Obama's opponent roughly the equivalent of a home-state advantage country-wide. Any votes Obama gained due to his race in the general election were not nearly enough to outweigh the cost of racial animus, meaning race was a large net negative for Obama," he adds.

The state with the highest racially charged search rate was West Virginia, where 41 per cent of voters chose Keith Judd, a white man who is also a convicted felon currently in prison in Texas, over Obama just this May. Louisiana, Pennsylvania, Mississippi, Kentucky, Michigan, Ohio, South Carolina, Alabama, and New Jersey rounded out the top 10 most-racist areas, according to the search queries used. Even in states that are considered fairly liberal, racism is prevalent enough in certain areas to put the entire state high up on the list. Other areas with high percentages included western Pennsylvania, eastern Ohio, upstate New York and southern Mississippi, Stephens-Davidowitz points out in his *New York Times* article.

The 10 states with the fewest racially charged searches were Utah, Hawaii, Colorado, New Mexico, Idaho, Washington DC, Minnesota, Oregon, Montana, and Wyoming. What does this mean for this year's contest? "Losing even two percentage points lowers the probability of a candidate's winning the popular vote by a third," Stephens-Davidowitz explains. "Prejudice could cost Mr. Obama crucial states like Ohio, Florida and even Pennsylvania."

In Phoenix a Reuters report from Tim Gaynor said that veteran Arizona lawman Joe Arpaio, self-described as America's toughest sheriff, denied that his deputies targeted people because of the color of their skin in a controversial crackdown on illegal immigration. Arpaio, sheriff of Arizona's Maricopa County, was testifying in a class-action lawsuit that will test whether police can target illegal immigrants without racially profiling Hispanic citizens and legal residents. "I am against anyone racial profiling ... today, as in my 50 years in law enforcement," Arpaio, a lawman who recently turned 80, told the court during cross-examination.

Arpaio was also asked about a news release he issued after a sweep targeting illegal immigrants in 2008, in which he noted criticism from former Phoenix Mayor Phil Gordon that his agency went after brown-skinned people with cracked windshields. "We do not arrest people because of the color of their skin," said Arpaio. The sheriff, who is seeking re-election to a sixth term in November, has been a lightning rod for controversy over his aggressive enforcement of immigration laws in the border state with Mexico, as well as his investigation into the validity of President Barack Obama's birth certificate.

The suit was brought against Arpaio and his office on behalf of five Hispanic plaintiffs who say they were stopped by deputies because they were Latino, which Arpaio denies. The trial focuses attention on Arizona, which was in the news when the U.S. Supreme Court upheld a key element of the state's crackdown on illegal immigrants requiring police to investigate those they stop and suspect of being in the country illegally. The Obama administration had challenged the crackdown in court, saying the U.S. Constitution gave the federal government sole authority over immigration policy. Arpaio faces a separate, broader lawsuit filed by the U.S. Justice Department in May, alleging systematic profiling, sloppy and indifferent police work and a disregard for minority rights. Protesters from both sides of the debate gathered outside the court toting flags and placards.

The United States is an enigma. Any one of the fifty states could act on its own to create a sense that there is freedom in the life of a state or a parish. What I have in mind is the report from Alon Harish of ABC News that a Mississippi Church on 28 July 2012 refused to marry a black couple. They had booked their wedding far in advance. The invitations had been sent, the programs printed. But one day before Charles and Te'Andrea Wilson were to be married at the Mississippi church they frequented, they said the pastor told them they would have to find another venue – because they are black. There has never been a black wedding at the First Baptist Church in Crystal Springs, Miss., since its founding in 1883. According to Pastor Stan Weatherford, some church members objected so strongly to breaking that precedent, they threatened to oust him from his pastorship. Rather than risk his job, Weatherford, who is white, said he decided to marry the pair at a black church down the road.

"My 9-year-old was going to the church with us. How would you say to your 9-year-old daughter, We cannot get married here because, guess what, sweetie, we're black," Charles Wilson told ABC's affiliate WAPT-TV.

Outrage over the wedding's forced relocation swept the Jackson suburb of about 5,000 into a media firestorm. The vast majority of Crystal Springs residents, blacks and whites alike, were "blown away" by the church's decision, said Theresa Norwood, 48, who was born in Crystal Springs and has lived there her entire life. Norwood said she believes Weatherford should have married the Wilsons regardless of the risk to his job. "That church was their home," she said. "What would Jesus have done? He would have married them, without a doubt, because it's the right thing to do. We're all God's children."

While the Wilsons were not members of the church, they often attended services there, and Te'Andrea's uncle is an employee of the church, and her father is a member. Charles Wilson told WAPT that the couple had planned to join as members after their wedding, which was held July 20.

Weatherford told WLBT-TV in Jackson that he would have liked to marry the couple as planned, but he decided to perform the ceremony elsewhere as a compromise to ensure that the Wilsons could be married while "addressing a need within our congregation."

Norwood, who is black, said her nephew came to worship at First Baptist Church while he was temporarily living with her, having been evacuated from New Orleans after Hurricane Katrina. The church "made him feel at home," she said, but now she wonders whether he would return there when he visits Crystal Springs.

The church is now holding internal meetings to figure out how it should respond to future requests by black couples to be married there, Weatherford told WLBT-TV. For her part, though, Norwood, who is dating a white man, said that if she and her boyfriend decide to get married, they will likely look for a different venue.

XIII

SLAVERY IN America, according to History.com channel, began when the first African slaves were brought to the North American colony of Jamestown, Virginia, in 1619, to aid in the production of such lucrative crops as tobacco. Slavery was practiced throughout the American colonies in the 17th and 18th centuries, and African-American slaves helped build the economic foundations of the new nation. The invention of the cotton gin in 1793 solidified the central importance of slavery to the South's economy. By the mid-19th century, America's westward expansion, along with a growing abolition movement in the North, would provoke a great debate over slavery that would tear the nation apart in the bloody American Civil War (1861-65). Though the Union victory freed the nation's 4 million slaves, the legacy of slavery continued to influence American history, from the tumultuous years of Reconstruction (1865-77) to the civil rights movement that emerged in the 1960s, a century after emancipation. And the attitudes of many white Americans seem to be that the system is still in place and black Americans continue to feel like second-class citizens. The absurdity seems to have no end in sight.

A Reuters report from Daniel Trotta from Fayetteville in North Carolina said that the U.S. Army is battling racists within its own ranks. They call it "rahowa", he said, – short for racial holy war – and they are preparing for it by joining the ranks of the world's fiercest fighting machine, the U.S. military. White supremacists, neo-Nazis and skinhead groups encourage followers to enlist in the Army and Marine

Corps to acquire the skills to overthrow what some call the ZOG – the Zionist Occupation Government. Get in, get trained and get out to brace for the coming race war.

If this scenario seems like fantasy or bluster, civil rights organizations take it as deadly serious, especially given recent events. The U.S. Defense Department as well has stepped up efforts to purge violent racists from its ranks, earning praise from organizations such as the Southern Poverty Law Center, which has tracked and exposed hate groups since the 1970s. No one knows how many white supremacists have served since then. A 2008 report commissioned by the Justice Department found half of all right-wing extremists in the United States had military experience.

Experts have identified the presence of street gang members as a more widespread problem. Even so, the Pentagon has launched three major pushes in recent decades to crack down on racist extremists. The first directive was issued in 1986, when Defense Secretary Casper Weinberger ordered military personnel to reject supremacist organizations. That failed to stop former Marine T.J. Leyden, with two-inch SS bolts tattooed above his collar, from serving from 1988 to 1991 while openly supporting neo-Nazi causes. A member of the Hammerskin Nation, a skinhead group, he said he hung a swastika from his locker, taking it down only when his commander politely asked him to ahead of inspections by the commanding general. "I went into the Marine Corps for one specific reason: I would learn how to shoot," Leyden told Reuters. "I also learned how to use C-4 (explosives), blow things up. I took all my military skills and said I could use these to train other people," said Leyden, 46, who has since renounced the white power movement and is a consultant for the anti-Nazi Simon Wiesenthal Center.

In 1995, eight months before the Fort Bragg murders, two former Army soldiers bombed the Oklahoma City federal building, killing 168 people. With a growing awareness of the spreading militia movement, the Pentagon in 1996 banned military personnel from participating in supremacist causes and authorized commanders to cashier personnel for rallying, recruiting or training racists.

The Pentagon's third directive against white supremacists was issued in 2009 after a Department of Homeland Security report expressed concern that right-wing extremists were recruiting veterans returning from wars overseas. The Pentagon's 2009 instruction, updated in February 2012, directs commanders to remain alert for signs of racist activity and to intervene when they see it. It bans soldiers from blogging or chatting on racist websites while on duty. "This is the best we've ever seen," said Heidi Beirich, leader of the Southern Poverty Law Center's intelligence project, referring to the Pentagon's attitude. "It was really disheartening under the Bush administration how lightly they took it, so this is a major advance." The Southern Poverty Law Center and the Anti-Defamation League (ADL), another civil rights monitor, have helped train officers on how to spot extremists, although Mark Pitcavage, director of investigative research at the ADL, says the military lacks comprehensive training for recruiters and commanders. He called the military's reaction when alerted to white supremacists "patchy".

The Army showed Reuters a one-hour presentation it says was designed to educate soldiers and Army leaders about its extremism policy and how to respond, including to white supremacy groups. Penalties for extremist ideology may include being removed from the military, having security clearances yanked or being demoted. "The standard hateful message has not been replaced, just packaged differently with issues like freedom of speech, anti-gun control themes, tax reform and oppression," the presentation says, noting that recruitment may be difficult to detect, occurring quietly "in bars and break areas" on bases. The presentation instructs Army leaders to look out for tattooed symbols of lightning bolts, skulls, swastikas, eagles and Nordic warriors. Skinheads may have tattoos showing barbed wire, hobnailed boots and hammers. In a detailed flowchart called a "Tattoo Decision Support Matrix", Army leaders are shown how to respond to various tattoos. Academics who study white supremacists say proponents of the "infiltration strategy" of joining the U.S. military have adapted, telling skinheads to deceive military recruiters by letting their hair grow, avoiding or covering tattoos, and suppressing their racist views.

There is no end however to the fight against discrimination. According to a Reuters report a federal appeals court has ruled that Alabama and Georgia could enforce key aspects of their laws against illegal immigration that allow police to check the status of criminal suspects. The decisions were in line with the U.S. Supreme Court ruling on a similar Arizona law, but the U.S. Court of Appeals for the 11th Circuit in Atlanta continued to block other parts of the two Southern states' laws, which have been challenged by the federal government and civil rights groups. Judges said the laws' opponents were likely to prevail in their fight against provisions in both states that would make it a crime in some cases to knowingly harbor or transport an illegal immigrant. The court also barred Alabama from requiring schools to check the immigration status of children upon enrollment and from requiring all immigrants to carry a registration document at all times. "We conclude that most of the challenged provisions cannot stand," the court said regarding the Obama administration's case against Alabama. The rulings follow a split Supreme Court decision in June on Arizona's first-of-its-kind crackdown on people who are in the country illegally in which the court upheld a measure requiring police to check the immigration status of people they stop and suspect are in the country illegally. But the top U.S. court struck down provisions requiring immigrants to always carry immigration papers, banning illegal immigrants from soliciting work in public places, and allowing police arrests of immigrants without warrants if officers believed they committed crimes that would make them deportable.

Other states that used Arizona's example in crafting immigrations laws have been waiting for rulings of their own in light of that decision. The mixed opinions from the appeals court drew praise from both sides of the issue. The House speaker in Alabama said the court had upheld the "real teeth" of that state's law, while critics hailed the injunction against the schools provision. "The essence of Alabama's immigration law has been upheld by today's ruling," Republican Governor Robert Bentley said in a statement. "The Court is recognizing the state's authority to inquire on immigration status in certain circumstances." Opponents vowed to keep fighting what have been dubbed the "show me your papers" provisions, which they argue cannot be enforced without racial profiling.

Was this arrogance, ignorance or much ado about nothing Lylah M. Alphonse, Senior Editor of Yahoo! Shine/Fashion wanted to know on 16 October 2012 when she had finished writing that Gap had pulled a T-Shirt with the words "Manifest Destiny" written across it.

338

The fact is clothing giant pulled the controversial T-shirt off its warehouse shelves after outraged consumers lashed out via social media. The T-shirt with "MANIFEST DESTINY" printed on it in stark white letters was part of the "Gap x GQ" collection, a joint effort between Gap and GQ magazine to showcase America's best new designers. Adding fuel to the fire, the shirt's designer, Mark McNairy, tweeted "MANIFEST DESTINY. SURVIVAL OF THE FITTEST" in response to customer complaints. He quickly deleted his tweet, but not before it was widely circulated, and then he followed up three days later with an all-caps semi-apology. "Unfortunately, the meaning of my 'Manifest Destiny' T shirt has been misconstrued and the sentiment behind it grossly misunderstood," McNairy posted on Twitter. "I first learned of Manifest Destiny in American History in Junior High School. To me it has always meant that one could set goals, work hard, and achieve their dreams. Having the opportunity to design for the Gap was the realization of one of my dreams. This phrase and the way I used it was in no way meant to be offensive or hurtful, and I apologize to those who might have interpreted it in that manner."

The term "Manifest Destiny", as was pointed out to McNairy, actually refers to the mid-19th century mindset that white Americans had a divine obligation to claim as much of the continent as possible for themselves, slaughtering and oppressing native people in the process. As Ms. Alphonse stated the term was coined in 1845 by John O'Sullivan, a newspaper editor at the *Democratic Review*, who wrote that the United states should annex Texas and claim the Oregon Country because "that claim is by the right of our manifest destiny to overspread and to possess the whole of the continent which Providence has given us for the development of the great experiment of liberty and federated self-government entrusted to us." It also was used to justify the idea that people with darker skin were "heathen," "backwards," and otherwise less than human.

Needless to say, Gap experienced a bit of a backlash. More than 4,700 people have signed a petition at Change.org calling on Gap to discontinue the shirt and issue a formal apology, and there are Facebook protests aplenty. While the $30 shirt is no longer available on gap.com, it is still available in some stores. "This article of clothing promotes a belief that has resulted in the mass genocide of indigenous people, and it serves to normalize oppression," wrote Dorit I, who launched the petition. "This shirt is marketed to teens and young adults, and it gives no context for the racism and inequality that persists in our society, to this day, as a result of this doctrine."

"Manifest destiny was the symbolic banner settler colonizers marched behind while waging genocidal wars against Indigenous Peoples," wrote Klee Benally of IndigenousAction.org. "This shirt design is grossly offensive and should be immediately removed. I certainly don't think *Arbeit macht frei* would have made it this far. Gap Inc. has been under serious scrutiny for exploitative labor practices within the past couple of decades, maybe they are just now making their intentions more clear?"

But not everyone is offended by the shirt. "Manifest destiny is the reason our country even exists," Casey Jo Adams-Carlisle, who describes herself as "a racial mutt," wrote on Facebook. "If you don't like it, pack up, and get out. Simple."

It's possible that the shirt is more about ignorance than arrogance, but if that's the case, it goes all the way to the top. Online, Gap lauds the shirt as "rebellious and playful." And in their write-up of the Gap x GQ launch event, GQ described McNairy's "left-of-center spirit" and his "tech sports jacket with pop yellow, trim, Bengal stripe daisy print boxers, and wool camo cargo pants" but didn't mention the "Manifest Destiny" shirt, even though both the designer and an African American model were wearing it in photos from the event.

The trouble is every racist protest is never much ado about nothing as Congresswoman Bachmann should understand by now.

Chapter Five – New Technologies

A number of global forces have gradually, sometimes almost clandestinely, altered the world as we know it. The most visible to most of us has been the increasing transformation of everyday life by cell phones, personal computers, email, BlackBerries, and the Internet. – Alan Greenspan in *The Age of Turbulence*

SAN FRANCISCO. – Before we left for the United States on 1 September 2011, Rhona had diligently sent the manuscript of *The Concubine*, one of the four books I had written in China, to a number of publishers in the United States and in the United Kingdom. It was, Simon had said, the thing to do and in fact he had given her the newest *Agents Directory*, the bible of Rachel Vater which proclaims itself as "the essential Writer's Reference". The book is supposed to contain "everything you need to know to sell your book or script". But the truth is I had long ago lost faith in the industry and I remembered when I was in York, England in 2008, and went every day to the library to use its computers I used to walk from bookshelf to bookshelf reading the recent titles and I couldn't find a single new book that I would want to join the books in my own library. I wondered every time who had decided on the selection of books to be published. But Rhona was convinced that this was the way to go and she sent off as directed portions of *The Concubine* to publishers. The funny thing is since we had gone to China to live and work, she had self-published a number of books in Hong Kong and in the United States, but I had not followed this route and perhaps had thought that my books were good enough to be grabbed up by a well-known publisher. It was not just vanity; I was sure that I did not want to have anything to do with the marketing of my books. That was not my expertise.

The Concubine did not draw blood. Oh, yes, it was generally well-received – a euphemism for rejecting an author's work with the hope perhaps that one day he would write something spectacular. It was not the kind of book the publishers were doing they explained. On 25 June 2012, for example, Penny Thomas, Fiction Editor of Seren, Well Chosen Words, wrote me: *"Dear Owen Baptiste, Many thanks for letting us see the opening chapters of The Concubine and many apologies for the long delay in replying to you, which is due to the large number of submissions which we have received over the last year. This is a very interesting concept for a work of fiction. However I'm afraid there is very little space on our fiction list and competition is intense, so I'm afraid I'm not able to publish your novel. I am sorry to have to reply in the negative and do wish you luck with this novel elsewhere. With best wishes. Penny Thomas."*

Poor, overworked Penny Thomas had taken almost a year to reply to the submission of *The Concubine* to be published and I assumed I was lucky to hear from her. My spirits were buoyed up however by the fact that there is still a great amount of interest in old-fashioned publishing according to Ms. Thomas. But I felt that there was really no reason for Ms. Thomas to say twice that she was afraid. A rejection notice would not have ended my interest in writing. It was clear that the alternative to her industry, Printing on Demand, what CreateSpace offered, was as yet not threatening her living. But should it if it takes so long to respond to the queries of writers? Let me explain with this story from the *Wall Street Journal*'s point of view.

Darcie Chan's debut novel became an unexpected hit last summer, wrote Alexandra Alter in the *Wall Street Journal* on 9 December 2011. The book sold more than 400,000 copies and landed on the bestseller lists alongside brand-name authors like Michael Connelly, James Patterson and Kathryn Stockett. It's been a success by any measure, save one. Ms. Chan still hasn't found a publisher. Five years ago, Ms. Chan's novel, *The Mill River Recluse*, which tells the story of a wealthy Vermont widow who bestows her fortune on town residents who barely knew her, would have languished in a drawer. A dozen publishers and more than 100 literary agents rejected it. "Nobody was willing to take a chance," says Ms. Chan, a 37-year-old lawyer who drafts environmental legislation. "It was too much of a publishing risk." In May 2011, Ms. Chan decided to digitally publish it herself, hoping to gain a few readers and some feedback. She bought some ads on Web sites targeting e-book readers, paid for a review from Kirkus Reviews, and strategically priced her book at 99 cents to encourage readers to try it. She's now attracting bids from foreign imprints, movie studios and audio-book publishers, without selling a single copy in print.

The *Wall Street Journal* and Ms. Alter tell the story of how Ms. Chan joined the ranks of bestsellers is as much a tale of digital marketing savvy and strategic pricing as one of artistic triumph. Her breakout signals a monumental shift in the way books are packaged, priced and sold in the digital era. Just as music executives have been sidestepped by YouTube sensations and indie iTunes hits, book publishers are losing ground to independent authors and watching their powerful status as literary gatekeepers wither. Self-publishing has long been derided as a last resort for authors who lack the talent or savvy to hack it in the publishing business but it has gained legitimacy as a growing number of self-published authors land on bestseller lists. In 2010, 133,036 self-published titles were released, up from 51,237 in 2006, according to Bowker, a company that tracks publishing trends.

As I have done elsewhere in this book, I am quoting from sources on line that I trust and my naiveté here reveals my Achilles' heel more completely than anywhere else. I had no previous opportunity to investigate the industry in the United States and I am relying on published accounts. My aim here and elsewhere is to present enough information from the news media to help America-watchers to discover the Soul of Americans, that is, what makes them Americans. I say this because there are critics outside there, people incapable of writing as I am incapable of bungee-diving, waiting for the chance to pounce on uninformed writers. All I could be accused of I think is "an excess of liberty" in quoting from these sources; I have no intention to pass off the work as my own. Readers might find fault with the selection of material but not with the transparency of my motive. I am trying real hard to give a kaleidoscopic view of American experience and to show what authenticates the American character and this is the reason for long, unedited pieces from time to time. Besides, if you haven't read it before here is your chance to understand the work other Americans are doing.

The truth is often what I am doing is unabashedly the work of a reviewer. For example, according to news reports a handful of self-published authors have achieved blockbuster status, selling more than a million copies of their books on the Kindle. While they represent a tiny minority of independent authors, the ranks of the successful are growing. Thirty authors have sold more than 100,000 copies of their books through Amazon's Kindle self-publishing program, and a dozen have sold more than 200,000 copies, according to Amazon. The program, which Amazon launched in 2007, allows authors to upload their books directly to Amazon's Kindle store, set their own prices and publish in multiple languages. Barnes & Noble followed suit in 2010 with a similar program for its Nook e-reader. And self-published titles have been buoyed by an explosion in digital book sales. E-book sales totaled $878 million in 2010, compared to $287 million in 2009, according to the Association of American Publishers. Some analysts project that e-book sales will pass $2 billion in 2013. The march of self-published authors has put publishers and literary agents on guard. Publishing houses like Penguin and Perseus have recently launched their own digital self-publishing programs in an effort to capture a slice of the mushrooming market. Some agents, including Scott Waxman, have started their own digital imprints.

Digital self-publishing still has serious drawbacks they say. Though e-books are the fastest-growing segment of the book market, they still make up less than 10 per cent of overall trade book sales, according to the Association of American Publishers. Book reviewers tend to ignore self-published works, and brick-and-mortar bookstores have long shunned them. And very few authors have a marketing and advertising budget equal to a publisher's. However several successful self-published authors have gone on to cut deals with major publishers. After selling around 1.5 million digital copies of her books on her own, 27-year-old fantasy writer Amanda Hocking signed with St. Martin's Press. She won a $2 million advance for a new four-book fantasy series called *Watersong*. St. Martin's will also reprint her best-selling self-published *Trylle* trilogy about attractive teenage trolls.

Devices such as the Kindle and iPad are changing the way the public think about books but who will control the future of reading? Victor Keegan wrote on 15 October 2010 in the guardian.co.uk that books have come late to the digital party, but change is now happening at such a furious pace that even conservative members of the trade are starting to realize that their industry is being snatched away from them before their eyes. The undisputed leader in the race to sell digital books is Amazon. Its Kindle e-reader was a late entry into the race but it used its redoubtable marketing muscle to gain a 76 per cent share of all digital books sold. It could have been much more but for the arrival of the iPad, which now has a 5 per cent market share; Apple's iPad is good for Amazon's Kindle, which has 76 per cent of eBooks market, says the Cowen report, though rising fast. Traditional booksellers such as Barnes and Noble which has released a new Wi-Fi reader and Waterstones are still in the race, but it looks as though book distribution is being sewn up by existing digital giants. Is this what writers really want? asked Keegan. Why hasn't a horizontal model emerged in which networks of readers and authors can interact and buy and exchange favorite works on a global scale? Where is the Facebook of books? This vertical model, of course, brings terrific benefits having a virtual library of thousands of books you can read when and where you want. Do we want reading, which ought to be a truly communal experience, migrating into a handful of digital silos, each imposing their own rules about what we can read, where we can read it and making it impossible to lend a book if you don't lend the device as well?

The story goes on: Amazon doesn't just own Kindle. Its tentacles have spread out into a series of worrying monopolies. Instead of using its formidable base in selling traditional books to build up a similar position with second-hand books, it purchased the biggest existing seller of second-hand books on the internet, Abebooks.com. Instead of building up its own presence in audio books, it purchased Audible.com, which had over 90 per cent of the audio market. It also bought a 40 per cent stake in Librarything.com, one of the admirable online book clubs, which has just released a kind of mobile public library in the US and Ireland. There are lots of interesting experiments in the online book world, including Nick Cave's novel *Bunny Munro*, sold as a multimedia iPhone app; Google's massive scanning of out-of-copyright books; the now venerable Gutenberg project, which has over 33,000 out-of-copyright books uploaded by volunteers; and numerous book clubs not to mention the *Guardian*'s own. The video book publisher Vook.com has just celebrated its first anniversary. And still to come is 24Symbols, which aims to be the Spotify of books by streaming them for free over the web (with adverts paying) as well as traditional paid-for downloads.

No one knows where all this will end up. Digital devices such as the Kindle and the iPad have media companies quivering with excitement but will people really use them to read newspapers and magazines? Over at Screen Digest, one of the better research firms, they reckon that Apple will sell 1 million iPads by the end of the year and that iPad penetration will reach about 10-11 per cent (6 to 6.5 million) of the British population by 2014, which is about as far as anybody can reasonably forecast.

Speculation continues even though it is still too easy to jump from one news source to another, because digital has fundamentally changed people's relationship with printed news sources. There is also this development as Stu Woo wrote in *The Wall Street Journal* on 21 December 2012 that behind the piles of smiley-faced Amazon.com Inc. boxes arriving on doorsteps this holiday season in Fernley, Nev., are workers like Ray and Sarann Williams. The retired couple is part of the swarm of seasonal employees taking up temporary residence in this small desert city – home to one of Amazon's warehouses – to help the online-retail giant fulfill its influx of holiday orders. The Williamses migrated from their home in Hurricane, Utah, to take the two-month warehouse gig. "The money always helps" and the physical labor "always makes me feel better," Mr. Williams said as he walked his miniature schnauzer, Maya, around the Desert Rose RV park, where the couple is currently residing. The 75-year-old said this was his second stint as a seasonal Amazon worker, after spending last autumn at Amazon's Campbellsville, Ky., location.

Amazon, the world's biggest e-commerce purveyor, sees a sales spike every fourth quarter, when it makes nearly 40 per cent of its more than $34 billion in annual revenue. To meet that surge, the Seattle-based company hires hundreds of temporary workers at each of its 34 U.S. warehouses. A spokeswoman for Amazon, which has

51,000 staffers excluding seasonal workers world-wide, said it hires "thousands" of temporary workers for the holidays, but declined to disclose specific numbers. It said it quadrupled its staff at its warehouse in Phoenix to 1,200 to handle the end-of-year rush. Many of these employees belong to the community of "workampers", a sort of modern-day migrant worker. Many of them are retirees who spend all or part of the year living in RVs and taking odd seasonal jobs around the country.

Many current and former seasonal workers said Amazon pays decent wages – about $12 an hour plus overtime in Fernley, which is about 50 per cent better than minimum wage. But that is in exchange for long hours and tedious labor. "It's like the best place to work and the worst place to work," said Kelly Andrus, a 50-year-old Fernley resident who served as an Amazon holiday employee seven years ago. "It's good pay, and they're safety oriented," but she said the managers were strict and the labor was physically demanding. Workers can be on their feet for hours fetching items from shelves, packing boxes and preparing incoming items for storage. Many said they lose five pounds or more in a few weeks."

II

IN A WORLD where Amazon can track your next book purchase and you must register to buy allergy medicine, wrote Nicholas Riccardi of the Associated Press after the Denver shooting, James Holmes spent months stockpiling thousands of bullets and head-to-toe ballistic gear without raising any red flags with authorities. Holmes, the 24-year-old university student, availed himself of an unregulated online marketplace that allows consumers to acquire some of the tools of modern warfare as if they were pieces of a new wardrobe. Make no mistake about it: The Internet is awash in sites ranging from BulkAmmo.com, which listed a sale on a thousand rifle rounds for $335, to eBay, where bidding on one armored Special Forces helmet has risen to $799. "We're different than other cultures," said Dudley Brown, executive director of Rocky Mountain Gun Owners, which advocates for firearms owners' rights. "We do allow Americans to possess the accoutrements that our military generally has." Gun rights activists like Brown celebrate that freedom, but even some involved in the trade are troubled by how easily Holmes stocked up for his rampage.

Chad Weinman runs TacticalGear.com that caters to police officers looking to augment their equipment, members of the military who don't want to wait on permission from the bureaucracy for new combat gear, and hobbyists like survivalists and paintballers. The site receives "thousands" of orders daily, sometimes from entire platoons that are about to deploy to war zones. On 2 July 2012, Holmes placed a $306 order with the site for a combat vest, magazine holders and a knife, paying extra for expedited two-day shipping to his Aurora apartment. The order, Weinman said, didn't stand out. "There's a whole range of consumers who have an appetite for these products, and 99.9 per cent of them are law-abiding citizens," Weinman said. He added that he doesn't sell guns or ammunition and that he was "shocked" at the amount of bullets that Holmes allegedly bought online.

Authorities say all of Holmes' purchases were legal – and there is no official system to track whether people are stockpiling vast amounts of firepower. There is no restriction on the sale of bullets in the United States, except for armor-piercing rounds, which can only be bought by law enforcement, said Ginger Colbrun, a spokeswoman for the Bureau of Alcohol, Tobacco and Firearms. Hence the proliferation of websites offering Amazon.com-style wish-lists for hollow-point rifle rounds or tracer bullets. There is a federal law that bars selling body armor to violent felons – which Holmes was not – but it is rarely used because there is no requirement to check whether purchasers of the material have criminal records, according to Dan Gross, president of the Brady Campaign Against Gun Violence. Over four months, authorities said, Holmes received more than 50 packages at his Aurora apartment and the University of Colorado medical school, where he was studying neuroscience. As the boxes piled up, he began to shop for guns at sporting goods stores – because of the need to pass a background check to buy a firearm; they are still generally bought at brick-and-mortar locations.

Rep Carolyn McCarthy (D-NY), whose husband was killed in a mass shooting on the Long Island Railroad in 1993, has proposed a ban on high-capacity magazines in Congress but acknowledges it has little chance of passage. She said she was horrified by the shooting but most shocked by the other material that Holmes allegedly accumulated – the bullets and combat gear. "It befuddles me to think those things should be sold to the general public," she said. Colorado State Rep. Mike Waller cautioned against trying to limit purchases of ammunition. He noted that Holmes reportedly bought 300 rounds for his shotgun. "My 13-year-old son and I go out to the shooting range all the time," said Waller, a Republican. "I buy more than 300 rounds of shotgun shells when I do that." He said there may be discussion of limiting the sale of the sort of protective clothing that Holmes allegedly donned. "Is that what the right to bear arms means, that you can purchase tactical gear to stop law enforcement from preventing you from perpetrating a crime?" Waller asked. "In the days and weeks to come, this is going to be a significant conversation."

But gun enthusiasts caution against over-reacting to the massacre. Brown, of Rocky Mountain Gun Owners, said he thinks citizen's access to weaponry has made the United States "a stronger country." And he doesn't see anything unusual about many of Holmes' purchases. "If I only had 6,000 rounds for my AR-15s, I'd literally feel naked," Brown said. Then he totaled up Holmes' firearms purchases: "Two handguns, a shotgun and a rifle. That's the average male in Colorado."

According to Russell Goldman of ABC News the family of gunman James Holmes said they will support the Ph.D. student accused of entering a movie theatre on 20 July 2012 and not leaving until he had killed 12 people and wounded another 58. Asked if they stand by Holmes, lawyer and family spokeswoman Lisa Damiani said at a press conference, "Yes they do. He's their son." Damiani said the family was holding up "as well as anyone could under the circumstances. I think everyone can imagine how they're feeling," Damiani said, "anyone who's ever been a parent." The spokeswoman said the family had spoken to investigators from California, but had not been contacted by police in Colorado. "No one from the Aurora Police Department has contacted us, or asked for assistance," she said. Through Damiani, the suspect's mother Arlene Holmes wanted to clarify a statement she made to ABC News in the immediate aftermath of the shooting. ABC News phoned Arlene Holmes at 5 am PST, at her home in San Diego, Calif., according to notes and email records by

ABC News producer Matthew Mosk, who placed the call. Through her lawyer, Holmes sought to clarify the remarks she made in that phone interview. "I did not know anything about a shooting in Aurora at that time," Arlene Holmes said in statement read by her lawyer. "He [Mosk] asked if I was Arlene Holmes and if my son was James Holmes, who lives in Aurora, Colorado. I answered yes, you have the right person. I was referring to myself. I asked him to tell me why he was calling and he told me about a shooting in Aurora. He asked for a comment. I told him I could not comment because I did not know if the person he was talking about was my son and I would need to find out."

As President Obama and Mitt Romney face up to the issue of gun control, it is easier for them to turn their attention to the evils of the Internet as British Prime Minister David Cameron did in August 2011 when he was faced with riots in London. Dylan Stableford wrote in The Cutline on 11 August 2011 that Mr. Cameron said that he is considering a limit on social media use in an attempt to curtail the riots that had spread throughout England. Cameron told Parliament that it is the clear the rioters used social media sites such as Facebook and Twitter to mobilize themselves – and to spread disorder. "Everyone watching these horrific actions will be stuck by how they were organized via social media," Cameron said. "Free flow of information can be used for good. But it can also be used for ill." And his government was expected to meet with executives from Facebook, Twitter and Research in Motion (the company behind BlackBerry Messenger, a key organizing device in the spread of the riots), Cameron said. He continued: "We are working with the police, the intelligence services and industry to look at whether it would be right to stop people communicating via these websites and services when we know they are plotting violence, disorder and criminality." In a statement posted on the 10 Downing Street website, Cameron said, "When people are using social media for violence, we need to stop them."

Cameron's comments recall Egypt government's response to the uprising this spring, when access to Facebook and mobile Internet services was blocked during the height of protests in Cairo. "We are making technology work for us," Cameron said. "By capturing the images of the perpetrators on CCTV, even if they haven't yet been arrested, their faces are known and they will not escape the law. And as I said, no human rights concerns about publishing photographs will get in the way of bringing these criminals to justice. Anyone charged with violent disorder and other serious offenses should expect to be remanded in custody, and anyone convicted should expect to go to jail." Cameron said that police have made more than 1,200 arrests since the riots began.

The London riots, at least initially, appeared to have been fueled by rioters using something not technically social: BlackBerry Messenger. Young protestors in Tottenham used the free instant message service – which requires BlackBerry users to exchange pin numbers – to mobilize their numbers during their clash with police because it is a private channel, unlike Facebook and Twitter. According to TechCrunchEurope, the BlackBerry is "by far the most popular handset" among British youth. Meanwhile, Twitter has been instrumental in the clean-up of London. A Twitter feed called Clean Up London (@Riotcleanup) has more than 87,000 followers while providing frequent, crowd-sourced updates on locations where volunteers are most needed. The feed also spawned the trending hashtag "#riotcleanup". BlackBerry announced that it would cooperate with police in their investigations of the riots. Twitter, though it has refused to close the accounts of London rioters, insisting that "freedom of expression" be protected, reiterating what the company said in January during the revolution in Egypt: "tweets must flow."

III

SEVEN STATES won a share of $200 million in federal "Race to the Top" money to improve K-12 education programs, the Education Department announced on 22 December 2011. The Associated Press said the winners were Arizona, $25.1 million; Colorado, $17.9 million; Illinois, $42.8 million; Kentucky, $17 million; Louisiana, $17.5 million; Pennsylvania, $41.3 million; and New Jersey, $37.9 million. The Obama administration has awarded billions of dollars in such competitions to encourage changes in education that it favors. The seven states competing in this round were all runners-up last year, and the Education Department has said it wants to encourage them to finish and carry out many of the changes proposed in their earlier applications. Competing states committed to make changes such as improving principal and teacher evaluation systems and turning around under-performing schools. They also were asked to show specifically how they would improve science, technology, engineering and math instruction. Education Secretary Arne Duncan said the money was driving dramatic improvements. "We've had broken teacher-evaluation systems in many places, unfortunately for five, or six or seven decades," Duncan said. "You've seen more effort there and more movement in a short amount of time than in a long time prior to that, and many states are using Race to the Top resources to do that." Two other states, South Carolina and California, were also eligible. South Carolina opted not to compete, while California submitted an incomplete application. Earlier, nine states were announced as winners of a share of $500 million in grants under a similar competition focused on improving early learning programs.

Duncan also said federal officials are monitoring states to ensure that they follow through on their plans to improve schools with "Race to the Top" money. For example, he said he has warned Hawaii that it's in danger of losing funding. "We're going to look for some pretty significant improvements early in the New Year," Duncan said. "There's not a hard-and-fast date. If we see things turning around, that would be fantastic. If we don't see things turning around, then we've got some tough decisions to make."

Meanwhile Christina Des Marais of Inc. wrote on 2 December 2011 that for a number of tech start-ups, it's the Gallatin Valley – not the Silicon Valley – that offers the best environment for growth. According to Jerry Nettuno he didn't found his startup Schedulicity in Silicon Valley because he didn't see the point. For one thing, he really likes where he lives. With a population of only 38,000, Bozeman, Montana, is barely a blip on the map compared with some of the other places cranking out tech start-ups. But Nettuno says the area attracts bright minds – increasingly more of them from the San Francisco Bay area itself. "It's a small town in southwestern Montana right in the mountains with fantastic schools and unbelievable opportunities for recreation, so we have people that come here from all over."

Nettuno launched Schedulicity, an online appointment booking platform, to the public in 2010. He wouldn't reveal the company's revenue figures but says the platform now facilitates $500 million worth of business each year. It helps small businesses, such as hair salons or massage therapists, fill up their appointment books on the Web and slot last-minute cancellations by marketing "pop-up offers" to customers. The company makes money by charging businesses $19 a month for a single user account or $39 for a multiple-user plan. Schedulicity isn't the only tech company to prefer the quiet life. Bozeman is home to social media e-learning platform Wisetail, CRM software provider RightNow Technologies (which Oracle just acquired for $1.5 billion), and TechRanch, an advisory organization that has helped more than 60 tech start-ups get off the ground in the area. "People [in Bozeman] aren't agitated and they aren't in a hurry all the time," says Nettuno. "So finding support people that are happy and enjoy talking to customers is really easy." Nettuno admits there are benefits to inclusion in the Silicon Valley club and recently hired one of its own, Diana Vincent-Galvan, to work from the Bay Area as VP of Communications and raise its profile within the tech community. So far, it's working; she helped the company land a DEMOgod Award at DEMO Fall 2011 for those pop-up offers. But when asked to talk about the culture of Silicon Valley – since she has spent her career working there for the likes of Yahoo and Cisco – she raved about the Gallatin Valley instead, even going as far as calling her first trip to Bozeman a "Twilight Zone experience". "Everyone and not just the people at the company, but everyone at the restaurants, the stores, and the hotels have a completely different attitude. Everybody was so nice and so catering and so willing to help."

On the investor front, Bozeman boasts a network of angels who hail from all over the country, but the area still has some catching up to do. "Bozeman isn't home to any institutional firms, which is very different from the Silicon Valley where you can find several within a three-block radius," says Nettuno, referring to Sand Hill Road. So for Series A funding, which the company aims to close in the next 60 days, he pitched angels in Bozeman, but he also went west to pitch institutional investors. Still, he says he's been hearing some feedback that should bode well for other so-called "Silicon Prairie" start-ups: "There are VC firms that prefer to invest in companies outside of the

Valley because, according to them, they seem to be better connected to their product and more committed to their customers." And that much, building a product with a solid business model, Nettuno says his company has gotten right. "I think we could have done that anywhere," he says. "But we're lucky enough to be in a place where we love to live. We love everything that comes with living here in Montana, except maybe minus 25 degrees in January," he says.

Chris Moody wrote in The Ticket on 29 July 2011 that the software company Apple has more cash on hand than the United States federal government, according to the company's financial records. Apple's quarterly financial report shows that the company responsible for the iPad, iPod and the iPhone now has $76.4 billion in reserve cash, while the Treasury Department is sitting on just $73.7 billion. The feds he wrote could probably learn a thing or two from Apple's success. Congress remains embroiled in a debate over spending and whether the federal government, which currently owes trillions in debt, should be allowed to borrow even more. International credit rating agencies had threatened to downgrade the national debt for the first time in the nation's history if Washington didn't come up with a solution to lift the $14.3 trillion debt ceiling while implementing a concrete plan to get the nation's financial house in order. Meanwhile, Apple's financial report shows that the company's profits, even through the last recession, are booming. The truth is, as Scott Ard reported in Yahoo! News on 15 March 2012 Apple is riding a wave of popularity and success seldom seen in the tech industry – or any other industry. With the company's recent white-hot success, including today's release of a new model of the market-leading iPad, it's easy to forget that it wasn't always this way.

The company's history is well-known to anyone even remotely interested in Silicon Valley lore. Apple was launched in 1976 by the affable and brilliant Steve Wozniak and the charismatic visionary Steve Jobs in a garage in Los Altos, California. Its first line of PCs, the Apple II, is credited with igniting the personal computer revolution and became a mainstay in schools and homes throughout the 1980s. The Mac, introduced in 1984, forever changed the interface between humans and computers, bringing to the mass market advances that today we take for granted, including the mouse, the graphical interface, and tiled windows. The 1990s, however, were not so kind:

Innovative products like the Newton failed to catch on, the Mac languished as an overpriced, niche PC (with less than 5 per cent market share), and a misguided strategy to allow manufacturers to clone Macs pushed the company to the precipice of irrelevancy and bankruptcy. Jobs's 11-year exile ended in 1996, when Apple purchased his NeXT Computer company. Back in control of his baby, he slashed product lines and employees, focused on form and function, and soon introduced another hit, the bulbous Bondi-blue iMac. With some cash in the bank and a rejuvenated fan base, Jobs orchestrated a string of hits – iPod, iTunes, iPhone, and iPad – that have swelled Apple's bank account to more than $100 billion and made it the most valuable company ever.

But what do you really know about Apple and how it operates? If you are like most people, and even most of the company's 50,000 employees, you know precious little about what goes on inside 1 Infinite Loop, Cupertino. Competitors, analysts, investors, employees, the press, retailers – everyone – are kept in the dark about what's coming until the very last minute. Hoping to shed light on how Apple operates, *Fortune* magazine reporter Adam Lashinsky interviewed numerous former and current executives and employees. His findings, which have surely upset Apple, were published in his book *Inside Apple: How America's Most Admired – and Secretive – Company Really Works*. Yahoo! talked with Lashinsky in late February, the same day Apple sent out invitations to an event that turned out to be the unveiling of its newest iPad. Given the timing, Lashinsky was asked to talk about the findings in his book in the context of Apple's mysterious product-development cycle. As people read the interview, long lines were snaking around Apple stores, consumers receiving their iPads via FedEx were breathlessly tweeting their joy, and tech blogs, newspapers, and the evening news were eagerly covering Apple's latest big product release. Indeed, the day marked the culmination of months of detailed planning, exquisite execution, and masterful media manipulation. As uncovered by Lashinsky, this is how Apple does it.

Yahoo!: Talk about the genesis of a product formation at Apple. How does a product idea get bubbled up? At what level is it being approved?

Adam: Apple has relatively few products, first of all. For many years, the company would say that it could fit all of its products on a conference room table. That's not completely true anymore. But in spirit, it is true that Apple has a simple lineup compared with so many other companies. The products that Apple has had over the last 15 years have been part of a larger strategy, part of this digital-hub strategy, starting with the Macintosh, extending out to iTunes and iPod, and so on. So each product has to fit with the previous products. And the very first thing that happens once Apple is going to do a product is to do the design of the product. This is very unusual compared with other companies. The design is so pre-eminent.

IV

ON 16 FEBRUARY 2012 Andrew Couts of Digital Trends wrote that the Federal Bureau of Investigation may be forced to shut down a number of key Domain Name System (DNS) servers, which would cut Internet access for millions of Web users around the world, reports BetaBeat. The DNS servers were installed by the FBI last year in an effort to stop the spread of a piece of malware known as DNSCharger Trojan. But the court order that allowed the set-up of the replacement servers expires on March 8. In November of last year, authorities arrested six men in Estonia for the creation and spread of DNSCharger, which re-configures infected computers' Internet settings, and re-routes users to websites that contain malware, or other illegal sites. DNSCharger also blocks access to websites that might offer solutions for how to rid the computer of its worm, and often comes bundled with other types of malicious software.

By the time the FBI stepped in, DNSCharger had taken over computers in more than 100 countries, including half-a-million computers in the US alone. To help eradicate the widespread malware, the FBI replaced infected servers with new, clean servers, which gave companies and individuals with infected computers time to clean DNSCharger off their machines. Unfortunately, DNSCharger is still running on computers "at half of the Fortune 500 companies," and at "27 out of 55 major government entities," reports cybersecurity journalist Brian Krebs. These computers rely on the FBI-installed DNS servers to access the Web. But if the court order is not extended, the FBI will be legally required to remove the clean servers, which would cut off the Internet for users still infected with DNSCharger. Companies or other agencies that are unsure whether their systems are infected with DNSCharger can get free assistance here. And private users can find out if they are infected using instructions provided here, according to Digital Trends.

Ned Potter of ABC News reported on 18 January 2012 that even in his last months, Steve Jobs, who had already masterminded the iPad and iPhone, reimagined digital music, animated films and done so much more in modern technology, said he had new projects on his mind. In New York, Apple was holding what it calls "an education announcement in the Big Apple." Word all over the digital world was that the company has been working on one of Jobs' pet projects: to re-invent the old-fashioned American school textbook. Gene Munster, the technology analyst who closely follows Apple for Piper Jaffray, said Apple will offer a series of software tools to make it possible to move education from textbooks to interactive digital lessons, easily prepared by publishers, teachers or others interested in creating learning materials. "Instead of a textbook, we call it a 'native digital learning experience'," Munster said. "I know that's a lot of words. People will call it a textbook, but it's really not just an e-book or digital book."

Jobs is cited by his biographer, Walter Isaacson, as saying textbooks were just waiting to be transformed. Not only were they dull and sometimes outdated, they were heavy (just ask any seventh-grader with a backpack full of them). In *Steve Jobs*, Isaacson wrote, "His idea was to hire great textbook writers to create digital versions, and make them a feature of the iPad. In addition, he held meetings with the major publishers, such as Pearson Education, about partnering with Apple. 'The process by which states certify textbooks is corrupt,' he said. 'But if we can make the textbooks free, and they come with the iPad, then they don't have to be certified. The crappy economy at the state level will last for a decade, and we can give them an opportunity to circumvent that whole process and save money.'"

Jobs had apparently been thinking about the educational market for a long time. Munster pointed to an interview Jobs did in 1996 in which "he was very cynical about getting education on board with technology. I think the Isaacson book reflects his later thinking." Munster said Piper Jaffray surveyed 25 computer-system managers from schools teaching kindergarten to 12th grade. "The biggest reason iPads are not in schools is not a lack of content, but that school I.T. departments can't manage hundreds of iPads," he said. "They can't control them the way they control computers." It's not a matter of cost for schools, he said. Instead, they worry about students using school equipment to roam online instead of study. With Apple's new tools, he said, teachers, publishers and others should be able to create new learning materials even if they're not tech-savvy. A line being used is that 'it's the Garage Band of textbooks'," said Munster. (Garage Band is an app sold by Apple that helps one create music.) Who is threatened if Apple succeeds? The answer is, publishers who don't embrace the change, said Munster, as well as sellers of school backpacks, since students will have less to carry.

Nearly all of the information in this chapter is from published accounts but I am not making any excuse for my formidable lack of knowledge of the IT business as I continue my search for America's Soul. I wished I had done all the research, read all the reports, studied all the books, talked to all the experts. But this was not possible. My abysmal ignorance is a shame really because in 1994 I set up Caribbean Information Systems & Services to do just this – that is to make Trinidadians and Tobagonians more aware of the IT revolution. But the media and big business took little interest in what I was doing and wished it seemed for the venture to fail – as it did. But my work continues and while I share Oscar Wilde's feelings that everything published is public property I have no wish to present other people's work as my own. I know that the likelihood of abuse for my attempts to reveal the Soul of America in this way is what scared She Xiuling when we discussed the new route we had to take to get the work done. She was aware of the accusations of literary piracy aimed at Chinese businessmen and of the charges of plagiarism that have plagued journalists, academics and politicians in the United States and in Europe.

So, to continue, what does the US advanced technology tell us about America and Americans? In one word, it is innovation. See for yourself. For example, is the video game industry Apple's next victim? Chris Morris of Plugged In wonders on 19 March 2012. While Apple has a well-earned reputation as the inventor of new markets, it's also something of a serial killer he said. The company's advances in digital music players made the Walkman an afterthought. The introduction of iTunes sounded a virtual death knell for many record retailers. The iPad cut the legs out from under the once fast-growing netbook PC market. And the iPhone has put Motorola in a fight for its life. Now, the company looks to be focusing on the video game industry – and plenty of people are rightfully scared. The sheer numbers are overwhelming. In 2011 alone, the company says it sold 172 million "post PC" devices, an Apple term encompassing the iPhone, iPad and iPod. To put that into context, that's nearly 30 million more than the lifetime sales of the Xbox 360, PlayStation 3, Nintendo 3DS and PlayStation Vita added together.

And it's worth noting that for the last two years, Apple has chosen to unveil the latest iPad smack in the middle of the video game industry's Game Developer Conference. Adding insult to injury, they made the announcement right across the street from the GDC's main convention hall. Last year, Nintendo's global president Satoru Iwata spoke passionately about the danger Apple (and other mobile companies) represent to the industry. "Game development is drowning," he said. "Until now, there has always been the ability to make a living [making games]. Will that still be the case moving forward?" Ben Cousins, the general manager of mobile game maker ngmoco Sweden, furthered that argument at this year's GDC. "I believe that mobile devices and mobile platforms are the disruptive technologies that are going to cut a slice through the Western market," he said in a talk called, "When The Consoles Die, What Comes Next?"

To say Apple could outright kill the video game industry is a bit hyperbolic. A diminished market is not a dead one, and there will likely always be a demand for bleeding-edge products which can't be played on an Apple device. "There's always going to be a market for the very high end, whatever that high end is," says Ubisoft Toronto managing director Jade Raymond. "If consoles eventually become the holodeck and I can only have that at home I'm going to want that. It's going to be something you can't get walking to the bus. ... That high-end experience needs to be beefed up with our top hardware but more and more we're going to have to think about what people's experiences are." There is, however, no doubt that Apple's having a transformative effect.

Sony has seen the Vita struggle a bit since its February debut, and Nintendo was forced to deeply cut the retail price of the 3DS when it failed to quickly stir gamer passions. All the while, gaming apps have continued to see sales increase, even finding success by crossing over to console. One of the most successful games on Xbox Live Arcade, Fruit Ninja, got its start as an app. And it's virtually mandatory for publishers to release an app companion to major console games these days to capitalize on both markets. Cousins says he expects this trend to continue, and suggests that some franchises may abandon consoles for the App store. He notes that after televisions were introduced in the mid-1960s, cinema attendance plunged and theaters suffered terribly. Content producers, though, managed the transition by bringing movies to TV (and later home video). "They moved their content to the lower-res, free-to-play TV channels," he says. "Games content developers need to do the same. They need to move their content to these low-resolution platforms." The irony, of course, is that the company that's revolutionizing video games is Apple, which only a few years ago was lampooned for its lack of gaming options. The company stumbled into its powerful position in the gaming world and didn't seem to embrace it until the fall of 2009, when Steve Jobs, in one of his famous keynotes, referred to the iPod Touch as "the number one portable game player in the world." A year and a half later, console companies are wringing their hands as talk of an Apple TV swirls and the new Angry Birds is getting more attention than the new Halo. To some, it's really just a matter of time. "It is quite easy to imagine a world where an iPad is more powerful than a home console, where it wirelessly talks to your TV and wirelessly talks to your controller and becomes your new console," Mike Capps, president of Epic Games, recently told Reuters. "Apple is definitely building their devices as if they care a lot about 'triple-A' games."

Amazon said that it sold more than one million Kindles a week in December with the new Kindle Fire tablet computer its top-selling item. This year saw "the best holiday ever for the Kindle family as customers purchased millions of Kindle Fires and millions of Kindle e-readers," the Seattle-based online retail giant said in a statement. Amazon said the Kindle Fire has been the "number one best-selling, most gifted and most wished for product" on Amazon.com since it went on sale 13 weeks ago. Besides the Kindle Fire, Amazon offers a range of Kindle electronic book readers. Amazon said it sold "well over" one million Kindle devices per week in December with the Kindle Touch and basic Kindle taking the top two spots after the Fire. Amazon said the Kindle is its best-selling item in Britain, France, Germany, Italy and Spain in addition to the United States. The company said "gifting" of Kindle books between November 25 and Christmas Day rose 175 per cent compared to the holiday period in 2010 with Christmas Day the biggest day ever for Kindle book downloads.

Despite the rosy sales numbers for the gadgets, Goldman Sachs said in a research note that the online titan may fall short of fourth-quarter earnings expectations. Industry tracker comScore found that US online spending for the first 56 days of the November-December holiday season rose 15 per cent over the same period last year to $35.3 billion. "On average, Amazon's year-over-year sales growth in the fourth quarter has outpaced holiday season eCommerce by 23 points," Goldman Sachs said. "As such, the comScore data released today would imply top line growth of 38 per cent year-over-year to $17.87 billion, slightly below current consensus of $18.19 billion, up 40 per cent year-over-year."

The Kindle Fire costs $199, less than half the price of the cheapest iPad from tablet market leader Apple. It has a seven-inch (17.78-centimeter) screen, smaller than the iPad's 9.7 inches (24.6 centimeters), connects to the Web using Wi-Fi and is powered by Google's Android software. It does not have a camera or the 3G connectivity featured on other tablets but gives buyers easy access to Amazon's online store, which sells books, music, movies, television shows, games and other content.

Anyone would feel bad about missing the new Apple iPad pre-order period, writes Tecca in *Today in Tech* on 16 March 2012. It's pretty annoying having to stand in line to get your tablet, especially if you're at the end of a long and winding queue. But there was one person who lined up for the new iPad on his own volition when he could've easily got his hands on Apple's newest device. That is Steve Wozniak, also known as "the other Steve" of Apple. Wozniak co-founded Apple with Steve Jobs in 1976. While he doesn't work full time for the company anymore, he's still an employee and a stockholder. His lining up outside an Apple Store doesn't mean it's excessively hard to find a device, though it's a ritual that he's been doing for years. But while he's been first in line for many prior Apple devices, this time, there was someone else who got there before he did – his wife. "I want to be one of the people lined up and wait all night," he said in an interview.

On 14 February 2012, the Associated Press reported that President Obama signed legislation that modernizes the nation's aviation system, speeding up the nation's switch from radar to an air traffic control system based on GPS technology. The law also opens up the skies to military, commercial and privately-owned unmanned drones. The legislation faced opposition from some labor unions because it set new rules governing union organizing elections at airlines and railroads. However, the Senate passed the bill, completing action after a struggle that shut down the Federal Aviation Administration for two weeks. The law authorizes $63.4 billion for the FAA over four years, including about $11 billion toward the air traffic system and its modernization. It sets a deadline of June 2015 for the FAA to develop new arrival procedures at the nation's 35 busiest airports. "This critical effort to shift from our antiquated air traffic control technology to a GPS-based system will improve air traffic efficiency and safety, reduce fuel burn and pollution from aircraft, and bring costs down for consumers," said Republican Rep. John Mica of Florida, the chairman of the House Transportation and Infrastructure Committee.

In a compromise, the legislation set some new requirements for union organizing elections. While some unions accepted the changes, others called for it to be rejected. Among those opposing the legislation were the Teamsters, Communications Workers, Machinists and Flight Attendants. The president of the National Air Traffic Controllers Association, Paul Rinaldi, praised the new law. "This new technology will help reduce delays, give controllers better tools with which to perform their jobs even more efficiently and provide a platform for further technological and safety enhancements," he said in a statement. Under the new law, the FAA must by 30 September 2015 begin permitting unmanned drones controlled by remote operators on the ground to fly in the same airspace as airliners, cargo planes, business jets and private aircraft.

The Class of 2012 may have few reasons to celebrate this year. Along with the long-term unemployed, experts say their prospects are the bleakest among all job-seekers. The U.S. economy added a lower-than-expected 80,000 jobs last month, according to data from the Labor Department. Though the overall unemployment rate remained unchanged at 8.2 per cent, experts say this year's 1.8 million college graduates have a rough job search ahead. "Over the last five years, the jobs situation has gotten increasingly intense for each successive graduating class," says Paul T. Conway, president of Generation Opportunity, a non-profit think-tank based in Arlington, Va. "Their concern is now palpable."

The last half-decade has not been good to graduates. Only a half of those who graduated since 2006 are now employed full time, according to a recent Rutgers University survey. More college graduates are settling for jobs that in years past would have gone to those without degrees, while people in their 30s are now occupying jobs once taken by recent graduates, says Carl Van Horn, professor of public policy and director of Rutgers' John J. Heldrich Center for Workforce Development. But if all the young people who have already given up looking for jobs are included – the 1.7 million people aged 18-29 who have been out of work for more than a year – the latest 8.2 per cent unemployment figure would be closer to 16.8 per cent for that age group, Conway says. That's the highest unemployment rate for that age group since World War II. "Their story is one of few opportunities, delayed dreams, and stalled careers," he says.

The faltering economic recovery prompted students from the class of 2012 to apply for jobs much earlier than graduates of earlier years. More than half of college seniors reported they applied for a job prior to graduating, according to a survey of 48,000 graduating seniors by National Association of Colleges and Employers, and more than a quarter of those that applied for a job found one, the survey found. Some majors fared far better than others: Over half of those who accounting, engineering, computer science, economics and business administration graduates received at least one offer. But faced with competition from older workers, young professionals are accepting jobs for less money. College graduates who obtained their first job between 2009 and 2011 earned $27,000 a year or 10 per cent less than those who entered the workforce in the two previous years, the Rutgers survey found. Van Horn says many of this year's graduates lucky enough to find employment will be disappointed with their salary.

Mark Mulholland, 22, a history major from the University of Virginia, graduated in May 2012 and is now looking for work in communications. "My hope is to gain valuable experience rather than a massive salary," he says. His target is $40,000 a year.

Online Shoe retailer Zappos told customers on 16 January 2012 that it had been the victim of a cyber-attack affecting more than 24 million customer accounts in its database, according to a Reuters report. The popular retailer, which is owned by Amazon.com, said customers' names, email addresses, billing and shipping addresses, phone numbers and the last four digits of credit cards numbers and scrambled passwords were stolen. But it said the hackers had not been able to access servers that held customers critical credit card and other payment data. "We were recently the victim of a cyber-attack by a criminal who gained access to parts of our internal network and systems through one of our servers in Kentucky," Zappos chief executive Tony Hsieh said in an email to staff which was posted on the company's blog. "We are cooperating with law enforcement to undergo an exhaustive investigation," he added. Zappos said it was recommending that customers change their passwords including on any other website where they use the same or similar password. The company, which is well known for its customer service, said due to the high volume of customer calls it is expecting it will temporarily switch off its phones and direct customers to contact via email.

V

THE SAN FRANCISCO-OAKLAND BAY Bridge will have a Made-in-China label according to *The New York Times* on 25 June 2011. At a sprawling manufacturing complex, in Shanghai Zhenhua hundreds of Chinese laborers were completing work on the San Francisco-Oakland Bay Bridge. In July, the last four of more than two dozen giant steel modules – each with a roadbed segment about half the size of a football field – would be loaded onto a huge ship and transported 6,500 miles to Oakland. There, they will be assembled to fit into the eastern span of the new Bay Bridge. The project is part of China's continual move up the global economic value chain – from cheap toys to Apple iPads to commercial jetliners – as it aims to become the world's civil engineer. The assembly work in California, and the pouring of the concrete road surface, will be done by Americans. But construction of the bridge decks and the materials that went into them are a Made-in-China affair. California officials say the state saved hundreds of millions of dollars by turning to China. "They've produced a pretty impressive bridge for us," Tony Anziano, a program manager at the California Department of Transportation, said a few weeks ago. He was touring the 1.2-square-mile manufacturing site that the Chinese company created to do the bridge work. "Four years ago, there were just steel plates here and lots of orange groves."

On the reputation of showcase projects like Beijing's Olympic-size airport terminal and the mammoth hydroelectric Three Gorges Dam, Chinese companies have been hired to build copper mines in the Congo, high-speed rail lines in Brazil and huge apartment complexes in Saudi Arabia. In New York City alone, Chinese companies have won contracts to help renovate the subway system, refurbish the Alexander Hamilton Bridge over the Harlem River and build a new Metro-North train platform near Yankee Stadium. And as it is with the Bay Bridge, American union labor would carry out most of the work done on United States soil. However, American steelworker unions have disparaged the Bay Bridge contract by accusing the state of California of sending good jobs overseas and settling for what they deride as poor-quality Chinese steel. Industry groups in the United States and other countries have raised questions about the safety and quality of Chinese workmanship on such projects. Indeed, China has had quality control problems ranging from tainted milk to poorly built schools. But executives and officials who have awarded the various Chinese contracts say their audits have convinced them of the projects' engineering integrity. And they note that with the full financial force of the Chinese government behind its infrastructure companies, the monumental scale of the work, and the prices bid, are hard for private industry elsewhere to beat.

The new Bay Bridge, expected to open to traffic in 2013, will replace a structure that has never been quite the same since the 1989 Bay Area earthquake. At $7.2 billion, it will be one of the most expensive structures ever built. But California officials estimate that they will save at least $400 million by having so much of the work done in China. California had issued bonds to finance the project, and will look to recoup the cost through tolls. And California authorities say they had little choice but to rebuild major sections of the bridge, despite repairs made after the earthquake caused a section of the eastern span to collapse onto the lower deck. Seismic safety testing persuaded the state that much of the bridge needed to be overhauled and made more quake-resistant. Eventually, the California Department of Transportation decided to revamp the western span of the bridge (which connects San Francisco to Yerba Buena Island) and replace the 2.2-mile eastern span (which links Yerba Buena to Oakland). On the eastern span, officials decided to build a suspension bridge with a complex design. The span will have a single, 525-foot tower, anchored to bedrock and supported by a single, enormous steel-wire cable that threads through the suspension bridge. "We wanted something strong and secure, but we also wanted something iconic," said Bart Ney, a transportation department spokesman.

A joint venture between two American companies, American Bridge and Fluor Enterprises, won the prime contract for the project in early 2006. Their bid specified getting much of the fabricated steel from overseas, to save money. California decided not to apply for federal funding for the project because the "Buy America" provisos would probably have required purchasing more expensive steel and fabrication from United States manufacturers. China, the world's biggest steel maker, was the front-runner, particularly because it has dominated bridge building for the last decade. Several years ago, Shanghai opened a 20-mile sea bridge; the country is now planning a much longer one near Hong Kong. The selection of the state-owned Shanghai Zhenhua Heavy Industries Company was a surprise, though, because the company made port cranes and had no bridge building experience. But California officials and executives at American Bridge said Zhenhua's advantages included its huge steel fabrication facilities, its large low-cost work force and its solid finances. The company even had its own port and ships. "I don't think the U.S. fabrication industry could put a project like this together," Brian A. Petersen, project director for the American Bridge/Fluor Enterprises joint venture, said in a telephone interview. "Most U.S. companies don't have these types of warehouses, equipment or the cash flow. The Chinese load the ships, and it's their ships that deliver to our piers."

Despite the American union complaints, former California Gov. Arnold Schwarzenegger, a Republican, strongly backed the project and even visited Zhenhua's plant last September, praising "the workers that are building our Bay Bridge." Zhenhua put 3,000 employees to work on the project: steel-cutters, welders, polishers and engineers. The company built the main bridge tower, which was shipped in mid-2009, and a total of 28 bridge decks – the massive triangular steel structures that will serve as the roadway platform. Pan Zhongwang, a 55-year-old steel polisher, is a typical Zhenhua worker. He arrives at 7 a.m. and leaves at 11 p.m., often working seven days a week. He lives in a company dorm and earns about $12 a day. "It used to be $9 a day, now it's $12," he said, while polishing one of the decks for the new Bay Bridge. "Everything is getting more expensive. They should raise our pay." To ensure the bridge meets safety standards, 250 employees and consultants working for the state of California and American Bridge/ Fluor also took up residence in Shanghai.

On 21 December 2011 Lee Chyen Yee reported that China had become the world's top patent filer in 2011, surpassing the United States and Japan as it steps up innovation to improve its intellectual property rights track record, a Thomson Reuters research report showed. The report said the world's second-largest economy aimed to transform from a "Made in China" to a "Designed in China" market, with the government pushing for innovation in sectors such as automobiles, pharmaceuticals and technology. However, legal experts said China would need to do more before it can lead the world in innovation as the quality of patents needed to improve. The government provided attractive incentives for companies in China to file patent applications, regardless of whether a patent was eventually granted, they said. "The idea of subsidizing patents is not bad in itself, however it is a blunt instrument because you get high figures for filings, but it does not tell you anything about the quality of the patents filed," said Elliot Papageorgiou, a Partner and Executive at law firm Rouse Legal (China). "One thing is volume, quality is quite another. The return or the percentage of grants of the patents is still not as high in China as, say, in the U.S., Japan or some places in Europe," he said.

The Thomson Reuters report said published patent applications from China were expected to total nearly 500,000 in 2015, following by the United States with close to 400,000 and Japan with almost

300,000. Published applications from China's patent office have risen by an average of 16.7 per cent annually from 171,000 in 2006 to nearly 314,000 in 2010, data from Thomson Reuters Derwent World Patents Index showed. During the period, Japan had the highest volume, followed by the United States, China, Korea and Europe, the report said. It did not give figures for 2011. "The striking difference among these regions is China – it is experiencing the most rapid growth and is poised to lead the pack in the very near future," it said.

Of total patents filed in China, the percentage of domestic applications rose to nearly 73 per cent in 2010 from less than 52 per cent in 2006, indicating that Chinese companies have outpaced foreign entities in the patent boom. In terms of patents overseas, Chinese companies have also been climbing in the rankings, according to data from the World Intellectual Property Office (WIPO). In 2010, China's No.2 telecommunications equipment maker ZTE Corp was second on the list of applicants, ranking just behind Japan's Panasonic Corp. U.S. chip maker Qualcomm Inc. came in third, while China's Huawei Technologies Co Ltd, the world's second-largest telecom gear maker, was fourth, according to WIPO. Chinese companies have been trying to be more innovative as they transform from contract manufacturers to regional and global brand names producing higher end products to improve margins. Patent filings have also increased among Chinese companies due to legal battles that they have had to fight, especially in the telecommunications sector. For instance, Huawei and ZTE have been embroiled in patent disputes over fourth-generation wireless technology.

The *Blaze* on 5 January 2012 reported that although it happened back in September, 2011, it appears many American taxpayers are unaware that General Motors struck a deal in Shanghai wherein the company has agreed to develop an electric vehicle (EV) platform with its longtime Chinese partner SAIC. What else was included in this deal? GM has agreed to effectively move all future EV development to China. It could also mean that production of the vehicle itself will be moved overseas. The agreement is the result of the Chinese government coercing foreign automakers into giving Chinese companies the EV technology they lack, according to the Associated Press. Unsurprisingly, some U.S. lawmakers have voiced concerns that the deal is little more than a "shake down" from the Chinese to get GM's Volt secrets. GM has denied reports that it will hand over the intellectual property underlying the Volt. GM Vice Chairman Steve Girsky, in a conference call from Shanghai, said that neither SAIC nor the Chinese government have demanded Volt technology but that any future EV developments would, of course, draw on GM's Volt "experience and technology," according to a *USA Today* report first published in September, 2011.

Under the deal, SAIC and GM will equally share the cost of developing a new all-electric vehicle, Girsky said. As per the arrangement, GM started exporting Michigan-made Volts to China. However, it is highly unlikely that GM will sell many of the unsuccessful vehicles. "The Chinese government is pushing electrics with a subsidy that amounts to about $19,000 per car – but only if the car is made in China. No imports allowed," writes Chris Woodyard of *USA Today*. "There also are tariffs on cars imported to China, which lawmakers argue are unfair and may violate world trade rules." But what has some people truly upset is the fact that Girsky hinted that the Volt could eventually be built in China. "If we localize, eventually it won't have a tariff and it will get the subsidy. We have made no decision on if, when or where we build Volt in the future," Girsky said.

The push for more advanced technology reflects China's frustrations with its continued weakness in automotive technology, analysts say. After 25 years of auto joint ventures that require local partners to hold at least a 50 percent stake, domestic automakers still lag behind global rivals in automotive engineering. "China is not a technology leader in virtually any industry. The country has developed around low-cost production," said Bill Russo of consultancy Synergistics. "This is the irony, that the largest and biggest growth market has relatively weak domestic manufacturers." It was because of the sudden growth in Chinese demand and faltering sales in the recession-stricken West that China was able to surpass the U.S. as the largest car market in 2009. Just this year, sales of passenger vehicles, excluding large buses, jumped by a third to 13.7 million vehicles.

VI

AN ASSOCIATED Press report by Raphael Satter from London on 12 July 2012 stated that some 450,000 Yahoo users' email addresses and passwords have been leaked because of a security breach, the company confirmed, adding that just a small fraction of the stolen passwords were valid. The company said in a statement that an "old file" from the Yahoo Contributor Network was compromised. Among the stolen emails and passwords were many from Yahoo's own email service along with those of other companies. The Yahoo Contributor Network is a content-sharing platform. Yahoo said it was fixing the vulnerability that led to the disclosure, changing the passwords of affected Yahoo users, and notifying other companies whose users' accounts might have been compromised. "We apologize to all affected users," the company statement said. Technology news websites including CNET, Ars Technica, and Mashable identified the hackers behind the attack as a little-known outfit calling itself the D33D Company. The group was quoted as saying it had stolen the unencrypted passwords using an SQL injection – the name given to a commonly used attack in which hackers use rogue commands to extract data from vulnerable websites. "We hope that the parties responsible for managing the security of this subdomain will take this as a wake-up call," the group was quoted as saying. And online security experts said Yahoo might have done more to protect the stored passwords, with Ohio-based TrustedSec describing the Internet giant's decision not to encrypt them as "most alarming." Nevertheless, the haul does not appear as useful to hackers as they might have thought. Yahoo cautioned that only 5 percent of passwords associated with its account holders were valid.

On 18 April 2012 the Associated Press reported from New York that revenue from Internet advertising in the U.S. hit a record $31 billion last year, according to a study released that month. That's up 22 percent from $26 billion in 2010, the previous record. The Interactive Advertising Bureau, an industry group, conducted the quarterly study with PricewaterhouseCoopers. About half of the ad revenue, $14.8 billion, came from the search category. Those are the text-based ads that are sold by Google and others and that are targeted to search terms and other keywords. The fastest-growing category was mobile, with revenue of $1.6 billion in 2011, more than double the $600 million a year earlier. It's still a small part of overall Internet advertising, however. David Silverman, a partner with PricewaterhouseCoopers, said the growth in mobile should continue given its ability "to deliver timely, targeted, relevant and local advertisements in a manner that was not previously possible." According to the study, retail advertisers were the largest spenders, accounting for 22 per cent, or $7.1 billion, of the total last year. Internet ad revenue in the final three months of 2011 totaled $9 billion, a 20 per cent increase from the same period in 2010. That is also a record, beating the $7.8 billion in the third quarter of 2011.

But Dan Graziano of BGR News revealed on 16 April 2012 that the Pew Internet & American Life Project's latest poll indicates that one in five adults in the United States still does not use the Internet. "Senior citizens, those who prefer to take our interviews in Spanish rather than English, adults with less than a high school education, and those living in households earning less than $30,000 per year are the least likely adults to have Internet access," Pew Internet said. Almost half of those adults who don't use the Internet found the technology irrelevant to them, with most having never used it before. About one in five adults claimed they didn't know enough about technology to start using the Internet on their own and only 10 per cent were interested in using the Internet or email in the future. Overall Internet adoption rates have leveled off, however adults already online are using the Web more often than ever before. Pew's study also showed that 88 per cent of American adults have a cell phone, 57 per cent have a laptop, 19 per cent own an eReader, 19 per cent have a tablet and 63 per cent access the Internet wirelessly with one of these devices.

However Sydney Lupkin of ABC News found a Mom who did and who was arrested for hacking school computers to change her kids' grades. A Pennsylvania mom writes Lupkin faces six felony charges for allegedly hacking into her children's school computer to change their grades and read school officials' emails. Catherine Venusto, 45, worked for the Northwestern Lehigh School District from 2008 through April 2011 and has at least two children in the district, according to the District Attorney's office. She has been accused of changing her daughter's failing grade from an F to an M for "medical" in June 2010, and then changing her son's 98 to a 99 in February 2012, nearly a year after she quit her job as an administrative office secretary to work at another school district. Venusto was arraigned in Lehigh County Magisterial Court on three counts of unlawful use of a computer and three counts of computer trespassing and altering data.

All six charges are third degree felonies. When ABCNews.com attempted to contact Venusto at her current job as an event coordinator at Lehigh University, a school employee said her employment had ended.

"I'm concerned on numerous levels," said Jennifer Holman, Northwestern Lehigh School District's assistant superintendent. "When we say systems, there were three difference systems violated... There were 10 different users that at some point had their email violated." Holman told ABCNews.com that she first realized something was wrong when a teacher asked why Superintendent Mary Ann Wright was in that teacher's online grade book. Once Wright explained she was never in the grade book, administrators and state police began looking for whoever used Wright's username and password without permission. State police discovered Venusto used Wright's username and password 110 times to access the district's online grading system, according to the District Attorney's office. Venusto also allegedly accessed nine other faculty members' email accounts without permission, and accessed the human resources "H-drive" to view "thousands of files associated with district policy, contract information, employee reports and personnel issues."

Wright released a statement in anticipation of Venusto's arraignment. "We deeply regret this incident and that this unauthorized access occurred, and we sincerely regret any inconvenience this may cause," Wright wrote. "We are doing everything we can to prevent this from happening again, and new security procedures are in place to better assure that our systems are protected from such attempts." Holman said the district's news release and email purposefully left Venusto's name out to protect her children, but the District Attorney's press release revealed the name. "It's not their fault," Holman said of Venusto's children. "If the students continue to go to school here, which I assume they will, we need to do our best to support them in whatever way they need." The court set bail at $30,000, but Venusto will not have to pay it unless she does not appear in court for her preliminary hearing on July 26, according a District Attorney's office spokeswoman. If convicted, Venusto could face fines, jail time, and restitution payments. Venusto could face a maximum of 42 years in prison or a $90,000 fine, according to District Attorney's office spokeswoman Debbie Garlicki, who said the maximum penalty on each count is seven years or a $15,000.

VII

ACCORDING TO a Reuters report by Bill Rigby Microsoft Corp reported its first quarterly loss as a public company as it took a previously announced hit for writing down the value of its ailing online unit, but held up better than expected in the face of stagnant computer sales. Excluding the multibillion-dollar write-down, which was signaled earlier, and factoring in some deferred Windows revenue, the world's largest software company actually exceeded Wall Street's expectations, boosting its shares in after-market trading. "It looks good, given the dicey economic environment and the weakness we already know about in PCs," said Brendan Barnicle, an analyst at Pacific Crest Securities.

After several years of stumbling behind mobile and Internet trailblazers Apple Inc. and Google Inc., and a decade-long static share price, some expectation is building that Microsoft can re-establish itself as a tech leader with its new, touch-friendly Windows 8 system, due out on October 26, and an accompanying tablet of its own design. "There's a lot of anticipation for the next Microsoft products. They are regaining credibility with enterprises," said Trip Chowdhry, an analyst at Global Equities Research. Alongside Windows 8 and its new Surface tablet – which it hopes will challenge Apple's all-conquering iPad – Microsoft is set to release new phone software and a new web-oriented version of its highly profitable Office suite of applications over the next 12 months. These and other products "will drive our business forward and provide unprecedented opportunity to our customers and partners" said Chief Executive Steve Ballmer, in a statement.

The Redmond, Washington-based company reported a net loss of $492 million, or 6 cents per share, for its fiscal fourth quarter, compared with a profit of $5.87 billion, or 69 cents per share, in the year-ago quarter. The loss was expected after Microsoft said earlier this month that it would take a $6.2 billion write-down for the value of its online unit after an ill-fated acquisition of a digital advertising agency five years ago. Microsoft has not suffered a quarterly loss since going public in 1986. Revenue rose 4 per cent to $18 billion, slightly below analysts' estimates, helped by strong growth in its Office unit, but dampened by slowing computer sales featuring its flagship Windows operating system. Global PC sales, which have been stagnant for the last two years, fell 0.1 per cent last quarter, according to tech research firms Gartner and IDC.

Microsoft deferred $540 million of Windows revenue in the quarter due to an upgrade discount it is offering customers who buy machines running Windows 7 before the launch of Windows 8 in October. Excluding the deferred revenue, the company's flagship Windows unit posted only a 1 per cent drop in sales, which was better than some analysts had expected in the uncertain economy and the run-up to the launch of Windows 8. "PC sales could have been much worse," said Mark Moerdler, senior research analyst at Sanford C. Bernstein. "Usually people hold off buying new PCs when there is new software coming out." Excluding the write-down, but factoring in the loss of deferred revenue, Microsoft said it earned 67 cents per share in the quarter. On that basis, Wall Street expected profit of 62 cents per share, according to Thomson Reuters I/B/E/S. Microsoft's shares rose 2.5 per cent in post-market trading after closing at $30.67 on NASDAQ. The stock is up 10 per cent so far this year, compared to a 14 per cent gain in the tech-heavy NASDAQ. But it has remained locked around the $30 level, which it has not exceeded for any prolonged period since the tech stock boom 12 years ago.

VIII

THE SENATE failed to pass legislation to protect the U.S. electrical grid, water supplies and other critical industries from cyber-attack and electronic espionage, despite dire warnings from top national security officials about the potential for devastating assaults on American computer networks, wrote Richard Lardner of the Associated Press. Both Republicans and Democrats said they are committed to approving a final bill when they return in September from a monthlong recess.

But deep divisions between the two parties over the right approach to cybersecurity will make it difficult to forge a compromise.

And there is very little time left to get a deal done with presidential and congressional elections coming up in November. The White House and Senate Democrats blamed Republicans for blocking what they called the only comprehensive piece of cybersecurity legislation that would have given the federal government and businesses the tools they need to deal with vulnerabilities in the nation's critical infrastructure. More than 80 per cent of the infrastructure, which includes financial networks, transportation systems and chemical plants, are owned and operated by the private sector. "The politics of obstructionism, driven by special interest groups seeking to avoid accountability, prevented Congress from passing legislation to better protect our nation from potentially catastrophic cyber-attacks," White House Press Secretary Jay Carney said in a statement.

Failure to approve the Senate's Cyber security Act of 2012 before the August congressional recess amounted to a rejection of advice from senior national security officials, including Gen. Martin Dempsey, the chairman of the Joint Chiefs of Staff, who have been calling for Congress to act now on comprehensive legislation to deal with cyberthreats. "The uncomfortable reality of our world today is that bits and bytes can be as threatening as bullets and bombs," Dempsey said in a 1 August letter to Sen. Jay Rockefeller, D-W.Va.

The principal stumbling block on Capitol Hill is what role the Homeland Security Department and other federal agencies should play in protecting U.S. businesses from cyberattacks. Republicans argued the bill would have led to rules imposed by Washington that would only increase the private sector's costs without substantially reducing its risks. They also said Democrats who control the Senate tried to ram the bill through without adequate time for debate. "No one doubts the need to strengthen our nation's cyber security defenses," said Senate Minority Leader Mitch McConnell, R-Ky. The issue, he added, is how the Democratic leadership "has tried to steamroll a bill that would address it."

A closure motion filed by Senate Majority Leader Harry Reid, D-Nevada, to limit debate and force a vote on the bill fell well short of the 60 votes needed to pass, failing 52-46. The White House and Senate Democrats criticized Republicans for allowing the pro-business U.S. Chamber of Commerce to have such a prominent voice in a debate over a pressing national security issue. Democrats said they made substantial revisions to the legislation after the GOP and the Chamber complained it would expand the federal government's regulatory authority over businesses already struggling in a tough economy. The new version of the bill offered incentives, such as liability protection and technical assistance, to businesses that voluntarily participated in a government-managed cybersecurity program. Industry associations and groups would be involved in developing the standards needed to blunt the risks of cyber-attacks, according to the revised legislation. But the chamber said the voluntary program was nothing more than a "springboard" to federal regulations that would take time and money away from efforts businesses already have under way to protect their networks. Once a "government-driven 'voluntary' standards system is enacted," the Chamber said on its FreeEnterprise blog, "it's only a short hop to a mandatory one because the administration has the intent and regulatory leverage."

The Cybersecurity Act would also create a framework for federal agencies and the private sector to exchanges information about cyberthreats or malicious software that can destroy computer networks if it's not detected. Provisions were included in the bill to ensure privacy and civil liberties aren't violated, said the bill's primary sponsors, Sens. Susan Collins, R-Maine, and Joe Lieberman, I-Conn. But the Chamber and other Republicans support a competing bill drafted by Sen. John McCain, R-Ariz., that is similar to legislation passed by the House in late April. Those bills are focused only on the sharing of threat information between the federal government and private sector. The White House threatened to veto the House bill, however, over concerns the bill didn't do enough to protect privacy rights.

Dempsey and other national security officials said more than just information sharing is needed. Key to addressing the threat is the adoption of basic security requirements that will harden critical infrastructure networks and make it more difficult for cyberattackers to succeed. "Minimum standards will help ensure there is no weak link in our infrastructure," Dempsey wrote in his letter to Rockefeller. Speaking to reporters after the vote, Lieberman said he's not optimistic an agreement can be reached, but is open to discussions.

"The threat is so real," he said. "None of us are going to walk away from the table."

IX

A REUTERS report by Jim Finkle and Nicola Leske in August from Boston and New York stated that Hewlett Packard Co. warned of a mammoth quarterly loss after writing down $8 billion on the value of its services business, most of which it acquired four years ago with its $14 billion purchase of EDS. The world's largest computer maker also plans to replace its head of services, a vast but sluggish division that new CEO Meg Whitman wants to reshape into a stronger competitor to the likes of IBM. Whitman, the former eBay CEO who took up the computing giant's helm in 2011 to some skepticism about her technology and hardware credentials, is trying to turn around the company. HP's stock has lost more than half its value in the two years since CEO Mark Hurd unexpectedly resigned amid a scandal over his relationship with a female marketing contractor.

In a sign that Whitman's efforts to trim costs and bolster the company's prospects were succeeding, HP raised its quarterly outlook for profit, after excluding one-time items such as the goodwill write-down. It did not provide reasons. HP's stock rose 2.4 per cent to end at $19.41 after the increase in the company's outlook relieved investors, who had been expecting another bad quarter with global IT spending on the wane. "Everybody was expecting them to miss the quarter. Now they said they are going to beat their forecast. That's why the stock is up," said Shaw Wu, an analyst with Sterne Agee. But analysts cautioned that it is premature to say that HP's darkest days have passed, especially because the company did not explain why it raised its outlook for profit, excluding items. "There are a lot of unanswered questions," said Stifel Nicolaus analyst Aaron Rakers. "It is hard for me to get too terribly positive on it." HP said it decided to take the $8 billion non-cash charge in its fiscal third quarter ended July 31 following a review prompted by declines in its stock price, changing market conditions and the services division's financial performance. "When indicators of potential impairment are identified, companies are required to conduct a review of the carrying amounts of goodwill and other long-lived assets to determine if an impairment exists," HP said in a statement. Analysts said that charge confirmed what has long been widely known by investors: HP paid too much for EDS, one of the pioneers of the outsourcing of technology services. The deal was unpopular on Wall Street from the day it was announced in May 2008 as critics questioned whether then-CEO Hurd was paying too dearly for a slow-growing company. "Is this a huge write-off? Yes," said Global Equities Research analyst Trip Chowdhry. "Management is undoing the things that Hurd did – overpaying for something that is not right."

The company is scheduled to release quarterly earnings on August 22 after the closing bell. HP also said that it had moved faster than it previously anticipated with plans announced in May to reduce 27,000 jobs, or 8 per cent of its workforce. Because of this, it raised its estimate of a third-quarter pre-tax restructuring charge to as much as $1.7 billion from its previous estimate of $1 billion As a consequence of the impairment charge and the restructuring charge, HP said it expected to post a third-quarter loss of $4.31 to $4.49 per share. HP, which employs more than 300,000 people globally, posted a 31 percent drop in second-quarter profit and a 3 per cent decline in revenue. Analysts said the company's long-term success depends on efforts to rejuvenate its products, such as developing goods that can compete with the likes of Apple Inc.'s iPads and phones that run on Google Inc.'s Android operating system. "Write-offs don't do it," said Fred Hickey, editor of *The High-Tech Strategist* newsletter. "You need revenue growth."

Wall Street analysts expect HP's sales to fall 3.4 per cent to $123 billion in its current fiscal year, according to Thomson Reuters I/B/E/S. Wu, the analyst with Sterne Agee, said it will be tough to get sales growing at a healthy clip, noting that about 30 per cent of revenue comes from HP's ailing PC division and at least 20 per cent from its sluggish printer business. "They've got at least 50 per cent of their company that's still under pressure. Restructuring doesn't help that out," Wu said. "They still have a lot to do." HP said it now expects third-quarter earnings, excluding one-time items, of about $1.00 per share, compared with analysts' average estimate of 97 cents. The company had previously forecast earnings of 94 cents to 97 cents per share. Whitman, a Silicon Valley veteran who waged an unsuccessful bid for governor of California in 2010, has said she plans to use some of savings from the restructuring to develop new products, especially in printing and PCs.

The industry news about Apple continued however to be rosy. Barely a year after supplanting ExxonMobil as the largest stock in the current marketplace, Apple entered the record books, becoming the most valuable stock to have ever traded, reports Robert Hum of CNBC. Apple retail store in New York City.Apple closed at another historic high of $665.15, ending the day with a record market cap of $623.5 billion. With the gain, Apple (AAPL) eclipsed Microsoft's (MSFT) peak market cap of $618.9 billion, a level that Microsoft hit more than 12 1/2 years ago, on 30 December 1999. That happened at the height of the dot-com boom and just three months before the NASDAQ Composite peaked at its all-time high of 5,132.52.

Nothing seems to be slowing down Apple's stock these days. Shares have been on the rise over the past three months in high anticipation of new iPhone and iPad models that have been predicted to hit stores during the second half of this year. Even a disappointing earnings report did little to spook investors as they remained focused on the widely expected, but not yet formally announced, iPhone launch next month. Despite paying a dividend for the first time since 1995, Apple's stock quietly closed at historic highs and saw its market cap close above $600 billion for the first time. In fact, Apple has seen its market cap double from $300 billion to $600 billion in a mere 19 months. Now, Apple's colossal market cap is roughly equivalent to the combined market caps of tech titans IBM (IBM), Google (GOOG), Intel (INTC), and Hewlett-Packard (HPQ).

As Apple's stock continues to push higher, the gap between its market cap and that of the second largest company, ExxonMobil (XOM), continues to widen. Apple's stock is now more than 50 per cent bigger than ExxonMobil, with over $200 billion now separating the two companies' market caps. That's a large gap, considering only nine stocks in the S&P 500 have a market cap of $200 billion or more. The difference between Apple and ExxonMobil's market caps is bigger than the individual market caps of 98 per cent of the S&P 500 companies.

Apple's record market cap also comes almost exactly a year after co-founder Steve Jobs abruptly resigned as CEO due to ongoing health issues. When he resigned on 24 August 2011, some people grew concerned that Apple's growth could slow without Jobs' intrepid and visionary leadership. Despite the change in leadership, Apple's stock has continued to soar over the past year. Since Tim Cook succeeded Jobs last August, shares of Apple have risen 76 per cent. During this period, only five stocks on the NASDAQ 100 and 12 stocks on the S&P 500 have outperformed Apple. Additionally, while Apple remains absent from the Dow Industrials, it should not go unnoticed that Apple has outperformed all of the 30 Dow stocks since Cook's tenure.

And on 24 August 2012 Matt Nesto of Breakout reported that it was one year ago that Steve Jobs' temporary leave of absence turned into his actual retirement: when the late and legendary founder of Apple (AAPL) announced he was losing his fight against cancer and would not be returning to the company he loved. As shocking and sad and unsettling as the news was at the time, Nesto wrote, the actual hand-off was seamless, considering chief operating officer Tim Cook was already seven months into his second stint as interim CEO. Even so, the doubts were many and the concerns were plentiful, as loyal consumers, devoted employees, and beholden investors were forced to acknowledge that things would never be the same. After all, no one could ever replace Steve Jobs. Depending on whom you ask or how you look at it, Cook has either a lot or very little to show for the past 12 months of work, says Nesto.

"What stands out is how little stands out," says Adam Lashinsky, author of *Inside Apple* and senior editor-at-large for *FORTUNE*. "It's been a year of continuation of everything Apple had been doing in the previous two years," he adds in an attached video, pointing out that the real measure of the Cook era won't begin until a brand new product category is launched that is as "mind-blowingly revolutionary as the last few." While the latest iteration of the iPhone (version 5) is expected to be unveiled in September, brand new products such as a much-anticipated TV or iPad mini might not come to market for another quarter or two. As much as that seems like a lifetime to some device devotees and technophiles, company historians like Lashinsky point out that it's only been two-and-a-half years since the iPad debut, which itself came three years after the iPhone was first unveiled. "So they're about on schedule," Lashinsky says, "assuming we get something cool this fall or spring."

In the meantime, Lashinsky characterizes Cook's tenure as being a caretaker of the "rocket ship company" he inherited from his former boss. He also calls Cook a good steward of Apple's culture, a corporate climate he says is famous for being very product focused, intensely secretive, and unapologetic about "doing things its own way." To be sure, investors in Apple must be nothing short of thrilled with the past year. It has been a 12-month joyride that has seen the stock go from about $375 to over $650. To put that into perspective, that gain of roughly 80 per cent amounts to more than $250 billion worth of new market cap. That's equivalent to growing a brand new Microsoft (MSFT) in a single year or about what it would cost to acquire all of Coca-Cola (KO) and Intel (INTC)! But such is life when you're running the largest company in the world – one that's now worth over $600 billion.

Another inaugural accomplishment Cook can claim is ending Apple's 17-year drought of dividends after agreeing in March to use about $10 billion, or 10 per cent, of the company's cash stockpile to placate investors. Analysts still love the stock, 90 per cent of whom rate it a "buy", while sales and earnings continue to set records. Despite the July quarter coming in below expectations, the stock has regained all the ground and then some in the past few weeks. "Not much has changed," Lashinsky says of year one. "The company is still going on the same trajectory that it was on while Steve Jobs was alive."

Tech stocks continue to make Americans rich and the trend is not confined to Apple. As Alexie Oreskovic of Reuters reported Facebook Inc. director Peter Thiel sold roughly $400 million worth of shares in the Internet social networking company in August, cashing out most of his stake, according to a regulatory filing. Thiel sold his shares on a Thursday and Friday at average prices ranging between $19.27 and $20.69 per share after the end of the first lockup, which barred early investors and insiders from selling shares following the initial public offering. The sales, in which Thiel sold roughly 20 million Facebook shares, were conducted as a result of a trading plan that Thiel entered into on May 18, according to the filing. Thiel, who co-founded PayPal and was among Facebook's earliest backers, still owns roughly 5.6 million shares of Facebook. Accel Partners, a Silicon Valley venture capital firm that was also an early backer of Facebook, distributed roughly 57.8 million Facebook shares to the limited partners and general partners of its various funds, according to another filing. The move allows those partners to sell or hold on to their distributed Facebook shares as they see fit.

There is fear however in some quarters as tech possibilities expand to include Online education writes Ryan Lytle of *U.S. News and World Report* on 6 July 2012 and as Online education continues its meteoric rise on college campuses, and many faculty members are frightened by its growth and prevalence, notes a recent study by Inside Higher Ed and the Babson Survey Research Group, which has spent more than a decade studying online education. The report, which surveyed 4,564 faculty members, reveals that 58 per cent of respondents "described themselves as filled more with fear than with excitement" over the growth of online courses within higher education. The fears of college faculty are sustained by the consistent rise in popularity of online education during the past decade. The number of college students enrolled in at least one online course increased for the ninth straight year, with more than 6.1 million students taking an online course during fall 2010 – a 10.1 per cent increase over fall 2009, according to a separate Babson report. While some of these fears could be attributed to professors not seeing the benefits of digital education, others may worry that instructors could be replaced altogether by online courses, says Dan Johnson, a senior lecturer at Wake Forest University. "It's the idea of being able to do with technology what has been done with people in the past," Johnson says. "There is a very real fear that this will be cutting into the education system and actually not just supplementing instructors but replacing them."

Although opinions differ between professors who have worked with an online component and those who have not, 66 per cent of all faculty members surveyed say that the learning outcomes of online courses are inferior compared to traditional courses. Among faculty members who teach online courses exclusively, 39 per cent note that online courses produce inferior learning outcomes. But instead of making comparisons on learning outcomes between online courses and classroom courses, educators should base opinions on the actual course design, says Diane Johnson, assistant director of faculty services at the Center for Online Learning at St. Leo University. "It's all based on how the course is designed," she says. "You can't compare one course with another without looking at instructional design, whether it's face to face or online."

Wake Forest's Johnson agrees, noting that educators are making judgments and comparisons between traditional courses and online courses, when each requires "different assessments and evaluations." He says, "I could easily put together a series of assessments that would look at online [courses] versus brick-and-mortar [courses], and you would see much better outcomes for online. I could also create a different set of evaluations, and we would clearly see better benefits in a brick-and-mortar environment. We just don't know what we're looking for."

The future of online education looks bright, though, according to some full-time professors which accounted for roughly three-fourths of all faculties surveyed. Forty per cent reported that online courses have the potential to match in-class instruction for learning outcomes. But, much like in face-to-face learning environments, the success of the course is dependent on the quality of the instructor, notes Julanna Gilbert, executive director of the Office of Teaching and Learning at the University of Denver. "For the future, it's about getting enough people enough professional development so they can also teach high-quality online courses," Gilbert says. "You still need a faculty member because you still need feedback."

In order for faculty members to fully embrace online education in traditional settings, though, they must stop resisting these changes in technology, Wake Forest's Johnson says. "We can argue against it all we want," he says. "But if we're spending all our time arguing ... we lose the ability to help shape it so that it goes in the direction that's helpful for the students. We can turn online learning into a marvel of the 21st century, or we can turn it into a horrible mistake."

According to an Associated Press report on 6 September, Amazon.com will update its Kindle Fire tablet computer in an effort to take a larger share of a tablet computer market dominated by Apple's iPad. It could help Amazon.com Inc. boost sales of digital goods such as e-books and movies. The announcement at a former airplane hangar in Santa Monica, Calif., will feature CEO Jeff Bezos. He announced the first Kindle Fire in New York less than a year ago. The price tag was $199, about half the price of the cheapest iPad now available.

Amazon has pursued the strategy of selling lower-priced tablets at razor-thin, if any, profit margins in order to boost sales of digital items from its online store. The Kindle Fire has a smaller screen than the iPad.

X

OLIVIER KNOX, reporting for Yahoo! News / The Ticket, wrote on 26 October 2012 that President Barack Obama told MTV in an interview on that day that he wished there were more overtly political music today and said that he is not as concerned about elder daughter Malia dating or driving as he is about her being on Facebook. Interviewer Sway Calloway had asked the Commander-in-chief whether he was more worried about seeing his daughters go out with boys, get behind the wheel, or join the social networking site. "I'd worry about Facebook right now," he said. "I know the folks at Facebook obviously they've revolutionized, you know, the social networks. But Malia, because she's well known, I'm very keen on her protecting her privacy. She can make her own decisions obviously later as she gets older, but right now, even just for security reasons, she doesn't have a Facebook page. Dates, that's fine, because she's got Secret Service protection," he added with a smile. Obama said he hoped his girls would date "boys who respect them and value them and understand their worth. (It's the) driver's license that always worries a parent. But you know, sooner or later they've got to leave the nest, so we'll have to figure out how she gets the license," he said.

The half-hour exchange, broadcast live on MTV and on the channel's website, was one of 10 interviews Obama did, most of them targeting pivotal battleground states or key demographics like young voters. Calloway pointed to politically engaged musicians like Bob Marley, Bob Dylan, Public Enemy and Rage Against the Machine and asked the president who, today, best "inspired and informed" young people. "We haven't seen as much directly political music. I think the most vibrant musical art form right now, over the last 10-15 years, has been hip-hop. And there have been some folks that have kind of dabbled in political statements," Obama replied. "But a lot of it has been more cultural than political. You've got folks like Springsteen who are still putting out very strong political statements, but I'd like to see a more explicit discussion of the issues that are out there right now," he said.

"You just mentioned Bob Marley, I can remember when I was in college listening and not agreeing with his whole philosophy necessarily, but raising my awareness about how people outside of our country were thinking about the struggles for jobs, and dignity and freedom," Obama said. "You think about a lot of music of the 70s, there was a sense of engagement in what was happening with the anti-war movement, what was happening with respect to the civil rights movement. And so I would hope that we're going to see more of that, because young people, they communicate in a lot of different ways and everything moves so fast today that you can set the world on fire in a positive way just through a message that goes through the Internet," he said, adding with a smile that when he bought music in years past "I had to go buy an album or a cartridge."

XI

AMAZON PRIDES itself on unraveling the established order. This fall, signs of Amazon-inspired disruption are everywhere. There is the slow-motion crackup of electronics showroom Best Buy. There is Amazon's rumored entry into the wine business, which is already agitating competitors. And there is the merger of Random House and Penguin, an effort to create a mega-publisher sufficiently hefty to negotiate with the retailer on equal terms. Amazon inspires anxiety just about everywhere, but its publishing arm is getting pushback from all sorts of booksellers, who are scorning the imprint's most prominent title, Timothy Ferriss's *The 4-Hour Chef.* That book is coming out just before Thanksgiving into a fragmented book-selling landscape that Amazon has done much to create but that eludes its control.

Timothy Ferriss is the best-selling author of *The 4-Hour Workweek.* Mr. Ferriss's first book, *The 4-Hour Workweek,* sold nearly a half-million copies in its original print edition, according to Nielsen BookScan. A follow-up devoted to the body did nearly as well. Those books about finding success without trying too hard were a particular hit with young men, who identified with their quasi-scientific entrepreneurial spirit. Signing Mr. Ferriss was seen as a smart choice by Amazon, which wanted books that would make a splash in both the digital and physical worlds. When the seven-figure deal was announced in August 2011, Mr. Ferriss, a former nutritional supplements marketer, said this was "a chance to really show what the future of books looks like." Now that publication is at hand, that future looks messy and angry. Barnes & Noble, struggling to remain relevant in Amazon's shadow, has been emphatic that it will not carry its competitor's books. Other large physical and digital stores seem to be uninterested or even opposed to the book. Many independent stores feel betrayed by Mr. Ferriss, whom they had championed. They will do nothing to help him if it involves helping a company they feel is hell-bent on their destruction. "At a certain point you have to decide how far you want to nail your own coffin shut," said Michael Tucker, owner of the Books Inc. chain. "Amazon wants to completely control the entire book trade. You're crazy if you want to play that game with them."

Bill Petrocelli, co-owner of Book Passage, a large store in suburban Marin County, expressed similar reservations. "We don't think it's in our best interests to do business with Amazon," he said. Crown, a division of Random House, took on Mr. Ferriss in 2007, after more than two dozen publishers said no to him. "Crown put in a lot of effort to promote those books," Mr. Petrocelli said. "He decided to walk away. That's his decision to make but I can't say I applaud it. I think writers should be supportive of publishers that are supportive of them." This isn't a full-fledged boycott. Books Inc. and Book Passage said they would special order *The 4-Hour Chef* for anyone who wanted one. And some independent stores will even display it, if not enthusiastically. Green Apple, another big independent San Francisco store, said it would stock the book, figuring that if there was money to be made on its sale, better Green Apple make it than Amazon. But Kevin Ryan, the store's buyer, said there were limits. "We're not going to go out of our way to promote something from Amazon," he said. "We're not going to stretch." When Mr. Ferriss signed with Amazon, he celebrated the new at the expense of the old. "I don't feel like I'm giving up anything, financially or otherwise," he said. He has a somewhat different view these days. "By signing with Amazon, I expected this type of blowback," he said. "I've been girding my loins." The irony, he added, is that the $35 book was meant to be inviting to the casual browser. Amazon can do many things, but it still cannot let readers examine a book before buying. "This is the kind of book that physical booksellers would be most excited to sell," Mr. Ferriss said.

Only a few years ago, culture was delivered in discrete doses. *The 4-Hour Chef* would have been in the chain bookstores by the stacks and in independents by the handful. You wanted a book, you went to the bookstore. Now the technology overlords – Amazon, Google and Apple – are competing among themselves and with other players to control how the culture is consumed. Amazon's Kindle Fire was introduced last year to carve out some space from Apple's iPad; since then, Google and Microsoft have brought out their own tablets. There is constant jockeying for position. Amazon, for instance, is at odds with Wal-Mart and Target, both of which have stopped selling the Kindle, worried that it is a Trojan horse that will lure their customers away.

All the technology companies hope to bind users to their devices as tablet use explodes. There are about 70,000 activations every day of tablets powered by Google's Android software. That is a vast number of potential readers, but Google Play, a media store for these devices, does not offer the big books Amazon published this fall. It does, however, offer downloads of a popular book Amazon published several years ago, *The Hangman's Daughter*. A Google spokeswoman referred calls to Amazon. "We're going to decline to participate," an Amazon spokeswoman said. Wal-Mart, asked if it would be selling *The 4-Hour Chef*, said only that it would be offered online through Walmart.com. Target said it isn't carrying the book, although it is carrying both online and in stores other new cookbooks published by the traditional presses, like Lidia Matticchio Bastianich's *Lidia's Favorite Recipes*.

Amazon has been publishing books since 2009. Most of its imprints are run out of its Seattle offices, including lines for mysteries and romances. Authors who write for these imprints say they are doing well, sometimes extremely well. Their sales are largely digital. They live within the Amazon ecosystem, selling their books from the retailer's Web site. For the moment, though, a book that aspires to be a genuine national best seller needs more than that. And that is where the books being acquired by Amazon in New York, which are distributed to the book trade by Houghton Mifflin Harcourt under the New Harvest imprint, are faltering. Its editors, led by a longtime publishing operative, Laurence Kirshbaum, seem to have backed off, at least for the time being, from buying prominent books. "I had expected more," said Sucharita Mulpuru, a Forrester technology analyst. "I expected them to find the next *Hunger Games*. I expected the next Harry Potter to come through Amazon. They have not changed the world like many assumed they would."

In September, Amazon published the movie director Penny Marshall's *My Mother Was Nuts*. According to Nielsen BookScan, it has sold 8,000 hardcover copies. "That should have sold 50,000, but they couldn't go through the brick and mortar stores," said Mr. Tucker of Books Inc. He declined to sell that one too, and so apparently did just about everyone that wasn't Amazon. Ms. Marshall's agent did not respond to an e-mail requesting comment.

As publication approaches, Mr. Ferriss has started aggressively promoting *The 4-Hour Chef* on his blog, announcing a weight-loss contest. The book might need all of his considerable promotional talents. It has not yet generated instant heat even on Amazon; it was ranked No. 597 in books and 4,318 in the Kindle Store. The 4-Hour Workweek," in an updated edition published in 2009, was by contrast No. 328 in books and 2,723 in Kindle. "The nature of experiments is that sometimes you succeed and sometimes you fail," Mr. Ferriss said. "This could be a landmark in a lot of ways, for better or worse."

Chapter Six – Celebrities

In the 1990s, the now-defunct magazine *George,* started by the late John F. Kennedy, Jr., demonstrated how all politics had become entertainment and how pop culture had become political. In this era of politics as entertainment and entertainment as politics, what has become of the political process, and what has become of popular culture? In a time when the deaths of Princess Diana and John F. Kennedy, Jr., are covered around the globe, the distinction between public life and pop culture has virtually disappeared. Celebrities run for political office (or lobby those who do), and operatives such as George Stephanopoulos, Geraldine Ferraro, Oliver North, and Jesse Ventura become celebrated figures. With popular culture merging with the political system, the press has moved toward a style of reporting that emphasizes Hollywood style gossip and scandal, to the detriment of traditional politicians and political parties. – David M. West and John Orman in *Celebrity Politics*

LOS ANGELES. – When Marc and Simon had graduated from university they had opted to spend the year that the US Immigration and the Internal Revenue Service had allowed them as non-immigrants to stay unmolested in the United States to go to the City of Angels to realize part of their American dream. I was mad as hell because I had expected that they would join me at CISS, the online information company we had started with their involvement in mind. However Marc was after a career as a script writer and Simon was infatuated with the entertainment industry, a dream that had been born after his part in YouthFest. This was a stellar four-day art and craft event we had promoted in 1991 at the National Stadium while we were at the Trinidad Express Newspapers Ltd. But as an indulgent father I accommodated their wish and the star-dust I saw in their eyes. I had remembered that when I had visited the state of California for the first time in 1971 how I fell in love with first San Francisco and then Los Angeles and the climate of these places. I had even the thought that Marc, who was then just three years old, would one day go to Stanford University where Ms. Condoleezza Rice, the nation's 66th Secretary of State, is nowadays a political science professor and Provost. But at the time I had no idea of Ms. Rice. I knew however many of Hollywood's box office stars from my trips to the cinema.

Actor and director Clint Eastwood was one of them. He had made his career in what was called "spaghetti westerns" and "Dirty Harry" movies. I didn't know his ties to the Republican Party until this year when he performed at the Republican National Convention in Tampa, Florida. Then he gave a speech in which he laid out what he sees as the good, the bad and the ugly state of American political affairs, according to Halimah Abdullah of CNN. And he did it all, while addressing an "invisible" President Barack Obama sitting in an empty chair. Eastwood fired up the party base when he said he cried when Obama was elected and cried even harder years later when millions were out of work. "It's a national disgrace," Eastwood said. "It may be time for someone else to come along and solve the problem." At times, Eastwood sent the crowd into laughing fits when he pretended Obama was offering colorful objections. "What do you want me to tell Romney?" Eastwood asked the empty chair. "I can't tell him to do that to himself ... you're getting as bad as Biden ..."

The RNC had left room for a "mystery guest" on its Thursday schedule and announced on that day that Eastwood would speak. Late Thursday afternoon, Eastwood walked through the convention floor for a brief rundown of the night's events. His ad-libbed speech later in the evening was decidedly political, bitingly satirical and more than a bit, well ... rambling. "I think if you just step aside and Mr. Romney can kind of take over. You can maybe still use a plane," Eastwood said.

Seconds after Eastwood finished his speech, the Twittersphere was buzzing with response. Larry Sabato, director of the University of Virginia's Center for Politics tweeted: "I'd feel better if I knew for sure that Clint doesn't see anyone in the chair. :)" Comedian Roseanne Barr tweeted: "clint eastwood is CRAY". Actor George Takei tweeted that he could use the Eastwood tactic at next week's Democratic National Convention. "I'm drafting a DNC speech to imaginary Romney in an empty factory," Takei's tweet said. Actress Mia Farrow tweeted that she thought Florida Sen. Marco Rubio, who introduced Mitt Romney later in the evening, was the night's best speaker – with one problem: "Rude to ignore invisible Obama sitting right there."

The Twitter handle "Invisible Obama", which said it was sitting "Stage left of Clint Eastwood," quipped that "The GOP built me." An hour after Eastwood's speech, it already had 20,000 followers. The move spawned a new trend with people posting photos of themselves pointing at empty chairs with the hashtag "eastwooding".

Comedic takes on Eastwood's speech went viral and all of a sudden, what might have been for some younger viewers a ho-hum speech by an octogenarian actor became both a national joke and a means to engage in the political process, political experts said. "It was campaign malpractice that the Romney managers sent out a dithering, clueless Clint Eastwood. The Romney campaign will be lucky if Eastwood's antics don't linger as a national punch line," Sabato wrote on his *Crystal Ball* blog. Sabato also noted that fallout from Eastwood's vaudevillian like schtick overshadowed "Sen. Marco Rubio, whose dazzling speech to his home state conclave might end up being as nationally invisible as the imaginary Barack Obama sitting in Clint's stage chair."

A Romney campaign aide addressed Romney's appearance later, saying, "Judging an American icon like Clint Eastwood through a typical political lens doesn't work. His ad-libbing was a break from all the political speeches, and the crowd enjoyed it. He rightly pointed out that 23 million Americans out of work or underemployed is a national disgrace and it's time for a change." But political fact checkers immediately pounced on the 23 million unemployment figure. The U.S. Labor Department says there are 12.8 million unemployed people – not 23 million.

Eastwood had endorsed Romney at an Idaho fundraiser at the beginning of August, where he told reporters that he was backing the GOP presidential candidate "because I think the country needs a boost somewhere." He had endorsed Sen. John McCain in the 2008 presidential election. Earlier this year in an ad that aired during the Super Bowl, Eastwood's familiar, sandpaper voice, says one reviewer, spoke to Americans about the nation's economic woes. The ad featured close-up shots of factory workers and black-and-white photos of Midwest families – images some political watchers flagged as subtly political. "It's halftime in America, too," said the 81-year-old Hollywood legend. "People are out of work, and they're hurting. And they're all wondering what they're gonna do to make a comeback. And we're all scared because this isn't a game. The people of Detroit know a little something about this. They almost lost everything. But we all pulled together, now Motor City is fighting again."

What about the Democrats and the Stars? Jocelyn Noveck of the Associated Press wrote that the Celebrity presence at their convention would be smaller. Four years ago she recalled Ben Affleck was a familiar presence around the Democratic convention, packing produce for charity and even winning a poker tournament. Singer Fergie performed with her Black Eyed Peas. Sheryl Crow sang, too, with Susan Sarandon joining in from the audience. But none of these celebrities is planning a similar trip to Charlotte this year, she wrote and that's likely true for a number of other A-listers who were in Denver as well. In terms of star wattage, this gathering will be decidedly less sparkly. Some reasons are obvious. A re-election bid is hardly as exciting as the historic anointment of the first black nominee, on his way to becoming the first black president. And Barack Obama is no longer a rising star: He's, well, an incumbent.

Also different is the general tone of this year's campaign – not so full of lofty thoughts about hope and change, but focused on evoking doubts about Mitt Romney. Romney is trying to do the same with Obama. "This is a campaign based on raising questions about the other candidate," says Democratic consultant Chris Lehane. "It's a whole different narrative this time." There's also the possibility that some Hollywood celebrities have lost a measure of their enthusiasm for the candidate they warmly embraced four years ago. The most public of these has been actor Matt Damon, who as recently as last month repeated his disappointment with the president – while adding that he was still the "clear choice."

At the same time, there's a sense that the struggling economy, the central preoccupation of most voters, has cast a pall over the celebratory nature of the conventions – and that both campaigns need to be wary of too much partying, with or without celebrities. "Both the Democrats and the Republicans are cognizant of not looking decadent when the rest of the country is hurting," says Lehane. Still, it can't be denied that parties – and if they involve celebrities, as the best ones do, so much the better – are an essential part of conventions. "They're a natural part of the process," says Michael Steele, the former RNC chairman. "I don't think anyone expects the conventioneers to show up in sackcloth. Parties celebrate the grueling process that has gotten us this far. They celebrate the nominee. And they fire up the troops." He adds, though, that he expects the parties to be tasteful – "not in-your-face, not ostentatious."

The Democrats in particular have made a point of saying that this convention has a different mood. They are spending significantly less than four years ago, they say, and they point out that they have limited corporate and special interest money. They also say their parties will have a more public feel. "Instead of the exclusive, closed-door, party-insider-only events of the past, we're opening and closing the convention with public events that will allow more people than ever before to participate," says Democratic National Convention Committee spokeswoman Joanne Peters. As for the Republicans, "I don't see any scaling back," says James Davis, communications director for the Republican National Convention in Tampa. "We've got Republicans coming from across the country, some 70-plus venues being booked for events. This is going to be really big for us. I think it shows the excitement of where our party is right now."

As usual, there will be high-profile entertainment at both conventions. The RNC announced that the Mississippi band 3 Doors Down, Lynyrd Skynyrd and The Oak Ridge Boys would be among the official entertainers in Tampa. The Democrats announced that folk icon James Taylor would perform on the final night in Charlotte. On the sidelines, the arts advocacy group Creative Coalition will present the band Journey in Tampa – cue the perfect campaign song, *Don't Stop Believin'* – and the B-52s in Charlotte. Given the state of the economy, "I was concerned," says the coalition's CEO, Robin Bronk, of the high-profile fundraisers. "But happily we are almost sold out already. This is a celebration of the arts in America." And the Recording Industry Association of America is presenting, along with the Auto Alliance of

America and others, pop star Gavin DeGraw in Tampa and the rapper Common in Charlotte. "We're feeling what everyone has been feeling," says Cara Duckworth, spokeswoman for the RIAA, of the economic concerns. "But this is about celebrating music."

In a way, the relative lack of high-wattage celebrity guests this year may benefit the Democrats. In 2008, the John McCain campaign tried to use Obama's considerable celebrity appeal against him, most memorably with an ad likening him to Britney Spears and Paris Hilton: i.e. all splash and no substance. Earlier this year, the pro-GOP super PAC American Crossroads put out an ad asking: "After 4 years of a celebrity president is your life any better?" Obama's campaign did try to downplay celebrity presence in Denver, keeping it on the sidelines. But still, luminaries of the entertainment world were there in droves.

The AP called representatives of a number of celebrities who were in Denver to ask if they were coming this year. Of those who responded, all said no, except for Jessica Alba. The actress will be headlining a final-night party with her husband, Cash Warren, featuring performances by Pitbull and Scissor Sisters. Also, Eva Longoria, a co-chair of Obama's campaign, will be speaking at the convention.

Traditionally there have been fewer celebrities at Republican conventions. Two past attendees are skipping Tampa, though, according to their representatives: former California Governor Arnold Schwarzenegger and actor Robert Downey Jr., who was at the last GOP convention, but also attended an Obama fundraiser in May at George Clooney's home. Many powerful Hollywood boosters of Obama simply prefer to stay away from conventions but maintain their strong support nonetheless. Like Clooney, Sarah Jessica Parker and movie mogul Harvey Weinstein, all of whom have hosted major fundraisers recently, some obviously feel they can be of greater use in other ways than hanging out in Charlotte. And the most important thing is what happens after the convention, says Steele, who notes he worked hard when he was RNC chairman to create relationships with celebrities. "Of course, the real goal is to have these stars then go out on the road for you in the fall," Steele says.

II

AN AFP Relax News report said on 7 August 2012 that candid Marilyn Monroe photos would go public in Poland as fans worldwide mark 50 years since her untimely death. A collection of rare Marilyn Monroe photographs immortalizing the American blonde bombshell went on display in Warsaw. Poland's State Treasury obtained the candid shots of Monroe by a friend, Milton Green, in a collection of nearly 4,000 photographs it received as part of a 1995 foreign debt settlement. The collection also contained images of Frank Sinatra, Liza Minnelli, Marlon Brando, Judy Garland and Marlene Dietrich and will be auctioned off later this year. Monroe is snapped dressed in jeans fixing her lipstick and hair, eating a meal and coyly chatting on the phone in several photos, which will be on display until 6 September at the Association of Polish Artistic Photographers on Warsaw's Royal Castle square. According to the association, some of the images of Monroe have not been seen before. No date was fixed for the auction, but Poland's treasury expects it to go ahead before the end of the year and fetch upwards of $680,000 (560,000 euros). Some 300 Monroe fans gathered at the Los Angeles cemetery where she is buried, commemorating the iconic sex symbol on the 50th anniversary of her death. The actress died on 5 August 1962 from a barbiturate overdose at her home it is said.

Another famous name in the news is that of Scout Willis who at 20 is already mimicking the body-baring ways of her 50-year-old mother, Demi Moore, writes Sheila Marikar for ABC News Blogs on 8 December 2011. In a new editorial for the website StyleLikeU, Willis poses in a pair of bottomless chaps and flashes her full, naked rear end while sitting on the back of a motorcycle. She gives the finger to the camera in another shot that shows her backside in profile. She wears little more than a coat or a blanket in some of the other photographs. The Brown University student is ahead of the game. Moore posed nude for the August 1991 issue of *Vanity Fair* when she was 28 and seven months pregnant. Another one: StyleCaster.com's photo gallery of Willis' shoot is sponsored by Nikon, whose celebrity endorser is Ashton Kutcher, Moore's soon to be third ex-husband.

Tim Kenneally of Reuters wrote on 17 February 2012 that Jennifer Aniston had her naked boobs pulled from her new movie

Wanderlust, putting a last-minute ban on a frontal topless scene out of consideration for her boyfriend and *Wanderlust* co-star, Justin Theroux, an insider tells TheWrap. The former *Friends* star demanded that the topless scene from the Judd Apatow-produced film, which hit theaters on 24 February 2012, be replaced with a tamer version, an individual with knowledge of the movie told TheWrap. A spokeswoman for Universal, which released the movie, said: "The scene was shot a bunch of different ways and we have the best possible version." Aniston's publicist, Stephen Huvane, denies that the scene was altered at the actress' behest. "The scene is how it was always supposed to be," Huvane told TheWrap.

The scene in question features Aniston going topless in front of TV news cameras. In the version that will be included in the film, Aniston will be seen topless from behind, with her bare breasts shown pixelated on TV screens, as they would appear on a TV news broadcast. But the movie insider who spoke to TheWrap said that when the film was edited with the frontal nudity in it, Aniston pleaded for an alternate version due to her blossoming relationship with Theroux, whom she met on the set of the film. The 43-year-old actress, it seems, decided it just wouldn't be right to share her naked breasts with anyone except her new beau. In the film, Aniston and Paul Rudd play a Manhattan couple who suddenly become unemployed and seek an alternative living situation, ultimately landing on a rural, free-love commune. Theroux, 40, plays commune inhabitant Seth. Aniston performed a brief, semi-topless scene – though her breasts were concealed by an open lab coat – in her recent comedy *Horrible Bosses*. The actress has also displayed a penchant for skin-happy photo-shoots on the pages of magazines such as *Rolling Stone* and *GQ*. Her most recent appearance in the latter, for its March 2012 issue, featured Aniston posing in little more than a black bra with her co-star Rudd.

On 7 February 2012 Reuters reported that talk show host Ellen DeGeneres said she was "proud and happy" that retail store JCPenney had stood by her in the face of a conservative anti-gay campaign, and said there was no such thing as a "pro-gay bandwagon." Breaking her silence on the furor, DeGeneres, one of America's best known gay celebrities, also poked fun at the One Million Moms group who had urged JCPenney to drop her as a spokeswoman because she is a lesbian and said they would boycott the store. "For those of you are just tuning in for the first time, it's true. I'm gay. I hope you were sitting down," DeGeneres told viewers of *The Ellen DeGeneres Show*. "They (One Million Moms) wanted to get me fired and I am proud and happy to say that JCPenney stuck by their decision to make me their spokesperson," she said.

The group, a division of the socially conservative American Family Association, claimed that JCPenney was trying to gain a new target market by "jumping on the pro-gay bandwagon" with its hiring of DeGeneres to revamp their clothing and household brand. "Being gay or pro-gay isn't a bandwagon. You don't get a free ride anywhere. There's no music. And occasionally we'll sing 'We Are Family' but that's about it," she said. She also noted that the One Million Moms group "only has 40,000 members on their (Facebook) page. So they're rounding up to the nearest million and I get that." DeGeneres, who has some 9 million followers on Twitter, said she preferred to avoid talking about such matters on her show "and normally I try not to pay attention to my haters, but this time I'd like to talk about it because my haters are my motivators."

Natalie Wood's daughter Courtney Wagner was arrested for cocaine and heroin possession writes Suzy Byrne of Now: Your Daily Dose of Celebrity News on 30 April 2012. Courtney, the only daughter of the late Natalie Wood and actor Robert Wagner, was arrested after police responded to a domestic dispute at her home that involved gunfire. The 38-year-old former jewelry designer who was just 7 years old when her famous mother drowned on a weekend trip to Catalina Island in California was taken into custody at her Malibu home when officers responded to a call that a woman at the residence was screaming and there was gunfire, reports TMZ. Courtney was arrested on suspicion of felony drug possession for reportedly having cocaine and heroin. The other person involved, an unidentified male, was also arrested for negligent discharge of a firearm.

If you had to choose a new challenge to deal with in life, the ramifications of being named the sexiest woman alive sounds like a good one ... and happens to be the exact problem actress Kate Beckinsale has faced since the title was bestowed upon her by *Esquire* magazine in 2009, writes Lizbeth Scordo for A-Line: Celebrity Style. "I think the risk of being the sexiest woman alive is that you don't want to ever have sex again," she tells *Allure*. "You don't want to wear a bikini again. You want to wear some nice overalls and a trucker's hat." Whether or not she's over those hang-ups remains to be seen, but there's another issue the British beauty is dealing with these days: the public's perception of a 38-year-old mom of a teenager ... a real-life role Beckinsale just happens to have. "It's more of the thing of being embarrassing to somebody. I haven't been embarrassed before. I can't dance at a party where there are teenagers without clearing the dance floor," she confesses in the magazine's August issue. "Those are the things that make me go, F***, I'm old ."

It may be hard to believe, but Beckinsale is indeed the parent of a teenager, 13-year-old Lily, the daughter she had with fellow actor Michael Sheen. The couple's relationship ended in 2003 after eight years together. Since 2004, Beckinsale has been married to director and producer Len Wiseman, whom she met on the set of the 2003 thriller *Underworld* and credits with helping her finally feel beautiful. "Feeling attractive didn't come until I was 29 and with Len ... At the time it was partly perceived as if I'd gone all Hollywood, but it wasn't like that at all," she explains. "It was just OK for me to walk around and feel feminine and attractive. I like feeling liberated like this." And at the ripe old age of 38, Beckinsale indeed feels like she's doing a decent job of keeping it together. "I haven't experienced a full facial collapse, I haven't suddenly gained 20 pounds that won't go away, or a beard," she jokes in the interview. "That probably will happen, but it hasn't yet."

According to Greg Risling of the Associated Press on 7 November 2011 Lindsay Lohan was released from a Los Angeles County jail less than five hours after she arrived at the crowded women's lockup to serve a 30-day sentence for violating probation. The *Mean Girls* actress was booked into the Century Regional Detention facility in Lynwood in what was expected to be a short stay because of jail overcrowding. News crews staking out the jail said she left in a black Cadillac Escalade sport utility vehicle, and that she was in her Venice home by 2 a.m. It's Lohan's fifth jail sentence since being arrested twice for drunken driving in 2007. Her brief return to jail came after Lohan completed an interview and photo shoot for *Playboy* magazine that will appear in the January/February issue, her spokesman Steve Honig wrote in an email. A judge ordered jail time because Lohan recently violated court orders by getting booted from a community service assignment at a women's shelter. The judge imposed a complicated sentence, telling Lohan that she will now have to perform all of her community service at the county morgue or risk serving an additional 270 days in jail.

Lohan will have to serve 423 hours at the county morgue, where for nearly two weeks she has been mopping floors, cleaning bathrooms and washing dirty sheets. The sentence also requires Lohan to undergo psychotherapy sessions and appear monthly at court hearings between December and March. The judge also said Lohan can no longer leave the country and needs the permission of her new "no-nonsense" probation officer to travel outside California. Jail overcrowding has led to significantly shortened jail terms. In 2007, Lohan spent 84 minutes at the jail before being released, and in the past she has served about 20 per cent of her sentence, which is roughly six days. "As pathetic as it sounds, this is not necessarily special treatment," said Adam H. Braun, a defense attorney who was not involved in the case. "It just depends how full the jail is when someone surrenders. If it is filled to capacity or nearly full, offenders like her are the first ones let go so more serious offenders can be held. Even so, she was not likely to do more than 20 per cent of the 30 days under the jail crowding formulas being used because her offense was not a crime of violence," he added in an email.

Bunnies and Stewardesses will be TV's racy slant when the new season begins, writes Tim Kenneally of Fall TV. There will be a marked increase in the number of actresses populating new series this fall. On the other hand, they appear to have packed pretty light when it comes to wardrobe. From the tight uniforms sported by the stewardesses on ABC's *Pan Am* and the Alphabet Network's sexy re-commissioned *Charlie's Angels* crime-fighters, to the fluffy-tailed servers of NBC's *The Playboy Club*, the fashion trend of the season appears to be flesh, and plenty of it. Call it the resurgence of Jiggle TV, a titillating genre that briefly blossomed in the 1970s with the original *Charlie's Angels*, before giving way with the exit of *Baywatch*.

Though none of the series have yet to debut, the trend of new shows featuring female leads in little clothing and subservient positions has already been met with criticism. Gloria Steinem, who gained notoriety by going undercover as a bunny at the Playboy Club in New York in 1960s and writing an exposé about the working conditions, has said that she's hoping for a boycott of NBC's *The Playboy Club*, claiming, "It normalizes a passive-dominant idea of gender. So, it normalizes prostitution and male dominance."

Christine Baranski, co-star of *The Good Wife*, has similarly chimed in, telling *New York* magazine, "I'm rather appalled that they're now making television shows about Playboy bunnies and stewardesses... I think, 'Really? Haven't we gone past that, well past that?'" Apparently not. But why now, in particular, does there seem to be a resurgence in flesh-centric TV fare. Certainly, AMC's *Mad Men* seems to have loosened the jar lid with its highly successful exercise in flesh-friendly, misogyny-laced nostalgia. And it might be no coincidence that the upcoming series – like *Mad Men* – all have retro elements to them.

Martha M. Lauzen, Ph.D., the executive director for Center for the Study of Women in Television and Film, suggests that, particularly in dour financial times, male viewers – not to mention the overwhelmingly male decision-makers at the networks – might be looking to retreat into less complicated, more comforting times. "In times of economic and social upheaval and difficulty, nostalgia and a longing for an era when life seemed simpler tend to bloom," Lauzen said. That could be especially true in an era when men – at least the ones not on TV, anyway – find themselves losing economic and social ground to the fairer sex. "As women continue to gain economic, social and political power, there is always some sort of backlash, a desire to put women 'back in their place,'" Lauzen adds. "These programs may reflect that type of wishful thinking."

Naturally, those involved with the series have a different take on the matter. At the Television Critics' Association press tour earlier this month, *Pan Am* star Christina Ricci dismissed cries of sexism, claiming that her series provides "a really great message for young girls and women... [Air travel] is something that's exciting for these women. We're as excited as the passengers are." Never mind that the Pan Am stewardesses were subjected to mandatory girdle-wearing and weigh-ins. Or that the trailer for the series prominently features a clip of one of the stewardesses stripped down to her bra as she frantically changes clothes in the back of a taxi. Similarly, Amber Heard, who portrays Maureen on *The Playboy Club*, praised the original Playboy

Bunnies as pioneers of women's lib. "[They] wanted their own fortune and they went out into the work force doing what they wanted to do," she told E! Online. "I could not be more empowered by that example, and I think denying women their sexuality is just as chauvinistic, if not worse." A lofty sentiment – but one that might fall, um, flat when it comes wrapped in a skin-tight, cleavage-baring Playboy Bunny outfit.

Whether *The Playboy Club* and its ilk serve as crass exploitation or lessons in empowerment wrapped in an attractive package, Lauzen said that there will probably be more of the same coming, particularly if the current trend toward fewer women behind the scenes continues. "The percentage of women working as writers on broadcast programs plummeted last season, declining from 29 per cent in 2009-2010 to 15 per cent in 2010-2011," she said. "The industry remains mostly male, and these programs may reflect the behind-the-scenes gender ratios." Looking at the credits for the shows in question, Lauzen noted, "Many of the important behind-the-scenes roles on these shows are filled by males." Indeed, Drew Barrymore's executive-producer role on *Charlie's Angels* stands as a prominent exception to the general rule – along with Nancy Ganis, a former Pan Am stewardess who serves as an executive producer of *Pan Am*.

ABC declined to comment to TheWrap for this story, while NBC and its series producers did not provide comment before publication. So can viewers look forward to – or look askance at, depending on the perspective – reboots of *Three's Company*, *The Love Boat* and other jiggle-TV mainstays of yore? But if the new crop of plots and character development end up as skimpy as the outfits, audiences just might decide to bounce elsewhere says this critic.

III

CHINA'S BOOMING movie industry is attracting interest from Hollywood heavyweights, as they chase bigger box-office returns to offset tighter margins at home, reports AFP Relax News on 13 April 2012. Films with Asian and especially Chinese themes are becoming more prominent after Hollywood hit a 16-year low in movie tickets sales last year, while some of its biggest studios are setting up shop in the country.

DreamWorks Animation is setting up a China base while Legendary, the studio behind Christopher Nolan's wildly successful *Batman* series as well as *Clash of the Titans* and *The Hangover* franchises, is also developing a venture. Keanu Reeves is making his directorial debut with *Man of Tai Chi* which is currently filming in China and Hong Kong, while Aamir Khan's Bollywood comedy drama *3 Idiots* is in talks for a Hollywood remake. "It's a hugely interesting time now," said executive producer Tracey Trench, whose projects have included *Just Married* and *Ever After*. "The United States is still the biggest market. Within the next 10 years, we are not going to be the biggest market place, everything is going to change," she told a forum at the Hong Kong International Film and Television Market (FILMART) in March.

According to the experts China's rapidly expanding film industry continues to break new ground and set new records, collecting an estimated 13.1 billion yuan ($2.07 billion) in 2011 – up by around 30 per cent on-year. Around 2,500 more cinema screens are expected to be unveiled across the country this year, with its market now the third largest behind Japan and the United States. This compares with a clear slowdown in North America. The Motion Picture Association (MPA) says box office takings from 2007 to 2011 in the United States and Canada grew only 6.3 per cent to $10.2 billion, while the Asia-Pacific region saw 38 per cent growth to $9 billion.

Zhang Yimou's *The Flowers of War* was China's biggest box office smash of the past 12 months, starring Oscar-winning American actor Christian Bale. It collected around $90 million from the Chinese box office while picking up a nomination for best foreign language film at the prestigious Golden Globes in the United States. It comes as Hollywood looks to increasingly give a Chinese angle to its output. "There are so many stories that you can tell and right now China is hot, so many people want to know more," said screenwriter Glenn Berger, who wrote the popular 2008 animated Hollywood comedy, *Kung Fu Panda*, and its 2011 sequel. A box-office hit in China, the film told the story of Po, an oversize and unfit panda who dreams of becoming a martial arts hero. But Berger said the movie was never really about China or Kung Fu. "We were just trying to tell a classic underdog story, not particularly a Chinese story," he said of the film.

"But it was very well received in the Chinese market because they thought it was very respectful of Chinese culture," he said. *Kung Fu Panda* raked in an estimated $630 million, with $26 million from the Chinese mainland alone.

Hong Kong's FILMART exhibition is Asia's major entertainment industry market and one of the top three events of its kind in the world. This year it attracted a record 648 exhibitors and more than 5,700 buyers, up 14 per cent from last year. The US pavilion had over 40 US exhibitors or about 25 per cent more than last year. Industry veterans say Chinese audiences are particularly drawn to movies that include Chinese references or elements of Chinese culture. "People want to feel connected," said Chinese American writer Rita Hsiao, who wrote the screenplay for *Toy Story 2* and the 1998 animated musical, *Mulan*, a story about a legendary Chinese girl-warrior. "If you have that universal message and it's interesting, everybody everywhere can connect with it," she said. One of the main obstacles for foreign filmmakers wanting to crack the Chinese market is a law limiting the number of international films that can be screened in the country to just 20 a year. It forces studios to co-produce films with Chinese partners or risk having their films blocked at the border. But all the pandas in the world won't guarantee a hit in China. "It has to succeed on all the fundamentals of a movie, not just because it is shot in China," Berger said.

On 25 October 2012 an Associated Press report from Las Vegas said that Katy Perry was doing her best get-out-the vote effort: At a rally for President Barack Obama, she wore a tight white dress imprinted like a ballot, and a square box on her right hip filled in the names of Obama and Joe Biden. Perry gave a free concert at a park in a historically minority neighborhood just northwest of downtown Las Vegas to screaming fans at about 9 p.m., the same time Air Force One landed at McCarran International Airport across town. Obama later told the crowd, "I believe in you. I need you to keep believing in me." The Las Vegas campaign event drew more than 10,000 people, according to fire officials and organizers, with long lines still on sidewalks during Perry's 30-minute performance before Obama arrived. The singer opened with a rendition of Al Green's soul hit, *Let's Stay Together*, and played five songs, including *Teenage Dream*, before ending with a thumping bass drum version of *Firework.* Perry, who recently also played a free concert at an Obama event in Los Angeles, paused before the last song to exhort people in the Las Vegas crowd to vote early. "Don't wait. Go tomorrow," she said. "How many of you are 18 here? It's going to be your first time, right?"

And on the same day, 25 October 2012, and according to Dylan Stableford of Yahoo! News and The Lookout, Barbara Walters had a message for Donald Trump on *The View*, a day after the real estate mogul made his widely-mocked offer to donate $5 million to charity if President Obama agreed to release his college and passport applications. "You and I have known each other for many years," Ms. Walters said in a message to Trump. "And you know that I am your friend, and I think you are a brilliant businessman, and you are great on television, and you have a fascinating personality. Donald, you're making a fool of yourself. You're not hurting Obama. You're hurting Donald, and that hurts me because you're a decent man. Stop it. Get off it, Donald."

Trump was apparently watching, and fired off a series of Twitter messages to Walters in response. "Barbara, unfortunately you've missed the entire point of my announcement," Trump wrote. "You just don't get it!" [Walters] will apologize to me just like she did when I was right about @Rosie," Trump continued. "Besides, I get great ratings on *The View*." He added: "Why did you choose me as one of the 10 Most Fascinating People of the Year last season (and more than once?)" There is at least one television personality supporting Trump: Ann Coulter, herself the target of some public scorn after she referred to President Obama as "the retard" during Monday's presidential debate. "Our side needs Donald Trump," Coulter said on Fox News. "Thanks Ann," Trump tweeted. Meanwhile, a reporter for the *Guardian* newspaper called Trump's offices asking to see the "Celebrity Apprentice" star's own college and passport application records, but was rebuffed. "I think what you're doing, whether you're trying to be funny, intentionally or not, actually it's a stupid request on your behalf," Michael Cohen, Trump Organization executive vice president and special counsel to Trump, told the *Guardian* reporter. "The president of the United States is the least transparent president that we've ever had. He may be the least transparent politician we've ever come across."

With all indications that the presidential election will be extremely close, one factor in the race clearly isn't: the money Hollywood is giving to the two presidential candidates, writes Michael Janofsky of The Wrap. Through 21 October 198 "celebrity" donors have given $684,006 to the Barack Obama campaign compared with 14 donors who have given $43,250 to Mitt Romney's camp, according to the Center for Responsive Politics, the leading organization that tracks donations. For those keeping score, that's a 16-to-1 advantage for the incumbent over the Massachusetts governor.

Veteran women's rights campaigner Gloria Steinem said in August 2011 she hoped TV viewers would boycott *The Playboy Club*, calling the 1960s nightclubs tacky and far from the glamorous places depicted in the show, Jill Serjeant reported. "Clearly *The Playboy Club* is not going to be accurate. It was the tackiest place on earth. It was not glamorous at all," Steinem told Reuters in an interview. Steinem, one of America's leading crusaders for women's rights for 40 years, went undercover to work as a Bunny at the New York City Playboy Club in 1963 and wrote a ground-breaking exposé about the onerous conditions for women who worked there. "When I was working there and writing the exposé, one of the things they had to change because of my exposé was that they required all the Bunnies, who were just waitresses, to have an internal exam and a test for venereal disease," she said. Steinem said she regards the Emmy Award-winning drama *Mad Men*, which is also set in the 1960s as "a net plus, because it shows the world of the early 1960s with some realism. But she added; "I expect that *The Playboy Club* will be a net minus and I hope people boycott it. It's just not telling the truth about the era."

The Playboy Club, set in the first Playboy Club in Chicago, debuts in September as one of the centerpieces of NBC's new fall television season. Speaking to TV reporters in Los Angeles, network executives, producers and the show's cast all rejected opinions by critics who feel the series will glamorize the porn industry and is demeaning to modern women. NBC entertainment chairman Robert Greenblatt called the show a "really fun soap opera" while executive producer Chad Hodge told TV reporters that the program was "all about empowering these women to be whatever they want to be." One NBC affiliate, in Salt Lake City, has already said it will not broadcast the show but NBC says it does not expect others to follow.

Steinem, 77, said that it was important to reject the TV series, despite the fact that it is set 40 years ago. "It normalizes a passive dominant idea of gender. So it normalizes prostitution and male dominance... I just know that over the years, women have called me and told me horror stories of what they experienced at the Playboy Club and at the Playboy Mansion," she said. Steinem was speaking ahead of the premiere of an HBO documentary about her life, Gloria: In her Own Words, on 15 August 2012.

When you say "Kardashian" the name alone elicits such drastically different reactions, writes Suzy Byrne for A-Line Celebrity Style. But – love them or hate them – the family is certainly a success story in the entertainment world. Behind it all is matriarch Kris Jenner, who was able to capitalize on the public interest in her daughter Kim after what most families would deem a humiliating situation and turn it into a successful reality TV series. Now the 56-year-old is at the helm of a multimillion dollar business empire, which includes spin-offs, boutiques, a clothing line, a fragrance, and just about any other product you can conjure up in your mind. So what is behind America's fascination with the *Keeping Up With The Kardashians* stars? Jenner herself credits their reliability. "There are so many of us in my entire family that everybody finds someone who they can relate to or connect with," she tells *Interview* magazine. "At the end of the day, our show is just about our family and what happens, and over the last seven seasons, you've watched my little girls grow up, you've watched people get married and have babies and graduate from school and go to college. You know, it's like so much that goes on in any family, but it's magnified and dramatic, because that's who we are. So I think everyone can look at us and go, 'Wow! I can relate to them.'"

According to Jenner, it also has to do with spontaneity. Many so-called reality shows are actually scripted, but *Keeping Up With The Kardashians* isn't, giving it that you-never-know-what-will-happen-next feeling. Also, the family has never instructed the cameramen to stop rolling in an attempt to hide anything from the audience. "We don't have writers. We don't have scripts. We don't have storylines that we preconceive before we start filming," Jenner notes. "We do have a big meeting at the beginning of a season and say, 'What is everybody doing?' We all have about five full-time jobs apiece. So I think the beauty is that there are so many of us and there are so many things going on that we don't have to sit and think, 'Oh, what would be interesting?' I mean, you can't make up Lamar [Odom] getting traded and Kourtney giving birth and the kids getting married – you can't write that stuff. Or Khloé going to jail." After the show goes off the air – whenever that may be – Jenner's plans, other than counting her fortune, will focus more on her personal interests. "I actually enjoy working on the clothing line that I have on QVC, so I think I'd like to concentrate on growing that brand and just doing my own thing," she tells *Interview*. "My motivation is to be creative and have fun. You want to do something that keeps you on your toes the rest of your life and keeps you busy. That's why we're creating these clothing lines and the kids' fragrances and all the things we have our hands in. I'm really good at multitasking, but I always look at the amazing opportunity that we've been given. ... You know, at this point, we've filmed more seasons of *Keeping Up With The Kardashians* than they did of *I Love Lucy*."

Among the actors, producers and directors who have given the Obama campaign at least $5,000 are Cameron Crowe, Will Ferrell, Ron Howard, Scarlett Johansson, Julia Louis-Dreyfus, Eddie Murphy, George Clooney, J.J. Abrams, Ellen DeGeneres, Leonardo DiCaprio, Robert Downey Jr., Jamie Foxx, Brian Grazer, Adrian Grenier, Tom Hanks, Mariska Hargitay, Will Smith, Aaron Sorkin, Steven Spielberg, Barbra Streisand, Quentin Tarantino, Marlo Thomas, Sam Waterston and Rita Wilson. Among singers and songwriters, Don Henley and Randy Newman have given Obama $5,000 each. Dozens more from the industry have given lesser amounts. The list of Hollywood campaign contributors has grown so long that, for the first time, The Center for Responsive Politics has established "celebrity" lists with the names of well-known people giving to each campaign. The list, which is based on filings with the Federal Election Commission, includes entertainers but also professional athletes, authors and fashion designers. "It's new for us," says Russ Choma, a Center spokesman. "We started it a couple of weeks ago, mostly out of demand, but also because there are so many people on it."

Lady Gaga and Brad Pitt have weighed in on one side, evangelist icon Billy Graham on the other as a four-state showdown over same-sex marriage reaches its Election Day conclusion with the potential for a historic breakthrough, writes David Crary of the Associated Press on

6 November 2012. Until now, he wrote, same-sex marriage has been rejected in all 32 states that have held popular votes on the issue. Gay-rights advocates believe they have a chance to break that streak as Maine, Maryland and Washington state vote on whether to legalize same-sex marriage, and Minnesota votes on whether to place a ban on gay marriage in the state constitution.

In all, there are 176 measures on the ballots in 38 states, according to the Initiative and Referendum Institute at the University of Southern California. Washington, Oregon and Colorado could become the first states to legalize recreational use of marijuana; Massachusetts is considering whether to allow physician-assisted suicide; Californians have a chance to repeal the death penalty. But no other issue has generated the star power or multistate intensity of the same-sex marriage measures.

In just the past week, Lady Gaga released a video backing same-sex marriage, while Pitt donated $100,000 to support the cause. On the other side, Graham, 93, took out newspaper ads asking voters to support "the biblical definition of marriage between a man and a woman." President Barack Obama also has entered the debate, endorsing the three gay-marriage measures and urging a "No" vote on the proposed ban in Minnesota. Brian Brown of the National Organization for Marriage, which has spent more than $5.5 million in the four states opposing same-sex marriage, predicted Obama's stance wouldn't be enough to break the 32-state streak. "People's personal conviction that marriage is the union of husband and wife is too strong to be swayed by what the president says," Brown said. All four elections are expected to be close. In Maine, the latest poll showed gay-marriage supporters with a lead of 13 percentage points, down from a 21-point lead in September. The referendum in Maine marks the first time that gay-marriage supporters have put the issue to a popular vote there. They collected enough signatures over the summer to schedule the vote, hoping to reverse the outcome of a 2009 referendum that quashed a gay-marriage law enacted by the Legislature. A TV ad by gay-marriage supporters in Maine featured Republican state Rep. Stacey Fitts, who was opposed in 2009 but now plans to vote for it. "Society in general has come to the idea of why would we ostracize people for something that's part of who they are," Fitts said.

In both Maryland and Washington State, gay-marriage laws were approved by lawmakers and signed by the governors earlier this year, but opponents gathered enough signatures to challenge the laws. In Minnesota, the question is whether the state will join 30 others in placing a ban on gay marriage in its constitution. Even if the ban is defeated, same-sex marriage will remain illegal under a current statute in Minnesota. Gay marriage is legal in six states and Washington, DC. In each case it is the result of legislation or court orders, not by a vote of the people.

Of the other issues on the ballot in multiple states, marijuana is perhaps the highest-profile. Voters in Washington state, Oregon and Colorado have a chance to do what no state has done before – legalize the recreational use of pot by allowing adults to possess small amounts under a regimen of state regulation and taxation. The Oregon proposal has lagged, but the Washington and Colorado measures have a decent chance of passage. If approved, the measures would set up a direct challenge to federal drug law. "If one of these initiatives passes, it will be a watershed moment in the decades-long struggle to end failed marijuana prohibition policies in this country," said Ethan Nadelmann of the Drug Policy Alliance, a critic of the so-called war on drugs. In Arkansas and Massachusetts, voters will be deciding whether to allow marijuana use for medical reasons, as 17 states have done previously. Arkansas would be the first Southern state to join the group.

Over the last two years, Obama has outraised Romney from what the Center calls the "TV/Movies/Music" industry, by nearly 5-1, with $4,518,742 in donations to the President and $836,038 to the Romney campaign. But those figures do not include money raised by the usual entertainment industry bundlers, people like Jeffrey Katzenberg, Harvey Weinstein and Ron and Kelly Meyer, who collect money from friends, relatives and business associates and combine it into one gift. Three actors are also among the top bundlers for the President this cycle – Wendell Pierce, Tyler Perry and Eva Longoria, who almost has to be there: She's a co-chair of the Obama campaign.

All of them collected at least $500,000 each, according to the Center, which shows that altogether, 41 bundlers from "TV/Movies/ Music" have given Obama $11.4 million. Other bundlers have raised lesser amounts. The Center provides no comparable figures for Romney. Also, the bundling figures do not include individual contributions or money given to SuperPacs, which are not required to reveal their donors. The Center's data shows that among celebrity donors, Bill Maher stands at the top, with contributions of $1,010,000, almost all of it (99 per cent) to Priorities USA Action, the SuperPac working for President Obama. Next is Morgan Freeman, who gave all his money, $1,001,000, to the same group. Magic Johnson, the former Laker star who is a businessman and part owner of the Dodgers, has given all of his $111,600 in campaign contributions to Democrats.

As for Romney, his list of bold-faced Hollywood names includes only Scott Baio, Jerry Bruckheimer, Neil Simon, Orson Bean and John O'Hurley. His supporters also include the McMahons of Connecticut, from the wrestling division of the entertainment business. Linda McMahon is now a Republican candidate for the Senate. Romney also got $250 from Alex Rodriguez who has five years to go on his 10-year, $275 million contract with the New York Yankees.

Chapter Seven – Sex and Society

America is close to rotten. The entertainment media are loose. Bare belly-buttons pop onto every TV screen, as open in their statement as wild animals' eyes. The kids are getting to the point where they can't read, but they sure can screw. – Norman Mailer in *Why Are We At War?*

LAS VEGAS. – There is a kind of bewilderment among Republican politicians about morality in America and this acute moral disorder gives birth to a pharisaic denial of sex in their society that many Americans must live with every day. This hypocrisy is also the cause of the shallowness of lives that produces an unbridled appetite for money and a liberal life-style, what many see as the twin pillars of the American Dream. It is the mythology of generations of Americans that has its genesis in the black past of slavery with its secret lusts and the lies it told that failed to create heroes and heroines except among the slaves white Americans brutalized in their greed for property and power. The truth is this infirmity characterizes the highest examples of men in the land and the fact is neither the Constitution nor Hollywood nor Marvel Comics has succeeded in changing the American archetype. "The practice of modern politics itself seems to be value-free," Barack Obama wrote despairingly in *The Audacity of Hope*, his own apology and quest for the American Dream.

It is not however a truth that has gone unnoticed by the general public. Nowadays more and more Americans are seeing that it is a risk to put their trust in their leaders as a record 64 per cent of American adults surveyed by Gallup rated the honesty and ethical standards for members of Congress as "low" or "very low". Most Americans believe that it is not surprising that Congress ranked so low on ethics and the popular analysis is that a growing number of Americans are labeling their rating "low" or "very low" with a corresponding decline in "high" or "very high" ratings based on the ineffectiveness of the government and this low ethics rating, wrote Rachel Rose Hartman of The Ticket in December 2011, is in line with the overall low regard the American public has for its lawmakers.

Every American parent Obama wrote in 2006 complains about "the coarsening of the culture, the promotion of easy materialism and instant gratification, the severing of sexuality from intimacy," and this morose indictment was a declaration of war against the excesses of American degeneracy. Examples of this notoriety in American behavior are easily seen in every city but especially in the desert metropolis that Wikipedia says was built on gambling, vice and other forms of entertainment. The fact is the America that is still burdened with the guilt of slavery, as is portrayed in Hollywood film after Hollywood film, is struggling also with the lack of honor in universities, churches and public offices. It is clear that Greek democracy has failed to inspire Americans with the values necessary to build a benevolent empire and, instead, the country remains a marketplace of meanness, bigotry and hate. Seeing these flaws in the national character a hundred years ago, Walter Lippmann wrote that the new freedom erred grievously because it failed to recognize that the profit motive was a poor incentive for creating a good society. And yet for years this poison was what fuelled the American Dream.

Let us look first at the country's obsession with gambling nurtured in modern times by tourist invasions from the East. After twelve years in China, teaching in Guangzhou and Beijing, I had come to see that gambling is an addiction for a majority of Chinese and this explained, perhaps, the invasion into Macao of Las Vegas-type casinos. The lure of money has no borders. I remember that students in

Guangzhou used to relate tragic stories of family members who had lost everything because of their fidelity to spending on government lotteries and of family members who had quit their jobs to play the stock market from home. I should not have been surprised by this passion however; in Trinidad, one of the four countries in the Caribbean that the Chinese had come to early in the nineteenth century, those poor immigrants had brought with them a numbers game that a hundred and fifty years later the Trinidad and Tobago Government legitimized to raise funds for its National Insurance Scheme. All of this came together for me in Las Vegas where thousands of Asians, young and old, male and female, played poker and black jack and spent thousands and thousands of dollars on slot machines.

But we could scarcely blame the Chinese for this native-born American hunger for gold and silver. Wikipedia says that in just a century of existence Las Vegas has drawn millions of visitors and trillions of dollars in wealth to southern Nevada. The city it says was founded by ranchers and railroad workers but quickly found that its greatest asset was not its springs but its casinos. Las Vegas's embrace of Old West-style freedoms – gambling and prostitution – provided a perfect home for East Coast organized crime. Beginning in the 1940s, money from drugs and racketeering built casinos and was laundered within them. Visitors came to partake in what the casinos offered: low-cost luxury and the thrill of fantasies fulfilled. It was natural therefore that the city would be a magnet for Chinese coming to the United States on holidays and when I set foot in Las Vegas for the first time in 1990 I should not have been astonished at the number of Asian people I saw everywhere on The Strip. The majority of them were like me, I guessed later, curious visitors going in and out of the casinos and looking to fulfill their fantasies of returning home with pockets full of American dollars.

But it is not possible to avoid the other face of Las Vegas as Wikipedia points out: its prostitution and the business of sex. I remember coming away with dozens of business cards of women inviting me to spend time with them in bed. In Kowloon there are always men on the streets handing out business cards and you could take them if you were interested in having a suit made in a day by a good tailor. But in Las Vegas the men who handed out business cards of nude women were not looking at your crumpled suit or sloppy clothes; they hoped in fact that your interest was not sartorial but sexual and the nude on the card, more daring than any of the models in *Sports Illustrated*'s 2012 swimsuit issue, barred the 20-year-old Kate Upton, shouted for immediate and intimate attention. Only a eunuch or a misogynist would walk away from the promise of such female pulchritude.

The veneer of respectability of the White American Male conceals however a heart with a history of disrespect of and cruelty to women, especially black women. In *Lincoln* Gore Vidal relates the story of Eliza who had belonged to a well-to-do family. When the family died out, Eliza was put up for sale by their distant heirs. Ordinarily, wrote Vidal, it would have been a familiar if depressing story, but the case of Eliza was much discussed in the press because she was a lovely white girl of eighteen who happened to be one sixty-fourth Negro. At the auction, wrote Vidal, the Reverend Calvin Fairbank had bid against a Frenchman from New Orleans who, it was rumored, kept a brothel. "The courthouse square was crowded. People had come from miles around. Abolitionists had threatened violence." In the book Mrs. Lincoln tells Salmon P. Chase, one of Lincoln's Cabinet ministers, that she had watched the bidding. She herself was only a few years older than the girl who stood, shuddering, on the block, the tall auctioneer beside her. When the Frenchman's bids began to flag – the price had gone to a thousand dollars – the auctioneer had shouted, "Come on, you mean-hearted gentlemen! Look at what I've got!" With that he pulled down the girl's blouse. Mary Lincoln remembered the horrified gasp from the crowd. "Many ladies turned away. Yet when a black woman was stripped, no one had ever noticed," she said. The bidding resumed, then flagged again. This time the auctioneer pulled up the girl's skirt to show her naked thighs. There were now shouts of anger from a part of the crowd, and raucous shouts and whistles from the other. Finally the girl was sold to the Reverend Fairbank. And when Fairbank went to take down the weeping girl from the block, a loud voice shouted, "What're you going to do with her now?" "I am going to set her free," shouted Fairbank And as Mary Lincoln recalled there was almost a civil war right there and then in Lexington's courthouse square.

And yet, the truth is many American behave as though this history is not part of their lives and that this New World version of

Sodom and Gomorrah in the heart of the Nevada desert does not exist on American soil. I guess it is the same ethic that hoped in the time of Lincoln to spread slavery to other states because politicians and the public closed their eyes to the ruthlessness of slavery's masters. Whatever the defect, graying American politicians would like us to think that the country is without the stain of original sin. As Adam and Eve did in the garden after they had eaten the forbidden fruit and when they heard God's approaching footsteps, these politicians hide behind their banana leaves every time the safe-guarding of women's dignity is mentioned by the media or by an abused woman. I would have thought that Las Vegas is all the proof they need to admit that Americans do not really have to conceal their liberal views of sex. And the fact is when these men do so their dishonesty creates at once an environment of hypocrisy and loathing for leaders whose job Americans see as setting standards of truth and morality.

But look what is happening in God's new Promised Land:

Mitt Romney called on Congressman Todd Akin to drop out of the Missouri Senate race because of remarks he had made about "legitimate rape". It requires a heart and mind made of asbestos not to sneer every time a Republican talks about sex. Drop out. Was that it? Mr. Romney hadn't given any hint for instance that he should reprimand Rush Limbaugh for calling Sandra Fluke a slut. Dyland Stableford of Yahoo! News / The Ticket reported on the aftermath of Romney's call that the embattled Republican Congressman released a new campaign ad asking for "forgiveness". Facing a fury of calls from his own party to drop out of the Missouri Senate race Akin released a new campaign ad apologizing for his comments and asking for forgiveness. "Rape is an evil act," Akin says in the 30-second ad. "I used the wrong words in the wrong way and for that I apologize. As the father of two daughters, I want tough justice for predators. I have a compassionate heart for the victims of sexual assault. I pray for them. The fact is rape can lead to pregnancy. The truth is rape has many victims. The mistake I made was in the words I said, not in the heart I hold. I ask for your forgiveness."

Can you believe this idiot?

Republican leaders had called for Akin to abandon his campaign against Democratic incumbent Claire McCaskill, and Romney condemned the "legitimate rape" remarks. "Congressman's Akin comments on rape are insulting, inexcusable and, frankly, wrong," Romney said. "Like millions of other Americans, we found them to be offensive." Akin then canceled a scheduled interview with CNN's Piers Morgan who proceeded to open his primetime show with a shot of Akin's empty chair, calling the Republican Senate candidate a "gutless little twerp" for cancelling the sit-down. "Congressman, you have an open invitation to join me in that chair whenever you feel up to it," Morgan said. "Because if you don't keep your promise to appear on the show, then you are, what we would call in Britain, a gutless little twerp." I didn't like Morgan's language either but I guessed he could have been as angry and disappointed with the member of the Congress as most people were. In an interview on Mike Huckabee's radio show, Akin apologized for his "legitimate rape" comments, but he had the gall to say that he wouldn't drop out of the race. "I'm not a quitter," Akin said. And following the Huckabee interview, Akin tweeted: "I am in this race to win. We need a conservative Senate." No; Morgan was on the right track. What America needs are men who respect women. And women who would not allow men to slander other women as happened in the case of Sandra Fluke.

Akins' new campaign ad hit the airwaves a day after the powerful conservative super PAC Crossroads GPS announced it was pulling its advertising money from the Missouri Senate race amid the political firestorm Akin's comments created. "First of all, from what I understand from doctors (is that) pregnancy after rape is really rare," Akin told St. Louis' KTVI-TV Fox affiliate in an interview broadcast. "If it's a legitimate rape, the female body has ways to try to shut that whole thing down." Akin said that even if a rape victim does somehow become pregnant, "there should be some punishment, but the punishment ought to be on the rapist and not attacking the child." I think it's time to send this man to Las Vegas for re-education. And maybe it is time to do the same for Mitt Romney. Hear this:

On 25 October, President Obama made repeated, though indirect, references to Indiana Republican Richard Mourdock's controversial comment on rape and pregnancy. "We've seen again this week, I don't think any male politicians should be making health care decisions for women," Obama told a crowd of about 15,000 in Richmond, Va. The president's aides pressed further, using a web video to highlight Romney's endorsement of Mourdock and to accuse the GOP nominee of kowtowing to his party's extreme elements. Romney, who appeared in a television advertisement declaring his support for Mourdock, ignored repeated questions on the matter. He centered his efforts instead on turning his campaign's claims of momentum into a more practical – and ultimately necessary – road map to winning the required 270 Electoral College votes. Ohio, where he spent all of Thursday and will return Friday evening following the Iowa speech, is crucial to that effort. Romney disavowed Mourdock's comments, but his campaign said he continues to support the Indiana Republican's Senate candidacy.

II

WHAT IS THE problem Americans could ask that Republicans have with women? Rush Limbaugh issued an apology on 3 March 2012 to the Georgetown law student he branded a "slut" in three days of attacks, after she argued to Congress that the expense for her birth control should be covered by her employer's health care plan, Dean Schabner and Matt Negrin of ABC News reported. He said he "did not mean a personal attack" on Sandra Fluke, the Georgetown student. "My choice of words was not the best, and in the attempt to be humorous, I created a national stir. I sincerely apologize to Ms. Fluke for the insulting word choices." The conservative radio host said that throughout his career he has "illustrated the absurd with absurdity, three hours a day, five days a week. In this instance, I chose the wrong words in my analogy of the situation." But Limbaugh mocked President Obama after the president called the young woman to thank her for testifying before Congress on the issue. Shortly before Ms. Fluke gave an interview on the cable network MSNBC, Obama called her to tell her that her parents should be proud of her for speaking out for women. After learning of the president's phone call during his radio show, a day after he chided Fluke over her sex life, Limbaugh made a kissing noise with his lips and mocked Obama. "That is so compassionate. What a great guy," Limbaugh said. "The president called her to make sure she's OK. What is she, 30 years old? Thirty years old, student at Georgetown Law who admits to having so much sex she can't afford it."

In response to a question from ABC News Jake Tapper, White House press secretary Jay Carney said Obama called Fluke to "express his disappointment that she has been the subject of inappropriate personal attacks and to thank her for exercising her rights as a citizen to speak out on an issue of public policy." Limbaugh replied by arguing that Obama should return the $1 million donation that comedian Bill Maher gave his super PAC. "Will President Obama now give back the $1 million that Bill Maher just gave his super PAC?" Limbaugh said on his show. "You want to get some of the tapes that Bill Maher has called Sarah Palin? The 'c' word over and over again?" Limbaugh continued to focus on Fluke, saying she "hilariously" testified to Congress that "she's having so much sex" that health insurance should cover her birth control. "Not one person says, 'Well, did you ever think about maybe backing off the amount of sex you have?'" Limbaugh said. Limbaugh first thrust himself into the center of the contraception debate when he called Fluke a "slut" on his radio show for arguing to Congress that the expense for her birth control should be covered by her employer's health care plan. As the Senate voted down a Republican effort that would have allowed employers not to cover contraception in their health plans, Limbaugh enraged the left by saying that Fluke was "having so much sex she can't afford her own birth control pills and she agrees that Obama should provide them, or the pope."

In an interview with Tapper, Ms. Fluke expressed great appreciation for support she had got across the country. At her Georgetown campus, many students sided with her. "I think everybody on campus, or pretty much everybody I know, was pretty horrified by them," Hannah Dee, a senior, said of Limbaugh's comments. Georgetown President John J. DeGioia praised Fluke's "civil discourse" in a letter to the school and at the same time took a shot at Limbaugh's stance, writing, "And yet, some of those who disagreed with her position – including Rush Limbaugh and commentators throughout the blogosphere and in various other media channels – responded with behavior that can only be described as misogynistic, vitriolic, and a misrepresentation of the position of our student." Limbaugh, who mocked DeGioia's statement repeatedly on his show, appeared to have suffered immediate backlash, at least financially. Two national advertisers – Sleep Number and Quicken Loans – say they have "suspended" their advertising on his show, and a third, ProFlowers, says it is "re-evaluating" its marketing plan.

Democrats see the controversy over contraception funding as a major opportunity to show the Republican Party as bogged down fighting social battles that mainstream America has moved past. Before the Senate debated the legislation that would have repealed President Obama's contraception mandate requiring employers or their insurance companies to cover the cost of contraceptives, Rick Santorum had emerged in the GOP primary largely because of his positions against birth control, women in combat, gay marriage and abortion. In a letter to supporters, House Minority Leader Nancy Pelosi said Democrats had raised more than $1 million in an effort to preserve what they say are women's rights to contraception coverage. The party is also circulating a petition asking supporters to sign a request asking House Republicans to condemn Limbaugh's tirade against Fluke. Boehner's spokesman, Michael Steel, declined to say whether Boehner thinks Limbaugh should apologize. "The speaker obviously believes the use of those words was inappropriate, as is trying to raise money off the situation," Steel said.

Mitt Romney, then the Republican front-runner for the presidential nomination, also waded into the controversy when he told an Ohio reporter that he didn't support the so-called Blunt amendment in the Senate, which would have undermined Obama's proposed mandate, and then said shortly after that he did. Romney's reversal garnered widespread attention, despite his assertion in the same interview that he preferred not to talk about birth control. "The idea of presidential candidates getting into questions about contraception within a relationship between a man and a woman, a husband and wife – I'm not going there," he said in the interview.

The furor was undoubtedly a pleasant event for Obama, who, even after drawing criticism for a rule that required religious groups to cover contraceptive services, has avoided the spotlight as the GOP and prominent conservative voices like Limbaugh focused on cultural matters rather than highlighting many Americans' dissatisfaction about the state of the economy. The willingness to move away from the economy conversation likely reflects the importance of key Southern states that will vote in the Republican primaries on "Super Tuesday", where social issues remain important to conservative and religious voters.

The focus on divisive cultural issues is reminiscent of the political sparring over gay marriage during the 2004 presidential race that drove Republicans to the polls in many Southern states to oppose efforts to make it legal. President Bush's 2004 campaign manager, Ken Mehlman, who announced in 2010 that he is gay, said in an interview with Salon that he wished he "had spoken out against the effort" to enact an amendment banning gay marriage. "As I've been involved in the fight for marriage equality, one of the things I've learned is how many people were harmed by the campaigns in which I was involved," he said. "I apologize to them and tell them I am sorry. While there have been recent victories, this could still be a long struggle in which there will be setbacks, and I'll do my part to be helpful."

The absurdity of this war on women that Republicans seemed to like was reflected in a University of Vermont fraternity that was suspended over a survey that asked members who they would like to rape. According to an Associated Press report from Burlington, Vt., on 14 December 2011 the fraternity was to get a visit from a representative of the fraternity's national headquarters. The national Sigma Phi Epsilon organization says in a statement that it has instructed the chapter to cease all operation, pending further investigation. It says that any behavior that demeans women is not tolerated. University officials say the survey question was "incredibly offensive and inappropriate." They are investigating where the survey came from, who saw it and how it was used. Officials say a student reported the survey to the university. School officials contacted the national fraternity and police to determine if any crimes have been committed.

III

AND YET Romney is hoping not just to win the black vote but also the women's vote from Obama. Aware of this Liz Goodwin of Yahoo! News | The Ticket explained three myths about women voters that didn't go away in 2012. "In the bitterly fought battle for women voters this election season," she wrote, "both candidates dwelled on issues like equal pay, abortion, access to contraception and women's unemployment." And the news media eagerly speculated on the candidates' chance of success with female voters, who made up 53 per cent of the electorate in 2008. "In the process, a few major myths emerged about the female voter, from their views on abortion to whether their dating life influences them in the voting booth." Here are three of the biggest ones that I quote verbatim and for the historical record:

Myth No. 1: Women are more in favor of abortion rights than men are. For the past year Democrats argued Republicans are waging a 'war on women' for wanting to make all abortions illegal, while Republicans countered that Democrats don't want any restrictions on abortion. Each side is attempting to paint the other as extreme, hoping to pick up on-the-fence women voters in the process. But, despite how they are sometimes portrayed in the news media and by political candidates, female voters are about as divided on abortion as men are. "One of the central myths in American politics is that women are more pro-choice than men," Karen Kaufman, an associate professor at the University of Maryland who has researched the gender gap, told Yahoo News. In 2011, 59 per cent of men and 56 per cent of women said in a Gallup poll that abortion should be legal in no circumstances or only in a few. Men and women are much more divided on the issue of war (women oppose military interventions) and the role of government (women are more wary of federal spending cuts) than on abortion.

That fact may come as a surprise in this election in particular, as abortion and reproductive issues took on a huge role. Mitt Romney criticized President Barack Obama for requiring employers' insurance plans to provide free contraception, calling the health care reform's mandate an infringement on employers' freedom of religion. Meanwhile, to paint Romney as extreme and out of touch, Obama seized on the abortion-related comments of a handful of Republicans like Missouri Senate candidate Todd Akin, who said women who are raped should not be allowed to access legal abortions because he believed, falsely, that they could not physically become pregnant. Rutgers political scientist Susan Carroll told Yahoo News she has not seen a presidential election contest as focused on abortion and reproductive rights since 1972, the year before Roe v. Wade was decided. "Candidates have wanted to run away from abortion in previous elections," Carroll sad. "When you talk about it, you alienate someone."

Despite the fact that women are about equally split on abortion, it still makes sense that the Obama campaign has relentlessly highlighted comments from Akin, Indiana Senate candidate Richard Mourdock, and a few other Republicans explaining why they think abortions should be illegal in all circumstances. The majority of both men and women think abortions should be legal in cases of rape or the health of the mother, so the ads paint the candidates, and by extension, Romney, as outside of the mainstream. Playing defense, Romney put up TV ads in three key swing states saying he would not outlaw abortion in these cases and does not oppose contraception. An anti-abortion group, meanwhile, bought ads in swing states calling Obama "an abortion radical" for sending federal funding to clinics that perform abortions.

According to a CBS News poll, more women than men (38 per cent) will only support a candidate who shares their views on abortion. One such voter is Susan Moore, an anti-abortion physical education teacher in the Columbus, Ohio, suburb of Groveport. She told Yahoo News that she's voting for Romney even though she disagrees with the Republicans' tough line on teachers' unions. "It's economics versus values," she said. "I'd vote conviction over jobs, I guess." Moore said she would support Obama if he were against abortion. Polls suggest that birth control and funding for Planned Parenthood are more clearly winning issues for the Obama campaign. A majority of both women and men in a Gallup/*USA Today* poll rate Obama higher than Romney on his handling of birth control policy. The poll found that more than 30 per cent of women in 12 swing states said a candidate's birth control policy would be "very important" for how they vote.

Myth No. 2: The gender gap is about the "war on women." Carroll says the Obama campaign's focus on reproductive rights is ultimately a way to motivate women who already support Obama to vote on Election Day, rather than a way to sway women in the middle away from Romney. "The people in the base turn out the vote and they need to mobilize them," Carroll said. "Those issues, the fact that women might not be able to get contraception, that can help to motivate women in the base." That prediction seems to be supported by polling. The latest ABC News/*Washington Post* tracking poll shows that the female gender gap in favor of Obama has held steady at 7 percentage points. Meanwhile, men back Romney by six points more than women, which keep the race at a dead heat. The 7-point female gap in favor of Obama is in line with the female-male spread that political scientists have observed for 30 years. Women began consistently voting for Democrats in higher proportions than men starting in the 1980 presidential election between Jimmy Carter and Ronald Reagan. But you wouldn't know that if you turned on cable news, where pundits wonder whether women don't support Romney because Democrats say he and other Republicans are waging a "war on women", on abortion and contraception.

Right now, "the average gender gap is approximately the average of the past nine presidential elections," ABC News/*Washington Post* pollster Gary Langer told Yahoo News. "It doesn't come from any dynamic in this election. Women are about 10 percentage points more likely to describe themselves as Democrats than Republicans. [The gap] comes from a substantial sense among women that the Democratic Party is better attuned to women's issues." Political scientists say more women than men vote Democratic in part because men and women see the role of government fundamentally differently. Women are more wary of federal spending cuts, and tend to support safety net programs more than the average male voter. Women are also more opposed to military interventions than men. Shirley Hutner, a manager at a manufacturing company in Indiana, told Yahoo News she voted for John McCain in 2008 but is voting for Obama this time around in part because of his stance on welfare programs. "I've never been unemployed, I've always been lucky, I've always had a job," Hutner, 40, said. "But if I ever needed help, I would feel like I would be able to get help from the Obama administration and not so much from Romney." Hutner said she also worries about older workers who were laid off and can't get companies to hire them. Two of Hutner's female friends adamantly disagreed, however, saying many people on welfare feel "entitled" and are riding the system. "The problem is, everybody counts on that," said Hutner's friend Beverly Brouse, who is voting for Romney. "At some point, that's going to blow up."

Myth No. 3: Women vote like they date. Pundits often conflate a woman's voting and dating preferences. Matthew Dowd, a former aide to President George W. Bush, wrote in an ABC News article (*What women want in a president*) that women "want to be in a relationship with a man who is clear, strong, kind ... and can make a woman feel protected and safe." Dowd used this dating prism to postulate that women voters moved to Romney after the first presidential debate in Denver because he came across as strong and the president as weak. Kevin D. Williamson at *National Review* argued that because women select reproductive mates for their "status", Romney should emphasize his personal wealth to win the female vote by a landslide. "From an evolutionary point of view, Mitt Romney should get 100 per cent of the female vote. ... You can insert your own Mormon polygamy joke here, but the ladies do tend to flock to successful executives and entrepreneurs," Williamson wrote.

Here's the conclusion to these myths: We're not quite sure where the trope that women approach the ballot box like it's an episode of *The Bachelorette* comes from, but pollsters are skeptical of the claims. "I don't know where that comes from," Langer said. "I think women base their political attitudes on substantive issues." Studies have shown that both men and women tend to unconsciously vote for more attractive candidates, which fits in with a large body of research that shows physical attractiveness is rewarded in the workplace. Because the major presidential candidates over the past 20 years have been wealthy, there's not much research on how a candidate's personal wealth affects voters, male or female.

IV

WRITING FROM Defiance, Ohio, on 26 October 2012 Julie Pace and Steve Peoples of the Associated Press reported that Romney is renewing his focus on the nation's economy while facing continued pressure to break his silence on a GOP Senate candidate's statement that any pregnancy resulting from rape is "something God intended." As Election Day looms less than two weeks away, the Republican presidential contender is also trying to move past new questions about his role in a key supporter's divorce. Court documents released on 24

October revealed that Romney created a special class of company stock for Staples founder Tom Stemberg's then-wife as a "favor".

Romney has so far ignored the criticism and is instead accusing President Obama of playing partisan politics in an "incredibly shrinking campaign." He said, "This campaign is growing. The momentum is building. We're taking back America." Romney told 12,000 supporters in Ohio the same night that media trackers confirmed the Republican's campaign was expanding its television advertising into Minnesota. The economy was to play prominently in the presidential contest on 26 October. And as Obama takes a break from the campaign trail, Romney was to deliver what his campaign billed as a significant economic address in swing state Iowa. While he was not expected to break new ground, his campaign said Romney would use the speech to help crystalize the differences between each candidate's economic approach on the same day the government issues its final report on GDP growth before the 6 November election. The report was expected to show that growth picked up only slightly in the third quarter. Tepid growth has given Romney an opening to challenge Obama's assessment that the economy is moving in the right direction.

Obama arrived back in Washington late on 25 October following a 40-hour battleground state blitz that took him to eight states. He was taking a brief break from the campaign trail the next day and planned to spend much of the day at the White House. But the Democratic campaign wasn't ceding the spotlight to Romney. Obama had a series of interviews scheduled, including several with local television stations in swing states. And the campaign announced on 26 October that the president will travel next week to Colorado, Wisconsin and Ohio for a series of campaign rallies and events. The president was also using a trio of national interviews to reach key constituencies, including an MTV interview aimed at rallying the youth vote and a sit-down with American Urban Radio Networks, which has a largely black audience. The president was also scheduled to talk with Michael Smerconish, the conservative-leaning radio host who backed Obama in the 2008 election.

The Republican Party still believed it had to have a plan to neutralize President Obama's success with women voters and not surprisingly it felt it had to get a woman to say what a great fellow Mitt Romney is. He had said that he felt he wasn't liked so how would he overcome this disadvantage? Simply by getting someone whom the American public could trust to list his good points. And the person to do this was the candidate's wife, Ann Romney. At the Republican National Convention Mrs. Romney began her address with the words, "I want to talk to you tonight not about politics and not about party. And while there are many important issues we'll hear discussed in this convention and throughout this campaign, tonight I want to talk to you from my heart about our hearts. I want to talk not about what divides us, but what holds us together as an American family. I want to talk to you tonight about that one great thing that unites us, that one thing that brings us our greatest joy when times are good and the deepest solace in our dark hours. Tonight I want to talk to you about love. I want to talk to you about the deep and abiding love I have for a man I met at a dance many years ago. And the profound love I have, and I know we share, for this country. I want to talk to you about that love so deep only a mother can fathom it – the love we have for our children and our children's children. And I want us to think tonight about the love we all share for those Americans, our brothers and sisters, who are going through difficult times, whose days are never easy, nights are always long, and whose work never seems done.

"They are here among us tonight in this hall; they are here in neighborhoods across Tampa and all across America. The parents who lie awake at night side by side wondering how they'll be able to pay the mortgage or make the rent; the single dad who's working extra hours tonight so that his kids can buy some new clothes to go back to school, can take a school trip or play a sport, so his kids can feel... like the other kids; and the working moms who love their jobs but who would like to work just a little less to spend more time with the kids. But that's just out of the question with this economy. Or that couple who would like to have another child, but wonder how they will afford it. I've been all across this country for the past year and a half and heard these stories of how hard it is to get ahead now. I've heard your voices: 'I'm running in place', 'we just can't get ahead.'

"Sometimes I think that late at night, if we were all silent for just a few moments and listened carefully, we could hear a great collective sigh from the moms and dads across America who made it through another day, and know that they'll make it through another one

426

tomorrow. But in that end of the day moment, they just aren't sure how. And if you listen carefully, you'll hear the women sighing a little bit more than the men. It's how it is, isn't it? It's the moms who always have to work a little harder, to make everything right. It's the moms of this nation – single, married, widowed – who really hold this country together. We're the mothers, we're the wives, we're the grandmothers, we're the big sisters, we're the little sisters, we're the daughters. You know it's true, don't you?

"You're the ones who always have to do a little more. You know what it's like to work a little harder during the day to earn the respect you deserve at work and then come home to help with that book report which just has to be done. You know what those late night phone calls with an elderly parent are like and the long weekend drives just to see how they're doing. You know the fastest route to the local emergency room and which doctors actually answer the phone when you call at night. You know what it's like to sit in that graduation ceremony and wonder how it was that so many long days turned into years that went by so quickly. You are the best of America. You are the hope of America. There would not be an America without you. Tonight, we salute you and sing your praises.

"I'm not sure if men really understand this, but I don't think there's a woman in America who really expects her life to be easy. In our own ways, we all know better! And that's fine. We don't want easy. But these last few years have been harder than they needed to be. It's all the little things – that price at the pump you just can't believe, the grocery bills that just get bigger; all those things that used to be free, like school sports, are now one more bill to pay. It's all the little things that pile up to become big things. And the big things – the good jobs, the chance at college, that home you want to buy, just get harder. Everything has become harder.

"We're too smart to know there aren't easy answers. But we're not dumb enough to accept that there aren't better answers. And that is where this boy I met at a high school dance comes in. His name is Mitt Romney and you really should get to know him. I could tell you why I fell in love with him – he was tall, laughed a lot, was nervous – girls like that, it shows the guy's a little intimidated – and he was nice to my parents but he was really glad when my parents weren't around. That's a good thing. And he made me laugh.

"I am the granddaughter of a Welsh coal miner who was determined that his kids get out of the mines. My dad got his first job when he was six years old, in a little village in Wales called Nantyffyllon, cleaning bottles at the Colliers Arms. When he was 15, Dad came to America. In our country, he saw hope and an opportunity to escape from poverty. He moved to a small town in the great state of Michigan. There, he started a business – one he built himself, by the way. He raised a family. And he became mayor of our town. My dad would often remind my brothers and me how fortunate we were to grow up in a place like America. He wanted us to have every opportunity that came with life in this country – and so he pushed us to be our best and give our all. Inside the houses that lined the streets of our town, there were a lot of good fathers teaching their sons and daughters those same values. I didn't know it at the time, but one of those dads was my future father-in-law, George Romney. Mitt's dad never graduated from college. Instead, he became a carpenter. He worked hard, and he became the head of a car company, and then the governor of Michigan. When Mitt and I met and fell in love, we were determined not to let anything stand in the way of our life together. I was an Episcopalian. He was a Mormon. We were very young. Both still in college. There were many reasons to delay marriage, and, you know, we just didn't care. We got married and moved into a basement apartment. We walked to class together, shared the housekeeping, and ate a lot of pasta and tuna fish. Our desk was a door propped up on sawhorses. Our dining room table was a fold-down ironing board in the kitchen. Those were very special days.

"Then our first son came along. All at once I'm 22 years old, with a baby and a husband who's going to business school and law school at the same time, and I can tell you, probably like every other girl who finds herself in a new life far from family and friends, with a new baby and a new husband, that it dawned on me that I had absolutely no idea what I was getting into. That was 42 years ago. Now we have five sons and 18 grandchildren and I'm still in love with that boy I met at a high school dance. I read somewhere that Mitt and I have a 'storybook marriage'. Well, in the storybooks I read, there were never long, long, rainy winter afternoons in a house with five boys screaming at once. And those storybooks never seemed to have chapters called MS or Breast Cancer. A storybook marriage? No, not at all. What Mitt Romney and I have is a real marriage.

"I know this good and decent man for what he is – warm and loving and patient. He has tried to live his life with a set of values centered on family, faith, and love of one's fellow man. From the time we were first married, I've seen him spend countless hours helping others. I've seen him drop everything to help a friend in trouble, and been there when late-night calls of panic came from a member of our church whose child had been taken to the hospital. You may not agree with Mitt's positions on issues or his politics. Massachusetts is only 13 per cent Republican, so it's not like that's a shock. But let me say this to every American who is thinking about who should be our next President: No one will work harder. No one will care more. No one will move heaven and earth like Mitt Romney to make this country a better place to live!

"It's true that Mitt has been successful at each new challenge he has taken on. It amazes me to see his history of success actually being attacked. Are those really the values that made our country great? As a mom of five boys, do we want to raise our children to be afraid of success? Do we send our children out in the world with the advice 'Try to do... okay?' And let's be honest. If the last four years had been more successful, do we really think there would be this attack on Mitt Romney's success? Of course not.

"Mitt will be the first to tell you that he is the most fortunate man in the world. He had two loving parents who gave him strong values and taught him the value of work. He had the chance to get the education his father never had. But as his partner on this amazing journey, I can tell you Mitt Romney was not handed success. He built it. He stayed in Massachusetts after graduate school and got a job. I saw the long hours that started with that first job. I was there when he and a small group of friends talked about starting a new company. I was there when they struggled and wondered if the whole idea just wasn't going to work. Mitt's reaction was to work harder and press on. Today that company has become another great American success story.

"Has it made those who started the company successful beyond their dreams? Yes, it has. It allowed us to give our sons the chance at good educations and made all those long hours of book reports and homework worth every minute. It's given us the deep satisfaction of being able to help others in ways that we could never have imagined.

Mitt doesn't like to talk about how he has helped others because he sees it as a privilege, not a political talking point. And we're no different than the millions of Americans who quietly help their neighbors, their churches and their communities. They don't do it so that others will think more of them. They do it because there is no greater joy. 'Give and it shall be given unto you.' But because this is America, that small company which grew has helped so many others lead better lives. The jobs that grew from the risks they took have become college educations, first homes. That success has helped fund scholarships, pensions, and retirement funds. This is the genius of America: dreams fulfilled help others launch new dreams.

"At every turn in his life, this man I met at a high school dance, has helped lift up others. He did it with the Olympics, when many wanted to give up. He did it in Massachusetts, where he guided a state from economic crisis to unemployment of just 4.7 percent. Under Mitt, Massachusetts's schools were the best in the nation. The best. He started the John and Abigail Adams scholarships, which give the top 25 percent of high school graduates a four-year tuition-free scholarship. This is the man America needs. This is the man who will wake up every day with the determination to solve the problems that others say can't be solved, to fix what others say is beyond repair. This is the man who will work harder than anyone so that we can work a little less hard.

"I can't tell you what will happen over the next four years. But I can only stand here tonight, as a wife, a mother, a grandmother, an American, and make you this solemn commitment: This man will not fail. This man will not let us down. This man will lift up America! It has been 47 years since that tall, kind of charming young man brought me home from our first dance. Not every day since has been easy. But he still makes me laugh. And never once did I have a single reason to doubt that I was the luckiest woman in the world. I said tonight I wanted to talk to you about love. Look into your hearts. This is our country. This is our future. These are our children and grandchildren.

"You can trust Mitt. He loves America. He will take us to a better place, just as he took me home safely from that dance. Give him that chance. Give America that chance."

V

ACCORDING TO a report released in September 2010 and quoted by Susan Heavey of Reuters, America's middle class has shrunk drastically over the last 10 years as Americans' net worth has plunged, wages declined and standards of living slipped away, Middle-income earners, long seen as the solid center of the country, are pessimistic and place the blame squarely on U.S. lawmakers, banks and big business, the findings by the Pew Research Center showed. "America's middle class has endured its worst decade in modern history," researchers wrote. Since 2001, median household income has fallen from $72,956 to $69,487 in 2010, the report said. The median household net worth, which is the value of assets minus debt, dropped from $129,582 to $93,150 over the same 10-year period, according to Pew, which analyzed U.S. data along with its own survey of nearly 1,300 adults who consider themselves middle class.

The nonpartisan research group's snapshot comes in the midst of a close presidential campaign that has become in part a referendum on whether President Barack Obama's policies over the last few years have helped Americans as the nation struggles to recover from deep economic woes. His Republican rival Mitt Romney, a multi-millionaire former private equity executive who is one of the richest men ever to run for president, has based his campaign on his pledge to build jobs and boost the economy. The Pew survey found more of the middle class support Obama's policies than Romney's. More than half (52 per cent) of those polled said Obama's policies would help the middle class in a second term, while 39 per cent say they would not. Forty-two per cent said Romney would benefit middle income Americans if elected, while 40 per cent say his policies would not help, the survey showed. Researchers said they found that "neither candidate has sealed the deal with them, but that President Obama is in somewhat better shape than his Republican challenger, Mitt Romney."

The plight of the middle class has become a bellwether of the U.S. economy in the wake of the recent Great Recession that officially ran from December 2007 to June 2009, ending just six months into Obama's first term. According to the poll, 62 per cent of respondents said Congress deserved "a lot" of the blame for the nation's economic troubles over the past decade, while 29 per cent blamed lawmakers "a little". Banks and financial institutions as well as large corporations were also largely at fault, respondents told Pew. Various surveys have shown Americans – particularly women, minorities, children and young adults – are still struggling amid the slowest economic recovery since the 1980-81 period. Pew's analysis is based on data from the Census Bureau as well as the Federal Reserve Bank and is broadly in line with separate reports from the two government entities that were released in June. According to the Census Bureau, household wealth declined by 35 per cent to $66,740 between 2005 and 2010 as home values and share prices plummeted. The Fed report showed median family net worth plunged to $77,300 in 2010 from $126,400 in 2007.

For its report, Pew defined middle class as households with incomes from $39,000 to $118,000, a range that is between two-thirds and double the national median. Its survey is based on telephone interviews from July 16 to July 26 with 1,287 U.S. adults who identified as middle class and has a margin of error of plus-or-minus 2.8 percentage points.

But there is more from the Pew poll says Hope Yen of the Associated Press. As the income gap between rich and poor widens, a majority of Americans say the growing divide is bad for the country and believe that wealthy people are paying too little in taxes, according to the survey. The poll released by the Pew Research Center points to a particular challenge for Republican presidential candidate Mitt Romney, whose party's policies are viewed by a wide majority as favoring the rich over the middle class and poor. The poll found that many Americans believe rich people to be intelligent and hardworking but also greedy and less honest than the average American. Nearly six in 10, or 58 per cent, say the rich don't pay enough in taxes, while 26 per cent believe the rich pay their fair share and 8 per cent say they pay too much. Even among those who describe themselves as "upper class" or "upper middle class", more than half – or 52 per cent – said upper-income Americans don't pay enough in taxes; only 10 per cent said they paid too much. This upper tier was more likely to say they are more financially secure now than 10 years ago – 62 per cent, compared to 44 per cent for those who identified themselves as middle class and 29 per cent for the lower class. They are less likely to report problems in paying rent or mortgage, losing a job, paying for medical care or other bills and cutting back on household expenses.

The findings came at the start of the week's Republican National Convention and as both Romney and President Barack Obama seek to appeal to a broad swath of financially struggling voters who identify as middle class. Romney supports an extension of Bush-era tax cuts for everyone including the wealthiest 2 per cent, and says his policies will benefit the middle class by boosting the economy and creating jobs. "The fact that Romney may be viewed as wealthy doesn't necessarily pose problems for his candidacy," said Kim Parker, associate director of Pew Social & Demographic Trends, noting that people see the wealthy as having both positive and negative attributes. "The challenge for Romney lies more in the fact that large majorities say if he is elected president, his policies would likely benefit the wealthy."

The results reinforce a tide of recent economic data showing a widening economic divide. America's middle class has been shrinking in the stagnant economy and poverty is now approaching 1960s highs, while wealth concentrates at the top. A separate Pew survey earlier this year found that tensions between the rich and poor were increasing and at their most intense level in nearly a quarter-century. In fact, well-off people do shoulder a big share of the tax burden. Though households earning over $1 million annually comprise just 0.3 per cent of all taxpayers, they pay 20 per cent of all federal taxes the government is projected to collect this year, according to the Tax Policy Center, a nonpartisan group that studies tax policy. The figures included income, payroll and estate taxes. In contrast, households earning $50,000 to $75,000 a year accounted for 12 per cent of taxpayers and contributed 9 per cent of federal taxes, the center's data showed. Some 46 per cent of households pay no federal income tax at all, although they do pay payroll, excise and other taxes.

VI

IN HER SPEECH to the Democratic National Convention, Massachusetts Senate candidate Elizabeth Warren said that the American system of government is "rigged" against the middle class, according to Chris Moody of Yahoo! News. "People feel like the system is rigged against them. And here's the painful part: they're right," Warren said in her first address to a party convention. "The system is rigged. Look around. Oil companies guzzle down billions in subsidies. Billionaires pay lower tax rates than their secretaries. Wall Street CEOs – the same ones who wrecked our economy and destroyed millions of jobs – still strut around Congress, no shame, demanding favors, and acting like we should thank them. Anyone here has a problem with that? Well I do."

Warren is running against Republican Massachusetts Sen. Scott Brown, who won the seat in a 2010 special election following the death of former Sen. Edward Kennedy. She said, "I'm here tonight to talk about hard-working people: people who get up early, stay up late, cook dinner and help out with homework; people who can be counted on to help their kids, their parents, their neighbors, and the lady down the street whose car broke down; people who work their hearts out but are up against a hard truth -- the game is rigged against them. It wasn't always this way. Like a lot of you, I grew up in a family on the ragged edge of the middle class. My daddy sold carpeting and ended up as a maintenance man. After he had a heart attack, my mom worked the phones at Sears so we could hang on to our house. My three brothers all served in the military. One was career. The second worked a good union job in construction. The third started a small business.

"Me, I was waiting tables at 13 and married at 19. I graduated from public schools and taught elementary school. I have a wonderful husband, two great children, and three beautiful grandchildren. And I'm grateful, down to my toes, for every opportunity that America gave me. This is a great country. I grew up in an America that invested in its kids and built a strong middle class; that allowed millions of children to rise from poverty and establish secure lives; an America that created Social Security and Medicare so that seniors could live with dignity; an America in which each generation built something solid so that the next generation could build something better.

"But for many years now, our middle class has been chipped, squeezed, and hammered. Talk to the construction worker I met from Malden, Massachusetts, who went nine months without finding work. Talk to the head of a manufacturing company in Franklin trying to protect jobs but worried about rising costs. Talk to the student in Worcester who worked hard to finish his college degree, and now he's drowning in debt. Their fight is my fight, and it's Barack Obama's fight too. People feel like the system is rigged against them. And here's the painful part: they're right. The system is rigged. Look around. Oil companies guzzle down billions in subsidies. Billionaires pay lower tax rates than their secretaries. Wall Street CEOs – the same ones who wrecked our economy and destroyed millions of jobs – still strut around Congress, no shame, demanding favors, and acting like we should thank them.

"Anyone here has a problem with that? Well I do. I talk to small business owners all across Massachusetts. Not one of them – not one – made big bucks from the risky Wall Street bets that brought down our economy. I talk to nurses and programmers, salespeople and firefighters – people who bust their tails every day. Not one of them – not one – stashes their money in the Cayman Islands to avoid paying their fair share of taxes. These folks don't resent that someone else makes more money. We're Americans. We celebrate success. We just don't want the game to be rigged. We've fought to level the playing field before. About a century ago, when corrosive greed threatened our economy and our way of life, the American people came together under the leadership of Teddy Roosevelt and other progressives, to bring our nation back from the brink.

"We started to take children out of factories and put them in schools. We began to give meaning to the words 'consumer protection' by making our food and medicine safe. And we gave the little guys a better chance to compete by preventing the big guys from rigging the markets. We turned adversity into progress because that's what we do.

"Americans are fighters. We are tough, resourceful and creative. If we have the chance to fight on a level playing field – where everyone pays a fair share and everyone has a real shot – then no one can stop us. President Obama gets it because he's spent his life fighting for the middle class. And now he's fighting to level that playing field – because we know that the economy doesn't grow from the top down, but from the middle class out and the bottom up. That's how we create jobs and reduce the debt.

"And Mitt Romney? He wants to give tax cuts to millionaires and billionaires. But for middle-class families who are hanging on by their fingernails? His plans will hammer them with a new tax hike of up to 2,000 dollars. Mitt Romney wants to give billions in breaks to big corporations – but he and Paul Ryan would pulverize financial reform, voucher-ize Medicare, and vaporize Obamacare. The Republican vision is clear: 'I've got mine, the rest of you are on your own.' Republicans say they don't believe in government. Sure they do. They believe in government to help themselves and their powerful friends. After all, Mitt Romney's the guy who said corporations are people.

"No, Governor Romney, corporations are not people. People have hearts, they have kids, they get jobs, they get sick, they cry, they dance. They live, they love, and they die. And that matters. That matters because we don't run this country for corporations, we run it for people. And that's why we need Barack Obama.

"After the financial crisis, President Obama knew that we had to clean up Wall Street. For years, families had been tricked by credit cards, fooled by student loans and cheated on mortgages. I had an idea for a consumer financial protection agency to stop the rip-offs. The big banks sure didn't like it, and they marshaled one of the biggest lobbying forces on earth to destroy the agency before it ever saw the light of day. American families didn't have an army of lobbyists on our side, but what we had was a president – President Obama leading the way. And when the lobbyists were closing in for the kill, Barack Obama squared his shoulders, planted his feet, and stood firm. And that's how we won. By the way, just a few weeks ago, that little agency caught one of the biggest credit card companies cheating its customers and made it give people back every penny it took, plus millions of dollars in fines. That's what happens when you have a president on the side of the middle class.

"President Obama believes in a level playing field. He believes in a country where nobody gets a free ride or a golden parachute. A country where anyone who has a great idea and rolls up their sleeves has a chance to build a business, and anyone who works hard can build some security and raise a family. President Obama believes in a country where billionaires pay their taxes just like their secretaries do, and – I can't believe I have to say this in 2012 – a country where women get equal pay for equal work.

"He believes in a country where everyone is held accountable, where no one can steal your purse on Main Street or your pension on Wall Street. President Obama believes in a country where we invest in education, in roads and bridges, in science, and in the future, so we can create new opportunities, so the next kid can make it big, and the kid after that, and the kid after that. That's what president Obama believes. And that's how we build the economy of the future. An economy with more jobs and less debt. We root it in fairness. We grow it with opportunity. And we build it together.

"I grew up in the Methodist Church and taught Sunday school. One of my favorite passages of scripture is: 'Inasmuch as ye have done it unto one of the least of these my brethren, ye have done it unto me'. Matthew 25:40. The passage teaches about God in each of us, that we are bound to each other and called to act. Not to sit, not to wait, but to act – all of us together.

"Senator Kennedy understood that call. Four years ago, he addressed our convention for the last time. He said, 'We have never lost our belief that we are all called to a better country and a newer world.' Generation after generation, Americans have answered that call. And now we are called again. We are called to restore opportunity for every American. We are called to give America's working families a fighting chance. We are called to build something solid so the next generation can build something better.

"So let me ask you – let me ask you, America: are you ready to answer this call? Are you ready to fight for good jobs and a strong middle class? Are you ready to work for a level playing field? Are you ready to prove to another generation of Americans that we can build a better country and a newer world?

"Joe Biden is ready. Barack Obama is ready. I'm ready. You're ready. America's ready. Thank you! And God bless America!"

VII

THE AMERICAN income tax system has long been designed to be progressive, meaning higher earners are expected to pay a greater share of their income than those making less. In this year's tax battle in Washington, President Barack Obama wants to let the current top rate of 35 per cent for high earners rise to 39.6 per cent next year. Congressional Republicans would reduce the top rate to 25 per cent, while Republican Mitt Romney would reduce it to 28 per cent. Romney and GOP lawmakers have said they would eliminate some deductions to pay for the rate reductions, but have not specified which ones. According to Pew's latest findings, about 63 per cent of Americans say the GOP favors the rich over the middle class and poor, and 71 per cent say Romney's election would be good for wealthy people. A smaller share, 20 per cent, says the same about the Democratic Party. More Americans – 60 per cent – say if Obama is re-elected his policies will benefit the poor, while half say they will help the middle class and 37 per cent say they will boost the wealthy.

"The Great Recession was not an equal opportunity disemployer," said Sheldon Danziger, a public policy professor at the University of Michigan who describes the gap between rich and poor as the widest in decades. "College graduates, whites and middle-aged workers had fewer and shorter layoffs than high school graduates, blacks, Hispanics and younger workers. And, only a small percentage of the rich work in the hardest-hit industries, like construction and manufacturing."

About 65 per cent of Americans say the gap between rich and poor has gotten wider in the past decade, while 20 per cent believe it has stayed the same and 7 per cent say the gap has gotten smaller. Separately, 57 per cent say a widening income gap is a bad thing for society; just 3 per cent say it is a good thing. Asked to estimate how much a family of four would need to earn to be considered wealthy in their area, the median amount given by survey respondents was $150,000. For middle class, the median amount was $70,000. Many Americans see rich people as more likely to be intelligent (43 per cent) and hardworking (42 per cent) than average Americans. But the rich are also seen as more likely to be greedy (55 per cent). Thirty-four per cent of those surveyed say the rich are less likely to be honest than the average person; just 12 per cent say the rich are more likely to be honest.

But this is not the end of the debate on the middle class. Henry Blodget of the Daily Ticker said that the Pew study revealed the real problem with the economy. One of the most important stories in the U.S. economy these days he said is the rise of extreme inequality. "Over the past 30 years, a larger and larger portion of America's income growth has gone to those in the top 10 per cent of incomes, and especially those in the top 1 per cent. This is a major change from the prior 60 years, in which the top 10 per cent and the bottom 90 per cent shared in the income gains." A stark and startling example of this trend is the fact that, adjusted for inflation, "average hourly earnings" in the United States have not increased in 50 years. As reports show the recent Pew study confirms that America's middle class has recently experienced a "lost decade". Since 2000, the Pew study says, "the middle class has shrunk in size, fallen backward in income and wealth, and shed some – but by no means all – of its characteristic faith in the future." Pew cites statistics showing that middle class earnings and net worth have plummeted since the mid-2000s and that about 85 per cent of the middle class say it is harder to maintain their standard of living than it was 10 years ago.

The reason the decline of the middle class is important is not just about fairness. It's about the health of the economy as a whole. Collectively, the middle class represents enormous buying and spending power, and in the past 60 years this spending power has helped the U.S. economy become the envy of the world. But now, however, the middle class is increasingly strapped. And the resulting impact on spending is constraining the growth of companies that sell products and services to American consumers. The causes of this middle-class decline are many, from globalization (jobs being shipped overseas), to the decline of private-sector unions, to the wholesale embrace of a "shareholder value" religion that values profit over everything else that companies produce. But the result of the trend can be seen vividly in two charts. First, wages are now at an all-time low as a percentage of the economy. Second, corporate profits are now at an all-time high.

To truly "fix" the U.S. economy, corporations are going to have to be persuaded to invest more of their excess profits in their employees, both by hiring new employees and paying existing employees more. "Wages" to employees become spending money for those employees, and the spending produces revenue for other companies. If corporations can collectively be persuaded to reinvest more of their profits in their people, in other words, they will help restore their own revenue growth. Henry Ford famously decided to pay his workers more than he had to to keep them. One result of this was that the workers made enough money to be able to buy Ford's cars, and this made Ford more successful. Another result, which is considered irrelevant in some business circles, is that Ford employees were able to live middle class lives. This helped not only Ford, but the country.

VIII

ACCORDING TO Tim Skillern of The Lookout going hungry in America is distressing, humbling and scary. Skillern spoke with a number of Americans to illustrate the point. One of the people he spoke with was Dave Krepcho, director of the Second Harvest Food Bank, who checks inventory at the food bank warehouse in Orlando, Fla. "In the past four years, food distribution to 500 pantries, shelters, and other relief agencies in the six-county area has jumped about 60 per cent. In the last year alone, that amounted to 36 million pounds of food." Krepcho estimates about 30 per cent of those seeking help are first-timers. They are blue-collar and white-collar, many middle class, even some upper middle class. They include college-educated couples and professionals, according to John Raoux of Associated Press. Their stories contradict the view of plenty that the rest of the world has of America and I quote liberally from their findings.

Cheryl Preston knows that others are worse off. But she's still hungry. As grocery prices creep higher and her income sags, rationing her family's food is a daily task. The 54-year-old mother of three and grandmother of three in Roanoke, Va., says there are days she skips meals so her husband and son can eat. If they notice, she says, she'll let them think she's fasting. She waters down the milk and juice to make it last longer. She visits food pantries, but it's not enough. "Who would think that in the land of plenty, hard-working families would go hungry? But I am living proof it is true," Preston writes in a first-person account for Yahoo!

In the last three years, she hasn't been able to replace a $500 loss in monthly income. Her husband's job can't always guarantee 40 hours a week; his second job lasted only through Christmas. So mealtime suffers: Her family eats in one day what they used to eat at one meal. Often, they manage on a nearly barren cupboard for five or six days until the next pay day. They sometimes skip family gatherings at restaurants because they can't pay the tab. "It is distressing," Preston writes. "When you get a check for $250, and your basic needs require at least $400, you are already defeated. You can only cut back so much and then you have no choice but to do without. I long for the days when I could pay my bills on time, buy more than enough groceries and have money left over."

She's not alone. Eighteen per cent of Americans say there have been times this year that they couldn't afford the food they needed, according to a Gallup poll. In particularly hard-hit regions of the United States, like the South, at least one in five didn't have enough money for food. In Preston's Virginia, 15.2 per cent of state residents are affected.

To put a face on hunger in America, Yahoo! asked readers and contributors to share their personal stories: Are they going hungry? How are they coping with higher food prices? Did they ever think they'd be in this position? Here are more personal stories shared with Yahoo! News:

Six years ago, Robert Watkins and his wife earned more than $100,000 combined. Groceries comprised 5 per cent of their budget. They kept an emergency fund – good for three months' expenses – in a money market. Now, Watkins writes, they keep a "rainy day" jar of about $250 in assorted change by the bedside. "If I had to travel to the market and buy groceries for dinner tonight, would I have the money to do so? The truth is, yes, I would," Watkins writes. "Yet it's strange to think that this is life in America today. Like tens of millions of other people in the United States, we look closely at an expenditure that we took for granted just a few years ago – the cost of food."

Seventeen months ago, Watkins was downsized from his job and while he works contractually and part-time, his income "pales in comparison" to two years ago. Couple their one-income family with inflated food prices, and their grocery budget is almost 10 percent of their net income. At 46, he says "it's a humbling exercise." To make due, they have taken advantage of living in a farming community in Lancaster, Pa. Fruits and veggies are affordable; there's plenty of corn on the cob, red potatoes, lettuce, and tomatoes. They create their own dressing and get water from a well. And they eat lots of pasta. "Is it scary sometimes? You bet it is," Watkins writes. "However, it could always be a whole lot worse."

In Arizona, Jeremy Shapiro lives on a nutrition assistance program, receiving $50 a week for food. It's significantly altered his eating habits: less food, less often. "I have reduced my portion sizes and meal frequency," he writes. "Creativity and flexibility is key." Shapiro, 35, says he has always tried to eat healthy. When he was employed and food prices were more reasonable, it was easy. Now it's tricky with less money. "I only shop sales. I hunt for online and paper ads and cut coupons. I also do not stock food unless it's extremely fiscally prudent," Shapiro writes. That means no more fresh fruit; canned and concentrate must suffice. Only frozen chicken, beef and fish are affordable. Brand-name cereals are out. Milk must be on sale, and hormone-free varieties aren't "financially feasible." Generics and store brands have replaced Tillamook cheese, Boar's Head meats and Laura Scudder's peanut butter. "One day, I will have gainful employment and afford more and better again," Shapiro writes. "However for today, I keep my head up and spirits high as best I can."

Here's a taste of Tom Servo's bare-bones grocery list according to Yahoo!: "A few bags of dried beans. Breakfast cereal of some kind – usually whatever's on sale. A large canister of dried oats. Lots of bananas – typically a few pounds. A bag of apples. Other miscellaneous fresh fruits and veggies – whatever's in season and on sale." The 29-year-old college student in Tampa, Fla., says his grocery list is written for nutrition, not taste. He sticks to bare essentials and buys in bulk. But two weeks of groceries used to cost him $50; now it's almost $100. For example: "I used to pay 99 cents for one pound of dried black beans; now they cost $1.49 or more. Two years ago I paid $2.39 for a 16-ounce jar of generic peanut butter; now the same peanut butter costs $3.99. For the first time in my life, I've recently had to make a choice between groceries or some other expense," he writes.

Michelle Zanatta once spoiled her husband with her elaborate Italian meals of fresh vegetables and heaps of garlic bread. They were expensive, too: Her four-cheese lasagna cost $18 to make. The Italian ham and cheese rolls set them back $20. But after her once-successful business started failing and their home went into foreclosure, she faced the reality of food prices. She and her husband are also dealing with higher food costs in Atlanta after a move from Delaware. ("The cost of a fresh-baked loaf of Italian bread was 98 cents from the local Wal-Mart, while here in Georgia it's a $1.49 – plus food tax!") "I at no time thought about how much money I spent grocery shopping, until we had to set a very tight budget," she writes. "I was also never a huge fan of couponing because I thought it was time-consuming; however, at 34, my perspective on coupons has changed greatly." Her family visits local food banks and shaves costs off milk, eggs, cereal and cheese through a WIC program. "Though times seem tough, and my lavish meals have dwindled down to two times a month, my children learned to appreciate those special meals," Zanatta writes, "and I have learned to use my resources and shop smartly."

When she worked as a Wal-Mart cashier, Michelle Croy remembers watching seniors decide between buying food and buying medicine. "Their medicine often ranked first so that meant that Vienna sausages and crackers sufficed for the month for sustenance," she writes. "I never really entertained the thought that someday that would be me." The single mother in Huntington, W.V., says she is shocked she must scramble to pay bills and feed her children. Milk runs upward of $4 a gallon, and a pack of hamburger costs $9. "This is why my family settles with a banana or cereal for breakfast, skips lunches entirely, eats a dinner that is produced almost entirely from our garden, and hardly ever eats out." Croy, now a student teacher in Huntington ("where jobs are as scarce as rain in the Sahara"), writes that while groceries trump other needs and wants, they could be in worse shape. "My case is nowhere near as disheartening as those of the children who go to bed hungry every night, or the families who survive solely on donations from food banks," she writes, "but it's indicative of the reality that most of us middle-class Americans face: We are all just one paycheck away from going hungry or living homeless out on the streets."

But there is another aspect to America's economic troubles. Many Americans writes Bernice Napach of The Daily Ticker / Yahoo! Finance / Parade are not happy in their jobs. According to a joint survey of 26,000 Americans almost 60 per cent would choose a different career. "Now we have the McJob that for so many people in the economy goes nowhere," says The Daily Ticker's Henry Blodget. "The whole idea is that [those jobs] are a stepping stone to something else, and it never is. You can understand why they would be unhappy with that."

It's not just the jobs like those at McDonald's that's upsetting America workers, says Aaron Task of The Daily Ticker. "There are also people working white collar jobs... and feeling like they're just on a treadmill, not getting anywhere." Maybe that's because they're not good at playing office politics. Just over 50 per cent of those surveyed said workers get ahead because of internal politics. Twenty-seven per cent cited hard work and the rest credited initiative or creativity for getting ahead. Despite their unhappiness with work, many Americans expect to work past age 65, according to the survey. Only 33 per cent of respondents expect to retire before they turn 65 years old and 43 per cent plan on retiring between ages 65 and 70. That's almost 80 per cent by the time they turn 71. "That's a tough number," says Task given what's going on with people having to work longer because of their savings situation. "If you don't have any savings, how will you retire at any age?" There will probably still be social security, says Blodget, "but you'll probably get less than what we have now and the retirement age will probably go up."

The survey didn't have details about respondents' retirement savings but found that 53 per cent of workers had just three months' worth of savings to tide them over if they lost their jobs tomorrow. Another 15 per cent had enough savings to last four to six months. Perhaps that's why more than half said they would choose a 5 per cent raise over two weeks more of vacation.

IX

A NEW REPORT outlines the reasons teens give for not taking precautions against pregnancy according to LiveScience. Of teen moms who reported not using birth control, 31 per cent said they did not believe they could get pregnant at the time. To decrease teen birth rates, teens need factual information about the conditions under which pregnancy can occur, along with public health efforts aimed at reducing or delaying teens' sexual activities, according to the report released on 19 January 2012 by researchers for the Centers for Disease and Control and Prevention. Others gave various reasons for not using birth control – 24 per cent said their partner did not want to use contraception, 13 per cent said they had trouble getting birth control, 9 per cent said they experienced side effects from using contraception and 8 per cent said they thought their sex partner was sterile. Twenty-two per cent of the teens said they did not mind getting pregnant. Health care providers and parents can work to prevent teen pregnancy by increasing teens' motivation to avoid pregnancy; providing access to contraception and encouraging the use of more effective methods, and strengthening the skills of teens to negotiate contraceptive use with their partners.

Of all teens who gave birth, 21 per cent reported using a highly effective contraceptive method, such as an intra-uterine device, and an additional 24 per cent reported used condoms. Inconsistent use of contraception may explain how these teens became pregnant, according to the report. Research has shown that teens who report using birth control do not use it consistently, the report noted. One survey found that among sexually active teens who reported using condoms only 52 per cent said they used a condom every time they had sex. The rates of not using birth control did not vary among teens of different racial groups – whether white, black or Hispanic; about half the teens reported not using birth control when they became pregnant. There were some differences among the groups in terms of the reasons teens gave for not using birth control. Forty-two per cent of Hispanic teens reported not using contraception because they did not think they could get pregnant at the time, whereas 32 per cent of black teens gave that reason and 27 per cent of white teens did. Previous research has shown that 17 per cent of all sexually active teens report not using birth control when they last had sex.

About 400,000 U.S. teens ages 15 to 19 give birth each year, which gives the United States the highest teen birth rate in the developed world, according to the report. Teen mothers are more likely than others to drop out of school, and infants born to teens are more likely to have low birth weight, putting them at risk for a number of health conditions, and lower academic achievement, according to the report. The researchers used data from the Pregnancy Risk Assessment Monitoring System, which gathers data on maternal attitudes and experiences before, during and after pregnancy. Thirty-seven states and New York City contribute data to the system. The data used in the report were gathered from 2004 to 2008.

However, birth and abortion rates among U.S. teens fell to record lows in 2008 as increased use of contraceptives sent the overall teen pregnancy rate to its lowest level since at least 1972, a study showed in

February 2012, according to a Reuters report on 8 February 2012 by James B. Kelleher. But disparities among racial and ethnic groups continued to persist, with black and Hispanic teens experiencing pregnancy and abortion rates two to four times higher than their white peers, the Guttmacher Institute, the nonprofit sexual health research group that conducted the analysis, said. The Guttmacher researchers looked at government statistics on teen-age sex, pregnancies and births, as well as the institute's own data on abortions for 2008, the most recent year for which all the numbers were available. They found that nearly 750,000 U.S. women under the age of 20 became pregnant in 2008 – nearly 98 per cent of them between the ages of 15 and 19. That translated into a pregnancy rate of 67.8 pregnancies per 1,000 women aged 15 to 19, the researchers said, the lowest pregnancy rate seen since 1972, the year before the Supreme Court decision in Roe v. Wade that established a woman's right to an abortion. It was also down 42 per cent from 1990, when teen pregnancies peaked at 116.9 per 1,000 teen girls and women. The teen abortion rate in 2008 dropped to the lowest rate seen since 1972 at 17.8 per 1,000 teen girls and women, the analysis found, and was down 59 per cent from 1988 when the abortion rate peaked at 43.5 per 1,000 teen women.

The Guttmacher researchers said the decline in teen birthrates was largely attributable to increased contraceptive use by teens of both genders. "Teens are also using more effective forms of contraception," said Kathryn Kost, a demographer with the Guttmacher Institute who co-authored the analysis. Among women aged 15 to 17, about a quarter of the long-term decline in pregnancies, births and abortions could be attributable to reduced sexual activity, the researchers said. But pregnancy, birth and abortion rates remained much higher for teens that belonged to minority groups, even though their overall rates have fallen over the past four decades. Birth rates for black and Hispanic teens were more than twice those of their white peers in 2008, the researchers found. The abortion rate among black teens, meanwhile, was four times higher than the rate for their Caucasian counterparts. Abortion rates for Hispanic teens were twice as high as for their white peers.

Republican politicians are treading into murky (read: sexist) waters in the contraception debate, writes Jen Doll in The Atlantic Wire on 16 February 2012. Earlier, in protest of House Oversight

Committee Chairman Rep. Darrell Issa's refusal to allow women onto a panel of witnesses at the hearing on the White House mandate to require employers and insurers to provide contraception coverage, Reps. Carolyn Maloney (D-NY) and Eleanor Holmes Norton (D-DC) walked out, garnering a significant amount of media attention and setting off an ensuing furor among women and men. Why no women? Issa said, "The hearing is not about reproductive rights and contraception but instead about the Administration's actions as they relate to freedom of religion and conscience."

Currently under the Obama plan, in cases where religious groups are involved contraception coverage will be offered to women by their employers' insurance companies directly, so that religious employers who oppose contraception don't have to be involved with that nasty business. What Issa means is that the hearing is about whether requiring insurers to cover birth control violates the religious freedom of people who don't believe that birth control should, essentially, exist. The people on his panel, then, were men. Two women appeared on a second panel at the hearing. Both spoke against contraception. How do you take "reproductive rights and contraception" out of a conversation about birth control? You can't. You might try to ignore those parts of the conversation because you want to get a specific answer, for a specific purpose. And allowing women on a panel to talk about how and why they need birth control – and how and why they need insurers to pay for it – detracts from that mission.

In tackier, more sensational headlines, Rick Santorum's pal Foster Friess announced on MSNBC that back in the old days the "gals" used to just put some Bayer Aspirin between their knees as a handy contraception method. In addition to winning "most moronic statement of the day", Friess went on to further belittle the issue of birth control, insinuating that all this focus on stupid lady crap when there are more important issues at stake (like wars), is the marking of a randy, sex-obsessed culture. Here we have millions of our fellow Americans unemployed, we have jihadist camps being set up, which Rick has been warning about, and people seem to be so preoccupied with sex. I think it says something about our culture. We maybe need a massive therapy session so we can concentrate on what the real issues are. Rush Limbaugh comes down on this side, with a bit more of a conspiracy angle, saying Democrats "ginned up" the contraception debate to divide the GOP and distract from the real issues. But what are the real issues? Sex, and everything related to it – you could argue that very little is not related to sex in some way. Surely Friess knows that.

Friess, Limbaugh, and Issa, each in different ways, are trying to de-sexualize and downplay the importance of an issue that is at its core not only about sex but also about men and women, power, religion, socio-economics, relationships, healthcare, equal rights, and, not to speak too broadly, but pretty much our entire global future. This particular hearing is also about freedom of religion and conscience – things that women have opinions on just as much as men do, just like men should care about birth control just as much as women do. But, two facts: Men don't actually get pregnant, and we have nothing to gain from a one-sided conversation about an issue that impacts us all. It's doubly insulting when women, who have been dealing with birth control on their own for years, are left out of the conversation or added as an afterthought.

The simple answer of why men are dominating the conversation on birth control is that, regardless of strides made, men continue to largely dominate the conversation in politics. The more complicated answer is that the men who are dominating the conversation on birth control – and you can count Mitt Romney, Rick Santorum, and Florida Senator Marco Rubio among those who have come out against the White House contraception plan – are deeply afraid of losing the conservative vote, and, it seems, conservatives continue to be deeply afraid of women having free and equal control over their own bodies and all that follows from that. Like having sex; creating fewer unwanted children; and women taking care of themselves.

But there is this too: Roughly 200 million people worldwide use illicit drugs such as marijuana, amphetamines, cocaine and opioids each year, according to a new study. The figure represents about one in 20 people between the ages of 15 and 64, wrote Katie Moisse in ABC News Blog on 6 January 2012. Using a review of published studies, Australian researchers estimated that as many as 203 million people use marijuana, 56 million people use amphetamines including meth, 21 million people use cocaine and 21 million people use opioids like heroin. The use of all four drug classes was highest in developed countries. "Intelligent policy responses to drug problems need better data for the prevalence of different types of illicit drug use and the harms that their use causes globally," reads the report, published in The Lancet. "This need is especially urgent in high-income countries with substantial rates of illicit drug use and in low-income and middle-income countries close to illicit drug production areas."

The 200-million number does not include people who use ecstasy, hallucinogenic drugs, inhalants, benzodiazepines or anabolic steroids – just one reason it's likely a vast underestimate of illicit drug use, according to lead author Louisa Degenhardt of the Sydney-based National Drug and Alcohol Research Center. Drug use is often hidden, particularly when people fear the consequences of being discovered for using drugs, such as being imprisoned, Degenhardt said in a press conference. Up to 39 million people are considered "problematic" or dependent drug users and up to 21 million people inject drugs, according to the report. "It's likely that injectable drug users have increased," said Degenhardt, adding that the practice "is a major direct cause of HIV, hepatitis C and to some extent hepatitis B transmission globally." Cocaine, amphetamine and heroin can be injected either alone or in combination.

Illicit drugs can have dangerous health effects, including overdosing, accidental injury caused by intoxication, dependence and long-term organ damage. While they may not cause immediate death, they're thought to shave 13 million years of the life spans of users worldwide, according to the report. A 2000 report by the World Health Organization attributed roughly 241,000 deaths to illicit drug use – double the number from 1990.

X

IN THIS swamp of bad news there are still examples of personal fortitude among Americans and following reports of some of these, Sue Shellenbarger of *The Wall Street Journal* asked the question, Who Is Likely to Step Up or Freeze Up in a Crisis? Who, for example, will act like Stephen St. Bernard who caught a 7-year-old child who fell from the third floor of a building? How, indeed, would we react in an emergency? Would we risk our lives to help someone in danger? Laurie Ann Eldridge found out last year. Looking up from her garden one evening at her Cameron, N.Y., home, Ms. Eldridge saw a confused 81-year-old driver stuck at a railroad crossing nearby, oblivious of the train speeding toward her car. Ms. Eldridge raced barefoot to the car, wrestled out the disoriented woman, rolled with her down the railway embankment and covered her with her body, just seconds before the train demolished the automobile. Ms. Eldridge's feet were bloody and riddled with splinters. The elderly woman, Angeline C. Pascucci of Le Roy, N.Y., was unhurt.

It is hard to know for sure who will step up and who will freeze up in a crisis. But, amid growing interest in positive psychology, the study of human strengths and virtues, research in recent years has shed light on the qualities and attitudes that distinguish heroes from the rest of us, writes Ms. Shellenbarger. Certain traits she says make it more likely that a person will make a split-second decision to take a heroic risk. People who like to take charge of situations, who respond sympathetically to others, and who have a strong sense of moral and social responsibility are more likely to intervene than people who lack those traits, research shows. Heroes tend by nature to be hopeful, believing events will turn out well. They consciously try to keep fear from hampering their pursuit of goals, and they tend to block out the possibility of injury or material loss.

People who are otherwise good and caring may still shrink back in a crisis. Their responses depend partly on whether they perceive the situation as an emergency and whether they know how to help; someone who doesn't know anything about electrical wiring probably won't rush to save a person tangled in a power line. How you're feeling that day makes a difference, too. "People who are in a good mood are more likely to help," says Julie M. Hupp, an assistant professor of psychology at Ohio State University in Newark. Context also matters; some researchers say a large crowd makes it less likely that an individual hero will step up. Of course, it helps to be physically able. In a 1981 study of 32 people who had intervened to help victims of assaults, robberies or other serious crimes, researchers found the heroes were taller, heavier and more likely to have had training in rescuing people or responding to emergencies than a comparison group of people who hadn't intervened in a crime or emergency for 10 years.

But heroism is far more complex than that. Some heroes have qualities that enable them to blast through obstacles, recent research shows. Empathy, or care or concern for others, runs high in people with heroic tendencies, according to a 2009 study led by Sara Staats, a professor emeritus of psychology at Ohio State University in Newark. Ms. Eldridge was an unlikely hero. She had no rescue training. At 5-foot-8 and 115 pounds, she was outweighed by the woman she saved. The biggest surprise to Ms. Eldridge, a single mother of two teenage boys, was that she was able to run at all. Until the day of the rescue, she hadn't run for 10 years because of a disabling back injury. "All I could think about was the lady's face. She looked lost. She needed help, and she needed help right then," says Ms. Eldridge, who received a medal from the Carnegie Hero Fund Commission, which honors civilians who risk their lives to save others, last June.

A tendency to frame events positively and expect good outcomes is another hallmark of heroes, says Jeremy Frimer, an assistant professor of psychology at the University of Winnipeg. In a 2010 study, 25 Canadians who had won awards for risking their lives to save others were asked to tell stories about their lives. Heroes were more likely to "take something that's bad and turn it into something that's good," says Dr. Frimer, a co-author of the study with Lawrence Walker, a psychology professor at the University of British Columbia, and others. In an example from another study, Dr. Frimer says, a woman diagnosed with breast cancer described the disease as "re-energizing her creative side," saying her return to creating art was "a gift that came from the tragedy."

When Stephen St. Bernard came home from work last month to his Brooklyn, N.Y., apartment building, neighbors had gathered outside. A 7-year-old child had squeezed out of her family's third-floor apartment window and was dancing on the air-conditioning unit outside, some 25 feet above the pavement. All Mr. St. Bernard was thinking was "maybe I can catch her," says the 53-year-old bus driver for the Metropolitan Transportation Authority. "The weight of the child, how hard she was going to hit me – none of that crossed my mind," he says. "I was just hoping, praying, 'God, please don't let me miss.'" As he moved beneath the window, the girl slipped and plummeted into his outstretched arms with an estimated 600 pounds of force, nearly ripping his arm off. He has had surgery to repair the torn muscles, tendons and nerves and will need months of painful physical therapy. But in describing the incident, he focuses on the fact that the child escaped injury or death. "Not a scratch was on that baby," he says.

Heroic people also tend to have a strong sense of ethics and above-average coping skills – a belief in their ability to tackle challenges and beat the odds, research shows. On the battlefield in Afghanistan last January, Navy nurse James Gennari knew, when he saw an injured Marine arrive on a stretcher at his medical facility, that standard procedures wouldn't work. The Marine had a live rocket-propelled grenade embedded in his body, from his thigh through his buttocks. A surgeon told Lt. Cmdr. Gennari he didn't have to intervene; a bomb squad could remove the grenade. But Lt. Cmdr. Gennari stepped up to the stretcher, took the Marine's hand and told him, "I promise you, no matter what, I won't leave you until that thing is out of your leg." He administered a sedative so an explosives specialist could pull out the bomb. It was later detonated in a huge blast outside the base. Lt. Cmdr. Gennari kept the Marine alive by pumping a manual respirator during a power failure on a helicopter flight to another camp. He was awarded a Bronze Star for valor this month.

Values that inspire heroism are often taught in childhood. "Children who grew up watching their parents stick their necks out for others, are likely to do the same," says Dr. Hupp. Lt. Cmdr. Gennari says his parents taught him "that every good thing that happens to you is a blessing, and you're supposed to give back." His father Gilbert, a Staff Sergeant in the Army who won a Bronze Star in the Korean War for meritorious service, taught him that "a man's word is a measure of his character," he adds. Thus when he gave the Marine his word that he wouldn't leave him, he says, "that was the way it was going to be."

Residents of Plaquemines Parish in Louisiana were shocked by Hurricane Isaac when ocean water burst over the Mississippi River levee, covering their town and leaving thousands trapped in attics and on roofs, said Jennifer Abbey of ABC News. Jesse Shaffer, 25, and his father, also named Jesse Shaffer, 53, both of Braithwaite, La., stayed behind in their town to rescue their friends. While police and the fire department were unable to reach some stranded people using their vehicles, the Shaffers were able to save lives using boats. "We rescued a lot of people, saw a lot of things you never thought you'd see," the older Shaffer told ABC News, beginning to cry.

Each Shaffer controlled a boat, in which the pair saved a combined 120 people in 12 hours, as well as animals. Their rescue mission began at five a.m. Wednesday at a local auditorium, where they rescued 10 people including a baby and an elderly man, they said. The Shaffers had to break through the attic ventilation system to reach the victims. "They'd call me and didn't know the water was coming up until it was late, and they'd call me to come get them," the older Shaffer said. "We had to scramble and try to find a boat because none of the sheriff's department or anybody could come to this end of the parish." The Shaffers rescued a family of five, including three children under the age of 6, from the roof of their trailer home just minutes before water overtopped it. The rescue was the older Shaffer's most memorable of the day. "They were all on there, screaming their lungs out," he said. The rapid rate at which water gushed over the 18-mile levee, into their town was "unexpected", the younger Shaffer said. Their home had 12 feet of water in it and they had to stash their belongings in the attic, which was then flooded. Water rose six inches every four minutes, the older Shaffer said. "There were a lot of houses we saw that were in spots that we know where they're supposed to be and they were maybe a half a mile down the road, floating down the highway."

The Shaffers fought through debris, rough water, wind and downed power lines to save their stranded friends. The older Shaffer insisted they are not heroes and they were never afraid. "I guess we were just going on adrenaline," the younger Shaffer said. But the most emotional part of their day was not the difficulty of their rescue mission, but the thought of knowing their town has to re-build. "It's just the people you know that you know that are not going to come back," the older Shaffer said.

XI

HEROISM CHOOSES its people and police in Anaheim, Californian, maintained a heavy presence on the streets of Anaheim to guard against further violent protests in the wake of the fatal shooting of an unarmed man by officers, according to an Associated Press report by Gillian Flaccus and Amy Taxin on 25 July 2012. The mother of Manuel Diaz condemned the unrest that has roiled the city, saying she did not want them to become her son's legacy. "I watched as my son took his last breath. I watched as his heart stopped beating for the last time," Genevieve Huizar said, breaking into sobs. "Please, please, please stop the violence. It's not going to bring my son back, and this is the worst thing any mother could go through."

Her news conference followed a night of protests where as many as 600 demonstrators surged through downtown, smashing shop windows, setting trash fires and hurling rocks and bottles at riot-clad officers who used batons, pepper balls and beanbag rounds. Twenty-four people, including four minors, were arrested on suspicion of crimes ranging from failure to disperse to assault with a deadly weapon, Police Chief John Welter said. The violence downtown left 20 stores with shattered windows, authorities said Mayor Tom Tait also appealed for calm and said the U.S. attorney's office had agreed to review two officer-involved shootings – including the one that left Diaz dead – and that he planned to meet with members of that office and the FBI. "We will have a clear and complete understanding of these incidents," followed by a public dialogue on what actions should be taken, Tait said at a news conference.

Police were out in force and there were no immediate reports of problems. Police said Diaz was shot Saturday after two officers approached three men who were acting suspiciously in an alley before running away. One officer chased Diaz to the front of an apartment complex. The second shooting occurred Sunday when officers spotted a suspected gang member in a stolen sport utility vehicle. After a brief pursuit, police said 21-year-old Joel Mathew Acevedo fired at an officer who returned fire and killed him. The back-to-back deaths were the fourth and fifth fatal police shooting in this Orange County city this year. The shootings and resulting demonstrations marred the image of the Orange County city, which is home to Disneyland and the Angels baseball team but also has neighborhoods teeming with gritty apartments. Like much of California, the city of more than 330,000 has changed significantly since Disneyland put it on the map in 1955. With its growth spurt, the once mostly white population is now more than 50 percent Hispanic and there's a sense of disenfranchisement from some in the Latino community.

The lawyer for Diaz's family said Hispanics feel they are disproportionately singled out by police and instinctively avoid police. "White kids in a rich white neighborhood don't get rousted by police and when they do, they don't have to fear the police. But that's not true with brown kids in a poor neighborhood," said Dana Douglas, the attorney. "Frankly, when it's brown kids in a poor area just standing there having a conversation, it's considered suspicious." Police would not say what led the officer to shoot Diaz. But Welter said Diaz failed to heed orders to stop and threw something on the roof of the complex that contained what officers believe was heroin. Both officers were placed on paid leave pending an investigation.

XII

MEANWHILE THE worst U.S. housing crisis since the Great Depression has been declared over, but is it asked Michelle Conlin and Leah Schnurr of Reuters in an analysis of the U.S. housing market. What some of Wall Street's forecasts for a recovery may be underestimating what they write are tectonic shifts in the U.S. economy that makes the housing market a different place from a decade ago. "Record levels of student debt, 15 years of flat incomes and the fact that nearly half of homeowners are effectively stranded in their houses look likely to weigh on prices into the indefinite future." Several housing experts have said the market is in danger of drifting for years. In a bleaker scenario, the fragile U.S. economic recovery could slip back into recession if Europe's crisis deepens or the political impasse in Washington triggers a new budget crisis, putting the housing market at risk again. "We've gone through half of a lost decade since the crisis started in 2007," said Robert Shiller, co-founder of the Case-Shiller U.S. housing price index and an economics professor at Yale University. The so-called Lost Decade in Japan occurred after the speculative bubble in the 1980s when abnormally low interest rates fueled soaring property values. The ensuing crash has continued to afflict the Japanese economy ever since. "It seems to me that a plausible forecast is, given our inability to do stimulus now, for

Japan-like slow growth for the next five years in the economy. Therefore, if there is an increase in home prices, it's modest," said Shiller.

A Reuters poll showed most economists think the U.S. housing market has now bottomed and prices should rise nearly 2 per cent in 2013 after a flat 2012. Cities such as New York and San Francisco have joined other world cities, like London and Hong Kong, to form a global housing market that aligns its fortunes with the wealthy elite. Then there's Stockton, the California city that filed for bankruptcy in June. A recent Rockefeller Institute of Government research report suggested it could turn into a ghost town with its lack of jobs and abundance of abandoned, foreclosed homes. Still, there's no doubt that in most places the housing market appears to have bottomed out and is now gathering strength.

"I don't think it's a head-fake, because when you look across all your price measures and construction measures on the starts side, you're seeing broad-based indication of improvement," says Beata Caranci, deputy chief economist at TD Bank Group in Toronto. But even those who say the recovery is on are subdued. "We have to be a little bit cautious," said Caranci. "It's the beginning of a recovery." The Case-Shiller home price index, considered a bellwether of the U.S. housing markets, rose in May for the third consecutive month. Those price hikes, however, reversed just a sliver of the wealth lost since the housing peak: $200 billion of the $6.7 trillion that has evaporated since 2006, according to a recent Bank of America report. Some of the biggest jumps – such as the 10 per cent year-over-year price gains in foreclosure-filled cities like Phoenix and Miami – were largely due to banks holding back inventory. That's because of lingering legal problems from the so-called robo-signing foreclosure scandal as well as a reluctance to flood the market, according to CoreLogic's Khater. "Don't let the volatility in prices fool you," he said. "Yes, prices are increasing in some markets, but in the longer term it has to come back to incomes, and unless incomes are increasing, price increases are not sustainable."

At this point in a typical cycle, executives at the home-building companies are usually the loudest members of the housing recovery pep squad. Yet the mood has been subdued in the most recent round of earnings conference calls with home-builder executives. In late June,

Lennar, the third-largest home-builder in the United States, reported a rise in new orders for the fifth straight quarter, helping to push share price to a year high in July. Executives had foreseen that, after the housing crash, family members would start to live together as a way to save. Lennar started designing a new home that included a 600-square-foot apartment with its own entrance called the "Multi Gen Home". It has been a hit. Nonetheless, Lennar's chief executive officer, Stuart A. Miller, told analysts in June that he was nervous about uttering the word recovery. "I don't think that there's reason for exuberance right now – except for the fact that the beatings have stopped."

XIII

THE RANKS of America's poor says an Associated Press report are on track to climb to levels unseen in nearly half a century, erasing gains from the war on poverty in the 1960s amid a weak economy and fraying government safety net. Census figures for 2011 will be released this fall in the critical weeks ahead of the November elections. The Associated Press surveyed more than a dozen economists, think tanks and academics, both nonpartisan and those with known liberal or conservative leanings, and found a broad consensus: The official poverty rate will rise from 15.1 per cent in 2010, climbing as high as 15.7 per cent. Several predicted a more modest gain, but even a 0.1 percentage point increase would put poverty at the highest level since 1965. The AP report was written by Hope Yen assisted by Kristen Wyatt in Lakewood, Colo., Ken Ritter and Michelle Rindels in Las Vegas, Laura Wides-Munoz in Miami, and AP Deputy Director of Polling Jennifer Agiesta.

"Poverty is spreading at record levels across many groups, from underemployed workers and suburban families to the poorest poor." More discouraged workers are giving up on the job market, leaving them vulnerable as unemployment aid begins to run out. Suburbs are seeing increases in poverty, including in such political battlegrounds as Colorado, Florida and Nevada, where voters are coping with a new norm of living hand to mouth. "I grew up going to Hawaii every summer. Now I'm here, applying for assistance because it's hard to make ends meet. It's very hard to adjust," said Laura Fritz, 27, of

Wheat Ridge, Colo., describing her slide from rich to poor as she filled out aid forms at a county center. Since 2000, large swaths of Jefferson County just outside Denver have seen poverty nearly double.

Fritz says she grew up wealthy in the Denver suburb of Highlands Ranch, but fortunes turned after her parents lost a significant amount of money in the housing bust. Stuck in a half-million dollar house, her parents began living off food stamps and Fritz's college money evaporated. She tried joining the Army but was injured during basic training. Now she's living on disability, with an infant daughter and a boyfriend, Garrett Goudeseune, 25, who can't find work as a landscaper. They are struggling to pay their $650 rent on his unemployment checks and don't know how they would get by without the extra help as they hope for the job market to improve.

In an election year dominated by discussion of the middle class, Fritz's case highlights a dim reality for the growing group in poverty. Millions could fall through the cracks as government aid from unemployment insurance, Medicaid, welfare and food stamps diminishes. "The issues aren't just with public benefits. We have some deep problems in the economy," said Peter Edelman, director of the Georgetown Center on Poverty, Inequality and Public Policy. He pointed to the recent recession but also longer-term changes in the economy such as globalization, automation, outsourcing, immigration, and less unionization that have pushed median household income lower. Even after strong economic growth in the 1990s, poverty never fell below a 1973 low of 11.1 per cent. That low point came after President Lyndon Johnson's war on poverty, launched in 1964, that created Medicaid, Medicare and other social welfare programs. "I'm reluctant to say that we've gone back to where we were in the 1960s. The programs we enacted make a big difference. The problem is that the tidal wave of low-wage jobs is dragging us down and the wage problem is not going to go away anytime soon," Edelman said.

Stacey Mazer of the National Association of State Budget Officers said states will be watching for poverty increases when figures are released in September as they make decisions about the Medicaid expansion. Most states generally assume poverty levels will hold mostly steady and they will hesitate if the findings show otherwise. "It's a constant tension in the budget," she said. The predictions for 2011 are based on separate AP interviews, supplemented with research on suburban poverty from Alan Berube of the Brookings Institution and an analysis of federal spending by the Congressional Research Service and Elise Gould of the Economic Policy Institute. The analysts' estimates suggest that some 47 million people in the U.S., or 1 in 6, were poor last year. An increase of one-tenth of a percentage point to 15.2 per cent would tie the 1983 rate, the highest since 1965. The highest level on record was 22.4 per cent in 1959, when the government began calculating poverty figures.

"Poverty is closely tied to joblessness. While the unemployment rate improved from 9.6 per cent in 2010 to 8.9 per cent in 2011, the employment-population ratio remained largely unchanged, meaning many discouraged workers simply stopped looking for work. Food stamp rolls, another indicator of poverty, also grew." Analysts also believe that the poorest poor, defined as those at 50 per cent or less of the poverty level, will remain near its peak level of 6.7 per cent.

"I've always been the guy who could find a job. Now I'm not," said Dale Szymanski, 56, a Teamsters Union forklift operator and convention hand who lives outside Las Vegas in Clark County. In a state where unemployment ranks highest in the nation, the Las Vegas suburbs have seen a particularly rapid increase in poverty from 9.7 per cent in 2007 to 14.7 per cent. Szymanski, who moved from Wisconsin in 2000, said he used to make a decent living of more than $40,000 a year but now doesn't work enough hours to qualify for union health care. He changed apartments several months ago and sold his aging 2001 Chrysler Sebring in April to pay expenses. "You keep thinking it's going to turn around. But I'm stuck," he said.

The 2010 poverty level was $22,314 for a family of four, and $11,139 for an individual, based on an official government calculation that includes only cash income, before tax deductions. It excludes capital gains or accumulated wealth, such as home ownership, as well as non-cash aid such as food stamps and tax credits, which were expanded substantially under President Barack Obama's stimulus package. "An additional 9 million people in 2010 would have been counted above the poverty line if food stamps and tax credits were taken into account." Robert Rector, a senior research fellow at the conservative Heritage Foundation, believes the social safety net has worked and it is now time to cut back. He worries that advocates may use a rising poverty rate to justify additional spending on the poor, when in fact, he says, many live in decent-size homes, drive cars and own wide-screen TVs. A new census measure accounts for non-cash aid, but that supplemental poverty figure isn't expected to be released until after the November election. Since that measure is relatively new, the official rate remains the best gauge of year-to-year changes in poverty dating back to 1959.

Few people advocate cuts in anti-poverty programs. Roughly 79 per cent of Americans think the gap between rich and poor has grown in the past two decades, according to a Public Religion Research Institute/RNS Religion News survey from November 2011. The same poll found that about 67 per cent oppose "cutting federal funding for social programs that help the poor" to help reduce the budget deficit. "Outside of Medicaid, federal spending on major low-income assistance programs such as food stamps, disability aid and tax credits have been mostly flat at roughly 1.5 per cent of the gross domestic product from 1975 to the 1990s." Spending it was reported spiked higher to 2.3 per cent of GDP after President Obama's stimulus program in 2009 temporarily expanded unemployment, insurance, and tax credits for the poor.

And yet, the U.S. safety net may soon offer little comfort to people such as Jose Gorrin, 52, who lives in the western Miami suburb of Hialeah Gardens. Arriving from Cuba in 1980, he was able to earn a decent living as a plumber for years, providing for his children and ex-wife. But things turned sour in 2007 and in the past two years he has barely worked, surviving on the occasional odd job. His unemployment aid has run out, and he's too young to draw Social Security. Holding a paper bag of still-warm bread he had just bought for lunch, Gorrin said he hasn't decided whom he will vote for in November, expressing little confidence the presidential candidates can solve the nation's economic problems. "They all promise to help when they're candidates," Gorrin said, adding, "I hope things turn around. I already left Cuba. I don't know where else I can go."

XIV

IN HIS BROADEST remarks on gun control in the aftermath of the mass shooting at a Colorado movie theater, President Obama called

460

for tougher background checks designed to keep guns out of the hands of criminals and the mentally ill, writes Olivier Knox of Yahoo! News / The Ticket. "A lot of gun owners would agree that AK-47s belong in the hands of soldiers, not in the hands of criminals – that they belong on the battlefield of war, not on the streets of our cities," the president, who has called for re-imposing the Assault Weapons Ban, said in a speech to the National Urban League. "I believe the majority of gun owners would agree that we should do everything possible to prevent criminals and fugitives from purchasing weapons; that we should check someone's criminal record before they can check out a gun seller; that a mentally unbalanced individual should not be able to get his hands on a gun so easily," he said. "These steps shouldn't be controversial. They should be common sense."

But Obama also offered a nod to the difficult politics of gun control, portraying himself as a believer in the individual right to bear arms, and acknowledging that calls to action after an incident like the one in Aurora often fade. "When there is an extraordinarily heartbreaking tragedy like the one we saw, there's always an outcry immediately after for action. And there's talk of new reforms, and there's talk of new legislation," Obama said in his speech. "And too often, those efforts are defeated by politics and by lobbying and eventually by the pull of our collective attention elsewhere. And I, like most Americans, believe that the Second Amendment guarantees an individual the right to bear arms. And we recognize the traditions of gun ownership that passed on from generation to generation – that hunting and shooting are part of a cherished national heritage," he said.

The president also singled out youth violence, and warned that government can only do so much. "It's up to us, as parents and as neighbors and as teachers and as mentors, to make sure our young people don't have that void inside them," he said. On a lighter note, Obama warned American school kids that they have to "hit the books" if they want to compete with their peers in rising economic powers – and avoid temptations like TV's Real Housewives. "You're competing against young people in Beijing and Bangalore. They're not hanging out. They're not getting over. They're not playing video games. They're not watching Real Housewives. I'm just saying: It's a two-way street. You've got to earn success," he said. "That wasn't in my prepared remarks," he said, to laughter from the crowd. "But I'm just saying."

There is however a gun culture in the United States and people acquire guns, are proud of their purchases, and sometimes use them to kill other Americans. Two guns believed seized from gangsters Bonnie and Clyde in 1933 after a deadly Missouri shootout with police sold for a combined $210,000 to an unnamed online bidder at an auction in Kansas City, according to Kevin Murphy of Reuters on 21 January 2012. The bidder paid $130,000 for a .45-caliber Thompson submachine gun, known as a "Tommy gun" in gangster slang. The same bidder paid $80,000 for an 1897 12-gauge Winchester shotgun. "We're happy," said auctioneer Robert Mayo, owner of Mayo Auction & Realty, which held the auction attended by more than 100 people. As for the bid prices, Mayo said, "Nothing ever surprises me." Mayo had not put an estimated value on the guns but said pre-auction online bids had reached $35,000 for the Tommy gun. Three weeks ago, a Missouri gun dealer who once sold a pistol owned by 19th-century outlaw Frank James predicted the Tommy gun would bring at least $25,000.

The guns were seized after a police shootout with Bonnie Parker and Clyde Barrow in Joplin, Missouri, on April 13, 1933. Police raided an apartment where the couple was hiding out. Bonnie and Clyde escaped, but two officers died in the shootout. A police officer later gave the weapons to Mark Lairmore, a Tulsa police officer, and they remained in the Lairmore family, according to a Mayo account of the guns' history. A great-grandson of Lairmore, also named Mark Lairmore, said the family no longer saw a need for the guns, which had been in a police museum in Springfield, Missouri, from 1973 until late last year.

Several people bid in person on the guns, including Michael Brown, who said he was representing a group that wanted the guns for a gangster museum planned in Las Vegas. He bid nearly as much as the winning bidder on each gun and said he especially wanted the Tommy gun. "There are very few guns with the historic value of that one," Brown said as he left the building to catch a plane back to Las Vegas. Brown said he hadn't planned to bid on the second gun but did so after losing out on the Tommy gun. He said he was surprised the second gun went so high. Mayo talked up the Tommy gun during the bidding as a "unique opportunity to own a piece of history" and he predicted the weapons would sell for much more in the years ahead. Bonnie and Clyde history buff John Mahoney of Overland Park, Kansas, said he couldn't resist attending the auction, though he said he had no plans to make a bid. "Curiosity got the best of me," Mahoney said. "I'd love to own one, but they are out of my price range."

Guns however are never out of other Americans' price range and eight people were wounded and at least two people are dead after a shooting outside the Empire State Building in the Midtown area of Manhattan on a Friday morning in September, according to a report from Jason Sickles of Yahoo! / The Lookout. The shooting occurred at Fifth Avenue and West 34th Street around 9 a.m. ET. The New York Post reported that the incident was the result of a co-worker's dispute; the gunman was fired from his job on Thursday and returned to his office to target his boss, local and federal officials told NBC News. The gunman, who was shot by police at the scene, and a bystander were dead. The shooter followed his co-worker down 33rd Street, and shot him outside of Legend's Bar, the Post reported. It was unclear if he fired into a crowd of pedestrians outside of the landmark building, or if pedestrians were caught in crossfire, reported the New York Daily News. Police shot and killed the gunman near the tourist entrance of the Empire State Building.

Police cordoned off a one-block perimeter around the Empire State Building after the shooting. Around 10 a.m., a lone tourist bus headed down Fifth Avenue, and a guide could be heard over the bus's microphone explaining they were nearing the landmark. As police waved the bus to detour down 36th Street, the guide was openly mystified. "I don't know what's going on, folks," he said, as the bus turned. By then the bus's passengers were looking up at the sky at a news helicopter floating overhead. Some stood, clutching their cameras. Along 35th street, hundreds of people stood photographing the scene with iPhones and iPads. Officers could be seen standing in the middle of 34th street around a scene surrounded by police tape. Television producers roamed the crowd looking for eyewitnesses. It is a scene that Americans have grown accustomed with.

XV

THE DEADLY shootings at a movie theater in Colorado briefly silenced the presidential campaign, prompting both President Obama and Republican challenger Romney to cut short their schedules and pull advertising in the state out of respect for the victims and their families, writes Ken Thomas of the Associated Press. Obama said on 21 July in his weekly radio and Internet address that he hopes everyone takes time on the weekend "for prayer and reflection – for the victims of this terrible tragedy, for the people who knew them and loved them, for those who are still struggling to recover." The president said Americans should also think about "all the victims of the less publicized acts of violence that plague our communities on a daily basis. Let us keep all these Americans in our prayers."

Obama and Romney used campaign appearances on 20 July to focus attention on the need for national unity in the aftermath of the shootings in Aurora. Their campaign teams re-scheduled Sunday show appearances by top aides and surrogates, essentially providing a break in what has been an increasingly testy campaign. The rampage injected a new tone into the campaign after Obama and Romney had clashed repeatedly over the economy, Medicare and tax returns. Obama was set to start his second day of events in Florida when the shootings occurred, prompting his team to address the violence at a previously scheduled rally in Fort Myers, Fla., and scrapping an event in suburban Orlando. Obama told supporters in Fort Myers that the shootings served as a "reminder that life is very fragile." He said, "Our time here is limited and it is precious. And what matters at the end of the day is not the small things, it's not the trivial things. Ultimately, it's how we choose to treat one another and how we love one another." Romney echoed Obama's call for unity, saying at a previously scheduled event in Bow, N.H., that he joined with the president and First Lady in offering condolences for those whose lives were shattered in a few moments, a few moments of evil in Colorado. "The answer is that we can come together. We will show our fellow citizens the good heart of the America we know and love," Romney said. Other prominent lawmakers called the shootings a time for unity. House Speaker John Boehner, R-Ohio, said in the Republican address that lawmakers joined Obama in offering condolences and prayers to the loved ones of those who were killed and wounded. "I know that when confronted with evil we cannot comprehend, Americans pull together and embrace our national family more tightly," Boehner said.

However, beyond the calls for a higher purpose, the shootings could raise the profile of gun rights in the presidential campaign, an issue which has played a minor role so far. As a senator Obama voted to leave gun makers and dealers open to civil lawsuits, and as an Illinois state lawmaker he supported a ban on all forms of semi-automatic weapons and tighter state restrictions generally on firearms. Following the killing of six people and wounding of then-Rep. Gabrielle Giffords in Tucson, Ariz., in 2011, Obama called for a series of steps to "keep those irresponsible, law-breaking few from getting their hands on a gun in the first place." Among those steps was a better federal background check system. The administration said that it has indeed improved the amount and quality of information poured into that system, allowing background checks to be more thorough. But the administration has offered no detailed, public explanation of how it is following up on all of Obama's previous promises, and it had no comment about any need for new legislation. "The president believes that we need to take common-sense measures that protect Second Amendment rights of Americans, while ensuring that those who should not have guns under existing law do not get them," said White House press secretary Jay Carney. Romney backed some gun control measures when he was governor of Massachusetts. When he challenged Sen. Edward M. Kennedy in 1994 he declared, "I don't line up with the NRA." In April, Romney told the National Rifle Association he was a guardian of the Second Amendment. Romney spokeswoman Andrea Saul said the Republican candidate believes that the "best way to prevent gun violence is to vigorously enforce our laws."

New York Mayor Michael Bloomberg, in a radio interview, urged the president and his challenger to address gun violence forcefully. "You know, soothing words are nice," Bloomberg said, "but maybe it's time that the two people who want to be president of the United States to stand up and tell us what they are going to do about it, because this is obviously a problem across the country." Bloomberg's warning gained strength when a gunman shot and killed six people in Sikh temple in Oak Creek, Wis., south of Milwaukee on 5 August.

According to Dylan Stableford of Yahoo! News / The Lookout the suspected gunman also was shot dead. Police said that a 911 dispatcher received multiple calls from the temple at approximately 10:25 a.m. local time. An officer who responded to the scene engaged with the suspected gunman in the parking lot. The veteran officer was shot multiple times and is in surgery at Milwaukee's Froedtert Hospital, according to Greenfield (Wis.) Police Chief Bradley Wentlandt. His condition is not known. The suspect was "put down" and is presumed dead, Wentlandt said. Tactical units conducting a sweep of the 17,000-square-foot temple discovered four bodies inside and three, including the gunman, in the parking lot. "We have not identified additional shooters," Wentlandt said. A spokesman for Froedtert Hospital said a total of three victims were admitted in critical condition, two with gunshot wounds to the face and one with gunshot wounds to the abdomen. Other area hospitals were told to prepare for as many as 20 victims. Dozens of worshipers, including women and children, were gathering for a meal before an 11:30 a.m. service when the shooting occurred. There are about 500 members in the congregation, officials say. Sikhism is a 500-year-old monotheist faith with about 27 million followers worldwide, and 500,000 in the United States.

In a statement, Wis. Gov. Scott Walker said his office is working with the FBI and local law enforcement in its investigation. According to ABC News, federal agents from the Alcohol, Tobacco and Firearms bureau were sent to the scene of the shooting. "Our hearts go out to the victims and their families as we all struggle to comprehend the evil that begets this terrible violence," Walker said. "At the same time, we are filled with gratitude for our first responders, who show bravery and selflessness as they put aside their own safety to protect our neighbors and friends." The Indian Embassy in Washington called it a "tragic incident" and said it has been in touch with the National Security Council and local authorities to monitor the situation. Since 9/11, Sikh rights groups in the United States have reported a rise in bias attacks. There have been more than 700 incidents since the Sept. 11, 2001, terror attacks, according to the Associated Press. "Sikhs don't practice the same religion as Muslims," the AP noted, "but their long beards and turbans often cause them to be mistaken for Muslims, advocates say."

The FBI said Liz Goodman of Yahoo! News / The Lookout is treating a mass shooting at the Milwaukee-area Sikh Temple as a possible act of domestic terrorism, officials announced in a press conference. Wade Michael Page, a 40-year-old Army veteran and suspected white supremacist, is believed to be the gunman and was killed at the scene of the crime. Domestic terrorism is defined by the U.S. Patriot Act as a dangerous action that is intended to intimidate or coerce a "civilian population", influence government policy by intimidation or affect a government's actions by "mass destruction, assassination or kidnapping." Terrorism can be the work of one isolated individual, or a larger network of criminals. While authorities haven't disclosed a possible motive for Page to open fire in a Sikh temple an hour before services began, law enforcement sources and advocacy groups say that Page was a longtime white supremacist who played in a white power band called "End Apathy". However, Page's alleged crime could have been designed to send a message that the government should exclude non-white people from America, or any number of anti-minority messages. Since the September 11 attacks, Sikhs have sometimes been mistaken for Muslims and have increasingly found themselves the target of anti-Muslim hate crimes in America. It's possible that Page could have mixed up the temple with a mosque and started his attack as a way to make a political statement against Muslims – another political act that seems to fit the bill of terrorism.

Prabhjot Singh, the co-founder of the Sikh Coalition in New York, told Yahoo News that he thinks it's too soon to talk about whether the attack should be treated as terrorism or a hate crime. "How we categorize it is not so important right now," Singh said. "It's that the nation comes to heal collectively." The coalition was founded when hate crimes against Sikhs escalated after 2001, including the murder of gas station owner Balbir Singh Sodhi in Mesa, Ariz., by Frank Roque. The discussion around what counts as terrorism has been charged since 9/11, when Muslim-American communities were subjected to surveillance and heightened scrutiny out of fear that more terror attacks were on the way.

Domestic terrorism is actually at a four-decade low, according to Gary LaFree at the University of Maryland's National Consortium for the Study of Terrorism and Responses to Terrorism. Between 1980 and

2001, non-Islamic American extremists carried out about two-thirds of all terrorism in the United States, according to FBI statistics cited by the Council on Foreign Relations and between 2002 and 2005, that figure jumped to 95 percent. In the 10 years following 2001, only 6 percent of terrorist acts in America have been the work of Islamic extremists. Even so, some scholars say the common perception is that most homegrown terrorists in America are Muslims adhering to a violent brand of Islamist extremism. People are less likely to understand that violent white supremacism can also be terrorism. "I think that [white supremacist attacks] should quality as terrorism just as much as an individual who's a Muslim who abuses that faith to say 'I want to kill these people to further my political agenda,'" said Sahar Aziz, an associate professor at Texas Wesleyan University School of Law. White supremacy is also a political message, she added.

Aziz says that since the September 11 attacks, the government has shifted to focusing law enforcement resources on Islamic extremism, possibly to the detriment of preventing white supremacist attacks and other dangerous extremists. "I think one of the issues that had bothered me in the aftermath of the Colorado incident and that has bothered ... many Muslim, Sikh, Arab and South Asian civil rights advocates is the ease with which the terrorism label applies to some individuals and some incidents and the assumption that if you have a person who isn't from certain communities then that label isn't appropriate," Dawinder "Dave" Sidhu, a Sikh-American law professor at the University of New Mexico, told Yahoo News. Sidhu added that he thinks terrorism should be re-defined to focus on a perpetrator's actions, not his or her motivations. Terrorism represents "a disregard for human life and a killing of innocents," he says, not the rationale of a killer that may be unknowable.

The Associated Press also reported that suspects in deputy killings in New Orleans have been linked to extremists. At least some of the seven people arrested in the fatal shootout with Louisiana deputies writes Cain Burdeau have been linked to violent anarchists on the FBI's domestic terrorism watch list. Detectives had been monitoring the group before Thursday's shootout in Laplace in which two deputies were killed and two more wounded, said DeSoto Parish Sheriff Rodney Arbuckle. His detectives and other law enforcement discovered the suspects were heavily armed adherents to an ideology known as the "Sovereign Citizens" movement. The FBI has classified "sovereign citizens" as people who believe they are free from all duties of a U.S. citizen, like paying taxes. The FBI considers the group's members a danger for making threats to judges and law enforcement, using fake currency and impersonating police officers. The seven suspects have been charged in the shooting of Deputy Michael Scott Boyington, who survived. But authorities have said murder charges are pending.

Detectives in Tennessee, Nebraska and Louisiana have sketched a portrait of an outlaw gang led by a 44-year-old accused molester named Terry Smith, who has a criminal record dating to 1984 in Morehouse Parish, the *Times-Picayune* reported. Morehouse Parish Sheriff Mike Stubbs said the Smith family was notorious. He said they lived for a long time in a house on the outskirts of Bastrop. "We had a good bit of dealings with them," he said. The Smith brothers had been involved in theft and drugs.

Sovereign citizens are a loosely organized movement founded in the 1970s and more fully developed in the 1980s, according to the Anti-Defamation League website. Sovereign citizens believe that all levels of government have no jurisdiction over them and resist – sometimes with violence – authority including police, the website said. They also like to use what is dubbed "paper terrorism". It involves using frivolous lawsuits and fake documents and of using genuine documents such as IRS forms to intimidate, harass and coerce public officials, law enforcement officers and private citizens.

From Washington Matt Spetalnick of Reuters reported that President Obama said that mass killings like the shooting rampage at a Sikh temple in Wisconsin were occurring with "too much regularity" and should prompt soul searching by all Americans, but he stopped short of calling for new gun-control laws. "All of us are heart-broken by what happened," Obama told reporters at the White House a day after a gunman opened fire on Sikh worshippers preparing for religious services, killing six before he was shot dead by a police officer. But when asked whether he would push for further gun-control measures in the wake of the shootings, Obama said only that he wanted to bring together leaders at all levels of American society to examine ways to curb gun violence. That echoed his pledge last month in a speech in New Orleans to work broadly to "arrive at a consensus" on the contentious issue after a deadly Colorado shooting spree highlighted the problem in an election year. But like his earlier comments, Obama offered no timetable or specifics for such discussions and did not call outright for tighter gun control laws.

Talk of reining in America's gun culture is considered politically risky for Obama. "All of us recognize that these kinds of terrible, tragic events are happening with too much regularity for us not to do some soul searching to examine additional ways that we can reduce violence," Obama said at an Oval Office ceremony to sign an unrelated bill. But he added, "As I've already said, there are a lot of elements involved in it." The Democratic president has made a point of emphasizing his support for the U.S. Constitution's Second Amendment, which covers the right to bear arms. White House spokesman Jay Carney reiterated, however, that Obama remained in favor of renewing an assault weapons ban but pointed out "there has been reluctance by Congress" to pass it.

Obama said the FBI was still investigating the temple shooting, but if it turned out it was ethnically motivated, the American people would immediately recoil. "It would be very important for us to re-affirm once again that in this country, regardless of what we look like, where we come from, who we worship, we are all one people," he said.

In a show of respect for the victims of the shooting in a Milwaukee suburb of Oak Creek, Obama ordered flags at all U.S. government facilities at home and abroad to be flown at half-staff until sunset.

XVI

EVER SINCE Al Gore's defeat in 2000, it has become hardened conventional wisdom among Democrats that gun control is a losing issue for the party, writes Ronald Brownstein in the *National Journal*. And there's no question that public opinion since 2000 has tilted toward greater skepticism of restrictions on gun ownership. But those basic facts he wrote omit some other factors relevant to the debate. One is that the key elements of the Democratic coalition, though wavering somewhat since 2000, still preponderantly prioritize restrictions on gun ownership over protecting the rights of gun owners. The other is that support for gun control actually increased during the 1990s, when President Clinton waged and won two pitched battles with the National Rifle Association, and has declined in this decade, when no president (and virtually no congressional leader) has made a case to the public for gun restrictions.

Results from the nonpartisan Pew Research Center offer a good long-term gauge of the change and stability in attitudes toward regulating access to guns. For two decades, Pew has asked a fundamental question: "What do you think is more important: to protect the right of Americans to own guns, or to control gun ownership?" In 1993, 57 per cent of adults said it was more important to control gun ownership while only 34 per cent said it was more important to protect gun rights. Those attitudes remained largely stable through the 1990s, when Clinton drove through Congress two major gun-control initiatives: the Brady Bill in 1993, which required a waiting period for handgun purchases and a ban on assault weapons in 1994. After the 1999 Columbine high school massacre in Littleton, Colo., (not far from Friday's shooting in Aurora, another blue-collar Denver suburb), Clinton failed in an effort to pass further limits on purchases at gun shows. But as Clinton completed his term in 2000, Pew polling still showed that a solid majority of Americans placed greater priority on restricting gun ownership than protecting gun rights (with 57 per cent picking the gun control side in one 2000 survey and 66 per cent in another).

Despite those overall attitudes, after George W. Bush defeated Gore in 2000, largely by routing him in rural areas and among blue-collar whites, many if not most Democratic strategists concluded that gun control was a losing issue for the party. No less a political authority than Clinton himself once said he believed Gore lost the election in states where the AFL-CIO lacked the ground presence to neutralize the NRA campaign against Gore among blue-collar whites. Coming after a similar rural/blue-collar uprising keyed the GOP takeover of Congress in 1994, following the passage of Clinton's two big gun-control initiatives, the 2000 election solidified the attitude among Democrats that the intensity on the gun-control issue tilted overwhelmingly toward the conservative side – that those opposed to gun control were much more likely to vote on the issue than those who supported it.

Even so, most Americans continued to place a higher priority on controlling gun ownership than protecting gun rights in Pew polling through the George W. Bush years when Congress, with Bush's support, allowed Clinton's assault-weapon ban to lapse. It was only around the time of President Obama's election that the lines in Pew's polling converged and then crossed: In the most recent survey that asked the question (April 2012), 49 per cent of adults said it was most important to protect gun rights, compared with 45 per cent who placed the higher priority on controlling gun ownership. The polling data doesn't fully explain why attitudes toward guns have shifted so far toward the conservative side in the Obama years. From the outset, he has almost never discussed the subject; after the shooting of then-Rep. Gabrielle Giffords in 2011, Obama promised to lead a national conversation about guns, but he has been almost completely AWOL since. Even after the Aurora massacre, his first comments never raised the issue.

But one clue may be that attitudes toward gun control, while cooling among all key groups in the electorate, have shifted most dramatically among the portions of the white electorate expressing the broadest unease about Obama – particularly his vision of a more expansive role for Washington across an array of issues. Figures provided by Michael Dimock, Pew's associate research director, show that the biggest shifts toward opposition to gun control have come among the same blue-collar whites who have displayed the greatest alienation to Obama across the board. From 2000 to 2008, the share of non-college white men who prioritized gun rights over gun control soared from 55 per cent to 73 per cent; non-college white women moved comparably, shifting from 32 per cent emphasizing gun rights to 52 per cent. "Whether related to the economy or the uncertainty that's creating for people or the arrival of a president that certain groups have felt uncomfortable with from day one, this issue has really has come to symbolize something powerful for these voters," says Dimock.

The change was somewhat more restrained among college-educated white men: The share of them prioritizing gun ownership increased from 46 per cent to 59 per cent. Among college-educated white women, the most Democratic-leaning component of the white electorate, support for gun rights increased 11 percentage points; among all minority adults, it rose a relatively modest 9 percentage points over the period. But even after those changes, those key pillars of the modern Democratic coalition still lean heavily toward gun control: In the April 2012 Pew survey, 61 per cent of both college-educated white women and all nonwhite adults said it was more important to control gun ownership than to protect gun rights. Young people, another pillar of the modern Democratic coalition, do not tilt as overwhelmingly toward the gun-control side, but are still more supportive than older generations.

What this means is that gun control is now overwhelmingly unpopular among the portions of the white electorate Obama is least likely to win anyway – and maintains solid majority support among the Americans most likely to actually vote for him. For individual Democratic senators or House members representing rural or heavily blue-collar states, the equation may look very different. But at the national level, Obama's reluctance to address gun control means he is failing to articulate what remains a strong preference within his coalition. Gun control, in fact, remains a majority position with the same groups generally most enthusiastic about Obama's recent embrace of gay marriage, free access to contraception in health insurance, and an administration version of the Dream Act for young illegal immigrants. It's also possible that if Obama or other leading Democrats made a more forceful case for gun control, support for it in Obama's coalition would rise further, back toward its levels when Clinton was articulating the argument for limits.

If Obama or other leading Democrats identified more strongly with the gun-control cause, there would undoubtedly be political costs: Such an emphasis would sharpen the cultural, class, and regional divides that already define American politics. It could help the president in places like Northern Virginia or the Denver and Philadelphia suburbs (all places where economic discontent threatens to erode his decisive 2008 support), and hurt him in more rural areas of the same states. But it's a myth that there is no longer any audience for gun control: it is, in fact, the same audience that the president is pursuing with almost everything else he does. But even as the issue of guns shifts to the forefront of the presidential campaign, the White

House and the Senate's top Democrat made it clear that new gun legislation will not be on the political agenda this year, writes Julie Pace of the Associated Press. Instead, President Obama intends to focus on other ways to combat gun violence – a position not unlike that of his rival, Mitt Romney. Days after the mass shootings in Colorado, White House spokesman Jay Carney said Obama still supports a ban on the sale of assault weapons, a restriction that expired in 2004. But he added: "There are things we can do short of legislation and short of gun laws that can reduce violence in our society." Carney's comments came the day after Obama, in a speech to an African-American group in New Orleans, embraced some degree of additional restrictions on guns. He acknowledged that not enough had been done to keep weapons out of the hands of criminals and pledged to work with lawmakers from both parties to move forward on the matter. Carney also spoke as a prominent gun control group called on Obama and Romney to lead a search for solutions to gun violence. The Brady Campaign to Prevent Gun Violence said both candidates owe voters concrete plans and appealed to them not to duck the issue.

In the Senate, Majority Leader Harry Reid said that the Senate would not consider the gun issue this year, even though he agreed with Obama's remarks in New Orleans. "With the schedule we have, we're not going to even have a debate on gun control," Reid told reporters. The White House and Reid's stance illustrate a reality in Washington, where advocating for restrictions on gun ownership is viewed as a political liability. Acknowledging opposition in Congress to new limits, Carney said Obama will work to enhance existing gun laws. "While there is that stalemate in Congress there are other things we can do," he said. Obama told the National Urban League in New Orleans that he was willing to work with both parties in Congress to find a national consensus that addresses violence. That speech came six days after the shooting in an Aurora, Col., movie theater that left 12 people dead and injured dozens more.

In an interview with CNN, Romney said new laws won't keep people from carrying out "terrible acts". He cited the case of Timothy McVeigh, who was convicted and put to death for the 1995 bombing of a federal building in Oklahoma City that killed 168 people. "How many people did he kill with fertilizer, with products that can be purchased legally anywhere in the world? He was able to carry out vast mayhem," Romney said. "Somehow thinking that laws against the instruments of violence will make violence go away, I think is misguided." In another interview, Romney said many weapons used by the shooting suspect in Aurora, Colo., were obtained illegally, though authorities have said the firearms used were purchased legally. "The illegality the governor is referencing is the ordinances, the devices that were in the home," said campaign spokesman Danny Diaz. "He was not referencing the weapons carried to the theater."

Obama called for stepped-up background checks for people who want to buy guns and restrictions to keep mentally unbalanced individuals from buying weapons. He said those steps "shouldn't be controversial." Despite the Second Amendment's protection of gun rights, Obama said: "I also believe that a lot of gun owners would agree that an AK-47 belongs in the hands of soldiers, not in the hands of criminals – that they belong on the battlefield of war, not on the streets of our cities."

Neither candidate strayed significantly from previously held positions on gun violence. But their pointed comments revived a debate – if perhaps only briefly – that has steadily faded to the background in national politics and been virtually non-existent in the 2012 campaign. The White House in particular has faced fresh questions since the shootings about whether Obama, a strong supporter of gun control as a senator from Illinois, would make an election-year push for stricter measures.

Following last year's killing of six people and the wounding of then-Rep. Gabrielle Giffords in Arizona, Obama called for steps to "keep those irresponsible, law-breaking few from getting their hands on a gun in the first place." But he has advanced no legislative proposals since then. It's been more than a decade since gun control advocates had a realistic hope of getting the type of legislation they seek, despite predictions that each shocking outburst of violence would lead to action. In his remarks, Obama acknowledged a national pattern of calling for tougher gun restrictions in the wake of violent crimes but not following through. "Too often, those efforts are defeated by politics and by lobbying and eventually by the pull of our collective attention elsewhere," he said.

Romney was pressed on gun control during an interview with NBC News in London, where he was attending the Olympics and kicking off a three-country foreign trip. The presumptive Republican nominee said changing laws won't "make all bad things go away." Asked about his tenure as Massachusetts governor, when he signed a bill that banned some assault-style weapons like the type the Colorado shooter is alleged to have used, Romney described such guns as "instruments of destruction with the sole purpose of hunting down and killing people." Asked if he stood by those comments, Romney mentioned the Massachusetts ban but said he didn't think current laws needed to change. "I don't happen to believe that America needs new gun laws. A lot of what this ... young man did was clearly against the law. But the fact that it was against the law did not prevent it from happening," Romney said.

Obama addressed the nationwide troubles in front of the Urban League in part because blacks, who make up the bulk of the organization's membership, have been disproportionately affected by gun violence. While mass shootings like the one in Colorado receive widespread attention, Obama said roughly the same number of young people are killed in the U.S. by guns every day and a half. "For every Columbine or Virginia Tech, there are dozens gunned down on the streets of Chicago and Atlanta, and here in New Orleans," he said. "For every Tucson or Aurora, there is daily heartbreak over young Americans shot in Milwaukee or Cleveland."

XVII

PRESIDENT OBAMA blamed Republicans for a stalemate that could increase taxes on Americans next year while a leading Senate Republican cast Obama and his Democratic Party as obstructionists who want to place the tax burden on businesses during an economic slowdown. In his weekly radio and online address, says Jim Kuhnhenn of the Associated Press, Obama pressed the Republican-controlled House to extend Bush-era tax cuts for households making $250,000 or less while letting lower rates on wealthier taxpayers expire and go up. The Democratic-controlled Senate narrowly passed such a measure earlier in the week, but the House is not expected to follow suit. "Instead of doing what's right for middle-class families and small-business owners, Republicans in Congress are holding these tax cuts hostage until we extend tax cuts for the wealthiest Americans," Obama said. Responding on behalf of the congressional GOP, Sen. Orrin Hatch of Utah, the top Republican on the Senate Finance Committee, said Obama's plan would do more harm to the economy and criticized him with almost identical language. He called for extending current tax rates for all taxpayers and spending 2013 overhauling and simplifying the tax code. "Raising taxes as our economy continues to struggle is not a solution, and the majority of Americans and businesses understand that," Hatch said. "The president and his Washington allies need to stop holding America's economy hostage in order to raise taxes on those trying to lead our economic recovery."

The competing views frame today's Washington political debate and the presidential contest. With the economy standing as the main issue on voters' minds, Obama, rival Mitt Romney and lawmakers of both parties are engaged in brinkmanship and political test votes ahead of the November election and the 31 December deadline when the Bush-era tax rates expire. Obama used his address to take a rare swipe at Romney, even though he didn't mention his challenger by name. "Republicans in Congress and their nominee for president believe that the best way to create prosperity in America is to let it trickle down from the top," he said. "They believe that if our country spends trillions more on tax cuts for the wealthy, we'll somehow create jobs – even if we have to pay for it by gutting things like education and training and by raising middle-class taxes. They're wrong." Saturday's dueling addresses come a day after the government reported that weak consumer spending held growth to an annual rate of just 1.5 per cent in the second quarter. That was lower than the 2 per cent rate of the first quarter and less than what's necessary to help drive down the unemployment rate, now stuck at 8.2 per cent. The White House budget office also predicted that the economy for this year will grow at a modest 2.6 per cent annual rate and that the jobless rate will average 8 per cent. It forecasts 2.6 per cent growth next year, down from the 3.0 per cent it predicted in February.

Elsewhere the news is that hundreds of bailed-out banks are still struggling to repay taxpayers and will soon find it even harder to make required dividend payments to the Treasury, according to a report by the watchdog for the government bailout program. Of the 707 banks that received taxpayers' money from the government's Troubled Asset

Relief Program starting in 2008, also known as TARP, about half have repaid the Treasury, says Rachelle Younglai of Reuters. However, 137 of those banks used a government-loan program to repay their taxpayer debts, according to the watchdog's quarterly report to Congress. And of the 325 banks still propped up with taxpayer money, 203 have missed dividend or interest payments, with some missing as many as 13 payments since receiving capital injections at the height of the financial crisis, said the report. Adding to their woes, the dividend that the bailed-out banks are required to pay to Treasury is set to increase to 9 per cent from the current 5 per cent as early as 2013. "Those banks are not able to raise the capital that is required to get out of TARP," said Christy Romero, the special inspector general for the bailout program. "We are very concerned about those banks, and want those banks to stand on their own feet without government assistance," she said.

The Treasury has been trying to exit the bailout programs that have been criticized by Republican lawmakers for excessive government intervention. And Obama administration officials repeatedly stress that the bank bailouts, including the one used to directly inject capital into banks, have earned taxpayers more than $19 billion. This week, the Treasury said it would sell preferred stock and debt in 12 of the bailed-out banks. In June, Treasury successfully raised some $200 million from the sale of preferred stock in seven bailed-out banks. Treasury has been careful in saying that it will exit programs when the time is right and would not make decisions for political reasons. "We're continuing to balance exiting our investments as soon as practicable and maximizing value for taxpayers," said Treasury spokesman Matt Anderson. But Romero said it appears the Treasury wants to exit their investments as soon as possible. "If they want to do a swift government exit, (Treasury) has to ensure that financial stability continues otherwise the purpose of TARP is not met," Romero said, adding that she has not seen the analysis from Treasury that she thinks is necessary to make decisions on whether to exit a TARP bank. According to the inspector general's report, taxpayers have now lost $5.5 billion on its investment in insurer American International Group. The government's remaining investment in the company is $30 billion, down from the initial $180 billion.

XVIII

THE MOST respected investor and capitalist on the planet, Warren Buffett, took to the pages of *The New York Times* on 15 August 2011 to bust a myth that has dominated political discourse in recent months: The idea that raising taxes on super-rich people would hurt the economy. According to Henry Blodget of the Daily Ticker, Buffett said that his own personal taxes as a percentage of his income have plummeted in the past decade, to all-time lows. He observes, as he has done before, that he pays a much lower tax rate than his secretary. He calls out the absurdity of hedge-fund managers and other professional investors playing "long-term capital gains" rates on short-term trading profits. And then he takes aim at the biggest rationale for preserving these astonishing tax breaks, if taxes on deca-millionaire and billionaires were increased, these super-rich Americans would stop investing, thus clobbering the economy and hurting job growth.

"Back in the 1980s and 1990s, tax rates for the rich were far higher, and my percentage rate was in the middle of the pack. According to a theory I sometimes hear, I should have thrown a fit and refused to invest because of the elevated tax rates on capital gains and dividends. I didn't refuse, nor did others. I have worked with investors for 60 years and I have yet to see anyone – not even when capital gains rates were 39.9 per cent in 1976-77 – shy away from a sensible investment because of the tax rate on the potential gain. People invest to make money, and potential taxes have never scared them off. And to those who argue that higher rates hurt job creation, I would note that a net of nearly 40 million jobs were added between 1980 and 2000. You know what's happened since then: lower tax rates and far lower job creation.

"When presented with these facts, those who argue against tax increases on the super-rich – or, even more absurdly, for more tax cuts – often point to President Ronald Reagan, observing that he cut taxes for the wealthy, helping usher in a long economic boom. "This ignores the point that Reagan also raised taxes. And, more importantly, it ignores how high tax rates on super-rich people were when Reagan cut them: In 1980, the top bracket was a startling 70 per cent. It also ignores how Bill Clinton raised taxes and then took the US from the perpetual deficits of the Reagan years to a surplus. It ignores how

George Bush cut taxes, plunged the budget back into a deficit, encouraged the wild borrowing spree that inflated the housing bubble, and then oversaw the worst recession since the Depression. It ignores how the US prospered all through the 1950s and 1960s, when marginal tax rates were super-high. And so on. In short, it ignores almost all the economic data we have. And it appears to be based on a rigid ideology, rather than common sense."

Buffett isn't proposing a blanket increase on today's entire top tax bracket, those making over $379,150, many of whom protest against the idea that they are "rich". Buffett is suggesting the implementation of two new brackets – one for taxpayers making over $1 million, of whom there are 237,000 in the country, and one for taxpayers making over $10 million, of whom there are only 8,000. In other words, Buffett's tax-increase-on-the-super-rich would affect 1 in 1,253 Americans, less than 1/10th of 1 per cent of the population.

The House and the Senate are in a state of near-paralysis over the country's finances. Even conservatives who generally embrace Thoreau's maxim that the government that governs best governs least show signs of fear and alarm about the government's inability to get things done. The United States has an aging population that is depending on underfunded federal health and pension programs during a time of sluggish economic growth, unrelenting international challenges, soaring debt, and pertinacious division. "If we keep kicking the can down the road, and ducking ... and pushing responsibility off to the next Congress, then we'll have a European-type situation on our hands: We'll have a debt crisis," warns Rep. Paul Ryan, the Republican from Wisconsin who chairs the House Budget Committee. And that procrastination will mean "bitter austerity ... sudden, disruptive cuts ... slow economic growth ... [and huge] tax increases."

The 435 members of the House are as polarized as their Senate colleagues. Only six Republicans – Chris Smith of New Jersey, Tim Johnson of Illinois, Justin Amash of Michigan, Ron Paul of Texas, Steven LaTourette of Ohio, and Walter Jones of North Carolina – compiled a slightly more "liberal" voting record than the most conservative Democrat, Rep. Dan Boren of Oklahoma. And Ron Paul makes the list only because his libertarianism takes him so far right that on some issues he runs off the screen, Pac-Man like, and pops up on the other side. Continued polarization could lead to awful consequences. "The country is in dire straits, and ... we are tied down like Gulliver by the Lilliputians. We can't do squat," said Keith Poole, an expert on political polarization from the University of Georgia. "The tea party whack jobs are right: We're bankrupt... But we're just drifting, drifting toward the falls."

"There is a mismatch between our new, parliamentary-style parties and the governing system in which they have to operate," says Thomas Mann, a congressional scholar at the Brookings Institution and the co-author with Norman Ornstein of the American Enterprise Institute of *The Road to Obstructionism*, an upcoming book on the dismal state of Congress. "The Framers had in mind, with the Constitution's separation of powers and checks and balances, a process of negotiation. But now these negotiations don't take place. The inclination is to oppose, obstruct, discredit, and nullify."

Few in Washington believe that Cantor's Republicans will respect President Obama's mandate if he wins re-election. Their GOP counterparts in 1992 and 2008, as well as their Democratic counterparts in 2000, barely recognized the legitimacy of the newly elected chief executive, and there is little reason to think that the current crop of congressional Republicans or Democrats would defer to a leader from the rival party. Would Cantor honor the electorate's verdict if Obama wins in November? "That is a hypothetical I am not answering," the majority leader says. "It is disappointing to me that the Republicans give so little cooperation to President Obama, when we gave so much cooperation to President Bush," says Rep. Nancy Pelosi of California, the House Democratic leader – an assertion that draws guffaws from Republicans. The Democrats "rammed 'Obamacare' through the House, using every trick in the book to stifle dissent and circumvent the will of the American people," Speaker John Boehner told CPAC. "We are allowing a wide-open process to repeal it."

XIX

PRESIDENT OBAMA had warned in his State of the Union address on 26 January 2012 that the nation's middle class is at risk because of growing economic inequality, and argued that the government must do to preserve the basic American dream, says Holly Bailey, Senior Political Reporter of The Ticket. In a speech that is likely to set the theme of his 2012 re-election bid, Obama said "the basic American promise" that hard work can allow one to own a home and support a family are at risk if the government doesn't do more to balance the scale between the nation's rich and poor. "The defining issue of our time is how to keep that promise alive. No challenge is more urgent. No debate is more important," Obama declared. "We can either settle for a country where a shrinking number of people do really well, while a growing number of Americans barely get by. Or we can restore an economy where everyone gets a fair shot, everyone does their fair share, and everyone plays by the same set of rules. What's at stake are not Democratic values or Republican values, but American values. We have to reclaim them."

In his third such address to the Congress, Obama's focus was not just on the future – as he laid out broad proposals to boost an "economy built to last, where hard work pays off and responsibility is rewarded." But in a message that was unmistakably aimed at voters in the upcoming presidential election, Obama reminded his audience that the nation's economic troubles began long before he arrived at the White House, starting with the collapse of the nation's leading banks in 2008 due to lax regulation and "bad behavior". "In the six months before I took office, we lost nearly four million jobs. And we lost another four million before our policies were in full effect," Obama said. But he argued that the country is turning around under his policies, pointing to 3 million jobs created in the last 22 months. In a sign that Obama will campaign against the Republican-led Congress as much as his eventual GOP presidential rival, the president indicated he will take a hard stand against lawmakers determined to block his economic agenda.

"The state of our union is getting stronger, and we've come too far to turn back now," Obama insisted. "As long as I'm president, I will work with anyone in this chamber to build on this momentum. But I intend to fight obstruction with action, and I will oppose any effort to return to the very same policies that brought on this economic crisis in the first place." The president argued that he's laying out a "blueprint for an economy that's built to last" based on four main themes: American manufacturing, American energy, skills for American workers and "a renewal of American values."

Among other things, Obama called for a rollback for tax breaks for American companies that outsource jobs overseas and proposed new tax cuts for manufacturers that build their products stateside – a proposal that generated muted applause among Republican lawmakers in the House chamber. He also announced the creation of a "trade enforcement unit" that would investigate unfair trade practices in counties including China, an issue that has been a big issue on the 2012 campaign trail. "Our workers are the most productive on Earth, and if the playing field is level, I promise you, America will always win," Obama declared. Tackling an issue that will be big in the general election, Obama called on Republicans to pass immigration reform, including the DREAM Act. "If election-year politics keeps Congress from acting on a comprehensive plan, let's at least agree to stop expelling responsible young people who want to staff our labs, start new businesses, and defend this country," Obama said. "Send me a law that gives them the chance to earn their citizenship. I will sign it right away."

Obama also called for aid to boost the nation's struggling housing market, proposing new tax incentives to help homeowners save $3,000 a year on their mortgages. He also announced the creation of a federal task force to monitor banks, mortgage lenders and credit card companies for fraud. "Millions of Americans who work hard and play by the rules every day deserve a government and a financial system that do the same," Obama said. "It's time to apply the same rules from top to bottom: No bailouts, no handouts, and no copouts. An America built to last insists on responsibility from everybody."

Obama sounded familiar themes on energy, calling for a rollback of tax cuts on oil companies in favor of investments in clean energy sources. He announced a federal incentive to build clean energy projects on government land. On education, he called on states to pass laws to mandate that all minors stay in school until they graduate or turn 18. He also called on Congress to enact measures to ensure student aid but he also warned higher education institutions to crack down on skyrocketing education costs. "If you can't stop tuition from going up, the funding you get from taxpayers will go down," Obama said. "Higher education can't be a luxury – it's an economic imperative that every family in America should be able to afford." He repeated a call for investment in the nation's crumbling infrastructure, announcing that he will sign an executive order to clear the "red tape" slowing federal construction projects. "But you need to fund these projects. Take the money we're no longer spending at war, use half of it to pay down our debt, and use the rest to do some nation-building right here at home," Obama said.

The White House has been signaling for weeks that Obama would embrace populist themes about the economy, as a way of drawing a line in the sand between him and his Republican rivals ahead of his 2012 re-election push. Like other presidents before him, he was joined in the House chamber by individuals aimed at personifying elements of his speech, including Debbie Bosanek, the secretary to billionaire financier Warren Buffett, whose argument that he shouldn't be paying a lower tax rate than average workers has become a rallying cry for the White House. "We don't begrudge financial success in this country. We admire it," Obama insisted. "When Americans talk about folks like me paying my fair share of taxes, it's not because they envy the rich. It's because they understand that when I get tax breaks I don't need and the country can't afford, it either adds to the deficit, or somebody else has to make up the difference." But the larger message of Obama's remarks was obvious, as the president at one point returned to one of the major themes of his 2008 presidential bid: Rising above cynicism and partisan gridlock to enact real change in Washington. He noted that the "greatest blow to confidence in our economy" came during last year's combative debt ceiling talks. "Who benefited from that fiasco?" Obama asked. "I've talked tonight about the deficit of trust between Main Street and Wall Street. But the divide between this city and the rest of the country is at least as bad – and it seems to get worse every year."

He called for lawmakers to "lower the temperature" and "end the notion" that Democrats and Republicans must be locked in a "perpetual campaign of mutual destruction." At the same time, he warned again that he wouldn't wait for Congress to enact major reforms in Washington. "With or without this Congress, I will keep taking actions that help the economy grow," Obama said. "But I can do a whole lot more with your help. Because when we act together, there is nothing the United States of America can't achieve."

XX

ABOUT ONE THIRD of all American adults are taking care of their ill or disabled relatives, the National Alliance for Caregiving estimates, and that number is expected to grow as more people find themselves sandwiched between their own young kids and their rapidly-aging parents, writes Lylah M. Alphonse, Senior Editor of Yahoo! Shine / Vitality on 11 January 2012 after examining a study on Stress in America released by the American Psychological Association. Obviously, it's a stressful situation, but according to the American Psychological Association's latest report on stress, it's even tougher than most people think. Caregivers (who are usually women) are more likely to report stress than the general population – and they're more likely to suffer from chronic illness themselves, even though they're the ones taking care of people who are chronically ill.

In the newly released report, "Stress in America: Our Health at Risk", 1,226 U.S. residents ranked their stress levels and discussed their beliefs about stress and health. While the average stress rating dropped slightly since 2010 – from 5.4 to 5.2 on a 10-point scale – 39 per cent of respondents said that their stress levels had increased over the past year, and 44 per cent said that theirs had increased over the past five years. Meanwhile, just 29 per cent of respondents said that they thought they were doing an "excellent" or "very good" job managing or reducing their stress levels. But what's causing the stress? According to the report, money (75 per cent), work (70 per cent), and the economy (67 per cent) top the list, though the severity depends on where you live. People in the East were more stressed about money, relationships, and job stability than those in the West, and those in the South were most concerned about family responsibilities.

Numerous studies have shown the link between stress and chronic illnesses like diabetes, high blood pressure, heart disease, obesity, and depression. And those who care for people with chronic illnesses, ironically, are more likely – 82 per cent compared to 61 per cent for non-caregivers – to develop chronic illness themselves. They also tend to manage their stress in less-healthy ways, like smoking (20 per cent, compared to 10 per cent of non-caregivers), and 55 per cent of caregivers surveyed admitted that they felt "overwhelmed" by the amount of care their aging or ill family member required. "We are caught in a vicious cycle where our stress exceeds our own definition of what is healthy, and those who are already living with a chronic illness report even higher levels of stress," psychologist Norman B. Anderson, the American Psychological Association's CEO and executive vice president, said in a statement. "Given the persistent nature of our stress and the serious physical health consequences associated with it, stress has the potential to become the country's next public health crisis."

In his White House memoir, *Courage and Consequence*, Karl Rove recalls being the lone non-lawyer among the group of George W. Bush aides who initially interviewed John Roberts for the Supreme Court in 2005. Rove asked Roberts to go back in history to name the justice whom he most revered. Roberts' answer, Robert Jackson, intrigued and re-assured Rove. When appointed in 1941, Jackson was serving as Franklin Roosevelt's attorney-general and had been expected to be a pro-New Deal rubber-stamp on the court. But, as Rove put it, Jackson "instead demonstrated a fidelity to the Constitution that Roberts admired." And in a jaw-dropping turnabout worthy of Justice Jackson, Roberts provided the swing vote in a 5-to-4 decision that upheld the constitutionality of almost all of Obamacare, the president's signature legislative achievement. While an army of armchair court watchers expected Justice Anthony Kennedy to determine the fate of the Affordable Care Act (a recent *TIME* cover called him "The Decider"), it was Roberts who took his fidelity to the Constitution in an ideologically surprising direction. Kennedy voted with three other conservative justices to overturn the health insurance mandate at the heart of the law.

Constitutional law seminars and unlicensed political psychologists will spend years speculating about Roberts' motivations in joining the liberal bloc in probably the most important Supreme Court decision since Bush v. Gore in 2000. While we may wait decades to know for certain, it does seem plausible that Roberts may have been partly triggered by a desire to prevent the court from being seen as overtly political. Polls showing public respect for the Supreme Court at a quarter-century low reflect the growing view that the justices pursue partisan agendas. One of the most important passages in Roberts' majority decision was the chief justice's assertion: "We do not consider whether the act embodied sound policies. That judgment is entrusted to the Nation's elected leaders. We ask only whether Congress has the power under the Constitution to enact the challenge provisions." In short, if you want a national referendum on the health-care law, then the proper arena is the 2012 campaign – and not the inner sanctums of the Supreme Court.

The majority opinion in the health care case points up the inadequacy of the political clichés used in the heat of an election year to describe the Supreme Court. Phrases like "strict constructionist" and "not making law from the bench" do not clarify complex Supreme Court opinions. Romney's campaign website declares, "As president, Mitt will nominate judges in the mold of Chief Justice Roberts and Justices Scalia, Thomas and Alito." There's only one problem with this formulation: Roberts went in one direction and Scalia, Thomas and Alito went in the opposite on the constitutionality of the health care bill.

Obama's own ability at prophecy is limited, as well. In 2005, the former constitutional law professor declared in a Senate address that he was opposing Roberts' nomination to the Supreme Court because "I ultimately have to give more weight to his deeds and overarching political philosophy ... than to the assuring words he provided me in our meeting." While Obama has sharply disagreed with major decisions of the Roberts Court (particularly the anything-goes Citizen United ruling on campaign finance), it is tempting to wonder if the president now feels that he misjudged the man who saved his legislative legacy. It is almost part of the job description of a president that he will make, at least, one blunder when picking Supreme Court justices. Harry Truman called one of his nominees, Tom Clark, a "damn fool from Texas." When George H.W. Bush tapped New Hampshire jurist David Souter in 1990, the president never expected that he would be reinforcing the court's liberal wing. Now it is Roberts who has refused to stay in his pre-determined ideological cubbyhole.

With four current justices over the age of 70, it is likely that whoever is elected president this November will get an opportunity to put his stamp on the Supreme Court. But the potential for Lucy-and-the-football surprises endures. About the only ways a president can achieve some measure of certainty about the court are either to nominate fire-breathing ideologues like Antonin Scalia or political cronies like Abe Fortas, who kept open a back channel to Lyndon

Johnson during his brief tenure as a justice. But even the Scalia precedent no longer works, because anyone with a sharply articulated judicial philosophy probably could not make it through today's hyperpartisan Senate.

XXI

THOUSANDS OF people gathered at dawn 17 October 2012 to give the new Martin Luther King Jr. Memorial a proper dedication on the National Mall after its opening in August, according to an Associated Press report by Brett Zongkier from Washington, DC. Aretha Franklin, poet Nikki Giovanni and President Barack Obama were among those honoring the legacy of the nation's foremost civil rights leader during a ceremony scheduled to run more than four hours. Cherry Hawkins traveled from Houston with her cousins and arrived at 6 a.m. to be part of the dedication. They postponed earlier plans to attend the August dedication, which was postponed because of Hurricane Irene. "I wanted to do this for my kids and grandkids," Hawkins said. She expects the memorial will be in their history books someday. "They can say, 'Oh, my granny did that.'" Hawkins, her cousin DeAndrea Cooper and Cooper's daughter Brittani Jones, 23, visited the King Memorial after joining a march with the Rev. Al Sharpton to urge Congress to pass a jobs bill. "You see his face in the memorial, and it's kind of an emotional moment," Cooper said. "It's beautiful. They did a wonderful job."

A stage for speakers and thousands of folding chairs were set up on a field near the memorial along with large TV screens. Some attendees started lining up at 5 a.m. and even earlier Sunday morning. Organizers anticipate as many as 50,000 people will attend. By 9 a.m., thousands of seats were filled, and attendees were greeted with bright sunlight. The August ceremony had been expected to draw 250,000. Even with the smaller crowd, King Memorial foundation president Harry Johnson called Sunday "a day of fulfillment". About 1.5 million people are estimated to have visited the 30-foot-tall statue of King and the granite walls where 14 of his quotations are carved in stone. The memorial is the first on the National Mall honoring a black leader. The sculpture of King with his arms crossed appears to emerge from a stone extracted from a mountain. It was carved by Chinese artist Lei Yixin. The design was inspired by a line from the famous "I Have a Dream" speech in 1963: "Out of the mountain of despair, a stone of hope." King's "Dream" speech during the March on Washington galvanized the civil rights movement. King's older sister, Christine King Farris, said she witnessed a baby become "a great hero to humanity." She said the memorial will ensure her brother's legacy will provide a source of inspiration worldwide for generations. "He was my little brother, and I watched him grow and develop into a man who was destined for a special kind of greatness," she said. To young people in the crowd, she said King's message is that "Great dreams can come true and America is the place where you can make it happen." King's daughter, the Rev. Bernice King, said her family is proud to witness the memorial's dedication. She said it was a long time coming and had been a priority for her mother, Coretta Scott King, who died in 2006. "Today represents another milestone in the life of America," Bernice King said. King's son Martin Luther King III also was to speak. The choir from King's historic Ebenezer Baptist Church in Atlanta was scheduled to sing.

The nation's first black president, who was just 6 years old when King was assassinated in April 1968 in Memphis, Tenn., will speak about the man he has said "gave his life serving others." Giovanni planned to read her poem, "In the Spirit of Martin", and Franklin was to sing. Early in the ceremony, during a rendition of "Lift Every Voice and Sing", the crowd cheered when images on screen showed Obama on the night he won the 2008 presidential election. A concert followed the dedication, featuring Stevie Wonder, James Taylor, Sheryl Crow and others.

XXII

HOUSE SPEAKER John Boehner and members of his Republican leadership team scoffed at the positive jobs data, suggesting that despite new signals that the economy is improving, the president's economic agenda has failed and the country would be better off if the GOP's policies are implemented. Boehner bluntly advised President

Obama's re-election campaign to prod Senate Democrats to "get off their rear ends" in order to bring the unemployment rate down even further. He once again called on the president to pressure Senate Democrats to consider more of the GOP's House-passed legislation, 27 of which the speaker said are stalled in the upper chamber. "The president asked us to work with [Senate Democrats]. We have worked with them," Boehner, R-Ohio, said. "If president really wants to get the economy moving again, really wants to improve his own chances for reelection, maybe he'll pick up the phone and call Senator Reid and ask Senate Democrats to get off their rear ends." Boehner ripped President Obama for promising that the stimulus bill would keep the unemployment rate from ever exceeding 8 percent. The speaker said that the Obama administration had also promised that this far along into the recovery, the unemployment rate should have fallen to 6 percent by now as a result of the Recovery Act.

Affluent black Americans who are leaving industrial cities for the suburbs and the South are shifting traditional lines between rich and poor, according to new census data, writes Hope Yen of the Associated Press. Their migration is widening the income gap between whites and the inner-city blacks who remain behind, while making blacks less monolithic as a group and subject to greater income disparities. "Reverse migration is changing the South and its race relations," said Roderick Harrison, a Howard University sociologist and former chief of racial statistics at the Census Bureau. He said a rising black middle class is promoting a growing belief among some black conservatives that problems of the disadvantaged are now rooted more in character or cultural problems, rather than race. But Harrison said most black Americans maintain a strong racial identity, focused on redressing perceived lack of opportunities, in part because many of them maintain close ties to siblings or other blacks who are less successful. "I don't think suburban blacks are yet driven by their higher income or new locations, although this might have a greater effect in a generation or two," he said.

The typical white person last year earned income roughly 1.7 times higher than that of blacks, the widest ratio since the 1990s. Census figures show that cities such as Detroit, Chicago, Philadelphia, Cleveland and Milwaukee in particular saw increases in inequality, hurt by an exodus of middle-class minorities while lower-skilled blacks stayed in the cities. Low-income blacks also slipped further behind. The share of black households ranking among the poorest poor – those earning less than $15,000 – climbed from 20 per cent to 26 per cent over the past decade; other race and ethnic groups posted smaller increases. At the same time, African-Americans making $200,000 or more a year were unchanged from 2000 at about 1.1 per cent, even after a deep recession.

Many affluent blacks are moving to the South, seeking a return to their ancestral homeland after a decades-long Great Migration to the North. Pursuing a better quality of life, they are opting for more upscale metropolitan locales rather than the traditional rural communities of the old South in places such as Louisiana, Mississippi and Arkansas, which remain home to larger shares of minority farmers, construction and other low-wage workers. Since 1990, blacks living in Southern urban locations such as Atlanta, Dallas, Washington, D.C., and Miami, where incomes rose in the last decade, have increased 70 per cent. William H. Frey, a Brookings Institution demographer who did a broad analysis of the race and income data, said the latest numbers reflect a longer-term trend of increased racial integration between blacks and whites. He said the changes could pose challenges in the coming months in political redistricting as well as courting the traditional black vote. Groups in states such as Texas, Florida, California and Maryland have gone to court or are now otherwise grappling with political maps being re-drawn based on the 2010 census, considering whether to preserve historically black legislative seats amid slowing population growth and black movement into traditionally white suburbs. The change also complicates strategy for President Obama, who is banking on blacks in key Southern states in the 2012 election. Obama is pushing a broader re-election theme of middle-class renewal, reciting his jobs agenda and his feud with Congress over extending a Social Security tax cut, while targeting outreach to black communities in hopes of remaining competitive in Southern and other battleground states.

"The Democratic Party will surely gain consistent support from these new black suburbanites, but the active support for traditional black issues like civil rights may take a back seat," Frey said, citing issues such as schools, housing and public safety that may rise to the forefront. According to census data, about 67 million Americans, or nearly 1 in 4, lived in neighborhoods with poverty rates of 20 per cent or higher; that's up from roughly 1 in 5 in 2000. The South in general had higher shares of people living in high-poverty areas, led by states including Mississippi, Louisiana, Texas and Kentucky. Despite some gains for middle-class blacks, African-Americans on average last year still had rising poverty and worsening economic situations compared with whites. The mostly suburban counties where blacks had growing and higher-than-average income make up about 19 per cent of the black population. That's compared with 45 per cent of blacks who lived in urban counties and small towns where black incomes fell relative to whites.

Part of the income divide falls along age and education, with higher unemployment rates for young men and those who lack a college degree. Last year, about 19 per cent of men ages 25 to 34 were "idle" – neither working nor attending school – up 5 percentage points from 2007, according to the Population Reference Bureau. About 31 per cent of young black adults were disconnected from school and work, compared with 27 per cent for Latinos and about 19 per cent each for whites and Asians. Blacks also were more likely than other groups to live in neighborhoods with poverty rates of 40 per cent or more, roughly 1 in 9.

XXIII

A MITT ROMNEY spokesman reprimanded reporters traveling with the candidate on his six-day foreign trip, telling them to "kiss my a**" after they shouted questions from behind a rope line, said Emily Friedman of ABC OTUS News. As Romney left the site of the Tomb of the Unknown Soldier in Warsaw and walked toward his motorcade parked in Pilsudski Square, reporters began shouting questions from the line where campaign staffers had told them to stay behind, prompting traveling press secretary Rick Gorka to tell a group of reporters to "kiss my a**" and "shove it." He later apologized.

As Romney wrapped up his visit to the historical site, a CNN reporter had yelled, "Governor Romney, are you concerned about some of the mishaps of your trip?"

"Governor Romney, do you have a statement for the Palestinians?" a *New York Times* reporter shouted.

"What about your gaffes?" yelled a *Washington Post* reporter, referring to a number of missteps the candidate has made during his trip, including one in which he said there were some "disconcerting" developments leading up to the London Olympics, drawing the ire of the British media, and another suggesting that culture was to blame for the difference in economic success between Israelis and Palestinians.

The Romney campaign has called the reports on the candidate's remarks about Palestinians a "gross mis-characterization."

Gorka told reporters answering questions to "show some respect. This is a holy site for the Polish people," he added.

"We haven't had another chance to ask a question," one reporter noted to Gorka.

Gorka told another journalist to "shove it."

Gorka later called both reporters to apologize for his remarks, telling one that he was "inappropriate".

Republican House Speaker John Boehner ripped into President Obama during an interview with Fox News Radio's *Kilmeade and Friends*, accusing him of never having "a real job," said Chris Moody of Yahoo! News / The Ticket. Boehner said, "Sometimes I have to catch my breath and slow down because the rhetoric in this campaign is just so over the top. And that's because the President's policies have failed. Listen: 93 per cent of Americans believe they're a part of the middle class. That's why you hear the President talk about the middle class every day, because he's talking to 93 per cent of the American people. But the President has never created a job. He's never even had a real job for [God's] sake. And I can tell you from my dealings with him, he has no idea how the real world, that we actually live in, works." The Ohio Republican was responding to a question about Obama's comments about building the economy "from the middle class" and not "from the top down."

But the U.S. economy added 163,000 jobs in July, the most in five months, wrote Christopher Rugaber, AP Economics writer. It was a hopeful sign after three months of sluggish hiring. July's hiring was the best since February. Still, the economy has added an average of 151,000 jobs a month this year – enough to keep up with population growth but not enough to drive down the unemployment rate. Stocks rose sharply in early trading. The Dow Jones industrial average added 219 points to 13,098, while Standard & Poor's 500 index rose 125 points to 1,390. The government uses two surveys to measure employment; a survey of businesses showing job gains is one. The unemployment rate comes from a survey of households and is calculated by dividing the number of unemployed people by the size of the labor force. In July, more people said they were unemployed, while the size of the labor force shrank even more. Economists say the business survey is more reliable. Stronger job creation could help President Barack Obama's re-election hopes. Still, the unemployment rate has been above 8 per cent since his first month in office – the longest stretch on record. No president since World War II has faced re-election with unemployment over 8 per cent.

A better outlook on hiring could make the Federal Reserve reluctant to take more action to spur growth. The Fed, which ended a two-day policy meeting, signaled in a statement a growing inclination to take further steps if hiring doesn't pick up. But some economists say the job gains need to be greater. Paul Ashworth, senior U.S. economist for Capital Economics, said July's job gains were a "vast improvement" over the past four months. Still, they were well below the average 252,000 jobs a month added from December through February. "It also isn't strong enough to drive the unemployment rate lower, which is what the Fed really wants to see. So, on balance, we doubt this would be enough to persuade the Fed to hold fire in September," Ashworth said. The job gains were broad-based. Manufacturing added 25,000 jobs, the most since March. Restaurants and bars added 29,000. Retailers hired 7,000 more workers. Education and health services gained 38,000. Governments cut 9,000 positions. Average hourly wages also increased by 2 cents to $23.52 an hour. Over the past year wages have increased 1.7 per cent – matching the rate of inflation. Despite July's gains, the economy remains weak more than three years after economists declared the recession had ended in June 2009. Growth slowed to an annual rate of 1.5 per cent in the April-June quarter, down from 2 per cent in the first quarter and 4.1 per cent in the final three months of 2011. Manufacturing activity shrank for the second straight month in July, a private survey said. Consumer confidence improved slightly last month but remains weak.

Rising pessimism about the future is taking a toll on businesses and consumers, many economists say. Europe's financial crisis has weakened that region's economy, hurting U.S. exports. Worries have also intensified that the U.S. economy will fall off a "fiscal cliff" at the end of the year. That's when tax increases and deep spending cuts will take effect unless Congress reaches a budget deal. A recession could follow, Fed Chairman Ben Bernanke has warned. Americans are responding by spending less and saving more. A big reason growth slowed in the second quarter was that consumer spending, which accounts for roughly 70 per cent of economic activity, slowed to an annual growth rate of 1.5 per cent. That was down from 2.4 per cent in the first quarter. The 2012 survey of Affluence and Wealth in America, from American Express Publishing and Harrison Group, finds that One Percenters, as the Occupy protesters named them, are hoarding three times as much cash as they were two years ago. Their savings rate soared to 34 per cent in the second quarter of 2012, up from 12 per cent in 2007 reported Robert Frank of CNBC on 8 August 2012. And, according to the poll, the fear and the lack of risk taking could be imposing real financial costs on the economy. Higher savings would normally be good for the economy. But not now, when capital is needed to invest in growth and jobs. The One Percenters put 56 per cent of their available cash into savings accounts and money markets in 2012 – that's up from 24 per cent in 2007. They are investing just 44 per cent in financial markets – down from 76 per cent in 2007. More One Percenters say the stock market is "a real risk" rather than a "real opportunity". That's a big switch from just last year, when 62 per cent said the market was an opportunity. In other words, One Percenters used to save less, and invest more. Now they are "basically stuffing money under the mattress," said Jim Taylor, vice chairman of Harrison Group.

That also means they are spending less – on everything from traditional luxury to second homes. Fully 82 per cent said they would spend more if they had more confidence in the future. "This has resulted in people managing their risk to a 'no loss' position rather a 'real gains' position," Taylor said. "That's not the great tradition of American investing." One respondent in the study said, "My savings rate has gone up and I'm not spending, which I realize is bad for the economy ... but I like having a wide moat around me so that nothing can bother me."

The Occupy movement, media coverage of inequality and the Obama campaign's "you didn't build it" attacks have all made the wealthy fearful of any outward signs of success. The survey showed that only 31 per cent of today's One Percenters "like it when others recognize me as wealthy." That's a huge drop from 2010, when 53 per cent liked the recognition. This jibes with another recent poll that showed One Percenters don't see themselves (and don't want to be seen) as One Percenters. The wealthy, in other words, are embarrassed to be wealthy. "We can't have a rise of an aristocracy without the aristocracy believing in it," Taylor said. As a result, today's wealthy are further isolating themselves from broader society. Only 46 per cent of One Percenters say "it is important for me to join social events in my community." That's a huge drop from 2010, when 64 per cent said community is important. Fully 90 per cent of the ultra-wealthy say they prefer to spend time with their closest friends and family.

Many Democrats might argue that all of this moat-building and cash hoarding and community-shunning by the rich is exactly why we should tax them more. They say the lack of mass consumer demand is the reason the wealthy aren't investing and creating jobs. At least the government would deploy that capital into the economy, rather than keep it under a Vividus mattress, they argue. Most One Percenters agree with them – at least when it comes to higher taxes. The survey found that 62 per cent of One Percenters are in favor of an income-tax increase. More than half say the increase should be imposed on people making $500,000 or more. Another 31 per cent say it should be imposed on filers making more than $250,000 – basically the Obama cut-off. Only 25 per cent think the income cut-off should be $1 million.

Taylor said that it's the uncertainty over tax policy rather than higher taxes themselves that is most affecting the spending and investing of the wealthy. He said this reality stands in stark contrast to the public perception that greed is preventing compromise in Washington. "All of this antagonism that is being created is not the fault of the people Obama says are being greedy," Taylor says. "If there is resistance to tax increases it's coming from others, perhaps lobbyists or Tea Party people or consultants. The One Percent accepts the reality." And they also understand, perhaps, the need for self-preservation.

XXIV

KAITLIN NOOTBAAR, the Oklahoma high school valedictorian who was denied her diploma after she used the word "hell" in her graduation speech, said she has no plans to apologize, wrote Dylan Stableford of Yahoo! News / The Lookout. "I'm still not gonna issue an apology, because I'm not sorry for that," Nootbaar said in an interview on the *Today* show. "I'm sorry for other things. I'm sorry for the problems that this has caused the school, especially the teachers. I've heard they've been getting calls from numerous people, and it would be nice if that would stop." Nootbaar graduated from Prague High School with a 4.0 grade point average, her father, David Nootbaar, told KFOR-TV. But school administrators told him that Kaitlin would have to submit a written apology in order to get her diploma. "We went to the office and asked for the diploma and the principal said, 'Your diploma is right here but you ain't getting it. Close the door, we have a problem,'" David Nootbaar said. She was inspired she said by a similar address in *Eclipse: The Twilight Saga*. But Kaitlin recounted how annoying it is to be constantly asked what she wants to do as graduation approached. "How the hell do I know?" she said. "I've changed my mind so many times."

A woman who helped a lost man ended up with a surprise $20,000 gift, Ron Recinto of the Sideshow reported. That's what happened last month when Jennifer Vasilakos guided Ty Warner when he stopped and asked for driving directions in Santa Barbara, Calif. While Warner didn't know exactly how to get to where he was going, Vasilakos didn't realize who she was helping. Warner is the billionaire founder of Ty Inc., the Beanie Baby company. Vasilakos was at the intersection trying to raise $20,000 for a stem cell procedure she needs to help save her life because she suffers from kidney failure and does not qualify for a transplant. She describes their encounter in her blog. "I often get asked by random strangers for directions. Not one to miss an opportunity, I handed him my flyer and he made a fifty dollar donation. As he drove off, I thought that was the end of our encounter.

He'd returned after an hour or so. Rolling down his window, he reached out his hand and introduced himself. I immediately recognized his name. He was kind and sincere as he looked directly into my eyes... I listened as he repeated over and over that he was going to help me; that my fundraising was done; that I didn't need to worry any longer. He said he would send a check after he returned to his offices during the week." He was true to his word. Vasilakos, an herbalist and Reiki teacher, received a package on July 16 with a $20,000 check and with a handwritten note from Warner. The note read in part, "Someone up there loves you because I was guided to meet you Saturday. I never lose my way, but fate had me lost and ask you for directions. The rest of the story I hope will be a wonderful new life for you."

Harvard University is investigating whether dozens of undergraduate students cheated on a take-home exam last spring, writes Jay Lindsay of Associated Press. School officials said they discovered students may have shared answers or plagiarized on a final exam. They declined to release the name of the class, the students' names or the exact number being investigated, citing privacy laws. The undergraduate class had a minimum of 250 students and possible cheating was discovered in roughly half the take-home exams, university officials said. "These allegations, if proven, represent totally unacceptable behavior that betrays the trust upon which intellectual inquiry at Harvard depends," President Drew Faust said. A Harvard spokesman said he knows of no incidents in recent memory of possible cheating at the university on this scale. Each student whose work is in question has been called to appear before a subcommittee of the Harvard College Administrative Board, which reviews issues of academic integrity, said Jay M. Harris, dean of undergraduate education. He emphasized that none of the allegations has been proven and said there's no evidence of widespread cheating at Harvard. "The facts that are before us are that we have a problem in this one course," Harris said. "I hope that doesn't sound overly naive, I don't want to be naive, but this is what we have. The rest would be speculation. Looking at the students we have and the work that they do, I would be loath to say this is something that represents Harvard students generally."

The spring course included undergraduates at all class levels, Harris said. A teaching assistant noticed some possible problems on the tests, including evidence that students collaborated on answers or used the same long, identical strings of words. The exam had clear instructions that no collaboration was allowed, Harris said. The assistant notified the professor, who referred the case in May to the administrative board. After interviewing some students, the board found what Harris characterized as "cause for concern."

A student was shot and critically wounded on the first day of classes at a Baltimore County high school, Alex Dominguez of the Associated Press reported. County police said the wounded Perry Hall High School student was flown to a hospital. The 17-year-old male student was in critical condition at Maryland Shock Trauma Center, a hospital spokeswoman said. A male suspect was taken into custody after the shooting, police said. The suspect is a student, but police did not say where he attended school. The school was evacuated, and students were escorted to a nearby shopping center and middle school. WJZ-TV showed video of a shirtless male with his hands behind his back being put into a police cruiser. Perry Hall is a middle-class community along the Interstate 95 corridor, northeast of Baltimore city. The school is the largest in the county, with 2,200 students. County Councilman David Marks, who lives next door to the school, said he had received dozens of phone calls and text messages from worried parents and residents. "This is a very comfortable, very safe community, and it's an excellent high school," said Marks, who graduated from Perry Hall. "I think this is an aberration, but clearly one that is horrifying, particularly on the first day of school." Television coverage showed scores of police cars surrounding the school and parked on neighborhood streets. A group of officers with weapons drawn staked out a corner of the building, one of them lying prone on the ground and appearing to cover a particular area of the campus. Hundreds of students streamed away from the school toward a nearby shopping center where they met their parents.

Nine persons were wounded and two people were killed outside the Empire State Building in Midtown Manhattan Friday after Jeffrey Johnson shot his 41-year-old former boss, Steven Ercolino. The two dead include the gunman, who was shot and killed by police near the tourist entrance of the landmark skyscraper. Jason Sickles of Yahoo!

News / The Lookout reported that Johnson, 53, lost his job last year during a corporate downsizing at Hazan Imports, where Ercolino was a vice president. He returned to his office to target his former supervisor. Johnson followed his former co-worker down 33rd Street and shot him outside of Legends Bar, according to the *New York Post*. It is unclear if he fired into a crowd of pedestrians outside of the Empire State Building, or if pedestrians were caught in crossfire, reported the *New York Daily News*. A construction worker who witnessed the shooting followed the suspect and then alerted police who were posted nearby. As the officers approached Johnson, he pulled his gun and fired on the officers. They returned fire and killed him, New York City Mayor Michael Bloomberg said. None of the other people who were shot were seriously wounded. Some of those wounded may have been hit by police gunfire, Bloomberg said. After the shooting, police immediately cordoned off a one-block perimeter around the Empire State Building. Around 10 a.m., a lone tourist bus headed down Fifth Avenue, and a guide could be heard over the bus's microphone explaining that they were nearing the landmark. As police waved the bus to detour down 36th Street, the guide was openly mystified. "I don't know what's going on, folks," he said, as the bus turned. The bus's passengers looked up at the sky at a news helicopter floated overhead. Some stood, clutching their cameras.

And on 24 October 2012 Shayndi Raice and Nick Timiraos of *The Wall Street Journal* reported that the federal government has filed a civil lawsuit against Bank of America Corp. (BAC), alleging the second-biggest U.S. bank by assets saddled taxpayers with losses by misrepresenting the quality of home loans it sold to mortgage-finance firms Fannie Mae (FNMA) and Freddie Mac (FMCC). The action, filed on 24 October 2012 in federal court in Manhattan, seeks at least $1 billion in damages. The filing represents a novel effort by the government to defray costs tied to the 2008 bailout of Fannie and Freddie, and potentially opens a new front against a banking industry already dealing with hefty legal costs.

According to *The Wall Street Journal* the government alleges Countrywide, which Bank of America acquired in 2008, dismembered quality control and checks on loan quality in 2007 through 2009, in a process called "the Hustle" that aimed to boost the speed at which it originated and sold loans to the companies. The mortgage unit falsely continued to claim the loans qualified for insurance from Fannie Mae and Freddie Mac, the complaint alleges. Bank of America shares, up 70 per cent this year, were up six cents in midday trading at $9.41. Fannie and Freddie, while backed by taxpayers since the 2008 bailout, aren't part of the government. Previous suits have been brought on behalf of government agencies such as Medicare and the FHA. Fannie and Freddie were publicly traded entities before their market funding evaporated in the early stages of the financial crisis, forcing their effective nationalization. Taxpayers have since poured $142 billion into the companies, which along with other government agencies financed nine out of 10 home loans written last year. Fannie and Freddie don't make loans but guarantee regular principal and interest payments to mortgage-bond investors. The suit was also brought under a federal statute known as the Financial Institutions Reform, Recovery and Enforcement Act, which was enacted in 1989 following a wave of bank failures triggered by the savings-and-loan crisis.

Last year Fannie and Freddie's regulator, the Federal Housing Finance Agency, sued 18 major banks including Bank of America, accusing them of violating federal securities law and other laws in the sale of residential private-label mortgage-backed securities. The seven biggest U.S. commercial banks have recognized or set aside $76 billion in mortgage-related legal costs since 2008, according to analysts at Credit Suisse Group (CSGN.VX). Fannie Mae stopped buying or guaranteeing new loans delivered by Bank of America this past February amid an impasse over billions in defaulted mortgages that Fannie said Bank of America was obligated to re-purchase. Negotiations over resolving the dispute are ongoing, according to both parties. Bank of America briefly became Fannie's top client following its acquisition of Countrywide. It accounted for 20 per cent of all loans Fannie bought or backed in 2009, but that share had fallen below 10 per cent by the third quarter of 2011, and below 3 per cent in the fourth quarter, according to Inside Mortgage Finance.

The action isn't Bank of America's first False Claims Act suit. In February, Bank of America agreed to a $1 billion settlement of False Claims Act fraud allegations tied to Federal Housing Administration-backed loans brought by the Eastern District of New York. The bank settled without admitting wrongdoing. Three other large banks have agreed to pay a total of more than $490 million in similar cases, each accepting responsibility for "certain conduct". The suit follows in a long line of legal headaches for Bank of America. Last month, the bank agreed to pay $2.43 billion to settle claims it misled investors about the acquisition of brokerage firm Merrill Lynch & Co., the largest settlement of a shareholder claim by a financial-services firm since the upheaval of 2008 and 2009. The lawsuits continue to underscore how the hasty acquisitions made during the height of the financial crisis by Kenneth Lewis, then the bank's chief executive, still haunt it today. Decisions to buy mortgage lender Countrywide and Merrill have forced Bank of America, run since 2010 by Chief Executive Brian Moynihan, to shoulder some $42 billion in litigation expenses, payouts and reserves, according to company figures.

In a remarkable policy shift, former Citigroup chairman and chief executive Sandy Weill now thinks that Wall Street should break up its big banks in an effort to regain the public's trust, according to Dylan Stableford of Yahoo! News / The Ticket. "What we should probably do is go and split up investment banking from banking," Weill said on CNBC's Squawk Box. "Have banks be deposit takers, have banks make commercial loans and real estate loans, have banks do something that's not going to risk the taxpayer dollars, that's not too big to fail. "I'm suggesting that they be broken up so that the taxpayer will never be at risk, the depositors won't be at risk, the leverage of the banks will be something reasonable, and the investment banks can do trading," he said. Weill essentially called for the return of the Glass-Steagall Act, CNBC said. The 1933 Depression-era legislation separated investment and commercial banking activities in the wake of the 1929 stock market crash and commercial bank failure, according to Investopedia. It was repealed in 1999 during the Clinton administration. Weill was one of the architects of the Gramm-Leach-Bliley Act, which helped repeal Glass-Steagall. The 79-year-old Wall Street legend also called for complete transparency in the banking industry. "There should be no such thing as off balance sheet," he said. "I want to see us be a leader, and what we're doing now is not going to make us a leader."

A wave of tax increases and billions of dollars in automatic spending cuts would cause "a lot of damage" to the fragile economy, Treasury Secretary Timothy Geithner has said, according to Julie Halpert in Ann Arbor, Mich. Tax breaks for all Americans are set to expire at the end of the year, and $100 billion in cuts to domestic and military programs are set to take effect in January if Congress does not agree on a new deficit-cutting deal. "Many people who look at this say that, yes, you'd at least get a recession out of this," Geithner said on PBS' Charlie Rose television show. "The cumulative size of those cuts, tax increases and spending cuts, are very, very large relative to the economy," he said.

The nonpartisan Congressional Budget Office forecasts that the mix of spending cuts and tax hikes would cause the U.S. economy to contract at an annual rate of 1.3 per cent for the first half of 2013 if lawmakers do not act. The White House is pushing Congress to extend for one year tax cuts for families earning less than $250,000 a year. Taxes for those earning more than that would increase in 2013 if Congress passes legislation the Obama administration wants. Republicans argue that all tax cuts should be extended to avoid hurting the tepid economy. Geithner warned lawmakers that investors could not stomach a repeat of last year's debt ceiling battle that increased the U.S. Treasury's borrowing costs and stripped the United States of its top credit rating. "You saw huge damage to consumer confidence, to business confidence, and to confidence around the world in the United States because you had people in public office threatening to default on our nation's obligations," Geithner said. President Barack Obama had said that Congress "ought to be able to come together and agree on a plan, a balanced approach" to avoid the steep automatic spending cuts.

Geithner reiterated that the domestic fiscal problems and the European Union's economic crisis were still the biggest threats to the U.S. economy. But he said he thought the 17-nation common currency would stay intact. "They've said, 'We will do everything it takes to hold the European Union together.' And you could say that's what they're trying to do," Geithner said. His comments came as Moody's Investors Service cited an increased chance that Greece could leave the euro zone, which would set off a chain of financial sector shocks. Although Geithner said European leaders had committed to do what it takes to hold their financial system together, he added they had to make that commitment credible to markets and investors. "If you leave Europe on the edge of the abyss, if you leave it just teetering on the edge of financial disaster, it'll be much harder for this strategy to work," he said.

An analysis of political spending by the *Wall Street Journal* found that organized labor groups dropped a combined $4.4 billion on political activities between 2006 and 2011, about four times more than previously estimated, writes Chris Moody in Yahoo! News and the Ticket on 10 July 2012. The *Journal* cast a wide net to determine what counted as "political spending", including activities that range from traditional candidate donations to the cost of hot dogs for union demonstrators at political rallies. To find the additional costs, the newspaper added spending reports filed with the Labor Department to Federal Election Commission spending data.

The usual measure of unions' clout encompasses chiefly what they spend supporting federal candidates through their political-action committees, which are funded with voluntary contributions, and lobbying Washington, which is a cost borne by the unions' own coffers. These kinds of spending, which unions report to the Federal Election Commission and to Congress, totaled $1.1 billion from 2005 through 2011, according to the nonpartisan Center for Responsive Politics. The unions' reports to the Labor Department capture an additional $3.3 billion that unions spent over the same period on political activity. The costs reported to the Labor Department range from polling fees, to money spent persuading union members to vote a certain way, to bratwursts to feed Wisconsin workers protesting at the state capitol last year. Much of this kind of spending comes not from members' contributions to a PAC but directly from unions' dues-funded coffers. There is no requirement that unions report all of this kind of spending to the Federal Election Commission, or FEC.

Union spending goes overwhelmingly to Democratic candidates and liberal causes. According to the Center for Responsive Politics, which tracks political spending, 92 per cent of the $58.5 million in direct candidate donations from 1990 to 2012 went toward Democratic candidates. Jeff Hauser, a spokesman for the AFL-CIO, responded to the *Journal* report, arguing that much of the union political activity on the local and state level cannot be equally compared to spending by super PACs:

The *Wall Street Journal* treats all advocacy for working people at the local, state and federal levels as "political" work. Everything from someone writing policy proposals to create jobs to working in a local community to elect a working families-friendly City Council is viewed as equivalent to corporations anonymously attacking President Obama. Providing expert input for the formulation of mine safety rules, assisting the civil rights community – be it the 1963 March on Washington or voting protection efforts year-round – everything labor works on is said to be a counter-weight to the Super PACs of Karl Rove, the Koch Brothers and more shadowy figures. By this definition, the entire budget of the Chamber of Commerce would be considered political, but the Chamber doesn't report its spending on Department of Labor forms or anywhere else. The *Journal* missed the central point that unions are advocacy organizations. The job of a union is to advocate on behalf of working men and women. Moreover, the *Journal* ignored the fact that corporations outspend unions by more than 10 to one but are free to hide their spending while unions disclose everything.

XXV

FORMER PRESIDENT Bill Clinton, seen once as a political foe of President Barack Obama, made a strong case that he's one of the nominee's best surrogates on 5 September 2012, especially when it comes to bringing independents into the Democratic re-election effort, writes Chris Moody of Yahoo! News / The Ticket. In a speech that was repeatedly interrupted by standing ovations and often veered from the prepared remarks on his Teleprompter, Clinton took on nearly every criticism that Republicans leveled at Obama at their party convention in Tampa the week before. Clinton's wide-ranging speech defended several aspects of Obama's record, including his health care law, the controversial Recovery Act, the restructuring of cash-strapped American auto companies and even his choice of Joe Biden as vice president. "We believe 'we're all in this together' is a far better philosophy than 'you're on your own'." Clinton said in a speech that went on for nearly an hour. "I want to nominate a man who's cool on the outside but burns for America on the inside." Clinton even took on the question that Republicans have used in their convention counter-programming, arguing that the country is better off than it was when Obama first took office. "Are we better off than we were when he took office? Listen to this, listen to this," he said, clearly enjoying an audience hanging on his every word. "When President Obama took office, the economy was in a free fall, we were losing 750,000 jobs a month. Are we doing better than that today? The answer is yes."

Speaking from experience, Clinton defended Obama from critics who blame him for overseeing what many have felt is a painstakingly slow recovery from the 2008 recession. "No president, not me or any of my predecessors, could have repaired all the damage in just four years," he said, going on to suggest that Obama's work was only half finished. The theme – that electing Republicans would stall the progress of an administration still struggling to turn around the economy – is one that has been repeated throughout the week. Clinton hammered the point home. "He inherited a deeply damaged economy," Clinton said (and) Obama "put a floor under the crash, began the long, hard road to recovery and laid the foundation for a more modern, more well-balanced economy that will produce millions of good new jobs, vibrant new businesses, and lots of new wealth for the innovators." The biggest problem for Democrats, according to Republicans, is that the country is still on that road – and looking for a fast way off. But during a Democratic convention that up until this point appeared to be geared toward the liberal wing of the party, Clinton's remarks were tailored to independents who might tune in during prime time. He made his arguments comprehensively, weaving personal stories in and out of his pitch for the President. "Conditions are improving, and if you'll renew the president's contract you will feel it," Clinton said.

When Clinton finished, he bowed to Obama, who joined him on the stage. The two embraced before walking offstage together. It was a scene that represented Lincoln's One America and which showed up the pessimism and absurdity of Mr. Eastwood's Empty Chair. This respect didn't happen every day in America and was probably happening less and less and I wondered if it was the gun in George Zimmerman's hand on the evening of 26 February 2012 that made the difference between law and peace, between hate and brotherhood, and between life and death. And even if a presidential election does bring a lot into the open of men and women's hopes and vanities, who could really tell what the Soul of America is today?

On 28 October 2012 *The New York Times* said it has endorsed Barack Obama for the Presidency. Connor Simpson of The Atlantic

Wire wrote that what ultimately led *The Times* to their decision was Obama's achievements, "including carrying out the economic stimulus, saving the auto industry, improving fuel efficiency standards, and making two very fine Supreme Court appointments." *The Times* argued that Romney, on the other hand, needs to start thinking for himself. He's campaigned "with a guile that allows him to say whatever he thinks an audience wants to hear," but his dedication to the ideas held by the base of the party, and not his own, are too much. This is the second time the paper has endorsed Obama. The last time wrote Simpson that *The Times* endorsed a Republican was President Eisenhower in 1956. And among other endorsements for President Obama was this one from the *Washington Post* Editorial Board: "The 2012 presidential campaign has dwelt on the past, but the key questions are who could better lead the country during the next four years – and, most urgently, who is likelier to put the government on a more sound financial footing. That second question will come rushing at the winner as soon as the votes are tallied. Absent any action, a series of tax hikes and spending cuts will take effect January 1 that might well knock the country back into recession. This will be a moment of peril but also of opportunity. How the president-elect navigates it will go a long way toward determining the success of his presidency and the health of the nation."

XXVI

FORMER FIRST LADY Mary Todd Lincoln will get a new trial to decide whether she was actually insane. One hundred and thirty years after her death, Mary Todd Lincoln will be retried for insanity writes Eric Pfeiffer in Yahoo! News / The Sideshow. The former first lady was declared insane 10 years after the assassination of Abraham Lincoln in 1865, when her son Robert Todd Lincoln had her committed. "Even today, historians disagree whether the evidence against the First Lady was 'trumped up', whether the procedures used constituted due process, and what would occur if today's modernized health laws were applied to the same facts," reads a statement from the Abraham Lincoln Presidential Library and Museum.

Mrs. Lincoln's mental stability was called into question after she suffered from depression following the deaths of not only her husband but also two of her young children. She allegedly spent the years after President Lincoln's death attempting to communicate with him via séance. But the *St. Louis Post-Dispatch* reports that the Illinois Supreme Court Historic Preservation Commission and the Lincoln Museum are set to give Mary Todd Lincoln a new trial, starting in October. The dueling legal teams will dress in period clothes from the era but will argue their case relying on current law. Actors will play the roles of Mary Todd Lincoln and Robert Todd Lincoln, but real-life judges will serve as lawyers for each side in the re-creation of the case. Former Illinois Gov. Jim Edgar will narrate the trial. And adding more theatricality to the performance, members of the audience will reportedly serve as jury.

Mary Todd Lincoln spent about four months in the Bellevue Place sanitarium after being declared insane in 1875. However, after secretly communicating with her lawyer and writing a letter to the *Chicago Times*, she was eventually released. In a letter written in August 1875, Mrs. Lincoln wondered why her son Robert had seemingly turned on her. She later came to believe that her son's actions were an attempt to take control of her finances: "It does not appear that God is good, to have placed me here. I endeavor to read my Bible and offer up my petitions three times a day," she wrote. "But my afflicted heart fails me and my voice often falters in prayer. I have worshipped my son and no unpleasant word ever passed between us, yet I cannot understand why I should have been brought out here." The letter is just one of 25 written by Mary Todd Lincoln during her "insanity period" and was believed to have been burned by Robert Todd Lincoln. However, the letters were discovered in 2006 in a steamer trunk owned by the children of Robert Todd Lincoln's attorney.

XXVII

PRESIDENT OBAMA, transformed from inspiring hope-and-change candidate into struggling stay-the-course incumbent, promised Americans wary of giving him another term that "our problems can be

508

solved" if only voters will grant him four more years, writes Olivier Knox of Yahoo News / The Ticket on 7 September 2012. "Know this, America: Our problems can be solved," he told thousands of delegates to the Democratic National Convention in Charlotte, N.C. "Our challenges can be met. The path we offer may be harder, but it leads to a better place. And I'm asking you to choose that future."

Obama's appeal aimed to build on a rousing speech from Michelle Obama and former president Bill Clinton. The first lady assured disenchanted voters who backed her husband in 2008 but are wary or wavering today that four years of political knife fights and hard compromises had not stripped her husband of his moral core. And Clinton cast the current president as the heir to the policies that charged the economy of the 1990s and yielded government surpluses. "I won't pretend the path I'm offering is quick or easy. I never have," Obama told the cheering crowd in the Time Warner Cable Arena and a television audience expected to number in the tens of millions. "You didn't elect me to tell you what you wanted to hear. You elected me to tell you the truth. And the truth is it will take more than a few years for us to solve challenges that have built up over a decade."

Obama's main vulnerability is the still-sputtering economy with a stubbornly high unemployment rate at 8.3 per cent nearly four years after he took office vowing to restore it to health. In Charlotte, he ridiculed the Republican approach championed by Mitt Romney. "All they have to offer is the same prescriptions they've had for the last thirty years: Have a surplus? Try a tax cut. Deficit too high? Try another. Feel a cold coming on? Take two tax cuts, roll back some regulations, and call us in the morning!" he said, to laughter and cheers from the crowd. And it was with ridicule, too, that he portrayed Romney and vice presidential candidate Paul Ryan as heirs to George W. Bush's foreign policy, and unfit to manage America's relations with the world. "My opponent and his running mate are new to foreign policy, but from all that we've seen and heard, they want to take us back to an era of blustering and blundering that cost America so dearly," he said. "After all, you don't call Russia our number one enemy – not al Qaeda, Russia – unless you're still stuck in a Cold War mind warp," he said. "You might not be ready for diplomacy with Beijing if you can't visit the Olympics without insulting our closest ally. My opponent said it was 'tragic' to end the war in Iraq, and he won't tell us how he'll end the war in Afghanistan. I have, and I will." In fact, wrote Knox, Romney has supported an Obama-endorsed, NATO-approved timetable to withdraw the alliance's combat troops by the end of 2014.

The speech reflected Obama's drive to convince voters to see the election as a choice and not as a referendum on an embattled incumbent whose job approval ratings are below the 50-percent mark, a traditional danger zone. "On every issue, the choice you face won't be just between two candidates or two parties. It will be a choice between two different paths for America. A choice between two fundamentally different visions for the future," he said. At the same time, he did not spell out in detail his plans for a second term should he get one – even as he acknowledged that he is not the candidate he was when he pursued his history-making 2008 drive for the White House. "You know, I recognize that times have changed since I first spoke to this convention. Times have changed – and so have I," he said. "If you turn away now – if you buy into the cynicism that the change we fought for isn't possible, well, change will not happen."

Obama's speech came after an evening studded with stars, from Hollywood's Scarlett Johansson, who pressed young voters to register and cast ballots in November, to James Taylor, who quipped, "I'm an old white guy and I love Barack Obama" in between renditions of his folksy classics. And he was preceded onstage by Vice President Joe Biden, who gave a long-form version of this memorable re-election slogan: "Osama Bin Laden is dead and General Motors is alive." In addition to the economy, the president highlighted his support for access to abortion, and offered his longest remarks on the fight against climate change in recent memory. "Yes, my plan will continue to reduce the carbon pollution that is heating our planet – because climate change is not a hoax. More droughts and floods and wildfires are not a joke. They're a threat to our children's future. And in this election, you can do something about it." Obama had moved his speech from nearby Bank of America Stadium into the Time Warner Cable Arena citing concerns about the weather. Republicans charged he merely feared not being able to fill the 74,000-seat space. Democrats countered that they had more than 65,000 ticket holders.

But the President had some other bad news to confront. The United States wrote Ansuya Harjani of CNBC had slipped further down a global ranking of the world's most competitive economies, according to a World Economic Forum (WEF) survey released on 5 September 2012. The world's largest economy, which was placed 5th last year, fell two positions to the 7th spot – marking its fourth year of decline. A lack of macroeconomic stability, the business community's continued mistrust of the government and concerns over its fiscal health were some of the reasons for the downgrade, according to the annual survey. "A number of weaknesses are chipping away at its competitiveness... the U.S. fiscal imbalances and continued political deadlock over resolving these challenges," said Jennifer Blanke, Economist at the Geneva-based WEF.

Political deadlock over reducing the unsustainable federal government budget deficit – projected to hit $1.1 trillion this year – prompted Standard & Poor's to downgrade the country's credit rating by one notch to AA+ from AAA last August. A mix of U.S. tax hikes and spending cuts – referred to as the "fiscal cliff" – are set to come into force in January unless lawmakers reach a compromise for avoiding them. The survey, which has been conducted annually for over three decades, ranks the competitiveness of 144 countries based on 12 key indicators including infrastructure, macroeconomic environment, labor market efficiency and innovation. Despite declining in the overall ranking, the forum highlighted that the U.S. remains one of the world's top innovators – supported by an "excellent" university system – and continues to offer vast opportunities because of the sheer size of its domestic economy.

Switzerland and Singapore retained their positions as the most competitive economies, coming in 1st and 2nd respectively. Switzerland's top spot was achieved as a result of its strong performance across the board, according to WEF, with notable labor market efficiency, sophistication of its business sector and its innovative capacity. The country has among the highest rates of patents per capita globally. "Switzerland's productivity is further enhanced by a business sector that offers excellent on-the-job-training opportunities and labor markets that balance employee protection with the interests of employers," the report said. Among the large emerging economies, China was ranked highest at 26, thanks to favourable macroeconomic conditions. This was significantly higher than Brazil, India and Russia which came in at 53, 56 and 66, respectively. China runs a moderate budget deficit, boasts a low government debt-to-GDP ratio of 26 percent and its gross savings rate remains above 50 per cent of GDP, the forum said. In addition, the rating of its sovereign debt (AA-) is significantly better than that of the other BRICs and of many advanced economies. However, the world's second largest economy has slipped two notches from last year's ranking, owing to a deterioration in the development of its financial markets and technological readiness. "Insufficient domestic and foreign competition is of particular concern, as the various barriers to entry appear to be more prevalent and more important than in previous years," WEF report said.

XXVIII

IN CHARLOTTE Michelle Obama said that "Barack knows the American dream because he's lived it," reported Holly Bailey, Senior Political Reporter of Yahoo! News / The Ticket. Said Ms. Bailey, First Lady Michelle Obama never once mentioned Mitt Romney's name. But in her speech before the Democratic National Convention on Monday night, she offered a dramatic contrast between her husband, Barack Obama, and his Republican opponent, insisting he understands the struggles of average Americans because he's lived through those tough times, too. "Barack knows the American Dream because he's lived it, and he wants everyone in this country to have that same opportunity, no matter who we are, or where we're from, or what we look like, or who we love," Michelle Obama said. "He believes that when you've worked hard, and done well, and walked through that doorway of opportunity, you do not slam it shut behind you. You reach back, and you give other folks the same chances that helped you succeed."

It was a speech meant to bolster her husband's legislative accomplishments and it did as the first lady touted the president's push for health care reform, the auto industry bailout and efforts to keep down student loan interest rates. But not unlike Ann Romney's speech on behalf of her husband at the Republican National Convention, Michelle Obama also sought to humanize the president, and to remind voters of the working class background she and her husband came from. With tears in her eyes, she spoke of her father, a pump operator at a Chicago water plant, and how her husband was raised by a single mother and by his grandparents. "We learned about dignity and decency – that how hard you work matters more than how much you make, that helping others means more than just getting ahead yourself. We learned about honesty and integrity; that the truth matters; that you don't take shortcuts or play by your own set of rules, and success doesn't count unless you earn it fair and square," she said. "We learned about gratitude and humility; that so many people had a hand in our success, from the teachers who inspired us to the janitors who kept our school clean, and we were taught to value everyone's contribution and treat everyone with respect."

Those are the values they are trying to pass on to their own children – and values that inform her husband's job as president, she said. "After so many struggles and triumphs and moments that have tested my husband in ways I never could have imagined, I have seen firsthand that being president doesn't change who you are – it reveals who you are," said Michelle Obama. "As president, you can get all kinds of advice from all kinds of people. But at the end of the day, when it comes time to make that decision, as president, all you have to guide you are your values, and your vision, and the life experiences that make you who you are." Her husband, she said, "is thinking about folks like my dad and his grandmother" and is "thinking about the pride that comes from a hard day's work." It was a line meant to push back against Romney's claims that Obama doesn't understand how to create jobs because he's never worked in the private sector. But it also offered a subtle contrast between her husband and Romney, who came from a well-off background.

She spoke of the student loan debts they incurred as a young married couple. "We were so young, so in love, and so in debt," she said. And she spoke of her husband's skills as a father, which she insisted have been unchanged even despite the pressures of the presidency. "People ask me whether being in the White House has changed my husband, I can honestly say that when it comes to his character, and his convictions, and his heart, Barack Obama is still the same man I fell in love with all those years ago," she said, her eyes wet with tears. Pushing back against GOP charges that her husband is driven by politics, Mrs. Obama insisted there is no "us and them" for the president, that "he doesn't care whether you're a Democrat, a

Republican or none of the above." She told voters her husband never lets himself "get distracted by the chatter and the noise." He just keeps "getting up and moving forward," she said. "He reminds me that we are playing a long game here, and that change is hard, and change is slow, and it never happens all at once," she said. "Many of us stand here tonight because of their sacrifice, and longing, and steadfast love because time and again, they swallowed their fears and doubts and did what was hard." That has been the story of the American dream, the first lady said. "That is what has made my story, and Barack's story, and so many other American stories possible."

XXIX

A VOTE FOR Mitt Romney, House Minority Leader Nancy Pelosi said at the Democratic National Convention, is a vote to end Social Security and Medicare, according to Chris Moody, of Yahoo! News / The Ticket. Ms. Pelosi he said urged Democrats to re-elect President Barack Obama, tying a vote for him to a means to preserving the nation's main entitlement programs, Social Security and Medicare. "Social Security is on the ballot. Democrats enacted it. Democrats will fight to preserve it," Pelosi said. "Some Republicans want to replace the guarantee of Social Security with the gamble of private accounts. It's just plain wrong. When you go to the polls, vote for Social Security. Vote for President Obama."

Said Ms. Pelosi: "Fellow Democrats! That American Dream is the story of America. We are here to re-ignite the American Dream. I'm pleased to see so many young people the future of our party, the hope of America. I stand before you as the first mother and grandmother to serve as Democratic leader and speaker of the House. For 25 years, it has been my privilege to represent the city of San Francisco and the great state of California; to work to strengthen our vibrant middle class; to secure opportunity and equality. We stand together in our 'drive for 25' – 25 seats to win back the House – as we re-elect President Barack Obama!

"Democrats believe in re-igniting the American Dream by removing barriers to success and building ladders of opportunity for all, so everyone can succeed. Jobs are central to the American Dream and President Obama has focused on jobs from day one. Under President Obama, we've gone from losing 800,000 jobs a month to adding 4.5 million private sector jobs over the last 29 months. The American Dream is about freedom. Jobs mean freedom for workers to support their families.

"Working with President Obama, Democrats passed the Lilly Ledbetter Fair Pay Act to strengthen the rights of women in the workplace; repealed 'don't ask, don't tell' so our troops can serve the country they love regardless of whom they love; made college more affordable. House Democrats passed the Dream Act, but Senate Republicans blocked it. With President Obama, Democrats enacted the toughest consumer safeguards in history to protect Main Street from recklessness on Wall Street. Democrats passed health reform to allow Americans the freedom to pursue their passion; to make health care a right, not a privilege; to ensure that being a woman is no longer a 'pre-existing condition'!

"Freedom is secured every day by our men and women in uniform. We must build a future worthy of their sacrifice. We thank them for keeping America the land of the free and the home of the brave.

"This year, we are determined to re-elect an extraordinary president who, in no ordinary time, led America back from the brink of depression while Republicans tried to block him at every turn. This election offers the clearest choice of our time. Many names are on the ballot. So, too, is the character of our country. Medicare is on the ballot. Democrats will preserve and strengthen Medicare. Republicans will end the Medicare guarantee. It's just plain wrong. When you go to the polls, vote for Medicare. Vote for President Obama!

"Social Security is on the ballot. Democrats enacted it. Democrats will fight to preserve it. Some Republicans want to replace the guarantee of Social Security with the gamble of private accounts. It's just plain wrong. When you go to the polls, vote for Social Security. Vote for President Obama!

"The hard-won rights of women are on the ballot. Democrats trust the judgment of women. We reject the Republican assault on women's health. It's just plain wrong. When you go the polls, vote for women's rights. Vote for President Obama!

"Our democracy is on the ballot. Democrats believe we must curb the influence of special interests on our political institutions. To change policy for the middle class, we must change politics. Democrats believe we must create jobs, not protect the special interests; build the economy from the middle out, not the top down. Democrats will work to overturn Citizens United. Republicans support opening the floodgates to special interest money and suppressing the right to vote. It's just plain wrong. We believe in government of the many, not the privileged few. When you go to the polls, vote for democracy. Vote for President Obama!

"The American Dream is on the ballot. Ladders of opportunity for our middle class are on the ballot. And we have work to do. We must re-ignite the American Dream. With President Obama, we will move America forward. When you go to the polls, vote for strong Democratic majorities in the House and Senate! Vote for Vice President Joe Biden and President Barack Obama! God bless the United States of America."

"The country is better off", declared Stephanie Cutter, the president's deputy campaign manager, as the Democratic National Convention opened. When asked if the country is better off than it was four years ago, Obama campaign aides took the question head-on. Joined by fellow Obama campaign architects Ben LaBolt and Jim Messina, Cutter sat down with Yahoo News' Olivier Knox and ABC News' Diane Sawyer and Jake Tapper for a live Newsmakers broadcast, according to Torrey Anderson Schoepe of The Ticket.

Summing up their point, Obama's aides reinforced the "bumper sticker" line credited to Vice President Joe Biden: Osama bin Laden is dead, GM is alive.

"We broke the back of al-Qaeda," Cutter said. "The auto industry was on the verge of bankruptcy and now they're creating hundreds of thousands of jobs." Cutter also hit back at a Mitt Romney campaign aide's contention during *Newsmakers* at the Republican National Convention that "we're not going let our campaign be dictated by fact-checkers. We do care about fact checks. We do care about the honesty of our ads," she said.

At the RNC, Romney's wife, Ann, took the stage tasked with humanizing her husband, and the role is no different for Obama's wife, Michelle, who spoke.

"I think that what the first lady can do better than anybody else is give a lens into the values that drive the president," Cutter said.

Looking toward November, Obama's aides agreed that it's going to be a tight race that they're careful to characterize as a "choice" for voters. "We're confident in the choice, and we're confident when people understand that choice that we're going to win this election," Messina said.

XXX

SENATE MAJORITY LEADER Harry Reid lambasted Mitt Romney for refusing to release several years of tax returns, suggesting that no other presidential candidate in modern history has been as secretive, writes Holly Bailey of Yahoo! News and The Ticket. "Never in modern American history has a presidential candidate tried so hard to hide himself," Reid said in his speech at the Democratic National Convention. The Nevada senator said Romney has asked the country to "take his word" that there are no damaging revelations in his tax returns. Take his word? His word?" Reid said sarcastically. "Trust comes from transparency and Mitt Romney comes up short on both."

Reid's attacks came just weeks after he took to the Senate floor and accused Romney of not having paid taxes at all for the last decade. The Democratic leader cited a source close to Romney whom he wouldn't identify. Romney has denied Reid's accusations. Reid sought to contrast Romney with President Barack Obama, telling the crowd, "You know him." He praised Obama for bringing "courage and character" to the presidency and for doing the "right thing" even in the face of GOP opposition.

In a criticism of Romney, Reid praised Obama for bailing out the Detroit auto industry, a move Romney opposed. And Reid claimed "some said he shouldn't move heaven and earth" to find and kill Osama bin Laden. But Obama did, he said. He cast Obama as a president hobbled by Republicans whom he described as "naysayers" who embrace "couldn'ts and shouldn'ts". The Republican Party, Reid said, has become the party of the "wouldn'ts and won'ts," doing anything to block Obama instead of working together with Democrats on behalf of the country. "If they won't stand up to Rush Limbaugh or

Grover Norquist, what would make anyone think they would stand up for you?" Reid said.

XXXI

AS THE NATIONAL DEBT swelled past $16 trillion, Republican House Speaker John Boehner accused President Barack Obama of lacking the "courage" to work with his political foes to rein in entitlement spending and overhaul the tax code, writes Olivier Knox of Yahoo! News / The Ticket. Boehner also called passage of that symbolic threshold "another sad reminder of President Obama's broken promise to cut the deficit in half. "This debt is a drain on our economy and a crushing burden on our kids and grandkids, and it's yet another indication that the president's policies have made things worse," Boehner said in a written statement. The Obama campaign countered that when it comes to the debt, Republicans should be saying, "We built this."

Republicans have highlighted the fact that the national debt swelled about $5.3 trillion on Obama's watch, and accused him of adding to it with government spending like the $800 billion economic stimulus that was his first major initiative after taking office in 2009. In the past, Democrats have responded to such charges by saying that the principal tributaries to the flood of red ink have been the global economic collapse of 2007-2008, the wars in Iraq and Afghanistan, a Republican-crafted expansion of Medicare coverage, and the Bush-era tax cuts, which Obama extended in late 2010.

"To tackle the debt in a meaningful way and help our economy grow, we need pro-growth tax reform, and we need to strengthen and secure Medicare and other critical entitlement programs," said Boehner. "Unfortunately, President Obama hasn't had the courage to join us in working on these common sense reforms."

Democrats have also placed the blame on Republicans – including Boehner – for the political stalemate that has jammed up any ambitious bipartisan plan to cut the debt. The White House, specifically, has accused Republicans of killing any such deal by rejecting tax increases as a component of a plan that would also include painful spending cuts. Republicans have countered that tax hikes on the wealthy risk drying up investment income they say would help grow the economy.

"The debt clock at the Republican convention was appropriately placed next to a sign that said 'We Built This,'" Obama campaign national press secretary Ben LaBolt said at a forum organized by ABC and Yahoo News. "Congressman Ryan voted for the major drivers of the deficit during the Bush administration: those tax cuts for the wealthiest, the Medicare prescription plan that wasn't funded, and two unfunded wars," LaBolt said. "The president knows that we need to take a balanced approach, that we need to reduce our deficit, and he's been working for action on this over the course of the past few years," LaBolt said.

Chapter Eight – The Race in Space

We choose to go to the moon in this decade and do the other things, not because they are easy, but because they are hard, because the goal will serve to organize and measure the best of our energies and skills, because that challenge is one that we are willing to accept, one we are unwilling to postpone, and on which we intend to win, and the others, too. It is for these reasons that I regard the decision last year to shift our efforts in space from low to high gear as among the most important decisions that will be made during my incumbency in the office of the Presidency. – John F. Kennedy at Rice University, Houston, on 12 September 1962

MIAMI. – It was as if the Space Age in America was coming to an end as it seemed to have come to an end for Soviet Russia with Yuri Gagarin and the Sputniks gone and all that remains is the International Space Station. And for the Americans and for Rhona and for the boys and me it had begun in Florida at Cape Canaveral where with Marc and Simon we had spied on the base. I remembered when the Challenger had broken up a little more than a minute after lift-off killing Christa McAuliffe, the New Hampshire teacher who had won her place on the shuttle from thousands of other teachers. This I believe is what men mean about Fate and the uncertainties of life. And I remember in the early days of our experience at Disney World in Orlando when Marc and Simon, seeing the trail of vapor left by US airplanes, would run for shelter thinking that it was the start of World War III.

In 1968 when Marc was born it was a year before Neil Armstrong walked on the moon. And nearly a half century later on 25 August 2012 Armstrong died. He was 82 and until his death he remained the moon's mystery man. On the day he died, Virginia Heffernan of Yahoo! News / The Lookout recalled the words of Tom Wolfe, "A lot of people couldn't figure out Armstrong." With those words, wrote Ms. Heffernan, Tom Wolfe had introduced Neil Armstrong, the astronaut hero of his non-fiction masterpiece, *The Right Stuff*. Armstrong, of course, was the commander of the 1969 Apollo 11 mission and the first man ever to walk on the moon. Armstrong died from complications relating to heart surgery. Decades after his moon walk, Armstrong, the lunar Adam as Ms. Heffernan called him, has represented a code his admirers knew better than to try to crack. Wolfe had said, "You'd ask him a question, and he would just stare at you with those pale-blue eyes of his, and you'd start to ask the question again, figuring he hadn't understood, and – click – out of his mouth would come forth a sequence of long, quiet, perfectly formed, precisely thought-out sentences." So Wolfe warned against understanding Armstrong in *The Right Stuff*. And that warning was more or less heeded, somewhat miraculously, until Armstrong's dying day. Profilers kept their hands off him. Hollywood starlets didn't swoop in to wreck his family. And, Johnnie Carson and Merv Griffin and Dinah Shore and Ali G and Oprah Winfrey didn't demand that he couch-surf with them. So says Ms. Hefferman.

In the 1960s and 1970s, the national pastime was psychoanalyzing postwar celebrities – John F. Kennedy, Marilyn Monroe, and Muhammad Ali. And once a hero is cracked open by one *Vanity Fair* profile, the pile-on never ends. This one had a sex addiction; this one had a chip on her shoulder; this one could never live up to his big brother. Let's not do that to Armstrong, Wolfe pleaded. In any case, the great man simply would not succumb. In an era when everyone was expected to evince the adolescent emotionality of Marlon Brando or Allen Ginsberg, Armstrong was resolutely adult and elegantly square. He was a Navy pilot from a small town who married a home-economics major at Purdue whom he had no recollection of courting or even proposing to Janet Armstrong, with whom he had three children, evidently didn't remember any courtship either. Though astronauts in the time were represented as hard-partying matinee idols, Armstrong always described himself as a "white-socks, pocket-protector, nerdy engineer." He wasn't boasting, though engineers are, of course, the hotshots of today: the hackers and technologists who keep pushing into the new breach – the post final frontiers of cyberspace.

Once in 1969, Norman Mailer it is said bullied Armstrong into saying something romantic about going to the moon. Armstrong stood his ground like a Buddha. "I think we're going to the moon because it's in the nature of the human being to face challenges," he said, defying Mailer. "It's by the nature of his deep inner soul ... We're required to do these things just as salmon swim upstream." Michael Collins, an Apollo 11 crewmate, wrote that Armstrong "never transmits anything but the surface layer, and that only sparingly ... I like him, but I don't know what to make of him, or how to get to know him better." And so the story goes.

Almost a month before, on 23 July 2012, Sally Ride, the first US woman in space died after a 17-month battle with pancreatic cancer. She was 61. Ride first launched into space in 1983 aboard the Challenger shuttle, taking part in the seventh mission of US space shuttle program. President Obama called her a "national hero and a powerful role model" who "inspired generations of young girls to reach for the stars. Sally's life showed us that there are no limits to what we can achieve and I have no doubt that her legacy will endure for years to come," he added, in a statement offering condolences to Ride's family and friends. NASA administrator Charles Bolden said in a statement Ride "literally changed the face of America's space program" and that "the nation has lost one of its finest leaders, teachers, and explorers." The agency's deputy administrator Lori Garver added that the trailblazing astronaut was a "personal and professional role model to me and thousands of women around the world." Tributes quickly poured in on the micro-blogging website Twitter including from women who remembered learning as young girls of Ride's pioneering flight. "I was seven in the summer of 1983. Sally Ride was simply everything," read one. Another declared: "RIP Sally Ride – you inspired me to believe that, as a female, anything was possible. May your journey to the stars be swift."

In an interview marking the 25th anniversary of the mission, Ride said she was so dazzled that she only later "came to appreciate what an honor it was to be selected to be the first (US woman) to get a chance to go into space." Ride, born May 26, 1951, in southern California, earned degrees in physics and English from Stanford University. She applied to be an astronaut at US space agency NASA in 1977, after seeing an ad in her university's student newspaper. It was the first time the space agency had allowed applications from civilians – or from women. Ride was one of 35 people, including just six women, chosen from a pool of 8,000 applicants. She flew in two space missions, logging nearly 350 hours in space. However, after the Challenger explosion that killed all seven crew members, her third planned mission was grounded in 1986. Ride served on the commission to investigate the accident, and was then assigned to NASA headquarters. She retired from the agency in 1987. On her foundation's website, Ride said of her historic foray into space: "The thing I'll remember most about the flight is that it was fun." According to the foundation, Ride became an advocate "inspiring young people, especially girls, to stick with their interest in science, to become scientifically literate, and to consider careers in science and engineering. She founded Sally Ride Science in 2001, directed NASA-funded education projects, and also co-authored seven science books for children. Ride is survived by Tam O'Shaughnessy, her partner of 27 years, as well as by her mother, sister, niece and nephew.

More than a quarter century before these deaths, on 28 January 1986, the American shuttle orbiter Challenger broke up 73 seconds after liftoff, bringing a devastating end to the spacecraft's 10th mission. The disaster claimed the lives of all seven astronauts aboard, including Ms. McAuliffe who had been selected to join the mission and teach lessons from space to schoolchildren around the country. It was later determined that two rubber O-rings, which had been designed to separate the sections of the rocket booster, had failed due to cold temperatures on the morning of the launch. The tragedy and its aftermath received extensive media coverage and prompted NASA to temporarily suspend all shuttle missions. And seventeen years after the Challenger tragedy, on 1 February 2003, the Space Shuttle Columbia disaster occurred, when shortly before it was scheduled to conclude its 28th mission. Columbia disintegrated over Texas and Louisiana during re-entry into the Earth's atmosphere, resulting in the death of all seven crew members. Debris from Columbia fell to earth in Texas along a path stretching from Dallas suburb Trophy Club to Tyler, as well as into parts of Louisiana.

The loss of Columbia was a result of damage sustained during launch when a piece of foam insulation the size of a small briefcase broke off from the Space Shuttle external tank (the 'ET' main propellant tank) under the aerodynamic forces of launch. The debris struck the leading edge of the left wing, damaging the Shuttle's thermal protection system (TPS), which shields it from the intense heat generated from atmospheric compression during re-entry. While Columbia was still in orbit, some engineers suspected damage, but NASA managers limited the investigation, on the grounds that little could be done even if problems were found.

NASA's original shuttle design specifications stated that the external tank was not to shed foam or other debris; as such, strikes upon the shuttle itself were safety issues that needed to be resolved before a launch was cleared. Launches were often given the go-ahead as engineers came to see the foam shedding and debris strikes as inevitable and unresolvable, with the rationale that they were either not a threat to safety, or an acceptable risk. The majority of shuttle launches recorded such foam strikes and thermal tile scarring. On STS-112, two launches before, a chunk of foam broke away from the ET bipod ramp and hit the SRB-ET Attach Ring near the bottom of the left solid rocket booster (SRB) causing a dent four inches wide and three inches deep in it. After that mission, the situation was analyzed and NASA decided to press ahead under the justification that "The ET is safe to fly with no new concerns (and no added risk)" of further foam strikes, justification that was revisited while Columbia was still in orbit and Chair of the Mission Management Team (MMT) Linda Ham re-assessed, stating that the "Rationale was lousy then and still is". Ham as well as Shuttle Program Manager Ron Dittemore had both been present at the 31 October 2002 meeting where this decision to continue with launches was made. During re-entry of STS-107, the damaged area allowed hot gases to penetrate and destroy the internal wing structure, rapidly causing the in-flight breakup of the vehicle. An extensive ground search in parts of Texas, Louisiana, and Arkansas recovered crew remains and many vehicle fragments.

Mission STS-107 was the 113th Space Shuttle launch. It was delayed 18 times over the two years from its planned launch date of 11 January 2001, to its actual launch date of 16 January 2003. A launch delay due to cracks in the shuttle's propellant distribution system occurred one month before a 19 July 2002 launch date. The Columbia Accident Investigation Board (CAIB) determined that this delay had nothing to do with the catastrophic failure six months later.

The Columbia Accident Investigation Board's recommendations addressed both technical and organizational issues. Space Shuttle flight operations were delayed for over two years, similar to the delay following the Challenger accident. Construction of the International Space Station was put on hold, and for 29 months the station relied entirely on the Russian Federal Space Agency for re-supply until Shuttle flights resumed with STS-114 and 41 months for crew rotation until STS-121. Major changes to shuttle operations, after missions resumed, included a thorough on-orbit inspection to determine how well the shuttle's thermal protection system had endured the ascent, and keeping a designated rescue mission at the ready in case irreparable damage was found. Also it had been decided that all missions would be flown only to the ISS so that the crew could use that spacecraft as a "safe haven" if need be. Later NASA decided it would be an acceptable risk to make one exception to that policy for one final mission to repair Hubble in its high-altitude low-inclination orbit.

II

ON 8 AUGUST 2012 NASA scientists hailed the Mars rover Curiosity's flawless descent and landing as a "miracle of engineering", wrote Irene Klotz and Steve Gorman of Reuters, as they scanned early images of an ancient crater that may hold clues about whether life took hold on Earth's planetary cousin. The one-ton, six-wheeled laboratory made an intricate and risky touchdown late on Sunday, much to the relief and joy of scientists and engineers eager to conduct NASA's first astrobiology mission since the 1970s Viking probes. "We trained ourselves for eight years to think the worst all the time," Curiosity lead engineer Miguel San Martin said. "You can never turn that off."

Mission control engineers at the Jet Propulsion Laboratory near Los Angeles erupted in cheers when confirmation was received that Curiosity, touted as the first full-fledged mobile science lab sent to a distant world, had landed on the Martian surface. NASA engineers said the feat stands as the most challenging and elaborate achievement in the history of robotic spaceflight and opens the door to a new era in planetary exploration. President Barack Obama hailed the accomplishment as an historic "point of national pride." The landing also marked a much-welcome success and a major milestone for a U.S. space agency beset by budget cuts and the recent cancellation of its space shuttle program, NASA's centerpiece for 30 years. The landing was a major initial hurdle for a two-year, $2.5 billion project whose primary focus is chemistry and geology. The daredevil nature of getting the rover to Mars captured the public's imagination.

Encased in a capsule-like protective shell, the nuclear-powered rover capped an eight-month voyage as it streaked into the thin Martian atmosphere at 13,200 miles per-hour (21,243 kilometers per hour), 17 times the speed of sound. Plunging through the top of the atmosphere at an angle producing aerodynamic lift, the capsule's "guided entry" system used jet thrusters to steer the craft as it fell, making small course corrections and burning off most of its downward speed. Closer to the ground, the vessel was slowed further by a giant supersonic parachute before a jet backpack and flying "sky crane" took over to deliver Curiosity the last mile to the surface. The rover, about the size of a small sports car, came to rest as planned at the bottom of a vast, ancient impact bowl called Gale Crater, and near a towering mound of layered rock called Mount Sharp, which rises from the floor of the basin. A trio of orbiting satellites monitored what NASA had billed as the "seven minutes of terror," but the anxiety proved to be unfounded.

From an orbital perch 211 miles away, NASA's sharp-eyed Mars Reconnaissance Orbiter snapped a stunning and serene picture of Curiosity gracefully riding beneath its massive parachute en route to Gale Crater, located near the planet's equator in its southern hemisphere. At 10:32 p.m. PDT on Sunday (1:32 a.m. EDT on Monday/0532 GMT on Monday) flight controllers at JPL received the equivalent of a text message from Curiosity that its journey of 352 million miles (566 million km) had ended safely. Seven minutes later, the rover transmitted a picture, related by another Mars orbiter called Odyssey, showing one of Curiosity's wheels on the planet's gravel-strewn surface.

"When you see a picture of the surface of the planet with the spacecraft on it, that is the miracle of engineering," lead scientist John Grotzinger told reporters on Monday. With the late-afternoon sun slipping behind the crater's rim, Curiosity relayed six more sample pictures and the results of initial health checks of some of its 10 scientific instruments before shutting down for the Martian night. Curiosity touched down about 6.2 miles from the foot of Mount Sharp, a monstrous formation of sedimentary rock that rises like a stack of cards three miles from the floor of Gale Crater. Taller from base to summit than California's Mount Whitney, the tallest mountain in the continental United States, Mount Sharp crests above the northern rim of the crater. Scientists believe the mound may have formed from the remains of sediment that once completely filled the basin, offering a potentially valuable geologic record of the history of Mars, the planet most similar to Earth. For that reason it is a key focus of interest for Curiosity scientists looking for evidence of Martian habitats that may have supported microbial life. It may be months, however, before Curiosity heads over to Mount Sharp. "Our goal is not just to head for the hills," Grotzinger said. Added project manager Pete Theisinger: "We have a priceless asset and we're not going to screw it up."

The rover comes equipped with an array of sophisticated instruments capable of analyzing samples of soil, rocks and atmosphere on the spot and beaming results back to Earth. One is a laser gun that can zap a rock from 23 feet away to create a spark whose spectral image is analyzed by a special telescope to discern the mineral's chemical composition. Among Curiosity's first tasks will be to chemically analyze the soil near its landing site. "We're on gravel plain of Mars, a somewhat familiar scene," Grotzinger said, noting that the gravel seemed to be quite uniform in size. "We're a complex spacecraft, and simple geology is a good thing to start off with."

Scientists are also eager to explore rocks and pebbles that appear to have been transported by flowing water to a fan-shaped region near the landing site. On Monday, the rover was expected to unfurl its dish-shaped antenna so it could better communicate directly with Earth. "The surface mission of Curiosity has now begun," mission manager Mike Watkins said. "We built this rover not just to be launched or not just to land on Mars, but to actually drive on Mars and execute a very complex and beautiful science mission." Engineers said the tricky landing sequence, combining a giant parachute with a rocket-pack that lowered the rover to the Martian surface on a tether, allowed for zero margin for error. "I can't believe this. This is unbelievable," enthused Allen Chen, the deputy head of the rover's descent and landing team at the Jet Propulsion Laboratory near Los Angeles. Moments later, Curiosity beamed back its first three images from the Martian surface, one of them showing a wheel of the vehicle and the rover's shadow cast on the rocky terrain. NASA put the official landing time of Curiosity, touted as the first full-fledged mobile science laboratory sent to a distant world, at 10:32 p.m. Pacific time (1:32 a.m. EDT/ 0532 GMT). The landing marked a much-welcome success and a major milestone for a U.S. space agency beset by budget cuts and the recent cancellation of its space shuttle program, NASA's centerpiece for 30 years.

The $2.5 billion Curiosity project, formally called the Mars Science Laboratory, is NASA's first astrobiology mission since the 1970s-era Viking probes. "It's an enormous step forward in planetary exploration. Nobody has ever done anything like this," said John Holdren, the top science advisor to President Barack Obama, who was visiting JPL for the event. "It was an incredible performance." Obama himself issued a statement hailing the Curiosity landing as "an unprecedented feat of technology that will stand as a point of national pride far into the future. It proves that even the longest of odds are no match for our unique blend of ingenuity and determination," he said. NASA plans to put the one-ton, six-wheeled, nuclear-powered rover and its sophisticated instruments through several weeks of engineering checks before starting its two-year surface mission in earnest. "We're going to make sure that we're firing on all cylinders before we blaze out across the plains," lead scientist John Grotzinger said.

The rover's precise location had yet to be determined, but NASA said it came to rest in its planned landing zone near the foot of a tall mountain rising from the floor of a vast impact basin called Gale Crater, in Mars' southern hemisphere. Launched on 26 November from Cape Canaveral, Florida, the robotic lab sailed through space for more than eight months, covering 352 million miles (566 million km), before piercing Mars' thin atmosphere at 13,000 miles per hour – 17 times the speed of sound – and starting its descent. Encased in a protective capsule-like shell, the craft utilized a first-of-its kind automated flight-entry system to sharply reduce its speed. Then the probe rode a huge, supersonic parachute into the lower atmosphere before a jet-powered backpack NASA called a "sky crane" carried Curiosity most of the rest of the way to its destination, lowering it to the ground by nylon tethers.

When the rover's wheels were planted firmly on the ground, the cords were cut and the sky crane flew a safe distance away and crashed. The sequence also involved 79 pyrotechnic detonations to release exterior ballast weights, open the parachute, separate the heat shield, detach the craft's back shell, jettison the parachute and other functions. The failure of any one of those would have doomed the landing, JPL engineers said. NASA sardonically referred the unorthodox seven-minute descent and landing sequence as "seven minutes of terror." When Curiosity reached Mars it was not the first to set its wheels on the Red Planet, but it is the largest and most advanced robotic explorer that has ever been sent to our planetary neighbor, writes Denise Chow of SPACE.com. The Curiosity rover was designed to search for clues that Mars could be now, or in the ancient past, a habitable planet for microbial life.

NASA first set its sights on landing on the Red Planet in the 1970s. The agency achieved its first Mars landing in 1976 with the Viking 1 lander. Since then, the agency has had six spacecraft successfully touch-downs on the Martian surface. But with the impending arrival of Curiosity, NASA will showcase the most sophisticated Martian rover yet. "The Curiosity landing is the hardest NASA robotic mission ever attempted in the history of exploration of Mars, or any of our robot exploration," John Grunsfeld, associate administrator for NASA's Science Mission Directorate, said in a news briefing on 16 July 2012 at the agency's headquarters in Washington, D.C.

For starters, the way Curiosity lowered itself to the surface of Mars in less than 20 days was unprecedented. The rover used a new and complex sky crane system to slow its descent. According to Doug

McCuistion, director of the Mars Exploration Program at NASA Headquarters, Curiosity's landing "could arguably be the most important event – most significant event – in the history of planetary exploration." Previous Mars rovers, such as the twin Spirit and Opportunity rovers (collectively known as the Mars Exploration Rovers), used airbags to cushion their landing. Spirit and Opportunity arrived at the Red Planet about three weeks apart in January 2004. Each rover weighs about 384 pounds (174 kilograms), but since Curiosity tips the scales at 1 ton, it was deemed too heavy and too large for an airbag-assisted landing. "The mass of Spirit and Opportunity was just about at the limit for what that airbag design could handle," McCuistion said.

Spirit and Opportunity were designed for three-month missions on Mars, but both far outlived their warranties. After getting stuck in Martian sand and losing contact with Earth, Spirit was officially declared dead in May 2011. But, Opportunity is still alive and well, and is currently exploring a massive crater, called Endeavour. Since it landed on the Red Planet, Opportunity has logged an impressive 21.4 miles (34.4 km). Like its two predecessors, Curiosity is equipped with six wheels with individual driver motors and a suspension system to help it drive up inclines and combat the difficult Martian terrain. But Curiosity is also be able to move faster, with 3.35 miles per hour (5.39 kilometers per hour) being its top speed on flat, hard ground. For comparison, Opportunity's maximum speed is approximately 0.1 miles per hour. "Mars Science Lab [is the] most challenging mission we've ever sent to another planet, and certainly the most challenging we've sent to Mars," McCuistion said. "It truly is a major step forward both in technology and in potential science return and science capability, to unlock the mysteries of Mars in places that have never been accessible to humankind in the past."

Curiosity is designed to perform detailed analyses of Martian rocks and soil, including what lies beneath the surface. The rover is equipped with 10 different instruments that have a collective mass of 165 pounds (75 kilograms). Spirit and Opportunity each carried five instruments, totaling 11 pounds (5 kg). Curiosity will be able to dig, snap high-definition pictures of Mars, analyze chemical properties of soil and rock samples, study minerals, and even blast rocks with a laser to measure their chemical compositions. As one of the key indicators of potential habitability, Curiosity will investigate the presence of water around Gale Crater. "Over the last decade-and-a-half of exploration, we have found more water than expected," said Michael Meyer, lead scientist for NASA's Mars Program at NASA headquarters. "With the landing of Curiosity, the adventure begins as we explore the past and present of Gale Crater."

III

LOOKING BACK, NASA said that history had changed on 4 October 1957 when the Soviet Union successfully launched Sputnik I. The world's first artificial satellite was about the size of a beach ball (58 cm. or 22.8 inches in diameter), weighed only 83.6 kg. or 183.9 pounds, and took about 98 minutes to orbit the Earth on its elliptical path. That launch ushered in new political, military, technological, and scientific developments. While the Sputnik launch was a single event, it marked the start of the space age and the U.S.-U.S.S.R space race. The story began in 1952 when the International Council of Scientific Unions decided to establish July 1, 1957, to December 31, 1958, as the International Geophysical Year (IGY) because the scientists knew that the cycles of solar activity would be at a high point then. In October 1954, the council adopted a resolution calling for artificial satellites to be launched during the IGY to map the Earth's surface. In July 1955, the White House announced plans to launch an Earth-orbiting satellite for the IGY and solicited proposals from various Government research agencies to undertake development. In September 1955, the Naval Research Laboratory's Vanguard proposal was chosen to represent the U.S. during the IGY.

The Sputnik launch changed everything. As a technical achievement, Sputnik caught the world's attention and the American public off-guard. Its size was more impressive than Vanguard's intended 3.5-pound payload. In addition, the public feared that the Soviets' ability to launch satellites also translated into the capability to launch ballistic missiles that could carry nuclear weapons from Europe to the U.S. Then the Soviets struck again; on November 3, Sputnik II was launched, carrying a much heavier payload, including a dog named Laika. Immediately after the Sputnik I launch in October, the

U.S. Defense Department responded to the political furor by approving funding for another U.S. satellite project. As a simultaneous alternative to Vanguard, Wernher von Braun and his Army Redstone Arsenal team began work on the Explorer project. On January 31, 1958, the tide changed, when the United States successfully launched Explorer I. This satellite carried a small scientific payload that eventually discovered the magnetic radiation belts around the Earth, named after principal investigator James Van Allen. The Explorer program continued as a successful ongoing series of lightweight, scientifically useful spacecraft.

The Sputnik launch also led directly to the creation of National Aeronautics and Space Administration (NASA). In July 1958, Congress passed the National Aeronautics and Space Act (commonly called the "Space Act"), which created NASA as of October 1, 1958 from the National Advisory Committee for Aeronautics (NACA) and other government agencies. April 12 was already a huge day in space history twenty years before the launch of the first shuttle mission. On that day in 1961, Russian cosmonaut Yuri Gagarin became the first human in space, making a 108-minute orbital flight in his Vostok 1 spacecraft. Newspapers like *The Huntsville Times* trumpeted Gagarin's accomplishment. Mercury astronaut Alan Shepard became the first American in space less than a month later.

The first cooperative human space flight project between the United States and the Soviet Union took place in 1975. The Apollo-Soyuz Test Project was designed to test the compatibility of rendezvous and docking systems for American and Soviet spacecraft and to open the way for future joint manned flights.

Since 1993, the U.S. and Russia have worked together on a number of other space flight projects. The Space Shuttle began visiting the Russian Mir space station in 1994, and in 1995 Norm Thagard became the first U.S. astronaut to take up residency on Mir. Seven U.S. astronauts served with their Russian counterparts aboard the orbiting Mir laboratory from 1995 to 1998. The experience gained from the Mir cooperative effort, as well as lessons learned, paved the way for the International Space Station.

In 1961, U.S. President John F. Kennedy had a challenge for NASA. The challenge was to land a man on the moon before the end of the decade (before 1970). The race to meet his goal would require the greatest technological achievement the world has ever seen. The first Apollo missions were spent getting ready for the moon landing. Apollo 8 and Apollo 10 even flew all the way to the moon, around it, and back to Earth. Finally, everything was ready. On July 16, 1969, Apollo 11 launched from Kennedy Space Center in Florida. They traveled to the moon and arrived in lunar orbit on July 19.

Neil Armstrong was the first astronaut to step on the moon. He was soon joined by Buzz Aldrin. The two astronauts spent 21 hours on the moon. They did experiments and took pictures. They also brought back 46 pounds of moon rocks. After their stay on the moon, they blasted off in the top part of the lunar lander. They docked with "Columbia", the Command Module. Columbia was piloted by astronaut Michael Collins who stayed in orbit around the moon waiting for Neil and Buzz. Finally, all three astronauts rode back to the Earth in Columbia. They splashed down in the Pacific Ocean on July 24, 1969. While on the moon Neil and Buzz planted a United States flag and left a sign that read, "Here men from the planet Earth first set foot upon the Moon July 1969, A.D. We came in peace for all mankind."

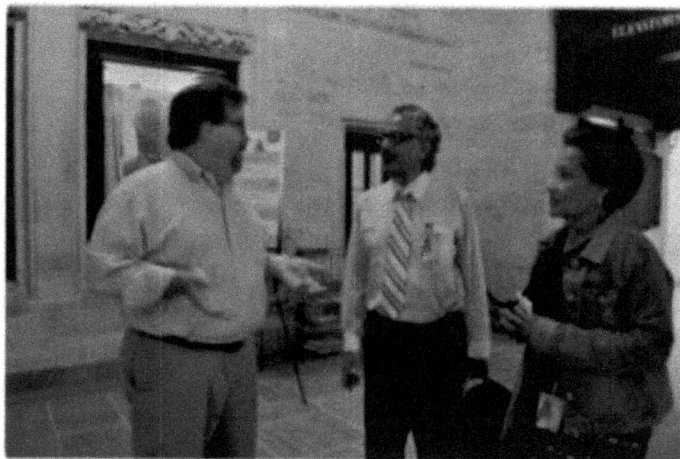

Epilogue – The Fourth Estate

The battle for us, in short, does not lie against crusted prejudice, but against the chaos of a new freedom. This chaos is our real problem. So if the younger critics are to meet the issues of their generation they must give their attention, not so much to the evils of authority, as to the weaknesses of democracy. But how is a man to go about doing such a task? He faces an enormously complicated world, full of stirring and confusion and ferment. He hears of movements and agitation, criticisms and reforms, knows people who are devoted to "causes", feels angry or hopeful at different times, goes to meetings, reads radical books, and accumulates a sense of uneasiness and pending change. – Walter Lippmann in *Drift & Mastery*

PORT OF SPAIN, TRINIDAD – And the winner is Barack Hussein Obama!

It was not however an election to augment American pride in themselves and in the world because it brought out the worst aspects in democracy and the lowest anthropological qualities in humans, racism and bigotry, and threats of anarchy if voting did not go the way of the conservatives. Neither Democrats nor Republicans could testify when the votes were finally counted that the race for the Presidency was fought in an arena free of spite and that the polling result on the night of 6 November 2012 while it gave Obama a second term in the Office of President had bestowed on Americans Gold, Silver and Bronze for the democracy that Administrations under George W. Bush and under Barack Hussein Obama have been trying to promote in countries that were once ruled by dictators, from Iraq to Libya to Egypt, and where Americans were trying to plant the flag of free and fair elections. It just wasn't so. The two-billion-dollar presidential race became a victim once more of fear and hate.

First the fear: Jason Sickles of Yahoo! / The Lookout reported the case of Judge Tom Head who was on a local TV news show making his case for a tax increase, when he said hiring extra sheriff's deputies would especially be needed if Obama wins in November. The report comes from Lubbock's Fox 34 News. "He's going to try to hand over the sovereignty of the United States to the U.N., and what is going to happen when that happens?" Head asked. "I'm thinking the worst: Civil unrest, civil disobedience, civil war maybe. And we're not just talking a few riots here and demonstrations, we're talking Lexington, Concord, take up arms and get rid of the guy. Now what's going to happen if we do that, if the public decides to do that? He's going to send in U.N. troops. I don't want 'em in Lubbock County. OK. So I'm going to stand in front of their armored personnel carrier and say 'you're not coming in here'. And the sheriff, I've already asked him, I said, 'you gonna back me?' and he said, 'yeah, I'll back you'." Sheriff Kelly Rowe told a Lubbock newspaper reporter however that he has never discussed any of the scenarios with the judge. But the evil done, Judge Head explained his remarks in a video interview with the Lubbock *Avalanche-Journal* saying his original comments were taken out of context. However as the county's emergency management director, he said, he has to keep a "worst case scenario" in mind if Obama returns to the White House and Democrats control the Senate. "I have some opinions what they're doing and what they're trying to do if they stay in power," he said. "And I have to prepare for that."

So shouldn't Americans worry when they read that Social Security needs 174,000 bullets? Stephen Ohlemacher of the Associated Press was puzzled by this order as he wrote on 2 September 2012, and it didn't take long for the Internet to start buzzing with conspiracy theories after the Social Security Administration posted a notice that it was purchasing 174,000 hollow-point bullets. Why is the agency that provides benefits to retirees, disabled workers, widows and children stockpiling ammunition? Whom are they going to use it on? "It's not outlandish to suggest that the Social Security Administration is purchasing the bullets as part of preparations for civil unrest," the website Infowars.com said. Another website, The Daily Caller, said the bullets must be for use against American citizens, "since the SSA has never been used overseas to help foreign countries maintain control of their citizens."

The clamor became such a distraction for the agency that it dedicated a website to explaining the purchase. The explanation, it turns out, isn't as tantalizing as an arms build-up to defend against unruly senior citizens. The bullets are for Social Security's office of inspector general, which has about 295 agents who investigate Social Security fraud and other crimes, said Jonathan L. Lasher, the agency's assistant IG for external relations. The agents carry guns and make arrests – 589 last year – Lasher said. They execute search warrants and respond to threats against Social Security offices, employees and customers. Agents carry .357 caliber pistols, Lasher said. The bullets, which add up to about 590 per agent, are for the upcoming fiscal year. Most will be expended on the firing range. Some bloggers have taken issue with the type of ammunition the agency is buying, questioning why agents need hollow-point bullets. Hollow-points are known for causing more tissue damage than other bullets when they hit a person because they expand when they enter the body.

The bullets, however, are standard issue for many law enforcement agencies, Lasher said, a fact confirmed by the directors of two law enforcement training centers. "For practice ammunition, they do not have to be hollow-points, but hollow-points are the normal police round used for duty ammunition due to their ability to stop when they hit an object as opposed to going through it and striking more objects," said William J. Muldoon, president of the International Association of Directors of Law Enforcement Standards and Training. "Six hundred rounds per year for training, qualification and I would assume to carry on duty is not out of line at all," said John W. Worden, director of the University of Missouri's Law Enforcement Training Institute. "Hollow points are carried by law enforcement all over the country and are probably the preferred type of ammo no matter what caliber."

The episode says the news source illustrates what can happen when a seemingly salacious tidbit gets amplified and embellished on the Internet. A few weeks ago, the National Oceanic and Atmospheric

Administration had a similar dustup when it solicited bids for 46,000 rounds of ammunition and shooting targets, seemingly to arm workers at the National Weather Service. It turns out the notice had a clerical error and the bullets were for NOAA's Fisheries Office of Law Enforcement, the agency said. And Social Security's turn in the pillory hit a crescendo when Jay Leno joked about it in a recent monologue on *The Tonight Show*. "What senior citizens are they worried about?" Leno asked. "I mean, who's going to storm the building?"

These were not isolated cases of anxiety in the United States and it is easy to conclude that the country is resting on a fault-line of catastrophe. In New York City, a significant majority of New Yorkers, say Michael M. Grynbaum and Marjorie Connelly, claim that the Police Department favors whites over blacks, according to a new poll by The New York Times. Criticism was leveled at the stop-and-frisk practice. The constitutionality of the police tactic has been questioned in New York City and elsewhere. But does it work? That view, as widespread now as it was in 2001 during the administration of Mayor Rudolph W. Giuliani, is particularly prevalent among black New Yorkers, 80 per cent of whom say the police favor one race over the other. A plurality of white residents – 48 per cent – agrees.

Concern about police favoritism came at a time of intensified scrutiny of the department's extensive practice of stopping, questioning and, in many instances, frisking people on the city's streets. Last year, the police made nearly 700,000 stops; about 85 per cent of the stops involved blacks or Hispanics. The poll found that a majority of black residents said the stop-and-frisk tactic had led to the harassment of innocent people, but most white residents viewed the practice as an acceptable way to improve urban safety. Among all New Yorkers, 48 per cent said the tactic was "acceptable to make New York City safer," while almost as many – 45 per cent – deemed the tactic "excessive". Most of those surveyed rejected Mayor Michael R. Bloomberg's chief rationale for the practice, saying they did not think that stopping and frisking suspicious people had lowered the crime rate or reduced the use of illegal guns. "Stop-and-frisk would be a good idea if they did it right," Jose Aponte, 64, a retired doorman who lives in the Bronx, said in a follow-up interview after the poll. "But it's not decreasing crime or guns. There are more shootings every day."

But Bloomberg and the police commissioner, Raymond W. Kelly, received high marks on the crime issue: 57 per cent of New Yorkers said they approved of the way the mayor was dealing with crime, and 61 per cent said they approved of the way the commissioner was handling his job. Even 50 per cent of the respondents who said they had been the target of a racially motivated police stop approved of Mr. Kelly's management. Mr. Bloomberg, who has overseen a significant rise in the number of stops during his nearly 11 years in office, scored slightly lower on his stewardship of race relations, with half of residents saying they approved and one-third saying they disapproved. Just 36 per cent of black residents said they approved of the mayor's handling of race relations.

James Westcott, a Bronx resident who has been unemployed for two years, said he had been stopped by the police on three occasions. "One right after the other, by three different patrol cars," Westcott, who is black, said. He also said the police had become less considerate, adding, "It started getting bad when Giuliani was mayor, and now it's getting worse and worse. You know it's excessive when you see people get stopped who really don't deserve to be stopped, like kids going to school," Mr. Westcott, 44, said. "The police just jump out, stop them, search them, take their names down, then get back in their car and leave, and the kids don't know what went on." But some New Yorkers, while conceding that the police show favoritism for one race over another, said the stop-and-frisk tactic's ends justified the means. "If that's what it takes, I find it acceptable," said Jani Kipness, 58, a special-education teacher from Brooklyn who is white. She said that she thought that officers "single out minority groups," but that "if you look at the crime in New York, it's less white people; that's just the way it is. I wouldn't want to be stopped and frisked," she added. "But if you look at cities like Detroit and other cities that have a way higher crime rate than New York, I think New York has to be doing something right."

The stop-and-frisk practice has come under harsh criticism from civil liberties groups and some lower court judges. The issue has become a subject of debate among elected officials and has apparently captured the attention of the public: more than three-quarters of New Yorkers interviewed for the poll said they had heard a lot or some about it.

But there's more bad news. An Associated Press report from New York has stated that Transportation Security Administration officers at Boston's Logan International Airport are alleging that a program intended to help flag possible terrorists based on passengers' mannerisms has led to rampant racial profiling, The New York Times reported on its website that in interviews and internal complaints it has obtained, more than 30 officers involved in the "behavior detection" program at Logan contend that the operation targets not only Middle Easterners, but also passengers who fit certain profiles – such as Hispanics traveling to Miami, or blacks wearing baseball caps backward. The TSA told the newspaper that it is investigating the officers' claims. At a meeting in July with the agency, officers provided written complaints, some of them anonymous, from 32 officers. The officers said their co-workers were increasingly targeting minorities, believing the stops would lead to the discovery of drugs, outstanding arrest warrants and immigration problems, in response to pressure from managers who wanted high numbers of stops, searches and criminal referrals, the NYT reported. "The behavior detection program is no longer a behavior-based program, but it is a racial profiling program," one officer wrote in an anonymous complaint. The program billed as a model for other airports across the country is intended to allow officers to stop, search and question passengers who seem suspicious. Specially trained "assessors" observe security lines for unusual activity and speak individually with each passenger, looking for inconsistencies in the passenger's responses to questions and behavior such as avoiding eye contact, fidgeting or sweating. Passengers considered suspicious can be taken aside for more intensive questioning.

At least one passenger filed a formal complaint with the TSA. Kenneth Boatner, a black psychologist and educational consultant who was traveling to Atlanta on business, said he was detained for nearly half an hour as agents examined his belongings, including his checkbook and his patients' clinical notes. In an interview with The Times, Boatner said he felt humiliated, and that the officers never explained why they were singling him out, but he suspected it was because of his race and attire. He was wearing sweat pants, a white T-shirt and high-top sneakers. "I had never been subjected to anything like that," Boatner said. But the TSA said the program at Logan "in no way encourages or tolerates profiling," and that passengers cannot be subjected to behavior assessments based on their nationality, race, ethnicity or religion. "If any of these claims prove accurate, we will take immediate and decisive action to ensure there are consequences to such activity," the agency said in a statement. The TSA said it did not compile information on passengers' race or ethnicity and could not provide a breakdown of passengers who may have been stopped on either basis through the program.

Next the hate: On 23 March 2012 in West Monroe, Louisiana, and at a campaign stop at a firing range, while Rick Santorum was firing off some rounds, a woman shouted, "Pretend it's Obama". Arlette Saenz reporting for ABC News said that Santorum, who was far from the woman, couldn't hear the comment as he proceeded with his target practice. Neither could his staffers. But the yell – the identity of the yeller is not clear, although the words were clearly audible – was in close proximity to journalists traveling with the candidate. "It's absurd," Santorum said of the woman's outburst when reporters told him about it. "No, we're not pretending it's anybody but shooting pistols. It's a very terrible and horrible remark and I'm glad I didn't hear it."

All of this makes a fraud and a farce of Republicans' support for free and fair elections. According to Reuters, House Speaker John Boehner is the most prominent Republican to admit that his party's strategy for winning in November doesn't suppose that the GOP can win over some black and Latino voters, but hopes they won't vote at all. Boehner wasn't talking about voter I.D. laws, which are being pushed by Republicans and criticized as disenfranchising minority and poor voters. He told a luncheon hosted by the Christian Science Monitor in Tampa that the Republican Party was counting on apathy from the Latinos and blacks who are choosing Democrats over Republicans by record margins in recent polls. As Talking Point Memo's Benjy Sarlin reports, Boehner said: "This election is about economics... These groups have been hit the hardest. They may not show up and vote for our candidate but I'd suggest to you they won't show up and vote for the president either."

Less prominent Republicans have made essentially the same case in other terms. Doug Priesse, chair of the Franklin County, Ohio, Republican Party, indicated restrictions on early voting hours and voter ID laws were meant to keep blacks from voting. In an email sent earlier this month to The Columbus Dispatch's Darrel Rowland, Priesse said, "I guess I really actually feel we shouldn't contort the voting process to accommodate the urban – read African-American – voter-turnout machine... Let's be fair and reasonable." Priesse is on the elections board and voted against keeping polls open in the weekends. In June, Pennsylvania House Republican leader Mike Turzai conceded the point of voter ID is to help Republicans win when he said, "Voter ID, which is gonna allow Governor Romney to win the state of Pennsylvania, done."

II

HOWEVER THESE predictions did not come true for Republicans and President Obama won 51 per cent of the popular vote to claim victory. Romney trailed with 47 per cent. Earlier, after congratulating Mitt Romney "on a spirited campaign" Obama had declared that he was "confident we've got the votes to win," Jim Kuhnhenn and Julie Pace of the Associated Press reported from Chicago. Closing down his campaign late Monday night with a nostalgia-filled rally in Iowa, Obama, the pair reported, went back to exhorting his supporters during a Tuesday morning visit to a campaign office near his South Side Chicago home. The president had headed into Election Day locked in a close race with Romney, according to national polls, but he appeared to have a slight edge in some of key battlegrounds that would decide the contest, including Ohio, Iowa and Wisconsin. Speaking to reporters, Obama said that after all the ads and electioneering "it comes down to one day" and declared that it was "a source of great optimism." And after offering congratulations to Romney, he added: "I know his supporters are just as engaged, just as enthusiastic."

According to news reports, Obama spent Monday night at the home where he lived with his family before moving to the White House. There was no traditional Election Day photo of Obama casting his ballot on Tuesday because he voted in Chicago the previous week, part of his campaign's efforts to promote early voting. First lady Michelle Obama voted by absentee ballot. One tradition Obama would keep, however, is an Election Day basketball game. In 2008, Obama played basketball with aides before winning the kickoff Iowa caucuses. The president and his aides decided to make the games an Election Day tradition after they lost the next contest – the New Hampshire primary – on a day when they didn't hit the court. "We made the mistake of not playing basketball once. I can assure you we will not repeat that," said Robert Gibbs, a longtime Obama aide who joined the president on the road for the campaign's waning days. The president planned to have lunch and dinner at his home but would spend other parts of the day at a downtown hotel, where he would be joined in the evening by family, friends and aides to await the election returns. He was expected to speak – delivering either a victory or concession speech – at his campaign's election night party at McCormick Place convention center.

In Pataskala, Ohio, there was relief that the election was over the Associated Press reported. If there was one thing the regulars at the Nutcracker restaurant could agree upon on Tuesday, AP said, it was that the presidential campaign went on for far too long. Like voters throughout Ohio, residents of this small town east of Columbus were inundated for months with ads, campaign mail and phone calls. Just Monday, both President Barack Obama and Republican challenger Mitt Romney stumped in central Ohio for the umpteenth time. "Overbearing," said 77-year-old Ken Armentrout, a retired truck driver who stopped in to eat after voting for Romney on a bright, frosty day. "It was the same thing over and over." "Annoying," added Jack Cruikshank, a 69-year-old retired heavy equipment operator who voted early for Romney. "They beat you over the head with it." Sitting between them was 61-year-old Lewie Hoskinson, a retired city worker who his friends claim is the only Obama supporter in the town of 14,000 souls. "I'm sure there are others, but I'm the only one who will admit it," Hoskins said, to belly laughs from his buddies. Pataskala and rural Licking County are so Republican that Hoskins twice had his Obama yard sign vandalized. Still, Hoskinson said he supported the president because he seemed more in touch with the working man and because he engineered the auto bailout, a big deal in a state where that industry looms large. His friends acknowledged they weren't exactly thrilled with Romney but said Obama hadn't done enough to get the economy moving.

And on that subject, Republicans and their Democratic companion could also find consensus. In Ohio and the rest of the country, they said, this Election Day was still all about the economy. After 102 years on this earth, after a life as an art teacher and a store owner, after seeing war and a Depression and presidents good and bad, Selma Friedman sees no reason to muffle her opinion, writes Mitch Stacy of the Associated Press from Boca Raton, Fla. What does this election mean? She'll give you an earful. She wants to see war ended and schools renewed, for manufacturing to return and women's rights to improve. She worries about health care and climate change and energy and fairness, and stops for only a moment before continuing her litany. Friedman's first presidential vote was for Franklin Roosevelt in 1932. When she voted Tuesday at St. Andrews South, her retirement community in Boca Raton, Fla., she went with a Democrat again, marking Obama on her ballot with no hesitation. "He couldn't do it all in four years," she said. In this vital swing state, Obama's hopes hinged on getting supporters to turn out en masse in Democrat-rich South Florida. And with a higher percentage of seniors than any other state, Florida's 29 electoral votes depend, in part, on older voters' approval. Around the breakfast table at St. Andrews, Romney supporters shook their heads when they considered the past four years. Doris Jacobsen, 76, a retired secretary, couldn't imagine why someone would give Obama their vote again. "What has he done?" she asked, a piece of bacon pinched between her fingers. Friedman has heard those arguments, along with her neighbors' thoughts on tax rates and foreign policy and abortion. She cannot convince them. She is a couple decades older than most here. Maybe, she thinks, it's just youthful ignorance.

In Apex, N.C. Matt Sedensky of the Associated Press writes that once laid-off, a voter says Obama deserves a chance to turn things around. A few miles outside of Raleigh, N.C., voters streamed into the Wake County Firearms Education & Training Center to cast ballots. They lined up along a hallway dominated by posters offering National Rifle Association classes and "ladies handgun leagues." As Jerome Gantt signed in at the registration table, a target stared at him from the wall beyond. The 34-year-old black independent voted for Republican John McCain four years ago, but not because he did not like Barack Obama. "I honestly didn't want a black man to be the first president coming into that bad a situation," said Gantt, who works for a pharmaceuticals company. Gantt is far from happy with how the last four years have turned out. He and his wife, Paquita, were laid off within months of each other. Both are now back at work, and he feels that many who remain unemployed either didn't want to take a step down or move out of their comfort zone. And, he added: "I don't think four years is enough time really to turn anything around." Pat Crosswhite couldn't disagree more. The 55-year-old Holly Springs woman thinks Obama, if re-elected, should be impeached over his handling of the consulate attack in Libya. "I think what he started is terrible," said Crosswhite, who does voice-overs for television commercials. "I don't want him to finish it." Four years ago, Gantt resisted the tug of "history." This time, he favored giving Obama the chance to live up to his promises. "I don't feel elation," he said. "Even if Obama wins, I won't go out celebrating tonight and say, 'Yes. We won.' Because we won't win until four years from now, when we can see what the results are of his actions."

In Little Ferry, N.J. Allen G. Breed of the Associated Press tells of voting in the shadow of the super storm Sandy. The Big Dipper hangs over Liberty Street he wrote as Frank Puzzo arrives to begin his Election Day duties. Just a week ago, rescuers were piloting boats through three feet of water that coursed past Memorial School and throughout this storm-scarred town. Now, it's 28 degrees; the first voters won't arrive for nearly an hour. But Puzzo, whose apartment still has no heat or hot water, whose car was claimed by storm surge, is the first to arrive to prepare and open the polls. "This is super important for the future of the country," says Puzzo, an accountant who has been out of work since July. The people of Little Ferry could be pardoned if they focused purely on their beleaguered present. Some arrived shivering and clearly exhausted, their long-held certainties about shelter and safety deeply shaken. But the future matters to the people lined up at the voting machines in the hallway outside Ms. Kukula's third-grade class. Agim Coma, a 25-year-old construction worker, is the first voter to arrive, 13 minutes before polls open. The storm claimed his apartment and car. "It's important because it's our day," he said, as Election Day in America got under way here and everywhere. "No matter what happens, hurricanes, tornados, it's our day to vote."

III

PRESIDENT OBAMA returned from the campaign trail on Wednesday with little time to savor victory, facing urgent economic and fiscal challenges and a still-divided Congress capable of blocking his every move, wrote Steve Holland and Matt Spetalnick of Reuters. Obama defeated Republican challenger Mitt Romney on Tuesday night after a grueling presidential race and used his acceptance speech in front of a huge cheering crowd in Chicago to strike a conciliatory note toward his political opponents. But in the cold light of the election's morning-after, it was clear that even though voters have given their stamp of approval for a second Obama term, he could have a hard time translating that into a mandate to push forward with his agenda. Americans chose to stick with a divided government in Washington by leaving the U.S. Congress as it has been since the midterm elections of 2010. Obama's fellow Democrats retained control of the Senate and Republicans kept the majority in the House of Representatives, giving them power to curb the president's legislative ambitions. This is the political reality that Obama – who won a far narrower victory over Romney than his historic election as the country's first black president in 2008 – faces when he returned to Washington later on Wednesday. But that did not stop him from basking in the glow of re-election together with thousands of elated supporters in his hometown of Chicago early on Wednesday.

"You voted for action, not politics as usual," Obama said, calling for compromise and pledging to work with leaders of both parties to reduce the deficit, to reform the tax code and immigration laws, and to cut dependence on foreign oil. Obama told the crowd he hoped to sit down with Romney in the coming weeks and examine ways to meet the challenges ahead. But the problems that dogged Obama in his first term, which cast a long shadow over his 2008 campaign message of hope and change, still confront him. He must tackle the $1 trillion annual deficits, rein in the $16 trillion national debt, overhaul expensive social programs and deal with the split Congress.

The immediate focus for Obama and U.S. lawmakers will be to confront the "fiscal cliff", a mix of tax increases and spending cuts due to extract some $600 billion from the economy at the end of the year barring a deal with Congress. House Majority Leader John Boehner moved swiftly on the fiscal cliff issue, saying he would issue a statement on it on Wednesday, citing "the need for both parties to find common ground and take steps together to help our economy grow and create jobs, which is critical to solving our debt." Obama also faces looming international challenges like the West's nuclear standoff with Iran, the civil war in Syria, the winding down of the war in Afghanistan and dealing with an increasingly assertive China.

Romney, a multimillionaire former private equity executive, came back from a series of campaign stumbles to fight a close battle after besting Obama in the first of three presidential debates. But the former Massachusetts governor failed to convince voters of his argument that his business experience made him the best candidate to repair a weak U.S. economy. The nationwide popular vote remained extremely close with Obama taking about 50 per cent to 49 per cent for Romney after a campaign in which the candidates and their party allies spent a combined $2 billion. But in the state-by-state system of electoral votes that decides the White House, Obama notched up a comfortable victory. By early on Wednesday, Obama had 303 electoral votes, well over the 270 needed to win, to Romney's 206. Florida's close race was not yet declared, leaving its 29 electoral votes still to be claimed. Romney, 65, conceded in a speech delivered to disappointed supporters at the Boston Convention Center. "This is a time of great challenge for our nation," he told the crowd. "I pray that the president will be successful in guiding our nation. He warned against partisan bickering and urged politicians on both sides to "put the people before the politics."

The Republican Party, after losing two presidential contests, is now likely to go through a period of painful soul-searching, especially over how it has alienated Hispanic voters, an important constituency in Obama's victory. In the election aftermath, there were signs that partisan gridlock would persist in Washington. Senate Republican leader Mitch McConnell gave no sign that he was willing to concede his conservative principles, in a sign of potential confrontations ahead. "The voters have not endorsed the failures or excesses of the president's first term, they have simply given him more time to finish the job they asked him to do together with a Congress that restored balance to Washington after two years of one-party control," McConnell said.

Obama's win puts to rest the prospect of wholesale repeal of his 2010 healthcare reform law, which aims to widen the availability of health insurance coverage to Americans, but it still leaves questions about how much of his signature domestic policy achievement will be implemented. Obama, who took office in 2009 as the ravages of the financial crisis were hitting the U.S. economy, must continue his efforts to ignite strong growth and recover from the worst downturn since the Great Depression of the 1930s. An uneven recovery has been showing some signs of strength but the country's jobless rate, currently at 7.9 per cent, remains stubbornly high.

In keeping control of the 100-member Senate, Democrats seized Republican-held seats in Massachusetts and Indiana while retaining most of those they already had, including in Virginia and Missouri. The Republican majority in the 435-member House means that Congress still faces a deep partisan divide as it turns to the fiscal cliff and other issues. "That means the same dynamic. That means the same people who couldn't figure out how to cut deals for the past three years," said Ethan Siegel, an analyst who tracks Washington politics for institutional investors. While the Senate result was no surprise, Republicans had given themselves an even chance of winning a majority, so the night represented a disappointment for them.

U.S. stock futures slipped, the dollar fell and benchmark Treasuries rose after Obama's victory, which investors took to mean no dramatic shift in U.S. economic policy.

International leaders offered their congratulations. Israeli Prime Minister Benjamin Netanyahu, who has had a testy relationship with the U.S. leader, vowed to work with Obama to ensure the interests that are vital for the security of Israel's citizens. British Prime Minister David Cameron said Britain and the United States should make finding a way to solve the Syrian crisis a priority following Obama's re-election. His lease renewed in trying economic times, President Obama claimed a second term from an incredibly divided electorate and immediately braced for daunting challenges and progress that comes only in fits and starts, wrote Nancy Benac of the Associated Press in Washington. "We have fought our way back and we know in our hearts that for the United States of America, the best is yet to come," Obama said. The same voters who gave Obama another four years also elected a divided Congress. Democrats retained control of the Senate;

Republicans renewed their majority in the House. However, it was a sweet victory for Obama, but nothing like the jubilant celebration of four years earlier, when his hope-and-change election as the nation's first black president captivated the world. This time, Obama ground out his win with a stay-the-course pitch that essentially boiled down to a plea for more time to make things right and a hope that Congress will be more accommodating than in the past.

The vanquished Republican, Mitt Romney, tried to set a more conciliatory tone on the way off the stage. "At a time like this, we can't risk partisan bickering," Romney said after a campaign filled with it. "Our leaders have to reach across the aisle to do the people's work." House Speaker John Boehner spoke of a dual mandate, saying, "If there is a mandate, it is a mandate for both parties to find common ground and take steps together to help our economy grow and create jobs."

Obama claimed a commanding electoral mandate – at least 303 electoral votes to 206 for Romney – and had a near-sweep of the nine most hotly contested battleground states. But the close breakdown in the popular vote showed Americans' differences over how best to meet the nation's challenges. With more than 90 per cent of precincts reporting, the popular vote went 50 per cent for Obama to 48.4 per cent for Romney, the businessman-turned-politician who had argued that Obama had failed to turn around the economy and said it was time for a new approach keyed to lower taxes and a less intrusive government. Obama's re-election assured certainty on some fronts: His signature health-care overhaul will endure, as will the Wall Street reforms enacted after the economic meltdown. The drawdown of troops in Afghanistan will continue apace. And with an aging Supreme Court, the president is likely to have at least one more nomination to the high court.

The challenges immediately ahead for the 44th president are all too familiar: an economy still baby-stepping its way toward full health, 23 million Americans still out of work or in search of better jobs, civil war in Syria, an ominous standoff over Iran's nuclear program, and more. Sharp differences with Republicans in Congress on taxes, spending, deficit reduction, immigration and more await. And even before Obama gets to his second inaugural on 20 January 2013, he must grapple with the threatened "fiscal cliff" – a combination of automatic tax increases and steep across-the-board spending cuts that are set to take effect in January if Washington doesn't quickly come up with a workaround budget deal. Economists have warned the economy could tip back into recession absent a deal.

Despite long lines at polls in many places, turnout overall looked to be down from four years ago as the president pieced together a winning coalition of women, young people, minorities and lower-income voters that reflected the country's changing demographics. Obama's superior ground organization in the battleground states was key to his success. The president's victory speech – he'd written a concession, too, just in case – reflected the realities of the rough road ahead. "By itself the recognition that we have common hopes and dreams won't end all the gridlock, or solve all our problems or substitute for the painstaking work of building consensus and making the difficult compromises needed to move this country forward," Obama said. "But that common bond is where we must begin. Our economy is recovering. A decade of war is ending. A long campaign is now over, and whether I earned your vote or not, I have listened to you, I have learned from you and you have made me a better president."

The president said he hoped to meet with Romney and discuss how they can work together. They may have battled fiercely, he said, "but it's only because we love this country deeply." Romney's short concession – with misplaced confidence, he'd only prepared an acceptance speech – was a gracious end note after a grueling campaign. He wished the president's family well and told subdued supporters in Boston, "I so wish that I had been able to fulfill your hopes to lead the country in a different direction, but the nation chose another leader and so Ann and I join with you to earnestly pray for him and for this great nation."

Obama's re-election was a remarkable achievement given that Americans are anything but enthusiastic about the state they're in: Only about 4 in 10 voters thought the economy is getting better, just one quarter thought they're better off financially than four years ago and a little more than half think the country is on the wrong track, exit polls showed. But even now, four years after George W. Bush left office, voters were more likely to blame Bush than Obama for the fix they're in. It wasn't just the president and Congress who were on the ballot. Voters around the country considered ballot measures on a number of divisive social issues, with Maine and Maryland becoming the first states to approve same-sex marriage by popular vote while Washington state and Colorado legalized recreational use of marijuana.

From the beginning, Obama had an easier path than Romney to the 270 electoral votes needed for victory. The most expensive campaign in history was narrowly targeted at people in nine battleground states that held the key to victory, and the two sides drenched voters there with more than a million ads, the overwhelming share of them negative. Obama claimed at least seven of the battleground states, most notably Ohio, the Ground Zero of campaign 2012. He also got Iowa, New Hampshire, Colorado, Nevada, Virginia and Wisconsin, and he was ahead in Florida. Romney got North Carolina. Overall, Obama won 25 states and the District of Columbia and was leading in too-close-to-call Florida. Romney won 24 states. It was a more measured victory than four years ago, when Obama claimed 365 electoral votes to McCain's 173, winning with 53 per cent of the popular vote.

Obama was judged to be more in touch with people like them. More good news for him: Six in 10 voters said that taxes should be increased. And nearly half of voters said taxes should be increased on income over $250,000, as Obama has called for. Obama's list of promises to keep includes many holdovers he was unable to deliver on in his first term: rolling back tax cuts for upper-income people, immigration reform, reducing federal deficits, and more. A second term is sure to produce turnover in his Cabinet: Treasury Secretary Timothy Geithner has made it clear he wants to leave at the end of Obama's first term but is expected to remain in the post until a successor is confirmed. Secretary of State Hillary Rodham Clinton, Obama's rival for the presidency four years ago, is ready to leave too. Defense Secretary Leon Panetta isn't expected to stay on.

To the end, the presidential race was a nail-biter. About 1 in 10 voters said they'd only settled on their presidential choice within the last few days or even on Election Day, and they were closely divided between Obama and Romney. Nearly 1 per cent of voters went for Libertarian Party candidate Gary Johnson, who was on the ballot in 48 states.

In an election offering sharply different views on the role of government, voters ultimately narrowly tilted toward Obama's approach. "We have seen growth in the economy," said 25-year-old Matt Wieczorek, a registered Republican from Cincinnati who backed the president. "Maybe not as fast as we want it to be, but Obama has made a difference and I don't want to see that growth come to an end."

Works Cited

Introduction

ABC *Good Morning America* 4 April 2012.

AP *Big shift in Big Oil: Exxon is now No. 3* MailTribune.com

Blackman, Courtney N. *The Practice of Economic Management* Jamaica: Ian Randle Publishers, 2006.

Bloomberg News *Bloomberg Billionaires Index* April 2012.

Bloomberg (*Occupy Wall Street protestors*)
www.bloomberg.com/.../u-s-mayors-crack-down-on-occupy-wall-str...

Boehner, John A. *The New York Times*, 16 May 2012.

Borchers, Callum. Globe correspondent: https://twitter.com/callumborchers

Brookings Institute study, 10 May 2012.

Bush, George W. Poll. CNN ORC. 8 June 2012.

Byrne, Suzy. *The Client List* Yahoo! TV – 19 April 2012.

Chomsky, Noam. *Hegemony or Survival* London: Penguin Books, 2003.

Cooke, Alistair. British journalist report, June 1993.

Council on Foreign Relations. "FBI Statistics" cited.

Christoff, Chris. "Detroit." Bloomberg News
www.bloomberglink.com/gatherings_participants_bio.php?

Dawinder, Sidhu. Interview. Yahoo! News
content.usatoday.com/communities/ondeadline/post/2012/

Cutter, Stephanie. "State of the Union." CNN August 2012.

Douglass, Frederick. *Narrative of the life of Frederick Douglass*. New York: Simon & Schuster, 2004.

Dwyer, Devin. "Man Arrested for Alleged Obama Threat." ABC OTUS News 22 August 2012.

FitzGerald, Frances. *America Revised*. New York: Random House, 1979.

Friedman, Thomas I. and Mandelbaum, Michael. *That Used To Be Us*. New York: Farrar, Straus and Giroux, 2011.

G-20 (nations must 'do what's necessary' to boost world economy)
wtvr.com/.../g-20-nations-must-do-whats-necessary-to-boost-world-e...
Gallup. The United States' Basic Index Score
www.gallup.com/.../americans-access-basic-necessities-recession-level...

Galston, William A. "Six Months to go..." Governance Studies at Brookings. 10 May 2012.

Garrett, Charles V. and Smith, Henry L. *Socialized History of the United States*. New York: C. Scribner's and sons, 1936.

Gaza, Monica. news.softpedia.com Gheit, Fadel. (The Energy report)
www.theenergyreport.com/pub/htdocs/expert.html?id=1601

Giuliani, Rudy. CBS *Face the Nation*. August 2012.

Goodwin, Liz. Yahoo! News /The Lookout. 8 August 2012.

Graddick, Herndon. Reuters Celebrities, General. February 2012.

Greenspan, Alan. *The Age of Turbulence*. New York: Penguin Books, 2007.

Gros, Daniel. (Center European Policy Studies in Brussels) Interview, CNBC.com.
www.ceps.eu/quotes?page=12

Halpert, Julie. Report. Reuters. July 2012.

Hefner, Hugh. *The War Against Sex*. Playboy. May 2012.

Huffington Post, NBCOlympics.com

Intelligence Report. Southern Law Center. Spring 2012.

Jindal, Bobby. Report. firstread.nbcnews.com/_nv/more/section/archive?year...

Johnson, Keith, Report. *The Detroit News* http://www.detnews.com

Kaplan, Robert D. *The Coming Anarchy*. New York: Random House Inc., 2000.

Kissinger, Henry. *Diplomacy*. New York: Simon & Schuster Paperbacks, 1994.

Klum and Seal Celebrity website TMZ.com

Klum, Heidi. ABC News Report.17 April 2012.

Korwin, Alan. Gun Laws of America. USA: Bloomfield Press, 2009.

Kovach, Bill and Rosenstiel, Tom. *The Elements of Journalism*. New York: Random House Inc., 2007.

Krieg, Gregory J. "Sarah Palin" ABC OTUS 24 October 2012.

LaFree, Gary. Report. University of Maryland National Consortium for the Study of Terrorism and Responses to Terrorism

Levi, Michael. (energy policy expert) Council on Foreign Relations. Macke, Jeffe. Breakout.17 July 2012.

Mailer, Norman. *Why are we at war?* New York: Random House Inc., 2003.

McKeown, Jennifer. Report CNBC.com 31 Aug. 2012.

Morgan, Piers. "Interview with Seal." CNNtranscripts.cnn.com/TRANSCRIPTS/1201/.../pmt.01.htm...

Morgan, Piers. CNN Tonight "Interview with Touré." 30 March 2012.

Moynihan, Brian. (Bank excesses) finance.fortune.cnn.com/tag/brian-moynihan/

Moynihan, Daniel P. and Glazer, Nathan. *Beyond the melting pot*. USA: MIT Press, 1970.

Obama, Barack. Interview. AP report, 15 July 2012.

Obama, Barack. *The Audacity of Hope*. New York: Random House. 2008.

Obama, Michelle. Address. AME church, Gaylord Opryland Resort, Nashville, Tenn. June 2012.

Penn, Mark. (public relations firm Burson-Marsteller) Interview AP www.thestar.com/.../1121102--davos-business-leaders-say-we...

PetroChina (ranks third behind Exxon and BP) www.guardian.co.uk

Potok, Mark. *The Year in Hate & Extremism*. Intelligence Report, Issue Number: 145 Spring 2012.

Rice, Condoleeza. Speech. Super PAC fundraiser. Washington. June 2012.

Romney, Mitt. Interview. CBS *Sunday Morning*. www.cbsnews.com/sunday-morning/

Romney, Mitt. Speech Democratic National Convention, Charlotte, NC April 2012.

Romney, Mitt. NY Times, 16 May 2012.

Roth, Zachary. Report. The Lookout, October 2011.

Rugg, Harold. *Problems of American Culture*, (An introduction to…) Ginn and Company, 1931.

Russell, Bertrand. *Power*. London: Unwin Books. 1971

Russell Simmons & GlobalGrind.com Announce the Acquisition of CelebrityTweet.com New York, Dec. 8 /PRNewswire/

Santorum, Rick. CBS *Face the Nation*. www.cbsnews.com/8301.../sunday-on-face-the-nation-rick-santorum/

Santorum, Rick. CNN *State of the Union*." August 2012.

Sauter, Michael B. /Ashley, C. Allen. /Stockdale, Charles. B. Report 25 Jan. 2012. homes.yahoo.com/.../states-most-homes-foreclosure-224... - United States

Schiff. Peter. *The real crash: America's coming bankruptcy*. John Wiley & Sons, 2007.

Shulman, Douglas. Address. National Press Club, Washington. April 1 /PRNewswire-USNewswire/

Sickles, Jason. Yahoo! / The Lookout. 22 Aug. 2012.

Singh, Prabhjot. Interview Yahoo! News news.yahoo.com/.../sikh-temple-shooting-domestic-terro...

Soros, George. Interview. *Financial Times*, 24 June 2012. www.georgesoros.com/

Stableford, Dylan. Report. The Cutline. 6 March 2012.

Stableford, Dylan. Yahoo! News / The Lookout, August 2012.

Stockdale (Girls' High school Varsity Report) 25 Jan. 2012.

Stowe, Harriet Beecher. *Uncle Tom's Cabin*. New York: Barnes & Noble Books, 2003.

Sullivan, Eileen and Gillum, Jack. AP Report. 19 October 2012.

Thompson, Bankole. "Restoring Hope" Michigan Chronicle. 23-29 May, 2012.

TIME magazine analysis *Islamophobia: Does America have a Muslim problem?* 30 August 2010.

Vidal, Gore. *Abraham Lincoln Selected Speeches and Writings*. New York: Penguin Books, 1992

Vidal, Gore. *Lincoln*. New York: Random House, Inc. / Ballantine Books, 1985.

Vidal, Gore. *Dreaming War, Blood for Oil and the Bush-Cheney Junta* New York: Thunder's Mouth Press, 2002.

Watchdog group "robo-signing" scandal 4closurefraud.org

Weinstein, Joshua L. *One Million Moms*. LA Reuters. 2 Feb. 2012.

Weiss, Phil. (Argus research analyst) www.guardian.co.uk

Wiesenthal, Joe. Business Insider. 5 April 2012

Wiedemer, David, Wiedemer, Robert A. and Spitzer, Cindy. *Aftershock*: New Jersey: John Wiley & Sons, 2010.

Wile, Rob. Business Insider, 5 April 2012.

Wood, Gabriel & Biller. *America its people and Values*. New York: Harcourt Brace Jovanovich, 1979.

Woodward, Bob. *Obama's Wars*. New York: Simon & Shuster, 2010.

The World Economic (Davos)
topics.nytimes.com/top/reference/timestopics/.../w/.../index.html

World Social Forum
wsftv.net/.../critics-of-the-green-economy-green-energ

Worstall, Tim. Interview with Jeffrey Goldberg. Forbes, December 2011.

Zakarias, Fareed. globalpublicsquare.blogs.cnn.com/ - United States

Zezima, Katie. AP Report (Playboy and Penthouse) 30 October 2012.

Zillow Inc. survivalandprosperity.com/tag/zillow

Chapter One

AP "Hard Lessons" news.yahoo.com/auditors-billions-likely-wasted-iraq-17...

AP midyear report 2012 "Occupy Protest lives on"

AP on Davos Jan. 2012.
www.weforum.org/.../world-economic-forum-annual-meeting-2012

Barroso, Jose-Manuel. (EU not to be lectured to) www.huffingtonpost.ca/...

Bachmann, Michelle. Core of Conviction USA: self-published, 2011.

Bellinski, Robert. Morningstar analyst
biz.yahoo.com/a/2/214665.html

Bernanke, Ben. (Stone Mountain Georgia) Reuters, 10 Apr. 2012.

Bloomberg Billionaire Index
topics.bloomberg.com/bloomberg-billionaires-index/

Bosworth, Barry. www.brookings.edu/experts/bosworthb

Burns, Robert. AP (paper trail)
bigstory.ap.org/content/robert-burns

California Reinvestment Coalition survey 2012
www.calreinvest.org/

Cooke, Alistair. *Letter from America*. London: Penguin Books, 2005.

Dealogic data provider. www.dealogic.com/

Department of Transportation. Data, DOT and FlightStats.com

Fitzgerald, John J. *New Morning Telegraph*, 1920

FlightStats.com and Department of Transportation DOT

Flightware.com

Friedman, Thomas L. and Mandelbaum, Michael. *That used to be us*. Farrar, Straus and Giroux, 2011.

Goldberg, Jeffrey. Worstall, Tim. Forbes. December 2011.

Gross, Daniel. Interview. CNBC.com

IATA 11 June 2012.

IATA Annual General Meeting Beijing (Tony Tyler).

JP Morgan Chase AP report 13 June 2012.

JP Morgan Finance: "Shares of JPMorgan Chase & Co. tumbled" finance.yahoo.com/.../report-jpmorgan-trading-losses-m... -

Korn, Morgan. Daily Ticker. 2 Feb. 2012.

Labaton Sucharow. (Whistleblowers) www.reuters.com/.../us-wallstreet-survey-idUSBRE86906G20120710

Lehmann, Andre. Agence France Presse. Jan. 2012

Lender Processing Services "US fore closers jumped" March 2012. 4closurefraud.org

Levi, Michael. Council on Foreign Relations. www.cfr.org

Lincoln, Robert. (relates the riot) Abraham Lincoln and New York - The Riots on July 13-16 www.mrlincolnandnewyork.org/inside.asp?ID=93&subjectID=4

Madoff, Bernard. en.wikipedia.org/wiki/Bernard_Madoff

Martin, Edward. *The Wayfarer Martin*, New York: Macmillan Co. 1909.

McCartney, Scott. *The Wall Street Journal*, 5 Jan 2012.
McKeown, Jennifer. Interview. CNBC.com

Morgan Stanley. "Facebook sketches out IPO-mess defence; CTO departs"
uk.mobile.reuters.com

Morgan Stanley. "Insight: Morgan Stanley cut Facebook estimates just ... " Reuters
www.reuters.com/.../2012/.../22/us-facebook-forecasts-...

Moussaoui, Zacarias. (takes the stand)
forums.randi.org › JREF Forum › General Topics

Neighborhood Economics Development report January 2012

Nicholas, Carlson. Business Insider
www.businessinsider.com/commenter?id...

New York History - NewYorkTribune.com
www.newyorktribune.com/gpage1.html

Obama, Barack. *The Audacity of Hope*. New York: Random House. 2008.

O' Reilly, Bill. Fox network
www.foxnews.com/on-air/oreilly/index.html

Peace Corps website: www.peacecorps.gov/

Penn, Mark. AP Interview "Burson-Marsteller" 11 April 2011.
www.bloomberg.com/.../68555988-burson-marsteller-...

Perdue, Bev. O'Malley, Martin. Le Bas, Guy. CNN Interview 27 Aug. 2011.

Quelch, John. Interview AFP, www.ceibs.edu/media/newsletter/101706.shtml

Rajaratnam, Raj. topics.wsj.com/person/R/raj-rajaratnam/5453

Read, Bill. Report U.S. National Hurricane Center, Reuters. Aug. 2011.

Reuters. Report, "Wall Street executives" 9 July 2012.

Reuters report "Facebook IPO"
www.reuters.com/.../net-us-citigroup-massachusetts-mahaney- ...
www.reuters.com/.../us-facebook-lawsuit-idUSBRE84M0RK2012052...

Sahadi, Jeanne. CNNMONEY.COM

http://money.cnn.com/2011/06/14/news/economy/debt_ceiling_demands/index.htm ...

Sanders, Bernier. The Daily Ticker
finance.yahoo.com/.../minister-state-bernier-celebrates-bdc-1215004

Satwant, Kaleka. Milwaukee Journal Sentinel.
www.jsonline.com ›

Schwab, Klaus. Report at annual World Economic Forum
www.weforum.org/contributors/klaus-schwab

Schulman, Douglas. Address at the National Press Club
press.org/news-multimedia/videos/npc-luncheon-douglas-shulman-0

Schultz, Howard. The Blog "How Can America Win This Election?" Posted:
06/29/2012

Serwer, Andy, Fortune magazine
en.wikipedia.org/wiki/Andrew_Serwer

Soros, George. Financial Times (warned that EU…) 12 Apr. 2012.

Stanford, Allan. (Ponzi scheme) www.jayblessed.com

Stiglitz, Joseph E. *The Price of Inequality*. W.W. Norton & Company, Inc. 2012.

Task, Aaron. The Daily Ticker
finance.yahoo.com/blogs/author/aaron-task/

The Atlanta Journal-Constitution. "Aubrey Lee Price planned to kill himself" 8 July
2012

The United States Basic Index Score
www.gallup.com/.../americans-access-basic-necessities-recession-level...

Tyler, Tony. IATA (hit out at controversial tax)
carboncredits.carboncapturereport.org/...//profiler_showlist?...tony_t...

Stephen Tindale. Interview CNBC.com

Wall Street Journal report "INA Drew JP Morgan's chief investment officer" 2011.

Weather Channel. www.weather.com/newscenter/hurricanecentral/2011/irene.html

Wells, Greg. Southwest Review. "Peace Corps" 2007.

Wikipedia, the free encyclopedia "Manhattan."

Zachary, Roth. The Lookout. October 2011

Zecchino, Emilia. Only in America.USA: Llumina Press, 2011.

Chapter Two

Alexander, David. Reuters 8 Jan. 2012.

Amanpour, Christiane. "Is the US committing superpower suicide against China?" 22 Feb 2012 news.yahoo.com/.../u-committing-superpower-suicide-a

American Civil Liberties Union www.aclu.org/

AP report "China" 11 October 2011.

AP "Russia issued new warnings" 23 March 2012.

Brown University "Cost of War" research project by Institute news.brown.edu/pressreleases/2012/09/911

Bush, Richard, Asian Studies, Brookings Institute www.brookings.edu/experts/bushr

DigitalGlobe Inc www.digitalglobe.com/

Dozier, Kimberly. Debate. AP Aspen Colorado, 27 July 2012 .

Federeman, Joseph AP 19 Feb. 2012.

Friedman, Thomaas L. and Madelbaum, Michael. That used to be us. Picador 2011.

Greenspan, Alan. *The Age of Turbulence*. New York: Penguin Books. 2007.

Hartman, Rachael Rose The Ticket. December 2011.

ISNA en.wikipedia.org/wiki/Iranian_Students_News_Agency

Jaffe, Alexnder. *The National Journal*, 11 March 2012.

Kazan, Robert. *The New Republic*, 11 Jan 2011.

Kissinger, Henry. *Diplomacy*. USA: Touchstone Books, 1994

Knox, Olivier. "US free trade deals…" AFP 22 July 2011.

Lasher, Jonathan L. "The bullets are for Social Security's office of inspector general
www.startribune.com/nation/168425646.html

Le Carre, John. Times of London
www.johnlecarre.com

Lester, Will. "The United States has reached a deal…" AP 31 Dec. 2011

Lutz, Catherine. Report. Reuters 29 June 2011.
rt.com/usa/news/us-trillion-study-war/

Mailer, Norman. *Why Are We at War?* New York: Random House, 2003.

Marchione, Marilynn. *Detroit News* www.detroitnews.com/section/lifestyle03

Mehr News Agency www.mehrnews.com/en/

Mueller, Robert. FBI Director testifying before Judiciary Committee
www.fbi.gov

Raddatz Martha, Lila, Muhammad Interview ABC *Good Morning America*
gma.yahoo.com/soldier-held-afghan-massacre-had-brai…

Reuters "Bangladesh" 14 Jan 2012.

Reuters Report "Sarkozy told Obama" overheard and confirmed Nov. 2011.

Ross, Brian. ABC News 5 March 2012. abcnews.go.com/Author/Brian_Ross

Rozen, Laura. The Envoy 18 Aug 2011 news.yahoo.com/rss-rozen/ - United States

Sullivan, Eileen. AP 2 Feb. 2012. www.salon.com/writer/eileen_sullivan/
The Blaze "Is This China's Secret Weapon?" - The Blaze, 15 Dec 2011
www.theblaze.com/stories/is-this-chinas-secret-weapon/

The Times of London website www.thetimes.co.uk/

Time European edition website poll
www.ft.com/home/europe

Wala, Raha. Counsel for Human Rights First

www.humanrightsfirst.org

Woodward, Bob. *Obama's Wars* New York: Simon and Schuster. 2010.

Chapter Three

ABC News / Yahoo! News "Internet users"
abcnews.go.com/US/abc-news-yahoo-news-announce-online...

AFP Agence France Presse 2 March 2012.
 www.iri.org/news-events-press-center/news/afp-us-urges...

Agiesta, Jennifer and Kellman, Laurie. AP 27 Feb. 2012.

Allen.Mike. Politico
www.politico.com/playbook

Axelrod, David. *Fox News Sunday*
www.foxnews.com/on-air/fox-news-sunday-chris-wallace/...

Baily. Holly. Yahoo! News /The Ticket, 11 August 2012.
Biloye, Holly. Yahoo! News /The Ticket, 17 April 2012.

Billeaud, Jacques "Arizona Schools' Mexican-American Studies Program Ruled ..."
AP 27 Dec 2011

Boehner, John. Agence France Presse 2 Feb. 2011.

Brownstein, Ronald. National Journal nationaljournal.com/reporters/bio/1

Buffett, Warren. *TIME* 18 Jan 2012

Burns, Robert and Lekic, Slobodan. AP 12 Jan 2012

Chait, Jonathan, *The New York Times*
nymag.com/author/jonathan%20chait

ABC World News July 2012. abcnews.go.com/WN

Dempsey, Martin. Interview. CNN 19 Feb 2012.
www.commentarymagazine.com/topic/martin-dempsey

Donovan, Ed. Interview ABC Radio
en.wikipedia.org/wiki/Ed_Donovan

Doubouzinskis, Alex. Reuters 13 Jan. 2012 .

Dwyer, Devin. ABC OTUS News
abcnews.go.com/Author/Devin Dwyer

Espo, David. "Republicans and ..." AP 8 July 2012.

Fehrnstrom, Eric. Interview CNN 22 March 2012.

Fluke Sandra, *Today Show*
www.washingtonpost.com/blogs/the-buzz/post/rush-limbaugh

Fouhy, Beth and Pace, Julie AP
bigstory.ap.org/author/beth-fouhyjulie-pace

Friend, David, Carbonite "CEO wrote on company Facebook page"
www.carbonite.com/en/blog/A-Message-from-Carbonite-CEO

Goldstein, Ken. Yahoo! News
goodmenproject.com/author/ken-goldstein/

Good, Chris. ABC OTUS News July 2012.

Jaffe, Alexandra. "Boehner on Fox news" *The National Journal* 23 Jan. 2012.

Khan, Naureen. *The National Journal* 11 Dec. 2011.

Knox, Oliver, Yahoo! News /Ticket 15 Feb. 2012.

Knox, Olivier. The Ticket 23 Feb. 2012.

Knox, Oliver. The Ticket 5 July 2012.

Krieg, Gregory J. ABC OTUS News
abcnews.go.com/author/Gregory J. Krieg

LaBolt Vanity Fair
www.vanityfair.com/.../Drama-Mitt-and-Barack-Are-Like-C...

Lippmann, Walter Interview with Herbert Croly *The New Republic*

Maher, Bill. *The Tonight Show with Jay Leno*, 15 Feb. 2012.
www.fearssecretsdesires.com/...tonight-show/.../bill-ma...

McIntyre, Douglas A. and Hess, Alexander. 5 July 2012.

finance.yahoo.com/.../the-ten-companies-making-the-bi...

Miller, Jonathan, *The National Journal* 6 March 2012.

Moody, Chris. The Ticket 8 Feb 2012.

Moody, Chris. Yahoo! News /The Ticket, 10 July 2012.

Munro, Neil. The Daily , 16 Oct 2011.

Page, Susan "Is the US headed toward bankruptcy?" *USA Today*
firstread.nbcnews.com/

Papps, Stephanie, LiveScience.com, 29 Jan. 2012.

Pfieffer, Eric. Yahoo! / The Ticket, 31 May 2012.

Poor, Jeff. The Daily Caller, 30 Nov 2011.
Presidential Polls 2012: Latest Gallup, Rasmussen, AP/Gfk, ABC/Washington Post
Nationwide and Swing States Polls

Reeve, Elspeth. The Atlantic Wire 25 Jan. 2012.

Reid, Harry. ABC News Today abcnews.go.com ›

Reston, Maeve. *LATimes*
www.latimes.com/.../dispatcher.front?...Maeve+Reston...adv...

Reuters "Voters turn out to drop" 28 Dec. 2011.

Rroschild, David. Yahoo! News /The Signal, 23 Aug. 2012.

Roubini, Nouriel. "Global economy" Twitter"

Ryan, Paul. Interview ABC News Cincinnati affiliate, 29 Aug 2012.

Ryan, Paul. WBZ News radio Ryan said two years ago boston.cbslocal.com/.../paul-
ryan-on-2010-dan-rea-app...

Russell, Bertrand. Leaders and Followers
thinkexist.com/quotation/most_political_leaders.../155038.html

Sebelius, Kathleen announced in Jan 2012 en.wikipedia.org/wiki/
Contraceptive_mandate_(United_States)

Sherman, Jake Report Politico reports
www.politico.com/politicopulse/

Smead, Bill. Interview "CEO Smead Capital Management" CNBC 25 July 2012.
video.cnbc.com/gallery/?video=3000104988

Snowe, Olympia. Washington Post website 2 March 2012

Stableford, Dylan. The Cutline 23 Feb 2012.

Stableford, Dylan, The Ticket 2 March 2012

Stableford, Dylan. "Obama's war on women". Cutline

Steel, Michael Interview CNN "Breaks the News" 1 March 2009.

Stephanopoulous, George. Interview Goldman, ABC 3 Oct. 2011.

Stevenson, Seth. Slate, 12 Jan. 2012
deadspin.com/.../what-we-can-learn-about-football-and-bill-belichick...

Tapper, Jake. "This Week" ABC News
abcnews.go.com

Wallace, Chris, Fox News
www.foxnews.com/on-air/fox-news-sunday-chris-wallace/index.html

Webber, Tammy. AP 22 Dec 2011.
https://www.examiner.org/~examiner/index.php?...

Wolchjover, Natalie. LiveScience.com 28 Feb. 2012.

Wolf, Z. Byron. ABC OTUS News. July 2012.
news.yahoo.com/romneys-rate-history-politics-olympics... - United States

Yahoo Contributor Network.17 Feb. 2012.
sports.yahoo.com/top/news?slug=ycn-10978230 - United States

Chapter Four

Alphonse, Lylah M. "Love and Sex".Yahoo!/Shine, 16 Feb. 2012.
goodandgreen.ca/blog/?cat=9

AP Quinnipiac poll "Obama leads on Mitt Romney" July 2012 .

www.legislativegazette.com/Articles-Top-Stories-c-2012-09-17-8208

AP NY Report "Transport secretary" NY Times website www.thetimes.co.uk/

AP "Papa John's Pizza" 8 Jan. 2012. article.wn.com/.../2012/.../
Korean_immigrant_sues_Hooters_restaura...

Avalanche-Journal
en.wikipedia.org/wiki/Lubbock_Avalanche-Journal

Boatner, Kenneth. Interview *The NY Times*, 11 Aug. 2012.
www.nytimes.com/.../racial-profiling-at-boston-airport-officials-say.h...

Borger, Gloria. Interview with Ron Paul, CNN Dec. 2011
emsnews.wordpress.com/.../ron-paul-versus-cnn-gloria-borger-and-h...

Brookings Institute "The Re-Emergence of Concentrated Poverty ..." 3 Nov. 2011.
www.brookings.edu/research/.../03-poverty-kneebone-nadeau-berub...

Brown, Tom. "Stand your ground" Reuters, 23 March 2012.

Dobnik, Verena. AP 26 Feb. 2012.
www.tumblr.com/tagged/nypd?before=1330375326

Dwyer, Devin. ABC OTUS News
abcnews.go.com › Politicsews

Eisenberg, Jeff. The Dagger, 20 March 2012.
sports.yahoo.com/...dagger/brittney-gri

Foley, Ryan J. AP 17 Feb. 2012.
www.benefitspro.com/author/ryan-j-foleyner-bec

Fonseca, Felicia "Who is Indian?"AP 26 Jan. 2012 .
Fox, Lubbock. Fox 32 News www.myfoxlubbock.com/news/...lubbock.../...

Gates, Verna. "Univesity of Alabama study new..." Reuters 1 Feb. 2012.

Gamboa, Suzanne. AP 29 Dec. 2011. dev.akronnewsnow.com/news/state/itemlist/
category/25-featured?

Hananel, Sam." Pepsi beverages will pay" AP, Jan 11, 2012.

Harish Alon. "Romney" ABC News, 28 July 2012.
abcnews.go.com

Hosenball, Mark and Jacobins, Samuel P. Reuters, 23 Dec. 2011.

Human Resource Survey 2012.
www.shrm.org/.../surveyfindings/articles/.../2012_empbenefits_repor...

Inram, Luan. Charlotte Observer, 21 March 2012.
www.zoominfo.com/#!search/profile/person?personId...targetid...

Jacobs, Sally. The Other Barack. USA: PublicAffairs, May 2011.

Jealous, Benjamin. NAACP Interview, NY Times, 24 Jan. 2012.

Kierstead, Bob. ABC News affiliate KOMO, 21 Aug. 2012.
abcnews.go.com/.../secret-service-arrests-armed-man-for-alleged-oba

Kneebone, Elizabeth. Senior Researcher. Brookings Institute.
www.brookings.edu/experts/kneebonee

Kirchick, Paul. The New Republic www.tnr.com/article/politics/98811/ron-paul-
libertarian-bigotry

LATimes Report "Facebook users". articles.latimes.com/.../la-fi-tn-consumer-
reports-facebook-users-mor...

Leyden, T.J. Interview Reuters www.secretnews-compact.com/index.php?...
rt.com/usa/news/military-extremist-supremacist-page-231/

Mason, Jeff. and Trotta, Daniel. "Trayvon Martin". Reuters, 25 March 2012.

Matthews, Chris "Morning Joe" MSNB www.youtube.com/watch?
v=nwNbLYoRzuQ

Midden, Ryan. Interview. Boston Observer larrybrownsports.com/tag/linsanity

Moffitt, Robert.Report "Professor at St Johns Hopkins" AP
www.minnpost.com/users/robert-moffitt?page=48

Ng Christina Report "Inter racial couples" 1 Dec. 2011.
abcnews.go.com

Obama, Michelle Interview CBS News, 1 Jan. 2012 .

Pace, Julie. AP, 15 Jan. 2012.
antiobamablog.com/author/julie-pace/

Pfeiffer, Eric. The Sideshow, 16 March 2012.

Preisse, Doug. The Columbus Dispatch
hinterlandgazette.com/.../ohio-republican-doug-preisse-voting-proces...

"Racist Taunts" The Dagger – Thu, Mar 15, 2012 4:53 PM EDT. /newyorktimes-poll

Reuters Zimmerman Florida courts records
www.reuters.com/.../us-usa-florida-shooting-trial-...

Romney, Mitt. Interview. "Meet the Press" NBC 2007

Sickles, Jason. "Texas Judge" Yahoo! / The Lookout, 22 April 2012.
www.yahoo.com/.../lookout/texas-judge-warns-possible

Skelding Conor.. Yahoo! News /The Ticket, 10 July 2012.
news.yahoo.com/blogs/author/conor-skelding/

UnicomBooty.com

Walvin, James. The Zong.Boston: Yale University Press: 29 July 2011.

Warner, David. Reuters www.linkedin.com/pub/dave-warner/12/68b/b49

Weatherford, Wilson. Interview. WLBT-TV
abcnews.go.com

Yen, Hope. Census"One in two people are poor" AP, 8 Dec. 2011.

Chapter Five

Alter Alexandra. *The Wall Street Journal*
www.linkedin.com/pub/alexandra-alter/5/245/b69

Association of American Publishers
www.publishers.org/

Abebooks.com

Audible.com

Capps, Mike. (Epic games Video Games Industry)
games.yahoo.com/.../video-game-industry-app...

Cave, Nick. *The death of Bunny Munro*. UK:Canongate Books 2009.

Chan, Darcie. *The Mill River reclused*. Self-published 2011.

Chen Yee L. Kee. Reuters, 21 Dec. 2011.

Chowdhry, Trip. (Global Equities Research)
investing.businessweek.com/research/stocks/private/snapshot.asp?...

Des Marais, Christina. Inc.com 2 Dec. 2011.

Finkle, K and Leske, Nicola. Reuters, August 2012.

Goldman, Russell. ABC News
abcnews.go.com/Author/Russell_Goldman

Graziano, Bill. BGR News 16 April 2012.

Greenspan, Alan. *The Age of Turbulence*. New York: Penguin Books. 2007.

Hocking, Amanda. (Four Book deal) NY: St Martin's Press, 2011.

Holman, Jennifer Interview ABC News, 19 July 2012.
abcnews.go.com

Keegan, Victor. "Chile Miners" UK Guardian, 15 October 2010.
www.guardian.co.uk

Lardner, Richard. AP
bigstory.ap.org/content/richard-lardner

Lashinsky, Adam. *Fortune* magazine
www.amazon.com/Inside-Apple-Americas-Admired.../145551215X

Librarything.com

Lupkin, Sydney. ABC News
www.wopular.com/newsracks/abc%20news%20sydney

Lytle, Ryan. *US News and World Report*, 6 July 2012.

Moody, Chris The Ticket, 29 July 2011.

Morris, Chris. Pluged In, 19 March 2012.

Neso, Matt. Breakout, 24 Aug. 2012.

Oreskovic, Alexie. Reuters
www.crunchbase.com

Potter, Ned. "Apple to Remake Textbooks…" ABC News, 18 Jan. 2012.
abcnews.go.com/…/2012/…/apple-to-remake-textbooks-project-begu…

Riccardi, Nicholas AP
https://twitter.com/NickRiccardi

Rigby, Bill. Reuters.
www.linkedin.com/pub/dir/Bill/Rigby

Russo, Bill. Synergistics
cn.linkedin.com/in/williamrusso

Rutgers University Survey
bcsr.rutgers.edu/

Satter, Raphael. AP 12 July 2012.

Scott, Maureen. Etherbooks.com.uk

Silverman, David (Price Waterhouse) AP New York, 18 April 2012.

Stableford, Dylan. The Cutline, 11 Aug. 2011.

Sabbagh, Dan. "The iPad" UK Guardian, 29 November 2010.

Tecca Today I Tech, 16 March 2012.
m.tecca.com/guides/future/

Thomas, Penny. "Editor's Letter" Seren Publishing: UK 2010.

Thomson Reuters Report. "World Patents Index".

USA Today Report. Sept. 2011.
www.usatoday.com/story/money/business/…/september…/1642183/

Weinman, Chad. TacticalG
chadweinman.com/

Woo, Stu. The Wall Street Journal 21 Dec. 2011.

Woodyard, Chris. *USA Today*
content.usatoday.com/topics/reporter/Chris+Woodyard

Chapter Six

Abdullah, Halimah.
CNN politicalticker.blogs.cnn.com/tag/cnns-halimah-abdullah/

AFP Relax "New support" 7 Aug. 2012.
AFP Relax news Report "HK Forum on International film and TV market", 13 April 2012.

Baranski, Christine Interview. "The good wife" New York Magazine, 22 Aug. 2012.
article.wn.com/.../Emmy_Watch_Christine_Baranski_Picks_Her_Fav

Berger, Glenn. *Kung fu Panda* www.comingsoon.net/films.php?
id=11931&offset=20

Byrne, Suzy. *Celebrity News*, 30 April 2012.

Cunningham, Todd. The Wrap, 29 July 2012. |
TheWrap.com

Degeneres, Ellen. *The Ellen Degeneres Show* Reuters, 7 Feb. 2012.

Duckworth, Cara. RIAA
www.riaa.com/news_room.php?content_selector=riaa-news-media...

Heard, Amber. Interview. "Playboy Club" E Online.
www.eonline.com/.../amber-heard-exposes-the-playboy

Honig, Steve. (email on Miss Lohan)
ohnotheydidnt.livejournal.com/73045353.html

Hsiao, Rita Tynsoty 2nd Mulan
www.imdb.com/name/nm0398763/

Huvane, Stephen. Interview. The Wrap
www.thewrap.com/media/node/20375?page=0,0

Kenneally, Tim. Reuters 17 Feb. 2012.
www.thewrap.com/media/articles/michael-jackson

Kenneally, Tim. Fall TV

www.thewrap.com/tv

Lee Tiffany. Stop the Presses music.yahoo.com/blogs/author/tiffany-lee/

Lehane Chris. (Dem consultant)
pipl.com/directory/name/Lehane/Chris

Luazen, Martha M. PhD Exec Dir Center for the study of women Television and film
womenintvfilm.sdsu.edu/.../2011-12%20Boxed%20In%...

Noveck, Jocelyn. AP
bigstory.ap.org/content/jocelyn-noveck

Ricci, Christinal. Television Critics Association PressTour. 8 May 2012

Risling, Greg. "Lindsay Lohan was released from a Los Angeles County jail early
Monday"AP, 7 Nov. 2011.

Sabato, Larry. University of Virginia www.centerforpolitics.org/staff_sabato.html

Scordo, Lizbeth A-Line Celebrity Style, 29 July 2011
omg.yahoo.com/blogs/author/lizbeth-scordo.../8.html

Steinheim Gloria. en.wikipedia.org/wiki/Gloria_Steinhem

West, Darrell M. and Orman, John M. Celebrity Politics Pearson 2002.

Chapter Seven

Abbey, Jennifer. ABC News
jenniferbabbey.wordpress.com/abc/

Bell, Jeffey. *The Case for Polarized Politics*. Encounter Books, 2012.

Berube, Alan. Brookings Institute
www.brookings.edu/experts/berubea

Boehner, John. Fox News radio "Kilmeade and friends" 2 Aug. 2012.
radio.foxnews.com/.../speakerboehner-says-senatorreid-is-just-makin...

Bronson, Po. and Merryman, Ashley. Nurture Shock Twelve, 2011.

Brownstein, Robert National Journal
www.nationaljournal.com/reporters/bio/1

Buffett, Warren. The New York Times 15 Aug 2011.

Bush, Laura. Interview. ABC 26 July 2012.

Conlin, Michelle and Schnurr, Leah.
Reuters.com

Danziger, Sheldon. (Univ.Michigan)
www.psc.isr.umich.edu/people/cv/danziger_sheldon_cv.pdf

Dimock, Michael. Pews (Assoc research director)
www.people-press.org/about/michael-dimock/

Ditthavong, Sitthixay. AP, 13 Aug. 2012.

Doll, Jen The Atlantic Wire, 16 Feb. 2012.

Evans, Kelly NBC, 11 July 2012.
Fairchild, Caroline. Bloomberg News, 8 Aug. 2012.

Flaccus, Gillian and Taxin, Amy. AP, 25 July 2012.

Frank, Robert CNBC 8 Aug. 2012.

Friedmann, Emily. ABC OTUS News
abcnews.go.com/Author/Emily_Friedman

Goldman, Russell. ABC News
abcnews.go.com/Author/Russell_Goldman

Green, Franziska. Babble.com 14 June 2011.

Griffin, Chad. (Human Rights campaign)
www.hrc.org/staff/profile/chad-griffin1

Guthrie, Savannah.
en.wikipedia.org/wiki/Savannah_Guthrie

Guttmacher Institute
www.guttmacher.org/

Huckabee, Mike. St Louis KTVI-TV Fox affiliate

Jenner, Kris. Interview magazine
www.interviewmagazine.com/culture/kris-jenner

Kelleher, James B. Reuters, 8 Feb. 2012.
Knox, Olive. Yahoo. News /The Ticket
news.yahoo.com/blogs/ticket/ United States

Laitmon, Steven. The Calendar Group
https://twitter.com/CalendarGroup

Leib, David A. and Salter, Jim. "Todd Akin is scary" AP ,29 Oct. 2012.

Lindsay, Jay. AP
https://twitter.com/JayLindsay_AP

Mailer, Norman. *Why Are We at War?* New York: Random House, 2003.

Mann, Thomas. *The road to Obstructionism.* Blackstone Audio, Inc. 1 May 2012

Moisse, Katie ABC News blog, 6 Jan. 2012.

Moody, Chris Yahoo! News /The Ticket
news.yahoo.com/blogs/author/chris-moody/

Murphy, Kevin. "Bonnie and Clyde guns…" Reuters, 21 Jan. 2012.

National Journal Ratings 1982.
www.nationaljournal.com/.../congress-hits-new-peak-in-pol...

Parker, Kim. Pew Social and Demographic Trends
www.pewsocialtrends.org/author/kparker/

Piers, Morgan CNN
piersmorgan.blogs.cnn.com/

Pig;iucci, Massimi, Journal of Peace Research CUNY Lehman Coll. Turchin, July 2012.

Pace Julie AP
newsbusters.org/people/julie-pace

Raoux, John . AP
interceder.net/latest_news/John-Raoux

Reuters poll
www.reuters.com/.../us-usa-campaign-poll-idUSBRE89K0A9201210...

RNS Religion News Survey "Public Religion Research Institute" publicreligion.org/?source=religion-news-survey

Rowe, Karl. *Courage and Consequence*. Bargain Books, 2010.

Slava, Rubin. Indiegogo.com

Shellenbarger, Sue. *Wall Street Journal*
topics.wsj.com/person/S/sue-shellenbarger/6492

Sickles, John. Yahoo! /The Lookout
news.yahoo.com/rss-lookout/

Skillern, Tim. The Lookout
news.yahoo.com/rss-lookout/

Stableford, Dyland. (Sandra Fluke), Yahoo! News / The Ticket
news.yahoo.com/.../ticket/obama-rings-limbau...

Stableford, Dylan. "The Rise of the Asian…" Yahoo! News / The Lookout, 19 June 2012.

Task, Aaron. The Daily Ticker finance.yahoo.com/blogs/daily-ticker

Yinka, Adegoke and Erman, Michael. "Stubbornly high U.S. unemployment, a weak housing market combined …." Reuters, 2 Aug. 2012.

Wolchoyer, Natalie, *LiveScience*
www.lifeslittlemysteries.com/2907-science-religion-god-physics.html

World Health Organization Report 2000.
www.who.int/whr/2000/en/

Yahooshine and *Vanity* 11 Jan. 2012.
culture.newsroster.com/sources/yahoo-entertainment/

Yen, Hope. AP writer
newsbusters.org/people/hope-yen

Chapter Eight

Anderson Torrey of The Ticket
www.spokeo.com/Torrey+Anderson

Armstrong, Neil. The Right Stuff

Avalanche-Journal. Lubbock on line interview 23 August 2012 "Head said the comments he made during the interview were taken out of ..."

Blazucki, Sarah. Philadelphia Gay News
www.epgn.com/

Bolden, Charles. "statement about Sally Ride"
spaceflightnow.com/news/n1207/23ride/

Browning, Bill. "gay blogger"
www.nctimes.com

Collins, Michael. "wrote on Apollo 11"
www.space.com/16971-michael-collins-apollo-11.html

Cooper Anderson. CNN Human Rights Campaign study
www.hrc.org/blog/entry/cnn-anchor-anderson-cooper-comes-out

Carrey, David. Interview with Grotzinger, John AP 25 July 2012.

dailycaller.com/2010/03/25/social-security-payout-to...

Hefferman, Virginia. Yahoo! News / The Lookout
news.yahoo.com/.../lookout/neil-armstrong-moon-myste...

Holdren, John. Science advisor to President Obama
zombietime.com/john_holdren/

Info wars report: www.infowars.com/social-security-administration-to

Kennedy, JFK, 12 Sept. 1962.
er.jsc.nasa.gov/seh/ricetalk.htm

Klotz, Irene and Gorman, Steve. "Mars rover Curiosity lands on surface of Red Pl..."
Reuters, 8 Aug. 2012 .

Mailer, Norman. 1969.
www.nytimes.com/2007/11/18/nyregion/18mailer.html

Moore, Bill. (Chief Operating Officer NASA)
media.delawarenorth.com/delaware+north.../william-moore.htm

Pearlman, Robert Z. SPACE.com

Russert, Tim. *Meet the press* NBC 1969.

Sainz, Fred. www.facebook.com/fred.sainz

Stacy, Mitch. AP "Selma Friedman sees no reason to muffle her opinion. What does this election mean?"

www.boston.com/news/politics/2012/11/06/america-casts...

Sullivan, Andrew. The Daily Beast
andrewsullivan.thedailybeast.com/

The Huntsville Times "Yuri Gagarin" 31 Jan. 1958.

The New York Times "Warren County equal voting" 15 August 2012.
Ocean, Fran. Tumblr
www.tumblr.com/tagged/fran-ocean

Watkins, Mike. (Mission manager)
news.yahoo.com/.../michael-watkins-msl-mission-manag...

Wolfe, Tim. *The Right Stuff.* New York: Farrar, Straus and Giroux, 1979 / Picador, 2008.

Zap, Claudine. The Lookout
www.tumblr.com/tagged/claudine-zap

Epilogue

A.P. New York "Racial Profiling Alleged ..." 11 August 2012.

Bailey, Holly. Yahoo! New / The Ticket
news.yahoo.com/blogs/ticket

Blanke, Jennifer. WEF
www.weforum.org/contributors/jennifer-blanke

Boehner, John. Reuters news.yahoo.com/boehner-minorities-wont-turn-obama...

Bynum, Russ." Prosecutors say a murder case "AP, 27 Aug. 2012.

Christoffersen, John. AP ,19 Dec. 2011.

Cutter, Stephanie "Interviews.Mitt Romney"
archive.org/details/tv?time=20121006-20121014&q=stephanie nat convention Yhoo

Dominigez, Alex. AP
bigstory.ap.org/author/alex-dominguezand

Harjani, Ansura. CNBC
www.pakdef.info Holland, Keating. Interview CNN.com

Infowars.com Paul Joseph Watson Monday, 30 July 2012. "It's not just the
Department of Homeland Security that is…"
www.infowars.com/u-s-army-purchases-riot-gear-as-fears...

Klein, Rick. ABC news
abcnews.go.com/Author/Rick_Klein

Knox, Oliver. Yahoo! News / The Ticket, 7 Sept. 2012.

Kuhnhenn, Jim. Interview "Obama" AP
bigstory.ap.org/content/jim-kuhnhenn

LaBolt, Ben. Forum ABC and Yahoo! News
abcnews.go.com/.../obama-campaigns-ben-labolt-previews-presidents...

Leighton, Kyle. TPM
talkingpointsmemo.com/kyle-leighton.php

Leno. Jay. *The Tonight Show*
www.nbc.com/the-tonight-show/ - United States

Lippmann, Walter. *Drift & Mastery*. USA: H. Holt & Company, 1917.

Lubbock Avalanche-Journal County Judge Tom Head
lubbockonline.com/.../county-judge-head-concerned-civil...

Lubbock Fox 34 News and video interview with the New York Times, 27 Aug. 2012.
www.nytimes.com/2012/08/28/us/lubbock-official-tom-head...

Moody, Chris. Yahoo! News / The Ticket
news.yahoo.com/blogs/author/chris-moody/

Muldoon William J. (law enforcement)
www.linkedin.com/pub/dir/Bill/Muldoon

Ohlemacher, Stephen. AP, 2 Sept. 2012.
newsbusters.org/people/stephen-ohlemacher

Pace, Julie. AP

newsbusters.org/people/julie-pace

Pauley, Isabel. "Interview videotaped" AP, 27 Aug. 2012.
www.peachpundit.com/.../ap-four-soldiers-in-terror-plot-targeting-pr...

Rose, Charlie. Charlie Rose television show, PBS TV, 23 July 2012.
www.charlierose.com/

Saenz, Arlette, ABC 23 March 2102 "Rick Santorum – firing range"

Sedensky, Matt. AP 18 October 2012 "arrival of President Barack Obama and Mitt
Romney on ... for the upcoming presidential debate."

Sickles, Jason. Yahoo News 6 November the 2012 "presidential election returns"

Stableford, Dylan. Yahoo! News. news.yahoo.com/blogs/author/dylan-stableford/ -

The Daily Caller website "The SSA"
www.aim.org/newswire/why-did-the-social-security...

The New York Times Poll "Police and race"
www.nytimes.com/.../64-of-new-yorkers-in-poll-say-police...

Weill, Sandy, (Geithner on Charlie Rose) PBS TV
www.charlierose.com/

Woodward, Bob. *The Price of Politics*. NY: Simon and Schuster, 2012.

Younglai, Rachelle. Reuters blogs.reuters.com/search/journalist.php?
n=rachelle.younglai

About the Author

OWEN BAPTISTE is a former Managing Director and Editor-in-Chief of the Trinidad Express and Editor-in-Chief of the Trinidad Guardian and Chief Executive Officer and Editor-in-Chief of the Jamaica Observer, which he launched in 1993. In 1998 he left Trinidad to teach in the People's Republic of China and in 2010 he returned to Trinidad and worked with COSTAATT (College of Science, Technology and Applied Arts of Trinidad and Tobago) to plan the Ken Gordon School of Journalism. He also published in 2012 *The Seagulls Won't Come Down*, the story of his twelve years' teaching in Guangzhou and Beijing. In 2011 and 2012 he undertook tours of the United States to write *In Search of America's Soul*. He is married to Rhona Baptiste (née Hunte) and they have two sons, Marc and Simon. Owen Baptiste was honoured in 2013 with the award of Media Icon in celebrationof the 50th Anniversary of Trinidad and Tobago.